# Purposes and Ideas

## Readings for University Writing

### Second Edition

**David A. Jolliffe,** *Editor*

*Editorial Team:*

Beatriz Badikian
Sandra Barnard
Harry Burke
Rance Conley
Jeanette Cook
Thomas Fiffer
Melinda Rooney Florsheim
Kathleen Gallagher
Mary Grantner
Patrick McGann
Ellen McManus
Marilyn Reppa
Carol Severino
Eve Weiderhold

*University of Illinois at Chicago*

**KENDALL/HUNT PUBLISHING COMPANY**
2460 Kerper Boulevard   P.O. Box 539   Dubuque, Iowa 52004-0539

Cover photo by Valentina von Schacht.
"Overlooking Arts Building to top floors of University Hall"
Courtesy of the Office of Public Affairs
University of Illinois at Chicago

Copyright © 1988, 1991 by Kendall/Hunt Publishing Company

Library of Congress Catalog Card Number: 90–64211

ISBN 0–8403–6343–5

Printed in the United States of America
10  9  8  7  6  5  4  3  2  1

# Contents

**Sequence Three**
Race and Ethnicity in Our Families and Lives  **207**

**Readings for Sequence Three**

**Sequence Four**
Solving Problems and the Scientific Method  **279**

## Sequence Five
Public Art and the Public Eye  **317**

Assignments  **318**

# An Introduction
# to University Writing

## On Being an Active Learner in Your Writing Class

This book contains sequences of reading-and-writing assignments for one of the two writing courses required for graduation from the University of Illinois at Chicago, English Composition I. "Comp 101," as people often abbreviate the course, is designed to prepare students to succeed in the kinds of reading and writing tasks they encounter in university studies. The course should be taken early in your college career, ideally in your first or second term of course work. That way, you can apply what you learn about critical reading, systematic thinking and clear, straightforward writing in your other courses at the university.

No matter what your intended major is, you *will* be required to read critically and to write clearly and directly in *many* of the courses that make up your undergraduate degree program. There might have been a time when students in some major fields could feel certain that they would be finished with writing once they completed Composition 101 and Composition 102. That time is past. Professors and students in all majors now realize that people who want to succeed in university studies must become *active learners* and take charge of their own education. And students who succeed do so, in large measure, by seeing critical reading and writing as vital to their learning and by *choosing* to take courses that require them to examine, analyze, and construct their knowledge by writing about it.

This notion of active learning—the idea that a student can consciously determine what he or she wants to know, decide specifically what steps must be taken to acquire and understand that knowledge, and then take those steps—is what can distinguish a university education from schooling that precedes it. Too often in earlier years students are simply led to follow someone else's set of educational directions: "Learn these facts and be prepared to take a test on them," students are told. "Follow steps one through ten and you'll be finished." Too often in such settings, the student becomes a passive placeholder.

In the class for which you are using this book, your instructor wants you to be an *active* participant in the learning process. This means that *you* must be your own leader as you read the selections in this book and write your essays and compositions for the class. Assuming this leadership role prompts you to examine each piece you read and each composition you write with a critical eye. It demands that you understand that a piece of writing—either your own or one published in this book—is designed to accomplish a purpose, that the form a piece of writing assumes is shaped by its author's sense of purpose and audience. As you read and write assignments for this class, consider carefully what kind of thinking went into the writing of each piece. Think how the sense of purpose and audience affected its form, and think how it might have been written differently if the purpose and audience were different. Assume an engaged, almost aggressive, critical attitude. It will pay great dividends.

# The Sequences: Looking at Your Own Education, and More

The sequences you'll encounter in this writing course contain reading selections that range from short stories meant to capture the reader's imagination to scholarly, academic articles meant primarily to persuade specialists in a field to think or act in a certain way. Though the latter are sometimes more difficult to read than the former, nonetheless we think they are important for students taking control of their own education to consider. The sequences also contain four writing assignments that are arranged so that one leads specifically to the next. Your instructor may not ask you to write all the assignments, or he or she may provide different assignments than those printed in this book. Whatever the case, read over the introductions to the sequences and the assignments, and think, even in a preliminary way, how you would go about completing them.

You'll see that the sequences are designed to discourage passivity and encourage active learning, a hallmark of a good college education. For this reason, two of the sequences (you may be asked to complete just one of the two) focus specifically on the nature and functions of education. These sequences will lead you to address the following questions openly and honestly: What does being in college mean to me? How exactly is a getting a college education different from going to high school? How do successful students succeed in college? How can I take charge of my education and become an active learner? The remaining four sequences address the nature and functions of higher education less directly by focusing on several serious ideas with which college-educated people must be concerned: issues of philosophy and life choices, the role of art in their lives, the nature of scientific activity, and the importance of race and ethnicity in their city and neighborhoods. None of the reading-and-writing sequences allows you simply to accept information passively and report it back to your instructor. All of the sequences lead you to consider your stance on the subject, to investigate some aspect of it, and to create *your own* knowledge about it.

# Purposes and Ideas in University Writing

As you prepare to begin this course, ask yourself three questions:

- What *purposes* does writing serve in a university education?
- How am I, as a university student, supposed to interact with the difficult *ideas* I encounter in my classes and my studying?
- How can I use *writing* about difficult ideas as a means of learning and understanding them?

If you're reading this introduction at the beginning of the term, you probably don't have concrete answers to these questions. One of the purposes of the course and this book is to help you answer them clearly for yourself.

Each sequence of reading and writing assignments leads you through a study of a difficult idea by directing you to write essays that accomplish different purposes. Each sequence contains four assignments, and each of the successive assignments builds directly on the reading and writing you do for the preceding ones.

For the first reading and writing assignment of each sequence, we ask you to consider an idea—the subject matter of the sequence—and to clarify for yourself what you think and believe and how you feel about it. For this assignment, you are the primary audience. Although your instructor will read your composition, and your classmates may as well, you need to write clearly to yourself to come to your own preliminary understanding of the subject matter. For the second assignment of each sequence, you are asked to learn something new about the subject—often by interviewing someone, visiting a site, conducting a survey, or observing some phenomenon or event—and then to write an essay reporting what you have learned. For the third assignment of each sequence, we direct you to take some aspect, some idea, some proposition about the subject matter and explain, prove, or demonstrate it to your readers. Finally, for the last assignment, we direct you to write a composition that is designed to persuade, to change people's minds or actions about the subject matter.

You should realize, as you approach these assignments, that a piece of writing rarely accomplishes just one purpose. A piece in which you clarify ideas for yourself can also demonstrate an idea for a reader. An essay that is primarily informative may also have great persuasive appeal. But as a writer you always ought to be able to answer the following questions for yourself as you begin an assignment: "What is my *primary* purpose in this composition? What is the *most important* thing I'm trying to accomplish?" Once you begin drafting a composition, you should feel free to see that you need to accomplish a different purpose than the one you initially had. But you should try at all times to keep the question of *your* purpose in writing in view.

Your instructor will tell you which of these sequences you'll be working with directly during the course, but let us give you a brief overview of the six sequences, all of which offer you the chance to come to grips intellectually with the kinds of ideas that circulate in a university community.

- Sequence One, "Culture, Education, and Expectations," leads you to examine who and what has influenced your decision to attend college—your family, your ethnic culture, your friends, your own personal will.
- Sequence Two, "Learning to Write: Cultural Influences," leads you to examine yourself as a person who wants to become an independent reader and writer and helps you to understand how aspects of your life and cultural background have influenced you as a student.
- Sequence Three, "Race and Ethnicity in Our Families and Lives," deals with an issue that is always important in Chicago, the way traditions of race and ethnic culture affect us.
- Sequence Four, "Solving Problems and the Scientific Method," helps you understand that one of the most important functions of a scientific education is that it teaches not just the content of the sciences but also the valuable ability to solve problems.
- Sequence Five, "Public Art and the Public Eye," ask you to examine public art and architectures—including famous structures in Chicago—and to explore how these artifacts reflect both personal and social values.
- Sequence Six, "Boundaries of the Individual," leads you to consider your sense of self, and to examine how issues of gender, work, and government influence how you feel about yourself.

# A Reading and Writing Course:
## The Center of a University Education

The course you are taking, one in which you must read challenging material and write critically about it, has been at the center of the university curriculum for centuries. Yet some people question the need for a required university writing course. According to these critics, students should have learned in high school how to read and write well enough to get through college. These people are wrong for two reasons. First, they fail to consider the differences between the kinds of subjects a high school student must learn and those a college student must deal with. The substance of a university education is more rigorous, more complex, more intellectually demanding than the substance of a high school education. And one of the best ways to approach and *learn* demanding, university-level subjects is by writing about them. Second, the critics seem to believe that "knowing how to write" consists of some finite set of skills that one can acquire and use at will. They don't realize that successful writing calls for the development and interaction of a complicated set of abilities, and that all writers must regularly practice their craft or their abilities will decay. At every point in his or her academic life, a successful student ought to be studying and practicing writing, either in a class, in a community of peers, or alone.

The purpose of Composition 101, thus, is to start you on your way to a successful college career by introducing you to university writing. The course will teach you to read difficult texts critically, to think systematically about the ideas in the texts and their importance in the world, to generate your own ideas about compelling subjects, to organize your ideas and present them in appropriate formats, and to write English prose that is clear, forceful, straightforward, and correct.

A word about how this course might differ from your high school English courses might be in order. Many of you may have received very good instruction in English composition prior to this course. In high schools across the country, more and more teachers are realizing that writing can be taught as a process. These teachers design assignments that allow students opportunities to plan their compositions carefully, draft them over a period of time, and then revise them before their final evaluation. Often these teachers encourage students to use writing to express ideas that are personally important.

If this description sounds like the English classes you've had prior to Composition 101, you're fortunate. But whether you've had a good experience in English, or whether you've had what you consider to be less enjoyable and stimulating classes, you need to think clearly about how Composition 101 may differ from earlier English classes you may have had. The major differences will probably be three.

First, you need to think about possible differences in the *function* of the compositions you wrote in high school and the ones you'll write in this class. In high school, students are usually asked to write pieces that accomplish two functions. As we suggested above, some assignments direct students to express whatever ideas are personally troubling, important, or relevant to them. Other assignments require that students report to the reader—usually the teacher—some body of facts, information, or ideas, either about literature or about some phenomenon in the world. What some teachers may call "critical interpretation" papers may actually lead the student to report on someone else's interpretation of a work, not the student's own.

Composition 101 will require you to use these two functions—self-expression and reporting—as starting points, but you will be asked to build on them and write papers that accomplish other functions as well. In a university education, you can't count on having any deeply personal feelings you need to express about the subject matters you must study, so you must learn to use writing in college to clarify for yourself what these subjects *mean* to you as you study them. You need to consider what you *think* and *believe* about subjects, not necessarily only how you *feel* about them. You'll be asked to report to your readers in this course, but ideally your readers won't already know the body of facts, information, and ideas you're reporting, as is too often the case in high school. After you've clarified for yourself what a subject matter means and reported something new about it, you'll be asked to use your writing to explain ideas or demonstrate a point about the subject. Perhaps you'll even be asked to write a piece that will change the way people think and act concerning your subject matter. In brief, the emphasis in this course is on writing that requires you to discover, discuss, and explain *new* knowledge.

Second, you need to give some thought to possible differences in the *form* of the papers you may have written in high school English and the papers you'll write in this class. Many students in high school are taught to write the five-paragraph theme, a composition that has an introductory paragraph with a thesis statement, three paragraphs of development, and a concluding paragraph that restates the thesis. There is surely nothing wrong with writing papers in this form. Indeed, the five-paragraph format may be one of the clearest ways to organize your thoughts about your subject matter in a preliminary way. But many college writers find the five-paragraph theme more restrictive than it is helpful. The five-paragraph theme, after all, suggests that all university writing must have a simple thesis and that there are only three things you can say about your subject matter. Your instructor will teach you to think about the form of your papers in ways that will enable you to explore ideas more deeply than the five-paragraph theme allows.

Third, you need to consider carefully some possible differences in your use of what writing teachers call the *modes* or *methods of development.* In earlier classes, teachers may have given you assignments that asked you to employ one of the modes or methods—description, narration, classification, division, definition, comparison and contrast, cause and effect, process analysis, and so on. If you have been taught about these modes and methods, that's good—you'll be able to use what you know in Composition 101. If you've never learned about them, you will in this class. But you'll need to bear in mind that the modes and methods are not ends in themselves, but instead are means to an end. In other words, they are tools of a writer's trade. They are always used in the service of accomplishing some *purpose* in writing. Teaching a person to write by emphasizing the modes and methods in isolation is like teaching a person to build a cabinet by asking him to study the hammer and the nails. As a writer, you need to learn how to use your tools to achieve your desired product. You have to see the modes and methods of development as devices you can use to accomplish a purpose in your writing.

# How to Do Well in Composition 101

Each of your instructors will help you to understand early in the term what you must to succeed in each section of this course, including how many papers you have to write and how many hours per week you should spend on homework for this class. But let us offer six general guidelines that you can follow if you want to do well:

*Guideline 1*—**Read and reread the essays upon which your assignments are based:** Read slowly and carefully. Highlight or underline important sections. Write yourself notes or questions in the margins. In short, develop an *active* relationship with the texts you're reading.

*Guideline 2*—**Think systematically about your reading and the events, objects, and phenomena you're observing in order to write about them:** Many successful students keep a reading/observation journal. They write one page a night in which they react to some aspect of their reading or observations, write a summary of what they know or don't know, or practice writing about their ideas to different audiences. Your instructor will be able to share with you a handout describing three methods of thinking systematically about your reading and observations and keeping a journal to record your thoughts.

*Guideline 3*—**When you get a writing assignment, begin drafting it early:** Successful writers realize that a good piece of writing must have time to grow. Rarely does a composition succeed that has been written hastily at the last moment.

*Guideline 4*—**Enlist the help of a reader before you hand in your composition for evaluation:** Many college students think they're now allowed to have someone else read their paper. Not only are you allowed, but you're encouraged to do so. Of course, you may not allow anyone else to do your writing for you, but a piece of writing always benefits from the careful commentary of someone who's willing to read it before you turn it in. The university's Writing Center in 107 Addams Hall is staffed by trained tutors, one of whose jobs is to read drafts of papers and help you revise them.

*Guideline 5*—**Be willing and prepared to rewrite:** James Thurber once wrote that the only good writing is rewriting. Don't overlook upon rewriting as simply cleaning up your mistakes and turning in a "final copy." See rewriting instead as an opportunity to make your composition as clear, effective, and purposeful as possible.

# Sequence One

# Culture, Education, and Expectations

Most students who take university writing courses do so within their first year, or sometimes first two years, of college, and college often seems like a very new experience to them. But if you discuss your experiences of starting college with your classmates, you'll probably find that everyone has a different story to tell about what it was like. These differences come about in part because students arrive at the university with different expectations. They have been influenced and prepared for college in varying ways by their families, their cultural backgrounds, and their previous educational experiences. When they arrive they discover that the university itself has many expectations of its students, not all of which it states explicitly in its catalogue and course descriptions. A university, after all, must respond both to tradition and to current social needs.

What college becomes for some students, thus, is a jumble of expectations. You may not be clear about what you yourself expect from your education, much less about what the university expects from you. These different sets of expectations may come into conflict, especially when they are left unexamined or unstated.

In this sequence, you will explore these different expectations and how they affect you. You will begin by exploring cultural and family influences on your attitudes toward college. Next, in collaboration with your classmates, you will examine how your high school experiences have prepared you for college. Then you will study several statements about what society in general expects from universities and what universities expect from students. Finally, you will analyze the relationships among these sets of expectations and make some recommendations based on your discoveries.

## Assignment One

*Readings:*

Vivian Gornick, from *Fierce Attachments*
Howard London, "Breaking Away: A Study of First-Generation College Students and their Families."

Even before we begin to think seriously about our own future, many of us become aware that our families—themselves influenced by their communities and cultures—have certain expectations about what we will do with our lives after high school. And these expectations inevitably

1

influence us, sometimes to the point of making us want to resist our family members' wishes. Our families may have education or career plans for us that we don't feel we can or want to meet. Or, more subtly, our family members may fear that our own educational goals will take us away from them, not only literally but emotionally and intellectually as well. Then again, if we're lucky, our families' expectations for us may nurture and reinforce our own.

Vivian Gornick uses a personal narrative to explore her own experiences with conflicts between cultural values, family expectations, and personal goals. Howard London draws on the life histories of fifteen students who were the first in their families to go to college. A sociologist by training, London uses methods from the social sciences to explore these same conflicts.

Write an essay using personal narrative to explore your family's expectations of you: how those expectations have been influenced by cultural values; how those expectations are conveyed to you, both openly and indirectly; and how you feel about those expectations. Even if you are not a first-generation college student, you may want to consider your experience in light of the concepts London uses. For example, in regard to education, what role are you expected to play in your family?

# Assignment Two

*Readings:*

Mike Rose, from *Lives on the Boundary*
Carl Grant and Christine Sleeter, "Race, Class, Gender, and Abandoned Dreams."
Martin Kramer, "Empty Chairs: What Happens to Students Who Don't Go to College?"

In the first assignment, you examined how families helped to form attitudes toward education. But a person's attitudes don't come only from his or her family. High school experiences can also have a profound impact on a student's future. Often a high school student's expectations are shaped by messages others send about what they think he or she is capable of accomplishing. For example, Mike Rose's narrative illustrates the impact that tracking had on him and the motivation he received from one particular mentor. In an article that reports field research, Carl Grant and Christine Sleeter also examine the influence—mostly negative in the case of these students—of high school on students' attitudes and goals.

Unlike the students in the Grant and Sleeter study, but like Gornick and Rose, you and your classmates probably had experiences that encouraged you to attend college. As a class project, explore the differences and similarities among the experiences of the members of the class, of Gornick and Rose, and of the students in the Grant and Sleeter study. Interview a classmate about how high school experiences affected his or her decision to attend college. You might want to ask your classmate to compare his or her experiences with one or more of those described in the readings. In addition, you might want to develop questions on some of the areas that Grant and Sleeter studied: the school itself, teachers, courses, peers, family, the surrounding community, race and ethnicity, social class, and gender. If your classmate attended high school in another country, ask about specific details of that experience and what influenced him or her to attend college in the United States. If your classmate did not attend college right after high school, ask about work-related experiences and what has motivated him or her now to pursue a college degree. Finally, taking your cue from the Kramer article, you might ask whether he or she ever considered *not* going to college and what changed his or her mind.

Write up the interview and distribute copies to the rest of class so you can inform them of what you learned. After reading each other's interviews, the class can try to arrive at some general conclusions about how high school experiences shaped the attitudes and decisions of the class as a whole.

# Assignment Three

*Readings:*

Otto Friedrich, "Five Ways to Wisdom."
Allan Bloom, "Our Listless Universities."
George Levine, "A Response to Bloom."
"What We Expect: Preparing for College—A Statement by 12 Deans."

So far in this sequence you have considered what has influenced your attitudes toward higher education and your decision to attend college. This assignment asks you to look at what society expects universities to do and what universities, therefore, expect students to do. Otto Friedrich identifies five possible (but in some cases conflicting) functions that a society might assign to higher education. Then Allan Bloom and George Levine offer different perspectives on what universities should expect and demand of their students and what students should expect and demand of their institutions. Finally, the deans of 12 colleges and universities describe specific expectations that they have for beginning students.

On the basis of these readings and your own developing ideas, write an essay in which you explain what American society should expect from higher education and what colleges and universities should therefore expect and demand of their students. You may want to present your explanation as a response to one or more of the readings.

OR

Write an essay in which you describe and analyze the implications of one specific conflict among the many expectations described in these readings. What do you think are the reasons for this conflict, and what impact could it have on students?

# Assignment Four

*Readings:*

> Juan Guerra, "Bridging the Gap Between Home and Academic Literacies."
> Fred M. Hechinger, "School-College Collaboration: An Essential to Improved Public Education."

Throughout this sequence you have explored potential and real conflicts among the many sets of expectations that surround higher education. Can any of these conflicts be resolved? Juan Guerra, a UIC alumnus, argues that the university must make a stronger effort to welcome and accommodate students from cultural backgrounds whose values are different from those of the traditional academic culture. Fred Hechinger argues that closer cooperation between high schools and colleges could make the transition less traumatic for all concerned.

Drawing on the ideas you've developed through reading and discussion in this sequence, write an essay in which you make one or more specific recommendations about how the university could better accommodate students from different cultures or about how the university could make the high school-college transition easier.

OR

On the basis of your own experience as well as all you've read and thought about for this sequence, write an essay that might be used in the next education of *Purposes and Ideas,* giving advice to future students in this course about what the university expects of them.

# *From* Fierce Attachments: A Memoir

*Vivian Gornick*

Mama and Nettie quarreled, and I entered City College. In feeling memory these events carry equal weight. Both inaugurated open conflict, both drove a wedge between me and the unknowing self, both were experienced as subversive and warlike in character. Certainly the conflict between Nettie and my mother seemed a strategic plan to surround and conquer. Incoherent as the war was, shot through with rage and deceit, its aims apparently confused and always denied, it never lost sight of the enemy: the intelligent heart of the girl who if not bonded to one would be lost to both. City College, as well, seemed no less concerned with laying siege, to the ignorant mind if not the intelligent heart. Benign in intent, only a passport to the promised land, City of course was the real invader. It did more violence to the emotions than either Mama or Nettie could have dreamed possible, divided me from them both, provoked and nourished an unshared life inside the head that became a piece of treason. I lived among my people, but I was no longer one of them.

I think this was true for most of us at City College. We still used the subways, still walked the familiar streets between classes, still returned to the neighborhood each night, talked to our high-school friends, and went to sleep in our own beds. But secretly we had begun to live in a world inside our heads where we read talked thought in a way that separated us from our parents, the life of the house and that of the street. We had been initiated, had learned the difference between hidden and expressed thought. This made us subversives in our own homes.

As thousands before me have said, "For us it was City College or nothing." I enjoyed the solidarity those words invoked but rejected the implied deprivation. At City College I sat talking in a basement cafeteria until ten or eleven at night with a half dozen others who also never wanted to go home to Brooklyn or the Bronx, and here in the cafeteria my education took root. Here I learned that Faulkner was America, Dickens was politics, Marx was sex, Jane Austen the idea of culture, that I came from a ghetto and D. H. Lawrence was a visionary. Here my love of literature named itself, and amazement over the life of the mind blossomed. I discovered that people were transformed by ideas, and that intellectual conversation was immensely erotic.

We never stopped talking. Perhaps because we did very little else (restricted by sexual fear and working-class economics, we didn't go to the theater and we didn't make love), but certainly we talked so much because most of us had been reading in bottled-

Vivian Gornick is a journalist and essayist who has written on culture and politics, especially feminist issues, for a number of newspapers and magazines. This essay is from her autobiographical memoir, *Fierce Attachments.*

up silence from the age of six on and City College was our great release. It was not from the faculty that City drew its reputation for intellectual goodness, it was from its students, it was from us. Not that we were intellectually distinguished, we weren't; but our hungry energy vitalized the place. The idea of intellectual life burned in us. While we pursued ideas we felt known, to ourselves and to one another. The world made sense, there was ground beneath our feet, a place in the universe to stand. City College made conscious in me inner cohesion as a first value.

I think my mother was very quickly of two minds about me and City, although she had wanted me to go to school, no question about that, had been energized by the determination that I do so (instructed me in the middle of her first year of widowhood to enter the academic not the commercial course of high-school study), and was even embattled when it became something of an issue in the family.

"Where is it written that a working-class widow's daughter should go to college?" one of my uncles said to her, drinking coffee at our kitchen table on a Saturday morning in my senior year in high school.

"Here it is written," she had replied, tapping the table hard with her middle finger. "Right here it is written. The girl goes to college."

"Why?" he had pursued.

"Because I say so."

"But why? What do you think will come of it?"

"I don't know. I only know she's clever, she deserves an education, and she's going to get one. This is America. The girls are not cows in the field only waiting for a bull to mate with." I stared at her. Where had *that* come from? My father had been dead only five years, she was in full widowhood swing.

The moment was filled with conflict and bravado. She felt the words she spoke but she did not mean them. She didn't even know what she meant by an education. When she discovered at my graduation that I wasn't a teacher she acted as though she'd been swindled. In her mind a girl child went in one door marked college and came out another marked teacher.

"You mean you're not a teacher?" she said to me, eyes widening as her two strong hands held my diploma down on the kitchen table.

"No," I said.

"What have you been doing there all these years?" she asked quietly.

"Reading novels," I replied.

She marveled silently at my chutzpah.

But it wasn't really a matter of what I could or could not do with the degree. We were people who knew how to stay alive, she never doubted I would find a way. No, what drove her, and divided us, was me thinking. She hadn't understood that going to school meant I would start thinking: coherently and out loud. She was taken by violent surprise. My sentences got longer within a month of those first classes. Longer, more complicated, formed by words whose meaning she did not always know. I had never before spoken a word she didn't know. Or made a sentence whose logic she couldn't follow. Or attempted an opinion that grew out of an abstraction. It made her crazy. Her face began to take on a look of animal cunning when I started a sentence that could not possibly be concluded before three clauses had hit the air. Cunning sparked anger, anger flamed into rage. "What are you talking about?" she would shout at me. "What *are* you talking about? Speak English, please! We all understand English in this house. Speak it!"

Her response stunned me. I didn't get it. Wasn't she pleased that I could say something she didn't understand? Wasn't that what it was all about? I was the advance guard. I was going to take her into the new world. All she had to do was adore what I was becoming, and here she was refusing. I'd speak my new sentences, and she would turn on me as though I'd performed a vile act right there at the kitchen table.

She, of course, was as confused as I. She didn't know why she was angry, and if she'd been told she was angry she would have denied it, would have found a way to persuade both herself and any interested listener that she was proud I was in school, only why did I have to be such a showoff? Was that what going to college was all about? Now, take Mr. Lewis, the insurance agent, an educated man if ever there was one, got a degree from City College in 1929, 1929 mind you, and never made you feel stupid, always spoke in simple sentences, but later you thought about what he had said. That's the way an educated person should talk. Here's this snotnose kid coming into the kitchen with all these big words, sentences you can't make head or tail of . . .

I was seventeen, she was fifty. I had not yet come into my own as a qualifying belligerent but I was a respectable contender and she, naturally, was at the top of her game. The lines were drawn, and we did not fail one another. Each of us rose repeatedly to the bait the other one tossed out. Our storms shook the apartment: paint blistered on the wall, linoleum cracked on the floor, glass shivered in the window frame. We

barely kept our hands off one another, and more than once we approached disaster.

One Saturday afternoon she was lying on the couch. I was reading in a nearby chair. Idly she asked, "What are you reading?" Idly I replied, "A comparative history of the idea of love over the last three hundred years." She looked at me for a moment. "That's ridiculous," she said slowly. "Love is love. It's the same everywhere, all the time. What's to compare?" "That's absolutely not true," I shot back. "You don't know what you're talking about. It's only an idea, Ma. That's all love is. Just an idea. You think it's a function of the mysterious immutable being, but it's not! There is, in fact, no such thing as the mysterious immutable being . . ." Her legs were off the couch so fast I didn't see them go down. She made fists of her hands, closed her eyes tight, and howled, "I'll kill you-u-u! Snake in my bosom, I'll kill you. How dare you talk to me that way?" And then she was coming at me. She was small and chunky. So was I. But I had thirty years on her. I was out of the chair faster than her arm could make contact, and running, running through the apartment, racing for the bathroom, the only room with a lock on it. The top half of the bathroom door was a panel of frosted glass. She arrived just as I turned the lock, and couldn't put the brakes on. She drove her fist through the glass, reaching for me. Blood, screams, shattered glass on both sides of the door. I thought that afternoon, One of us is going to die of this attachment.

7

# Breaking Away: A Study of First-Generation College Students and Their Families

*Howard B. London*

• • •

## Introduction

Several years ago the film *Breaking Away* was a box office success across America. On the surface it was the story of "town-gown" frictions between the "cutters" of Bloomington, Indiana—so called because they were the children of the men who mined the local limestone quarries—and the ostensibly more sophisticated but condescending students of Indiana University. The competition between them became centered on the annual campus bicycle race, the cutters for the first time entering a team of their own. The hero of the story, a cutter, trains excruciatingly hard, and at movie's end he breaks away from the pack of racers, and the locals triumph.

It was not, however, simply the tale of how some snobbish university students were put in their place. Rather, the story within the story was of the adolescent hero struggling to find his place and of his "breaking away" or

Reprinted from *American Journal of Education* 97 (1987): 144–170, © 1989 by The University of Chicago Press. Used with permission.

For several years, sociologist Howard London recorded the life histories of fifteen college students who were the first in their families to go to college.

separating from family and friends whom he loves but whose world he finds narrow and constricting. He wants more out of life, and even takes his college entrance examinations, though he would be the first among his family and friends to matriculate. Yet at the same time he fears losing what he already has. Growth, in other words, implies loss.[1]

• • •

Family Role Assignments and First-Generation Students

The concept of family role assignment, prominent in contemporary psychodynamically oriented family theory, envisions the family as having a division of emotional labor with different members responsible for designated psychological tasks. The living out of such role assignments—the martyred parent and the parentified, achieving, or mediating child are familiar examples—has important consequences for each family member's self-imagery, emotional life, and behavior. Though it is a theme to which we shall return, it should be said here that being in the psychological employ of others, such as one's parents, can form as well as deform emotional life (Miller 1981). Indeed, it is a tenet of modern family theory that messages about role assignments (mutable, diverse, and unconscious as these messages may be) are communicated in all families, and that they are related to the histories, psychologies, and family systems of our parents and their parents before them (Framo 1972; Boszormenyi-Nagy and Spark 1973; Napier and Whitaker 1978). . . .

Whether and to what extent role assignments are internalized, as well as how they find expression, varies from family to family, person to person, and over the life cycle. Their existence and effects, however, can usually be seen in bold relief during late adolescence and early adulthood, a phenomenon useful to our examination of first-generation students. In industrial societies these are years of heightened concern with identity (Erikson 1959) and increased disengagement or separation from parents.[4] The young adult typically strives to become more individuated and differentiated, that is, to acquire more independence and autonomy on various emotional, cognitive, and moral levels. This is often an erratic process, consisting of discontinuous episodes and even reversals as offspring variously accept, modify, or reject parental wishes or demands, and, since separation is a two-way street, as parents decide to "let go" or "hold on" as they move through their own life cycles. Separation can, of course, be "out of phase," occurring prematurely, later in life, or perhaps never at all. In most families, however, whatever roles have been assigned and whatever dramas are being played out, the plot almost always thickens as a child moves through adolescence toward adulthood.

As it became apparent during the first several interviews that family role assignments and separation dynamics were at the center of the drama of first-generation students, I was struck by how their stories paralleled the formulations of the psychoanalyst Helm Stierlin.[5] As a vehicle of separation, higher education seemed to bring into play the same elemental concerns and feelings that Stierlin believes are found in all separations: "losing and refinding what one holds dearest, deepest distress and joy, conflict and reconciliation . . . the nature of love, of obedience, and of mutual growth and liberation in families" (1974, pp. ix–x).

Stierlin's view of separation rests on his observation that family role assignments are generated by parental needs that are expressed through one of three "transactional modes":

Where the binding mode prevails, the parents interact with their offspring in ways that keep the latter tied to the parental orbit and locked in the "family ghetto."

Where the delegating mode is dominant, the child may move out of the parental orbit but remains tied to his parents by the long leash of loyalty. This delegate must then fulfill missions for his parents . . . that embroil him in various forms of conflict.

Where, finally, the expelling mode prevails, parents enduringly neglect and reject their children and consider them nuisances and hindrances to their own goals. A strong centrifugal force pushes many of these children into premature separations. [1974, pp. xii–xiii]

While one mode usually predominates, there are often blends of modes. . . . Before turning to the first student, however, it should be noted that in this study students are the sole source of information about their forebears. Thus what is said to be true of previous generations may be so only from a student's perspective. Whether or not they have their facts straight, however, may be less important than their belief that they do. It is, after all, their beliefs that shape—indeed, that constitute—their perceptions of their parents and grandparents.

Lorena Aguillas: Bound and Delegated

During infancy and childhood some binding is helpful and necessary, for the eventual emergence of the self requires an initial fastening to others (Mahler 1968; Bowlby 1969). Some parents, however, try to keep a child forever dependent on them; others, as in the situation described below, attempt to convince a child that they, the parents, are the ones who are dependent, and that unless the child provides essential satisfactions and securities the parents will suffer and wither (Stierlin 1974, p. 42). Once responsive to such needs, a child's sense of well-being becomes contingent on meeting them. To use Stierlin's metaphor, a child is then gripped by centripetal forces that tie him or her to the family orbit. Enjoying autonomy becomes virtually impossible, for any experimentation with independence raises the specter of treason against the parents. It would be anomalous to find students who were truly bound children, whether first generation or not, and indeed none were interviewed. However, some students did describe a combination of binding and delegation. In effect, they were given conflicting messages: one to stay at home, the other to achieve in the outside world.

Lorena Aguillas found herself facing precisely this dilemma.[6] From a small southwestern town straddling the border between Mexico and the United States, Lorena identified herself as Mexican-American. When interviewed she was a second-semester freshman at an elite, highly selective women's college. Lorena described herself as being considerably closer to and more influenced by her father, a man she characterized as often feeling inferior. He was the first and only child of a short-lived marriage, one still considered a skeleton in the family closet. Adopted by his mother's second husband he felt treated, according to Lorena, as "less important" and as "not really his step-

father's child" in comparison with the four children born of this second marriage. Furthermore, unlike his stepsisters he was not sent to schools across the border to learn English, without which he believed his prospects for success were greatly diminished. Instead, he was taken out of school after the eighth grade to help out in the family-owned bakery: "He still resents it. . . . He tells me that he wanted an education. He says that he's really dumb and stupid and stuff. . . . I think he is smart, but they never gave him a chance. He was very good in school [in Mexico] but when his father said, 'Now you're going to come working with me and sweep the floors,' there was nothing he could say. . . . That's just the way he was raised, that you do what your parents tell you to do."

Taking advantage of what the world had to offer while remaining loyal to his family was, according to Lorena, a lifelong conflict for her father. Indeed, Lorena later described a dramatic reenactment of this conflict in which Mr. Aguillas was torn over where *his* firstborn (Lorena) should be educated: "He always tells me I was born in the United States just in case. We moved back to Mexico for a while and he said he had to make a very tough decision when I was going into first grade, whether he wanted me to go to school in Mexico or go to school in the United States. You see, he thinks that girls or women in Mexico are much more conservative than they are in the States, and he was afraid that I would become too different than the Mexican women."

Despite his misgivings, he sent his young daughter to school on the "American side of town," but his conflicts over what was to become of Lorena—educationally, culturally, and otherwise—became her own: "I first started thinking about going to college when I was in junior high. I did pretty well in school but my parents wanted me to stay in state, so they're not really happy that I'm here. . . . But if my father's friends or somebody would ask if I'm going to school, he'd say 'Oh, yes, she wants to go to Harvard or Stanford,' or somewhere like that, and I never even wanted to go there, but he would say that. [She laughs.] Those were some pretty nice colleges he said I wanted to go to.''

Yet by the time Lorena was a high school senior she indeed did apply to some of this country's most exclusive colleges, receiving more assistance from her father than anyone else:

I didn't feel a lot of support from teachers at school or anything. They kept saying, "Well, why don't you just go to the University of [name of state]. You know, it's not such a bad school." I'm not saying that it is, but I didn't want to go there. I didn't think it was for me. . . . My mother never said anything either way. . . . I got all the applications done the night before each had to be mailed and my father took them to the post office the next morning and mailed them. . . . When I had to have interviews with _____ and _____ [names of colleges], I had to go to Santa Fe for them, and my father drove me and everything. So it seemed like he was really supportive about it, but it wasn't until after I got accepted that he changed and said, "You can't go!"

According to Lorena, her father's fears were the same as when she was a first grader, though with some contemporary twists: he was afraid, she laughed, "I would become too different, more independent, more liberal, join a religious cult and become a feminist." She added more seriously, "He was afraid of the influences I would have in America."

In addition to his fears for the loss of his daughter's cultural identity, there were other perhaps more self-serving appeals to her loyalty based on two roles Lorena played in the family system. The first was a constellation of confidante, comforter, and helper to her father: "My parents, you know, they get along, but they've never been the kind of couple who really talked to each other or anything, you know, who really discuss important issues about work or something. My dad would mostly talk to me if he had problems in work or something.'' This role met with tacit but apparently begrudging maternal consent: "My mother and I really used to fight a lot. I've never been able to talk to her as you would think you would be able to with a mother. . . . I think sometimes that she was jealous because I got along with my father. . . . I think my mother sort of resented that.''

It seems, then, that the side of Lorena's father that was threatened with the loss of her support refused to let her go. Indeed, during the months between her admission to college and her departure from home he became—for the first time in Lorena's memory—silent, sullen, brooding, and angry.

He was really upset. And, I don't know, we always got along real well, so it was hard for me, because for five months he was really weird with me. He was rude and didn't treat me nice. One day he told me, "Do whatever you want!" He got mad. He was angry because I wouldn't listen to reason and stay home. . . . He told me later that when he said that, he was sure that I was going to say, "Well, O.K., he doesn't want me to go, so I'll stay." I didn't, I said, "Well, I'm going to go." And so he said, "Well, I'm not going to give you any money to go to school. And I'm not going to sign any paper to let you go."

Though Lorena received generous financial aid, her father was unyielding. Their first protracted struggle was at a stalemate, and for Lorena it was agonizing. For her mother, however, who was still sitting quietly on the sidelines, their struggle offered an opportunity to be heard, rescue Lorena, and get Lorena out of the house, all at the same time:

My mother stepped in and I got the shock of my life because I had never seen my mother actually tell my dad, "You shouldn't." But one day my mom said, "If you weren't going to let her go you should not have let her apply." And I think he was sort of shocked too. He just looked at her like, [wide-eyed] "What are you saying?" Because my mom has been really settled down. She's been like most typical Mexican women are supposed to be. You're supposed to do whatever your husband says and you don't answer back to him or tell him anything. But she told him.

Apparently affected by his wife's assertiveness and the finality of his daughter's decision, Mr. Aguillas relented somewhat in the days before Lorena left. On her next to last day home, saying he was still angry, he presented her with a credit card to be used for emergency purchases, but especially if she wished to fly home. The following day he drove her to the airport.[7]

Mr. Aguillas could drive Lorena to the airport because her second role assignment was to be his delegate, with a mission of enhancing his self-imagery by fulfilling (exceeding, really) the unmet aspirations he once had for himself. This was the part of her father that prematurely boasted to his friends about her attending an elite college, that mailed her completed application forms, and that drove her to interviews. While seemingly contradictory, in one fundamental sense it was not, for it is the paradox of delegation (as discussed more fully in the next section) that the leaving itself is a sign of allegiance. In other words, Lorena's determination to go to college, especially an elite one, appealed to this second set of paternal needs and so satisfied one set of loyalty demands at the same time that it violated the other (that she remain at home).

Lorena, then, was pitted between incompatible role assignments. If she left she was disloyal in her role as a paternal comforter and confidante; if she stayed, she was disloyal in her role as an emissary. By leaving as she did, the conflict, of course, remained unresolved. Through the mail, over the telephone, and at home on vacation, Lorena endured an onslaught of entreaties from her father to withdraw from college and return to his side:

The thing that gets to me a lot when I go home is that my father continually, every day, tells me that he needs me to come home. He just tells me, "It's so silly for you to still be there. You should come home and go to [the local college]." You see, he owns a bakery store in Mexico also, but with the devaluation of the peso he has to sell out. Well, he owns two mortgages on the house and says they're going to take the house away from them, and he wants to open a restaurant. But he wants me to stay there next year and help him out with the store. But I don't really think I should stop my education to go and help him. Not because I don't want to help him, but because I'm not sure I would be able to get into the track of things again, come back and take up where I left off. . . . It makes me feel kind of in the middle with what I want and what he wants, because I do respect a lot at times what he wants and I would like to help him. But I don't think it's really fair of him to ask this of me, for me to stop. Because this is really what I want to do with my life now. I said I would help him all summer, seven days a week in the store [and forgo an undergraduate hospital internship to help her decide whether to be a premedical student]. . . . But he wants me to go to school nearby, help out at night and weekends, and I'm sure he wants me to live at home. . . . It's awfully hard because it makes me feel like I've been a bad daughter. It's hard.

As stated earlier, offspring paralyzed by "breakaway guilt" feel that one or both parents are so dependent on them that to leave is criminal; it is tantamount to abandonment and betrayal (Stierlin 1974, p. 50). Were Lorena so immobilized she would be unable to fend off her father's pleas, just as Mr. Aguillas was unable to fend off those of his father a generation earlier. Yet she is not wholly emancipated, feeling still burdened by the pain of the "bad daughter." Despite her ambivalence she intends neither to atone by ruefully returning home nor to sever ties with her father. Instead, she seeks ways to help him that do not require a forfeiture of self or a foreclosure of career, and that thereby avoid the resentment Mr. Aguillas knows all too well. To say it differently, she wishes to establish a "related individuation" or a "separated attachment," in which her connectedness is expressed through empathic caring, but her autonomy is respected.[8]

Two qualifications are in order. First, norms and values regulating separation—its style, timing, pace, extent, and desirability—are historically and culturally variable. There is no inherently superior process or outcome of separation apart from considerations of time and place. For example, in many traditional societies with extended local kinship systems, separation as described here is alien, devalued, and even stigmatized; and in those modern societies where the cultural ideal of a successful separation is a state of "related individuation," such an ideal can be seen as promoting individual achievement and mobility while deflecting the guilt of disloyalty to family or community. Thus, in both traditional and modern societies, norms and values surrounding separation have an ideological function in that they help buttress a particular social, economic, and political system. From this perspective, then, the emotions that tether children to the family or loosen them from it are themselves shaped by the larger culture.

The second qualification is prompted by the report of a white, urban, working-class student who described a series of appeals from his parents to drop out of college. Their appeals were similar in content and motive to those heard by Lorena: "It's your turn among the children to work," they pleaded, and "That's not our way." These two families, so different in culture and locale, remind us that while attempts to bind children and to undermine their education may not be typical of any group—Mexican-American, Anglo, or others—such attempts may be found in all groups.

Don Peatro: Delegate

The verb delegate—from the Latin *delegare,* to send out, to assign—means to be entrusted with the responsibility of acting for another. To act responsibly, to be a "good delegate," therefore, requires going out into the world to promote the interests, wishes, or needs of another rather than one's own, unless, of course, they coincide. Thus, while a delegate is sent out, he or she is also held on to by a "long leash of loyalty." Like Lorena Aguillas, offspring in this situation are subject to "conflicting tendencies and hence to centrifugal as well as centripetal pressures" (Stierlin 1974, p. 52). What distinguishes the delegated from the bound child, however, is that the former demonstrates loyalty by leaving the family, not by staying in it. Leaving, or, more accurately, leaving as a delegate, paradoxically becomes a proof of allegiance and even of love.

Delegation is by no means always enslaving or exploitative. "More often it is the expression of a necessary and legitimate process of relationship. . . . Delegation gives our lives direction and significance [and our parents' lives meaning and satisfaction]. . . . As delegates of our parents, we have the possibility of proving our loyalty and integrity and of fulfilling missions reaching beyond purely personal levels" (Stierlin 1980, pp. 23–24). Furthermore, many parents simply do not delegate. They may still want things for and from their children, and may tell them so, sometimes with great clarity and concern, but their sense of well-being does not rest on filial compliance. This in turn makes it more likely that tensions and conflicts between parent and child can be defined and settled and is what distinguishes parental aspirations for their children from parental delegations to their children. As it happened, there were no

13

"happily delegated" students among those I interviewed. This may well be a consequence of having a self-selected sample, with less troubled students being less likely to respond to an advertisement. The assumption here is that interviewees wanted to talk of some distress, a point covered earlier.[9]

A delegation becomes troublesome and potentially injurious when a child, regardless of age, is so weighed down by it that he follows his parents' needs and wishes at the expense of his own separation and growth; that is, he does not become a person in his own right. Usually this happens when a child attempts to bear, reconcile, redeem, or repair something for one or both parents; perhaps it is a conflict, a disowned feeling, or an inner doubt about the self. A person's sense of well-being, and in an extreme case even the foundation of a personality, may consequently rest on successfully carrying out a mission (Framo 1972, p. 281). Such a person is, in regard to parents at least, underindividuated (fused in the extreme case), having weak and porous psychological boundaries. Unable to stand separately, he or she cannot refuse parental delegations without experiencing much inner conflict. Don Peatro, as we shall soon see, is such a young man.

### Don Peatro: The Arrival

This is a favorite story of my dad's. My grandfather came from Palermo and worked in a sweatshop in the garment district in New York. They lived in the projects after a while. My grandfather had no schooling. . . . My dad really emphasizes how hard my grandfather worked in the sweatshop. My father became a letter carrier and he's hoping that [the name of his college] for me will be "the arrival."

Don is an 18-year-old second-semester freshman at an elite, academically demanding liberal arts college. He talks fluently and intensely about the three-generation family legacy he brings to campus. His grandfather's struggle to build a better life for his children is a familiar story in the American experience, better known perhaps than that of the ghosts such quests can visit on succeeding generations. "My grandfather was very, very strict. I think it bothered my dad. He told me how he would ask for money and my grandfather would say, 'Do you know how hard I worked for this?' and give this kind of doling out motion, very slowly, saying, 'I don't want you to work like this.'"

After graduating from high school, Mr. Peatro married and enrolled in a technical school but dropped out after a few months when Don, the first of his three children, was born. He then went to work in the local post office where he still works after 20 years. The passing on of the delegation is direct and clear.

My father feels pretty unhappy in his job. . . . He really feels very strongly that I should get out of the working class. He feels trapped in his job. That's something he never wants me to feel. Dad and I have had long talks about this. . . . My dad is very negative about being working class. . . . It's very apparent. I think he obviously feels he could have been more. . . . He feels he doesn't have enough and he should have more and I'm going to be the culmination of "the more." My dad definitely sees my going to college as a key to the doors of the life that he and my grandfather wanted. [Imitating his father]: "Don, your grandfather would be so proud to see you going to college. You don't understand how we lived when we were young." My going to college is playing out what he wishes he could have done. . . . What my father has always told me is, "Do you see these affluent people, Don? You can have that too." And I guess I really believe it.

Delegations frequently come more from one parent than the other, and in Don's case the mother seems to play a lesser role not because she is uninterested in his education, but because for her his education has no mission-like functions. Reports Don, "My mother is pretty satisfied with the way she is. I think she's happier than my dad is in her job (a store clerk) because she knows she should be. . . . My mom I don't see as having as much of an influence on my education, like having an ideal sort of view. But she is more practical, saying things like, 'Have you done your homework?' "

By contrast, Don's father is depicted as beseeching him to provide a sense of worthwhileness and completeness, nowhere more evident than in Don's reporting him to have said, "So study, go to a good college, *so I can feel like I did something*" (emphasis added). To say it differently, Mr. Peatro's hopes for his son seem not for the son alone, but rather appear to be mixed with a mission to heal some private doubt. Without speaking directly with Mr. Peatro it cannot be said with certainty that this doubt derives from some sense of failure regarding his own father's stern injunction ("I don't want you to work like this"). We do know, however, that Mr. Peatro feels unhappy and trapped in his work. If Don has been enlisted in an effort to ease his father's burden, then the voice of the now-dead grandfather still reverberates, for his name is still invoked as one who would have been proud. What remains unsaid is that Don's father can feel proud too, not only of his son, but of himself in the memory he holds of his father.

It is not surprising, then, that Don also reports that he knew at an early age that college was for him and he for college. For his part Don has played the attendant son, obeying parental entreaties by always having done well in school and by acquiring the confidence and self-imagery of an academically superior student. Of concern is whether the autonomy and sense of self thereby gained are to some extent false, fragile, or conflict laden as a result of resting so heavily on meeting his father's needs. There are indications that this is the case, and, further, that Don is aware of it. In one interview, for ex-

ample, Don several times seems to slide in and out of awareness of his father's self-serving motives and his (Don's) own skepticism about them. One minute he is sure his father is right about things and is "only doing what is best for me," yet in the next Don fears he has been overadaptive. For example:

My senior year [in high school] was a very pressured year and I felt that my dad was putting too much pressure on me. But the thing was he always showed me that I could achieve. I mean, my father's favorite line is "hit the books." But I wished he would say it a little bit less often, yet I felt that he was right. I felt that I could achieve, but I just wished he'd kind of shut up about it for a little while and give me the chance to believe it more for me, and make sure it was for me and not for him. . . . Sometimes I do feel that if I don't achieve—like first semester I wondered if I don't do well—who am I doing well for? Am I doing well for me or doing well for my dad? The answer is he's really right. He's pushing me to achieve. He really is looking out for my best interest, but if I did not finish college he would give me a hard time for a long while. To some point how I feel about me is related to it. I think that's because I respect what he is saying, but is it just because I respect him as my father or do I really believe in his principles? I don't think I have a good perspective on how much of it is his personal concern for me or his personal concern for himself, though I'd see more if I wanted to. I could see myself thinking more about it, but he's my dad and that's not something I would choose to do.

Accepting a delegation so completely risks a diminished individuation, creating the soft, easily penetrable boundaries referred to earlier. Parental voices may come to sound stronger than one's own and can easily drown it out: "I am very concerned with whether I am making decisions for me, or am I making them for my girlfriend, or am I being influenced by my roommate, my mom and my dad? I listen too much. I listen too hard. I take too much personally. I listen to everything everyone else says. I guess I have to learn not to listen to everything, just to be more selective.''

While Don expressed some skepticism about his father's delegation and his own acceptance of it, there remains the possibility of someday repudiating, altering, or fleeing his mission. That further developmental progress—that is, further intellectual, psychological, and emotional maturation and sophistication—may lead to a greater questioning of family matters is considered in a later section.

## Betty Smith: Expelled and Delegated

Stierlin's third and last mode of intergenerational separation is an expelling one. Expelling has a positive and legitimate function, as when a child is pushed from the nest to progress toward a more mature independence. However, it can ''become malignant when directed toward a child who still requires nurturant care and executive control and who, instead of needing exposure to the cold winds of autonomy and competition, needs shelter, caring intimacy and guidance in a bewildering world'' (Stierlin 1974, p. 126). The tensions that lead to expulsions of this kind typically fester for years, sometimes reaching an explosive climax, as when a child is thrown out or runs away; whether or not such a climax occurs, the child is usually emotionally and socially denied full family membership.

Betty Smith, a second-semester freshman at a state college, was so excluded. She was in her family but not of it, cast down but not out. In explaining, Betty referred to the circumstances of her birth: ''When my mother and father broke up, my mother didn't know she was pregnant with me, so I was a going-away present. I was the end, which as far as I know was not amicable. So I was not exactly welcomed as the flowers in spring, tra-la, tra-la. And I was two-and-a-half months early. And I was developmental-

ly delayed. I came into the world with all the odds against me. And I survived.''

Abandoned by her father whom she never saw or heard from, Betty went on to endure a sometimes subtle, sometimes overt, but always painful rejection. Her underlying sense of being unwanted is a common feeling among expelled children (Stierlin 1974, p. 66). More specifically, Betty described a lifetime of feeling apart and different, and of doubting that her apartness and differentness were respected. The following passage, necessarily lengthy, illustrates her position in the family as well as her deeply unsettled and mixed feelings about it. At one moment she exalts her apartness and differentness, proclaiming them as virtues; in the next she worries they are signs of being disowned and devalued, and she fears always having been disliked and seen as strange because of them:

I was never outfitted to stay at home. You know, the Mommy who bakes the brownies and the bread. I knew that when I was a little kid, but more so when I went into _____ High School [a public school with the highest competitive admissions standards in her city]. We [Betty and her classmates] did not have any home economics courses at all. None. Not even how to cook an egg. Nothing. No sewing courses either. Because it was expected we were going to college. . . . I didn't learn to cook or sew like my [five] sisters did at home. . . . They were just more homebodied because they were taught to do those things. When I was a young girl you couldn't get me outside to play. I didn't like to play. I didn't like board games. Nothing! Chutes and Ladders, Monopoly. Nothing. I don't like games. I don't like cards [said proudly]. I liked to sit in a corner and read, and that's what I always did as a kid . . . Greek myths, or black history. Anything. I just loved to read. I've always liked to be left alone. . . . I was too different from my sisters. I didn't have anything in common with them. . . . My mother would make us dress, not all exactly alike; the same material, but a different style. Mine might have one bow, but theirs would have two. . . . And their beds were together [in the same room] and mine was separate. . . . But I was always sort of like separate and different. . . . I've always felt being different was bad, because I was always made to feel so bad for being different. And I hated it, and I always said I just wanted to be normal. People pick on you if you're very, very smart. People pick on you. They think you're a Miss-Know-It-All. They think you're a wiseass, or, "Here's the dictionary.. Here comes the walking encyclopedia." And I was already getting teased about wearing glasses, being light-skinned, not being able to play sports. I mean I couldn't do anything to please these people. Everything you do is wrong. You get tired of that. Honey, I did back flips when Vanessa Williams won her [Miss America] title. I said, "Hot damn. A light-skinned black." I was in heaven. I said, "Yea! One of us won." I just get so sick of being teased about everything. I mean the skin color was wrong, my hair color was wrong, and it wasn't nappy enough. I wasn't black enough. I wasn't white enough. I was too smart for my own good. I had a big mouth. And I was shaped wrong. This is part of the reason I came back to school [after working a few years], because I couldn't deal with that anymore.

Though Betty recognized that her intellectualism contributed to her exclusion, it was a trait of which she was nonetheless proud. Indeed, Betty appeared to be swinging between two poles without stopping at either, never sure whether she was excluded because she was different, or different because she was excluded. Yet to whatever extent her siblings conspired in her ostracism, it was difficult not to see their mother's inspiration. Nowhere was this more forcefully and painfully dramatized than when after remarrying, Betty's mother changed her children's last name from her first to her second husband's, but excluded Betty: "I was jealous of them. They got their last names changed and I didn't. I was very jealous. They get a new name, why didn't I get one? It sounds kind of, it's crazy."

Another facet of Betty's exclusion was her loneliness, both in the family and on campus. Like other children who experience some form of expulsion, Betty felt unlikable and was highly vulnerable to rejection, and so perpetuated her loneliness: "I never was really that close [with her brothers and sisters]. I don't get close to people. . . . I'm just one of those people who don't like to reach out that much, because I figure if I reach out I might get hurt, so I just stay very New Englandish in that regard. . . . Before I moved out of my mother's house I was closest to myself. Basically, myself."

Betty's exclusion, however, was attenuated in at least two ways. First, in the curious workings of family life playing the role of the excluded one can itself be a form of involvement and hence inclusion: it does, after all, require the cooperation of family members to sustain the role, an activity necessitating considerable thought and expenditure of energy.[12] Second, Betty's mother recognized her academic abilities and insisted that they be cultivated. Reported Betty: "I wanted to go to a nice, normal, everyday high school where I could kick back and raise a little Cain. [Imitating her mother:] 'You need a challenge. You will go to [the most competitive high school in the city].' I didn't want to go, but she made me. . . . Later it got to be fun."

By demanding attendance at a superior high school her mother may have furthered Betty's exclusion, but this does not appear to be the action of a wholly callous and spiteful mother. (How much more insidious it would have been to deny Betty such opportunity!) Rather, it seems that her mother found through schooling a way of expressing both her resentment and her caring. Furthermore, in addition to being excluded Betty may well have been delegated the task of becoming formally educated: as reported by Betty, her mother also went to a competitive high school (that is, one which had academic entrance requirements), but was expelled when she became pregnant with Betty's older sister. Betty, though, did not state directly that by matriculating she felt she was acting on behalf of her mother, a requirement of delegation. However, she was the only one of her five sisters and three brothers to go to college.

Despite the costs Betty eventually responded to her exclusion by embracing her apartness and difference, expressing both through precocious academic achievement. I am brought back to her earlier words about her matriculation, words spoken after a litany of complaints about the penalties of being too smart, having too large a vocabulary, possessing the wrong physical characteristics—the penalties, in short, of being an outsider in her own family. Said Betty, "Part of the reason I came back to school, [was] because I couldn't deal with that anymore." She continued:

I think the fight with my sister last year is what did it. My sister said, "I'm not a fink like you. I didn't go to _____ [the name of Betty's selective high school]." Hell, she didn't graduate from any school. I got sick of being treated different and being made to feel like I did something wrong because I was different. Until last year [when Betty matriculated] I always felt it was bad. I don't care anymore. I've gotten to the point where I say, "I'm different. So what? Sue me. And if you're successful I want the name of your lawyer because I want to study under him."

In conclusion, over the years Betty's education helped her negotiate a potentially damaging separation, one which was, after all, adulterated, premature, and overly intense. Her loneliness never disappeared, but through her books was transformed into a thoughtful solitude. Reading and learning thus became a salve and finally a badge of specialness and honor. Education became the cloak that warmed her chilled heart, and school a house into which she could repair to build the strength to face her family, the world, herself.

## Qualifications

Some qualifications are in order. First, it should not be assumed that family forces are the only propelling ones. The full interviews reveal additional reasons for matriculation—career preparation, intellectual fulfillment, and social standing, for example—that are part of what probably is an ever-shifting hierarchy of motives. To omit the family from consideration, however, is to miss something of importance.

Second, during adolescence and early adulthood the maturation of intellectual and moral capacities may by itself help promote more differentiation and autonomy. Writes Stierlin of the adolescent: "He enlarges his vocabulary of human motives and increases his grasp of psychological complexity. And he now experiences emotions as states of the self rather than as correlates of external events. Therefore, he can increasingly differentiate and clarify conflicting attitudes, intentions, needs, and motives within himself, and importantly, within others" (1974, p. 11).

It may be that the students described here have only recently found and begun to use these enhanced abilities. Furthermore, they may well have been interviewed at some developmentally sensitive midpoint in their separation from family. I think here of the ambivalence and the sliding in and out of different levels of awareness of Don and Betty in particular, and of the latter's recent claim of emancipation. ("I'm different. So what? Sue me!")

Third, college-educated parents also bind, delegate, and expel their children. However, when separation struggles occur in such families, they are, I suspect, less likely played out around whether to go to college (unless the child decides not to go) than around where to go to college, choice of academic major, grades, life-style, personal appearance, or some other idiosyncratic matter (Sacks 1978; London 1986).

## Conclusion

By their very presence on campus the students described here have beaten the statistical odds. It is, of course, of great concern that there are odds to beat in the first place; indeed, sociologists have long been investigating the structural sources and functions of inequality in general, and educational inequality in particular. Rather than enter that argument, I have instead attempted to widen its dimensions by detailing some of the more intimate dynamics and circumstances of educational mobility.

From a wider cultural perspective the stories of these first-generation students dramatize the consequences for individuals of the shift from a traditional to a modern society. In traditional societies intergenerational continuity—in the areas of work, family, religion, and community—encourages the formation of a secure identity. Industrial societies, however, permit and even require the making of choices in these areas, so that people are less certain of how and where and with whom they will find themselves. Thus the past is no longer as effective a guide to the present or the future, and the ethic of individual achievement and upward mobility that we, on the one hand, extol can, on the other, produce a discontinuity that cleaves families and friends. It is only when we see that mobility involves not just gain but loss—most of all the loss of a familiar past, including a past self—that we can begin to understand the attendant periods of confusion, conflict, isolation, and even anguish that first-generation students report here. To say it differently, for the students who are the subject of this article modernity creates

the potential for biographical and social dislocation, so that freedom of choice, to whatever extent it exists, can also be the agony of choice.

While some first-generation students no doubt experience smooth transitions, others, like those described here, find the going rough. As educators we do these latter students no great favor should they become—out of our own unawareness—confused, frightened, and alienated, only to drift away and drop out. If we—faculty, administrators, and support staff—mean for them to stay and not become attrition statistics, we need a keener understanding of the sensibilities and concerns they bring with them and of the difficulties they encounter along the way. In this regard I hope this article is helpful.

## Notes

For their various forms of inspiration and helpful criticism I would like to thank Barbara Spivak, Barbara Schildkrout, David Riesman, Sophie Freud, Helen Reinherz, Bill Levin, David Karp, and two anonymous reviewers. To the students who gave of themselves, here are your stories, respectfully told.

1. An extensive discussion of the relationships between separation, loss, and growth is found in John Bowlby's *Attachment and Loss* (1969). A more recent treatment is Judith Viorst's *Necessary Losses* (1986), a book whose topic is of such appeal to college students that it remained on campus best-seller lists throughout 1987 and 1988 *(Chronicle of Higher Education* 1987, 1988). A sensitive autobiographical account of education as a vehicle of separation is Richard Rodriguez's *Hunger of Memory* (1982).

2. The composition of the "sample" by sex and type of college is:

| Type of College | Male | Female |
|---|---|---|
| State colleges/universities | 2 | 3 |
| Private women's colleges | ... | 2 |
| Private colleges/universities | 4 | 4 |

3. Paraphrased from the comment of an anonymous reviewer.

4. In many cultures separation from parents—geographically, emotionally, cognitively, morally, or in terms of fealty—is less extensive and sometimes

proscribed. This is discussed in a later section describing a first-generation student who comes from such a culture.

5. Stierlin focuses on how separation can go awry—especially in the families of runaway, schizophrenic, and "wayward" adolescents—in the belief that faulty cases more clearly show what is at stake, and because they provide important insights into the separation process in general. So that there is no mistake, this is not at all to imply that being the first in one's family to go to college is a sign of poor family functioning. It may in fact be quite the opposite, since individuation and separation may be negotiated well or not in any family regardless of the educational attainment of its members. Thus it is important to keep in mind that when this paper focuses on conflict and loss it is because these inhere in the separation process, not because there is necessarily something "wrong" with the families under scrutiny.

6. Names and identifying information have been changed. Quotations are verbatim except for minor editorial changes for clarity's sake. A series of periods indicates nonessential material has been omitted.

7. With these shifts in family life Lorena reported a steadily improved relationship with her mother.

8. Other forms of individuation are over- and underindividuation. The former refers to fusion with others, the latter to isolation from others. The next section considers these concepts further.

9. Two twists are provided by David Riesman (in personal correspondence). First, some students may attend universities so remote from parental imagination that their parents leave them alone to do what they want. Second, education is not the only road up, and delegations can and do take many noneducational forms.

10. This raises the question (not pursued in the interviews) of Lisa also being delegated the incompatible task of expressing her mother's longings. By dwelling on the differences between Lisa and herself, Mrs. Collins may have been subtly encouraging Lisa to "act out," thus making Lisa's separation all the more difficult. See Stierlin for an interesting discussion of this kind of dynamic (1974, p. 83).

11. Writes Alice Miller of children who awaken from such circumstances; " 'What would have happened if I had appeared before you, bad, ugly, angry, jealous, lazy, dirty, smelly? Where would your love have been then? And I was all these things as well. Does this mean that it was not really me whom you loved, but only what I pretended to be? The well-behaved, reliable, empathic, understanding, and convenient child, who in fact was never a child at all? What became of my childhood? Have I not been cheated out of it? I can never return to it. I can never make up for it. From the beginning I have

been a little adult. My abilities—were they simply misused?' These questions are accompanied by much grief and pain'' (1981, p. 15).

12. This applies to the role of the physically expelled as well as the socially excluded: one need not be physically present to play a part in the lives of others, or they in ours.

# References

Boszormenyi-Nagy, Ivan, and B. Spark. *Invisible Loyalties.* New York: Hoeber & Harper, 1973.

Bowlby, John. *Attachment and Loss,* vol. 1. London: Hogarth Press, 1969.

Eliot, T. S. "The Family Reunion." In *T. S. Eliot: The Complete Poems and Plays, 1909–1950.* New York: Harcourt, Brace & World, 1952.

Erikson, Erik. "Identity and the Lifecycle." In *Psychological Issues,* vol. 1. New York: International Universities Press, 1959.

Framo, James, M.D. "Symptoms from a Family Transactional Viewpoint." In *Progress in Group and Family Therapy,* edited by C. Sager and H. Kaplan. New York: Brunner-Mazel, 1972.

Kahl, Joseph. *The American Class Structure.* New York: Holt, Rinehart & Winston, 1957.

London, Howard. "Strangers to Our Shores." In *The Community College and Its Critics,* edited by L. S. Zwerling (New Directions for Community Colleges no. 54). San Francisco: Jossey-Bass, 1986.

Mahler, Margaret. *On Human Symbiosis and the Vicissitudes of Individuation.* New York: International Universities Press, 1968.

Miller, Alice. *The Drama of the Gifted Child.* New York: Basic, 1981.

Napier, Augustus, and Carl Whitaker. *The Family Crucible.* New York: Harper & Row, 1978.

Rodriguez, Richard. *Hunger of Memory: The Education of Richard Rodriguez.* Boston: Godine, 1982.

Sacks, Herbert, M.D. "Bloody Monday: The Crisis of the High School Senior." In *Hurdles: The Admissions Dilemma in American Higher Education,* edited by H. Sacks. New York: Atheneum, 1978.

Stierlin, Helm. *Separating Parents and Adolescents.* New York: Quadrangle, 1974.

Stierlin, Helm, et al. *The First Interview with the Family.* New York: Brunner-Mazel, 1980.

Viorst, Judith. *Necessary Losses.* New York: Ballantine, 1986.

Weber, Max. *Economy and Society.* New York: Bedminster, 1968.

# From *Lives on the Boundary*

*Mike Rose*

• • •

It took two buses to get to Our Lady of Mercy. The first started deep in South Los Angeles and caught me at midpoint. The second drifted through the neighborhoods with trees, parks, big lawns, and lots of flowers. The rides were long but were livened up by a group of South L.A. veterans whose parents also thought that Hope had set up shop in the west end of the county. There was Christy Biggars, who, at sixteen, was dealing and was, according to rumor, a pimp as well. There were Bill Cobb and Johnny Gonzales, grease-pencil artists extraordinaire, who left Nembutal-enhanced swirls of "Cobb" and "Johnny" on the corrugated walls of the bus. And then there was Tyrrell Wilson. Tyrrell was the coolest kid I knew. He ran the dozens like a metric halfback, laid down a rap that outrhymed and outpointed Cobb, whose rap was good but not great— the curse of a moderately soulful kid trapped in white skin. But it was Cobb who would sneak a radio onto the bus, and thus underwrote his patter with Little Richard, Fats

Mike Rose, associate director of UCLA Writing Programs, has written extensively on issues of language and literacy. This excerpt is from his own educational autobiography.

Domino, Chuck Berry, the Coasters, and Ernie K. Doe's mother-in-law, an awful woman who was "sent from down below." And so it was that Christy and Cobb and Johnny G. and Tyrrell and I and assorted others picked up along the way passed our days in the back of the bus, a funny mix brought together by geography and parental desire.

Entrance to school brings with it forms and releases and assessments. Mercy relied on a series of tests, mostly the Stanford-Binet, for placement, and somehow the results of my tests got confused with those of another student named Rose. The other Rose apparently didn't do very well, for I was placed in the vocational track, a euphemism for the bottom level. Neither I nor my parents realized what this meant. We had no sense that Business Math, Typing, and English-Level D were dead ends. The current spate of reports on the schools criticizes parents for not involving themselves in the education of their children. But how would someone like Tommy Rose, with his two years of Italian schooling, know what to ask? And what sort of pressure could an exhausted waitress apply? The error went undetected, and I remained in the vocational track for two years. What a place.

My homeroom was supervised by Brother Dill, a troubled and unstable man who also taught freshman English. When his class drifted away from him, which was often, his voice would rise in paranoid accusations, and occasionally he would lose control and shake or smack us. I hadn't been there two months when one of his brisk, face-turning slaps had my glasses sliding down the aisle. Physical education was also pretty harsh. Our teacher was a stubby ex-lineman who had played old-time pro ball in the Midwest. He routinely had us grabbing our ankles to receive his stinging paddle across our butts. He did that, he said, to make men of us. "Rose," he bellowed on our first encounter, me standing geeky in line in my baggy shorts. " 'Rose'? What the hell kind of name is that?"

"Italian, sir," I squeaked.

"Italian! Ho. Rose, do you know the sound a bag of shit makes when it hits the wall?"

"No, sir."

"Wop!"

Sophomore English was taught by Mr. Mitropetros. He was a large, bejeweled man who managed the parking lot at the Shrine Auditorium. He would crow and preen and list for us the stars he'd brushed against. We'd ask questions and glance knowingly and snicker, and all that fueled the poor guy to brag some more. Parking cars was his night job. He had little training in English, so his lesson plan for his day work had us reading the district's required text, *Julius Caesar,* aloud for the semester. We'd finish the play way before the twenty weeks was up, so he'd have us switch parts again and again and start again: David Snyder, the fastest guy at Mercy, muscling through Caesar to the breathless squeals of Calpurnia, as interpreted by Steve Fusco, a surfer who owned the school's most envied paneled wagon. Week ten and Dave and Steve would take on new roles, as would we all, and render a water-logged Cassius and a Brutus that are beyond my powers of description.

Spanish I—taken in the second year—fell into the hands of a new recruit. Mr.

Montez was a tiny man, slight, five foot six at the most, soft-spoken and delicate. Spanish was a particularly rowdy class, and Mr. Montez was as prepared for it as a doily maker at a hammer throw. He would tap his pencil to a room in which Steve Fusco was propelling spitballs from his heavy lips, in which Mike Dweetz was taunting Billy Hawk, a half-Indian, half-Spanish, reed-thin, quietly explosive boy. The vocational track at Our Lady of Mercy mixed kids traveling in from South L.A. with South Bay surfers and a few Slavs and Chicanos from the harbors of San Pedro. This was a dangerous miscellany: surfers and hodads and South-Central blacks all ablaze to the metronomic tapping of Hector Montez's pencil.

One day Billy lost it. Out of the corner of my eye I saw him strike out with his right arm and catch Dweetz across the neck. Quick as a spasm, Dweetz was out of his seat, scattering desks, cracking Billy on the side of the head, right behind the eye. Snyder and Fusco and others broke it up, but the room felt hot and close and naked. Mr. Montez's tenuous authority was finally ripped to shreds, and I think everyone felt a little strange about that. The charade was over, and when it came down to it, I don't think any of the kids really wanted it to end this way. They had pushed and pushed and bullied their way into a freedom that both scared and embarrassed them.

Students will float to the mark you set. I and the others in the vocational classes were bobbing in pretty shallow water. Vocational education has aimed at increasing the economic opportunities of students who do not do well in our schools. Some serious programs succeed in doing that, and through exceptional teachers—like Mr. Gross in *Horace's Compromise*—students learn to develop hypotheses and troubleshoot, reason through a problem, and communicate effectively—the true job skills. The vocational track, however, is most often a place for those who are just not making it, a dumping ground for the disaffected. There were a few teachers who worked hard at education; young Brother Slattery, for example, combined a stern voice with weekly quizzes to try to pass along to us a skeletal outline of world history. But mostly the teachers had no idea of how to engage the imaginations of us kids who were scuttling along at the bottom of the pond.

And the teachers would have needed some inventiveness, for none of us was groomed for the classroom. It wasn't just that I didn't know things—didn't know how to simplify algebraic fractions, couldn't identify different kinds of clauses, bungled Spanish translations—but that I had developed various faulty and inadequate ways of doing algebra and making sense of Spanish. Worse yet, the years of defensive tuning out in elementary school had given me a way to escape quickly while seeming at least half alert. During my time in Voc. Ed., I developed further into a mediocre student and a somnambulant problem solver, and that affected the subjects I did have the wherewithal to handle: I detested Shakespeare; I got bored with history. My attention flitted here and there. I fooled around in class and read my books indifferently—the intellectual equivalent of playing with your food. I did what I had to do to get by, and I did it with half a mind.

But I did learn things about people and eventually came into my own socially. I liked the guys in Voc. Ed. Growing up where I did, I understood and admired physical prowess, and there was an abundance of muscle here. There was Dave Snyder, a sprinter and halfback of true quality. Dave's ability and his quick wit gave him a natural appeal, and he was welcome in any clique, though he always kept a little independent. He enjoyed acting the fool and could care

less about studies, but he possessed a certain maturity and never caused the faculty much trouble. It was a testament to his independence that he included me among his friends—I eventually went out for track, but I was no jock. Owing to the Latin alphabet and a dearth of *Rs* and *Ss,* Snyder sat behind Rose, and we started exchanging one-liners and became friends.

There was Ted Richard, a much-touted Little League pitcher. He was chunky and had a baby face and came to Our Lady of Mercy as a seasoned street fighter. Ted was quick to laugh and he had a loud, jolly laugh, but when he got angry he'd smile a little smile, the kind that simply raises the corner of the mouth a quarter of an inch. For those who knew, it was an eerie signal. Those who didn't found themselves in big trouble, for Ted was very quick. He loved to carry on what we would come to call philosophical discussions: What is courage? Does God exist? He also loved words, enjoyed picking up big ones like *salubrious* and *equivocal* and using them in our conversations—laughing at himself as the word hit a chuckhole rolling off his tongue. Ted didn't do all that well in school—baseball and parties and testing the courage he'd speculated about took up his time. His textbooks were *Argosy* and *Field and Stream,* whatever newspapers he'd find on the bus stop—from *the Daily Worker* to pornography—conversations with uncles or hobos or businessmen he'd meet in a coffee shop, *The Old Man and the Sea.* With hindsight, I can see that Ted was developing into one of those rough-hewn intellectuals whose sources are a mix of the learned and the apocryphal, whose discussions are both assured and sad.

And then there was Ken Harvey. Ken was good-looking in a puffy way and had a full and oily ducktail and was a car enthusiast . . . a hodad. One day in religion class, he said the sentence that turned out to be one of the most memorable of the hundreds of thousands I heard in those Voc. Ed. years. We were talking about the parable of the talents, about achievement, working hard, doing the best you can do, blah-blah-blah, when the teacher called on the restive Ken Harvey for an opinion. Ken thought about it, but just for a second, and said (with studied, minimal affect), "I just wanna be average." That woke me up. Average?! Who wants to be average? Then the athletes chimed in with the clichés that make you want to laryngectomize them, and the exchange became a platitudinous melee. At the time, I thought Ken's assertion was stupid, and I wrote him off. But his sentence has stayed with me all these years, and I think I am finally coming to understand it.

Ken Harvey was gasping for air. School can be a tremendously disorienting place. No matter how bad the school, you're going to encounter notions that don't fit with the assumptions and beliefs that you grew up with—maybe you'll hear these dissonant notions from teachers, maybe from the other students, and maybe you'll read them. You'll also be thrown in with all kinds of kids from all kinds of backgrounds, and that can be unsettling—this is especially true in places of rich ethnic and linguistic mix, like the L.A. basin. You'll see a handful of students far excel you in courses that sound exotic and that are only in the curriculum of the elite: French, physics, trigonometry. And all this is happening while you're trying to shape an identity, your body is changing, and your emotions are running wild. If you're a working-class kid in the vocational track, the options you'll have to deal with this will be constrained in certain ways: You're defined by your school as "slow"; you're placed in a curriculum that isn't designed to liberate you but to occupy you, or, if you're lucky, train you, though the training is for work the society does not esteem; other students are picking up the cues from your school and your curriculum and interacting with you in particular ways. If you're a kid like Ted Richard, you turn your back on all this and let your mind roam where it may. But youngsters like Ted are rare. What Ken and so many others do is protect themselves from such suffocating madness by taking on with a vengeance the identity implied in the vocational track. Reject the confusion and frustration by openly defining yourself as the Common Joe. Champion the average. Rely on your own good sense. Fuck this bullshit. Bullshit, of course, is everything you—and the others—fear is beyond you: books, essays, tests, academic scrambling, complexity, scientific reasoning, philosophical inquiry.

The tragedy is that you have to twist the knife in your own gray matter to make this defense work. You'll have to shut down, have to reject intellectual stimuli or diffuse them with sarcasm, have to cultivate stupidity, have to convert boredom from a malady into a way of confronting the world. Keep your vocabulary simple, act stoned when you're not or act more stoned than you are, flaunt ignorance, materialize your dreams. It is a powerful and effective defense—it neutralizes the insult and the frustration of being a vocational kid and, when perfected, it drives teachers up the wall, a delightful secondary effect. But like all strong magic, it exacts a price.

My own deliverance from the Voc. Ed. world began with sophomore biology. Every student, college prep to vocational, had to take biology, and unlike the other courses, the same person taught all sections. When teaching the vocational group, Brother Clint probably slowed down a bit or omitted a little of the fundamental biochemistry, but he used the same book and more or less the same syllabus across the board. If one class got tough, he could get tougher. He was young and powerful and very handsome, and looks and physical strength were high currency. No one gave him any trouble.

I was pretty bad at the dissecting table, but the lectures and the textbook were interesting: plastic overlays that, with each turned page, peeled away skin, then veins and muscle, then organs, down to the very bones that Brother Clint, pointer in hand, would tap out on our hanging skeleton. Dave Snyder was in big trouble, for the study of life—versus the living of it—was sticking in his craw. We worked out a code for our multiple-choice exams. He'd poke me in the back: once for the answer under *A,* twice for *B,* and so on; and when he'd hit the right one, I'd look up to the ceiling as though I were lost in thought. Poke: cytoplasm. Poke, poke: methane. Poke, poke, poke: William Harvey. Poke, poke, poke, poke: islets of Langerhans. This didn't work out perfectly, but Dave passed the course, and I mastered the dreamy look of a guy on a record jacket. And something else happened. Brother Clint puzzled over this Voc. Ed. kid who was racking up 98s and 99s on his tests. He checked the school's records and discovered the error. He recommended that I begin my junior year in the College Prep program. According to all I've read since, such a shift, as one report put it, is virtually impossible. Kids at that level rarely cross tracks. The telling thing is how chancy both my placement into and exit from Voc. Ed. was; neither I nor my parents had anything to do with it. I lived in one world during spring semester, and when I came back to school in the fall, I was living in another.

Switching to College Prep was a mixed blessing. I was an erratic student. I was undisciplined. And I hadn't caught onto the rules of the game: Why work hard in a class that didn't grab my fancy? I was also hopelessly behind in math. Chemistry was hard; toying with my chemistry set years before hadn't prepared me for the chemist's equations. Fortunately, the priest who taught both chemistry and second-year algebra was also the school's athletic director. Membership on the track team covered me; I knew I wouldn't get lower than a C. U.S. history was taught pretty well, and I did okey. But civics was taken over by a football coach who had trouble reading the textbook aloud—and reading aloud was the centerpiece of his pedagogy. College Prep at Mercy was certainly an improvement over the vocational program—at least it carried some status—but the social science curriculum was weak, and the mathematics and physical sciences were simply beyond me. I had a miserable quantitative background and ended up copying some assignments and finessing the rest as best I could. Let me try to explain how it feels to see again and again material you should once have learned but didn't.

You are given a problem. It requires you to simplify algebraic fractions or to multiply expressions containing square roots. You know this is pretty basic material because you've seen it for years. Once a teacher took some time with you, and you learned how to carry out these operations. Simple versions, anyway. But that was a year or two or more in the past, and these are more complex versions, and now you're not sure. And this, you keep telling yourself, is ninth- or even eighth-grade stuff.

Next it's a word problem. This is also old hat. The basic elements are as familiar as story characters: trains speeding so many miles per hour or shadows of buildings angling so many degrees. Maybe you know enough, have sat through enough explanations, to be able to begin setting up the problem: "If one train is going this fast . . ." or "This shadow is really one line of a triangle. . . ." Then: "Let's see . . ." "How did Jones do this?" "Hmmmm." "No." "No, that won't work." Your attention wavers. You wonder about other things: a football game, a dance, that cute new checker at the market. You try to focus on the problem again. You scribble on paper for a while, but the tension wins out and your attention flits elsewhere. You crumple the paper and begin daydreaming to ease the frustration.

The particulars will vary, but in essence this is what a number of students go through, especially those in so-called remedial classes. They open their textbooks and see once again the familiar and impenetrable formulas and diagrams and terms that have stumped them for years. There is no excitement here. *No* excitement. Regardless of what the teacher says, this is not a new challenge. There is, rather, embarrassment and frustration and, not surprisingly, some anger in being reminded once again of long-standing inadequacies. No wonder so many students finally attribute their difficulties to something inborn, organic: "That part of my brain just doesn't work." Given the troubling histories many of these students have, it's miraculous that any of them can lift the shroud of hopelessness sufficiently to make deliverance from these classes possible.

· · ·

Jack MacFarland couldn't have come into my life at a better time. My father was dead, and I had logged up too many years of scholastic indifference. Mr. MacFarland had a master's degree from Columbia and decided, at twenty-six, to find a little school and teach his heart out. He never took any credentialing courses, couldn't bear to, he said, so he had to find employment in a private system. He ended up at Our Lady of Mercy teaching five sections of senior English. He was a beatnik who was born too late. His teeth were stained, he tucked his sorry tie in between the third and fourth buttons of his shirt, and his pants were chronically wrinkled. At first, we couldn't believe this guy, thought he slept

in his car. But within no time, he had us so startled with work that we didn't much worry about where he slept or if he slept at all. We wrote three or four essays a month. We read a book every two to three weeks, starting with the *Iliad* and ending up with Hemingway. He gave us a quiz on the reading every other day. He brought a prep school curriculum to Mercy High.

MacFarland's lectures were crafted, and as he delivered them he would pace the room jiggling a piece of chalk in his cupped hand, using it to scribble on the board the names of all the writers and philosophers and plays and novels he was weaving into his discussion. He asked questions often, raised everything from Zeno's paradox to the repeated last line of Frost's "Stopping by Woods on a Snowy Evening." He slowly and carefully built up our knowledge of Western intellectual history—with facts, with connections, with speculations. We learned about Greek philosophy, about Dante, the Elizabethan world view, the Age of Reason, existentialism. He analyzed poems with us, had us reading sections from John Ciardi's *How Does a Poem Mean?*, making a potentially difficult book accessible with his own explanations. We gave oral reports on poems Ciardi didn't cover. We imitated the styles of Conrad, Hemingway, and *Time* magazine. We wrote and talked, wrote and talked. The man immersed us in language.

Even MacFarland's barbs were literary. If Jim Fitzsimmons, hung over and irritable, tried to smart-ass him, he'd rejoin with a flourish that would spark the indomitable Skip Madison—who'd lost his front teeth in a hapless tackle—to flick his tongue through the gap and opine, "good chop," drawing out the single "o" in stinging indictment. Jack MacFarland, this tobacco-stained intellectual, brandished linguistic weapons of a kind I hadn't encountered before. Here was this *egghead*, for God's sake, keeping some pretty difficult people in line. And from what I heard, Mike Dweetz and Steve Fusco and all the notorious Voc. Ed. crowd settled down as well when MacFarland took the podium. Though a lot of guys groused in the schoolyard, it just seemed that giving trouble to this particular teacher was a silly thing to do. Tomfoolery, not to mention assault, had no place in the world he was trying to create for us, and instinctively everyone knew that. If nothing else, we all recognized MacFarland's considerable intelligence and respected the hours he put into his work. It came to this: The troublemaker would look foolish rather than daring. Even Jim Fitzsimmons was reading *On the Road* and turning his incipient alcoholism to literary ends.

There were some lives that were already beyond Jack MacFarland's ministrations, but mine was not. I started reading again as I hadn't since elementary school. I would go into our gloomy little bedroom or sit at the dinner table while, on the television, Danny McShane was paralyzing Mr. Moto with the atomic drop, and work slowly back through *Heart of Darkness,* trying to catch the words in Conrad's sentences. I certainly was not MacFarland's best student; most of the other guys in College Prep, even my fellow slackers, had better backgrounds than I did. But I worked very hard, for MacFarland had hooked me. He tapped my old interest in reading and creating stories. He gave me a way to feel special by using my mind. And he provided a role model that wasn't shaped on physical prowess alone, and something inside me that

I wasn't quite aware of responded to that. Jack MacFarland established a literacy club, to borrow a phrase of Frank Smith's, and invited me—invited all of us—to join.

There's been a good deal of research and speculation suggesting that the acknowledgment of school performance with extrinsic rewards—smiling faces, stars, numbers, grades—diminishes the intrinsic satisfaction children experience by engaging in reading or writing or problem solving. While it's certainly true that we've created an educational system that encourages our best and brightest to become cynical grade collectors and, in general, have developed an obsession with evaluation and assessment, I must tell you that venal though it may have been, I loved getting good grades from MacFarland. I now know how subjective grades can be, but then they came tucked in the back of essays like bits of scientific data, some sort of spectroscopic readout that said, objectively and publicly, that I had made something of value. I suppose I'd been mediocre for too long and enjoyed a public redefinition. And I suppose the workings of my mind, such as they were, had been private for too long. My linguistic play moved into the world; like the intergalactic stories I told years before on Frank's berry-splattered truck bed, these papers with their circled, red B-pluses and A-minuses linked my mind to something outside it. I carried them around like a club emblem.

• • •

# Race, Class, and Gender and Abandoned Dreams

*Carl A. Grant and Christine E. Sleeter*

• • •

## Student Culture and the Abandonment of Dreams

Our title suggests that the students [in the study] once had optimistic dreams of making it—finishing high school and possibly further education, getting a good job, making their families proud, and achieving personal satisfaction—and they slowly abandoned those dreams. To a large extent, this is true. What the title does not delineate, however, is what their dreams were, and why they were abandoned. First we will examine the students' dreams for education and work beyond high school. Then we will examine the effect of the school, the family, and the economy on their dreams. Finally their personal identities, and their view of the world in which they lived, will be considered before making a summary assessment.

## High School and Further Education

(9th grade, April 1981)

From 1979 to 1986, Carl Grant and Christine Sleeter followed the progress through junior high and high school of 24 students from lower-middle-class, racially diverse backgrounds.

Reprinted from *Teachers College Record* 90 (1988): 19–40, by permission of Teachers College, Columbia University.

ANNA: All the kids in our family who have graduated went on to vocational schools and I want to go to college.
R: What do you want to be?
ANNA: A lawyer.

(11th grade, May 1983)
R: What do you plan to do when you graduate?
ANNA: Go to the technical vocational institute.
R: What influenced you to make these plans?
ANNA: Well, I work at _____ Publishing, and they have word processing, so I'll take up that.
R: Is that what you would like to do most?
ANNA: Not really. I'd rather be a lawyer, but right now I can't afford to go to school.

(9th grade, March 1979)
R: You still want to be a lawyer, right?
HAZEL: Yeah, but I'm not sure, it's kind of one of my dreams. [It was a dream she talked about with us all year.]

(12th grade, May 1982)
R: What do you think about doing [next month when you graduate]?
HAZEL: Well, I think about dancing. I don't know if I should go to college right away and start that, or take dramatic

arts and communication. . . . And I just kinda want to dance for a year or something . . .

R: You've changed your mind since I talked to you last.

HAZEL: Yeah. That's true, it was law. I kinda gave up on law, I didn't think I had the brains for it.

The students voiced a variety of career goals over the time they were interviewed. Goals they discussed with interest included: lawyer (3 students), teacher (1), professional athlete (2), medical technologist (1), doctor (3), veterinarian (1), computer scientist (1), military (6), mechanic (4), truck driver (1), disc jockey (1), model (2), secretary (2), stewardess (3), beautician (1), and police officer (1). The numbers add up to more than twenty-four because most students changed their minds at least once, or toyed with alternatives. Their degree of conviction about these goals varied, but none of the twenty-four was without some goal.

College was a more immediate concern to many, since their career goals would require college. We asked the students in every interview about career goals and college. Since college is increasingly the "one important escalator" on the "elevation of a people," we will discuss their responses in detail.

While in junior high (eighth and ninth grades), thirteen of the twenty-four students said they definitely planned to attend college. Only one said definitely no to college; the rest (10) were undecided. The white students tended to voice about the same assurance as others about college: five of the eight white students definitely planned to attend college, and six of the eleven Hispanic students were definite, with two more discussing professional career goals without specifically discussing college. Of these thirteen, seven were girls and six were boys.

By the end of their senior year, however, only three of the thirteen who said they definitely had college plans were heading for a four-year college, and one dropped out his freshman year. What happened to the other twenty-one students? Three entered a community college and five planned to enroll in a vocational-technical institute; two of these were part of the thirteen who earlier planned on college, and two more had considered college rather briefly in high school. Three were flirting with the military, one viewing it as a possible career and two hoping to earn money for college. Four more graduated, but were still unsure of plans and talked of taking a "year off." Six did not graduate. Two of these took jobs as mechanics, a goal both had discussed with some interest since junior high; one is now working in a restaurant, a few credits shy of his diploma; one is working and living with her boyfriend; we lost track of one; and one dropped out of a school to which he was transferred, was shot on a city street, and now is a quadriplegic in a wheelchair.

What did students say about reasons for their decisions? This can best be answered by providing two representative examples.

Carmen's goals in junior high were very indefinite, although college was a possibility. For Christmas in ninth grade, her father gave her a typewriter. Her parents, both from Puerto Rico, had not graduated from high school, and saw secretarial work as a good employment opportunity for Carmen. In tenth grade she started taking clerical courses, receiving encouragement from her business teacher and talking about becoming a legal secretary. By eleventh grade she was thinking about community college to take legal secretarial courses, and reported that her accounting and shorthand teachers were very supportive. By her senior year, Carmen was sick of school—boy problems and boring classwork. She wanted just to work for a while—"business, they always need people like clerical workers and stuff." She felt her summer job in a company plus her business courses in high school had prepared her well enough to be a secretary. She simply wanted to be away from the hassles of school.

Larry's four older brothers were in the military, and while in junior high he figured he would follow suit, although he had not yet given it much thought. In tenth grade he was trying to take some of the harder courses because counselors had said these would help for college, although he was not too sure about college. Money was the main obstacle:

I know college will be maybe third [choice], after the service and going to a voc. tech.—'cause it's a lot of money. And I ain't got a lot of money. . . . Money just keeps going up and up! So a lot of people find different ways to get around it. Through the service you can get the same schooling for, you know, free.

During his senior year, Larry said he wanted to be a disk jockey. He knew people who had tried and one who made it. If that failed, he did not know; he felt his opportunities to be restricted by his lack of money for college, the unemployment rate, and the poor quality of his secondary schooling. We quote at length because he articulated well the frustration most of our sample felt:

LARRY: Every year there's a scarcity of finding jobs. All over the place. . . . If you go to college and have, like, four years, when you get out, there's gotta be something. . . . If you can't get a job, you just wasted a lot of time and a lot of money.

R: But many colleges say they usually place 60, 70, 80 percent of their people.

LARRY: Yeah, but there's always a chance that you ain't that 70, 80 percent that's gonna get a job. . . . If you're not a part of that percentage that

*does* get placed, say like me—I'm not a top quality guy in school. I don't think I could handle college right now. I mean, you get a lot of homework, and I haven't had homework for three years now in this school!

Most of the students felt that they were freely making their own choices about their futures. However, they were making choices within a particular set of social institutions: the school, the family, and the local economy in the community.

## The School

The school can best be described as taking a laissez-faire stand—some resources for college preparation were there, but it was left up to the individual, for the most part, to take advantage of them. In junior high, the academic demand made of students was fairly light; we have described this in detail elsewhere. Most classes gave easy work and no homework; the main person to talk seriously with students about their futures was a counselor who had grown up in the community. When students entered tenth grade, most said that the work was much harder. They were taking academic courses required for graduation (typically English, social studies, math, science, and two electives), and many were receiving homework (typically two or three times per week in math and science). Students also said that teachers explained or helped students with the work less, and expected them to figure it out more on their own. Students did not complain much about any of this—they described the high school as treating them more "grown up."

After tenth grade, things changed. We will describe the changes in relationship to three different categories of students. One category consisted of those who entered college or community college after graduation—

six students. These students continued to take demanding courses until they graduated (except one who had a half day of work/study his senior year), and continued to have some homework. These might be thought of as the college-bound, in that their teachers treated them as if they were bound for college. However, it was often not the school that advised them which courses to take; it was often friends and family who had been to college and knew what preparation was needed. These students made the following kinds of comments about the counseling they received in high school:

(Senior Year)

R:    What did [the counselors] tell you that made you take Chemistry and Physics:

LIN-SU: They didn't tell me anything. I just decided.

R:    Did you know that those kinds of things are good for you to have if you're going to go to college?

LIN-SU: Yeah, that's why I took them.

R:    Who told you you should be taking them in order to go to college?

LIN-SU: Some of my teachers. My mom and dad. And my older sister—she's going to college and she took those classes.

(Junior Year)

R:    Why are you taking so many academic courses?

RAKIA: Mm, I don't know. I don't really like gym. I just like classes where you can sit and do your work [History, French, Algebra-Trig., Computers, Biology]. . . .

R:    Has anyone told you that you need the math and the algebra and science courses in order to go to college and become a doctor?

RAKIA: Yeah, my advisor. They usually ask you, "What do you plan to do after

high school?" I said, "Go to college." And they said, "O.K., you need a lot of math and English and stuff like science."

R:    Are most of your friends planning to go to college?

RAKIA: . . . Sandra, she wants to be a veterinarian.

R:    Is she taking courses like yours?

RAKIA: Not at all. . . . I don't think she really talks to people about what she's going to do.

(Senior Year)

RAKIA: I don't like the counselor. 'Cause instead of boosting up, he'll kinda put you down. He said that I wouldn't get in _____ College with my test scores. But I did. . . . I just got the letter back [from the college] that just proved him wrong.

The picture that emerged was that around tenth grade, counselors asked students what they planned to do after graduation. If they said "college," they were advised to take more math and science; three girls told us counselors "made" them stick with math and science at that point. After that, students seemed to be on their own. Some of their teachers told them which classes to take, and they got advice from counselors if they purposely sought it, but most of the advice they got came from outside the school.

A second group of five students consisted of those who were fairly certain they would become secretaries or mechanics. Little academic demand was placed on them in school. They were advised into secretarial or autoshop courses, and felt the school was helping them in that sense. These students reported getting advice and being made to work and think in their vocational classes. The other thirteen—the largest group— floated through with only minimal demands made on them after tenth grade. Several thought they were going to college, others were unsure. Either way, it appeared that no one in the school seriously thought they were headed for college; the school took steps mainly to help them fit into the blue-collar labor market. These students reported having little or no homework. Their senior English class was aimed, in one student's words, at "trying to make sure that our grammar's right." Their course schedules were filled with electives such as ceramics, office helper, bookstore worker, chorus, and gym; during their senior year several participated in half-day on-the-job training programs. They reported that virtually no one in the school talked to them about the future; they were free to select their own courses, and counselors did not talk to them unless they sought the counselors out. There was not even much attempt to let students know what information might be available through the counselors, so few students voluntarily went to ask; one pointed out that counselors "gotta let you know that it's there [information about a college], for you to come and see, you know."

By their senior year, many of these students were bitter, and many were simply bored with school. For example, one who took the easy way through told us the following, one month before graduating.

R:      You went through easy.
PABLO: Yeah.
R:      Do you ever regret that now?
PABLO: Yeah, 'cause—I feel like I coulda learned more if I went, if I took some harder classes. . . . There's a lot of kids that just, they're smart, but they just take easy classes and not, you know, they're not learning nothing. Once you get into senior high, you don't even have to take math, you know, not at all.

Their experience with school, and particularly the last two years, left many ambivalent about any future schooling: On the one hand, it would help them, but on the other hand it would probably be boring and they were not prepared for it. Some blamed the school for being too lax, others blamed themselves.

We wondered whether the school offered any other kinds of opportunities for learning how to "make it" in society, such as leadership development. We looked for this in our study of the junior high, and examined interviews from the senior high for comments. We found very little. The student council was one avenue for developing leadership skills; one of our sample had been president of the junior high student body, another was senior class president. Even here, however, student leadership did not seem to be taken seriously. The student council did not have authority over anything very important or consequential, and the senior class president spent half of her senior year in on-the-job training. One social studies teacher made a concerted effort to involve his students in school and community political events, but his singular effort did not seem to make a great impact on the students. The only other comment we found related to leadership development—and it is a weak one at that—was a shy student commenting that English classes that require students to make speeches had helped her learn to speak up more.

## The Family

The family was a second institution within which students constructed perceptions of their futures.

R:      How do your parents feel about you going to school in general?

ALVIN: They want me to finish school and get a good education and get good grades, too.

This comment illustrates the way these students' parents felt about school achievement. Discussions with counselors, teachers, administrators, and students on this topic were of one kind: Parents sent their kids to school to learn and expected them not to fool around while learning was going on. Parents were very supportive of the school and left their children's education, guidance, and course selection almost solely in school's hands. We have reason to assume that because most of the parents had not attended college, and were familiar mostly with traditional blue- and pink-collar jobs, they were reluctant to give career advice or to lobby strongly for a certain course selection if they believed the school had endorsed their child's program. There were a few exceptions. For example, Ron's father and uncle were mechanics and encouraged him to follow suit. During the study his goal did not change. Notice his comment in his sophomore year.

R:      What do you want to do when you graduate?
RON:   My Dad tells me I should be a mechanic 'cause he is.

Ron left school in his junior year and is now working as a mechanic.

Juan, who early in the study said he wanted to be a doctor, often spoke of receiving advice from his uncle, who was a doctor, as to which courses to take and the need to work really hard in school in order to achieve the goal.

Since most of the students did not have homework on a regular basis, parents did not set up home study hours or have identifiable opportunities to discuss schoolwork with their children. The role that the parents played in helping their children fulfill their

academic expectations was very small. Besides helping with homework, several ways to help children in academics include providing them with experiences such as museums, plays, and travel, and reading books, magazines, and newspapers. Most students when asked reported doing very little of the above either with parents or alone.

## The Economy

The local economy was a third institution within which the students constructed beliefs about their future. One important characteristic of the local economy was that neither the students nor their parents had extra money for things like college. This was, in fact, the main barrier to college cited by students. Many also discussed ways of dealing with it. The students' perception of reality may have been limited and even inaccurate, but it was based on available information and guided their behavior.

"Taking a year off" to work was an alternative several mentioned. None laid out a specific plan for doing this, but several felt they needed to work to save some money before they could go to college. Six students were more specific about how they would finance further education: They would join the military and either save their pay for college later, or receive their education "free" while in the military. They based this plan on talks given by military recruiters who came to the senior high school. Few students mentioned loans or scholarships for college. We asked them about this in interviews, and they had very little knowledge of this option—it was as if the option did not exist; no one had talked to most of them about it.

Another feature of the local economy that students perceived was the relatively high unemployment rate. It made students feel uncertain about the future, and caused several to view four years of college with some skepticism. Although Rakia, for example, enrolled in a community college, she said about the unemployment situation: "I'm kinda worried about it. I don't have a job right now, but that doesn't bother me. But it does worry me because when I get out of college I don't know what the situation's gonna be like." Other students were more worried about having a job right now, and felt some sense of security if they had at least their summer job or were involved in on-the-job-training. The unemployment situation made it risky to give up a job, expect financial support from parents, or incur debt to secure further schooling.

Students' career goals were wide-ranging, but their knowledge of the job market was based on jobs they or their parents actually held. Several distinguished between dreams and reality: One could dream of what one would like to do, but one would have to settle for a job that is really there, and that one can really get. Students commented about their own job experience:

R:      What do you plan to do when you graduate? [Earlier goal had been veterinarian.]
LINDA:  I'm going on to the technical-vocational institute. I'm either gonna take computers, or data processing, office fields, general accounting, or accounting.
R:      What influenced you to do that?
LINDA:  I work in 3M, in general accounting, so I'd like to get a job there.
R:      Oh. How'd you get the job at 3M?
LINDA:  Through on-the-job-training.
R:      Do you think about the current unemployment rate at all?
LINDA:  Yes! I'll probably end up being one of them if I don't get some training to keep my job.

Finally, we must consider the peer group itself. When we met the students in junior high school, we were struck by the strong division in their lives between school and the rest of the day. Most of their classwork was boring, but school could be tolerated from 8:00 A.M. to 2:30 P.M. After that, it could be forgotten, especially since few had homework. Students spent their free time either at home, playing sports, or "hanging around" with each other. They cared about passing their classes, but few cared which passing grade they received. It was considered neither "in" nor "out" to be smart—this was viewed in the peer group as irrelevant. Since high school did not offer much change, the peer group did not change much. Students spent less time playing and more time in jobs, but no more time with schoolwork. They became used to investing a prescribed number of hours in a work-type setting, and enjoying the rest of the day in social activities. This life-style fit the demands placed on them. The students also used each other as sources of information about future plans, quite possibly more than they used the counselors. Thus, their perceptions were widely shared, both because students encountered similar experiences and because they helped each other make sense of their futures.

## Personal Identities and View of the World

We wondered how the students viewed their identities as members of particular racial, social-class, and gender groups, and how they viewed the position of those groups in society. We were interested in the extent to which the students embraced the strengths offered by group membership without being constrained by social stereotypes or stigmas, and the extent to which their understanding of oppression developed, if at all. We also wondered what effect views of race, class, and gender had on their dreams. We learned about their personal and group identities by asking about their neighborhood, their views of each other, their views about cultural practices within the home, and their views about choices they made for themselves. We learned about their understanding of racism, classism, and sexism by asking them directly about these things.

## Race and Ethnicity

The students identified culturally with their community. The community was composed of working-class people of varied ethnic backgrounds, but the students viewed them as culturally all "the same." Households varied somewhat in menu, religion, strictness, and so forth, but the students did not see the various ethnic groups in the community as culturally distinct from one another. To the students, a distinguishing feature of their community was the fact that the people were different colors—this was positive, and students talked openly and eagerly about it. Culturally, however, they were not different from one another. Over the time of this study, we saw no change in this pattern.

What fascinated us was the extent to which many students disagreed with their parents on this. Several of their parents had moved from elsewhere (such as Puerto Rico, Egypt, Texas, Mexico), and saw different ethnic groups as culturally different. Some of the parents who had lived in the community a long time also saw them as different. These parents tended to want their children to date and marry members of their own ethnic group and some tried to discourage them from associating in any way with a particular ethnic group. The students did not see it this way, for the most part, and some argued with their parents about it. To the students, interracial dating and marriage were completely acceptable because color did not matter.

A few students commented on their parents' wanting them to retain their ethnic culture. Some saw this as important, but also saw no conflict between it and marrying someone of another ethnic group. Others did not see it as particularly important. For example, two Mexican-American students whose parents were from Texas told us they were not interested in learning Spanish, even though their parents wanted them to do so.

The students' acceptance of racial diversity seemed almost to interfere with their developing an understanding of racism. Only about half of the students believed any form of racism exists in society, and examples they described were, with two exceptions, individual prejudice. For example, a Mexican-American girl said that the students in an all-white school had said they were having an "invasion" when she visited there; a white girl said some of the police were racially prejudiced. A few students described their parents as racially prejudiced, but the only generalization they offered was that times have changed and younger people are not prejudiced any more. Students saw most prejudice away from the community; the main examples of prejudice in the community were offered by a Puerto Rican and an Arab-American (both of whom said people lumped them together with Mexicans, which they resented), and a Vietnamese-American, who commented on prejudice against newly arrived Hmongs.

Only two students attempted to describe institutional racism. One Mexican-American boy said that "just about everything is for white people," explaining that television, for example, is all white. A white boy explained that whites are upper class and Mexicans are lower class because Mexicans have not been able to afford college and therefore do not get good jobs.

The students of color had, as a group, no more understanding of racism than the white students. Nine of the sixteen students of color believed some racial prejudice exists in society as did four of the eight white students, but the explanations or understanding of prejudice offered by the students of color were no more informed than were those of the white students. Since most students had not experienced overt discrimination in the community and many of the students had not ventured very far outside the community, they assumed race relations in society are similar to race relations in that community. Neither school nor parents taught them much about racism beyond what they experienced. One teacher in the junior high taught about it and a few students mentioned this while in junior high, but seemed to forget it in high school since the race relations where they lived were positive. We did not study their parents directly to find out what they taught about race relations, but the main thing students ever said about their parents was whether parents were prejudiced against their friends.

## Social Class

Students defined themselves as middle class (with the exception of one who said her family was poor, and one who said his was upper middle class). They said they were middle class because, in the words of one student, "We don't make a lot, but then we still have enough to make ends meet." Earlier we described the community as working class but as having two neighborhoods differentiated by racial composition and somewhat by income level; to most of the students, it was all one middle-class community.

The students generated this common self-definition on the basis of several interrelated factors. Geographically, the community was cut off by a river from most of the rest of the city, and residents tended not to venture out. The range of incomes in the community was not great, and the schools served the entire community from kindergarten through graduation. Thus, the students grew up together, and associated with others who shared their economic circumstances, their neighborhood, their school. Lacking much firsthand contact with people of diverse social classes, they figured they were middle class since few lived in poverty but none had much money for luxuries.

Their knowledge of the social class structure in society was very thin, even after taking Sociology in high school, in which social class was a topic they studied. When we asked students about social class, we often had to explain what we meant, and even then students sometimes did not know how to respond. Students believed anyone could achieve upward mobility by hard work, getting a good education, and—two girls said—marriage. Most students did not want to move up; a white boy said he would like more money but wanted to stay in the same community, and a few others suggested this.

## Gender and Sexism

Students' gender self-definitions were more complex and less shared. The patterns we will describe only very roughly follow ethnic group membership, with the Hispanic students tending slightly more than whites to adhere to traditional gender identities. All students saw themselves as potential job-holders regardless of sex. Students believed both sexes could hold almost any job, although several ruled out construction for women (they lack the strength) and child care for men (men lack patience). Their aspirations tended to follow sex-stereotypic patterns, particularly as they approached graduation. The aspiring mechanics, truck drivers, and professional football players were male; the aspiring secretaries, stewardesses, and models were female—but the girls also envisioned themselves as lawyers, doctors, and computer technologists, at least until they confronted the problem of paying for college.

Students identified males more than females as providers, and this increased as they got older. Before they started dating, providing was not an issue—when same-sex groups went out, sex did not determine who initiated or paid. Dating changed this. Six of the boys from the time they started dating expected to initiate dates and pay for them, although most were flexible about who could initiate phone calls. By their senior year, the three who graduated, plus a fourth who had not dated much, saw themselves as providers for their future families—their wives *could* work but would not have to, especially if there were children. One boy initially advocated flexible roles, but by his senior year he was paying for all his dates, and referred to a wife's paycheck as "extra money." Interestingly, only two of these eight boys had a firm career goal in mind all during the study; the rest were unsure what they would do. Five of the girls, by high school, also saw the male as the main provider: Their boyfriends initiated and paid for dates, and they expected the man to be the main family breadwinner. This was a relationship they seemed to learn partly through dating; one had offered to pay for dates but the offer was turned down; others thought hypothetically that girls could pay but knew boys preferred it the other way around. Two of these five girls earlier expressed a strong career orientation, but by their senior year were uncertain about their futures. One of them entertained the idea of herself as provider and her husband staying at home, but did not expect this. A sixth girl saw the male as the main provider but was also preparing for a good career in computer science.

On the other hand, three girls and one boy definitely saw initiating and providing as shared responsibilities, and had worked this out in date relationships. Two more girls expressed ambivalence about providing: They questioned but did not reject outright traditional dating roles, and saw themselves as career-bound. The remaining four students did not address this issue.

All students but one saw themselves as present and future workers in the home. Most divided chores by sex; the girls wrestled with this more than the boys. Eleven of the twenty-four students expected and preferred to divide domestic chores by sex, and did not debate or question this during the study; four were girls, seven were boys. These tended to be the same students who saw males as providers. Most engaged in these roles at home, although in one boy's home chores were not divided by sex and he thought they should be. Only one boy and two girls completely rejected sex roles at home throughout the study. The two girls were rejecting roles learned at home, and one felt very strongly about this, saying she *hated* it that guys want women to stay in the house.

The other nine students were less certain. Three (1 boy, 2 girls) simply said it depended on whether the wife holds a job; if she does, they would expect to divide chores fifty-fifty. Four more students (1 boy, 3 girls) questioned domestic roles while in junior high, two girls having been angry about how chores were divided at home; but by their senior year all three of these girls seemed content to adopt traditional sex roles. Two more girls wanted to divide things fifty-fifty, but did not expect a man to go along with that.

Students justified role definition primarily based on masculine strength. Eleven students maintained that boys are the stronger sex, and therefore better in sports and heavy work; five disagreed, and two girls changed their minds on this during the study. What was particularly interesting was that approximately equal proportions of both sexes defined themselves as athletic, but many boys, and the girls as they got older, defined boys as naturally stronger and more athletic than girls.

With respect to sexism in society, students knew very little. They saw equal opportunity in the work place as an accomplished fact, with the exception of one girl who knew a woman who had filed a sex-discrimination grievance. The fact that many jobs are not sex-balanced was attributed mainly to individual choice or to ability to do the job. Several girls wrestled for a short period with sexism at home, but they saw this as a personal rather than a collective struggle, or as something women simply have to put up with. For example, one girl complained that men like to be outside until mealtime, and expect to come in and find dinner ready; this was an inconvenient male characteristic more than an arena for struggle. In fact, as students matured, they tended more and more to accept rather than resist sex-divided domestic work roles and supporting sex stereotypes. The only social issue any of the students discussed was whether women should fight in the military. Three boys brought this up, arguing that if women want equal rights they should be willing to fight in combat. This issue was being debated in the news, and seemed to be one of concern to boys who had considered entering the military.

The students generated gender self-definitions and their understandings of social relations between the sexes on the basis of several factors. A major one was observation. For example, a boy commented that girls must prefer sewing to cars because he had never seen roles switched, although another said girls in his autoshop class demonstrated that girls could be mechanical. As another example, a girl commented that she had seen traditional sex roles at home all her life. A related factor was doing: All but one student had chores at home, and most became used to and comfortable with those they were assigned, although a few rebelled against them. The local economy seemed to reinforce students' observations—girls were hired as babysitters and typists, boys as outdoor laborers, paper carriers, janitors, and mechanics. The school was a laissez-faire factor. It made available all courses and activities to both sexes, enabling many girls to develop an interest in sports, but hardly anyone in school (or at home), with the exception of one or two teachers, discussed gender or sexism. So students who questioned or rebelled against roles or expectations had to work these through themselves, and they tended to resolve them in favor of the status quo. A final, very important factor was the peer group itself. When students began to think about courtship, they began to shape their behavior and expectations in a way that would complement expectations of the opposite sex. The boys had fewer questions about role and gender-identity, and the girls tended to resolve their own questions by accepting the boys' definitions. This facilitated courtship, although it also tended to help reproduce existing gender relations.

## Discussion

This study has shown, particularly because it was longitudinal, that race, class, and gender relations in society are not reproduced simply because the young absorb and inherit the status and beliefs of their parents. It is a more complex process than this. As the young work through their dreams and questions in a particular context, the range of possibilities that seem open and real to them gradually narrows and tends to mirror the lives of their parents. The culture the young construct from the fabric of everyday life provides a set of answers and a sense of certainty for their questions and dreams. To the extent that everyday life embodies unequal social relationships, the culture students generate and regenerate over time gradually accepts and "explains" existing social relationships. The process may appear inevitable, but it is not. We will argue that at least part of the context within which the young grow up can be changed (the school), and can propel them in directions that diverge from the status quo. The school can be the key catalyst in this process. Unfortunately, in our study it did not perform this function well.

Let us review the students' dreams, particularly while they were in junior high and saw their futures as relatively open. In junior high, the students visualized themselves in a wide variety of career roles, unrestricted by race, social class, or, for the girls, gender. Over half aspired to college and only one rejected it. Their dreams of careers and college were, in fact, quite different from the lives of their parents. Elsewhere we have noted that this was particularly true for the girls, whose career goals tended to be more ambitious than those of the boys. In junior high, students seemed to adopt portions of the lives of adults around them that they liked (such as mechanical arts for those who liked working with their hands) and reject that which they did not like (such as housework for those girls who had become fed up with it).

The culture students generated out of everyday life, however, tended to hold them in their community and return them to lives very much like their parents'. One feature of everyday life they discussed often was their racial diversity. The students generated a common culture among themselves that transcended race. Many of their parents had also done this; others, particularly those who had grown up elsewhere, had not. Rather

than adopting their parents' racism, however, the students resisted it. Their own daily experience with each other convinced them that racism was incorrect. It also tended to convince them that their own community was the best place to live. They frequently told us that schools or neighborhoods of one race would be dull, uninteresting. The students' common culture that transcended race was like a magnet keeping them in their community, and also keeping them somewhat ignorant of race relations in the broader society. The student culture did not recognize institutional racism; individual prejudice was the main manifestation of racism that the students saw in their daily lives.

The culture students generated out of everyday life was also nonacademic. Students believed in school and valued education, seeing it as a route to their dreams, but on a day-to-day basis, they invested minimal effort in it. Unwittingly, in fact, they played a role in limiting their academic empowerment, in that they never actively resisted the school's low demand of them. In junior high, for example, they recognized that homework demands were light, and several said they thought they should get more homework, but they did nothing about this. We found it interesting to contrast this with students' active resistance toward parents' racism. Why did the students resist their parents' racism but not the school's low expectations of them? Their everyday experience taught them that their parents were wrong, and that racism would interfere with enjoyment of daily life. (Mexicans aren't lazy because my friend Diego isn't lazy, and if I avoided Diego, I'd lose a good buddy.) Students' everyday experience with school taught them that it was boring and that the content was irrelevant to daily life. It may be important for attaining a career goal, but if the medicine is bitter, why ask for more than the doctor prescribes, especially if more time devoted to school would lessen time with friends? So the students accepted minimal homework and a low involvement with classwork, and developed other interests and behavior patterns, centering largely around sports, that filled their time and probably would have caused them to resist a sudden increase in school work (a "what if" they never faced).

The students generated a distorted version of social class, which they used to help answer questions about college as well as goals in general. The inaccuracies and distortions in their beliefs were striking. They believed themselves to be middle class, and when asked many said they did not want to move up in the class structure, particularly if it meant moving away from the community. A white male student put it as follows: "I'd like to probably move upward in money, but not out of the neighborhood." Students seemed to believe middle-class people cannot afford college these days, and since jobs are limited, it is better to get a job now than take a chance that one will find a job after college. They did not seem to see college as improving their chance of obtaining a job, only as opening doors to certain kinds of jobs. The students did not seem to see a great difference in the pay and power that accrue from different occupations. They believed hard work was the best route to upward mobility; the role capital plays in the economy seemed completely unknown. Finally, they seemed to believe that race and gender have nothing to do with one's place in the economic structure. While this belief encouraged them to aspire to any career, it also produced false insights into opportunities available to them. Ultimately, the main beneficiaries of students' beliefs would be local employers: The student culture helped produce workers who were fairly content with their lot and willing to work hard to maintain their lives.

Everyday life with friends and family provided considerable material for generating an understanding of gender. Most homes placed the young in a sex-divided domestic work role from an early age. This was a role that few of the boys seriously questioned, probably because they grew up in it and it provided routes to attaining some status: being strong, supporting a family, taking a lead in courtship. The boys had experienced only part of this role; supporting a family, which eventually could be difficult for them, was not yet a reality. The girls raised more questions about the female role, mainly when they found themselves working while their brothers played outside. Regardless of ethnic background, at one time or another most girls believed it to be unfair and demeaning. There were rewards to adhering to a traditional female role: dates, especially with the popular boys; harmonious relationships at home; and admiration achievable through fashion. Students' questions about gender were never used to help them understand sexism. Thus, they answered their own questions by generating stereotypes (boys are just stronger than girls), accepting things as inevitable (men are just like that, nothing you can do about it), and interpreting conflicts as individual rather than collective. Many resolved the question of dividing labor by sex by insisting that both partners in a marriage should do as much work, even though the work is different. We stress that there appeared to be little or no relationship between ethnicity and the questions the girls raised. The Hispanic homes were more likely to adhere to traditional sex roles than the white homes, but Hispanic girls were just as likely to question their role—temporarily, at any rate—as were white girls raised in traditional homes.

That portion of the context of students' lives that could be changed most readily was the school. In fact, the school had a very important role to play in students' abandonment of their dreams. The school staff, much more so than the parents or the students themselves, knew how the education system works—what kind of preparation is needed for college, how to obtain scholarships and loans, what the differences are between a four-year college degree and job training in the military, and so forth. They also knew more than the students about social class, race relations, and gender. Let us first consider their abdication of the job for which they were hired: promoting academic learning.

In spite of students' interest in further education, in spite of their good behavior in school, and in spite of the fact that the majority had normal learning ability, both the junior and senior high school faculty (with the exception of a very few individuals) accepted students' failure to empower themselves through education, and in so doing, ensured that they would fail. This was particularly true after the tenth grade. Prior to the tenth grade students were required to take academic courses to meet graduation requirements. While few of these courses rigorously challenged them, at least to a limited degree students were receiving an education. After tenth grade two things happened: The students started raising serious questions about their futures (a major one being whether they could afford college) and the school pulled out of their lives as much as it could, expending its academic energies on only those few who for one reason or another continued to take the more difficult classes. For the majority of the students, advising virtually ceased once graduation requirements had been met, and any homework they might have had in the tenth grade came to an end. The school's main effort became equipping them to take a minimum-wage job after graduation. The school staff may have viewed it as inevitable that these students would not continue schooling—interviews with the junior high teachers found strong acceptance of this belief—but there was no inevitability here; the school actively helped it to happen.

• • •

# Empty Chairs:
## What Happens to Students Who Don't Go to College
*Martin Kramer*

If expected guests do not show up at a dinner party, the host may react variously. The reaction may be irritation, hurt feelings, or worry. Have the guests been in an accident? Have they lost their way? Has an opportunity come up that is so urgent they can think of nothing else?

A good many likely guests are not showing up at the higher education banquet, and the Grant Foundation Commission on Youth and America's Future has been doing some of our worrying for us. Its report is entitled *The Forgotten Half,* itself a half-misnomer: young people who do not go on to college indeed tend to be forgotten when programs are devised and funded. They are not forgotten, however, but reported in our newspapers every day, when their problems become our national problems of low productivity, dependency, and overtaxed social services.

The good news is that most noncollege youth are working: the great bulk of them are either finishing school or in the labor force. The bad news is that working is not getting them ahead. The average constant-dollar earnings of men aged 20 to 24 fell by a

Martin Kramer is editor-in-chief of *New Directions in Higher Education.*

*Change* 21 (January–February 1989): 6–7. Reprinted with permission of the Helen Dwight Reid Educational Foundation. Published by Heldref Publications, 4000 Albemarle St., N. W., Washington, D.C. 20016. Copyright © 1989.

quarter from 1973 to 1986. The proportion able to support a family of three above the poverty level fell from over half to under half.

One of the reasons why the economic return from gaining a bachelor's degree has risen this decade is that this is a *relative* figure; it has risen, in part, because those who do not go to college are earning less.

There has not been much structure to forestall this decline. The amounts spent by public treasuries are minute compared with what is spent on college students. For the most part, high school graduates who do not go on to college are simply cut adrift in a world of casual career choices and often scandalous trade schools. For many, it must be pretty lonely and scary out there. Look at recruiting for the armed forces: it emphasizes that someone will be there to invest in your future, that there will be something to belong to, and a path to be on. That must sound pretty appealing.

The situation would be much, much worse but for the training—and, yes, education—employers provide out of their obvious interest in worker productivity. The employer incentive can be great in periods of very low unemployment, such as the present. The trouble is that the incentive tends to be much reduced when unemployment is high. The business cycle aside, it is weaker in industries where workers carry most of the skills they acquire out the door with them when they change jobs, or where the skills employers want can readily be taught and convincingly credentialed by formal educational institutions. In either case, employers would rather the employee—or someone else—bear the cost of investment in human capital. We deceive ourselves if we think this calculus is changing desirably and consistently for all occupations just because it appears to be changing for some in a period of low unemployment.

The bleakness of the general picture drawn by the commission gives new life to the debate of the 1960s about how nearly universal we want higher education to be. The debate seemed to become moot in the 1970s. An overeducated labor force came to be seen as just as real a possibility as an undereducated one because returns from a college education declined for a while. Besides, it was pointed out that more education could not, for youth as a whole, be *both* a means to greater equality of income and to social mobility at the same time. Anyway, many of the additional college entrants seemed to have great difficulty in making much of college opportunities.

But can the debate be moot when not going to college turns out to be so prejudicial?

If the debate is to be resumed, it will be best to do without the extravagant assumption that college is good for all young people and would be chosen by all if they only knew. A great merit of the commission's report lies in emphasizing that those who drop out of formal education do not drop out of life. Almost all of them are trying to make something of their lives, but in a great variety of circumstances. Many are well organized, even academically competent. They have just decided to do something else: fortunately, for the rest of us if we ever want to encounter a first-rate me-

chanic or technician again. The National Longitudinal Study (NLS) and the High School and Beyond (HSB) surveys (of the high school classes of 1972 and 1980) identify a considerable pocket of highly talented young men who do not go to college. They are young men in the next to highest quartile of academic ability and in the next to lowest socioeconomic quartile. In other words, they are neither so bright that their teachers will push them into going to college or so socially slotted that their parents will. Fifty-eight percent of them did not go to college in 1972, and 51 percent did not in 1980. Some of these young men had found work they loved and were good at, and that should always be ground for social rejoicing. Others had simply found where their economic advantage lay: a good many of them probably saw themselves in line to inherit a farm or a small business or a union card that would make academic credentials financially irrelevant.

The point, then, is not that society loses the talents of young people who do not go on to college, but that it tends to underinvest in those talents. Higher education must come to terms with the fact that it is the principal vehicle of public investment in the country's young adults—and perhaps of private investment also. The student who does not enroll, the student who drops out, the student who fails to make good use of what is available is quite likely not going to be given much by any other system for investing in the individual's skills. The marginal student stands at the margin of a cliff.

The commission's report lists the many, many ways our society could arrange matters better for noncollege youth, but does not. Some of them are innovations; some are, in effect, restorations of attitudes, opportunities, and practices that existed before it came to be so widely assumed that all young people who could make something of themselves would go to college.

In its own self-interest, higher education should be concerned that society find other vehicles for providing guidance and investment. Just as mass higher education involved great costs to the structure and quality of higher education itself, so universal higher education—resulting merely from lack of alternatives—would surely have its costs also. We already have some unwilling, ill-served, and frustrated students. Would we not have many more?

Yet the short-run conclusion one must draw is quite different. *As things are,* getting more young people prepared for college and in college is the best option for them and for society. Nowhere else are the resources likely to be made available to invest in their talents, let alone to transmit to them their cultural heritage. We can congratulate the few who have a better invitation. Most do not.

# Five Ways to Wisdom

*Otto Friedrich*

Opening day! In front of the brick dormitory, the dust-streaked family car lurches to a halt with its load of indispensable college supplies: one Sony stereo with headphones, two gooseneck lamps, five pairs of blue jeans, two down parkas (one old, one new), one pair of Rossignol skis . . . and one nervous freshman wondering whether anybody will like him. The older students have an easier time of it, needing only to unpack what they left in storage over the summer: more lamps, more blue jeans, boots, bicycles, one unused thesaurus donated by an out-of-date uncle. . . . And now, from any reopening dormitory window on any campus from Chapel Hill to Santa Cruz, can be heard the thrumming, insistent sound of the contemporary campus: *Tattoo You . . . Vacation . . . Hold Me . . .*

These are the rites of initiation. Orientation meetings on subjects like time management. Tryouts for the glee club or the football team. Beer bashes. Join the struggle to save Lebanon; join the struggle to save Israel. At Princeton the freshmen and sophomores meet each other in a traditional series of games and rope pulls known as Cane

Otto Friedrich is a journalist and writer who works for *Time Magazine*. His books on history and biography include *Before the Deluge: A Portrait of Berlin in the 1920s* and *Clover: The Tragic Love of Clover and Henry Adams.*

Spree, which custom decrees that the freshmen lose. At Gettysburg College, the rituals of getting acquainted are even more folksy: a "shoe scramble" determines who will dance with whom. At Carleton, there is a fried-chicken picnic and square dancing on the grassy area known as the Bald Spot.

Along with the social games, though, a lot of intellectual choices have to be made, courses picked, books bought. Will it be the class known as "Slums and Bums" (Urban Government) or "Nuts and Sluts" (Abnormal Psychology)? The students joke about these things because they know the choices are serious; their future lives depend on them, and so does much else besides. It has been said that every nation has only a few years in which to civilize an onrushing horde of barbarians, its own children.

The barbarian hordes beginning their classes this month may be the largest in U.S. history, a tribute to both parental prodigality and the ideal of universal education. Though the crest of the 1950s baby boom has passed the college years, a larger percentage of high school graduates now goes to college (61%, *vs* 40% a generation ago), and the number of older and part-time students keeps increasing (34% of students are over 25). All in all, the number of Americans who are signing up for some form of higher education this fall totals a mind-boggling 12.5 million. Mind-boggling not only because of the quantity, but because there is very little agreement on what they are learning or should be learning.

Under the dappling elms of Harvard, which likes to think that it sets the national tone in such matters, President Derek Bok traditionally welcomes each graduating class into "the company of educated men and women." The phrase goes trippingly on the tongue, but what does it mean? Does any such community exist? Are the millions of people now engaged in earning diplomas really being educated?

The statistics of growth, unfortunately, are also the statistics of glut. When the 2.4 million college students of 1949 swelled into today's 12.5 million, the educational system was all but overwhelmed. The most prestigious institutions took easy pride in the numbers they turned away, but the states, somewhat idealistically committed to a policy of open admissions, had to double the number of public colleges, from some 600 to more than 1,250. Most of the new schools were two-year community colleges that featured remedial and vocational classes.

The overall quality of education almost inevitably sank. "Every generation since Roman days has decried the weakening of educational standards," sighs one Midwestern university dean, but the statistics provide sad evidence that there has been a genuine decline. Average scores in reading on the Scholastic Aptitude Tests (SATS) have dropped from 466 out of a possible 800 in 1968 to 424 in 1981, when the decline leveled out; mathematics scores over the same period sank from 492 to 466. A study conducted at the University of Wisconsin reported that at least 20% of last year's entering freshmen "lack the skill to write [acceptably] and 50% are not ready to succeed in college algebra."

"They don't know how to write, they don't read, they have little contact with culture," says Professor Norman Land, who teaches art history at the University of Missouri, in a typical complaint. "Every so often

I give them a list of names, and they can identify Timothy Leary or The Who but not Dante or Vivaldi. They haven't received an education: they've just had baby sitting." Nor are the criticisms entirely about intellectual shortcomings. "I think students are becoming less reflective, less concerned about fellow human beings, more greedy, more materialistic," says Alexander Astin, professor of higher education at U. C. L. A. "They're interested in making money and in finding a job that gives them a lot of power and a lot of status."

College officials tend to blame student shortcomings on the high schools, which undeniably need reform and renewal, but the high schools can blame the elementary schools, the elementary schools the family at home, and everybody blames TV. Wisconsin's President Robert O'Neil, however, argues that the colleges are "in part to blame." Says he: "Having diluted the requirements and expectations, they indicated that students could succeed in college with less rigorous preparation." Mark H. Curtis, president of the Association of American Colleges, is more caustic: "We might begin to define the educated person as one who can overcome the deficiencies in our educational system."

The traditional curriculum, such as it was, virtually disintegrated during the campus upheavals of the 1960s, when millions of students demanded and won the right to get academic credit for studying whatever they pleased. There were courses in soap operas and witchcraft. Even more fundamental, and even more damaging, was the spread of the "egalitarian" notion that everybody was entitled to a college degree, and that it was undemocratic to base that degree on any differentiations of intellect or learning. "The idea that cosmetology is just as important as physics is still with us but is being challenged," says Curtis.

"Quality," argues Chester E. Finn Jr., professor of education and public policy at Vanderbilt, "is almost certainly going to turn out to be the foremost national education concern of the 1980s, much as equity was the premier issue of the 1960s and 1970s." The counterrevolution has actually been well under way for some time. In 1978 Harvard announced with great fanfare a controversial new core curriculum, and in 1980 Stanford inaugurated an elaborate system of seven tracks that would carry every student through the basics of Western civilization. "A miracle has happened among Stanford undergraduates," Charles Lyons, director of the Western-culture program, proudly told the faculty senate last spring. "They do talk about Plato at dinner and about Shakespeare on the lawns."

Other colleges followed suit. Amherst now requires all freshmen to take an interdisciplinary program called Introduction to Liberal Studies. At Washington University in St. Louis, the science and math requirements, which were cut in half during the heady days of student power, have been restored to the old levels (four semester-long courses). "The students were evading the real purpose of their education," says Associate Dean Harold Levin, adding, in the language of deans everywhere, "The product we were turning out was not what we wanted." All told, according to a survey of 272 universities and colleges last spring, 88% are engaged in revising their curriculums, and 59% of these are increasing their programs of required courses in general education. That, presumably, will improve the "product."

While the educators reorganize their methods, the fundamental goals of the process—truth, knowledge, the understanding of the world—remain somewhere just beyond the horizon. It was said of Goethe, after his death in 1832, that he was the last man to know everything worth knowing. Today's cliché is that 90% of all scientists in the history of the world are alive now. Yet their knowledge has become hopelessly fragmented; the specialist in recombinant DNA feels no more obligation to understand laser surgery than to hear the latest composition by Pierre Boulez.

As scientific specialties spawn subspecialties, the rapidly growing mass of information has confused the arts and humanities as well. Historical research now presupposes a mastery of old tax records and population movements, and anyone who ventures into such popular fields as American literature or impressionist art must wade into a rising tide of studies, analyses, psychographic portraits and sheer verbiage. In addition, all the political trends of the past two decades have tended to multiply the demands for studies in fields once ignored: Chinese history, the languages of Africa, the traffic in slaves, the thwarted ambitions of women.

Not everyone is overawed by the so-called knowledge explosion. "What happens," says Computer Scientist Joseph Weizenbaum of M. I. T., "is that educators, all of us, are deluged by a flood of messages disguised as valuable information, most of which is trivial and irrelevant to any substantive concern. This is the elite's equivalent of junk mail, but many educators can't see through it because they are not sufficiently educated to deal with such random complexity." To many experts, the computer seems a symbol of both the problem and its solution. "What the computer has done," according to Stephen White of the Alfred P. Sloan Foundation, "is to provide scope for analytical skills that never before existed, and in so doing it has altered the world in which the student will live as well as the manner in which he will think about the world. . . . No adult is truly civilized unless he is acquainted with the civilization of which he is a member, and the liberal arts curriculum of 50 years ago no longer provides that acquaintance."

Acquaintance seems a bare minimum, and even that is difficult enough to attain in a world where millions cannot read and millions more read mainly falsehoods or formulas. Yet the basic questions of education still reach deep into every aspect of life: What is it essential to learn—to know—and why? Everyone seems to have his own answer, but there are interesting patterns among those answers. They can be organized into five main ideas:

## I: Education Means Careers

Today's most popular answer is the practical one, on which students are most likely to agree with parents virtually impoverished by tuition bills: an education should enable a student to get a better job than he would otherwise be able to find or fill. In a Carnegie Council poll, 67% of students cited this as an "essential" purpose of their education. A 9.8% unemployment rate makes this purpose seem all the more essential. Michael Adelson, 23, who studied psychology at U. C. L. A., has been unable to find a job in this field for a year and a half, and he now wishes he had chosen engineering. He calls his bachelor of arts degree "completely useless."

The idea that education has a basically social purpose derives more or less from Plato. In his *Republic,* the philosopher portrayed a utopia governed by an intellectual elite specially trained for that purpose. This form of education was both stern and profoundly conservative. Children who attempt innovations, warned Socrates, acting as Plato's narrator, will desire a different sort of life when they grow up to be men, with other institutions and laws. And this "is full of danger to the whole state." To prevent any innovations, Socrates forthrightly demanded

censorship so that students could not "hear any casual tales which may be devised by casual persons." When asked whose works he would ban, Socrates specifically named Homer. The poet's crime, he said, was to provide "an erroneous representation of the nature of gods and heroes."

Political pressure of this kind has never been far from the campus, but the overwhelming influence of U.S. education has been not politics but economics: the need for a technologically trained managerial caste. The very first Land Grant Act, in 1862, handed out 30,000 acres per Congressman for the building of state colleges at which "the leading object shall be . . . to teach such branches of learning as are related to agriculture and the mechanic arts." These needs keep changing, of course, and over the decades the U.S. economy demanded of its universities not only chemists and engineers but lawyers and accountants and personnel analysts, and then, after Sputnik's shocking revelation of the Soviet lead in space, yet more engineers.

Students naturally respond to the economy's needs. The Rev. Theodore Hesburgh, president of Notre Dame, complained last year that "the most popular course on the American college campus is not literature or history but accounting." This criticism reflects the fact that less than half the nation's swarm of college students go to liberal arts colleges; the rest are seeking not just jobs but entry into the middle class.

There are now thousands of Ph.D.s unable to find anyone willing to pay them for the hard-earned knowledge of Renaissance painting or the history of French monasticism, but any Sunday newspaper overflows with ads appealing for experts in electromagnetic capability, integrated logistics support, or laser electro-optics. Says George W. Valsa, supervisor of the college-recruiting section at Ford: "We are not ready to sign a petition to burn down liberal arts colleges, but don't expect us to go out and hire many liberal arts graduates.'' Ford does hire nearly 1,000 graduates a year, and most of them are engineers or M.B.A.s.

This is not the old argument between the "two cultures" of science and the humanities, for science too is often forced to defer to technical and vocational training. In 1979, according to one Carnegie study, 58% of all undergraduates pursued "professional" majors (up from 38% a decade earlier), in contrast to 11% in social sciences, 7% in biological sciences, 6% in the arts and 4% in physical sciences. Rich and prestigious private universities can resist this rush toward vocational training, but public and smaller private colleges are more vulnerable. "The bulk of the institutions will have to give in to a form of consumerism," says U. C. L. A.'s Astin, "in that they need applications and will therefore have to offer students what they want."

Says Paul Ginsberg, dean of students at Wisconsin: "It's becoming increasingly difficult to persuade a student to take courses that will contribute to his intellectual development in addition to those that will make him a good accountant." Quite apart from the pros and cons of professional training, the idea of educating oneself in order to rise in the world is a perfectly legitimate goal. But Ginsberg has been receiving letters from high school freshmen asking about the prospects for professional schools and job opportunities when they graduate from college seven years hence. Says he: "I don't know at what point foresight ends and panic sets in."

## II: Education Transmits Civilization

Jill Ker Conway, president of Smith, echoes the prevailing view of contemporary technology when she says that "anyone in today's world who doesn't understand data processing is not educated." But she insists that the increasing emphasis on these matters leaves certain gaps. Says she: "The very strongly utilitarian emphasis in education, which is an effect of Sputnik and the cold war, has really removed from this culture something that was very profound in its 18th and 19th century roots, which was a sense that literacy and learning were ends in themselves for a democratic republic."

In contrast to Plato's claim for the social value of education, a quite different idea of intellectual purposes was propounded by the Renaissance humanists. Intoxicated with their rediscovery of the classical learning that was thought to have disappeared during the Dark Ages, they argued that the imparting of knowledge needs no justification—religious, social, economic, or political. Its purpose, to the extent that it has one, is to pass on from generation to generation the corpus of knowledge that constitutes civilization. "What could man acquire, by virtuous striving, that is more valuable than knowledge?" asked Erasmus, perhaps the greatest scholar of the early 16th century. That idea has acquired a tradition of its own. "The educational process has no end beyond itself," said John Dewey. "It is its own end."

But what exactly is the corpus of knowledge to be passed on? In simpler times, it was all included in the medieval universities' *quadrivium* (arithmetic, geometry, astronomy, music) and *trivium* (grammar, rhetoric, logic). As recently as the last century, when less than 5% of Americans went to college at all, students in New England establishments were compelled mainly to memorize and recite various Latin texts, and crusty professors angrily opposed the introduction of any new scientific discoveries or modern European languages. "They felt," said Charles Francis Adams Jr., the Union

Pacific Railroad president who devoted his later years to writing history, "that a classical education was the important distinction between a man who had been to college and a man who had not been to college, and that anything that diminished the importance of this distinction was essentially revolutionary and tended to anarchy."

Such a view was eventually overcome by the practical demands of both students and society, yet it does not die. In academia, where every professor is accustomed to drawing up lists of required reading, it can even be played as a game. Must an educated man have read Dostoevsky, Rimbaud, Tacitus, Kafka? (Yes.) Must he know both Bach's *Goldberg Variations* and Schoenberg's *Gurrelieder?* (Perhaps.) Must he know the Carnot Cycle and Boole's Inequality? (Well . . .) And then languages—can someone who reads only Constance Garnett's rather wooden version of *Anna Karenina* really know Tolstoy's masterpiece any better than some Frenchman can know Shakespeare by reading André Gide's translation of *Hamlet?* Every scholar likes to defend his own specialty as a cornerstone of Western civilization, and any restraints can seem philistine. George Steiner approvingly quotes, in *Language and Silence,* a suggestion that "an acquaintance with a Chinese novel or a Persian lyric is almost indispensable to contemporary literacy." On a slightly more practical level, intellectual codifiers like to draw up lists of masterworks that will educate any reader who is strong enough to survive them—thus Charles Eliot's famous five-foot shelf of Harvard Classics and all its weighty sequels.

It was the immensely influential Eliot, deeply impressed with the specialized scholarly and scientific research performed at German universities, who proclaimed in 1869, upon becoming president of Harvard, the abolition of its rigid traditional curriculum.

Basic education should be performed by the high schools, Eliot declared; anyone who went on to college should be free to make his own choice among myriad elective courses. The students chose the practical. "In the end, it was the sciences that triumphed, guided by the hidden hand of capitalism and legitimated by the binding ideology of positivism," Ernest Boyer and Martin Kaplan observe in *Educating for Survival.* Before long, however, the inevitable counterrevolution against the elective system began; there was a "core" of certain things that every student must learn. Columbia established required courses in contemporary civilization; the University of Chicago and St. John's College duly followed with programs solidly based on required readings of classic texts.

St. John's, which is based in Annapolis, Md., and has a smaller campus in Santa Fe, N. Mex., is a remarkable example of an institution resolutely taking this approach. Ever since 1937, all of St. John's students (683 this fall on both campuses) have been required to read and discuss a list of 130 great books drawn heavily from the classics and philosophy but also from the ranks of modern novelists like Faulkner and Conrad. The students must take four years of math, three of a laboratory science, two of music and two years each of Greek and French. That is just about it. This modern liberal arts version of the *trivium* and *quadrivium* includes no such novelties as psychology (except what can be learned in the works of Freud and William James) and no sociology (except perhaps Jane Austen).

St. John's is aware of the obvious criticism that its approach is "elitist" and even "irrelevant" to the real world. But President Edwin DeLattre's mild voice turns a bit sharp when he retorts, "If knowing the foundations of one's country—the foundations of one's civilization—if understanding and learning how to gain access to the en-

*Kendra George*

gines of political and economic power in the world—if knowing how to learn in mathematics and the sciences, the languages, the humanities—if having access to the methods that have advanced civilizations since the dawn of human intelligence . . . If all those things are irrelevant, then boy, are we irrelevant!'' De Lattre is a philosopher by training, and he offers one definition that has an ominous but compelling reverberation in the thermonuclear age: "Don't forget the notion of an educated person as someone who would understand how to refound his or her own civilization."

## III: Education Teaches How to Think

Aristotle was one of those who could found a civilization, and while he thought of education as both a social value and an end in itself, he ascribed its chief importance to what might be considered a third basic concept of education: to train the mind to think, regardless of what it is thinking about. The key is not what it knows but how it evaluates any new fact or argument. "An educated man," Aristotle wrote in *On the Parts of Animals,* "should be able to form a fair offhand judgment as to the goodness or badness of the method used by a professor in his exposition. To be educated is in fact to be able to do this."

The Aristotelian view of education as a process has become the conventionally worthy answer today whenever college presidents and other academic leaders are asked what an education should be. An educated man, says Harvard President Bok, taking a deep breath, must have a "curiosity in exploring the unfamiliar and unexpected, an open-mindedness in entertaining opposing points of view, tolerance for the ambiguity that surrounds so many important issues, and a willingness to make the best decisions

he can in the face of uncertainty and doubt. . . ."

"The educated person," says University of Chicago President Hanna Holborn Gray, taking an equally deep breath, "is a person who has a respect for rationality, and who understands some of the limits of rationality as well, who has acquired independent critical intelligence, and a sense not only for the complexity of the world and different points of view but of the standards he or she would thoughtfully want to be pursuing in making judgments."

This is an approach that appears to attach more importance to the process of learning than to the substance of what is learned, but it does provide a way of coping with the vast increase of knowledge. "The old notion of the generalists who could comprehend all subjects is an impossibility, and it was even in past ages," says Chicago's Gray. "Renaissance humanism concentrated on social living and aesthetic engagement but left out most of science. To know all about today's physics, biology and mathematics, or even the general principles of all these fields, would be impossible." To make matters still more difficult, the fields of knowledge keep changing. Says Harvard's Henry Rosovsky, dean of the faculty of arts and sciences: "We can't prepare students for an explosion of knowledge because we don't know what is going to explode next. The best we can do is to make students capable of gaining new knowledge."

The old Aristotelian idea, combined with a contemporary sense of desperation about coping with the knowledge explosion, helped inspire a complete reorganization—yet again—of Harvard's curriculum. At the end of World War II, Harvard had curtailed Eliot's electives and launched a series of general education courses that were supposed to teach everyone the rudiments of science and the humanities. But by the 1960s, when

51

rebellious students seized an administration building, that whole system had broken down. "At the moment," a saddened Dean Rosovsky later wrote to his colleagues, "to be an educated man or woman doesn't mean anything. . . . The world has become a Tower of Babel."

Out of Rosovsky's unhappiness came what Harvard somewhat misleadingly calls its core curriculum. Inaugurated in 1979, after much faculty debate and amid considerable press attention, this core turned out to be a rather sprawling collection of 122 different courses, ranging from Abstraction in Modern Art to Microbial and Molecular Biology. Students are required to select eight of their 32 courses from five general areas of knowledge (science, history, the arts, ethics and foreign cultures).

Harvard's eminence exerts a wide influence, but other first-rate institutions, like Columbia, Chicago, and Princeton, point out that they have taught a more concentrated core and steadfastly continued doing so throughout the 1960s. "It makes me unhappy when people think that Harvard has done some innovative curriculum work," says Columbia College Associate Dean Michael Rosenthal (a Harvard graduate). "They have millions of courses, none of which, you could argue, represents any fundamental effort to introduce people to a kind of thinking or to a discipline."

But that is exactly what Harvard does claim to be doing. "The student should have an understanding of the major ways mankind organizes knowledge," says Rosovsky. "That is done in identifiable ways: in sciences by experiment, conducted essentially in mathematics; in social science through quantitative and historical analysis; in the humanities by studying the great traditions. We are not ignoring content but simply recognizing that because of the knowledge explosion, it

makes sense to emphasize the gaining of knowledge."

If anyone objects that it is still perfectly possible to graduate from Harvard without having read a word of Shakespeare, Rosovsky is totally unfazed. Says he: "That's not necessary."

## IV: Education Liberates the Individual

The current trend toward required subjects—a kind of intellectual law-and-order—reflects contemporary political conservatism. It implies not only that there is a basic body of knowledge to be learned but also that there is a right way to think. It implies that a certain amount of uniformity is both socially and intellectually desirable.

Perhaps, but the excesses of the 1960s should not be used to besmirch reforms that were valuable. They too derived from a distinguished intellectual tradition. Its founding father was Jean-Jacques Rousseau, who argued in his novel *Emile* that children are not miniature adults and should not be drilled into becoming full-grown robots. "Everything is good as it comes from the hand of the Creator," said Rousseau; "everything degenerates in the hands of man."

Isolated from the corrupting world, Rousseau's young Emile was given no books but encouraged to educate himself by observing the workings of nature. Not until the age of twelve, the age of reason, was he provided with explanations in the form of astronomy or chemistry, and not until the social age of 15 was he introduced to aesthetics, religion, and, eventually, female company. That was how Emile met Sophie and lived happily every after. It is a silly tale, and yet there is considerable power to the idea that a student should be primarily educated not to hold a job or to memorize literary monuments or even to think like Aristotle, but simply to develop the potentialities of his own self—and that everyone's self is different.

While there is probably not a single university that has not retreated somewhat from the experimentation of the 1960s, and while the rhetoric of that decade is now wildly out of fashion, a few small institutions have tried to keep the faith. For them, education is, in a sense, liberation, personal liberation. At Evergreen State College in Washington, which has no course requirements of any kind and no letter grades, a college spokesman describes a class on democracy and tyranny by saying, "We will try to find out who we are, and what kind of human beings we should become." At Hampshire College, founded in Massachusetts in 1970 as a resolutely experimental school, students still design their own curriculums, take no exams and talk of changing the world. "I don't see myself as giving a body of knowledge or even 'a way of learning,' " says Physics Professor Herbert Bernstein, "but as involved in something beyond that—to help people find their own path and the fullness of who they are."

The times have not been easy for such colleges. Not only do costs keep rising, but many students now prefer conventional courses and grades that will look impressive on job applications. Antioch, which expanded into an unmanageable national network of 32 experimental institutions, stumbled to the verge of bankruptcy in the 1970s, and is drastically cutting costs to survive. But the spirit of Rousseau flickers on. Rollins, which has sometimes been dismissed as a Florida tennis school, is trying to organize a conference for such like-minded colleges as Bard, Bennington, Sarah Lawrence, and Scripps on how best to pursue the goal of "making higher education more personal and developmental rather than formalistic."

Even when these enthusiasts do bend to the current pressures for law-and-order, they tend to do it in their own dreamy way. At Bard, where President Leon Botstein decided last year that all students should attend an intensive three-week workshop on how to think and write, the students pondered such questions as the nature of justice. What color is justice? What shape is it? What sound does it make? What does it eat? "I can't think of anything," one student protested at the first such writing class. "Don't worry about it," the teacher soothingly answered. Among the students' offerings: "Justice is navy blue, it's square. It weaves in and out and backs up . . . Justice is black and white, round . . . It has the sound of the cracked Liberty Bell ringing." Workshop Director Peter Elbow's conclusion: "We're trying an experiment here, and we're not pretending that we have it under control or that we know how it works."

## V: Education Teaches Morals

The U.S. Supreme Court has forbidden prayers in public schools, but many Americans cling to the idea that their educational system has a moral purpose. It is an idea common to both the Greeks and the medieval church ("O Lord my King," St. Augustine wrote in his *Confessions,* "whatsoever I speak or write, or read, or number, let all serve Thee"). In a secular age, the moral purpose of education takes secular forms: racial integration, sex education, good citizenship. At the college level, the ambiguities become more complex. Should a morally objectionable person be allowed to teach? (Not Timothy Leary, said Harvard.) Should a morally objectionable doctrine be permitted? (Not Arthur Jensen's claims of racial differences in intelligence, said student protesters at Berkeley.)

Many people are understandably dismayed by such censorship. But would they prefer ethical neutrality? Should engineers be trained to build highways without being taught any concern for the homes they displace? Should prospective corporate managers learn how to increase profits regardless of pollution or unemployment? Just the opposite, according to *Beyond the Ivory Tower,* a new book by Harvard's Bok, which calls for increased emphasis on "applied ethics." (Writes Bok: "A university that refuses to take ethical dilemmas seriously violates its basic obligations to society.")

Religious colleges have always practiced a similar preaching. But some 500 schools now offer courses in the field. The Government supports such studies with a program known as EVIST, which stands for Ethics and Values in Science and Technology (and which sounds as though a computer had already taken charge of the matter). "The modern university is rooted in the scientific method, having essentially turned its back on religion," says Steven Muller, president of Johns Hopkins. "The scientific method is a marvelous means of inquiry, but it really doesn't provide a value system. The biggest failing in higher education today is that we fall short in exposing students to values."

Charles Muscatine, a professor of English at Berkeley and member of a committee that is analyzing liberal arts curriculums for the Association of American Colleges, is even harsher. He calls today's educational programs "a marvelous convenience for a mediocre society." The key goal of education, says Muscatine, should be "informed decision making that recognizes there is a moral and ethical component to life." Instead, he says most universities are "propagating the dangerous myth that technical skills are more important than ethical reasoning."

Psychiatrist Robert Coles, who teaches at both Harvard and Duke, is still more emphatic in summing up the need: "Reading, writing, and arithmetic. That's what we've got to start with, and all that implies, at every level. If people can't use good, strong language, they can't think clearly, and if they haven't been trained to use good, strong language, they become vulnerable to all the junk that comes their way. They should be taught philosophy, moral philosophy and theology. They ought to be asked to think about moral issues, especially about what use is going to be make of knowledge, and why—a kind of moral reflection that I think has been supplanted by a more technological education. Replacing moral philosophy with psychology has been a disaster, an absolute disaster!"

Each of these five ways to wisdom has its strengths and weaknesses, of course. The idea that education provides better jobs promises practical rewards for both the student and the society that trains him, but it can leave him undernourished in the possibilities of life away from work. The idea that education means the acquisition of a cultural heritage does give the student some grasp of that heritage, but it can also turn into glib superficialities or sterile erudition. The idea that education consists mainly of training the mind does provide a method for further education, but it can also make method seem more important than knowledge. So can the idea that education is a form of self-development. And the teaching of ethics can unfortunately become a teaching of conventional pieties.

To define is to limit, as we all learned in school, and to categorize is to oversimplify. To some extent, the five ways to wisdom all overlap and blend, and though every educator has his own sense of priorities, none would admit that he does not aspire to all five goals. Thus the student who has mastered the riches of Western civilization has probably also learned to think for himself and to see the moral purposes of life. And surely such a paragon can find a good job even in the recession of 1982.

Are there specific ways to come nearer to achieving these goals? The most obvious is money. Good teachers cost money; libraries costs money; so do remedial classes for those who were short-changed in earlier years. Only mediocrity comes cheap. Those who groan at the rising price of college tuition (up as much as $7,000 since 1972) may not realize that overall, taking enrollment growth into account, college budgets have just barely kept up with inflation. Indeed, adjusted for inflation, four years of college today costs less than a decade ago, and faculty salaries in real dollars declined about 20% during the 1970s. Crocodile tears over the costs of higher education come in waves from the federal government, which has so far held spending to roughly 1981 levels, and proposes deep cuts (e.g., nearly 40% in basic grants) by 1985. This is an economy comparable to skimping on the maintenance of an expensive machine.

But money alone will not solve all problems, as is often said, and this is particularly true in the field of education. If improving the quality of American education is a matter of urgent national concern—and it should be—then what is required besides more dollars is more sense: a widespread rededication to a number of obvious but somewhat neglected principles. That probing research and hard thinking be demanded of students (and of teachers too). That academic results be tested and measured. That intellectual excellence be not just acknowledged but rewarded.

These principles admittedly did serve the system that educated primarily those few who were born into the governing classes, but the fact that elitist education once supported elitist politics does not mean that egalitarian politics requires egalitarian education. Neither minds nor ideas are all the same.

All that the schools can be asked to promise is that everyone will be educated to the limit of his capacities. Exactly what this means, everyone must discover for himself. At the community college minimum, it may have to mean teaching basic skills, at least until the weakened high schools begin doing their job properly, as Philosopher Mortimer Adler urges in his new *Paideia Proposal*. This calls for a standardized high school curriculum in three categories: fundamental knowledge such as history, science, and arts; basic skills such as reading and mathematical computation; and critical understanding of ideas and values. These essentials must really be taught, not just certified with a passing grade. Beyond such practical benefits, though, and beyond the benefits that come from exercising the muscles of the mind, higher education must ultimately serve the higher purpose of perpetuating whatever it is in civilization that is worth perpetuating. Or as Ezra Pound once said of the craft that he later betrayed, "The function of literature is precisely that it does incite humanity to continue living."

This is the core of the core idea, and surely it is by now indisputable that every college student improves by learning the fundamentals of science, literature, art, history. Harvard's Rosovsky may be right in suggesting that it is "not necessary" to have read Shakespeare as part of the process of learning how to think, but he is probably wrong. Not because anyone really *needs* to have shared in Lear's howling rage or because anyone can earn a better salary from having heard Macbeth declaim "Tomorrow and tomorrow and tomorrow . . ." But he is enriched by knowing these things, impoverished by not knowing them. And *The Marriage of Figaro* enriches. *The Cherry Orchard* enriches. *The City of God* enriches. So does a mastery of Greek, or of subnuclear particles, or of Gödel's theorem.

In a sense, there really is no core, except as a series of arbitrary choices, for there is no limit to the possibilities of learning. There are times when these possibilities seem overwhelming, and one hears echoes of Socrates' confession, "All I know is that I know nothing." Yet that too is a challenge. "We shall not cease from exploration," as T. S. Eliot put it, "and the end of our exploring/Will be to arrive where we started/And know the place for the first time." The seemingly momentous years of schooling, then, are only the beginning.

Henry Adams, who said in *The Education of Henry Adams* that Harvard "taught little and that little ill," was 37 when he took up the study of Saxon legal codes and 42 when he first turned to writing the history of the Jefferson and Madison Administrations, and 49 when he laboriously began on Chinese. In his 50s, a tiny, wiry figure with a graying beard, the future master of Gothic architecture solemnly learned to ride a bicycle.

# Our Listless Universities

*Allan Bloom*

I begin with my conclusions: students in our best universities do not believe in anything, and those universities are doing nothing about it, nor can they. An easy-going American kind of nihilism has descended upon us, a nihilism without terror of the abyss. The great questions—God, freedom, and immortality, according to Kant—hardly touch the young. And the universities, which should encourage the quest for the clarification of such questions, are the very source of the doctrine which makes that quest appear futile.

The heads of the young are stuffed with a jargon derived from the despair of European thinkers, gaily repackaged for American consumption and presented as the foundation for a pluralistic society. That jargon becomes a substitute for real experiences and instinct; one suspects that modern thought has produced an artificial soul to replace the old one supplied by nature, which was full of dangerous longings, loves, hates, and awes. The new soul's language consists of terms like *value, ideology, self, commitment, identity*—every word derived from recent German philosophy, and each carrying a heavy baggage of dubious theoretical interpretation of which its users are blissfully unaware. They

Allan Bloom is co-director of the John M. Olin Center for Inquiry into the Theory and Practice of Democracy at the University of Chicago, where he is also a Professor in the Committee on Social Thought.

take such language to be as unproblematic and immediate as night and day. It now constitutes our peculiar common sense.

The new language subtly injects into our system the perspective of "do your own thing" as the only plausible way of life. I know that sounds vaguely passé, a remnant leftover from the Sixties. But it is precisely the routinization of the passions of the Sixties that is the core of what is going on now, just as the Sixties were merely a radicalization of earlier tendencies.

The American regime has always attempted to palliate extreme beliefs that lead to civil strife, particularly religious beliefs. The members of sects had to obey the laws and be loyal to the Constitution; if they did so, others had to leave them alone. To make things work, it was thought helpful that men's beliefs be moderated. There was a conscious, if covert, effort to weaken religious fervor by assigning religion to the realm of opinion as opposed to knowledge. But everyone had to have an intense belief in the right of freedom of religion; the existence of that natural right was not to be treated as a matter of opinion.

The insatiable appetite for freedom to live as one pleases thrives on this aspect of modern democratic thought. The expansion of the area exempt from legitimate regulation is effected by contracting the claims to moral and political knowledge. It appears that full freedom can be attained only when there is no such knowledge. The effective way to defang oppressors is to persuade them that they are ignorant of the good. There are no absolutes: freedom is absolute.

A doctrine that gives equal rights to any way of life whatsoever has the double advantage of licensing one's own way of life and of giving one a democratic good conscience. The very lack of morality is a morality and permits what Saul Bellow has called "easy virtue," a mixture of egotism and highmindedness. Now, in feeling as well as in speech, a large segment of our young are open, open to every "lifestyle." But the fatal consequence of this openness has been the withering of their belief in their own way of life and of their capacity to generate goals. The palliation of beliefs culminates in pallid belief. A soul which esteems indiscriminately must be an artificial soul, and that, to repeat, is what we are coming near to constituting, not by some inevitable historical process but by a conscious education project. This project masquerades as the essential democratic theory without which we would collapse into tyranny or the war of all prejudices against all. Its premise is that truth itself must be prejudice or at least treated as such.

The tendency toward indiscriminateness—the currently negative connotation of the word *discrimination* tells us much—is apparently perennial in democracy. The need to subordinate the more refined sensibilities to a common denominator and the unwillingness to order the soul's desires according to their rank conduce to easygoingness. The democratic ethos obscures the reason for the desirability of such self-mastery. This is the moral problem of democracy and why fortuitous external necessities like war or poverty seem to bring out the best in us. Plato describes the natural bent of the democratic man thus:

He . . . also lives along day by day, gratifying the desire that occurs to him, at one time drinking and listening to the flute, at another downing water and reducing; now practicing gymnastics, and again idling and neglecting everything; and sometimes spending his time as though he were occupied with philosophy. Often he engages in politics and, jumping up, says and does whatever chances to come to him; and if he ever admires any soldiers, he turns in that direction; and if it's moneymakers, in that one. And there is neither order nor necessity in his life, but calling this life sweet, free, and blessed he follows it throughout.

This account is easily recognizable when applied to the middle-class youth who attend America's top colleges and universities. But Plato's description omits a more sinister element in our situation. Plato's young man believes that each of the lives he follows is really good, at least when he follows it. His problem is that he cannot keep his mind made up. Our young person, by contrast, is always plagued by a gnawing doubt as to whether the activity he undertakes is worth anything, whether this end is not just another "value," an illusion that men once believed in but which our "historical consciousness" reveals as only a cultural phenomenon. There are a thousand and one such goals; they are not believed in because they exist, they exist because one believes in them. Since we now know this, we can no longer believe. The veil of illusion has been town away forever. The trendy language for this alleged experience is *demystification* or *demythologization*. This teaching now has the status of dogma. It leads to a loss of immediacy in all experience and a suspicion that every way of life is a "role." The substitution of the expression "lifestyle," which we can change at will, for the good life, the rational quest for which is the origin of philosophy, tells the story. That is what I mean by nihilism, and this nihilism has resulted from a questionable doctrine that we seem no longer to question.

All of us who are under sixty know something about this doctrine and its transmission, for since the Thirties it is what the schools have been teaching. For fifty years the only spiritual substance they have been trying to convey is openness, the disdain for the ethnocentric. Of course, they have also been teaching the three Rs, but their moral and intellectual energy has been turned almost exclusively in this direction. Schools once produced citizens, or gentlemen, or believers; now they produce the unprejudiced. A university professor confronting entering freshmen can be almost certain that most of them will know that there are no absolutes and that one cannot say that one culture is superior to another. They can scarcely believe that someone might seriously argue the contrary; the attempt to do so meets either self-satisfied smiles at something so old-fashioned or outbursts of anger at a threat to decent respect for other human beings. In the Thirties this teaching was actually warring against some real prejudices of race, religion, or nation; but what remains now is mostly the means for weakening conviction when convictions have disappeared.

The doctrine of cultural relativism did not emerge from the study of cultures. It was a philosophic doctrine that gave a special interpretation of the meaning of culture and had a special political attractiveness. It could appeal to the taste for diversity as opposed to our principled homogeneity. All kinds of people climbed aboard—disaffected Southern snobs who had never accepted the Declaration and Constitution anyhow, Stalinists who wanted us to love Soviet tyranny without being too explicit about it, and similar types. No choices would have to be made. We could have the charms of old cultures, of what one now calls roots, along with democratic liberties. All that was required was an education making other ways attractive and disenchanting one's own. It is not so much the knowledge of other cultures that is important, but the consciousness that one loves one's own way because it is one's own, not

because it is good. People must understand that they are what they are and what they believe only because of accidents of time and place.

The equality of values seemed to be a decisive step in the march of equality. So sure were our social scientists of the truth and vigor of democracy that they did not even dimly perceive what Weber knew, that this view undermined democracy, which stands or falls with reason. Only democracy traces all its authority to reason; other kinds of regimes can more or less explicitly appeal to other sources. When we talk about the West's lack of conviction or lack of will, we show that we are beginning to recognize what has happened to us. Exhortations to believe, however, are useless. It is only by thinking ideas through again that we can determine whether our reason can any longer give assent to our principles.

But this serious reconsideration is not taking place in the universities.

## II

Today a young person does not generally go off to the university with the expectation of having an intellectual adventure, of discovering strange new worlds, of finding out what the comprehensive truth about man is. This is partly because he thinks he already knows, partly because he thinks such truth unavailable. And the university does not try to persuade him that he is coming to it for the purpose of being liberally educated, at least in any meaningful sense of the term—to study how to be free, to be able to think for himself. The university has no vision, no view of what a human being must know in order to be considered educated. Its general purpose is lost amid the incoherent variety of special purposes that have accreted within it. Such a general purpose may be vague and undemonstrable, but for just this reason it requires the most study. The meaning of life is unclear, but that is why we must spend our lives clarifying it rather than letting the question go. The university's function is to remind students of the importance and urgency of the question and give them the means to pursue it. Universities do have other responsibilities, but this should be their highest priority.

They have, however, been so battered by modern doctrines, social demands, the requirements of the emancipated specialties, that they have tacitly agreed not to open Pandora's box and start a civil war. They provide a general framework that keeps the peace but they lack a goal of their own.

When the arriving student surveys the scene, he sees a bewildering variety of choices. The professional schools beckon him by providing him with an immediate motive: a lucrative and prestigious livelihood guaranteed by simply staying in the university to the conclusion of training. Medicine and law were always such possibilities; with the recent addition of the MBA, the temptation has radically increased. If the student decides to take this route, liberal education is practically over for him.

If he first turns his eye to what was traditionally thought to be the center of the university, he will confront—aside from a few hot programs like black studies, native studies, women's studies, which are largely exercises in consciousness-raising—the natural sciences, the social sciences, and the humanities.

The natural sciences thrive, full of good conscience and good works. But they are ever more specialized and ever more separate from the rest of the university; they have no need of it. They don't object to liberal education, if it doesn't get in the way of their research and training. And they have nothing to say, even about themselves or their role in the whole human picture, let alone about the kinds of questions that agitated Descartes, Newton, and Leibniz. Their results speak for themselves, but they do not say quite enough.

The social sciences are the source of much useful research and information, but they are long past the first effervescence of their Marxist-Freudian-Weberian period. Then they expected to find a new and more scientific way to answer the old questions of philosophy. Such hopes and claims quietly disappeared from the scene during the past 15 years. Their solid reasons for existence are in specialized study of interest rates, Iranian politics, or urban trends. Practically no economist conceives of doing what Adam Smith did, and the few who try produce petty and trivial stuff. The case is pretty much the same for the other social sciences. They are theoretically barren, and the literature read and used by them is mostly ephemera of the last fifty years.

The remainder is to be found in the humanities, the smallest, least funded, most dispirited part of the university. The humanities are the repository of the books that are at the foundation of our religion, our philosophy, our politics, our science, as well as our art. Here, if anywhere, one ought to find the means to doubt what seems most certain. Only here are the questions about knowledge, about the good life, about God and love and death, at home in the university. If, however, one looks at the humanistic side of the campus, one finds a hodgepodge of disciplines, not integrally related with one another and without much sense of common purpose. The books are divided up among language departments, according to the largely accidental fact of the language in which they were written. Such departments have as their primary responsibility the teaching of the language in question (a very depressing responsibility now that languages have fallen into particular disfavor with students).

Humanists in general are the guardians of great books, but rarely take seriously the naive notion that these books might contain the truth which has escaped us. Yet without the belief that from Plato one might learn how to live or that from Shakespeare one might get the deepest insight into the passions and the virtues, no one who is not professionally obligated will take them seriously. Try as they may, the humanities will fail to interest if they do not teach *the truth* even as natural and social science are supposed to do. To present the great writers and artists as representatives of cultures or examples of the way thought is related to society, or in any of the other modes common today, is to render them uninteresting to the healthy intellect. The comprehensive questions have their natural home in the humanities, but it is there that the historical-cultural doubt about the possibility of answering them is most acute. Professors of humanities more than any others wonder whether they have a truth to tell.

Philosophy should, of course, provide the focus for the most needful study. But it is just one department among many and, in the democracy of the specialties, it no longer has the will to insist that it is the queen of the sciences. Moreover, in most philosophy departments the study of the classic texts is not central. Professors "do" their own philosophy and do not try to pose the questions as they were posed by the old writers. This is especially the case for the dominant school of thought in the United States, the Oxford school.

Of all university members, humanists have the least self-confidence. The students are abandoning them, and they have difficulty speaking to the concerns of the age. They fear they may have to huckster—if they are not already doing so—in order to keep afloat. In their heart of hearts, many doubt that they have much to say. After all, most of the writers they promote can be convicted of elitism and sexism, the paramount sins of the day.

There are, to be sure, many dedicated individuals in the humanities who know what needs to be done and can draw students' attention to the impoverished state of their experience and show them that great texts address their concerns. But the endeavor of these professors is a lonely one with little corporate resonance. The students are not reading the same books and addressing the same questions, so that their common social life cannot be affected by a common intellectual life.

It should be added that the humanities are also the center of some of the fastest selling intellectual items of the day—structuralism, deconstructionism, and Marxist humanism. The members of these schools—particularly rampant in comparative literature—do read books and talk big ideas. In that sense they are the closest thing to what the university should be about. The problem with them, and all of them are alike in this respect, is that the books are not taken seriously on their own grounds but are used as vile bodies for the sake of demonstrating theses brought to them by the interpreters. They know what they are looking for before they begin. Their approaches are ultimately derived from Marx or Nietzsche, whose teachings are tacitly taken to be true.

It is small wonder that the student is bewildered about what it means to be educated. The new liberal education requirements some universities are instituting are little more than tours of what is being done in the various workshops. To be sure, they always add on a course requirement, in a non-Western civilization or culture, but that is just another bit of demagogy serving the indoctrination of openness. Serious physicists would never require a course in non-Western physics. Culture and civilization are irrelevant to the truth. One finds it where one can. Only if truth is relative to culture does this make sense. But, once again, this is our dogma, accepted for covert political reasons. This dogma is the greatest enemy of liberal education. It undermines the unity of man, our common humanity in the intellect, which makes the university possible and permits it to treat man as simply without distinction.

## III

Three conclusions have forced themselves on me about students, their characters and ways, conclusions that have to do with their education and their educability. They are not scientific generalizations based on survey research, but they are the result of long observation of, and careful listening to, young people in our better universities by one who is intensely interested in their real openness, their openness to higher learning.

1. *Books.* They are no longer an important part of the lives of students. "Information" is important, but profound and beautiful books are not where they go for it. They have no books that are companions and friends to which they look for counsel, companionship, inspiration, or pleasure. They do not expect to find in them sympathy for, or clarification of, their inmost desires and experiences. The link between the classic books and the young, which persisted for so long and in so many circumstances, and is the only means of connecting the here and the now with the always, this link has been broken. The Bible and Plutarch have ceased to be a part of the soul's furniture, an incalculable loss of fullness and awareness of which the victims are unaware.

The loss of the taste for reading has been blamed on television, the universal villain of social critics. But lack of reverence for antiquity and contempt for tradition are democratic tendencies. It should be the uni-

versity's business to provide a corrective to these tendencies; however, I believe that the universities are most to blame for them. After all, they taught the schoolteachers. For a very long time now the universities have been preoccupied with abstract modern schools of thought that were understood to have surpassed all earlier thought and rendered it obsolete. And their primary concern has been to indoctrinate social attitudes, to "socialize," rather than to educate. The old books are still around, but one "knows" that they contain mere opinions, no better than any others. The result is true philistinism, a withering of taste and a conformity to what is prevalent in the present. It means the young have no heroes, no objects of aspiration. It is all both relaxing and boring, a soft imprisonment.

2. *Music.* While I am not certain about the effects of television, I am quite certain about those of music. Many students do not watch much television while in college, but they do listen to music. From the time of puberty, and earlier, music has been the food of their souls. This is the audio generation. And classical music is dead, at least as a common taste. Rock is all there is.

There is now one culture for everyone, in music as in language. It is a music that moves the young powerfully and immediately. Its beat goes to the depth of their souls and inarticulately expresses their inarticulate longings. Those longings are sexual, and the beat appeals almost exclusively to that. It caters to kiddy sexuality, at best to puppy love. The first untutored feelings of adolescents are taken over by this music and given a form and a satisfaction. The words make little difference; they may be explicitly sexual, or sermons in favor of nuclear disarmament, or even religious—the motor of it all is eroticism. The youngsters know this perfectly well, even if their parents do not.

Rock music caused a great evolution in the relations between parents and children. Its success was the result of an amazing cooperation among lust, art, and commercial shrewdness. Without parents realizing it, their children were liberated from them. The children had money to spend. The record companies recognized as much and sold them music appealing to their secret desires. Never before was a form of art (however unquestionable) directed to so young an audience. This art gave children's feelings public respectability. The education of children had escaped their parents, no matter how hard they tried to prevent it. The most powerful formative influence on children between 12 and 18 is not the school, not the church, not the home, but rock music and all that goes with it. It is not an elevating but a leveling influence. The children have as their heroes banal, drug-, and sex-ridden guttersnipes who foment rebellion not only against parents but against all noble sentiments. This is the emotional nourishment they ingest in these precious years. It is the real junk food.

One thing I have no difficulty teaching students today is the passage in the *Republic* where Socrates explains that control over music is control over character and that the rhythm and the melody are more powerful than the words. They do not especially like Socrates's views on music, but they understand perfectly what he is about and the importance of the issue.

3. *Sex*. No change has been so rapid, so great and so surprising as the change in the last twenty years concerning sex and the relations between the sexes. Young people of college age are very much affected by the sexual passion and preoccupied with love, marriage, and the family (to use an old formula that is now painfully inadequate to what is really meant). It is an age of excitement and uncertainty, and much of the motivation for study and reflection of a broader sort comes from the will to adorn and clarify erotic longings.

It is, however, in this domain that the listless, nihilistic mood has its practical expression and most affects the life of the students. The prevailing atmosphere deprives sex of seriousness as well as of charm. And, what is more, it makes it very difficult to think about sex. In a permissive era, when it is almost respectable to think and even do the deeds of Oedipus, shame and guilt have taken refuge in a new redoubt and made certain things unthinkable. Terror grips man at the thought he might be sexist. For all other tastes there is sympathy and support in universities. Sexism, whatever it may mean, is unpardonable.

The great change in sexual behavior has taken place in two stages. The first is what was called the sexual revolution. This meant simply that pre- and extra-marital sex became much more common, and the various penalties for promiscuity were either much reduced or disappeared. In the middle Sixties I noticed that very nice students who previously would have hidden their affairs abandoned all pretense. They would invite their professors to dine in apartments where they lived together and not hesitate to give expression to physical intimacy in a way that even married couples would rarely do before their peers.

This kind of change, of course, implied a very different way of thinking about things. Desire always existed, but it used to war with conscience, shame, and modesty. These now had to be deprecated as prejudices, as pointing to nothing beyond themselves. Religious and philosophic moral teachings that supported such sentiments became old hat, and a certain materialism which justified bodily satisfaction seemed more plausible.

The world looks very different than it once did to young people entering college. The kinds of questions they ask, and the sensitivities they bring to these fresh circumstances, are vastly altered. The tension of high expectation has been relaxed; there is much they no longer have to find out. A significant minority of students couple off very early and live together throughout college with full awareness that they intend to go their separate ways afterward. They are just taking care of certain needs in a sensible way. There is, for a member of an older generation, an incomprehensible slackness of soul in all this. Certainly the adventurousness of such people, who are half-married but without the moral benefits of responsibility, is lamed. There is nothing wild, Dionysian, searching, in our promiscuity. It has a dull, sterilized, scientific character.

One must add that an increasing number of students come from divorced families and include in their calculation the possibility or the likelihood of divorce in their own future. The possibility of separation is not a neutral fact, allowing people to stay or go; it encourages separation because it establishes a psychology of separateness.

The result is inevitably egotism, not because the individuals are evil or naturally more prone to selfishness than those of another era. If there is no other thing to be attached to, the desires concerning ourselves are ever present. This tendency is particularly pronounced in an age when political ties are weak. People can hardly be blamed for not being attached when there is nothing that calls forth attachment. There can be no doubt that the sexual revolution plays a great role in dissolving the bonds founded on sexual relationships. What is not sufficiently understood is that in modern society there is little else that can be the basis for moral association. There is a repulsive lack of self-knowledge in those who attack the "nuclear family" and are rhapsodic about the "extended family" and real "community." Looseness is thus made into an ethical criti-

que of our society. The "extended family" is no more possible in our time or consonant with our principles than is feudalism, while the "nuclear family" is still a viable alternative, but one that needs support in theory and practice. It provides a natural basis for connectedness. One can give it up, but one has to know the price. There is simply nothing else that is generally operative in society at large.

But even more powerful than all of the above changes are the effects of feminism, which is still early in its career of reform and is the second stage of the great change of which I am speaking. The theme is too vast to treat properly, but one can say that it, much more than the sexual revolution, takes place on the level of thought rather than that of instinct. Consciousness must be altered. Women have been exploited and misused throughout the entire past, and only now can one find out their real potential. We are on the threshold of a whole new world and a whole new understanding. And Right and Left are in large measure united on the issue. There is an almost universal agreement, among those who count for university students, that feminism is simply justified as is.

The degree of common agreement comes home to me when I teach the Socrates fantasy in the *Republic* about the abolition of the difference between the sexes. Twenty years ago it was an occasion of laughter, and my problem was to get students to take it seriously. Today it seems perfectly commonplace, and students take it all too seriously, failing to catch the irony. They do not note the degree to which Socrates acts as though men and women have no bodies and lightly give up all the things that are one's own, particularly those one loves—parents, spouses, children. All of them are connected with the bisexuality of the species. In doing this, Socrates shows the ambiguity of our nature and the degree of tension between our common humanity and our sexual separateness. The balance between the two is always fraught with difficulties. One must decide which has primacy; and this decision must be made in full awareness of the loss entailed by it. Our students no longer understand this.

It is here that a great difference between the situation of women and that of men comes to light. Women today have, to use our new talk, an agenda. They want to have the opportunity to pursue careers, and they want to find ways to reconcile this goal with having families. Also, it is their movement, so they are involved and excited, have much to talk about. The men, on the other hand, are waiting to be told what is on the agenda and ready to conform to its demands. There is little inclination to resist. All the principles have been accepted; it only remains to see how to live by them. Women are to have careers just as do men and, if there is to be marriage, the wife's career is not to be sacrificed to the man's; home and children are a shared responsibility; when and if there are to be children is up to the woman, and the decision to terminate or complete a pregnancy is a woman's right. Above all, women are not to have a "role" imposed on them. They have a right of self-definition. The women were the victims and must be the leaders in their recovery from victimization. The men, as they themselves see it, have to be understanding and flexible. There are no guidelines; each case is individual. One can't know what to expect. Openness, again, is the virtue.

The result is a desexualization of life, all the while that a lot of sexual activity is going on, and a reduction of the differences between the sexes. Anger and spiritedness are definitely out. Men and women in universities frequently share common dwellings and common facilities. Sex is all right, but creates a problem. There are no forms in which it is to express itself, and it is a reminder of differentiation where there is supposed to be none. It is difficult to shift from the mode of sameness into that of romance. Therefore advances are tentative, nobody is quite sure where they are to begin, and men's fear of stereotyping women is ever-present. It is love that is being sacrificed, for it makes woman into an object to be possessed. Dating is almost a thing of the past. Men and women are together in what is supposed to be an easy camaraderie. If coupling takes place, it must not disturb the smooth surface of common human endeavor. Above all: no courtship or courtliness. Now there is friendship, mutual respect, communication; realism without foolish fabulation or hopes. One wonders what primal feelings and desires are pushed down beneath the pat uniformity of the speech they almost all use, a self-congratulatory speech which affirms that they are the first to have discovered how to relate to other people.

This conviction has as its first consequence that all old books are no longer relevant, because their authors were sexists (if they happened to be women, they were maimed by living in sexist society). There is little need of the commissars who are popping up all over the place to make the point that Eve, Cleopatra, Emma Bovary, and Anna Karenina are parts of male chauvinist propaganda. The students have gotten the point. These figures can't move their imaginations because their situations have nothing to do with situations in which students expect to find themselves. They need no inquisition to root out sexist heresies—although they will get one. And in the absence (temporary, of course) of a literature produced by feminism to rival the literature of Sophocles, Shakespeare, Racine, and Stendhal, students are without literary inspiration. Teaching romantic novels to university students (in spite of a healthy perseverance of this genre, as indicated by the success of the Harlequin romances—I find one free in every box of Hefty garbage bags I buy these days) is a quasi-impossibility. Students are either not interested or use it as grist for their ideological mill. Such books do not cause them to wonder whether they are missing something. All that passion seems pointless.

Notwithstanding all our relativism, there are certain things we know and which cannot be doubted. These are the tenets of the egalitarian creed, and today its primary tenet is that the past was sexist. This means that all the doubts which tradition should inspire in us in order to liberate us from the prejudices of our time are in principle closed to us. This is the source of the contentless certainty that is the hallmark of the young. This is what a teacher faces today. I do not say that the situation is impossible or worse than it ever was. The human condition is always beset by problems. But these are *our* problems, and we must face them clearly. They constitute a crisis for humane learning but also reaffirm the need for it. The bleak picture is often relieved by the rays of natural curiosity about a better way; it can happen any time a student confronts a great book.

# A Response to Bloom

*George Levine*

The phenomenon of Allan Bloom's *The Closing of the American Mind* is more important than the book. It is an intellectual's book—at least one half of it devoted to a survey and analysis of the history of political philosophy from Plato to Weber—so it is difficult to believe that the more than 300,000 people who have reported bought it have also actually read it through. Why has it been so successful?

The book's enthusiastic reception by neo-conservatives suggests some obvious political explanations, but these alone are not sufficient. It makes, in addition, a strong emotional appeal. Who, after all, does not share some of Bloom's complaints about the thinness of family and community life in America? I would guess, on the strength of my own experience, that few in the middle class have escaped, in the texture of their lives at home or in what passes for community in cities or suburbia, paying the price

Bloom's *The Closing of the American Mind* was widely and heatedly discussed in both the popular media (including *Nightline* and the *Oprah Winfrey Show*) and academic journals. (A collection of these reviews was recently published in book form.) This review by George Levine appeared in the Winter 1988 issue of *Raritan*, a quarterly review of literature and culture. Levine is Director of the Center for Critical Analysis of Contemporary Culture at Rutgers University. His recent books include *One Culture* and *Darwin and the Novelists*.

Reprinted by permission from *Raritan: A Quarterly Review*, Vol. VII, No. 3 (Winter 1988). Copyright © 1988 by *Raritan*, 165 College Ave., New Brunswick, NJ 08903

of economic and social organizations of American life. Bloom says what many want to hear about this malaise, and reassuringly does not locate some of the causes in the structure of the American economy and society. He tells the story as though from within, with an authority that seems to certify the argument, and with a rhetoric of considerable persuasiveness.

The rhetoric matters a great deal, suggesting a fearless confrontation with contemporary pieties, and implying emotionally satisfying arguments without actually making them. Bloom consistently pretends to reject positions his rhetoric shows him to be taking. After analyzing the failure of the contemporary family, for instance, he claims that he is not arguing "that the old family arrangements were good or that we should or could go back to them. I am only insisting that we not cloud our vision to such an extent," he says, "that we believe that there are viable substitutes for them just because we want or need them." But this, in fact, is what his whole book implies. By rhetorically condemning present social and cultural arrangements and mocking those who try to come to terms with them or improve them, he implies that the only way to go is backwards.

Similarly, he avoids explicitly blaming the failures of contemporary culture entirely on the University and its professoriate. Nonetheless, from the book's title to the final analysis of the inadequacies of the contemporary disciplinary structure of American universities, he implies that a cowardly and ignorant professoriate and the institutions that house them are to blame, and he takes a high moral line against them. The moral indignation that exudes from the rhetoric must be, for many, one of the pleasures of this text, allowing readers to relax into the belief that they can locate the culprits and, by forcing them to behave, make things all better.

One cannot condemn the book for the audience it has attracted nor for the play it has been getting on television, the medium its author unequivocally despises. It is a matter of interest, however, that it could be so quickly assimilated by a culture that Bloom derides. This is a *cri de coeur,* a scholar's letting himself go in a long lamentation about the way the world has turned away from everything he, as scholar, had imagined the University ought to embody. It sounds authentic, and the unacademic texture of the prose, its highly personal nature, makes much of it accessible and credible to a non-academic audience that values education but feels—fairly enough—that something is the matter with it.

The immediate attractiveness of Bloom's position to neo-conservatives is misguided. His arguments are in fact more conservative than neo-conservatives themselves would like: he wants great books universities, which would exclude technical and practically oriented schools. He wants the University to be a place of pure thought, and of pure thought about the fundamental issues of good and evil, life and death, self and other. He sounds like a nineteenth-century liberal in the mode of Matthew Arnold. Like Arnold, he argues that the great intellectual tradition of the West is to understand nature, to see the object as in itself it really is and, again like Arnold, he believes this is possible only by withdrawing from the world. He doesn't use the word, but along with Thomas Arnold, Coleridge, and Matthew Arnold himself, he seeks "a clerisy," disinterested, in touch with their best selves, learning the best that has been thought and said in the West. In this new old vision, the University would be the true church. There is no guarantee that Bloom's clerisy would be capitalists.

It would be unfortunate if, confusing Bloom with the New Right or William Bennett, one were to evade his nineteenth-century excesses by denying that anything is wrong in academia. The book will be invoked as support for all kinds of assaults on the Academy and all kinds of proposals to return to traditional ways of doing things; and it will certainly be used by the back-to-basics movement, although Bloom himself is obviously not interested in "basics." His concern is only with the best students at the best universities. Those who turn to Bloom for quick-answer conservative reforms and for easy condemnations of the universities aren't reading him right. They are building on shaky ground because the immediate strength of the book's rhetoric disguises the intellectual shakiness of its arguments.

Bloom in fact consistently disparages the audience to which his book makes its appeal most directly, and for them the question of the intellectual coherence of his arguments is likely to be secondary. For them, the strength and personal engagement in the analysis of the failings on all sides (except Bloom's) will be sufficient, accompanied as it is by a rhetoric implying that Bloom himself cares deeply both about his students and about the pedagogical goal of "human completeness." This alone is sufficient to establish the book's authority and its appeal for those whose education is as deficient as Bloom says it is. The testimony, on the dust jacket and in reviews, even by educated people I respect, that this book is important, that it will therefore be "savagely attacked," is obviously intended to disarm rejoinders by implying that they will all be motivated by political and partisan prejudice. But quite aside from the rhetorical implications of what Bloom has to say about society, history, and the Academy, none of which I like, the case I would make against the book is that despite Bloom's obvious learning and intelligence, it is intellectually shallow and incoherent. As an argument, his book is difficult to take seriously; it doesn't make sense.

One has a right to expect intellectual coherence of a book that appeals so unabashedly to the universal, the true, the rational, even as it elevates personal disappointment into general cultural analysis. But Bloom totally fails to connect his analysis of the failings of contemporary culture to the failings of the Academy. His argument derives from deeply irrational sources; in its support of "reason," it defies any reasonable standard of what reason might be; and it offers no adequate object of blame or direction for change. His allegations about modern students and his analysis of their "souls" (as one blurb puts it) is entirely anecdotal, Olympian, and condescendingly sentimental. His evidential grounds are outrageously inadequate; and since one of Bloom's major culprits is social science itself, it isn't hard to understand why he refuses to sustain his analysis with the kind of evidence social scientists might find acceptable. Moreover, the essential language, the apparently unself-conscious confidence with which Bloom can talk about "nature" and the "good" and the universal aspirations of "human nature" is of a sort that intelligent people have guarded against for decades and that John Stuart Mill was complaining about one hundred and fifty years ago. Bloom must know this, and perhaps he adopted his argumentative strategies and his essentialist language precisely to provoke responses like mine. What's wrong with the world for him is that it is dominated by social science mentalities and antiessentialist thinking.

Bloom's rhetoric, gracefully rejecting the hard abstract language of the disciplines and invoking the highest ideals of Western culture, disguises its own intellectual inconsistencies by implying that it is precisely the loss of his fully humane way of talking and thinking that has caused our present plight. What fuels this book is surely, among other things, Bloom's experience of the sixties, when he felt himself abused, surrounded by cowards and traitors, his beloved dream of the ideal university (or the University of Chicago) shattered. There is a venom and bitterness in his anecdotes about those bad old days that makes of this book an act of vengeance. The sixties have been mythologized and trashed since the end of the Vietnam War. Bloom has been nursing his wound since then, and like most commentators who have eased comfortably into the eighties, he has made the years between about 1967 and 1973 the age of the decline of the West, and certainly of the university.

Bloom insists early in the book that he is making no comparisons: "I do not claim that things were wonderful in the past. I am describing our present situation and do not intend any comparison with the past to be used as grounds for congratulating or blaming ourselves." But his title is *The Closing of the American Mind*, with the implication that there was a time when the American Mind was open. Surely, that was before 1968. And he chose, as well, the aggressive subtitle, "How higher education has failed democracy and impoverished the souls of today's students." Apparently, there was also a time when higher education wasn't doing this awful thing, and assuredly too that time was before 1968. For all of his apparently impressive grasp of history, Bloom seems astonishingly insensitive to a long tradition of American lamentation about the country's shallowness and intellectual poverty, its apparently inveterate anti-intellectualism. This didn't start in the sixties, and Bloom knows this. The cowardly professoriate he despises, the treasonable clerks who sold out the idea of education, according to him, for a handful of student approval, were not the caricatures he makes of them. Nor did they sell education down the river. They were part of another phase of a continuing struggle within American education, which began at the beginning and continues to this moment, to understand and to define the responsibilities of the University in a democracy.

Bloom's ahistoricism is intrinsic to his argument. Ideas are proof against history, and the issues are to be understood outside of history. Yet with its focus on the culpable sixties, history is nonetheless made to play a role in Bloom's telling of his painful story, and it emerges in his argument through anecdotes about students who provide silly and trivial answers to large moral problems or faculty members and administrators withering under Bloom's sharply intelligent questions. Outside of a few great philosophers, the world of this book is populated by a set of absurdly unintelligent (and hypocritical) intellectuals and painfully shallow and "nice" students. But anecdotes such as Bloom provides were commonplace, if I too may be anecdotal, when I began teaching in the late fifties. The sixties were a mere blip in the course of American history and the history of universities, although for Bloom they were the beginning of the end. The guns have long since disappeared from Cornell; my own experimental college, Livingston, has been absorbed—for better or worse—into the mainstream of Rutgers University. Indeed, all too little of what we learned in the years Bloom finds so terrible has remained part of the academic world.

While it is important to challenge the anecdotal evidence and Bloom's interpretation of the state of our souls and of contemporary culture, the most telling criticism of the book can be directed to its substantive intellectual argument. Let me try to formulate briefly what I take to be Bloom's position, avoiding as far as possible detours into the several thousand interesting but often maddening asides and supplementary arguments, the items that contribute to the book's wide appeal without really substantiating its argument. First of all, Bloom believes—with a passion that I respect but find difficult to comprehend—that ideas, and particularly the great ideas of great thinkers (as defined, of course, by Bloom) are the primary cause of our behavior, and of our society's. In all of his analysis of the malaise of contemporary culture, there is precisely nothing about economic, industrial, or political forces. Somehow—and Bloom ingeniously shows parallels between the language of the German philosophers and the language of pop psychology and pop culture—there is a direct line from Nietzsche to the man in the street (women get very short shrift in Bloom's world), and the mediator is the University. The man in the street, we are to believe, gets watered down Nietzsche and guides his life according to Nietzschean principles without knowing it. The determining factors are ideas, not economics, politics, or other subjects of the social sciences.

Cultural relativism, it appears, is the cause of all our woes. This sounds simple, even stupid, but Bloom begins with cultural relativism as the culprit, and he stays there. Cultural relativism is evil, first because every society requires a special faith in itself to insure its coherence and survival; second, because Western culture is superior to all other cultures; third, because all other cultures are entirely closed while ours is open, and they would destroy ours if they could; and fourth, because it means the end of the good, true, and beautiful, of universal verities, of nature itself. (The second point is not overtly stated; Bloom argues that we *can* find some things in other cultures that Western societies might use. But in our rationality and our very capacity to find some good things in other cultures we are clearly superior.) "Cultural relativism," he laments, "succeeds in destroying the West's universal or intellectually imperialistic claims, leaving it to be just another culture." It is a mark of the character of this book that this sentence is apparently intended to register loss, not gain.

Though it is true that sentences like this encourage charges of enthnocentricity, and though I find this book not only ethnocentric, but misogynist, and provincial (and therein lies another part of its grand appeal), I don't want my argument to rest on this kind of accusation. Bloom seems to have heard enough of name calling in the hated sixties, and that got nobody anywhere. More tamely and genially and I fear tediously I want to look at the epistemological implications of his argument.

Bloom believes Western culture is founded on the appeal to reason; cultural relativism denies the priority of reason. Western culture is founded on the understanding of nature; culture relativism denies the authority if not the reality of nature. Bloom is ready to defend in fairly cogent ways his positions on reason, truth, and nature, and he explicitly argues that these positions are truly antiethnocentric. Nevertheless, as a "cultural relativist" (and part of the problem), I find his language indefensible.

Bloom believes in nature, as opposed to convention, and thus he believes in philosophy as opposed to the social sciences. He argues that "Nature should be the standard by which we judge our own lives and the lives of the people." That sentence left me breathless when I first read it; it still does. The long history of the complexities of the word "nature" seems to have made no impression on Bloom. Whatever he means by it, his "nature" is out there absolutely to be

known. It is the standard of both truth and value. Among other things, the sentence suggests a stronger endorsement of sociobiology than Bloom may want to give. But since in his world humanity strives to transcend convention (the subject of the much despised social sciences) in order to get back to *nature,* he must mean, among other things that humans need to behave in accordance with their biological natures. There is no need to invoke here the various issues revolving around that idea, from sociobiology to behaviorism to the battle of I. Q. Testing to feminism.

Bloom argues, moreover, that "what is most characteristic of the West is science, . . . the quest to know nature and the consequent denigration of convention." Science, in this reading, becomes the path to all knowledge and all value, and insofar as it succumbs to cultural relativism and historicism—of the sort philosophers of science like Kuhn and philosophers like Rorty have been practicing—it destroys itself. The whole basis of reality, truth, value of Western society goes down with cultural relativism. While Bloom believes in the possibility of objective, disinterested and universal truth, the cultural relativist tends to believe in the cultural construction of knowledge.

In Bloom, that belief heralds the death of the West, manifested in such unlikely effects as his students' failure to make love adequately, or the culture's absorption in the dumb animal rhythms of rock music, or the excesses of feminism and ethnic studies. Believing very sensibly that some things are better than others, Bloom strenuously insists on the disasters caused in every aspect of the culture, from top to bottom, by the tendency he finds in his students and their teachers to argue that studying other cultures is the only way to transcend the limits of our own. I'm not sure that very many people really do insist that, and the prominence of American and Western studies in most curricula—along with the continued manifestations of racial bigotry on ivied campuses—leads me to think that this particular "threat" is greatly overestimated. Nevertheless, the point about the intellectual importance of cultural relativism and its impact on Bloom's kind of faith in absolute and eternal verities is a strong one. Indeed, it is one that I accept without at all being dismayed by its effects. Rather, I'm encouraged by it as a provocation to rethink our fundamental assumptions about values and knowledge.

What is most striking to me is that Bloom never once in the entire book confronts the intellectual substance of the arguments for cultural relativism. His position is, simply, that its *effects* are bad and that most of the people who espouse it don't know its sources in the great thinkers and therefore can't understand its full moral and intellectual price. The latter part of his argument I find persuasive but trivial. That is, it's probably true that all but the most sophisticated "cultural relativists" haven't read Nietzsche or Weber, let alone Rousseau and Kant. It also seems that the consequences of a genuine cultural relativism can be very painful. For Bloom, cultural relativism is the erasing of value distinctions between cultures (creating the belief that other cultures are not only as good as ours but perhaps even better). It is also, however, an epistemological notion—that all perception and thus all knowledge is conditioned if not created by the cultural assumptions built into our consciousness and perceptual equipment from the time we are born. The confusions, paradoxes, and creative difficulties issuing from these views are manifest in the dominant critical theories of our time. Bloom's very reduction of the complex ideas and states of mind he attacks in the phrase "cultural relativism" suggests how inadequate his critique of contemporary culture is. Any in-

tellectual systems that tend to subvert the possibility of absolute objective knowledge, of the essential reality of ideas like "the good," or "nature," are in his world "cultural relativism."

There are arguments that might begin to contend with the difficulties of contemporary epistemology, the problems of perspectivalism or what William James called the egocentric predicament. We get no such arguments from Bloom. Instead, he tells stories about the bad effects of such thinking. He implicitly urges that we go back to traditions we don't believe in because life was richer and more fulfilling when we did believe in them. Although he contends that cultural relativism subverts the authority of reason, he doesn't make a single argument to avert the conclusion or to explain why intelligent people might be relativists. Obviously, he doesn't think there are any such people, which accounts for his consistent caricaturing of any figures in his past who disagreed with him. He doesn't talk about the tradition of contemporary hermeneutics that finds all knowledge mediated through personal or cultural biases and distortions; he invokes only to dismiss the deconstructionists and Derrida, Lacan, the Freudians, and structuralists. And because he doesn't seriously consider the possible contamination of ideas by ideology, contemporary Marxist critics go the way of the deconstructionists.

Everyone from his perspective is intent on denying the importance of the old texts and engaging in a "furious effort" to be up-to-date. The phrase characteristically treats all serious activity of modern thought as faddish and trivial and every effort to deal with the Nietzschean insight into the death of the absolute as derivative and superficial. Bloom's one answer to all these problems is, read his great philosophers. And he justifies his persistence in essentialist language by implying its moral superiority. He talks about nature as if it is not only possible to know exactly what it is but to guide one's behavior in accordance with it. Whose nature? what aspects of it? under what conditions? Is it universal or historical? Can it ever be perceived without the distorting mediation of the perceiver? Does the word refer to some objective nonverbal entity, or does it carry in its very texture the significances, prejudices, ideals of some of the philosophers Bloom constantly invokes?

Yet in insisting on the disastrous consequences of cultural relativism—however foggily undefined along with other of his key words—Bloom is, in fact, putting his finger on a crisis in contemporary thought, the crisis of knowledge and value. Unquestionably, contemporary social dislocations reflected in the dislocations of contemporary epistemology have forced important variations on the questions of how we know, even how we know that we know, and how we affirm, justify, and share values. But Bloom trivializes this important subject by dismissing all who have tried to address it. In effect, he dismisses the crisis itself as the inevitable result of the faddish and cowardly behavior of intellectuals and Americans in general. All of this would have been avoided had we continued to read the great thinkers.

Bloom's language is a desperate retreat to a faith in something in which it is no longer possible to believe. I infer that Bloom doesn't believe in it either. For example, he reprimands Woody Allen in *Zelig* for making fun of the old Jewish dancing men and complains that for Allen "it goes without saying that a return to the old mode of adjustment and apparent health is neither possible nor desirable." But here Bloom is surely practicing the cultural relativism for which he blames his students, since he clearly does not believe in what those old Jewish men believed in, only in the state of "health" that went with the belief. His answer to cultural

relativism is to pretend a commitment to older traditions that were healthier. The same kind of answer comes from William Bennett and those of the back-to-basics school who believe that the problems of education can be solved by returning to the very methods and subjects that were so discredited by the late fifties as to inspire the hated sixties to rebel.

The intellectual emptiness of Bloom's high-culture intellectual's attack on what he takes to be the University establishment needs to be recognized. Which is not to say that all is well with the University. His attack would not be so popular if some things weren't very wrong. Obviously, the University is a thoroughly compromised place. It cannot address its curricular and pedagogical problems without contending with finances, entrenched structures, the vagaries of the American economy, immigration policies, professional ambition, self-interest, and innumerable practical exigencies that Bloom does not attend to. And obviously, there are serious curricular problems that follow from social and political changes (and their intellectual counterparts) marking increased democratization and social homogenization—not, I would think, necessarily bad things. The University can address its problems, and lots of faculty are thinking serious non-Bloomian thoughts about how to handle them that make a return to the Great Books University a parochial and even silly response. In many ways, the University is now a more intellectually stimulating and vigorous place than it has been for decades. Many of its most interesting people are dealing uncomfortably but excitingly with the issues that Bloom wants to shove under the table in deference to great ideas by great thinkers. "Cultural relativism" does create profound problems in the establishment and authority of value, and it disrupts the positivist ideal of objective representation of natural truths. It raises the most fundamental of issues—what is knowledge and how is it possible to acquire it? Many people in the University are thinking about these problems, even reading a few great books along the way. The fact that they do not seem to know with dogmatic certainty what nature, "human completeness," or even the ideal curriculum should be is a mark of the integrity not the faddishness of their thought.

Bloom's book is intellectually disreputable because it totally fails to address these issues while pretending that philosophy is the most important of all subjects. Moreover, it absurdly attributes the real crises and weaknesses of contemporary culture entirely to the cowardice and intellectual shabbiness of the Academy and to a professoriate intimidated by the sixties. One of the great ironies of the popularity of his book is that while it looks to be passionately and neoconservatively pro-American, and shows a charming devotion to knowledge and students, it denigrates *everything* American as shabby, faddish, derivative—except when he waves the flag over America's responsibility to the world. Bloom is, I believe, deeply anti-American in that while he celebrates democracy, the only thing he expressly values in it is what it borrowed from European Enlightenment philosophy when it established democratic government. A look at the index confirms that he makes not a single allusion to important American thinkers, say, Emerson, William James, or Pierce. (Dewey, to be fair, is mentioned three times, for the most part dismissed and belittled, but implicitly praised for boyish optimism). *All* important ideas in America have been borrowed (and watered down) from Europe, and particularly, from Germany. Bloom reveals no feeling for American history, not even American intellectual history, so that while describing the closing of the American mind he talks only about Plato, Aristotle, Locke, Kant, Rousseau, Nietzsche, and Weber. And

American universities were at their best when they were suddenly filled, in the 1950s, with European professors.

One last point, which is probably central to any discussion of the subject at state universities. Bloom never connects the failures of the University to larger failures of contemporary society and culture, which he blames implicitly on the University. He oversimplifies intellectual history by ignoring everything that went into producing it, except ideas. I wouldn't for a minute suggest that the American University is an ideal institution, but Bloom's total preoccupation with "great ideas" as the cause of social action and personal behavior leads him to attribute to it and to the people he resented in the sixties the collapse of the whole culture. If we are to do anything about weaknesses in contemporary education it is essential that we dismiss this absurd but forceful part of Bloom's argument. One of things universities must do is consider the limits of what is genuinely possible for them, within the social, economic, and political constraints of American culture.

Even if Bloom's analysis of the problems of contemporary culture were correct, it wouldn't be of much use to the vast majority of strong institutions of higher education. He is quite explicit at the start about being interested only in the best students at the best universities, and all his anecdotes (which are his evidence) are drawn from experiences at those universities. Not concerned with the state's responsibilities in higher education to the population at large, but only with the best ideas for the best students at the best places, Bloom can't have anything to say about the nature of the curriculum at universities to which financially constrained parents send their children for training that might help them survive after the BA. How many parents would be willing to send their children to universities only that they may think great thoughts, struggle to "human completeness," and contemplate or discover the unity of all knowledge—unless, of course, the university's name carried such weight that the diploma would assure employment whatever the actual content of the education. At most universities, questions of curriculum are necessarily compromised by economics, state politics, social and ethnic variation. The University has a moral and a legal responsibility to bring along weak and mediocre students as well as to cultivate the outstanding ones, even if it cannot let the shape of its curricula be determined by the weakest students.

While agreeing with Bloom that cultural relativism has made it very difficult to determine what the best curriculum might be, I welcome that difficulty as a goad to thinking hard and seriously and freshly about the problem. Unlike Bloom, I do not believe that those who argued for radical changes in traditional curricula (which, in any case, wouldn't have satisfied his objectives) are cowards and charlatans. (Some of these show up everywhere.) And courage seems to me to be the requisite for those willing to resist the political and emotional pressures to return to discredited traditions simply because to aban-don them caused pain and uncertainty. We should know, though Bloom doesn't, that changing the curriculum isn't in fact going to make much of a difference to the way the family exists in America, or to rock music, or television.

Bloom looks backward and away from the real conditions of American education. Like many in academia, he doesn't like the impurities of history and society as they thrust themselves between great ideas and their embodiment. Grudgingly he modifies at the end his apocalyptic and utopian rhetoric for a melancholy concession that nothing more can be hoped for than to keep the embers of true philosophy alive. I would be happy to fan the flames, but only if "true philosophy" entails coming to terms with the apparently unphilosophical forces that largely determine the shape of our lives, only if it forced Bloom to recognize how much of his American jeremiad is inspired by personal animus, bitterness, and frustration at an early stage of his career, and only if it included a genuine intellectual confrontation with cultural relativism. Otherwise, the best thing to do is to ignore this book and get back to serious business.

# What We Expect

## Preparing for College—A Statement by 12 Deans

Most freshmen entering highly competitive colleges arrive on campus with top ranked secondary school averages and impressive SAT scores. Some, from their first day in class, do well, fulfilling our high expectations for them. Others falter educationally, not sure why they are in college, or how to study, or what to study, or why. Some college students take several semesters to begin gaining full advantage of the opportunities for learning that surround them; some never gain that advantage.

Secondary school teachers and administrators see the same problem from their perspective, and some have shared their concerns with us. We think a major reason some students succeed and others are not as successful lies in the kind and character of their secondary school preparation, not in their test scores and grades.

We are sharing our observations for two purposes. First, we want to offer high school students guidance in their selection of courses. Second, we want to assist parents, faculty, administrators, and school boards as they seek to offer high school students an education that will serve them well in a challenging world. We believe that the pluralism of American higher education, beneficial though it is, confuses some college-bound students. Even among the institutions we serve, the requirements for admission and for graduation vary widely, as do the available majors and areas of specialization. Despite these differences, we, as academic deans, share a belief in a basic set of priorities for college-bound students.

Our concern here is with preparation for college-level work, and not with the requirements for admission to a college. Our concern is with the special skills, attitudes, and motivation which students bring to college that let them participate effectively in the learning experiences open to them. Securing admission to college is important; more important is whether the student is prepared to make the best use of that opportunity.

We hope students—especially those who plan to attend selective colleges—will accept our advice. We hope, too, that our views will form the basis of a new cooperative effort between colleges and secondary schools leading to the improvement of education at both levels. Toward that end, we began the preparation of this statement by talking with many secondary school educators. We applaud other such efforts.

We find that students who benefit most from our educational programs are those who enter with certain identifiable attitudes and

This statement comes from a 1984 national educational conference on the relationship between high school and college.

Reprinted from *NASSP Bulletin* (October 1984) by permission of the National Association of Secondary School Principals.

skills—such as persistent curiosity, broad intellectual interests, skill at analytical and critical thinking, a concern for exploring and applying values, an ability to manage time responsibly, and a willingness to work hard.

The development of such attributes is, of course, only partially within the influence of secondary schools. We believe, however, that the content and expectations of secondary school courses can be shaped to enhance those characteristics that students will later need. Critical thinking skills can be improved, for example, by the regular practice of writing papers that require analysis and interpretation of material. They can be improved, too, by examinations that require students to assess and integrate information and ideas, rather than repeating only what they have memorized. Students who must master demanding course material within a series of deadlines can learn to manage time responsibly and appreciate the rewards of hard work.

Participation in well-managed extracurricular and cocurricular activities can, as well, help students develop constructive attitudes and sharpen useful skills. Writing for the school newspaper, participating in forensic and theatrical activities, playing in musical organizations or on athletic teams can, if purposefully performed, contribute forcefully to the development of characteristics valuable to college students. We believe that most college-bound students have the capacity to complete the academic program we recommend and have ample time to participate in useful, substantial cocurricular and extracurricular activities.

*We believe strongly that our incoming students need to be well grounded in seven specific subject areas. These are the arts, English language, foreign language, history, literature, mathematics, and science. In fact, we recommend that in these areas students go beyond the typical minimum requirements both for secondary school graduation and for admission to college. Competence in each of these areas is crucial for productive study at the college level.*

We do not believe our colleges should be expected to provide general remedial work to overcome basic deficiencies in preparation. Some college students, by extra effort, do overcome inadequate preparation in these essential areas; for other students, however, an initial experience of inadequacy in the basics inhibits their intellectual growth during their entire college years. The stronger the secondary school preparation is, the more easily a college student can begin immediately to experience the benefits of serious academic pursuits.

Without being prescriptive or intrusive, we want to indicate briefly what we mean by solid preparation in each of the seven vital subject areas.

**The arts:** The arts provide a uniquely valuable mode of seeing ourselves and the world around us. In a bureaucratic and technological age, the arts present a necessary balance, a sensitive link to that which makes us more fully human. Students should be familiar with the work of some major artists. They should develop an awareness of artistic sensibility and judgment and an understanding of the creative process. Students should select one or two semester-long courses, taught in an exacting manner in the areas of music, theatre, and/or art.

**English language:** Students must have a command of English grammar and well-developed compositional skills. Students should take courses in several subject areas that require closely reasoned compositions involving both concrete and abstract thought, as well as some fundamental library research activities. Courses that develop student abilities to use writing to form and exchange ideas and to write and speak English with clarity and style are among the most important courses they can take.

**Foreign language:** Competency in a foreign language, modern or classical, through the third or fourth year of a demanding secondary school program develops a student's language resourcefulness in a world community that increasingly expects that capacity. Such competency improves the comprehension of a student's native language and culture, and enhances the student's understanding of humankind. Such competency, which is most efficiently gained at an early age, also provides a good basis for further language study in college and adds to students' scholarly capability by freeing them from dependency upon translations.

**History:** The study of American history and culture and of Western traditions, from the ancient world to the present, is important to an understanding of the contemporary world. Familiarity with a non-Western culture (or cultures) adds substantially to that comprehension. Further, an appreciation of good government and civic responsibility is characteristically rooted in an understanding of history. An appreciation of historical perspective is, itself, an important educational objective. Indeed, serious conversation is not possible when students are ignorant either of major historical events, movements, and people or of the general mode of historical discussion and explanation. Such references are fundamental to much of higher education. At least two years of historical study at the secondary school level are highly valuable.

**Literature:** The study of traditional literary texts adds greatly to a student's understanding of humankind and human associations. Systematic literary study can also better prepare a student for the reading of contemporary literature. The experience of reading, for example, the comedies and tragedies of ancient Greek playwrights, the Judaic and Christian scriptures, the writings of Shakespeare, and the work of more recent writers of enduring reputation, provides an excellent foundation for further literary inquiry and a fine context for study in many fields. The student is best prepared by confronting excellent works in all the major genres—plays, novels, essays, poetry, and short fiction. Some combination of four years of strong English language courses and literature courses is expected.

**Mathematics:** The field of mathematics grows ever more important. Quantitative analysis is crucial to understanding the complexities of the modern world. Valuing and decision-making activities often require quantitative judgments. The use of algebra, calculus, and statistics is now commonplace in the study of many disciplines in college. Computer literacy is useful even in the humanities. Sufficient preparation for this range of mathematical applications normally requires four years of secondary school study, resulting in a readiness for beginning college calculus.

**Science:** The study for one year each of biology, chemistry, and physics is highly desirable; at the very least, a student should take one year or two of these sciences and perhaps two years of one science. Familiarity with the basic sciences has long been a hallmark of the educated person and is now a common, practical necessity. To understand the relationships among science, technology, and public policy makes crucial some knowledge of the basic issues, nomenclature, and methods of science—not the least because the survival of humanity is at stake.

Circumstances may make it difficult for some students to take the maximum number of academic courses available in each of the seven subject areas. Some students may have to exercise choices—depending upon the strengths of the particular secondary school program, the aspirations of the individual students, and even the peculiarities of scheduling. Yet, despite these considerations, we stress that students should remain determined to complete a strong academic program and not substitute other courses for those that are fundamental and exacting.

The excitement of higher learning is more easily gained by those students who arrive on campus properly equipped for the challenge. Successful college students regularly cite with admiration secondary school teachers who helped prepare them well. Those students do, in fact, find the learning experience at each level of their education to be part of the same grand adventure.

George Allan, *Dean of the College,* Dickinson College

Mary Maples Dunn, *Dean of the Undergraduate College,* Bryn Mawr College

Frances D. Ferguson, *Vice President for Academic Affairs,* Bucknell University

Andrew T. Ford, *Dean of the College,* Allegheny College

Robert M. Gavin, Jr., *Provost,* Haverford College

Thomas J. Hershberger, *Dean of Faculty,* Chatham College

John W. Hunt, *Dean of the College of Arts and Science,* Lehigh University

William A. Jeffers, Jr., *Dean of the College,* Lafayette College

David B. Potts, *Dean of the College,* Gettysburg College

Richard P. Traina, *Dean of the College,* Franklin and Marshall College

Richard L. Van Horn, *Provost,* Carnegie-Mellon University

Harrison M. Wright, *Provost,* Swarthmore College

# Bridging the Gap Between Home and Academic Literacies

*Juan C. Guerra*

When I first came to the University of Illinois at Chicago (UIC) as a freshman in 1968, I was faced with the kind of dilemma which I am sure any minority student who has grown up in a non-mainstream culture with a language and a set of values totally alien to the world of academia must inevitably confront. Unlike Richard Rodriguez, who according to his autobiography, *Hunger of Memory,* assimilated into academic culture to the point where he alienated himself from his own home culture, from his parents and the values they had taught him, from the language that he had grown up with and which his parents still spoke, I, for reasons which are still not completely clear to me, was unwilling to totally give up the culture and the language I had brought with me to this university. Minority students who enter UIC

today, especially those who come directly from Chicago's inner city high schools or transfer in from the City Colleges of Chicago, must inevitably confront the same dilemma that Mr. Rodriguez and I encountered. What determines whether they decide to alienate themselves from their home culture and totally buy into academic culture as Mr. Rodriguez did, to find a balance between the two as I believe I have done, or to be completely unwilling or unable to assimilate to any degree and therefore end up dropping out of the university is one of the issues I would like to address today.

Personally, I prefer the middle ground. That is, I would not like to see a whole army of Richard Rodriguezes graduating from this university any more than I would like to see underrepresented students coming to UIC and then dropping out because the university was unwilling to accept their home culture as a valuable and worthwhile asset and they, in turn, were unwilling or unable to buy into academic culture. If we hope to avoid either of these extremes, we must find a way to create an environment in which the home cultures and the affiliated languages or dialects that ethnic minorities bring with them to this institution are not only respected but understood by the faculty who will inevitably face them in the classroom. Fortunately, for us, there has been a general shift in attitude both among theorists and re-

Juan Guerra, assistant professor of English at the University of Washington at Seattle, was both a student in the English Department and a lecturer in the Educational Assistance Program at UIC from 1968 to 1990. During his tenure at UIC, Guerra was very active in promoting Latino organizations on campus and was a founding member of the Association of Latino Workers, the Chancellor's Committee on the Status of Latinos, and the Latino Committee on University Affairs. Specifically, he worked with the latter group to encourage parent-student involvement in the university and to establish a community presence here. The original version of this paper was presented in March 1989 at a conference of composition and communication teachers.

Reprinted with permission of Juan C. Guerra

searchers who deal with language and literacy and among top ranking administrators at UIC in favor of multiple literacies and cultural diversity, respectively.

Until very recently, most theorists and researchers in literacy studies had, knowingly or otherwise, accepted Goody and Watt's view (1963) that so-called oral and literate cultures are diametrically opposed to one another because alphabetic literacy makes it possible for individuals to develop certain cognitive abilities which people who primarily use oral language do not possess. To make matters worse, many of them had also unwittingly accepted Olson's notion (1977) that the introduction of written language in western culture resulted in the development of certain logical processes which were absent in what Olson and others (Goody & Watt, 1963; Ong, 1982) refer to as non-literate cultures. As a result of this new development, thought and language were supposedly transformed to the point where it became possible for a writer to express his or her ideas in such a way that meaning became an inherent and inviolable part of the text itself. The result, Olson tells us, was "not an ordinary language, not a mother tongue, but rather a form of language specialized to serve the requirements of autonomous, written, formalized text" (p. 270).

In recent years, sociolinguists employing an ethnographic methodology borrowed from anthropology have questioned these assumptions. These researchers (Scribner & Cole, 1981; Street, 1984; Tannen, 1982; Heath, 1982, 1983; and Scollon & Scollon, 1981) have demonstrated the importance of examining and understanding the uses of language, both oral and written, in particular cultures to see how they are affected by the dynamics of the social, cultural, political, and economic systems which exist within or impact from without. As a consequence, Tannen (1982) and Heath (1982) have both recommended that we view orality and literacy as endpoints of a continuum. In this way, the discourse patterns of the different cultures can be examined as points along a continuum instead of as either absolutely oral or literate. Furthermore, Street (1984) has argued that alphabetic literacy by itself does not lead to the development of certain logical processes and should not be examined in isolation from the particular socio-cultural context in which it is acquired and used. To speak a language at all, Street has pointed out, is to employ abstraction and logic. Moreover, because it is "already embedded in an ideology," any literacy brings with it a way of looking at the world and acting in it which goes beyond the traditional notion of literacy as a set of value-free mechanical or technical skills. Literacy, then, is more than a technological tool; it is a social practice. And because it is a social practice, we can no longer speak of one literacy; we must instead speak of multiple literacies.

In my work with the Mexican-American Language and Literacy Project at UIC, I am currently involved in an ethnographic study of several families in the Pilsen and Little Village neighborhoods of Chicago. One of our goals in this project is to describe the patterns of language and literacy used by the social network members of recent-immigrant and native-born families of Mexican origin to see how they differ from those of the academic mainstream model. In so doing, we will be able to develop a better sense of the difficulties that young people from these discourse communities face when they come to a major university like UIC. In time, we also hope to develop strategies which will help them make the transition from their home culture and language to the academic culture and language that they will encounter at UIC.

In view of the work that we are doing and the research which has been undertaken and which we are encouraging others to undertake among the various non-mainstream groups represented at this university, the key question we now need to answer is this: Will the faculty and administration be willing to make use of this research to help members of the various non-mainstream cultures represented at this particular institution bridge the gap between their home and the university's academic literacies? Based on what I have heard in recent months, my answer is a reasonably definite yes, if what I have heard presented in theory, and especially in realization of the changing demographics at this institution, is systematically implemented and put into practice within a reasonable period of time. Let me explain.

During most of the twenty years that I have been a student and a lecturer at UIC, I have noticed that some members of the faculty and the administration have taken a rather dim view of the effect that the growing number of non-mainstream students is having on the reputation of this institution. This, of course, was not a problem in the beginning. When I first came to UIC in 1968, there were only a handful of Blacks and Latinos on this campus. As a matter of fact, there were so few of us that, try as I might, I have never been able to find any statistics on just how many of us there were. The fact of the matter is that they just did not keep statistics on us back then. And because we were so few for so many years, the prevailing attitude was that it was our responsibility as students to overcome the limitations of our home cultures so that we could be assimilated into the new academic culture to which we were being exposed. If we were going to survive, we were just going to have to adapt to the practices of academic literacy which form the backbone of university studies. And so we did. At least those of us who survived did. As far as many of the faculty were concerned, their one and only responsibility was

to make sure that they did everything in their power to expose us to the culture and literacy of academia. And if one of us was unwilling or unable to accept or adapt to academic culture and literacy? Well, then, it was clear that such an individual just didn't belong here. The administration, meanwhile, was busy trying to figure out whether this institution was going to become a Research I university or maintain its urban mission. At the time, the two seemed incompatible. That was then. How is it now?

Today, we have over 4,000 Blacks and Latinos on this campus. Today, we also have what is becoming an increasingly enlightened top administration. Just last month, for example, Dr. Ann Smith, UIC's Associate Chancellor, demonstrated this increasing enlightenment in her panel presentation at the Sixth Annual Minority Urban Higher Education Forum. In her presentation, Dr. Smith outlined two opposing models which clearly demonstrate the choices we have. To begin with, Dr. Smith criticized what she calls the "integration deficit model" and argued that it was no longer useful in helping us deal with the current problems that face minority students at this institution. Such a model, she pointed out, suggests that all problems are brought in by the student. Under this model, minority students are generally referred to as special need, high risk, underprepared and/or disadvantaged. In place of this deficit model, Dr. Smith proposed what she calls the "diversity asset model". Such a model emphasizes strengths and new perspectives and a two way exchange through collaboration. In Dr. Smith's view, her main job on this campus will be, first of all, to establish a framework for this model; secondly, to encourage the university's top administrators to provide leadership and support for it; and thirdly, to develop a central committee that will design, implement, monitor and evaluate a strategy for attaining the kind of affirmative action which does not demand that our students strip themselves of their cultural past.

Fortunately for underrepresented students on this campus, Dr. Smith is not alone in championing this new model. In a recent article in *Black Issues in Higher Education,* Dr. W. Clarke Douglas, UIC's Dean of Student Affairs, argued that "it is the role of the university to sensitize faculty to ethnic diversity, and if it is sincere about developing an educational climate that supports and reinforces the learning process, then it has the responsibility to modify attitudes and expectations" (1989, p. 24). At a recent President's meeting, I am told, Dr. Jay Levine, the Dean of the College of Liberal Arts and Sciences, also mentioned the need to design a method whereby faculty members can participate in sessions that will help them become more sensitive to the needs of a multicultural student body. Finally, in both private conversations and public discussions with Dr. James J. Stukel, the Executive Vice Chancellor and Vice Chancellor for Academic Affairs, and Dr. Louise Año Nuevo Kerr, the Associate Vice Chancellor for Academic Affairs here at UIC, I have heard and sensed the same concern for the needs of non-mainstream students on this campus. There is, then, a general mood developing at UIC which suggests that students need not surrender their own culture and language when they walk in the door and that faculty, in turn, need to sensitize themselves to the various cultures and languages that underrepresented students bring with them.

I am glad to note that the administration on this campus is not alone in arguing for greater acceptance of the diverse views which non-mainstream students bring with them when they enter an institution of higher learning. In a recent essay in *College English,* one of the more important journals in English studies, Patricia Bizzell argued that

"teaching literacy [must become] a process of constructing academic literacy, creating it anew in each class through the interaction of the professor's and the students' cultural resources" (1988, p. 150). And in a more recent essay in *College English,* Kurt Spellmeyer called for the development of a common ground so that "entry into a community of discourse [begins], not with a renunciation of the 'home language' or 'home culture,' but with those points of commonality that expose the alien within the familiar, the familiar within the alien" (1989, p. 266). We must, Spellmeyer argued "permit our students to bring their extratextual knowledge to bear upon every text we give them, and to provide them with strategies for using this knowledge to undertake a conversation which belongs to us all" (p. 275).

We must, of course, also keep in mind that this new road is fraught with dangers and that certain elements who still support the old integration deficit model which Dr. Smith so aptly described will use incidents which supposedly demonstrate those dangers to attack us. In his column in last Friday's *Chicago Tribune,* for example, William Pfaff criticized Britain, Australia, Canada and the United States for implementing policies which encourage multilingual education and the establishment of a multicultural society. Pfaff used the recent Salman Rushdie incident to suggest that too much diversity is a dangerous thing because "without a community of values and cultural assumptions there is no community at all" (1989, p. 21). We must be careful not to be swayed by extremists on either end. Our road is clear. It is through an interactive relationship which permits the voices of those who were once ignored to join us in our continuing conversation that we will forge a new and stronger academic community, one that is dynamic and vital and open to change.

Although the notion of discontinuity between the home and the school plays a key role in explaining the degree to which academic literacy or the lack thereof has become a problem for non-mainstream students at UIC, and indeed among underrepresented students across the nation, our analysis cannot stop there. A related issue is the question of how we define academic literacy and the effects this definition has on what students are taught in the classroom. In defining this concept, we must be careful not to automatically shift the burden of responsibility on to minority students by suggesting that it is they who are lacking as persons because they do not possess the minimal skills of an "educated" individual. We cannot begin the process of educating these students at the university level by demeaning the cultural knowledge and skills which they acquired in their homes and communities and which they use in their day-to-day lives.

If we hope to deal with this problem, we must begin at the beginning by examining the historical development of our current notions of literacy and then establishing a broad and open-ended conceptual definition which demonstrates the inherent qualities of the multiple literacies that exist among the various groups in this country. We must also analyze the development of literacy both in theory and practice against the backdrop of what is currently referred to as academic literacy—the kind of literacy which is taught in our universities and which determines who will obtain the kind of earning power that makes for a comfortable living in this country. Finally, we must examine the ideological roots of academic literacy as a concept. Such an analysis will help us see the degree to which the vested interests of those who define literacy determine the definition itself.

In view of the growing minority populations in this country, in this city, and at this university, it behooves us to adapt our teaching to the various needs of the increasingly diverse population that we are going to be serving in the coming decades. It is no longer enough to expect our students to buy into academic culture and surrender their own. We must find ways to bridge the gap between our students' home cultures and literacies and the academic culture and literacy that we believe it is so important for them to learn.

Presented
at the
Third UIC/CCC Partnership Program
Conference
entitled
"Cultural Diversity in the Curriculum and
in Campus Life"

March 10, 1989
Chicago Illini Union
University of Illinois at Chicago

(Revised and updated on January 31, 1990)

## Cited Literature

Bizzell, P. (1988). Arguing about literacy. *College English, 50*(2), 141–153.

Douglas, D. W., & Johnson, M. L. (1989). The classroom experience: The missing link in minority retention efforts. *Black Issues in Higher Education, 5*(22), 24.

Goody, J., & Watt, I. (1963). The consequences of literacy. *Comparative studies in society and history, 5.* (Reprinted in Pier Paolo Giglioli [Ed.]. 1972. *Language and social context.* New York: Penguin Books, pp. 311–357).

Heath, S. B. (1982). Protean shapes in literacy events: Ever-shifting oral and literate traditions. In D. Tannen (Ed.), *Spoken and written language: Exploring orality and literacy.* Norwood, New Jersey: Ablex, pp. 91–117.

Heath, S. B. (1983). *Ways with words.* Cambridge: Cambridge University Press.

Olson, D. R. (1977). From utterance to text: The bias of language in speech and writing. *Harvard Educational Review, 47,* 257–281.

Ong, W. (1982). *Orality and literacy: Technologizing of the Word.* London: Methuen.

Pfaff, W. (1989, March 3). A collision of beliefs that cannot coexist. *Chicago Tribune,* p. 21.

Rodriguez, R. (1982). *Hunger of memory*. Boston: D. R. Godine.

Scollon, S. B. K., & Scollon, R. (1981). *Narrative, literacy, and face in interethnic communication.* Norwood, New Jersey: Ablex.

Scribner, S., & Cole, M. (1981). *The psychology of literacy.* Cambridge, Massachusetts: Harvard University Press.

Smith, A. E. (1989, February 3). Panel presentation on leadership perspectives. *Sixth Annual Minority Urban Higher Education Forum,* University of Illinois at Chicago.

Spellmeyer, K. (1989). A common ground: The essay in the academy. *College English, 51*(3), 262–276.

Street, B. V. (1984). *Literacy in theory and practice.* Cambridge: Cambridge University Press.

Tannen, D. (1982). The oral/literate continuum in discourse. In D. Tannen (Ed.), *Spoken and written language: Exploring orality and literacy.* Norwood, New Jersey: Ablex, pp. 1–16.

# School-College Collaboration: An Essential To Improved Public Education

*Fred M. Hechinger*

I'VE BEEN COVERING education for a long time, and what occurs to me at meetings like this is that in some way I have heard all these problems before. I've written about most of them.

I would like to talk about what this conference has been all about by starting with a quote: Education is what you remember after you've forgotten what you've learned.

I think that might be a good framework within which to look at all the reform proposals that are now being made. How many of the proposals, how many of the new mandates, are going to make young people remember after they have forgotten what they've learned? If it passes that test, if it increases that portion, then that particular reform is worth considering.

## The Human Dimension

One of the things that stuck to my mind in listening for the past day is that in general, with a few exceptions, we talked about systems—we talked about how to im-

Fred M. Hechinger has been an education columnist for the *New York Times* for many years and is now the president of the New York Times Company Foundation.

Reprinted from *NASSP Bulletin* (October 1984) by permission of the National Association of Secondary School Principals.

prove the systems—and I think that's important because we deal with large systems of education. But even more important in efforts to reform education is something that goes beyond the system: the human dimension.

I am convinced that unless the human dimension within the system can be improved all the reform proposals are going to fail. We've been talking about the relationship between college and high school, high school and college, the issue of continuity. We are not very good at continuity, in general. In the schools and colleges the continuity is poor.

A few years ago, I looked with my younger son, who I guess was then about 12 years old, at a segment of "Roots II." In that particular segment, the young black petty officer was leaving a southern Navy base and was going home, together with his wife and his baby. They started to drive home, and as it got dark, they stopped at a motel. There was a big vacancy sign flashing outside, and he went inside in his uniform and was told that there was no room. And they drove on and stopped at another motel, and again there was a vacancy sign, and again the story was repeated. This went on three or four times. Finally they parked at the side of the road and spent the night, with the baby, sleeping in the car. My 12-year-old son turned to me and said "Daddy, that couldn't really have happened." And I looked at him and asked myself why should he have known? Why should he have known something that happened only maybe a decade ago?

We are not very good at continuity. We don't teach it, we don't establish it. Why should we expect our children to be good at it?

We are not very good at continuity. After all, that's what we are talking about at this meeting. As a result of that, American education during the past few decades has become a collection of disjointed parts that in the main fail to connect. It's like a play with a succession of scenes and acts, each written by a different playwright and staged by a different director. Now, within that kind of play or system, some good things do occur in some of the segments. But they don't add up to a satisfying whole. The central character in this play, the student, ends up without a sense of unity, goal, or belonging.

It seems to me that the fundamental question to be asked now is who is going to be responsible for what in this long procession of education. Who takes care of what? Who, for instance, takes care of general education?

We got into some debate this afternoon over the college preparatory and the non-college-preparatory students. I don't think we've solved the question, but it was raised and it is an important one. But there are some aspects of education that affect everybody. And who is responsible for those? We can't simply go on to the next level and blame the previous one for not having done anything about these important areas and for the fact that they are in disarray.

## Lack of Continuity a Problem

The lack of continuity that plagues American education is something that all of education needs to address. Instead of con-necting the separate levels, critics generally compound the spirit of separation by seeking scapegoats instead of remedies. Professionals at each level point accusing fingers at what ought to be their colleagues' responsibility at the preceding level. And so you go from graduate school down to the colleges, and from the colleges down to the high schools, from the high schools down to the elementary schools. And when there is nobody left to blame you've still got the parents. In the oldest game of American pedagogy, university academicians rail against the weaknesses of teacher training institutions and of high school teachers without taking an active hand in helping correct what in fact are serious deficiencies.

Recently there was a report in the paper about the decline in students' mathematical performance. I wanted to do a story about that. And so I got a list of noted university mathematics professors and I called them. I read them the story since they hadn't read it. I asked, did they have an idea why this was happening? They said they didn't know. "We don't know what's happening in the high schools." It seems to me they really told what the problem was. They weren't interested. They weren't lending a hand.

One of the flaws in most of the reports that you've all read—the science report is the one exception—the flaw is that they still think there are only two problem areas: the high schools and the colleges. And if we could only solve those, then things would be all right.

That is a terrible fallacy. Almost all of the complaints we register focus only on the high schools or colleges. But the sagging academic standards really begin long before that. If you go to the source, they begin at a time when parents don't read to their two or three-year-old children. And the flaws are compounded when elementary schools don't teach what subsequently the junior high schools and high schools and colleges must make up: the skills required to do the job.

We've been talking standards for children this afternoon. Well, what incentive is there for a high school student to try to cope with what is being offered if the whole thing is a mystery?

## Detection vs. Prevention

Let me digress from education for a minute. Not long ago I read a story in the *Washington Post* by a foreign correspondent who had interviewed a managing director of a high technology industry in Japan. He asked the Japanese manager to define what he thought was the difference in quality control in the United States and quality control in Japan. The Japanese industrialist, trying to be polite as he could, said the United States tries to control quality by detection, and they try to control it by prevention. I think being a little less polite he would have said, we try to make things work the first time around.

Detection, you see, is recall. We are very familiar with American industries' reliance on recall for its quality. But recall is not purely an industrial matter. The educational term for recall is remediation. And, like recall in industry, it is costly. It's costly not only in terms of money; it's even more costly in terms of human waste and human suffering.

There's nothing more frustrating for a young person than to be subjected to a curriculum without being able to function. I've often thought that those high school kids who are confined to the normal course of studies without being able to understand what is being said, without being able to read or write, if they're really smart they drop out.

None of you would subject yourself to the torture of spending your days in an office trying to cope with tasks for which you are simply not equipped. To me the entire question of continuity starts with the effort to make it work the first time around. To move away as rapidly as possible from the massive process of remediation.

Now, that's difficult. It's difficult not only because you can't make a sudden change without being even more inhumane, but it's difficult also because by now we build into each level of education a very substantial vested interest in the process of remediation. You would have to fire a large number of faculty members in many of our high schools and colleges if remediation were no longer necessary. So there is no incentive for college faculties to come down first to the high schools and for the high school people to go down to the elementary schools and try to find out how you can prevent the passing on of failure.

## Writing in the Schools

Somebody mentioned the problem of getting high school students to write. It is a problem. I can give you an example out of personal experience. Friends of ours spent 10 years living in England, and their children went to school there. When they moved back to the United States, one of the boys complained bitterly day after day. He liked to write. Yet, they never gave him any writing assignments. Finally, the mother went in to see the principal to present this complaint. And the principal said, yes, he understood what she was trying to say. But, he added, you have to understand: Our children write so badly we can't expect them to write very much.

Now, continuity. If the students we were talking about this afternoon find it difficult to write, if it's difficult to assign them writing assignments in school and, if it's found sort of unnecessary because they are not going to be asked to do very much writing in the colleges to which they subsequently go, you face a serious problem. Asking young people to start to write in high school may be too late. If they haven't learned to enjoy writing it's a lost cause. Continuity has already been lost.

Now, there are things that can be done about this. But they start earlier. They start before the point at which our topic started. This is crucial. Because I think reading and writing are part of the same problem. You can't enjoy everything you do in education, but if you don't enjoy things like reading and writing you are never going to be educated in high school, in college, in graduate school, anywhere. It's just that simple.

Professional writers make fun of this. Red Smith was asked how difficult it was to write his column every day. And he said it was not difficult at all. All he had to do was sit down at a typewriter and puncture a vein and let it drip out. A noted television commentator, at a private meeting, said he was asked if he enjoyed writing and he said: "I don't enjoy writing; I enjoy having written."

But that is not good enough. It moves in the right direction. If you can get your students to the point where they will enjoy having written it's better than what is happening now. But it's not good enough. There are answers to this, however.

I went into a classroom not long ago in PS 230 in Brooklyn. I started out in kindergarten the first hour and then went on to first grade. And in that kindergarten and in the first grade all the children were writers. They were writing because of continuity. They were writing because of a program, a theory, by now sufficiently tested to be more than a pilot project—a theory that all children, in our city, out of our city, suburb, anywhere, all children come to school already knowing how to write. Now, you may not be able to read what they write, but they know they are writing.

A scribbling, a painting, a drawing, a writing, they pick up a letter here or there. They are writing. They are writing just as they spoke, as they learned how to speak. If we started in kindergarten or first grade with the assumption that children don't know how to speak and we then started to teach them how to speak, we would raise a generation of deaf mutes.

The other assumption is that the teachers know how to write and like to write. No teacher is permitted to teach in this program without first having gone through a fairly extensive course in writing. And wanting to write.

These kindergarten youngsters presented me with little books of their writings. They weren't grammatical, but I understood what they were saying. And, most important, they wanted to write. After they finished writing they got together—they didn't have a teacher come around marking up their precious writing with a red pencil—they had editorial conferences with their teachers and they criticized each other's writing. And they all wrote, every child in those classrooms wrote. They won't have any problem when they get to high school if somebody doesn't stop them in the meantime.

The other absolute requirement was that they wrote what they wanted to write. They weren't assigned topics. They chose their topics. Translate this into books: If we got away from teaching children to read, if we taught them to write, we would not have to teach them to read at all. They'd read automatically, because if you write you read. If we only didn't teach them to read with books that offer absolutely no incentive to read another book ever again in your life. That's the beginning of reforming the schools.

Get children to want to do the learning. And then you don't have to worry in high school or in college whether you can afford to assign papers to them. They will want to write. They'll be proud of their writing.

Our youngest son is just 17 now. Once or twice a week he goes up to Harlem to teach in a place, The Children's Storefront; to teach and play with the children, eight or nine years old. All of them have dropped out of the public schools. They dropped out essentially because they were chronic truants. They just didn't attend. Where they are going now, they have a perfect attendance record. They have terrible problems. They are just beginning to learn things like writing and reading. But they know that the people who work with them care. There is a personal contact.

Our son was terribly worried. He said: "They were having great times throwing a frisbee with me but they don't really want to write." They've already, at that age, been conditioned that writing is something they don't want to do. I suggested to John to find something they might want to write about. So, he devised a system. He wrote a sentence. There was great agonizing at home what the sentence should be about.

I said, write about something that they know about. So he came up with a first sentence about a house fire. He knew enough about the neighborhood that there were lots of fires. He wrote that one sentence about the fire. Last week, he came home to show me how one of the eight-year-old boys had finished the essay. Only about five or six sentences. But they were great.

He had gone in to this burning house, and there was an elderly woman upstairs and he came in and tried to rescue her. The woman said to him, "Go away, you're going to rob me." And he said, "No I'm not going to rob you, I'm going to save you." Now there was a child, an eight-year-old child, who had never written before, but he was given a chance to write about something that was part of his experience and you could see

what kind of an experience it was. The incentive was that his writing would be put on a word processor and eventually his and the other children's writing would make up a little book.

That's the beginning of teaching. And that, I believe, is where the inner incentive must begin. Then, when children come to high school, you don't have to worry about the fact that they've never read or have never written. I believe that if they've never read, if they've never written by the time they go to high school, it's almost a lost cause. The best you can do is make them do the things that need to be done. But after they've finished, they'll never read or write again unless they're absolutely forced to.

## Foreign Languages

Foreign languages? Same problem. I don't believe for a minute that foreign languages disappeared from our schools because there was a major revolution against the idea of foreign languages. Young people didn't take foreign languages for a very simple reason: What they were taught didn't make any sense. When you take a child and teach a foreign language, and at the end of the two or three years that child can't speak a single sentence or understand a native speak it, that child—if he has any sense at all—asks what's this for?

To a child, language—foreign or domestic—has only one purpose: communication. If you can't communicate you haven't learned anything. As a matter of fact, our older son dropped Spanish after two years because, he said, he hadn't learned to speak any Spanish. He switched to Latin. At least he didn't have to speak Latin. He took five years of Latin and was very happy.

In reforming the curriculum, don't bring back tough requirements in languages if you don't have the teachers who can teach the children to speak. If you do, you're going to go back to the story of Heywood Broun, who wrote that when he went to high school he studied beginners French and, then, when he went to Paris for the first time, he found that nobody there spoke beginners French. It's that simple.

If we want to reform the schools, two things are essential: continuity all the way up the line; and understanding the "why" of every single course. Read Bruno Bettelheim on that. Whatever you teach, make the children understand why they are studying it. Don't tell them: "you'll need it later." Later doesn't exist.

I went through all kinds of requirements in mathematics. I passed all my courses. I did fairly well. I know absolutely no mathematics. I learned no mathematics whatsoever. Nobody, in all my schooling, ever made me understand what mathematics was for. By the time I graduated from school and college and read about mathematics and how important it was, it had passed me by. That, I think, should apply to every subject at every level of education.

Give all young people some kind of joined baggage. And that's for the high schools to do. For all children. Because if the high schools don't do it, you can't keep postponing it. We read a lot now about getting the humanities into law school and medical school. It's a hopeless cause. You'll never get medical or law students to take seriously what they should have been taught in high school. It's another case of remediation. And remediation in the humanities, or ethics in law or medical or business school is simply an impossibility. You'll never catch up. The distractions are too great.

## What People Need To Know

So the high schools need to—after the elementary schools have taken care of writing and reading—teach a general core of what all people need to know, whether they go to college or not. They need to know about themselves, about their country, about the past, about the Constitution, about the Bill of Rights. I shudder to think that if we had to write the Constitution or the Bill of Rights today, how many people, how many educated people, would be equipped to cope with the issues involved.

The only place to correct this is in the high schools. It is even more important for those who don't go to college to get that kind of instruction in high school, because if they don't get there, they will never get it. And they will be flawed citizens and create a flawed country.

I find that in the present discussion, there is excessive attention being paid to what's happening in other countries. I get very suspicious about that. It doesn't mean that we shouldn't look at other countries in order to learn something from them. But we are not another country; we are the United States. Our system, our goals, our aspirations, and, yes, our past achievements are different.

I remember when I was first the education editor of the *Times,* one of my first assignments was to cover the return of an American education mission from the Soviet Union, led by the then Commissioner of Education. They came back with a stirring report that the Soviet Union had (I remember the exact quote, it appeared in the headline), "a passion for education." And then, for a while, everything we did was geared to the great achievements of the Soviet Union.

We're doing the same thing now with Japan. Ernie Boyer, president of the Carnegie Foundation, said, looking back at Sputnik and the Soviet Union, that we probably would get the same result again if the Japanese put a Toyota in orbit.

The fact is that the Japanese are at the beginning of an extensive re-evaluation of their schools. I'm told that the French are coping with very serious educational problems and are at the beginning of a school reform movement. I've just come back from England, where there was enormous concern over the fact that German children were two years ahead in mathematics.

It all sounds very familiar. But we can't learn that much from other countries because we are different. Our goals are different, and we have to find our own solutions to our problems. Under ideal circumstances and in exceptional schools the American approach to educational problems in the past has out-distanced everything that has ever been tried anywhere. But in the past, American schools, even when they were successful, tended to lower their sights. And that has led to some of the problems that the hearing commission reports have cited. But the solutions ought to be within the American framework of the past, of our past successes.

## Tougher Is Not the Solution

The solutions can't be in simply making everything tougher. When I read the reports and now read the reaction to the reports, especially on the part of state legislatures, I shudder. When I read about new requirements in mathematics I look back at what happened in the past when similar demands were made. You double your mathematics requirements overnight and you're short of mathematics teachers. Then, a lot of social studies teachers will be called in and they will be given an overnight course in mathematics and they will be proclaimed mathematics teachers—and nothing will have changed except that more of the children's time will be wasted in bad instruction. There is only one way, I believe, to really implement school reforms, and that is to assure

that there will be an ample supply of truly good teachers.

## Preparing Teachers

That leads me to perhaps the central issue of the topic for this session: the relationship between the school and college. The most serious area in which the colleges have failed in the past has been in their task of providing the kind of teachers that are needed for better schools. Unless the colleges address themselves to that problem, there is no point in talking about any school reform reports. And I don't believe the problem can be solved merely by changing some of the courses in teacher training institutions. True collaboration is absolutely essential.

You've heard this afternoon about some wonderful initiatives. I happen to be familiar with the Yale/New Haven enterprise, and I think it's one of the best we have in the country today. It's interesting, it should be added, that Yale is one of the universities that doesn't have a school of education. And yet, many of our major schools of education have deliberately gotten out of the business of teacher training.

Now in changing that desperate failure, I repeat, more is needed than simply changing the courses in teacher training institutions. A collaborative effort must totally change the way our teachers are trained. I believe very strongly that the only way to give the schools better teachers is to move a very substantial part of the teacher training process out of the teacher colleges (and I don't mean out of their control)—out of the teachers college campuses and into the schools.

Train the teachers in the schools and have the training be a joint enterprise between the teacher college faculties and experienced school teachers. Teachers cannot be trained to deal with real children unless the training takes place with real children. Having done this, the new teachers must be brought into the schools in a way that allows them to develop as professionals, and that probably means at least three or four or five years of work under very careful supervision and with continued training both by master teachers of the schools and by some of the teacher training people from the colleges.

During that period, there ought to be a very serious weeding out of people who are not suited for teaching. This need not mean that they aren't bright enough; but teaching requires very special skills, very special personal attitudes, and that is the time to get rid of young people unsuitable for teaching.

That means two things. It means that you have to bring into internship or residency or whatever you want to call it perhaps twice as many people as you are eventually going to hire. You need a process of selecting the best. And, it means that we have to give up the absolutely idiotic way of introducing new teachers to their tasks. In virtually every school in the United States, when a new teacher arrives, he or she is instantly given a full load of teaching. Now, to teach five periods a day, even for an experienced teacher, is a considerable task.

But to introduce new teachers, unsure of themselves, untrained, to their career in that fashion virtually assures losing the best teachers in the first five years, which is exactly what has been happening. Again, it is a question of putting together the best efforts of the colleges and of the schools to create a truly new category of teachers who will be professionals and will act as professionals. That means that they will have to continue to be in touch, not just with their own communities, not just with their school administrators, but with the people who teach in their field on any level in elementary schools, in colleges and the universities.

I'll tell you a sad story which says a great deal about the problem. A year ago, the *Times* ran a Page One story about a reinterpretation of the exodus of the Israelites from Egypt based on extensive research by the chairman of the Mideastern Studies Department of Johns Hopkins University. About a week after that story ran, I got a letter from a high school science teacher in Connecticut. He wrote that he had read the story in the *Times* with particular interest because three years earlier, after considerable study, he had come to the same conclusions.

He had written an extensive paper on it but nobody—no scholarly organization, no scholarly journal—showed any interest because he said, after all, "I was only a high school teacher." To corroborate his point, he had enclosed three Xeroxed pages of his story which had eventually appeared in an obscure high school journal. And it was, in fact, very much the same as the highly valued academic discovery.

After I wrote about this incident, I got a number of letters, including one from a high school teacher who had also done some extensive research. And he had eventually got it published in a highly respected, scholarly journal. But in the identification box he was described, not as a high school science teacher, but as a doctoral candidate at Columbia University.

Those are areas of noncooperation, examples of the failure to make the connection, of the lack of continuity. They tell a lot about what needs to be done.

## Conclusion

Finally, if we want to save American public education, we must do a much better job teaching—in our schools, in our colleges, at all levels—the link between public education and the free society. All our schools are failing in that. All our historians are failing in that.

Our children are not taught about Jefferson and his great faith in the power to educate, to create aristocracy of talent instead of an aristocracy of inherited wealth and privilege. Our children are taught nothing about Horace Mann and his view of public universal education as a centerpiece of our democracy. We can't afford not to teach this. We can't afford it now because I do believe that our schools are in danger.

"A Nation at Risk"—a great title. The "rising tide of mediocrity." The tide of mediocrity was rising in the schools; but you can also get your examples anywhere you like—in corporate offices, on assembly lines. Somebody told the story, I guess he was a union member, about the chairman of one of the big steel companies who died and went to hell. Two days after he had arrived, the Devil contacted St. Peter and said: "You've got to take this guy off my hands, we just can't stand him here." And St. Peter said well, he belongs where he is, what's the problem? And the Devil answered: "This guy has been here for only two days and he's already shut down three furnaces."

There's a lot to the question of mediocrity. I believe the nation is at risk, but for totally different reasons than the ones given in the report. I think the nation is at risk because so many people in positions of power lost sight of the importance of public education. I think the nation is at risk because of the possibility of tax credits for private schools. I think the nation is at risk because it doesn't understand what is meant by the importance of public education. I believe that cooperation between schools and colleges must address itself to the importance of the schools to all the children. What we are in danger of losing is not the quality of education. The curriculum can be fixed.

Here is a whole room full of people who can fix the curriculum. You can do it; that's not a really serious problem. The really serious problem is what we do with the schools, what we all—colleges, secondary schools, elementary schools, kindergarten—what we do with the schools for all the children.

In 1820, a newspaper in Philadelphia ran an editorial which said that it was evil to expect people to spend their hard-earned money (which meant taxes) for the education of other people's children. It is all right to spend it for your own children, but not for other people's children. One of the key issues today is that our school reforms, through cooperation between colleges and universities and high schools, and between high schools and elementary schools, and between schools and teachers colleges, address themselves to the need to train and retrain the best possible teachers. The ideas and the money we are expending to this end must be for all the children, other people's as well as ours.

# Sequence Two

# Learning to Write: Cultural Influences

This sequence invites you to think in general ways about how people learn to write and to consider specifically how your own habits and processes as a writer have developed. In particular, the assignments should lead you to investigate how a person's writing is shaped by his or her family, gender, or culture.

The first assignment examines how children learn to read and write in three different family environments—white middle-class, African-American working class, and Chicano working class. The next assignment, for which you will not only read about writing but also interview people about how they write, aims to make you more aware of the ways successful writers draft and rewrite their compositions, only gradually gaining a feeling that now they're "getting it right." The third assignment leads you to explore the ways writing is taught in schools, especially considering the cultural and practical "realities" of writing unearthed in the first two assignments. The final assignment asks you to assume the role of a conscientious student (which should be natural for you!), a concerned parent, or perhaps even a teacher yourself, in order to propose different ways that reading and writing could be taught in the schools.

## Assignment One

*Readings*

> bell hooks, "Talking Back."
> Margaret M. Voss, " 'Make Way for Applesauce': The Literate World of a Three Year Old."
> Richard Rodriguez, "Aria."

Now that you are in college, you can look back over your experiences as a student, but you can also review your experiences as a member of a family and, more generally, as a participant in particular cultural traditions. Write an essay in which you explore these influences—educational, family, and cultural—on your development as a writer. You might want to consider the following questions, among others: Did someone tell you stories? What exactly are your memories of these events? Were you encouraged to keep a diary or to make up stories yourself?

Were you a reader yourself? In elementary school and high school, how did you become familiar with writing? Did you write your own stories in school? Did teachers assign you topics to write on or did you get to choose your own? Assess your attitude toward reading and writing today: Are reading and writing a big part of your life? Why or why not? How do you think your experiences in your family, educational, and cultural environments led to the ways in which you look at reading and writing today? What you write will be your own "writing history," and will provide you with a personal perspective on the issues this sequence addresses.

# Assignment Two

*Preliminary Readings:*

   Sondra Perl, "Understanding Composing."
   Carol Berkenkotter, "Student Writers and Their Sense of Authority over Texts."
   Nancy Sommers, "Revision Strategies of Student Writers and Experienced Adult Writers."

Exercises to prepare for the next essay:

1. Write a paragraph or two describing one of your earliest reading and writing experiences. Talk to another student about what guided your choices in composing the paragraph. In other words, why did you choose a particular memory, why choose to start with your first sentence, why choose to order your sentences the way you did, why choose to leave out what you did, and so on? Does Perl's notion of "felt-sense" play a role in your choices? How conscious are you of the choices you are making? How conscious should you be?

2. Get into a group with two or three other students and edit each other's paragraphs for revision. Read the paragraphs aloud, and after each reading, students in the group should make suggestions for improvement, ask the author questions about anything that is confusing, and indicate what is good about the piece of writing. Think about the suggestions made in response to your piece of writing. Do some suggestions seem more valid than others? Why? Do you feel you should follow all the suggestions? Do you think you are most like Stan, Pat, or Joann in Berkenkotter's article? Do you find the peer editing process helpful? Why? or why not?

3. Revise your paragraph. Have another student look at both your revision and the first draft of the paragraph to see if she can uncover and describe your revision process. What sort of changes were made? Changes for the audience? For meaning? Changes to improve the way the paragraph reads? Grammatical changes? Were there both large, global changes, and smaller, local changes? According to Sommers' study, is your revision more like that of a student writer, or an experienced adult writer, or somewhere in between?

*Readings*

   Donald Murray, "The Climate for Writing," Subsections: "Why Writing Isn't Taught Effectively" and "The Classroom: A writing Laboratory."
   Edgar H. Schuster, "Let's Get Off the Mythmobile."

Interview another student about her writing process, and her writing history, questioning her not only about how she writes, but also about who or what is responsible for shaping and molding her process. Here are some possible questions to ask:

- The Writing Process

1. How do you go about deciding on a topic?
2. Do you ever get blocked?
3. Is your writing process the same as when you were younger? What's changed, if anything?
4. Does your writing process differ depending on the kind of writing you're doing?
5. Does your writing differ depending on who your audience might be?
6. What are you most afraid of about the writing process?
7. Do you prefer to write completely alone, or get help and suggestions from others? At what point in the process do you usually ask for suggestions?
8. Do you pre-write? If so, what sort of pre-writing do you do? Does it vary?
9. Do you rewrite? How often? What sort of revisions do you usually find yourself making? How much time do you spend revising?
10. Do you find that using a computer affects your writing process? Writing in pen or pencil?
11. What sort of setting do you usually write in?

- Responsibility for the Writing Process

1. Did your parents help shape your writing process? Did they read to you when you were a child? Did they take you to the library? Tell you stories? Did they give you advice about writing papers when you were older?
2. How did your teachers affect your writing process? Did any of them influence you with any of the myths Schuster writes about?
3. Have any favorite books or magazines influenced your writing process? Have you used them as models?
4. Have you done writing outside of school that has affected your process? A journal or diary? Stories or poems?
5. Does the way you talk affect your writing process?
6. Has television affected your writing process in any way?
7. Have you frequently or infrequently spent time writing? Has this affected your writing process?
8. What about your writing process do you consider to be of your own making?

Once you have completed the interview write an essay informing your readers not only how the student writes but also the forces that have shaped her writing process.

# Assignment Three

*Readings:*

  Thomas C. Wheeler, "The Writing Crisis."
  Marilyn Wilson, "Critical Thinking: Repackaging or Revolution?"
  Harvey Daniels, "Is There Really a Language Crisis?"

Wheeler, Wilson, and Daniels imply that within our culture there are several views of what it means to be literate. Certainly it means more than just being able to spell correctly, if it means that at all. Based on the articles you have read and your understanding of your own and other writing processes, write an essay in which you explain what you think it means to be literate. Include in your essay an explanation of why the culture you live in might find your understanding of literacy meaningful and useful.

# Assignment Four

*Readings:*

  Henry Ottinger, "In Short, Why Did the Class Fail?"
  Theodore Sizer, "Prologue: Horace's Compromise."
  Brian Austin-Ward, "English, English Teaching and English Teachers: The Perceptions of
    16-Year-Olds."

Write an essay that addresses some failure or success in your education as a reader and a writer. Take into account your own "writing history" and those of your fellow students as you assess a successful or unsuccessful learning experience. Whether you choose to focus on success or failure, address your composition to the person or persons "responsible" for the experience—a teacher, a tutor, a parent or other relative, a department in your high school or college. You may take the position of an advisor, offering concrete suggestions about what you might have done differently to improve your own writing and English education. You may take the role of a concerned former student addressing a teacher or principal about what your school might have done well or what it might have done differently to help students learn to read and write effectively. Or you may take the position of a son or daughter addressing your parents about the ways they exposed you to reading or writing in your home.

Whether you choose to concentrate on a success or failure in your reading and writing education, think of the ways your specific experiences could form the basis of a persuasive message to your reader.

# Talking Back

*bell hooks*

In the world of the southern black community I grew up in, "back talk" and "talking back" meant speaking as an equal to an authority figure. It meant daring to disagree and sometimes it just meant having an opinion. In the "old school," children were meant to be seen and not heard. My great-grandparents, grandparents, and parents were all from the old school. To make yourself heard if you were a child was to invite punishment, the back-hand lick, the slap across the face that would catch you unaware, or the feel of switches stinging your arms and legs.

To speak then when one was not spoken to was a courageous act—an act of risk and daring. And yet it was hard not to speak in warm rooms where heated discussions began at the crack of dawn, women's voices filling the air, giving orders, making threats, fussing. Black men may have excelled in the art of poetic preaching in the male-dominated church, but in the church of the home, where the everyday rules of how to live and how to act were established, it was black women who preached. There, black women spoke in a language so rich, so

bell hooks has written *Ain't I a Woman: Black Women and Feminism* and *Feminist Theory from Margin to Center*. This excerpt is reprinted from her most recent book, *Talking Back: thinking feminist, thinking black* (1989).

bell hooks, Talking Back: thinking feminist, thinking black (1989). Reprinted with permission of South End Press, 116 St. Botolph St., Boston, MA 02115.

poetic, that it felt to me like being shut off from life, smothered to death if one were not allowed to participate.

It was in that world of woman talk (the men were often silent, often absent) that was born in me the craving to speak, to have a voice, and not just any voice but one that could be identified as belonging to me. To make my voice, I had to speak, to hear myself talk—and talk I did—darting in and out of grown folks' conversations and dialogues, answering questions that were not direct at me, endlessly asking questions, making speeches. Needless to say, the punishments for these acts of speech seemed endless. They were intended to silence me—the child—and more particularly the girl child. Had I been a boy, they might have encouraged me to speak believing that I might someday be called to preach. There was no "calling" for talking girls, no legitimized rewarded speech. The punishments I received for "talking back" were intended to suppress all possibility that I would create my own speech. That speech was to be suppressed so that the "right speech of womanhood" would emerge.

Within feminist circles, silence is often seen as the sexist "right speech of womanhood"—the sign of woman's submission to patriarchal authority. This emphasis on woman's silence may be an accurate remembering of what has taken place in the households of women from WASP backgrounds in the United States, but in black communities (and diverse ethnic communities), women have not been silent. Their voices can be heard. Certainly for black women, our struggle has not been to emerge from silence into speech but to change the nature and direction of our speech, to make a speech that compels listeners, one that is heard.

Our speech, "the right speech of womanhood," was often the soliloquy, the talking into thin air, the talking to ears that do not hear you—the talk that is simply not listened to. Unlike the black male preacher whose speech was to be heard, who was to be listened to, whose words were to be remembered, the voices of black women— giving orders, making threats, fussing—could be tuned out, could become a kind of background music, audible but not acknowledged as significant speech. Dialogue—the sharing of speech and recognition—took place not between mother and child or mother and male authority figure but among black women. I can remember watching fascinated as our mother talked with her mother, sisters, and women friends. The intimacy and intensity of their speech—the satisfaction they received from talking to one another, the pleasure, the joy. It was in this world of woman speech, loud talk, angry words, women with tongues quick and sharp, tender sweet tongues, touching our world with their words, that I made speech my birthright— and the right to voice, to authorship, a privilege I would not be denied. It was in that world and because of it that I came to dream of writing, to write.

Writing was a way to capture speech, to hold onto it, keep it close. And so I wrote down bits and pieces of conversations, confessing in cheap diaries that soon fell apart from too much handling, expressing the intensity of my sorrow, the anguish of speech—for I was always saying the wrong thing, asking the wrong questions. I could not confine my speech to the necessary corners and concerns of life. I hid these writings under my bed, in pillow stuffings, among faded underwear. When my sisters found and read them, they ridiculed and mocked me—poking fun. I felt violated, ashamed, as if the secret parts of my self had been exposed, brought into the open, and hung like newly clean laundry, out in the air for everyone to see! The fear of exposure, the fear that one's deepest emotions and innermost thoughts will be dismissed as mere nonsense, felt by so many young girls keeping diaries, holding and hiding speech, seems to me now one of the barriers that women have always needed and still need to destroy so that we are no longer pushed into secrecy or silence.

Despite my feelings of violation, of exposure, I continued to speak and write, choosing my hiding places well, learning to destroy work when no safe place could be found. I was never taught absolute silence, I was taught that it was important to speak but to talk a talk that was in itself a silence. Taught to speak and yet beware of the betrayal of too much heard speech, I experienced intense confusion and deep anxiety in my efforts to speak and write. Reciting poems at Sunday afternoon church service might be rewarded. Writing a poem (when one's time could be "better" spent sweeping, ironing, learning to cook) was luxurious activity, indulged in at the expense of others. Questioning authority, raising issues that were not deemed appropriate subjects brought pain, punishments—like telling mama I wanted to die before her because I could not live without her—that was crazy talk, crazy speech, the kind that would lead you to end up in a mental institution. "Little girl," I would be told, "if you don't stop all this crazy talk and crazy acting you are going to end up right out there at Western State."

Madness, not just physical abuse, was the punishment for too much talk if you were female. Yet even as this fear of madness haunted me, hanging over my writing like a monstrous shadow, I could not stop the words, making thought, writing speech. For this terrible madness which I feared, which I was sure was the destiny of daring women born to intense speech (after all, the authorities emphasized this point daily), was not as threatening as imposed silence, as suppressed speech.

Safety and sanity were to be sacrificed if I was to experience defiant speech. Though I risked them both, deep-seated fears and anxieties characterized my childhood days. I would speak but I would not ride a bike, play hardball, or hold the gray kitten. Writing about the ways we are traumatized in our growing-up years, psychoanalyst Alice Miller makes the point in *For Your Own Good* that it is not clear why childhood wounds become for some folk an opportunity to grow, to move forward rather than backward in the process of self-realization. Certainly, when I reflect on the trials of my growing-up years, the many punishments, I can see now that in resistance I learned to be vigilant in the nourishment of my spirit, to be tough, to courageously protect that spirit from forces that would break it.

While punishing me, my parents often spoke about the necessity of breaking my spirit. Now when I ponder the silences, the voices that are not heard, the voices of those wounded and/or oppressed individuals who do not speak or write, I contemplate the acts of persecution, torture—the terrorism that breaks spirits, that makes creativity impossible. I write these words to bear witness to the primacy of resistance struggle in any situation of domination (even within family life); to the strength and power that emerges from sustained resistance and the profound conviction that these forces can be healing, can protect us from dehumanization and despair.

These early trials, wherein I learned to stand my ground, to keep my spirit intact, came vividly to mind after I published *Ain't I A Woman* and the book was sharply and harshly criticized. While I had expected a climate of critical dialogue, I was not expecting a critical avalanche that had the power in its intensity to crush the spirit, to push one into silence. Since that time, I have heard stories about black women, about women of color, who write and publish (even when the work is quite successful) having nervous breakdowns, being made mad because they cannot bear the harsh responses of family, friends, and unknown critics, or becoming silent, unproductive. Surely, the absence of a humane critical response has tremendous impact on the writer from any oppressed, colonized group who endeavors to speak. For us, true speaking is not solely an expression of creative power; it is an act of resistance, a political gesture that challenges politics of domination that would render us nameless and voiceless. As such, it is a courageous act—as such, it represents a threat. To those who wield oppressive power, that which is threatening must necessarily be wiped out, annihilated, silenced.

Recently, efforts by black women writers to call attention to our work serve to highlight both our presence and absence. Whenever I peruse women's bookstores, I am struck not by the rapidly growing body of feminist writing by black women, but by the paucity of available published material. Those of us who write and are published remain few in number. The context of silence is varied and multi-dimensional. Most obvious are the ways racism, sexism, and class exploitation act to suppress and silence. Less obvious are the inner struggles, the efforts made to gain the necessary confidence to write, to re-write, to fully develop craft and skill—and the extent to which such efforts fail.

Although I have wanted writing to be my life-work since childhood, it has been difficult for me to claim "writer" as part of that which identifies and shapes my everyday reality. Even after publishing books, I would often speak of wanting to be a writer as though these works did not exist. And though I would be told, "you are a writer," I was not yet ready to fully affirm this truth. Part of myself was still held captive by domineering forces of history, of familial life that had charted a map of silence, of right speech. I had not completely let go of the fear of saying the wrong thing, of being punished. Somewhere in the deep recesses of my mind, I believed I could avoid both responsibility and punishment if I did not declare myself a writer.

One of the many reasons I chose to write using the pseudonym bell hooks, a family name (mother to Sarah Oldham, grandmother to Rosa Bell Oldham, great-grandmother to me), was to construct a writer-identity that would challenge and subdue all impulses leading me away from speech into silence. I was a young girl buying bubble gum at the corner store when I first really heard the full name bell hooks. I had just "talked back" to a grown person. Even now I can recall the surprised look, the mocking tones that informed me I must be kin to bell hooks—a sharp-tongued woman, a woman who spoke her mind, a woman who was not afraid to talk back. I claimed this legacy of defiance, of will, of courage, affirming my link to female ancestors who were bold and daring in their speech. Unlike my bold and daring mother and grandmother, who were not supportive of talking back, even though they were assertive and powerful in their speech, bell hooks as I discovered, claimed, and invented her was my ally, my support.

That initial act of talking back outside the home was empowering. It was the first of many acts of defiant speech that would make it possible for me to emerge as an independent thinker and writer. In retrospect, "talking back" became for me a rite of initiation, testing my courage, strengthening my commitment, preparing me for the days ahead—the days when writing, rejection notices, periods of silence, publication, ongoing development seem impossible but necessary.

Moving from silence into speech is for the oppressed, the colonized, the exploited, and those who stand and struggle side by side a gesture of defiance that heals, that makes new life and new growth possible. It is that act of speech, of "talking back," that is no mere gesture of empty words, that is the expression of our movement from object to subject—the liberated voice.

# "Make Way for Applesauce": The Literate World of a Three Year Old

*Margaret M. Voss*

One summer afternoon just a month before his third birthday, Nathaniel sat at the picnic table in our backyard. He had just enjoyed a treat, a jar of apple blueberry baby food. As I turned the jar to examine the label, wondering if I'd just given my son some added sugar, Nathaniel suddenly proclaimed, "Make way for applesauce." Amused and confused, I asked, "What?" "Make way for applesauce," he repeated, pointing to the label. Then he reached out and ran his fingers underneath some words, just as I sometimes do as I read book titles to him. He continued, pointing to and "reading" one word at a time: "It say, 'Make . . . way . . . for . . . applesauce.'"

What was going on? I wanted to laugh, for I could see what had happened . . . at least on one level. Nat's current favorite book, which I had read over and over in recent weeks, was *Make Way for Ducklings* (McCloskey 1941). I had the habit of reading every one of the book's several title pages, while pointing to each word. No wonder Nathaniel figured that print must say something about "making way."

Margaret M. Voss is a teacher in Marblehead, Massachusetts. This article was originally published in *Language Arts* (65 [1988]: 272–278), a journal for elementary and high school teachers.

But clearly there was more here than met the eye. Nathaniel was not just imitating. He knew that jar held, in his word, "applesauce," so he extrapolated from my oral reading of titles, modifying it to make sense in this situation. It seems that this young child already knew a great deal about printed language. He knew that letters and words hold messages and he knew that the messages make sense, they fit a context.

But I didn't have much time to deliberate about what Nathaniel knew, because he immediately replaced the cap on the baby food and announced, "I'm going to the miller." Still in a daze, I offered my usual motherly phrase: "What?" "I'm going to the miller," he repeated, hopping down from the table. "He make bread," As I chuckled to myself about how *The Little Red Hen* (Rosenberg, illus, 1984) had just appeared in our backyard, he continued, "It's down a hill. You come, too." So I followed.

Along the way he pretended to open and shut three imaginary gates for me, saying "open, shut them" each time in a singsong way reminiscent of the fingerplay song he learned at day care: open, shut them, give a little clap. Then, reaching the fence, he held the jar out through the bars and confided, "Miller gonna make it bread." Jar still in hand, he pivoted away from the fence, proceeded through the "gates" again, then turned back to the fence, where I expected to hear more about the miller. To my surprise, Nathaniel said, "At the store now. Got some more." He reached through the fence. "Where are we?" I asked. "Neverland," he replied.

Such a series of references to stories and song made me aware of what had probably been happening for some time in Nathaniel's world. Not only had he begun making connections between print and meaning, but he had been using what he learned from literature to expand his knowledge of the world and the richness of his play.

I decided to keep informal notes of other activities, comments, and incidents which showed how reading was influencing Nathaniel. By October I began to notice some patterns. Nathaniel was then three years, three months old. I could see that he learned many specific facts about the world from information in stories, rhymes, and songs. *Curious George,* for example, (Rey 1941) introduced jails to him and we had many long discussions about them, why people are put in them, and how in real life, George's mischief would not have landed him in jail. (I was not surprised when an angry Nathaniel one day asserted that unless I did what he wanted, I would have to go to jail.) Nathaniel learned about radishes and scarecrows from *Peter Rabbit* (Potter, n.d.). One day when a loud noise bothered him, Nat announced "I need those ear things." As usual, I queried, "What?" and he said, *"Sounds All Around,"* (Friedman 1974). After a moment I remembered. We had read that book one day in the summer. As we'd looked at the airport picture, we had discussed how airport workers wear earmuffs to muffle loud noises. Not only had Nathaniel learned something interesting, but he even remembered which book introduced him to it.

Books were helping Nat learn not only facts, but they were helping him to learn about feelings. I was charmed when he told me, "I love you just the way you are," but I was amazed when he reminded me that the girl tells that to Corduroy (Freeman 1968). More than once, I noticed ways that Nat used books to deal with his adjustment to a new preschool/day care center. In late October he sat by himself and "read" aloud the book, *Dog Goes to Nursery School* (Hammond 1982). First he carried on the dialogue between the dog and its mother in words almost identical to those in the book: "Today you go to Nursery School" . . . "No, I want to stay home" . . . "No, today you go to Nursery School." But then he "read" a new version in which the mother said, "Okay, you stay home." And he laughed. He showed me the picture of the school and pointing to the teacher, he explained, "She's the mommy. Those friends are all at his house." Nathaniel was composing; he was modifying the story to fit his wish about his own situation.

Another evening after rereading *Curious George,* Nathaniel blurted out, "I'm gonna put Kevin in jail!" Kevin, the roughest boy at Preschool, had caused Nat some anxious moments, but previously Nat had merely shied away from him and had not verbalized his feelings. We talked at length about Kevin and his behavior, about whether he was really "bad," and about ways Nat might talk to Kevin. I think it no coincidence that the day after our talk, Nathaniel settled in at school and said a calm goodbye to me in five minutes instead of twenty. *Curious George* had opened up a discussion for us which let Nathaniel explores his fears and feelings, helping him to feel more confident in an uneasy situation.

Adults, too, react emotionally to stories. No matter how many times I read or see the play, *The Miracle Worker* (Gibson 1957), I blink back tears when Helen, at the water pump, makes her breakthrough to understanding. I think the scene affects me so powerfully because I feel a personal connection with it: it inspires me, a teacher who wants to help others make similar, though smaller and less dramatic, breakthroughs. I like plays and novels that offer me that kind of emotional connection. I frequently choose authors—Elizabeth Hailey, Anne Tyler, Gail Godwin—whose characters I can understand and care about. I often find myself empathizing with a certain character or drawing comparisons between her life and mine.

Will these first episodes of Nathaniel's, in which he makes emotional connections between stories and his own life, lead him to similar meaningful literary moments in his later life? I hope so. I think of sixth graders I have taught who devour books, laughing and crying over characters and incidents, recommending books to their friends, and thoroughly enjoying reading—and writing. I think of other youngsters who resist reading, who claim sullenly that they don't like to read, who have "nothing to write about," and I realize how important those preschool lessons are.

Nathaniel in October was making other kinds of connections as well. He had developed a concept of "book." One day as he looked at the book, *What's Teddy Doing?* (Spanner, illus, 1983), I overheard him say, "This is not a book, not enough pages." Apparently, its several accordian pages did not fit his definition of a book. At the end of August we had read *The Very Busy Spider* (Carle 1985) and Nat noticed the raised letters spelling "Eric Carle" on the book's final page. He asked what it said, I told him, and he immediately said, "The birthday message," referring to *The Secret Birthday Message,* another Eric Carle book (1986) which we had read a few days before. I doubt that he was demonstrating more than a good memory, but since then, we have looked at book jackets to learn about the authors of the books, and I always read the author's name. A three year old is not too young to under-

stand that things to read have been written by someone, and that people write things for themselves and others to read.

I remember some of Nathaniel's earliest attempts at writing messages to others. He was not yet two (I suspect there were earlier attempts which I did not always recognize as such—lines scrawled on papers and on walls). Meticulously, he would mark tiny lines and circles on post-it notes or computer paper. Sometimes Nat explained what the marks said, but usually he did not. The process of writing letterlike shapes was much more interesting to him at that time.

By three, he had a more developed understanding of what letters are, though no one at home had consciously tried to teach him. He may have learned from *Sesame Street,* which he watched two or three times a week, or from preschool, but I think those were only incidental lessons. Rather, I theorize that he learned about letters because he is surrounded by print . . . and by writers. Mom and Dad write on wordprocessors, his teenage siblings do their homework at the kitchen table, and the whole family writes notes for all occasions—grocery lists posted on the refrigerator and reminders of all types littering the house. Plus we read to him, at least a couple of books almost every day.

At age three years, three months, Nathaniel one day played with the magnetic letters attached to the refrigerator. "That's my name, Mommy," he proclaimed; then seeking reinforcement, "Is that my name?" Interested, I looked at the letters he had arranged—R, E, and an upside-down G. It would have been so easy to notice that none of the letters he had chosen fit his name and to take charge, showing him N-A-T or "correcting" that G. But I was truly interested, and I responded as I might to a writer in one of my workshops, reflecting the idea back to him. "Oh, are you writing you name?" I replied. "Yes," he said. "See, it has three letters." How fascinating! I was suddenly in tune with what the child *did* know, instead of the things he had yet to discover. He could recognize letters as such, he knew that his name had three letters, he knew that he could actively put letters together to make his name, and he knew that it could be a message read by others.

Nathaniel continued to experiment with writing over the next days and months. As he wrote, he would announce that he was writing his name or mine. At three years, two months, he had occasionally mixed numbers and letters, but no more—he now had sorted out the categories and he could identify that a 3 was a number and a P was a letter. He made games for himself in which he arranged things into letter shapes. For example one day he used several small boxes of raisins to form an H and told me, "That's a G." Often he would write lines on a paper and give them to family members as notes or messages.

Nat had started to compose little stories as he played. He would make a sequence by stringing things together, list-fashion, with "and then" tying events together. "The car came up the hill. Crash. Then the car goes like this . . . (nonsense words) . . . And then the fire engine puts out the fire. . . ." I was surprised at how often the pretending was influenced by the literature he knew. In mid-October, without preamble, he said, "We are the three bears." (Webb, illus., 1962) "You mean the Papa, the Mama, and the Baby bears?" I asked. (I had gotten beyond "What?" but still tended to respond with a question.). "You the Gramma," he stated and laughed at his own joke. "Are you the baby bear?" I pursued. He implied assent by crowing, "My chair's broken," and pointing to a real chair. On another day he called his cereal "porridge" and brought an imaginary Goldilocks shopping with us. It seemed to me that all his cars and trucks were con-

tinually crashing and the people all got broken legs like Curious George (Rey 1947). When he played with his train I frequently overheard him chanting, "I think I can." (from *The Little Engine That Could,* Piper 1985) At other times he would appoint me to chase him, saying, "You Mr. 'Gregor'" and in one such chase when his slipper fell off, he chortled, "It's in the cabbage." (from *Peter Rabbit,* Potter)

Nathaniel continued to weave stories into his play, to read and tell stories, to learn about the world from books, and to experiment with writing. One day in February he composed his first book. He sat with a pad of paper and drew, making up a story to fit the drawing. Then saying, "And *off* he went," Nat flipped to the next page and continued drawing and composing. He went on for five pages, each one beginning, "And *off* he went." The story included some nonsense words (perhaps they made sense to Nathaniel or perhaps, to him, many stories include incomprehensible parts); but it had many elements which showed Nathaniel's concept of "story": characters, plot, repetition, a series of adventures, a match between illustrations and action. The results are shown in figures 1 to 5.

As I watched, fascinated at Nathaniel's writing process, I realized again what a powerful influence literature had already been in his young life. And I reminded myself of how natural it had been. His play, his learning about the world, his communications with others, his feelings—all had been influenced by books. I trust that Nathaniel will continue to love books and writing. May we parents and teachers provide the stimulating literate environment he needs, ask questions which challenge him and which show our genuine interest . . . and stay out of the way.

"Make way for Nathaniel," I thought. And off he went.

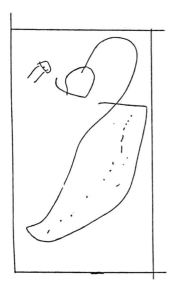

**Figure 1:** (drew a small face). "So happy. He was so happy. He got smaller, smaller. And he was so happy." (drew big lines). "Then he got bigger . . . and bigger . . . and then he was a grownup." (drew dots). "And he had lots of eyes."

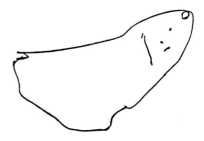

**Figure 3:** "And off they went . . . to Cherice (indistinct sense word). And they went to see what it was. It was people."

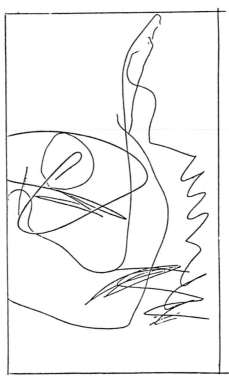

**Figure 4:** "And then off they went." (drew lines and sang nonsense syllables.)

**Figure 2:** "And then *off* he went." (drew person and added bits to it as he continued talking). "And then he fell fast asleep. He slept for miles. He saw the cats moving. He got out of bed. Know what happened? He been falling down the stairs. Look at the stairs." (drew scribbly line over picture to indicate stairs). "The stairs are on top of him cause he fell down the stairs. The stairs are over the place. I think I'll go see the doctor."

**Figure 5:** Said nonsense words as he drew, except for "And off they went. The end."

# References

Carle, Eric. *The Secret Birthday Message.* New York: Harper and Row, 1986.

_____. *The Very Busy Spider.* New York: Philomel Books, 1985.

Freeman, Don. *Corduroy.* New York: The Viking Press, 1968.

Friedman, Joy Troth. *Sounds All Around.* New York: Grosset and Dunlap, 1974.

Hammond, Eugenie. *Dog Goes to Nursery School.* Racine, Wisconsin: Western Publishing Company, Inc., 1982.

McCloskey, Robert. *Make Way for Ducklings.* New York: The Viking Press, 1941.

Piper, Watty. *The Little Engine That Could.* New York: Platt & Monk, Publishers, 1985.

Potter, Beatrix. *The Tale of Peter Rabbit.* New York: Frederick Warne & Co., Inc., n.d.

Rey, H. A. *Curious George.* New York: Scholastic Book Services, 1941.

_____. *Curious George Takes A Job.* New York: Scholastic Book Services, 1947.

Rosenberg, Amye, illus. *The Little Red Hen.* Racine, Wisconsin: The Western Publishing Company, Inc., 1984.

Spanner, Helmut, illus *What's Teddy Bear Doing?* Los Angeles: Price/Stern/Sloan, 1983.

Webb, Elizabeth, illus. *The Three Bears.* Chicago: Rand McNally & Company, 1962.

# Aria

*Richard Rodriquez*

## 1

I remember to start with the day in Sacramento—a California now nearly thirty years past—when I first entered a classroom, able to understand some fifty stray English words.

The third of four children, I had been preceded to a neighborhood Roman Catholic school by an older brother and sister. But neither of them had revealed very much about their classroom experiences. Each afternoon they returned, as they left in the morning, always together, speaking in Spanish as they climbed the five steps of the porch. And their mysterious books, wrapped in shopping-bag paper, remained on the table next to the door, closed firmly behind them.

An accident of geography sent me to a school where all my classmates were white, many the children of doctors and lawyers and business executives. All my classmates certainly must have been uneasy on that first day of school—as most children are uneasy—to find themselves apart from their families in the first institution of their lives. But I was astonished.

The nun said, in a friendly but oddly impersonal voice, 'Boys and girls, this is

Richard Rodriguez was born in San Francisco, the child of Spanish-speaking Mexican Americans. He received a Ph. D. in English from the University of California at Berkeley and later taught there. ''Aria'' comes from *Hunger of Memory*, Rodriguez's autobiography.

Richard Rodriguez.' (I heard her sound out: *Rich-heard Road-ree-guess.*) It was the first time I had heard anyone name me in English. 'Richard,' the nun repeated more slowly, writing my name down in her black leather book. Quickly I turned to see my mother's face dissolve in a watery blur behind the pebbled glass door.

Many years later there is something called bilingual education—a scheme proposed in the late 1960s by Hispanic-American social activists, later endorsed by a congressional vote. It is a program that seeks to permit non-English-speaking children, many from lower-class homes, to use their family language as the language of school. (Such is the goal its supporters announce.) I hear them and am forced to say no: It is not possible for a child—any child—ever to use his family's language in school. Not to understand this is to misunderstand the public uses of schooling and to trivialize the nature of intimate life—family's 'language.'

Memory teaches me what I know of these matters; the boy reminds the adult. I was a bilingual child, a certain kind—socially disadvantaged—the son of working-class parents, both Mexican immigrants.

In the early years of my boyhood, my parents coped very well in America. My father had steady work. My mother managed at home. They were nobody's victims. Optimism and ambition led them to a house (our home) many blocks from the Mexican south side of town. We lived among *gringos* and only a block from the biggest, whitest houses. It never occurred to my parents that they couldn't live wherever they chose. Not was the Sacramento of the fifties bent on teaching them a contrary lesson. My mother and father were more annoyed than intimidated by those two or three neighbors who tried initially to make us unwelcome. ('Keep your brats away from my sidewalk!') But despite all they achieved, perhaps because they had so much to achieve, any deep feeling of ease, the confidence of 'belonging' in public was withheld from them both. They regarded the people at work, the faces in crowds, as very distant from us. They were the others, *los gringos*. The term was interchangeable in their speech with another, even more telling, *los americanos*.

I grew up in a house where the only regular guests were my relations. For one day, enormous families of relatives would visit and there would be so many people that the noise and the bodies would spill out to the backyard and front porch. Then, for weeks, no one came by. (It was usually a salesman who rang the doorbell.) Our house stood apart. A gaudy yellow in a row of white bungalows. We were the people with the noisy dog. The people who raised pigeons and chickens. We were the foreigners on the block. A few neighbors smiled and waved. We waved back. But no one in the family knew the names of the old couple who lived next door; until I was seven years old, I did not know the names of the kids who lived across the street.

In public, my father and mother spoke a hesitant, accented, not always grammatical English. And they would have to strain—their bodies tense—to catch the sense of what was rapidly said by *los gringos*. At home they spoke Spanish. The language of their Mexican past sounded in counterpoint to the English of public society. The words

would come quickly, with ease. Conveyed through those sounds was the pleasing, soothing, consoling reminder of being at home.

During those years when first conscious of hearing, my mother and father addressed me only in Spanish; in Spanish I learned to reply. By contrast, English (*inglés*), rarely heard in the house, was the language I came to associate with *gringos*. I learned my first words of English overhearing my parents speak to strangers. At five years of age, I knew just enough English for my mother to trust me on errands to stores one block away. No more.

I was a listening child, careful to hear the very different sounds of Spanish and English. Wide-eyed with hearing, I'd listen to sounds more than words. First, there were English (*gringo*) sounds. So many words were still unknown that when the butcher or the lady at the drugstore said something to me exotic polysyllabic sounds would bloom in the midst of the sentences. Often, the speech of people in public seemed to me very loud, booming with confidence. The man behind the counter would literally ask, 'What can I do for you?' But by being so firm and so clear, the sound of his voice said that he was a *gringo*; he belonged in public society.

I would also hear then the high nasal notes of middle-class American speech. The air stirred with sound. Sometimes, even now, when I have been traveling abroad for several weeks, I will hear what I heard as a boy. In hotel lobbies or airports in Turkey or Brazil, some Americans will pass, and suddenly I will hear it again—the high sound of American voices. For a few seconds I will hear it with pleasure, for it is now the sound of *my* society—a reminder of home. But inevitably—already on the flight headed for home—the sound fades with repetition. I will be unable to hear it anymore.

When I was a boy, things were different. The accent of *los gringos* was never pleasing nor was it hard to hear. Crowds at Safeway or at bus stops would be noisy with sound. And I would be forced to edge away from the chirping chatter above me.

I was unable to hear my own sounds, but I knew very well that I spoke English poorly. My words could not stretch far enough to form complete thoughts. And the words I did speak I didn't know well enough to make into distinct sounds. (Listeners would usually lower their heads, better to hear what I was trying to say.) But it was one thing for *me* to speak English with difficulty. It was more troubling for me to hear my parents speak in public: their high-whining vowels and guttural consonants; their sentences that got stuck with 'eh' and 'ah' sounds; the confused syntax; the hesitant rhythm of sounds so different from the way *gringos* spoke. I'd notice, moreover, that my parents' voices were softer than those of *gringos* we'd meet.

I am tempted now to say that none of this mattered. In adulthood I am embarrassed by childhood fears. And, in a way, it didn't matter very much that my parents could not speak English with ease. Their linguistic difficulties had no serious consequences. My mother and father made themselves understood at the county hospital clinic and at government offices. And yet, in another way, it mattered very much—it was unsettling to hear my parents struggle with English. Hearing them, I'd grow nervous, my clutching trust in their protection and power weakened.

There were many times like the night at a brightly lit gasoline station (a blaring white memory) when I stood uneasily, hearing my father. He was talking to a teenaged attendant. I do not recall what they were saying, but I cannot forget the sounds my father made as he spoke. At one point his words slid together to form one word—sounds as confused as the threads of blue and green oil in the puddle next to my shoes. His voice rushed through what he had left to say. And, toward the end, reached falsetto notes, appealing to his listener's understanding. I looked away to the lights of passing automobiles. I tried not to hear anymore. But I heard only too well the calm, easy tones in the attendant's reply. Shortly afterward, walking toward home with my father, I shivered when he put his hand on my shoulder. The very first chance that I got, I evaded his grasp and ran on ahead into the dark, skipping with feigned boyish exuberance.

But then there was Spanish. *Español:* my family's language. *Español:* the language that seemed to me a private language. I'd hear strangers on the radio and in the Mexican Catholic church across town speaking in Spanish, but I couldn't really believe that Spanish was a public language, like English. Spanish speakers, rather, seemed related to me, for I sensed that we shared—through our language—the experience of feeling apart from *los gringos.* It was thus a ghetto Spanish that I heard and I spoke. Like those whose lives are bound by a barrio, I was reminded by Spanish of my separateness from *los otros, los gringos* in power. But more intensely than for most barrio children—because I did not live in a barrio—Spanish seemed to me the language of home. (Most days it was only at home that I'd hear it.) It became the language of joyful return.

A family member would say something to me and I would feel myself specially recognized. My parents would say something to me and I would feel embraced by the sounds of their words. Those sounds said: *I am speaking with ease in Spanish. I am addressing you in words I never use with* los gringos. *I recognize you as someone special, close, like no one outside. You belong with us. In the family.*

(*Ricardo.*)

At the age of five, six, well past the time when most other children no longer easily notice the difference between sounds uttered at home and words spoken in public, I had a different experience. I lived in a world magically compounded of sounds. I remained a child longer than most; I lingered too long, poised at the edge of language— often frightened by the sounds of *los gringos,* delighted by the sounds of Spanish at home. I shared with my family a language that was startlingly different from that used in the great city around us.

For me there were none of the gradations between public and private society so normal to a maturing child. Outside the house was public society; inside the house was private. Just opening or closing the screen door behind me was an important experience. I'd rarely leave home all alone or without reluctance. Walking down the sidewalk, under the canopy of tall trees, I'd warily notice the—suddenly—silent neighborhood kids who stood warily watching me. Nervously, I'd arrive at the grocery store to hear there the sounds of the *gringo*—foreign to me—reminding me that in this world so big, I was a foreigner. But then I'd return. Walking back toward our house, climbing the steps from the sidewalk, when the front door was open in summer, I'd hear voices beyond the screen door talking in Spanish. For a second or two, I'd stay, linger there, listening. Smiling, I'd hear my mother call out, saying in Spanish (words): 'Is that you, Richard?' All the while her sounds would assure me: *You are home now; come closer; inside. With us.*

*Sí,*' I'd reply.

Once more inside the house I would resume (assume) my place in the family. The sounds would dim, grow harder to hear. Once more at home, I would grow less aware of that fact. It required, however, no more than the blurt of the doorbell to alert me to listen to sounds all over again. The house would turn instantly still while my mother went to the door. I'd hear her hard English sounds. I'd wait to hear her voice return to soft-sounding Spanish, which assured me, as surely as did the clicking tongue of the lock on the door, that the stranger was gone.

Plainly, it is not healthy to hear such sounds so often. It is not healthy to distinguish public words from private sounds so easily. I remained cloistered by sounds, timid and shy in public, too dependent on voices at home. And yet it needs to be emphasized: I was an extremely happy child at home. I remember many nights when my father would come back from work, and I'd hear him call out to my mother in Spanish, sounding relieved. In Spanish, he's sound light and free notes he never could manage in English. Some nights I'd jump up just at hearing his voice. With *mis hermanos* I would come running into the room where he was with my mother. Our laughing (so deep was the pleasure!) became screaming. Like others who know the pain of public alienation, we transformed the knowledge of our public separateness and made it consoling—the reminder of intimacy. Excited, we joined our voices in a celebration of sounds. *We are speaking now the way we never speak out in public. We are alone—together,* voices sounded, surrounded to tell me. Some nights, no one seemed willing to loosen the hold sounds had on us. At dinner, we invented new words. (Ours sounded Spanish, but made sense only to us.) We pieced together new words by taking, say, an English verb and giving it Spanish endings. My mother's instructions at bedtime would be lacquered with mock-urgent tones. Or a word like *sí* would become, in several notes, able to convey added measures of feeling. Tongues explored the edges of words, especially the fat vowels. And we happily sounded that military drum roll, the twirling roar of the Spanish *r*. Family language: my family's sounds. The voices of my parents and sisters and brother. Their voices insisting: *You belong here. We are family members. Related. Special to one another. Listen!* Voices singing and sighing, rising, straining, then surging teeming with pleasure that burst syllables into fragments of laughter. At times it seemed there was steady quiet only when, from another room, the rustling whispers of my parents faded and I moved closer to sleep.

**2**

Supporters of bilingual education today imply that students like me miss a great deal by not being taught in their family's language. What they seem not to recognize is that, as a socially disadvantaged child, I considered Spanish to be a private language. What I needed to learn in school was that I had the right—and the obligation—to speak the public language of *los gringos*. The odd truth is that my first-grade classmates could have become bilingual, in the conventional sense of that word, more easily than I. Had they been taught (as upper-middle-class children are often taught early) a second language like Spanish or French, they could have regarded it simply as that: another public language. In my case such bilingualism could not have been so quickly achieved. What I did not believe was that I could speak a single public language.

Without question, it would have pleased me to hear my teachers address me in Spanish when I entered the classroom. I would have felt much less afraid. I would have trusted them and responded with ease. But I would have delayed—for how long postponed?—having to learn the language of public society. I would have evaded—and for how long could I have afforded to delay?—

learning the great lesson of school, that I had a public identity.

Fortunately, my teachers were unsentimental about their responsibility. What they understood was that I needed to speak a public language. So their voices would search me out, asking me questions. Each time I'd hear them, I'd look up in surprise to see a nun's face frowning at me. I'd mumble, not really meaning to answer. The nun would persist, 'Richard, stand up. Don't look at the floor. Speak up. Speak to the entire class, not just to me!' But I couldn't believe that the English language was mine to use. (In part, I did not want to believe it.) I continued to mumble. I resisted the teacher's demands. (Did I somehow suspect that once I learned public language my pleasing family life would be changed?) Silent, waiting for the bell to sound, I remained dazed, diffident, afraid.

Because I wrongly imagined that English was intrinsically a public language and Spanish an intrinsically private one, I easily noted the difference between classroom language and the language of home. At school, words were directed to a general audience of listeners. ('Boys and girls.') Words were meaningfully ordered. And the point was not self-expression alone but to make oneself understood by many others. The teacher quizzed: 'Boys and girls, why do we use that word in this sentence? Could we think of a better word to use there? Would the sentence change its meaning if the words were differently arranged? And wasn't there a better way of saying much the same thing?' (I couldn't say. I wouldn't try to say.)

Three months. Five. Half a year passed. Unsmiling, ever watchful, my teachers noted my silence. They began to connect my behavior with the difficult progress my older sister and brother were making. Until one Saturday morning three nuns arrived at the house to talk to our parents. Stiffly, they sat on the blue living room sofa. From the doorway of another room, spying the visitors, I noted the incongruity—the clash of two worlds, the faces and voices of school intruding upon the familiar setting of home. I overheard one voice gently wondering, 'Do your children speak only Spanish at home, Mrs. Rodriquez?' While another voice added, 'That Richard especially seems so timid and shy.'

*That Rich-heard!*

With great tact the visitors continued, 'Is it possible for you and your husband to encourage your children to practice their English when they are home?' Of course, my parents complied. What would they not do for their children's well-being? And how could they have questioned the Church's authority which those women represented? In an instant, they agreed to give up the language (the sounds) that had revealed and accentuated our family's closeness. The moment after the visitors left, the change was observed. *'Ahora,* speak to us *en inglés',* my father and mother united to tell us.

At first, it seemed a kind of game. After dinner each night, the family gathered to practice 'our' English. (It was still then *inglés,* a language foreign to us, so we felt drawn as strangers to it.) Laughing, we would try to define words we could not pronounce. We played with strange English sounds, often over-anglicizing our pronunciations. And we filled the smiling gaps of our sentences with familiar Spanish sounds. But that was cheating, somebody shouted. Everyone laughed. In school, meanwhile, like my brother and sister, I was required to attend a daily tutoring session. I needed a full year of special attention. I also needed my teachers to keep my attention from straying in class by calling out, *Rich-heard*—their English voices slowly prying loose my ties to my other name, its three notes, *Ri-car-do.* Most of all I needed to hear my mother and

father speak to me in a moment of seriousness in broken—suddenly heartbreaking English. The scene was inevitable: One Saturday morning I entered the kitchen where my parents were talking in Spanish. I did not realize that they were talking in Spanish however until, at the moment they saw me, I heard their voices change to speak English. Those *gringo* sounds they uttered startled me. Pushed me away. In that moment of trivial misunderstanding and profound insight, I felt my throat twisted by unsounded grief. I turned quickly and left the room. But I had no place to escape to with Spanish. (The spell was broken.) My brother and sisters were speaking English in another part of the house.

Again and again in the days following, increasingly angry, I was obliged to hear my mother and father: 'Speak to us *en inglés.'* (*Speak.*) Only then did I determine to learn classroom English. Weeks after, it happened: One day in school I raised my hand to volunteer an answer. I spoke out in a loud voice. And I did not think it remarkable when the entire class understood. That day, I moved very far from the disadvantaged child I had been only days earlier. The belief, the calming assurance that I belonged in public, had at last taken hold.

Shortly after, I stopped hearing the high and loud sounds of *los gringos.* A more and more confident speaker of English, I didn't trouble to listen to *how* strangers sounded, speaking to me. And there simply were too many English-speaking people in my day for me to hear American accents anymore. Conversations quickened. Listening to persons who sounded eccentrically pitched voices, I usually noted their sounds for an initial few seconds before I concentrated on *what* they were saying. Conversations became content-full. Transparent. Hearing someone's *tone* of voice—angry or questioning or sarcastic or happy or sad—I didn't distinguish it from the words it expressed. Sound and word were thus tightly wedded. At the end of a day, I was often bemused, always relieved, to realize how 'silent,' though crowded with words, my day in public had been. (This public silence measured and quickened the change in my life.)

At last, seven years old, I came to believe what had been technically true since my birth: I was an American citizen.

But the special feeling of closeness at home was diminished by then. Gone was the desperate, urgent, intense feeling of being at home; rare was the experience of feeling myself individualized by family intimates. We remained a loving family, but one greatly changed. No longer so close; no longer bound tight by the pleasing and troubling knowledge of our public separateness. Neither my older brother nor sister rushed home after school anymore. Nor did I. When I arrived home there would often be neighborhood kids in the house. Or the house would be empty of sounds.

Following the dramatic Americanization of their children, even my parents grew more publicly confident. Especially my mother. She learned the names of all the people on our block. And she decided we needed to have a telephone installed in the house. My father continued to use the word *gringo*. But it was no longer charged with the old bitterness or distrust. (Stripped of any emotional content, the word simply became a name for those Americans not of Hispanic descent.) Hearing him, sometimes, I wasn't sure if he was pronouncing the Spanish word *gringo* or saying gringo in English.

Matching the silence I started hearing in public was a new quiet at home. The family's quiet was partly due to the fact that, as we children learned more and more English, we shared fewer and fewer words with our parents. Sentences needed to be spoken slowly when a child addressed his mother or father. (Often the parent wouldn't understand.) The child would need to repeat himself. (Still the parent misunderstood.) The young voice, frustrated, would end up saying, 'Never mind'—the subject was closed. Dinners would be noisy with the clinking of knives and forks against dishes. My mother would smile softly between her remarks; my father at the other end of the table would chew and chew at his food, while he stared over the heads of his children.

My *mother!* My *father!* After English became my primary language, I no longer knew what words to use in addressing my parents. The old Spanish words (those tender accents of sound) I had used earlier—*mamá* and *papá*—I couldn't use anymore. They would have been too painful reminders of how much had changed in my life. On the other hand, the words I heard neighborhood kids call *their* parents seemed equally unsatisfactory. *Mother* and *Father; Ma, Papa, Pa, Dad, Pop* (how I hated the all-American sound of that last word especially)—all these terms I felt were unsuitable, not really terms of address for *my* parents. As a result, I never used them at home. Whenever I'd speak to my parents, I would try to get their attention with eye contact alone. In public conversations, I'd refer to 'my parents' or 'my mother and father.'

My mother and father, for their part, responded differently, as their children spoke to them less. She grew restless, seemed troubled and anxious at the scarcity of words exchanged in the house. It was she who would question me about my day when I came home from school. She smiled at small talk. She pried at the edges of my sentences to get me to say something more. (What?) She'd join conversations she overheard, but her intrusions often stopped her children's talking. By contrast, my father seemed reconciled to the new quiet. Though his English improved somewhat, he retired into silence.

At dinner he spoke very little. One night his children and even his wife helplessly giggled at his garbled English pronunciation of the Catholic Grace before Meals. Thereafter he made his wife recite the prayer at the start of each meal, even on formal occasions, when there were guests in the house. Hers became the public voice of the family. On official business, it was she, not my father, one would usually hear on the phone or in stores, talking to strangers. His children grew so accustomed to his silence that, years later, they would speak routinely of his shyness. (My mother would often try to explain: Both his parents died when he was eight. He was raised by an uncle who treated him like little more than a menial servant. He was never encouraged to speak. He grew up alone. A man of few words.) But my father was not shy, I realized, when I'd watch him speaking Spanish with relatives. Using Spanish, he was quickly effusive. Especially when talking with other men, his voice would spark, flicker, flare alive with sounds. In Spanish, he expressed ideas and feelings he rarely revealed in English. With firm Spanish sounds, he conveyed confidence and authority English would never allow him.

The silence at home, however, was finally more than a literal silence. Fewer words passed between parent and child, but more profound was the silence that resulted from my inattention to sounds. At about the time I no longer bothered to listen with care to the sounds of English in public, I grew careless about listening to the sounds family members made when they spoke. Most of the time I heard someone speaking at home and didn't distinguish his sounds from the words people uttered in public. I didn't even pay much attention to my parents' accented and ungrammatical speech. At least not at home. Only when I was with them in public would I grow alert to their accents. Though, even then, their sounds caused me less and less

concern. For I was increasingly confident of my own public identity.

I would have been happier about my public success had I not sometimes recalled what it had been like earlier, when my family had conveyed its intimacy through a set of conveniently private sounds. Sometimes in public, hearing a stranger, I'd hark back to my past. A Mexican farmworker approached me downtown to ask directions to somewhere '¿Hijito . . . ?' he said. And his voice summoned deep longing. Another time, standing beside my mother in the visiting room of a Carmelite convent, before the dense screen which rendered the nuns shadowy figures, I heard several Spanish-speaking nuns—their busy, singsong overlapping voices—assure us that yes, yes, we were remembered, all our family was remembered in their prayers. (Their voices echoed faraway family sounds.) Another day, a dark-faced old woman—her hand light on my shoulder—steadied herself against me as she boarded a bus. She murmured something I couldn't quite comprehend. Her Spanish voice came near, like the face of a never-before-seen relative in the instant before I was kissed. Her voice, like so many of the Spanish voices I'd hear in public, recalled the golden age of my youth. Hearing Spanish then, I continued to be a careful, if sad, listener to sounds. Hearing a Spanish-speaking family walking behind me, I turned to look. I smiled for an instant, before my glance found the Hispanic-looking faces of strangers in the crowd going by.

Today I hear bilingual educators say that children lose a degree of 'individuality' by becoming assimilated into public society. (Bilingual schooling was popularized in the seventies, that decade when middle-class ethnics began to resist the process of assimilation—the American melting pot.) But the bilingualists simplistically scorn the value and necessity of assimilation. They do not seem to realize that there are *two* ways a person is individualized. So they do not realize that while one suffers a diminished sense of *private* individuality by becoming assimilated into public society, such assimilation makes possible the achievement of *public* individuality.

The bilingualists insist that a student should be reminded of his difference from others in a mass society, his heritage. But they equate mere separateness with individuality. The fact is that only in private—with intimates—is separateness from the crowd a prerequisite for individuality. (An intimate draws me apart, tells me that I am unique, unlike all others.) In public, by contrast, full individuality is achieved, paradoxically, by those who are able to consider themselves members of the crowd. Thus it happened for me: Only when I was able to think of myself as an American, no longer an alien in *gringo* society, could I seek the rights of opportunities necessary for full public individuality. The social and political advantages I enjoy as a man result from the day that I came to believe that my name, indeed, is *Rich-heard Road-ree-guess.* It is true that my public society today is often impersonal. (My public society is usually mass society.) Yet despite the anonymity of the crowd and despite the fact that the individuality I achieve in public is often tenuous—because it depends on my being one in a crowd—I celebrate the day I acquired my new name. Those middle-class ethnics who scorn assimilation seem to me filled with decadent self-pity, obsessed by the burden of public life. Dangerously, they romanticize public separateness and they trivialize the dilemma of the socially disadvantaged.

My awkward childhood does not prove the necessity of bilingual education. My story discloses instead an essential myth of childhood—inevitable pain. If I rehearse here the changes in my private life after my Americanization, it is finally to emphasize the public gain. The loss implies the gain: The house I returned to each afternoon was quiet. Intimate sounds no longer rushed to the door to greet me. There were other noises inside. The telephone rang. Neighborhood kids ran past the door of the bedroom where I was reading my schoolbooks—covered with shopping-bag paper. Once I learned public language, it would never again be easy for me to hear intimate family voices. More and more of my day was spent hearing words. But that may only be a way of saying that the day I raised my hand in class and spoke loudly to an entire roomful of faces, my childhood started to end.

### 3

I grew up victim to a disabling confusion. As I grew fluent in English, I no longer could speak Spanish with confidence. I continued to understand spoken Spanish. And in high school, I learned how to read and write Spanish. But for many years I could not pronounce it. A powerful guilt blocked my spoken words; an essential glue was missing whenever I'd try to connect words to form sentences. I would be unable to break a barrier of sound, to speak freely. I would speak, or try to speak, Spanish, and I would manage to utter halting, hiccuping sounds that betrayed my unease.

When relatives and Spanish-speaking friends of my parents came to the house, my brother and sisters seemed reticent to use Spanish, but at least they managed to say a few necessary words before being excused. I never managed so gracefully. I was cursed with guilt. Each time I'd hear myself addressed in Spanish, I would be unable to respond with any success. I'd know the words I wanted to say, but I couldn't manage to say them. I would try to speak, but everything I said seemed to me horribly anglicized. My mouth would not form the words right. My jaw would tremble. After a phrase or two, I'd cough up a warm, silvery sound. And stop.

It surprised my listeners to hear me. They'd lower their heads, better to grasp what I was trying to say. They would repeat their questions in gentle, affectionate voices. But by then I would answer in English. No, no, they would say, we want you to speak to us in Spanish. ('. . . *en español.*') But I couldn't do it. *Pocho* then they called me. Sometimes playfully, teasingly, using the tender diminutive—*mi pochito.* Sometimes not so playfully, mocking, *Pocho.* (A Spanish dictionary defines that word as an adjective meaning 'colorless' or 'bland.' But I heard it as a noun, naming the Mexican-American who, in becoming an American, forgets his native society.) '¡*Pocho!*' the lady in the Mexican food store muttered, shaking her head. I looked up to the counter where red and green peppers were strung like Christmas tree lights and saw the frowning face of the stranger. My mother laughed somewhere behind me. (She said that her children didn't want to practice 'our Spanish' after they started going to school.) My mother's smiling voice made me suspect that the lady who faced me was not really angry at me. But, searching her face, I couldn't find the hint of a smile.

Embarrassed, my parents would regularly need to explain their children's inability to speak flowing Spanish during those years. My mother met the wrath of her brother, her only brother, when he came up from Mexico one summer with his family. He saw his nieces and nephews for the very first time. After listening to me, he looked away and said what a disgrace it was that I couldn't speak Spanish, '*su proprio idioma.*' He made that remark to my mother; I noticed, however, that he stared at my father.

I clearly remember one other visitor from those years. A long-time friend of my father from San Francisco would come to stay with us for several days in late August. He took great interest in me after he realized that I couldn't answer his questions in Spanish. He would grab me as I started to leave the kitchen. He would ask me something. Usually he wouldn't bother to wait for my mumbled response. Knowingly, he'd murmur: '¿*Ay Pocho, Pocho, adónde vas?*' And he would press his thumbs into the upper part of my arms, making me squirm with currents of pain. Dumbly, I'd stand there, waiting for his wife to notice us, for her to call him off with a benign smile. I'd giggle, hoping to deflate the tension between us, pretending that I hadn't seen the glittering scorn in his glance.

I remember that man now, but seek no revenge in this telling. I recount such incidents only because they suggest the fierce power Spanish had for many people I met at home; the way Spanish was associated with closeness. Most of those people who called me a *pocho* could have spoken English to me. But they would not. They seemed to think that Spanish was the only language we could use, that Spanish alone permitted our close association. (Such persons are vulnerable always to the ghetto merchant and the politician who have learned the value of speaking their clients' family language to gain immediate trust.) For my part, I felt that I had somehow committed a sin of betrayal by learning English. But betrayal against whom? Not against visitors to the house exactly. No, I felt that I had betrayed my immediate family. I *knew* that my parents had encouraged me to learn English. I *knew* that I had turned to English only with angry reluctance. But once I spoke English with ease, I came to *feel* guilty. (This guilt defied logic.) I felt that I had shattered the intimate bond that had once held the family close. This original sin against my family told whenever anyone addressed me in Spanish and I responded, confounded.

But even during those years of guilt, I was coming to sense certain consoling truths about language and intimacy. I remember playing with a friend in the backyard one day, when my grandmother appeared at the window. Her face was stern with suspicion when she saw the boy (the *gringo*) I was with. In Spanish she called out to me, sounding the whistle of her ancient breath. My companion looked up and watched her intently as she lowered the window and moved, still visible, behind the light curtain, watching us both. He wanted to know what she had said. I started to tell him, to say—to translate her Spanish words into English. The problem was, however, that though I knew how to translate exactly *what* she had told me, I realized that any translation would distort the deepest meaning of her message: It had been directed only to me. This message of intimacy could never be translated because it was not *in* the words she had used but passed *through* them. So any translation would have seemed wrong; her words would have been stripped of an essential meaning. Finally, I decided not to tell my friend anything. I told him that I didn't hear all she had said.

This insight unfolded in time. Making more and more friends outside my house, I began to distinguish intimate voices speaking through *English*. I'd listen at times to a close friend's confidential tone or secretive whisper. Even more remarkable were those instances when, for no special reason apparently, I'd become conscious of the fact that my companion was speaking only to me. I'd marvel just hearing his voice. It was a stunning event: to be able to break through his words, to be able to hear this voice of the other, to realize that it was directed only to me. After such moments of intimacy outside the house, I began to trust hearing intimacy conveyed through my family's English. Voices at home at last punctured sad confusion. I'd hear myself addressed as an intimate at home once again. Such moments were never as raucous with sound as past times had been when we had had 'private' Spanish to use. (Our English-sounding house was never to be as noisy as our Spanish-speaking house had been.) Intimate moments were usually soft moments of sound. My mother was in the dining room while I did my homework nearby. And she looked over at me. Smiled. Said something—her words said nothing very important. But her voice sounded to tell me (*We are together*) I was her son.

(*Richard!*)

Intimacy thus continued at home; intimacy was not stilled by English. It is true that I would never forget the great change of my life, the diminished occasions of intimacy. But there would also be times when I sensed the deepest truth about language and intimacy: *Intimacy is not created by a particular language; it is created by intimates.* The great change in my life was not linguistic but social. If, after becoming a successful student, I no longer heard intimate voices as often as I had earlier, it was not because I spoke English rather than Spanish. It was because I used public language for most of the day. I moved easily at last, a citizen in a crowded city of words.

# 4

This boy became a man. In private now, alone, I brood over language and intimacy—the great themes of my past. In public I expect most of the faces I meet to be the faces of strangers. (How do you do?) If meetings are quick and impersonal, they have been efficiently managed. I rush past the sounds of voices attending only to the words addressed to me. Voices seem planed to an even surface of sound, soundless. A business associate speaks in a deep baritone, but I pass through the timbre to attend to his words. The crazy man who sells me a newspaper every night mumbles something crazy, but I have time only to pretend that I have heard him say hello. Accented versions of English make little impression on me. In the rush-hour crowd a Japanese tourist asks me a question, and I inch past his accent to concentrate on what he is saying. The Eastern European immigrant in a neighborhood delicatessen speaks to me through a marinade of sounds, but I respond to his words. I note for only a second the Texas accent of the telephone operator or the Mississippi accent of the man who lives in the apartment below me.

My city seems silent until some ghetto black teenagers board the bus I am on. Because I do not take their presence for granted, I listen to the sounds of their voices. Of all the accented versions of English I hear in a day, I hear theirs most intently. They are *the* sounds of the outsider. They annoy me for being hard—so self-sufficient and unconcerned by my presence. Yet for the same reason they seem to me glamorous. (A romantic gesture against public acceptance.) Listening to their shouted laughter, I realize my own quiet. Their voices enclose my isolation. I feel envious, envious of their brazen intimacy.

I warn myself away from such envy, however. I remember the black political activists who have argued in favor of using black English in schools. (Their argument varies only slightly from that made by foreign-language bilingualists.) I have heard radical linguists make the point that black English is a complex and intricate version of English. And I do not doubt it. But neither do I think that black English should be a language of public instruction. What makes black English inappropriate in classrooms is not something *in* the language. It is rather what lower-class speakers make of it. Just as Spanish would have been a dangerous language for me to have used at the start of my education, so black English would be a dangerous language in use in the schooling of teenagers for whom it reenforces feeling of public separateness.

This seems to me an obvious point. But one that needs to be made. In recent years there have been attempts to make the language of the alien public language. 'Bilingual education, two ways to understand . . . ,' television and radio commercial glibly announce. Proponents of bilingual education are careful to say that they want students to acquire good schooling. Their argument goes something like this: Children permitted to use their family language in school will not be so alienated and will be better able to match the progress of English-speaking children in the crucial first months of instruction. (Increasingly confident of their abilities, such children will be more inclined to apply themselves to their studies in the future.) But then the bilingualists claim another, very different goal. They say that children who use their family language in school will retain a sense of their individuality—their ethnic heritage and culturalties. Supporters of bilingual education thus want it both ways. They propose bilingual schooling as a way of helping students acquire the skills of the classroom crucial for public success. But they likewise insist that bilingual instruction will give students a sense of their identity apart from the public.

Behind this screen there gleams an astonishing promise. One can become a public person while still remaining a private person. At the very same time one can be both! There need be no tension between the self in the crowd and the self apart from the crowd! Who would not want to believe such an idea? Who can be surprised that the scheme has won the support of many middle-class Americans? If the barrio or ghetto child can retain his separateness even while being publicly educated, then it is almost possible to believe that there is no private cost to be paid for public success. Such is the consolation offered by any of the current bilingual schemes. Consider, for example, the bilingual voters' ballot. In some American cities one can cast a ballot printed in several languages. Such a document implies that a person can exercise that most public of rights—the right to vote—while still keeping apart, unassimilated from public life.

It is not enough to say that these schemes are foolish and certainly doomed. Middle-class supporters of public bilingualism toy with the confusion of those Americans who cannot speak standard English as well as they can. Bilingual enthusiasts, moreover, sin against intimacy. An Hispanic-American writer tells me, 'I will never give up my family language; I would as soon give up my soul.' Thus he holds to his chest a thein of words, as though it were the source of his family ties. He credits to language what he should credit to family members. A convenient mistake. For as long as he holds on to words, he can ignore how much else has changed in his life.

It has happened before. In earlier decades, persons newly successful and ambitious for social mobility similarly seized upon certain 'family words.' Working-class men attempting political power took to calling one another 'brother.' By so doing they escaped oppressive public isolation and were able to unite with many others like themselves. But they paid a price for this union. It was a public union they forged. The word they coined to address one another could never be the sound (*brother*) exchanged by two in intimate greeting. In the union hall the word 'brother' became a vague metaphor;

with repetition a weak echo of the intimate sound. Context forced the change. Context could not be overruled. Context will always guard the realm of the intimate from public misuse.

Today nonwhite Americans call 'brother' to strangers. And white feminists refer to their mass union of 'sisters.' And white middle-class teenagers continue to prove the importance of context as they try to ignore it. They seize upon the idioms of the black ghetto. But their attempts to appropriate such expression invariably changes the words. As it becomes a public expression the ghetto idiom loses its sound—its message of public separateness and strident intimacy. It becomes with public repetition a series of words, increasingly lifeless.

The mystery remains: intimate utterance. The communication of intimacy passes through the word to enliven its sound. But it cannot be held by the word. Cannot be clutched or even quoted. It is too fluid. It depends not on word but on person.

My grandmother!

She stood among my other relations mocking me when I no longer spoke Spanish. '*Pocho*,' she said. But then it made no difference. (She'd laugh.) Our relationship continued. Language was never its source. She was a woman in her eighties during the first decade of my life. A mysterious woman to me, my only living grandparent. A woman of Mexico. The woman in long black dresses that reached down to her shoes. My one relative who spoke no word of English. She had no interest in *gringo* society. She remained completely aloof from the public. Protected by her daughters. Protected even by me when we went to Safeway together and I acted as her translator. Eccentric woman. Soft. Hard.

When my family visited my aunt's house in San Francisco, my grandmother searched for me among my man cousins. She'd chase them away. Pinching her granddaughters, she'd worn them all away from me. Then she'd take me to her room, where she had prepared for my coming. There would be a chair next to the bed. A dusty jellied candy nearby. And a copy of *Life en Español* for me to examine. 'There,' she'd say. I'd sit there content. A boy of eight. *Pocho.* Her favorite. I'd sift through the pictures of earthquake-destroyed Latin American names and blond-wigged Mexican movie stars. And all the while I'd listen to the sound of my grandmother's voice. She'd pace around the room, searching through closets and drawers, telling her stories of her life. Her past. They were stories so familiar to me that I couldn't remember the first time I'd heard them. I'd look up sometimes to listen. Other times she'd look over at me. But she never seemed to expect a response. Sometimes I'd smile or nod. (I understood exactly what she was saying.) But it never seemed to matter to her one way or another. It was though I was there. The words she spoke were almost irrelevant to the fact—the sounds she made. Content.

The mystery remained: intimate utterance.

I'd learn little about language and intimacy listening to those moral activists who propose using one's family language in public life. Listening to songs on the radio, or hearing a great voice at the opera, or overhearing the woman downstairs singing to herself at an open window, I learn much more. Singers celebrate the human voice. Their lyrics are words. But animated to voice those words are subsumed into sounds. I listen with excitement as the words yield their enormous power to sound although the words are never totally obliterated. In most songs the drama or tension results from the fact that the singer moves between word (sense) and note (song). At one moment the song simply 'says' something. At another moment

the voice stretches out the words—the heart cannot contain!—and the voice moves toward pure sound. Words take flight.

Singing out words, the singer suggests an experience of sound most intensely mine at intimate moments. Literally, most songs are about love. (Lost love; celebrations of loving; pleas.) By simply being occasions when sound escapes word, however, songs put me in mind of the most intimate moments of my life.

Finally, among all types of song, it is the song created by lyric poets that I find most compelling. There is no other public occasion of sound so important for me. Written poems exist on a page, at first glance, as a mere collection of words. And yet despite this, without musical accompaniment, the poet leads me to hear the sounds of the words that I read. As song, the poem passes between sound and sense, never belonging for long to one realm or the other. As public artifact, the poem can never duplicate intimate sound. But by imitating such sound, the poem helps me recall the intimate times of my life. I read in my room—alone—and grow conscious of being alone, sounding my voice, in search of another. The poem serves then as a memory device. It forces remembrance. And refreshes. It reminds me of the possibility of escaping public words, the possibility that awaits me in meeting the intimate.

The poems I read are not nonsense poems. But I read them for reasons which, I imagine, are similar to those that make children play with meaningless rhyme. I have watched them before: I have noticed the way children create private languages to keep away the adult; I have heard their chanting riddles that get nowhere in logic but harken back to some kingdom of sound. I have watched them listen to intricate nonsense rhymes, and I have noted their wonder. I was never such a child. Until I was six years old, I remained in a magical realm of sound. I didn't need to remember that realm because it was present to me. But then the screen door shut behind me as I left home for school. At last I began my movement toward words. On the other side of initial sadness would come the realization that intimacy cannot be held. With time would come the knowledge that intimacy must finally pass.

I would dishonor those I have loved and those I love now to claim anything else. I would dishonor our closeness by holding on to a particular language and calling it my family language. Intimacy is not trapped within words. It passes through words. It passes. The truth is that intimates leave the room. Doors close. Faces move away from the window. Time passes. Voices recede into the dark. Death finally quiets the voice. And there is no way to deny it. No way to stand in the crowd, uttering one's family language.

The last time I saw my grandmother I was nine years old. I can tell you some of the things she said to me as I stood by her bed. I cannot, however, quote the message of intimacy she conveyed with her voice. She laughed, holding my hand. Her voice illumined disjointed memories as it passed them again. She remembered her husband, his green eyes, the magic name of Narciso. His early death. She remembered the farm in Mexico. The eucalyptus nearby. (Its scent, she remembered, like incense.) She remembered the family cow, the bell round its neck heard miles away. A dog. She remembered working as a seamstress. How she'd leave her daughters and son for long hours to go into Guadalajara to work. And how my mother would come running toward her in the sun—her bright yellow dress—to see her return. *'Mmmaaaammmmáááá,'* the old lady mimicked her daughter (my mother) to her son. She laughed. There was the snap of a cough. An aunt came into the room and told me it was time I should leave. 'You can see her tomorrow,' she promised. And so I kissed my grandmother's cracked face. And the last thing I saw was her thin, oddly youthful thigh, as my aunt rearranged the sheet on the bed.

At the funeral parlor a few days after, I knelt with my relatives during the rosary. Among their voices but silent, I traced, then lost, the sounds of individual aunts in the surge of the common prayer. And I heard at the moment what I have since heard often again—the sounds the women in my family make when they are praying in sadness. When I went up to look at my grandmother, I saw her through the haze of a veil draped over the open lid of the casket. Her face appeared calm—but distant and unyielding to love. It was not the face I remembered seeing most often. It was the face she made in public when the clerk at Safeway asked her some question and I would have to respond. It was her public face the mortician had designed with his dubious art.

# Understanding Composing
*Sondra Perl*

Any psychological process, whether the development of thought or voluntary behavior, is a process undergoing changes right before one's eyes. . . . Under certain conditions it becomes possible to trace this development.[1]

L. S. Vygotsky

It's hard to begin this case study of myself as a writer because even as I'm searching for a beginning, a pattern of organization, I'm watching myself, trying to understand my behavior. As I sit here in silence, I can see lots of things happening that never made it onto my tapes. My mind leaps from the task at hand to what I need at the vegetable stand for tonight's soup to the threatening rain outside to ideas voiced in my writing group this morning, but in between "distractions" I hear myself trying out words I might use. It's as if the extraneous thoughts are a counterpoint to the more steady attention I'm giving to composing. This is all to point out that the process is more complex than I'm aware of, but I think my tapes reveal certain basic patterns that I tend to follow.

Anne
New York City Teacher

Anne is a teacher of writing. In 1979, she was among a group of twenty teachers who were taking a course in research and basic

Sondra Perl teaches at Herbert Lehman College of the City University of New York. This article was originally published in *College Composition and Communication,* a journal for college and university teachers.

writing at New York University.[2] One of the assignments in the course was for the teachers to tape their thoughts while composing aloud on the topic, "My Most Anxious Moment as a Writer." Everyone in the group was given the topic in the morning during class and told to compose later on that day in a place where they would be comfortable and relatively free from distraction. The result was a tape of composing aloud and a written product that formed the basis for class discussion over the next few days.

One of the purposes of this assignment was to provide teachers with an opportunity to see their own composing process at work. From the start of the course, we recognized that we were controlling the situation by assigning a topic and that we might be altering the process by asking writers to compose aloud. Nonetheless, we viewed the task as a way of capturing some of the flow of composing and, as Anne later observed in her analysis of her tape, she was able to detect certain basic patterns. This observation, made not only by Anne, leads me to ask, "What basic patterns seem to occur during composing?" and "What does this type of research have to tell us about the nature of the composing process?"

## Recursiveness in Writing

Perhaps the most challenging part of the answer is the recognition of recursiveness in writing. In recent years, many researchers including myself have questioned the traditional notion that writing is a linear process with a strict plan-write-revise sequence.[3] In its stead, we have advocated the idea that writing is a recursive process, that throughout the process of writing, writers return to substrands of the overall process, or subroutines (short successions of steps); writers use these to keep the process moving forward. In other words, recursiveness in writing implies that there is a forward-moving action that exists by virtue of a backward-moving action. The question that then need to be answered are, "To what do writers move back?" "What exactly is being repeated?" "What recurs?"

To answer these questions, it is important to look at what writers do while writing and what an analysis of their processes reveals. The descriptions that follow are based on my own observations of the composing processes of many types of writers including college students, graduate students, and English teachers like Anne.

Writing does appear to be recursive, yet the parts that recur seem to vary from writer to writer and from topic to topic. Furthermore, some recursive elements are easy to spot while others are not. The most visible recurring feature or backward movement involves rereading little bits of discourse. Few writers I have seen write for long periods of time without returning briefly to what is already down on the page. For some, like Anne, rereading occurs after every few phrases; for others, it occurs after every sentence; more frequently, it occurs after a "chunk" of information has been written. Thus, the unit that is reread is not necessarily a syntactic one, but rather a semantic one as defined by the writer.

The second recurring feature is some key word or item called up by the topic. Writers consistently return to their notion of the topic throughout the process of writing. Particularly when they are stuck, writers seem to use the topic or a key word in it as a way to get going again. Thus many times it is possible to see writers "going back," rereading the topic they were given, changing it to suit what they have been writing or changing what they have written to suit their notion of the topic.

There is also a third backward movement in writing, one that is not so easy to document. It is not easy because the move, itself, cannot immediately be identified with words. In fact, the move is not to any words on the page nor to the topic but to feeling or non-verbalized perceptions that surround the words, or to what the words already present evoke in the writer. The move draws on sense experience, and it can be observed if one pays close attention to what happens when writers pause and seem to listen or otherwise react to what is inside of them. The move occurs inside the writer, to what is physically felt. The term used to describe this focus of writers' attention is "felt sense."

The term "felt sense" has been coined and described by Eugene Gendlin, a philosopher at the University of Chicago. In his words, felt sense is

the soft underbelly of thought . . . a kind of bodily awareness that . . . can be used as a tool . . . a bodily awareness that . . . encompasses everything you feel and know about a given subject at a given time. . . . It is felt in the body, yet it has meanings. It is body and mind before they are split apart.[4]

This felt sense is always there, within us. It is unifying, and yet, when we bring words to it, it can break apart, shift, unravel, and become something else. Gendlin has spent many years showing people how to work with their felt sense. Here I am making connections between what he has done and what I have seen happen as people write.

When writers are given a topic, the topic itself evokes a felt sense in them. This topic calls forth images, words, ideas, and vague, fuzzy feelings that are anchored in the writer's body. What is elicited, then, is not solely the product of a mind but of a mind alive in a living, sensing body. When writers pause, when they go back and repeat key words, what they seem to be doing is waiting, paying attention to what is still vague and unclear. They are looking to their felt experience, and waiting for an image, a word, or a phrase to emerge that captures the sense they embody. Usually, when they make the decision to write, it is after they have a dawning awareness that something has clicked, that they have enough of a sense that if they begin with a few words heading in a certain direction, words will continue to come which will allow them to flesh out the sense they have.

The process of using what is sensed directly about a topic is a natural one. Many writers do it without any conscious awareness that that is what they are doing. For example, Anne repeats the words "anxious moments," using these key words as a way of allowing her sense of the topic to deepen. She asks herself, "Why are exams so anxiety provoking?" and waits until she has enough of a sense within her that she can go in a certain direction. She does not yet have the words, only the sense that she is able to begin. Once she writes, she stops to see what is there. She maintains a highly recursive composing style throughout, and she seems unable to go forward without first going back to see and to listen to what she has already created. In her own words, she says:

My disjointed style of composing is very striking to me. I almost never move from the writing of one sentence directly to the next. After each sentence I pause to read what I've written, assess, sometimes edit and think about what will come next. I often have to read the several preceding sentences a few times as if to gain momentum to carry me to the next sentence. I seem to depend a lot on the sound of my words and . . . while I'm hanging in the middle of this uncompleted thought, I may also start editing a previous sentence or get

an inspiration for something which I want to include later in the paper.

What tells Anne that she is ready to write? What is the feeling of "momentum" like for her? What is she hearing as she listens to the "sound" of her words? When she experiences "inspiration," how does she recognize it?

In the approach I am presenting, the ability to recognize what one needs to do or where one needs to go is informed by calling on felt sense. This is the internal criterion writers seem to use to guide them when they are planning, drafting, and revising.

## Drawing on the Felt Sense

The recursive move, then, that is hardest to document but is probably the most important to be aware of is the move to felt sense, to what is not yet in words but out of which images, words, and concepts emerge. The continuing presence of this felt sense, waiting for us to discover it and see where it leads, raises a number of questions.

Is "felt sense" another term for what professional writers call their "inner voice" or their feeling of "inspiration"?

Do skilled writers call on their capacity to sense more readily than unskilled writers?

Rather than merely reducing the complex act of writing to a neat formulation, can the term "felt sense" point us to an area of our experience from which we can evolve even richer and more accurate descriptions of composing?

Can learning how to work with felt sense teach us about creativity and release us from stultifyingly repetitive patterns?

My observations lead me to answer "yes" to all four questions. There seems to be a basic step in the process of composing that skilled writers rely on even when they are unaware of it and that less skilled writers can be taught. This process seems to rely on very careful attention to one's inner reflections and is often accompanied with bodily sensations. When it's working, this process allows us to say or write what we've never said before, to create something new and fresh, and occasionally it provides us with the experience of "newness" or "freshness," even when "old words" or images are used.

The basic process begins with paying attention. If we are given a topic, it begins with taking the topic in and attending to what it evokes in us. There is less "figuring out" an answer and more "waiting" to see what forms. Even without a predetermined topic, the process remains the same. We can ask ourselves, "What's on my mind?" or "Of all the things I know about, what would I most like to write about now?" and wait to see what comes. What we pay attention to is the part of our bodies where we experience ourselves directly. For many people, it's the area of their stomachs; for others, there is a more generalized response and they maintain a hovering attention to what they experience throughout their bodies.

Once a felt sense forms, we match words to it. As we begin to describe it, we get to see what is there for us. We get to see what we think, what we know. If we are writing about something that truly interests, the felt sense deepens. We know that we are writing out of a "centered" place.

If the process is working, we begin to move along, sometimes quickly. Other times, we need to return to the beginning, to reread, to see if we captured what we meant to say. Sometimes after rereading we move on again, picking up speed. Other times by rereading we realize we've gone off the track, that what we've written doesn't quite "say it," and we need to reassess. Sometimes the words are wrong and we need to change them. Other times we need to go back to the topic, to call up the sense it initially evoked

to see where and how our words led us astray. Sometimes in rereading we discover that the topic is "wrong," that the direction we discovered in writing is where we really want to go. It is important here to clarify that the terms "right" and "wrong" are not necessarily meant to refer to grammatical structures or to correctness.

What is "right" or "wrong" corresponds to our sense of our intention. We intend to write something, words come, and now we assess if those words adequately capture our intended meaning. Thus, the first question we ask ourselves is "Are these words right for me?" "Do they capture what I'm trying to say?" "If not, what's missing?" Once we ask "what's missing?" we need once again to wait, to let a felt sense of what is missing form, and then to write out of that sense.

*Retrospective Structuring*

I have labeled this process of attending, of calling up a felt sense, and of writing out of that place, the process of retrospective structuring. It is retrospective in that it begins with what is already there, inchoately, and brings whatever is there forward by using language in structured form.

It seems as though a felt sense has within it many possible structures or forms. As we shape what we intend to say, we are further structuring our sense while correspondingly shaping our piece of writing.

It is also important to note that what is there implicitly, without words, is not equivalent to what finally emerges. In the process of writing, we begin with what is inchoate and end with something that is tangible. In order to do so, we both discover and construct what we mean. Yet the term "discovery" ought not lead us to think that meaning exists fully formed inside of us and that all we need do is dig deep enough to release it. In writing, meaning cannot be discovered the way we discover an object on an archeological dig. In writing, meaning is crafted and constructed. It involves us in a process of coming-into-being. Once we have worked at shaping, through language, what is there inchoately, we can look at what we have written to see if it adequately captures what we intended. Often at this moment discovery occurs. We see something new in our writing that comes upon us as a surprise. We see in our words a further structuring of the sense we began with, and we recognize that in those words we have discovered something new about ourselves and our topic. Thus when we are successful at this process, we end up with a product that teaches us something, that clarifies what we know (or what we knew at one point only implicitly), and that lifts out or explicates or enlarges our experience. In this way, writing leads to discovery.

All the writers I have observed, skilled and unskilled alike, use the process of retrospective structuring while writing. Yet the degree to which they do so varies and seems, in fact, to depend upon the model of the writing process that they have internalized. Those who realize that writing can be a recursive process have an easier time with waiting, looking, and discovering. Those who subscribe to the linear model find themselves easily frustrated when what they write does not immediately correspond to what they planned or when what they produce leaves them with little sense of accomplishment. Since they have relied on a formulaic approach, they often produce writing that is formulaic as well, thereby cutting themselves off from the possibility of discovering something new.

## Projective Structuring

Such a result seems linked to another feature of the composing process, to what I call projective structuring, or the ability to craft what one intends to say so that it is intelligible to others. A number of concerns arise in regard to projective structuring; I will mention only a few that have been raised for me as I have watched different writers at work.

1. Although projective structuring is only one important part of the composing process, many writers act as if it is the whole process. These writers focus on what they think others want them to write rather than looking to see what it is they want to write. As a result, they often ignore their felt sense and they do not establish a living connection between themselves and their topic.

2. Many writers reduce projective structuring to a series of rules or criteria for evaluating finished discourse. These writers ask, "Is what I'm writing correct?" and "Does it conform to the rules I've been taught?" While these concerns are important, they often overshadow all others and lock the writer in the position of writing solely or primarily for the approval of readers.

Projective structuring, as I see it, involves much more than imagining a strict audience and maintaining a strict focus on correctness. It is true that to handle this part of the process well, writers need to know certain grammatical rules and evaluative criteria, but they also need to know how to call up a sense of their reader's needs and expectations.

For projective structuring to function fully, writers need to draw on their capacity to move away from their own words, to decenter from the page, and to project themselves into the role of the reader. In other words, projective structuring asks writers to attempt to become readers and to imagine what someone other than themselves will need before the writer's particular piece of writing can become intelligible and compelling. To do so, writers must have the experience of being readers. They cannot call up a felt sense of a reader unless they themselves have experienced what it means to be lost in a piece of writing or to be excited by it. When writers do not have such experiences, it is easy for them to accept that readers merely require correctness.

In closing, I would like to suggest that retrospective and projective structuring are two parts of the same basic process. Together they form the alternating mental postures writers assume as they move through the act of composing. The former relies on the ability to go inside, to attend to what is there, from that attending to place words upon a page, and then to assess if those words adequately capture one's meaning. The latter relies on the ability to assess how the words on that page will affect someone other than the writer: the reader. We rarely do one without the other entering in; in fact, again in these postures we can see the shuttling back-and-forth movements of the composing process, the move from sense to words and from words to sense, from inner experience to outer judgment and from judgment back to experience. As we move through this cycle, we are continually composing and recomposing our meanings and what we mean. And in doing so, we display some of the basic recursive patterns that writers who observe themselves closely seem to see in their own work.

After observing the process for a long time we may, like Anne, conclude that at any given moment the process is more complex than anything we are aware of; yet such insights, I believe, are important. They show us the fallacy of reducing the composing process to a simple linear scheme, and they leave us with the potential for creating even more powerful ways of understanding composing.

## Notes

1. L. S. Vygotsky, *Mind in Society,* trans. M. Cole, V. John-Steiner, S. Scribner, and E. Souberman (Cambridge, Mass.: Harvard University Press, 1978), 61.
2. This course was team-taught by myself and Gordon Pradl, associate professor of English Education at New York University.
3. See Janet Emig. *The Composing Process of Twelfth Graders,* NOTE Research Report No. 13 (Urbana, Ill.: NOTE, 1971); Linda Flower and J. R. Hayes, "The Cognition of Discovery," *College Composition and Communication 31* (February 1980): 21–32; Nancy Sommers, "The Need for Theory in Composition Research," *College Composition and Communication 30* (February 1979): 46–49.
4. Eugene Gendlin, *Focusing* (New York: Everest House, 1978), 35, 165.

# Student Writers and Their Sense of Authority over Texts

*Carol Berkenkotter*

One of the major difficulties most of us face is helping student writers write for a responsive audience other than the teacher-evaluator. As Nancy Sommers, Lil Brannon, and C.N. Knoblauch have shown, it is all too easy for teachers to appropriate student' texts and the responsibilities of authorship.[1] Donald M. Murray's solution to the problem is to ask teachers to serve students as "writing coaches" who encourage students to read their texts from the perspective of an inquiring reader.[2] Both Sommers and Murray have studied the writing processes of professional writers and recognize the problems that student writers confront when they feel that they lack both the authority over their texts and the means for gaining authorial control.[3]

Other teachers favor turning the classroom into a learning community in which students are each other's primary audience. They contend that students who receive feedback from peers as they move through the subprocesses of composing have a number of advantages: they will experience writing and revising for less threatening audiences than the teacher, and they will learn to discrim-

inate between useful and non-useful feedback and to use their awareness of anticipated audience response as they revise. A peer audience then, can help writers to negotiate a way between their readers' suggestions and their own imperatives.

Promising as this approach appears, it raises a number of provocative questions for researchers. For example, how do students interact in their writing groups when the teacher isn't there? How do the interactions between group members, teacher, and writer shape what the writer does when she revises? Can we assume that feedback from multiple audiences will help writers improve their texts? In order to study the relationships between student writers and their audiences, I asked ten volunteers from one of my freshman composition classes to think aloud on tape as they worked on multiple drafts of a single essay over a two-and-a-half-week period. I also listened to tapes of the subjects in their writing groups and of student/teacher conferences. I knew that I needed both kinds of data to gauge the extent to which students' readers' comments affected their revising behaviors. What I didn't anticipate was that the subjects would respond to their readers in significantly different ways depending on the writer's personality, level of maturity, and ability to handle writing problems. Nor did I realize that out of their transactions with their readers some students would assert their

Carol Berkenkotter teaches at Michigan Technological University. This article was originally published in *College Composition and Communication*, a journal for college and university teachers.

proprietary rights over their texts while others would gain—or lose—a sense of authority. The case of Stan, Pat, and Joann best illustrate how these distinctively different processes occur.

## Stan: The Resisting Revisor

Of all the subjects Stan was the most reluctant to alter any of the three drafts which followed his first, other than by substituting pronouns and adding or deleting words, phrases, and an occasional paragraph. None of his revisions altered the meaning of his text. Stan's essay dealt with "the good life" as it is pictured on television. He claimed that the medium projected a distorted view of reality by constantly showing beautiful people in luxurious settings out of the reach of most viewers. Having made this point in his first paragraph, he reiterated it throughout his essay using quotations from a television critic for support.

Upon reading his initial draft, his group told him that they liked his idea. They also advised him to incorporate many more examples (rather than quotations) as evidence. In response to their comments, Stan asserted in his first taped protocol that he didn't see the need to rewrite. With the exception of making a few references to his group's comments and jotting down minor lexical and spelling changes as he read his draft aloud, he appeared convinced that he had "said what I needed to say." Anticipating another writing group's response, Stan took the defensive: "None of the assholes in that class are going to agree with me. I hope to raise hell with this paper. Bull-shit. It's my opinion. Everyone has their own opinion." At the end of the protocol, however, his tone became less abrasive:

I hope I can. . . do better and better on the next tape. I don't figure I should get so bored on these . . . After I talk to Carol I will rewrite my

paper. Type it up. Then I'll get it back with comments and then do another protocol.

A week later Stan gave his second protocol after he had received criticism from a peer evaluation group. During that same session in his group protocols he was extremely critical of the papers the group read, frequently without reason. Finally, Dave S. suggested "Stan, you need to relax a bit." But Stan was not about to be deterred. "Bullshit," he replied. "I'm in a good mood for critiquing this morning." Stan's aggressive behavior and his use of expletives suggests that he enjoyed the feeling of power that the role of peer evaluator gave him.

Finding himself on the receiving end of another group's criticism, however, upset him. During his protocol he reports: "I don't really know what I am going to do today because in group critique in the peer evaluation group I got sucked to put it mildly." But he does not review the group's comments. Instead he decides to read his paper again and "look for weaknesses myself and correct a couple. So I really don't have that much to do today." He reads his paper, indicating his concern over his word choice at one point and adding two words at another. Finishing, he replays the tape following along with his paper and making a few grammatical changes. After hearing himself in tape he observes: "I really do think it is pretty good. . . just changed the pronoun. No big deal." After a pause he reviews what the peer evaluation group has written.

(Reading the questions on the evaluation report)[4] In the first part, it says *What do you see as the greatest strength in your paper?* They say my title and some good quotes. Big deal. That's all they wrote. Then on the back it says, *What do you see is the greatest weakness? Again, point out specific passages in your paper and discuss why. Let the reader/writer know what questions you have that still need to be addressed.* They say I have too many quotes. Not enough of my own opinion. This whole damn paper is my own opinion. I just use what other people have said to back me up because I title my paper, "What do you think?" You know, what do you think? Do you think that it is true or not true that t.v. does form the way you think? . . . It kind of goes along with the first paragraph too. But it is a two way title. I have always been taught to use quotes and shit to back up how you feel. You can't just go on the limb on your own intuition. . . and say "I think it does. Why? Just because I say so" . . . Now that don't work. You've got to have kind of proof or evidence and that's why I slipped in the 22,000 hours and the quotes. Now here the other groups say that I need more specific situations. More about a specific situation. . . I've got about a quarter of a page on a specific situation on a two page paper. I thought that was enough with the quote from Chris Stoer. I think that is a pretty good quote. I don't really feel the need to rewrite my paper. It's really a bunch of I think. . . shit.

Stan made a deliberate choice to disregard what his audience told him, a choice that he stuck with in his third protocol five days later even after I asked him in conference, "Where are you in this paper, Stan? I don't see you. All I see are quotations from someone else to support what you say. Can you make this more personal when you revise? Maybe use some examples from your own experiences." Instead, Stan decided to make his fourth draft "more personal" by changing the second person pronouns throughout to the first person, and adding a few passages about how his grandparents' values were not shaped by television the way he believes values of the current generation are. Throughout the protocol he insists on the primacy of the changes he has already made over any that might be suggested by his readers as he imagines their response. ". . . My own experience. They aren't going to believe it. They aren't going to know if it happened to me or not. Though it's close enough."

By making only the most minor surface-level changes in his text during the two and a half weeks he worked on it, Stan opted for the easiest solution to the problem of dealing with his readers. He never accepted the responsibility for critically reading his text, but was more concerned with defending his proprietary rights. Had he read it critically, he might have realized that his readers' suggestions to include examples and to draw them from personal experience would have helped him buttress his central point. Furthermore, Stan's insistent criticism of others' papers, criticism that was frequently unsupported by evidence or constructive suggestions for revision, seems linked with his inability to respond positively to the feedback he receives from peer readers and his instructor. Stan is locked in the myopia of his own perceptions. His response to his readers suggests that some student writers do not develop the sense of responsibility to their texts that we see in experienced adult writers.

## Pat: The Inner-directed Revisor

If Stan was too ego-centered to let his readers help him, Pat's case, in contrast, demonstrates that we cannot assume that peer feedback will necessarily help writers improve their text. Some students march to the beat of a different drummer. Once they discover their subject, they become their own best audience. Pat read to his group an account of the adventures he and a high school friend had on their motorcycles. His peers were pleased with that he had written and concurred that he had a good first draft which needed only more detail. Pat was not satisfied, however. Perhaps he sensed a latent intention he had not expressed. In conference a few days later, he voiced his dissatisfaction, yet he echoed his readers' asking if he should include more detail about his friend to "bind the whole thing together." "What did your friend look like," I asked. "I'd like to see him."

132

"Finn was two years older than I was." On the tape his voice becomes more empathic. "He'd been in trouble. Bad trouble. He had done some bad things. But he wasn't a bad guy." Shortly after reading me this Pat left my office and went to give his protocol. He began by saying:

I have decided to change my whole story around. The focus of my other story was very weak. The dates were hard to follow. It was lurchy. It was not me. There was one other main problem. It didn't seem very good to me. I was displeased with the way that it went and the way that it read. It was awfully short. I have decided to write about a person I mentioned in the first draft. It was Finn and me. I am going to write about him and some of the things we did.

Pat knew a great deal about Finn, his problems, and their friendship. Yet he did not initially realize that Finn was his subject; instead, he had internalized his readers' interest in seeing more detail about their adventures. My accidental question prompted him to name his friend, an act which triggered a powerful recollection. Sensing the gap between his vivid memories of their relationship and his description in the draft, he reconceived the subject of his paper.[5]

Once having determined to write about Finn and their friendship, Pat felt the first tug of resistance against his readers. While writing his third draft, he rejected my suggestion to rearrange his material:

It would be really hard to put this into chronological order in spite of what you said because you wouldn't be able to make entire paragraphs out of what was going on. . . that part there you couldn't make two paragraphs out of there. It would have to go in before the paragraph when I met him and that would. . . I don't like to follow a paper that way. That's great too but for now I think that I am just going to leave it that way.

After hearing his writing group criticize the narrative of another writer because it was too personal, he asserted,

If that is what a person wants to write about that's great because my paper is on reflections too, on my memories. If people don't like it, they don't have to read it, you know. It's important to me and it's important to her and there is nothing wrong with that and I just wanted to say that before I started my protocol.

It took Pat five drafts during the two-and-a-half-week period to complete his portrait of his friend. His sense of authority grew out of the early commitment he made to document their friendship. This commitment brought with it a feeling of responsibility to his text, so strong that he chose to make decisions independent of his readers' expectations. And although the readers might have helped him, they did not possess his clear sense of his subject. Pat demonstrates that some writers revise out of a sense of internal necessity. Other writers, however, may be other-directed. Extremely sensitive to the needs and expectations of their readers, they may be vulnerable to misdirected criticism. The effect that this kind of feedback can have on the sense of authority of the writer can best be seen in Joann's case.

## Joann: A Crisis of Authority

Of all the writers in the sample Joann was the most responsive to the comments of her readers and also spent the most time drafting to incorporate those responses directly into her work. Her keen awareness of her readers' needs made her willing to cooperate with her writing group's suggestion that she include more concrete detail in her paper, a description of her first trip in a canoe. She revised six times over the two and a half weeks to complete this task, each time rereading the essay, paragraph by paragraph, then adding more detail where she thought that it would help her readers, and deleting passages, sentences, or words she considered extraneous. Even when they asked her to include in dialogue form the "obscenities" that she and a friend had shouted at some water skiers who had nearly capsized their boat, Joann reluctantly scoured her memory. Unable to recall what they had said, she decided to make something up and spent several minutes on one protocol listing all the "vulgarity" she could think of. She jokingly concluded that she had "learned to write obscenities in English 101." Unfortunately for her, when a peer evaluation group read her final draft, they became overly zealous in their criticism. Observing that her paper contained some good description, they asked her for more, often in places where it was unnecessary or inappropriate. For example, as she watched from her canoe children fishing in an open culvert, Joann had observed, "Too bad we didn't bring our fishing poles." Her readers commented, "Dull! Must describe."

Joann found herself hard pressed to accommodate her readers' expectations. But in response to a similar suggestion she questioned their judgement, addressing them directly:

How can you say that? I don't understand. Okay (Reading their comments) *Show that "we relaxed awhile and set out again."* How can you show that? You just relax. . . Okay. . . How can you. . . I can see showing 'we were physically and mentally exhausted' (another suggestion), but. . . hmm. . . well sorry guys but I am gonna have to let that one go.

Finding many of her readers' expectations impossible to fulfill, Joann began to express doubt about the value of her work: "I am glad that I didn't put my name on my paper. . . oh I did. They know who I am. . . I don't like this paper. Wish I hadn't written on this." She managed to pull herself together, however, and as she read her paper aloud her feelings of confidence returned:

*The water gleamed in the evening sun reflecting every image surrounding it. Every tree, house, and cloud in the sky seemed to be taken in by the lake.*

*Warmed by a full day of sunshine the water seemed to caress our paddles as we glided along.* I am not going to touch that. I *like* that paragraph. (Emphasis mine).

These excerpts show Joann temporarily losing her authority because she took her readers' judgment seriously, even when she questioned it. Rather than taking the offensive (as Stan would have) or asserting her authority (as Pat did), she lost confidence. But Joann wasn't about to abandon her text. And as she reread her first page, she was able to reaffirm her faith in her prose. ("I'm not going to touch that. I *like* that.") Regaining her control over what she was doing, she then was in a position to assess which of her readers' suggestions she could use:

Let's see here. . . They wanted me to describe 'physically and mentally exhausted' How? (Reading) *When they finally left us alone, we were both physically and mentally exhausted.* How can I describe that? With tired limbs. . . I like that. Tired limbs. . . *We were both.* . . maybe I could just put 'exhausted'. No. . . *physically and mentally exhausted with tired limbs and foggy brains?* . . . How would your brain be when you are mentally exhausted? I always feel funny after a test. Fuzzy brains. That is a good way to describe a brain—fuzzy. What the heck. *And fuzzy brains.*

Joann easily retrieves the terms she needs to describe "physically and mentally exhausted." She is not so amenable, however, to her readers' next suggestion to show how she and her friend relaxed on an abandoned barge: "I am afraid folks. I can not show anymore details this time." Nevertheless, she tries:

Relaxed. What do you do when you relax? You lay down, right? We laid and relaxed, no we just relaxed. We sat there and drank a beer and had a cigarette. I am not going to put that in my paper. You aren't supposed to have beer out in the boats with you anyway.

Having initially invested her trust in her readers, Joann's relationship with them became adversarial when she realized that many of their suggestions were unwarranted. Unlike Stan, who shut his readers out as he declared his proprietary rights, Joann continued the dialogue, as in the passage above, determining where she could or could not accommodate their suggestions. In doing so she regained the authority over her text. Her experience suggests that in some cases peer feedback may not serve the best interests of the writer.

The responses that Stan, Pat, and Joann made to their readers varied considerably, as did their attitudes toward and approaches to the task of revising. Stan, too immature to develop any kind of rapport with his audience, could only assert his proprietary rights. Had he made more of a commitment of either his subject or his readers, he might have experienced a genuine need for authority over his text and consequently felt compelled to revise more frequently and thoroughly. Lacking a sense of responsibility to either, it was easy for him to opt for the simplest solution to the problem of accommodating his readers. Pat had the best relationship with his audience. He felt responsible to them, yet once he had experienced a commitment to his subject, he made a series of informed decisions about the usefulness of their comments. Joann appears to possess the keen sense of audience many of us would encourage. Yet her very receptivity to her readers' suggestions made her vulnerable to their unwarranted criticism. Having invested a great deal of time and energy on her essay, however, Joann didn't give up on her text readily; her tenacity brought her through a crisis of authority.

Together, the three cases suggest that students who write for peer readers as well as their teacher might not necessarily reap the advantages we'd like to imagine. It is true that peers can offer the writer additional perspectives, support, and, generally, less

threatening feedback than a teacher-evaluator. But it is a much more difficult matter to generalize about how writers respond to readers. These responses hinge on a number of subtle emotional and intellectual factors. We need to learn more about these factors and about the process through which writers gain a sense of authority over their texts. For example, under what conditions do they first experience the need for authority? How do they demonstrate it? How do they use it? Toward what end? And once having asserted their authority to their readers, are they likely to do so again to other readers? Finally, how might a writer with a newly awakened sense of authority be guided by others' advice. These are some of the questions researchers need to explore before we can begin to assess which kinds of writer/reader relationships best serve the writer, and how teachers may translate this information into an effective classroom pedagogy.

## Notes

1. See "Responding to Student Writing," and "On Students' Rights to Their Own Texts: A Model of Teacher Response," College Composition and Communication, 33 (May, 1982), 148-156 and 157-166.
2. "Teaching the Other Self: The Writer's First Reader." College Composition and Communication, 33 (May, 1982), 143-147.
3. Lil Brannon and C.H. Knoblauch point out that readers grant writers authority on numerous grounds including professional achievement and recognized skill in discourse. The investment of authority gives writers considerable freedom with their texts, while at the same time insuring that readers will subordinate judgment to the task of comprehension. See Brannon and Knoblauch, "On Students' Rights to Their Own Texts: A Model of Teacher Response," pp. 157-58.
4. The material italicized in the excerpts from these transcripts is text the subject is writ-

ing. The material italicized and underlined is material the subject is reading that had been written previously, by the author or others.

5. For a description of this process see Carol Berkenkotter, "Decisions and Revisions: The Planning Strategies of a Publishing Writer," College Composition and Communication, 3-4 (May, 1983), 162-163. I should note that Donald M. Murray frequently and systematically reread his text from the perspective of a critical reader. This behavior led him to reconceive his goals as he wrote.

# Revision Strategies of Student Writers and Experienced Adult Writers

*Nancy Sommers*

Although various aspects of the writing process have been studied extensively of late, research on revision has been notably absent. The reason for this, I suspect, is that current models of the writing process have directed attention away from revision. With few exceptions, these models are linear; they separate the writing process into discrete states. Two representative models are Gordon Rohman's suggestion that the composing process moves from prewriting to writing to rewriting and James Britton's model of the writing process as a series of stages described in metaphors of linear growth, conception—incubation—production.[1] What is striking about these theories of writing is that they model themselves on speech: Rohman defines the writer in a way that cannot distinguish him from a speaker ("A writer is a man who. . . puts [his] experience into words in his own mind"—p. 15); and Britton bases his theory of writing on what he calls (following Jakobson) the "expressiveness" of speech.[2] Moreover, Britton's study itself follows the "linear model" of the relation of thought and language in speech proposed by Vygotsky, a relationship embodied in the linear movement "from the motive which engenders a thought to the shaping of the thought, *first* in inner speech, *then* in meanings of words, and *finally* in words" (quoted in Britton, p.40). What this movement fails to take into account is its linear structure— "first. . . then. . . finally"—is the recursive shaping of thought by language; what it fails to take into account is *revision*. In these linear conceptions of the writing process revision is understood as a separate stage at the end of the process—a stage that comes after the completion of a first or second draft and one that is temporally distinct from the prewriting and writing stages of the process.[3]

• • •

## Methodology

I used a case study approach. The student writers were twenty freshman at Boston University and the University of Oklahoma with SAT verbal scores ranging from 450-600 in their first semester of composition. The twenty experienced adult writers from Boston and Oklahoma City included jour-

Nancy Sommers is the director of the Expository Writing Program at Harvard University. This article was originally published in *College Composition and Communication*, a journal for college and university teachers.

nalists, editors, and academics. To refer to the two groups, I use the terms *student writers* and *experienced writers* because the principal difference between these two groups is the amount of experience they have had in writing.

Each writer wrote three essays, expressive, explanatory, and persuasive, and rewrote each essay twice, producing nine written products in draft and final form. Each writer was interviewed three times after the final revision of each essay. And each writer suggested revisions for a composition written by an anonymous author. Thus extensive written and spoken documents were obtained from each writer.

The essays were analyzed by counting and categorizing the changes made. Four revision operations were identified: deletion, substitution, addition, and reordering. And four levels of changes were identified: word, phrase, sentence, theme (the extended statement of one idea). A coding system was developed for identifying the frequency of revision by level and operation. In addition, transcripts of the interviews in which the writers interpreted their revisions were used to develop what was called a *scale of concerns* for each writer. This scale enabled me to codify what were the writer's primary concerns, secondary concerns, tertiary concerns, and whether the writer used the same scale of concerns when revising the second or third drafts as they used in revising the first draft.

## Revision Strategies of Student Writers

Most of the students I studied did not use the terms *revision or rewriting*. In fact, they did not seem comfortable using the word *revision* and explained that revision was not a word they used, but the word their teachers used. Instead, most of the students had developed various functional terms to describe the type of changes they made. The following are samples of these definitions:

*Scratch Out and Do Over Again*: "I say scratch out and do over, and that means what it says. Scratching out and cutting out. I read what I have written and I cross out a word and put another word in, a more decent word or a better word. Then if there is somewhere to use a sentence that I have crossed out, I will put it there."

*Reviewing*: "Reviewing means just using better words and eliminating words that are not needed. I go over and change words around."

*Reviewing*: "I just review every word and make sure that everything is worded right. I see if I am rambling; I see if I can put a better word in or leave one out. Usually when I read what I have written, I say to myself, 'that word is so bland or so trite,' and then I go and get my thesaurus."

*Redoing*: "Redoing means cleaning up the paper and crossing out. It is looking at something and saying, no that has to go, or no, that is not right."

*Marking Out*: "I don't use the word rewriting because I only write one draft and the changes that I make are made on top of the draft. The changes that I make are usually just marking out words and putting different ones in."

*Slashing and Throwing Out*: "I throw things out and say they are not good. I like to write like Fitzgerald did by inspiration, and if I feel inspired then I don't need to slash and throw much out."

The predominant concern in these definitions is vocabulary. The students understand the revision process as a rewording activity. They do so because they perceive words as the unit of written discourse. That is, they concentrate on particular words apart from their role in the text. Thus one student quoted above thinks in terms of dictionaries, and, following the eighteenth century theory of words parodied in *Gulliver's Travels*, he imagines a load of things carried about to be exchanged. Lexical changes are the major revision activities of the student because economy is their goal. They are governed, like the linear model itself, by the Law of Occam's razor that prohibits logically needless repetition: redundancy and superfluity. Nothing governs speech more than such superfluities: speech constantly repeats itself precisely because spoken words, as Barthes writes, are expendable in the cause of communication. The aim of revision according to the students' own description is therefore to clean up speech; the redundancy of speech is unnecessary in writing, their logic suggests, because writing, unlike speech, can be re-read. Thus one student said, "Redoing means cleaning up the paper and crossing out." The remarkable contradiction of cleaning by marking might, indeed, stand for student revision as I have encountered it.

The students place a symbolic importance on their selection and rejection of words as the determiners of success or failure for their compositions. When revising, they primarily ask themselves: can I find a better word or phrase? A more impressive, not so cliched, or less hum-drum word? Am I repeating the same word or phrase too often? They approach the revision process with what could be labeled as a "thesaurus philosophy of writing": the students consider the thesaurus a harvest of lexical substitutions and believe that most problems in their essays can be solved by rewording. What is revealed in the students' use of the thesaurus is a governing attitude toward their writing: that the meaning to be communicated is already there, already finished, already produced, ready to be communicated, and all that is necessary is a better word "rightly worded." One student defined revision as "redoing"; "redoing" meant "just using better words and eliminating words that are not needed." For the students writing is translating: the thought to the page, the language of speech to the more formal language of prose, the word to its synonym. Whatever is translated, an original text already exists for students, one which need not be dis-covered or acted upon but simply communicated.[4]

The students list repetition as one of the elements they most worry about. This cue signals to them that they need to eliminate the repetition either by substituting or deleting words or phrases. Repetition occurs, in large part, because student writing imitates—transcribes—speech: attention to repetitious words is a manner of cleaning speech. Without a sense of the developmental possibilities of revision (and writing in general) students seek, on the authority of many textbooks, simply to clean up their language and prepare to type. What is curious, however, is that students are aware of lexical repetition, but not conceptual repetition. They only notice the repetition if they can "hear" it; they do not diagnose lexical repetition as symptomatic of problems on a deeper level. By rewording their sentences to avoid the lexical repetition, the students solve the immediate problem, but blind themselves to problems on a textual level; although they are using different words, they are sometimes merely restating the same idea with different words. Such blindness, as I discovered with student writers, is the inability to "see" revision as a process; the inability to "review" their work again, as it were, with different eyes, and to start over.

The revision strategies described above are consistent with the students' understanding of the revision process as requiring lexical changes but not semantic changes. For the students, the extent to which they revise is a function of their level of inspiration. In fact, they use the word *inspiration* to describe the ease or difficulty with which their essay is written, and the extent to which the essay needs to be revised. If students feel inspired, if the writing comes easily, and if they don't get stuck on individual words or phrases, then they say that they cannot see any reason to revise. Because students do not see revision as an activity in which they modify and develop perspectives and ideas, they feel that if they know what they want to say, then there is little reason for making revisions.

The only modification of ideas in the students' essays occurred when they tried out two or three introductory paragraphs. This results, in part, because the students have been taught in another version of the linear model of composing to use a thesis statement as a controlling device in their introductory paragraphs. Since they write their introductions and their thesis statements even before they have really discovered what they want to say, their early close attention to the thesis statement, and more generally the linear model, function to restrict and circumscribe not only the development of their ideas, but also their ability to change the direction of these ideas.

Too often as composition teachers we conclude that students do not willingly revise. The evidence from my research suggests that it is not that students are unwilling to revise, but rather that they do what they have been taught to do in a consistently narrow and predictable way. On every occasion when I asked students why they hadn't made any more changes, they essentially replied, "I knew something larger was wrong, but I didn't think it would help to move words around." The students have strategies for handling words and phrases and their strategies helped them on a word or sentence level. What they lack, however, is a set of strategies to help them identify the "something larger" that they sensed was wrong and work from there. The students do not have strategies for handling the whole essay. They lack procedures or heuristics to help them reorder lines of reasoning or ask questions about their purposes and readers. The students view their compositions in a linear way as a series of parts. Even such potentially useful concepts as "unity" or "form" are reduced to the rule that a composition, if it is to have form, must have an introduction, a body, and a conclusion, or the sum total of the necessary parts.

The students decide to stop revising when they decide that they have not violated any of the rules for revising. These rules, such as "Never begin a sentence with a conjunction" or "Never end a sentence with a preposition," are lexically cued and rigidly applied. In general, students will subordinate the demands of the specific problems of their text to the demands of the rules. Changes are made in compliance with abstract rules about the product, rules that quite often do not apply to the specific problems in the text. These revision strategies are teacher-based, directed towards a teacher-reader who expects compliance with rules—with pre-existing "conceptions"—and who will only examine parts of the composition (writing comments about those parts in the margins of their essays) and will cite any violations of rules in those parts. At best the students see their writing altogether passively through the eyes of former teachers or their surrogates, the textbooks, and are bound to the rules which they have been taught.

## Revision Strategies of Experienced Writers

One aim of my research has been to contrast how student writers define revision with how a group of experienced writers define their revision processes. Here is a sampling of the definitions from the experienced writers:

*Rewriting*: "It is a matter of looking at the kernel of what I have written, the content, and then thinking about it, responding to it, making decisions, and actually restructuring it."

*Rewriting*: "I rewrite as I write. It is hard to tell what is a first draft because it is not determined by time. In one draft, I might cross out three pages, write two, cross out a fourth, rewrite it, and call it a draft. I am constantly writing and rewriting. I can only conceptualize so much in my first draft—only so much information can be held in my head at one time; my rewriting efforts are a reflection of how much information I can encompass at one time. There are levels and agenda which I have to attend to in each draft.''

*Rewriting*: "Rewriting means on one level, finding the argument, and on another level, language changes to make the argument more effective. Most of the time I feel as if I can go on rewriting forever. There is always one part of a piece that I could keep working on. It is always difficult to know at what point to abandon a piece of writing. I like this idea that a piece of writing is never finished, just abandoned.''

*Rewriting*: "My first draft is usually very scattered. In rewriting, I find the line of argument. After the argument is resolved, I am much more interested in word choice and phrasing.''

*Revising*: "My cardinal rule in revising is never to fall in love with what I have written in a first or second draft. An idea, sentence, or even a phrase that looks catchy, I don't trust. Part of this idea is to wait a while. I am much more in love with something after I have written it than I am a day or two later. It is much easier to change anything with time.''

*Revising*: "It means taking apart what I have written and putting it back together again. I ask major theoretical questions of my ideas, respond to those questions, and think of proportion and structure, and try to find a controlling metaphor. I find out which ideas can be developed and which should be dropped. I am constantly chiseling and changing as I revise.''

The experienced writers describe their primary objectives when revising as finding the form or shape of their argument. Although the metaphors vary, the experienced writers often use structural expression such as "finding a framework,'' "a pattern,'' or "a design'' for their argument. When questioned about this emphasis, the experienced writers responded that since their first drafts are usually scattered attempts to define their territory, their objective in the second draft is to begin observing general patterns of development and deciding what should be included and what excluded. One writer explained, "I have learned from experience that I need to keep writing a first draft until I figure out what I want to say. Then in a second draft, I begin to see the structure of an argument and how all the various sub-arguments which are buried beneath the surface of all those sentences are related.'' What is described here is a process in which the writer is both agent and vehicle. "Writing,'' says Barthes, unlike speech, "develops like a seed, not a line,''[5] and like a seed it confuses beginning and end, conception and production. Thus, the experienced writers say their drafts are "not determined by time,'' that rewriting is a "constant process,'' that they feel as if (they) "can go on forever.'' Revising confuses the beginning and end, the agent and vehicle; it confuses, *in order to find*, the line of argument.

After a concern for form, the experienced writers have a second objective: a concern for their readership. In this way, "production'' precedes "conception.'' The experienced writers imagine a reader (reading their product) whose existence and whose expectations influence their revision process. They have abstracted the standards of a reader and this reader seems to be partially a reflection of themselves and functions as a critical and productive collaborator—a collaborator who has yet to love their work. The anticipation of a reader's judgment causes a feeling of dissonance when the writer recognized incongruities between intention and execution, and requires these writers to make revisions on all levels. Such a reader gives them just what the students lacked: new eyes to "re-view'' their work. The experienced writers believe that they have learned the causes and conditions, the product, which will influence their reader, and their revision strategies are geared towards creating these causes and conditions. They demonstrate a complex understanding of which examples, sentences, or phrases should be included or excluded. For example, one experienced writer decided to delete public examples and add private examples when writing about the energy crisis because "private examples would be less controversial and thus more persuasive." Another writer revised his transitional sentences because "some kinds of transitions are more easily recognized as transitions than others." These examples represent the type of strategic attempts these experienced writers use to manipulate the conventions of discourse in order to communicate to their reader.

But these revision strategies are a process of more than communication; they are part of the process of *discovering meaning* altogether. Here we can see the importance of dissonance; at the heart of revision is the process by which writers recognize and resolve the dissonance they sense in their writing. Ferdinand de Saussure had argued that meaning is differential or "diacritical," based on differences between terms rather than "essential" or inherent qualities of terms. "Phonemes," he said, "are characterized not, as one might think, by their own positive quality but simply by the fact that they are distinct."[6] In fact, Saussure bases his entire *Course in General Linguistics* on these differences, and such differences are dissonant; like musical dissonances which gain their significance from their relationship to the "key" of the composition which itself is determined by the whole language, specific language (parole) gains its meaning from the system of language (langue) of which it is a manifestation and part. The musical composition—a "composition" of parts—creates its "key" as in an over-all structure which determines the value (meaning) of its parts. The analogy with music is readily seen in the compositions of experienced writers: both

sorts of composition are based precisely on those structures experienced writers seek in their writing. It is this complicated relationship between the parts and the whole in the work of experienced writers which destroys the linear model; writing cannot develop "like a line" because each addition or deletion is a reordering of the whole. Explicating Saussure, Jonathan Culler asserts that "meaning depends on difference of meaning."[7] But student writers constantly struggle to bring their essays into congruence with a predefined meaning. The experienced writers do the opposite: they seek to discover (to create) meaning in the engagement with their writing, in revision. They seek to emphasize and exploit the lack of clarity, the differences of meaning, the dissonance, that writing as opposed to speech allows in the possibility of revision. Writing has spatial and temporal features not apparent in speech—words are recorded in space and fixed in time—which is why writing is susceptible to reordering and later addition. Such features make possible the dissonance that both provokes revision and promises, from itself, new meaning.

For the experienced writers the heaviest concentration of changes is on the sentence level, and the changes are predominantly by addition and deletion. But, unlike the students, experienced writers make changes on all levels and use all revision operations. Moreover, the operations the students fail to use—reordering and addition—seem to require a theory of the revision process as a totality—a theory which, in fact, encompasses the *whole* of the composition. Unlike the students, the experienced writers possess a non-linear theory in which a sense of the whole writing both precedes and grows out of an examination of the parts. As we saw, one writer said he needed "a first draft to figure out what to say," and "a second draft to see the structure of an argument buried beneath the surface." Such a "theory" is both theoretical and strategical; once again, strategy and theory are conflated in ways that are literally impossible for the linear model. Writing appears to be more like a seed than a line.

Two elements of the experienced writers' theory of the revision process are the adoption of a holistic perspective and the perception that revision is a recursive process. The writers ask: what does my essay as a *whole* need for form, balance, rhythm, or communication. Details are added, dropped, substituted, or reordered according to their sense of what the essay needs for emphasis and proportion. This sense, however, is constantly in flux as ideas are developed and modified; it is constantly "re-viewed" in relation to the parts. As their ideas change, revision becomes an attempt to make their writing consonant with that changing vision.

The experienced writers see their revision process as a recursive process—a process with significant recurring activities—with different levels of attention and different agenda for each cycle. During the first revision cycle their attention is primarily directed towards narrowing the topic and delimiting their ideas. At this point, they are not as concerned as they are later about vocabulary and style. The experienced writers explained that they get closer to their meaning by not limiting themselves too early to lexical concerns. As one writer commented to explain her revision process, a comment inspired by the summer 1977 New York power failure: "I feel like Con Edison cutting off certain states to keep the generators going. In first and second drafts, I try to cut off as much as I can of my editing generator, and in a third draft, I try to cut off some of my idea generators, so I can make sure that I will actually finish the essay." Although the experienced writers describe their revision process as a series of different levels of cycles, it is inaccurate to assume that they have only one objective for each cycle and that each cycle can be defined by a different objective. The same objectives and sub-processes are present in each cycle, but in different proportions. Even though these experienced writers place the predominate weight upon finding the form of their argument during the first cycle, other concerns exist as well. Conversely, during the later cycles, when the experienced writers' primary attention is focused upon stylistic concerns, they are still attuned, although in a reduced way, to the form of the argument. Since writers are limited in what they can attend to during each cycle (understandings are temporal), revision strategies help balance competing demands on attention. Thus, writers can concentrate on more than one objective at a time by developing strategies to sort out and organize their different concerns in successive cycles of revision.

It is a sense of writing as discovery—a repeated process of beginning over again, starting out new—that the students failed to have. I have used the notion of dissonance because such dissonance, the incongruities between intention and execution, governs both writing and meaning. Students do not see the incongruities. They need to rely on their own internalized sense of good writing and to see their writing with their "own" eyes. Seeing in revision—seeing beyond hearing—is at the root of the word *revision* and the process itself; current dicta on revising blind our students to what is actually involved in revision. In fact, they blind them to what constitutes good writing altogether. Good writing disturbs: it creates dissonance. Students need to seek the dissonance of discovery, utilizing in their writing, as the experienced writers do, the very difference between writing and speech—the possibility of revision.

# Notes

1. D. Gordon Rohman and Albert O. Wlecke, "Pre-writing: The Construction and Application of Models for Concept Formation in Writing," Cooperative Research Project No. 2174, U.S. Office of Education, Department of Health, Education, and Welfare; James Britton, Anthony Burgess, Nancy Martin, Alex McLeod, Harold Rosen, *The Development of Writing Abilities* (11-18) (London: Macmillan Education, 1975).

2. Britton is following Roman Jakobson, "Linguistics and Poetics," in T.A. Sebeok, *Style in Language* (Cambridge, Mass.: MIT Press, 1960).

3. For an extended discussion of this issue see Nancy Sommers, "The Need for Theory in Composition Research," *College Composition and Communication*, 30 (February, 1979), 46-49.

4. Nancy Sommers and Ronald Schleifer, "Means and Ends: Some Assumptions of Student Writers," *Composition and Teaching, II* (in press).

5. *Writing Degree Zero in Writing Degree Zero and Elements of Semiology*, trans. Annette Lavers and Colin Smith (New York: Hill and Wang, 1968), p. 20.

6. *Course in General Linguistics*, trans. Wade Baskin (New York, 1966), p. 119.

7. Jonathan Culler, *Saussure* (Penguin Modern Masters Series, London: Penguin Books, 1976), p. 70.

*Acknowledgement*: The author wishes to express her gratitude to Professor William Smith, University of Pittsburgh, for his vital assistance with the research reported in this article and to Patrick Hays, her husband, for extensive discussions and critical editorial help.

# The Climate for Writing

*Donald Murray*

In the usual classroom the teacher speaks and the students listen. In the writing class, the students speak and the teacher listens.

The climate of the writing workshop must encourage individual students to bring their own content to the course. During the class the students should not be passive receivers of information. They must be doers, writing and rewriting—discovering what they have to say, discovering what they need to know to say it effectively—until the students complete the act of writing by reaching a reader who understands what they have written.

The writing teacher should create a lesson plan which is flexible, disciplined, free, and demanding, all at the same time. Each student must be able to fail and try and fail and try again as he practices what he has come to understand is the normal process of the writer. Each student must face the lonely discipline of the empty page, the unsuccessful draft and the unknowing reader. The class environment must place the responsibility for learning on the student so that he feels the obligation and the opportunity to teach himself. The teacher must search for methods which prevent him from interrupting the natural progress of his students. The writing teacher who teaches least usually teaches most if his students work in an environment which allows them to teach themselves.

## Why Writing Isn't Taught Effectively

Most American high school graduates do not know how to write. This is one of the few statements on which most educators agree, and it is an opinion they share with employers and parents. Writing—the vital ability to express one's self with clarity and grace—is not taught in our schools.

Most students pass through twelve years of English courses, but few students ever have an intensive, concentrated opportunity to learn to write. They do write papers and their grades often depend on papers but the students are rarely taught how to write papers or given the chance to practice and develop composition skills.

There are many reasons writing is not taught in school. In the first place there are few writing teachers prepared to teach writing. English teachers are trained to be teachers of grammar or educated to be teachers of literature—if indeed they are prepared at all. A study by the National Council of Teachers of English revealed that only half of the English teachers majored in that subject at college and only a handful of English teachers had courses in composition

Donald Murray is a former journalist who recently retired as professor of English at the University of New Hampshire. "The Climate for Writing" comes from his book, *A Writer Teaches Writing*.

beyond Freshman English. There are many who never took that course.

We cannot say that our teachers of English are incompetent or irresponsible because they do not teach composition, when they are never educated to be composition teachers. They do not teach writing because they do not know how to teach writing, and it is the purpose of this book to attempt to help correct this lack.

There is another reason the English teacher simply does not attempt to teach writing, and that is because the English Department is a complicated collection of contradictory disciplines.

The English teacher each year is expected to teach or review the mechanics of the language. The approach may be through traditional grammar, transformational grammar, structural linguistics, the history of the language or a combination of all methods, but the result is the same. The teacher is expected to be an expert on the science of language, and he is expected to teach his students how language has been used in the past. This is a fine scholarly discipline but there is little evidence it has any relation to the student's ability to write. The study of language as language too often isolates language from meaning or use, and the experience in many classrooms shows that students who excel at analysis of the language cannot write, and students who can write do not necessarily have a scientific understanding of their language.

This situation is compounded by the fact that our students move from one method to another within a single school system and, of course, in a mobile society they move from one school system to another. The student is generally subjected to a confusing variety of grammatical approaches during his twelve years in school. The wise student attempts to forget these contradictions when he sits down to write. Many students who attempt to follow the contradictory language rules they have been taught are soon lost in a jungle of syntax. Most are never rescued.

The English teacher is also expected to be a reading teacher. In the beginning he teaches the students to recognize that black squiggles on the page are symbols for meaning. Eventually he teaches the students critical reading. Most of our students today are demonstrably better readers because of the time they have spent in careful analysis of a text. The ability to perform an act of critical analysis, however, does not mean that the student can write well. I can analyze a football play or a sonata but I can't score a touchdown or perform in Lincoln Center.

The English teacher not only teaches reading, he teaches literature. He is expected to make his students familiar with the historic context of English, American, and, frequently, world literature. He is supposed to introduce his students to the great writers and to the most common forms of literature. He may develop units on the myth, the lyric, the tragedy, showing how an attitude towards life has been expressed in many centuries and in many cultures.

In many school systems the English teacher is expected to design and operate courses in the humanities which integrate literature with history, philosophy, art and music. The teacher who can do this—and there are a surprising number of them—is indeed a Renaissance man. He is not often, however, a writing teacher. He is properly interested in great ideas and in illuminating humanistic visions of man's experience. He may be an exciting teacher but he is not, by training or temperament, prepared to coach his students in the fundamental skills of composition.

The English teacher often has other chores ladled into his curriculum by his supervisors. He may be expected to teach oral expression—public speaking, debate and even how to answer the telephone. He may teach business letter writing, advise the school paper, drive the debate club, lay out pictures for the yearbook, direct the school play and write school press releases. The English teacher must choose among the many demands placed on him and since he is not trained to be a writing teacher, he will rarely choose to emphasize writing.

In a survey of high school education, James Bryant Conant proposed that half the time spent in English courses in high school be spent on composition.[1] The College English Examination Board states that one-third of the time should be spent on writing. To a layman these proposals seem reasonable, even conservative. They are actually radical, for a United States Office of Education and National Council of Teachers of English survey of 168 high school English departments in forty-five states reported that composition was emphasized only 15.7 percent of the class time.[2]

The English teacher is not only the victim of his preparation and an overcrowded curriculum, he also suffers from a system which has made him believe—and made his supervisors believe—that a person is teaching only when he stands before the class talking. The role of preacher may be appropriate when you are lecturing on the history of a language, explicating a text, or synthesizing a century's literature. It is certainly not appropriate to the teaching of writing. There are a few things which need to be said about writing but once said, the student must spend his time in the lengthy process of discovering and solving his own writing problems. The teacher must be the student's most effective reader. When the English teacher is forced to stand before the class, period after period, day after day, talking, talking, talking, his students will not learn to write.

There are many other reasons students are not taught to write. Some of them may be

summarized in ten myths which have been passed on by generations of English teachers as articles of faith.

### Myth One: Correct Usage Comes First

For generations most English teachers have given first priority to correct usage. They feel compelled to mark every error on every draft, constantly focusing the students' attention on grammar and spelling rather than on content and form. Most students, and all writers, disagree with this emphasis. Language should be used correctly but the final, careful editing, cannot take place until the writer has discovered, by writing, what he has to say and how he wants to say it.

### Myth Two: Each Student Paper Must be Corrected by the Teacher

The English teacher is the faculty martyr. He lugs home, night after night, a cross of papers, all of which he believes have to be marked in red, the symbol of his own blood. He never escapes from the burden of papers to be corrected and his students, who glance only at the grade, never learn to write. Belief in the myth that the teacher must correct each student paper interrupts the necessary process of writing. The student must correct his own paper by drafting, rewriting and editing his own work until he is prepared to face the reader's stern evaluation of what he has said.

### Myth Three: Students Should Write a Few Papers but Write Them Well

As long as writing is an unnatural act which is performed rarely and only for an extremely critical audience, students will not learn to write. Writing must become the students' normal method of disciplined thinking. Students will not begin to write well until they are writing prolifically. The great writers have not hoarded their talents, but produced with a rich prodigality. Literature is the distillate of enormous failure.

## Myth Four: Students Do Not Want to Write

Writing is hard work and man is often lazy, so that students are not likely to write unless writing is required. But if students are both required and encouraged to write and if their teacher is a constructive reader, the students will frequently write more than is required. Man's drive to communicate is basic; he will write for a reader who will listen to what he has to say. He will seek criticism from an editor who is not attacking him but who is attacking the page with the clear, constructive purpose of trying to help the writer express himself more effectively.

## Myth Five: A Good Reader Will Become a Good Writer

Every student should be trained to be a perceptive reader, but it simply does not follow that the skillful reader will automatically become an effective writer. There are writers, both student and professional, who read relatively little and write very well. There are also many people, including English teachers, who read very well and write very poorly. The English curriculum in most secondary schools assumes that an emphasis on reading will produce effective writers. The ability to read well does not lead inevitably to the ability to write well. Because of the paperback revolution, students in English may be reading far more than in the past, but students writing has not greatly improved.

## Myth Six: The Best Subject Is a Literary Subject

It is a matter of dogma in many English departments that students have nothing to say until literature is poured into their heads. We cannot assume that literature is the primary interest of our students—or even that is should be. We must realize that the writing of literary analysis is but one form of writing. If we evaluate our students only on their ability to write literary analysis we will over-reward a minority and penalize a majority.

## Myth Seven: Grade Levels Are Significant in Teaching Writing

The English teacher should glory in the individual diversity of man. Too often, however, he falls into the fallacy that there is a group writing problem peculiar to the tenth grade, the seventh grade, or the twelfth grade. Students cannot be taught writing in a military manner, herded together by age, grade, height, or the development of secondary sexual characteristic. Students must be taught individually. Each student, when he meets a problem in his own writing, should have a teacher who is prepared to help him solve that problem. The order in which he strikes problems in writing will not correspond to his classmate's, and the time he takes to solve his problems will vary. That is not important. What is important is that the student solve his writing problems so that his writing becomes effective. The order in which he does this and the methods he uses are not the test of the course. The test of the writing course is the student's ability to write with clarity and grace when he graduates.

## Myth Eight: Students Learn Best by Imitating Models of Great Writing

The rhetorical teaching method used by the ancients is particulary attractive to the contemporary teacher who wants to make a science of composition. We do not, however, have a modern rhetoric which identifies and isolates the forms of discourse appropriate in modern society, with its diversity of rhetorical purposes, tones, appeals and audiences. And we have not yet found a method of applying the classical techniques of teaching oral discourse to mass education. Most students find isolated paragraphs, neatly labeled by rhetorical type, remote from their own writing problems. A student's ability to recognize his teacher's rhetorical classification has little effect on the student's own writing.

## Myth Nine: You Can Teach Writing by Talking

Some English teachers lecture about writing day after day, period after period, and become discouraged because the students listen but do not practice what their teachers preach. Other instructors feel guilty or inadequate because they do not know what to say about writing in hour-long classes. Both categories of teachers should understand there is not a great deal to say about writing. There are only a few skills, but it will take the students many years to master them. There is no content in the writing course in the conventional academic sense. And in the usual class period the student should not listen to lectures but write, rewrite, edit, or respond to student writing through individual conferences and small group discussions.

## Myth Ten: You Can't Teach Writing

There is a romantic belief, shared by too many English teachers, that writing is a mystical act, and that the ability to write is granted by God to a few students. This is an easy evasion of the teacher's responsibility. There is indeed a mystical element in great art, but writing is first of all a craft. It becomes an art when someone else places value on the product of the writer's craft. Writing can be taught to students if they are given the opportunity to discover for themselves the basic skills which each writer has to learn and practice while he aspires to art.

Finally, writing isn't taught in our schools because English teachers have the excuse of numbers. The majority of English teachers have a student load which makes it difficult and even, apparently, impossible to teach composition. Many English teachers have five or six class periods five days a week, in addition to study hall, lunchroom, and library monitoring duty. When parents, college administrators, and employers call for more instruction in writing they are answered with the English teacher's lament: "I have too many students."

Most English teachers agree that students should write a paper each week (they think of it as a maximum standard, while I believe it is a minimal one). If they correct a paper in the way they have been taught, identifying each grammatical and spelling error as well as marking it for logical thought, appropriate diction, tone and all the other ingredients of a good piece of writing, it is an intensive, exhausting task. One study has shown it takes at least 8.3 minutes to correct the average short high school composition. Ten minutes is more likely, and perhaps five papers an hour is possible under this system. Remember, that includes not only identifying all the student's problems, but writing comments which make those problems clear to the student and help him find working solutions. These comments should ideally, be made in an even more time-consuming individual conference.

Yet I have graduates with student loads of 170 and more. Five classes of thirty students each, or 150 students, is not an unusual load. A national average produced by one survey of good school systems revealed that the normal teacher of English had 130 students. If a teacher with 130 pupils corrects one paper each week per student in the conventional manner, spending just 10 minutes on each paper, he will work from seven to midnight, Monday night, Tuesday night, Wednesday night, and Thursday night. On Friday he will have to correct from seven o'clock to one o'clock Saturday morning if he wants to get the job done and take the weekend off. This schedule does not allow time for classroom preparation or extra duty, such as directing the school play.

Privileged school systems are trying to achieve a maximum goal of 100 students for each English teacher. Even with these "few" students, if the teacher corrects papers in the conventional manner from seven to midnight, Monday through Thursday, he can have Friday night off. When Dr. Conant first published his survey of secondary education, he advocated a hundred students as the standard load for each English teacher. But in the latest edition of his report, he admitted that only one-fourth of the 2000 schools surveyed reported a load of 120 or less. Reluctantly, he has accepted 120 as the norm for the English teacher.[3]

English teachers must fight vigorously for reasonable, workable class loads, but they should not use numbers as an excuse for not teaching composition. As a matter of fact, the higher the load the more important it is that they find ways of dealing with large numbers of papers so that their students can learn to write by writing. I have developed many of the techniques in this book because I found it impossible to do an adequate job of correcting each paper even with a university student load. These techniques allow me to assign nearly 6,000 papers this semester to my 119 students—96 at the University and 23 in a special non-credit course for teachers at Harvard sponsored by the New England School Development Council.

I evaluate every fourth paper in one course, and more than that in the other courses. I do not, however, do my students' job of rewriting. I have discovered that my students learn to write when I do not over-teach and over-correct. I help them diagnose their own programs, one at a time. English teachers must find methods which allow them to function despite their student load.

This book does not argue against the study of language and the study of literature. It does argue for an equivalent status for the teaching of composition. Writing is not taught in our school because writing is not taught. Writing can be taught if English teachers are educated to be teachers of writing, if they do not believe the myths about the teaching of composition, and if they face up to the problems of heavy student loads. Writing can be taught in our schools today without waiting for ideal conditions.

Departments of English ought to develop a curriculum which allows the student to concentrate on one phase of the discipline at a time under the direction of a teacher who is prepared to teach that particular specialty. We must develop English teachers who specialize in teaching language, others who prefer to teach literature and still others who are expert in teaching writing. We should not expect the student to go through a repetitive English course year after year which has a dibble of language study, a dollop of composition and a dabble of literature. Neither should we expect the teacher to be equally prepared to teach the entire curriculum. The discipline of English will not be well taught until we devise new ways of encouraging our students to learn. We cannot continue to blame our students for being bored by English when the courses are repetitive, and we cannot continue to blame teachers for boring their students when the faculty is expected to teach diverse subjects and to teach them all in one rigid manner. Writing will not be taught efficiently until we develop faculty members experienced in the teaching of writing who are given the authority to design a climate in which students can learn to write.

# The Classroom: A Writing Laboratory

If a classroom is designed for a sermon with row upon row of desks facing the pulpit, few teachers will have the courage to resist the temptation to preach. It's safer behind the desk, and, after all, the student congregation can't leave while you talk.

The writing teacher must understand that he does not need a classroom; he needs a laboratory. His students must have a place where they can work, and where the teacher can also do his work, which is to encourage them individually. The ideal writing laboratory should have these characteristics:

- Each student should have his own desk. These desks might face the walls so the students can concentrate on their own work, or the desk might be separated by soundproof partitions, as is often done in the language laboratory to provide small carrels, although I have not found partitions necessary in my writing laboratory at the University of New Hampshire.
- The teacher should have an office with a degree of acoustical privacy and a view of the classroom. He should be able to withdraw with a student and go over his paper, giving him individual criticism without the class hearing that personal criticism. It should be a place where both the teacher and the student feel free to be candid.
- It is important that the room be soundproofed so that the activity in the room will not disturb other classes, and so that various groups in the room can be working at the same time doing different things without disturbing each other.
- There may be an arrangement of tables in a hollow square or circle in the middle of the room so that a class can discuss student papers or mutual writing problems. There should not be a lectern. The teacher should not stand up, but sit around the table with his students.
- It should be possible to arrange the tables so that small groups of students can work editing each other's papers. The teacher may also want to use these tables for small group conferences, although he may use the table in his office.
- There should be a bulletin board where student and professional writing can be displayed.
- There ought to be a library of books on writing which students could read when they are waiting for conferences. Of course, there should be an unabridged dictionary and other basic research writing tools.
- There should be provision for an overhead projector, tape recorders, and other audio-visual aids.
- There should be adequate lighting for each student to work at his own desk.

The writing laboratory is not expensive, and the normal classroom can be turned into an effective laboratory quite easily. The important elements are: tables arranged so that the student can work individually; a place, perhaps in the corner of the room, where the teacher can hold conferences, an arrangement which encourages the students to discuss writing with the teacher as a fellow writer, not as a remote person lecturing about the subject.

The imaginative teacher can take an ordinary classroom and turn it into a writing laboratory. I've seen this done even in classrooms where the desks are nailed down. I've seen school libraries used for the same purpose. The teacher should remember that he is trying to create a climate, a place where the writer can do the jobs of writing, rewriting and editing which are central to learning how to write. The student should be shown by his surroundings and the way in which the equipment he is to use is arranged that he is discovering how to write on this own, with the aid of his classmates and his teacher.

## Notes

1. James Bryant Conant, *The American High School Today* (New York: McGraw-Hill) 1959).

2. *National Study of High School English Programs*, Cooperative Research Project No. 1994.

3. James Bryant Conant, *The Comprehensive High School: A Second Report to Interested Citizens* (New York: McGraw-Hill, 1967).

# Let's Get Off the Mythmobile

*Edgar H. Schuster*

The Mythmobile is a spaceship that many language arts teachers fly in. If you require students to follow "rules" that virtually no writer in the real world observes, you're a passenger. And the ship is crowded. In fact, judging from the college students I teach, many elementary and secondary schools are operating in outer space. Let us examine some of the nonrules students are taught in the hope of bringing the ship back to Earth.

## Myth One: Don't Use Contractions in Formal Writing

For a statement of Myth One, we do not have to apply at the door of an elementary school classroom. Here it is as stated in the best-selling *college* handbook in the country:

Contractions are common in informal English, especially in dialogue. But contracted forms are usually written out in a formal composition—which is not as casual or spontaneous as conversational English is. (Harbrace College Handbook, 9th Edition, p. 220)

Very well. Below is a quiz on those linguistic lice known as contractions. Can

Edgar Schuster supervises the English/Language Arts program for the Allentown, Pennsylvania, schools. This article was originally published in *English Journal*, a magazine for high school teachers.

you guess who wrote the phrases and where they appeared? Are they largely from "informal" sources? Scraps of dialogues, perhaps? Fragments from conversations or letters? Jottings from journals or scribblings by second-rate journalists?

Decide for yourself before checking the "answer key" below.

1. . . . most economists expect *they'll* be worse.
2. Even if it should be a fiction *it's* produced under pressure, *there's* a lot at stake.
3. If I had it to write over, *I'd* choose "relative."
4. We *don't* know who the speakers are. . . and we *can't* ask them for clarification.
5. . . . by an American resident of Paris I happen to know—Mathew Pillsbury, *who's* ten.
6. *I'm* sorry we asked . . . we starve ourselves and pray till *we're* blue.
7. Like many humanists, I hate to talk about money in connection with my profession. *It's* demeaning.
8. . . . others *aren't*, and *that's* that.
9. Frankly, we *don't* know, since the collected data does not address these question.
10. This melancholy judgment has hovered over every sentence *I've* written here.

Before going on, please note the *range* of contracted forms used here. When driven to admit that some good writers sometimes use contractions, many mythmobilists will take the position that some contractions are more acceptable than others.

Let us have a look at who these informal writers are and the informal publications that have printed them:

1. "Editorial," *New York Times*.
2. Anatole Broyard, in a book review, *New York Times*.
3. William Safire, "On Language," *New York Times Magazine*.
4. Geoffrey Nunberg, *Atlantic*.
5. Calvin Trillin, *New Yorker*.
6. Annie Dillard, *Teaching a Stone to Talk*.
7. Joseph H. Bourque, "Understanding and Evaluating: the Humanist as Computer Specialist," *College English*.
8. Linda Flower, *Problem-Solving Strategies for Writing*.
9. Donna Gorrell, "Toward Determining a Minimal Competency Entrance Examination," *Research in the Teaching of English*.
10. Joseph M. Williams, *Style: Ten Lessons in Clarity and Grace*.

Now if the *Times* and *Atlantic* and *New Yorker* are informal publications, if our best essayists write informal English, if professional journals and even research journals are informal, and if, finally, books on how to write are written in informal English, where is formal English to be found? And who writes it? And how many of our students are ever going to have to use it? We seem to be training our kids to write to some other planet.

## Myth Two: Every Paragraph Should Have a Topic/Clincher Sentence

This is two myths actually, and one is so absurd that we may dismiss it immediately. "Clincher sentences" in real-world prose are virtually nonexistent. The clincher about clinchers is that a writer who actually used them regularly would generate readers' migraine or migration.

Topic sentences, in contrast, are used in the real world—at least in some parts of it. We may note that *Harbrace* speaks as if there were no exceptions: "The paragraph," its editors say, "consists of a topic sentence (the controlling idea) and sentences that elaborate or qualify the topic sentence." (p. 347). The editors of this best seller evidently do not read fictional best sellers, which in fact virtually never make use of topic sentences. By way of example, here are the first and last sentences of six consecutive paragraphs in Anne Tyler's *Dinner at the Homesick Restaurant*:

They had thought she would be an old maid. . . . She felt that going to college would be an admission of defeat.

Oh, what was the trouble, exactly? . . . But Uncle Seward just puffed on his pipe and suggested a secretarial course.

Then she met Buck Tull. . . . She felt reckless and dashing, bursting with possibilities.

She met him at a church—at the Charity Baptist Church, which Pearl was only visiting because her girlfriend Emmaline was a member. . . . (Didn't that maybe, it occurred to her, imply some kind of faith after all?)

Courting her, he brought chocolates and flowers and then—more serious—pamphlets describing the products of Tanner Corporation. . . . Despite the reputation of salesmen, he was respectful to a fault and never grabbed at her the way some other men might.

Then he received his transfer and after that things sped up so. . . . Everything seemed so unsatisfying.

This is narrative. It moves in time. To clog it up with topic sentences would be unthinkable. When pointed out, this seems obvious; yet I cannot recall ever hearing a teacher or reading a textbook that qualified the assertion that every paragraph should have a topic sentence.

Suppose we focus on expository prose only. Indeed, let us overlook the expository prose of business and journalism and look only at the kind of exposition we are likely to find in essays published in the *Atlantic, Harper's, New Yorker, Reporter*, and *Saturday Review*. Surely every paragraph in such well-respected and well-edited magazines will contain a topic sentence.

It was precisely these magazines that were examined by Richard Braddock, one of the most respected researchers we've had in English education, who sought topic sentences in 889 paragraphs in 25 complete essays published in these excellent periodicals. ("The Frequency and Placement of Topic Sentences in Expository Prose," *Research in the Teaching of English*, Winter 1974, pp. 287-302.)

What Braddock discovered is not easily summarized because he found that he had to construct a sentence outline of each article to perform his research. However, it is reasonable to say that if we use the textbook definition of "topic sentence" Braddock found them in *fewer than one-third* of all the paragraphs he examined.

Granting these things, what accounts for the persistence of the myths of topic and clincher sentences? The answer, I think, is that they have a reality in one instance: where the paragraph is the whole discourse. That this mode of discourse is pervasive in the schools, no one can doubt. That it does not exist anywhere else on our planet is equally obvious.

## Myth Three: Don't Violate the Mystery Myth Rule

I'm calling this a "mystery myth" so that you may have the opportunity to take a quiz. What do the following phrases and sentences have in common?

We are such stuff as dreams are made on. (William Shakespeare)
Take the tone of the company that you are in. (Lord Chesterfield)
More things are wrought by prayer than this world dreams of. (Alfred, Lord Tennyson)
Spirit of Beauty, that dost consecrate with thine own hues all that thou dost shine upon. (Percy Bysshe Shelley)
Soil good to be born on, good to live on, good to die for and be buried in. (James Russell Lowell)
What a fine conformity would it starch us all into! (John Milton)

If your answer was "grace" or "eloquence," you were responding to meaning and the natural rhythms of the language. And you were ignoring the "rule" that one must never end a sentence with a preposition—the "fine conformity" that Milton is referring to. Actually, with so many examples in succession, it is remarkable that anyone misses the fact that a rule had been violated. How many readers have noticed how often I have violated it—including the second sentence in this paragraph and the first sentence in the article?

Writing in *The American Scholar* nearly fifteen years ago, linguist John Kenyon defended this "ancient" usage as "compact, simple, natural, and effective." Yet there are still many teachers who inveigh against it and force their students into writing sentences that are unnatural and ineffective.

## Myth Four: Avoid "I" and "You" in Formal Writing

Although I called the last the "Mystery Myth," it has always been truly a mystery to me that students enter college composition courses *actually believing* that they must never use the pronouns *I* and *you* in their composition. *I* (the author) and *you* (the reader) are, after all, the parties in transaction. Why should we not admit as much? *I* is the natural, honest pronoun to use when talking about oneself, and *you* is as natural and honest when talking about one's readers.

A glance at nearly anything written by good writers will show that they do not eschew either pronoun. In "What Is Science?" for example, George Orwell—a master of the essay—begins by citing a letter in a journal, and then writes:

As a general statement, *I* think most of us would agree with this, but *I* notice. . . .

He goes on to propose two distinct definitions of science, and then continues:

If *you* ask any scientist . . . "What is science?" *you* are likely to get an answer. . . [Italics mine.]

What about writers generally? Do they in fact tend to avoid speaking in the first person? I thought of a simple way of attempting to measure this. I took from my shelf *The Riverside Reader*, a collection of readings used quite widely in freshman composition courses across the United States. Edited by Joseph Trimmer and Maxine Hairston, it contains 50 essays, or parts of essays, which the editors consider models of good writing. The authors range widely but include such masters as E.B. White, George Orwell, Mark Twain, Dorothy Parker, Joan Didion, E.M. Forster, Loren Eiseley, Virginia Woolf, Henry David Thoreau, Jonathan Swift, Eudora Welty, and William Zinsser. Their essays are grouped under the following headings:

Narration

Description
Process Analysis
Comparison and
Contrast

Division and
Classification
Definition
Cause and Effect
Persuasion and
Argument
Essays for Further Reading
Essays for Reading and
Writing

Surely, Trimmer and Hairston were quite unconscious when they selected the essays of whether or not the writers used first person singular pronouns. They were simply trying to provide illustrations of good writing within the categories noted. How many of the 50 essays would you imagine made use of the first person singular pronoun? Guess.

Frankly, I would have guessed somewhere in the neighborhood of 50 percent, which, it turns out, only proves that I too am probably a victim of the false caveat to avoid *I* at all costs. The fact is that every writer I've just mentioned used *I* and that overall 82 percent (forty-one of the fifty) make use of first person singular pronouns referring to the author.

I haven't counted references to *you*, but that pronoun occurs with great frequency in the work of the best writers. In a preface of *A Dictionary of American-English Usage* (based on Fowler's *Modern English Usage*), editor Margaret Nicholson writes,

Fowler not only teaches *you* how to write, he is a demon on *your* shoulder, teaching *you* how not to write, pointing out and exhibiting, with terrifying clarity, *your* most cherished foibles. [Italics mine.]

How many of my misguided freshman English students would have used *one/one's* where Nicholson used *you/your*, and who would have written the better prose?

156

## Myth Five: Never Begin A Sentence with *and* or *but*

Stated fully, this myth insists that one should never begin a sentence with a coordinating conjunction—*and, but, for, nor, or, yet, or so.* Of all the myths discussed here, it is probably the one most frequently ignored by writers. It is, flatly, not a rule.

In a January 1984 article in *Learning* magazine, Susan Ohanian pointed out that George Orwell in *Homage to Catalonia* started at least 50 sentences with *and.* Conjunctions are repeatedly used at the beginning of sentences in the King James and Douay Bibles. Usage authority Bergen Evans, writing in the May 1962 *Atlantic* on the topic, "But What's a Dictionary for?" (a title that in five words exposes three of the five myths discussed here) used *and, but, yet,* or *so* to begin approximately 20 percent of his sentences.

It would be pointless to examine all the essays in *The Riverside Reader* to see how many writers begin sentences with *and* or *but* because anyone with eyes open needn't bother counting. Yet I did count the number of writers who began *paragraphs* with these conjunctions—which must surely be a capital offense. Thirty-one of the 50 writers, 62 percent, begin at least one paragraph with *and* or *but.* These authors included Dorothy Parker, John Ciardi, Joan Didion, E. M. Forster, Virginia Woolf, Isaac Asimov, Ralph Ellison, Jonathan Swift, Eudora Welty, and William Zinsser.

## Conclusion

If it is true that these are myths—and I trust I have proved that—then why do so many teachers continue teaching them? Why don't they get off the Mythmobile?

To begin with, I realize that not all teachers teach all the myths and that some teach none. Nevertheless, my observations of college freshman indicate that most students have been exposed to most of the myths and have been exposed to some frequently enough that they have accepted them as important "rules" of the language—which not one of them is.

In fairness, I should observe that there is a grain of truth in most of the myths. Contractions are found *less* frequently in research journals than in the popular press, and they are not as formal in tone as uncontracted forms. Topic sentences may be used to advantage to organize *some* paragraphs—as I have used one to organize this. A preposition at the end of a sentence *sometimes* sounds awkward, although usually only if the preposition is unnecessary to begin with. *Excessive* use of first person pronouns may give the impression of egotism, just as excessive attempts to avoid such pronouns may create pomposity. And any teacher can point out rhetorically ineffective uses of initial *and* and *but* in the work of students. But making an absolute rule to prevent such abuses is like banning water to prevent dysentery.

We should also recognize, in fairness, that students tend to make absolutes out of admonitions. Still, perhaps the main reason for the overcrowding on the Mythmobile is that three-quarters of our teachers teach as they were taught, to cite the percentage of Goodlad's researchers. And many assume that teachers in higher grades expect students to know the myths. Unfortunately, it is all too often true that teachers expect this, as my earlier citations from the *Harbrace College Handbook* demonstrate. But we must have the courage to follow the facts, not the false assumptions of others.

Finally, there are those who will insist that these myths are rules and that the writers who do not follow them are ignorant. But what is a "rule," after all, and why do we observe them? (The best discussion of this question that I know is Joseph M. William's

"The Phenomenology of Error" *College Composition and Communication*, May 1981.) If writers have communicated their meanings clearly and with grace, who's to say a rule has been broken? In the opening paragraph of this essay, I broke every one of the so-called rules I have been discussing. If they were rules rather than myths, you surely would have stopped reading, for any writer who violated five rules in the same paragraph must certainly not know how to write.

That you have come all this way with me instead must mean that you were not aboard the Mythmobile in the first place—or that you're ready to get off.

# The Writing Crisis

*Thomas Wheeler*

Language in America. What today inhibits the writing of citizens, scholars, and students? Americans, long vigorous and inventive in speech, object to the act of writing. Two out of three abilities expected from education—reading and writing—disintegrate as some insidious influence, thought by many to be television, captures succeeding generations of children. Many grade schools and high schools no longer encourage self-expression or sentences. Finding entering freshman unable to write clearly and coherently, colleges teach grammar and development of thought in a salvage operation called Remedial Writing. But even college graduates come into the job market unable to write, fearful of writing.

At the University of California at Berkeley, where students come from the top 12.5 percent of high school graduating classes, nearly half the entering freshmen display such inadequacies in writing that they are required to take remedial courses. At the University of Michigan and the University of Georgia, as at many colleges, remedial writing replaces the one term of freshman English common a decade ago. Even graduate students have writing problems. Purdue University tests all advanced-degree candidates with a written essay exam in order to determine whether they can write acceptable English.

A nationwide study of writing ability in 1969-70 that examined the passage submitted by 94,000 school children and young adults found that not many "moved beyond basic constructions and commonplace language." Five years later in 1975, a recheck found the essays of thirteen- and seventeen-year-olds more awkward, disorganized, and incoherent. These adjectives also describe the writing of many freshmen at the City University of New York, where I am a teacher.

The writing crisis has been getting worse. In defense of literacy, every wordsmith has his own horror story to tell. In a scrawled note, a bright girl, not long out of high school, wished me a "Mary Christmas." An editor of a national weekly told me she would be wary of hiring a copy editor under thirty, for fear of grammatical incompetence. A doctor, judging me physically fit and confiding a woe of his, deplored the inability of medical students he teaches to express themselves clearly in writing. An architect of my generation tells me that bright young architects he has hired cannot put a coherent report together. Although the young resent it, their elders utter more than the usual complaints of an older generation against the language of a new.

Thomas C. Wheeler teaches at York College of the City University of New York. He has written *The Great American Writing Block*, from which this article is taken, and has edited *A Vanishing America: The Life and Times of a Small Town* and *The Immigrant Experience*.

No one doubts that the high schools teach less than ever before. A colleague tells me that her son, who wrote imaginative short stories in a private elementary school, is not asked to write anything in one of New York City's special high schools for the academically superior. My students, from high schools lower on the scale, tell me more. They have never heard of a run-on sentence. Although some had been asked to write one-page essays every so often, the essays were apparently not corrected. The clumsiest, most incompetent writers have told me "English" was their best high school subject (a mystery I cannot unravel), while those who made the most conspicuous progress and began to write forcefully told me they had hardly ever written before. With the exception of private schools, with the exception of "good" high schools that put "gifted" students in writing classes—with the exception of the exceptions—high schools have, for all practical purposes, abandoned composition. Teaching students to write an essay and to handle ideas is now left to colleges, which find, inevitably, that they must begin with basics.

If students are assigned a "classic" in high school English, a survey by *The New York Times* found, few of them read much of it; but then, few long, serious books are assigned today. Though the problem of sustained reading is grave enough, the inability to write coherently is catastrophic. A people who cannot express their thoughts in writing are in greater trouble than a people who don't read "classics." Without clear thinking and coherent writing, no society can function properly. The widespread ability to write—the civilizing result of the industrial revolution—is an underpinning that the technological age tries to destroy but needs for its survival.

Certainly the reading crisis is one cause of the writing problem. Students who find reading a chore will inevitably find writing difficult. When students enjoy reading, they gain not only a familarity with language but respect for writing. Books that engage a student's interest enlarge his vocabulary and his mental experience. We should be concerned not only with declining reading scores but with the texts that are used to teach reading today. In many schools the reading of interesting books is replaced by technical training in "reading skills." Many of the reading texts are so jargon-filled and so divorced from real life that they discourage both reading and writing. Although reading is essential, writing requires more than an appreciation of books. Decent writing emerges from the mind's storage of words heard and read; it comes too from one's view of life. When, in the nineteenth century, Hawthorne "coldly" showed the young William Dean Howells his sparsely filled bookcase, Howells knew that Hawthorne prided himself in being a student of men more than of books. Search the shelves of many contemporary writers and find a modest collection of books that have shaped the writer's outlook and language. It is not the amount of reading a student has done but his involvement in it that helps his writing. To write—to write well or write adequately—is to draw from one's whole experience. To come into command of writing is, finally, to use one's own voice, to empower it with one's own identity.

"This generation has grown up without learning concentration—you don't develop that by switching channels. What can teachers do but pander to the rapid alteration of mood and attention." The view, from the chairman of an academic committee on literacy, puts the blame on television. The tube easily becomes the boob—and certainly is one of the culprits—keeping people from reading and writing. But television does something worse than shorten the attention span. As others have suggested, excessive viewing may finally destroy parts of the mind. The greater violence of TV is not the successive scenes of physical violence, harmful as they may be, but the primacy of the visual. In reading and listening the mind must decode, and drawing in a whole situation, reproduce within its own cavern the scene that language depicts. Language taxes the intellect. The more the mind works with words—words read, words heard, words spoken—the stronger it is, the more able to read and write. Television limits the mental work of the viewer. While it does use language, it is often of a simple order; and while it does make noise, it is often Muzak-type music that lulls the viewer along. Surely a point is reached in excessive television viewing where the child ceases to think at all. By not using his brain, the child may lose the function of part of it. The passivity of the TV viewer, noted since the inception of TV, produces a debilitation of the species. Unless the television picture is used like the set in a good play—as background for language and foreground for acting—it weakens the image making, the decoding capacity of the mind. Only a great picture is worth a thousand words and then only the way a great love affair is—condensing, representing a life of emotion. Even if, instead of watching TV, a child spent half of each day in art galleries, he still wouldn't be better off. As much of television uses it, the visual is a desert without sand.

But instead of resisting technology, schools have invited it into the classroom. Audiovisual equipment, on which millions of federal dollars have been spent, may be helpful to the handicapped, but it simplifies language in the way television does; and it implicitly discourages the use of books.

The writing and reading crises are too widespread among people of varying backgrounds to put the blame on television alone or primarily. The visual has come to dominate not only entertainment, but school books as well. Early reading texts once were dominated by words in bold letters, and used illustrations incidentally; now the visual often overwhelms the language. Comic books have orderly captions compared to some early reading texts whose sentences float in a sea of illustration. As does television, predominantly visual reading texts deprive the child of his own image making, and dissipate ideas into design. Action-oriented, even psychedelic in color—as if a child's attention could be arrested only by blinking neon—some texts become *Sesame Street* in print. If given relief from the visual assault, children could still find refuge and learning in the grip of unadulterated language. As some schools still do, all schools could build a world of books and language in which a child's mind could flourish. But the further grade school teaching goes, the more technological it becomes. To test a child's reading ability and to prepare him for test taking, purely informational texts replace the art of stories. Just as television breaks a half hour into bits, so reading texts offer only short, unrelated passages. Television presents the child with worlds with which he can have no real relationship, but the data-crammed paragraphs simply bore him. Other countries continue to educate with an emphasis on language and literature, but we have become too much of a "with it" nation to keep educational traditions.

As devastating an influence as television is the objective test system, introduced by higher learning—and now used in secondary education. Until the 1950s, students wrote essays in schools because they were expected to write essays on college entrance exams. But the university abandoned the essay requirement by adopting, a generation ago, the entirely objective test for admission, the Scholastic Aptitude Test (SAT).* Before World War II the objective SAT had been a supplement to written Achievement Tests in various subjects. But when the SAT became dominant, the Achievement Tests became objective too.** When the university dropped the essay requirement, it failed to recognize the power of the system it launched. Once the college entrance exams were objective, secondary schools asked for less writing. Urged on by text manufacturers, high schools began to use objective tests not only to prepare their students, but for their own examinations. The university, by sanctioning the objective system, bears the terrible responsibility for the decline of writing in the United States.

Today, the test manufacturers—led by the Educational Testing Service of Princeton, N.M.—are big businesses profiting from miseducation. ETS produces not only the SAT but a battery of tests used for secondary and graduate education. Although the tests have made writing seem unnecessary—although they have also damaged reading ability—they are too expensive to throw out or replace. Harmful though the tests are, the schools have submitted to a system that runs on its own power. Measuring students means measuring schools—according to the aggregate scores of the enrolled—and few schools dare

drop out of the spiral of relative standing. Public schools are also tied to the tests by school boards demanding measurement.

Developed first for the Army in World War II and widely used in World War II to test intelligence and ability, objective tests are gifts of war to civilian life. In the twenty-five years the SAT has been dominant, American education has been revolutionized. The marketplace has overturned the traditional foundations of learning—reading and writing—more completely than the efforts of any mechanistic theorist. Most Americans are probably tested more than they are taught. Composition, essay questions, term papers—vigorous thinking—all have yielded to one right answer out of four, to boxes to be checked, blanks to be filled. Objective tests not only carry the prestige of being scientifically accurate—when they aren't—but are also an easy way of handling the masses of machine. The results might have been predictable to an educational system that valued education. The national SAT Verbal Aptitude scores have shown a steady decline over a ten-year period. If the scores are worth anything, they show how poor teacher objective tests are. The American language—supple, imaginative, and alive—has lost ground to the pretense of measurement. "Nobody ever cared about my writing," is a refrain I, as a teacher, have heard in several accents. After two decades of objective education, the "educationally disadvantaged" are not merely the poor and minority groups, but the supposedly well-educated and well-to-do.

In the past, writing was not so much "taught" as shown. In the nineteenth century the Bible, widely read, influenced Americans to write declaratively, simply, imaginatively. Newspapers and radio played their roles in teaching as biblical Elizabethan, the origin of American language, lost its regular audience. Much nostalgic reverence is now given to

*Most American colleges use the SAT; some, mainly in the South and West, use the American College Test (ACT), developed later, modeled after the SAT, and produced by the American College Testing Program of Iowa City. Some colleges accept scores on either. Since the SAT is the prototype, it is this dominate test that is discussed in this book.

**The Achievement Tests also became optional. The change from the written essays to objective Achievement Test in History and the Social Sciences was catastrophic. Such subjects, drawing greater student interest than English, had required and brought forth solid writing abilities.

*McGuffey's Readers* and to New England primers in the name of honoring basics, but the old texts didn't preach grammatical rules; they presented young readers with lively, clear texts on American situations. Symptomatic of today's approach, most grammar books list rules and principles, amplifying the order of a dictionary. Grammar itself becomes a specialty divorced from its use. In the past, reading more, students enjoyed more of what they read, and hearing more conversation than a TV tube produces, soaked in the syntax of language. Since they were asked to write throughout school, they learned from writing, as well as from reading and hearing. The horrendous misspellings of freshmen today—*probaly, satify*; the endless confusions of *there* for *their*, of *where* for *were*, of *went* for *gone*—result not from the demise of the spelling bee, but from rarely having written words down.

When reading is not habitual but a forced drill, and when grammar is a distant abstraction, years of vacancy have to be filled by one, two, or three semesters of—to use the ugly word—remediation. At the college level no one has ever had to "teach" writing before. Even twenty years ago, a fair time for the literary teacher, freshman English was a literature course in which students who had been writing for ten years perfected style and punctuation. Today, faced with the need to teach the unpracticed, colleges turn the mute over to English faculties trained for literary scholarship, who are appalled by the new ignorance, and often temperamentally hostile to it. Teachers, however, can insist that students have meaningful experiences to write about; and experience can be explored in the first writing assignments. In spite of early resistance within the academic community, remedial teaching actually has gotten better and has begun to work. Adapting to a different job, more and more English faculty have come to recognize that education begins with and builds on what a student already knows, however invisible that knowledge may seem to be.

But, wherever they begin to write steadily and seriously, Americans encounter a subtle psychological barrier in the name still used for the practice of reading and writing—English. Our language is indisputable American—distinctive not in its grammar, when correct, but in its idiom and brisk pace. The student, young or old, faces a forbidding title for the tongue he is to write. The bold and well-educated can cope with it; but others, schooled badly or well, can be easily intimidated. It is not ethnicity that makes "English" a tough name to meet, it is the native Americanness of all of us. "English" encourages in many young Americans, unconsciously but doggedly, the evasion of a foreign tongue. For teachers upholding standards of "English," the title invites teaching by rules, regulations, and finally formulas. Colonial rule has to be imposed. Throughout American history there has been a smoldering rebellion against the "English" of the classroom. With only partial success, schoolmarms chided the country boys; and in cities, civil servants tried to cleanse the immigrants. Huck Finn was—and remains—a prototype of resistance to "correct" English, of loyalty to a spoken language. Against the language of technology, against "English" too, students now revolt in an anarchy of usage, a sloppiness of expression.

The illiteracy crisis is even more tragic in light of the old glory of the American language. (Because of American isolation, the influence of the Bible on our language lasted longer than on British English; in England new styles succeeded one another. Even in our earthiness we are still heirs of the Elizabethans.) Faced from the beginning with new conditions of life, the American has had to adapt English words to American necessities and to coin words of his own. Our idiom expresses our history, our humanity. First the English and then the American academics inveighed against American innovations, and then finally adopted them. Thomas Jefferson was flailed in a London review in 1787 for writing *to belittle*, but the verb, like so many brisk Americanisms, became so common in England that in 1862 it appeared in Trollope. As H.L. Mencken noted in *The American Language* (1937), " . . . the American, on his linguistic side, likes to make his language as he goes along, and not all the hard work of the schoolmarm can hold the business back. A novelty loses nothing by the fact that it is a novelty: it rather gains something, and particularly if it meets the national fancy for the terse, the vivid, and, above all, the bold and the imaginative." Commending "the superior imaginativeness revealed by Americans in meeting linguistic emergencies," Mencken charted the course of American creativity in response to a new environment, meeting the needs of a necessarily direct people. From the town meeting to the political caucus, from the backwoods to the frontier, from the railroad, the barroom, the jazz band, and now the ghetto (all previous terms are themselves mild examples of American inventions or conventions), the uneducated as well as the educated have created an American language fitting our circumstances and energy. The string of native idioms and compounds that trip off our American tongues, that no English or academic soap has been able to wash away, is infinite and ongoing. Consider *back talk* and *downtown*, to *peter out*, and *to fly off the handle* as nineteenth-century creations; *scofflaw* and *sit-in*, *splashdown* and *drop out* as twentieth-century word building. *Spellbinders* and *screwballs*, *shortstops* and *shortcuts*, and countless thousands of Americanisms have taken hold and are *here to stay*. Although the line must surely be held against American barbarisms, of which illiteracy is

one and useless slang another, some who teach "English" really teach American without appreciating the native genius.

As new usages came into speech, nineteenth-century American writers—leaving bad grammar to dialogue—took up the most useful and expressive of them. Literature, as it had in other nations, became the authority. If American literature were more consistently read in our schools, it might exercise some authority over student writing. But English is not only the name tag for composition courses; English literature is still the specialty of most teachers in colleges and in high schools. Though American literature has come more into favor in the classroom, it is still a body of work most students never meet.

The struggle to claim American language has gone on for a long time. Nineteenth-century American writers—Cooper, Howells, Twain, and Whitman—publicly pled the cause against native Anglophiles. In 1924 Rupert Hughes, the critic, was sufficiently outraged by the Anglophiles to write, in *Harper's Magazine*, "Let us put off the livery, cease to be the butlers of another people's language, and try to be the masters and creators of our own"—even while Hemingway, Fitzgerald, Dos Passos were doing just that. In 1923, Robert Frost, then perfecting an American idiom, denied that American partway came from either "the soil" or "the city," from "the native" or "the alien." He said in an interview, "Where there is life there is poetry, and just as much as our life is different from English life, so is our poetry different. . . . When he [the immigrant] becomes articulate and raises his voice in the outburst of song, he is singing an American lyric. He is an American. His poetry is American. He could not have sung that same song in the place from where he hails; he could not have sung it in any other country to which he might have emigrated. Be grateful for the individual note he contributes and adopt it for your own as he has adopted the country.''

Mencken noted in 1937, ''The popular speech is pulling the exacter speech along and no one familiar with it successes in the past can have much doubt that it will succeed again, soon or late.'' Decent American writing has always resulted from a tension between the vulgar—what Mencken called ''the great reservoir of the language''—and educated speech. But educated writing—often a product of graduate schools—veers from the popular language. Let the two separate entirely and the written language will fade further, the popular speech further decline. The two must be in some equilibrium for either to be safe.

Teaching American might bring better results than teaching English; and the least our professor should do is to call the language American English, as some already do, or call it the American language. Teaching writing—because writing is inevitably self-expression—is always touchy, because the student's ego is at stake and is easily offended. How terrible, then, to ignore his national history by giving him an English bath.

In his 1837 American Scholar Address, Emerson urged Americans to turn away from ''the courtly muses of Europe.'' That same year he noted in his *Journal*:

The language of the street is always strong. What can describe the folly and emptiness of scolding like the word *jawing*? I feel too the force of the double negative, though clean contrary to our grammar rules. And I confess to some pleasure from the stinging rhetoric or a rattling oath in the mouths of truckmen and teamsters. How laconic and brisk it is by the side of a page of The North Atlantic Review. Cut these words and they would bleed; they are vascular and alive; they walk and they run. Moreover they who speak have this elegancy, that they do not trip in their speech. It is a shower of bullets; whilst the Cambridge men and Yale men correct themselves and begin again in every half sentence.

The passage is a good example of the tendencies of written American. The sentences are declarative, falling without formula more to brevity than to length. American comes up short to clinch a point. One thinks of Thoreau surfacing from rivers of prose: ''The mass of men lead lives of quiet desperation.'' Even in the delicious lengths of Thoreau and W.E.B. Du Bois—the latter not yet valued as an American writer—American has a love for thrift of phrase. As in the Emerson passage, briskness comes from the verbs. *Cut, bleed, walk, run, trip*—active and plain—are metaphors lifted from a physical life. A nation, much of whose history is physical endeavor, has the physical in its language. The vernacular—*stinging, rattling, shower of bullets*—stands side by side with more formal terms; energy comes from the pairing. There is nothing dull or common about the passage because it reaches into letters and life. The language of the street will never write an essay, but the ear of the good writer is tuned by it. Students of writing, however, are usually drowned in vocabulary lists. They are not thought to have an ear or a language of their own. They think they must use big words, and their writing becomes, predictably, tedious and impersonal. They are taught only half the mixture.

Contemporary novelists, such as Ellison and Bellow, conscious heirs of Emerson's nationalism, honor the popular language as well as their educated vocabularies. The best American journalism today is also written in a mixture of the formal and colloquial. But in the classroom, as in textbooks, American language is edged out by academic jargon—the bulky phraseology of psychologists, the heavy abstractions of social science. At a faculty meeting, an English medievalist laces his talk with street language; but English professors, perhaps even the medievalist, preach the doctrine; *Never write as you speak.* In telling students to forget their natural speech, teachers ask them to forget everything, for their voices contain far more than slang. Under that academic prohibition, speech can never rise through the mind. In the speaking voice lies the miracle, the beginning of writing. Even the illiterate, when they talk of something they care about, perform feats of grammar and thought—by the sentence, by the paragraph.

Once, at an English Department meeting, I suggested that teaching primarily by rules and regulations blocked the powers of the mind. "How are you going to tell a student," one Ph.D. asked, "that the following sentence is wrong: "The reason for the student being late was because the subway broke down'?" Another Ph.D. replied, "Two noun clauses cannot go together." But these grammarians had lost sight of the power of the human voice. When students write, as they often do at the beginning, "the reason. . . was because," they only display that gap bred in their minds between written and spoken language. When I tell students to *write as directly as you speak* such contortions of language clear up. They invariably write, "The student was late because the subway broke down." To many academics, the speaking voice is a barbarous instrument, to be silenced in writing. But writing is not simply a transcription of the speaking voice; it is a heightening of it in that time that writing allows for thought.

Linguists—the "new linguists"—now believe that grammar is not an act of imitation but an innate ability, inborn, emerging in a child's first speech. When they first begin to speak, children use verbs and speak in sentences. Writers have guessed for a long time what linguists now postulate: Grammar is a set of names for the way the mind works with language. For descriptive purposes the names come in handy. But teaching by rules

alone does not give the student confidence in his own voice. The first emphasis must be on encouraging the student to use the voice. It contains the miracle of grammar. Particulars that the voice has not mastered must be learned through workbook exercises and through instruction. The more of this a student can do for himself, prodded by the instructor, the more he will learn.

One year when New York State budget cuts threatened York College—one of the four-year colleges in the City University of New York and the college where I teach—I acted upon an administrative suggestion and asked students to write letters to the legislature supporting full funding of the school. All the letters began, "It has come to my attention that . . . " When I pointed out the methodical beginnings, students who were now writing essays with competence and sometimes individuality replied, "That's the way we were taught in Business English."

Some subspecies of "Business English" is becoming more and more common. At the Watergate hearings, Nixon's bright young men with their points in time would *depart Camp David* and *arrive Key Biscayne* without knowing the difference between an intransitive verb, requiring a preposition, and a transitive one, capable of a direct object. Their verbs came from the airport terminal. Science, which has discovered its truths detail by detail, step by step, has become in the minds of nonscientists something to imitate— not its method but its labeling and classification system. The weak, alas, misunderstand the strong. Psychologists seeking categories, imitating science, write a jargon concealing all clarity; in some of their inventions—*cognitive imagery, perceptual dysfunction, personality feedback*—people are described like machines. Academic jargon is infected with computer terminology—*program feedback, committee input*—even while English professors are still caught in Latinate imitations.

From professional schools of education comes "educationese," such as this professional analysis of a classroom situation: "Her result was a confusion matrix showing how often these children confuse each letter with every other letter." The greater the oppression of language, the more assertive the folk language—and the more form is abused.

American English has fallen not just to sentence fragments but to incomplete talk. The young talk less well because they write less, because vigorous speech has been tested or stolen away.

Still, in spite of the colonial rule of English and the tyranny of tests, Americans haven't given up on literary expression. Today, Americans hanker after the act of individuality that writing should be. "To write" is even the dream of many who will, alas, continue to mangle the language. A young lady whom I had coached through a remedial course told me a couple of years later that she hoped to publish some of her "literary works." Colleges find that less pretentious students, once they have completed basic work, often want more courses in writing. English Departments, once snobbish even about creative writing and journalism courses but finding fewer students interested in English literature electives, now find that they can stay in business by offering courses in nonfiction writing. Some faculties, further losing the struggle for humanity in language, and catering to new fashion, call their courses "Communications." Here, it seems, students may learn at last, like radio towers, to send out impressive sounds. The flood of writers' conferences, writers' schools, and writing courses in and out of college attests to the frantic effort of many Americans to be somebody through language. Writing the novel, the play, or the poem has been the underground hope of businessmen as well as the vocation of Bohemians. In a country that reads little poetry, an enormous amount of poetry is written. American language has built American song, a street poetry, for generations. The best popular music has always had style and content. A decent respect for writing in our schools would strengthen many willing hands. Those who write well only exercise their individuality. Self-expression, in spite of our difficulty with the written word, still proves as fundamentally American as cutting down cherry trees.

When, in 1952, I left college with only a Mater's degree, an English professor swore that should I ever want to teach I'd be teaching nothing more than Freshman Composition. With some luck as a lubricant, I have wriggled out of the dreary prediction into the higher realms of advanced writing, of literature itself, but lately I have concentrated on the remedial job. When, after earning my living as a journalist, after free-lancing and not earning enough, I did turn to teaching, revelations occurred in the dramas of Freshman Composition. The longer I taught the more I was drawn toward teaching minorities to hear strong sounds of speech. At Brooklyn College, where I began teaching, a number of Orthodox Jews clad in sports coats and yarmulkes occupied one of my evening classes. Attending Yeshivas (religious schools) by day, they had been brought up on the Book, and in the endless talmudic dialogues had learned to ask questions. Wearing fedoras on top of yarmulkes in the secular hallways, they were self-confident exiles holding to a belief—one told me—that had saved their parents from the Nazi persecution. But it was not the power of God in them that drew me; it was their implicit identity. Identity—a cube of ice, unmeltable, at the center of oneself, formed from all sorts of sources—is a force that allows every writer—even students of writing—to write well. But some of the Orthodox Jews, like other students who had been "successful" in high school, were so hung up in formulas, had become such induction and deduction machines, that they had to remove their intellectual showcases before writing well.

Among other students, there were individuals who stood out, who brought identity to their writing. Out of the Vietnam war came a T-shirted, red-haired young man writing tales about his role in a tangled war. A slim, long-haired girl who considered herself inarticulate came to life—danced like the dancer she was—in a paper on Thoreau.

Then, as the admission policy broadened in the early 1970s, bringing students with low high school averages into the city colleges, I began teaching a course in a program called SEEK (Search for Education, Elevation, and Knowledge), designed for ill-prepared black and Puerto Rican students. I didn't have a romance with the nonstandard grammar called black dialect, but I was drawn by the identity in these aroused, committed students. Many of my students had failed in the educational system of tests—or had never learned to take them. But they were able to speak forcefully and could summon an eloquence, a lyricism, when encouraged to write. In many of the poor, spirit was accessible; it hadn't been taught away. And spirit, of course, is the song of identity. Both, I knew, had something to do with suffering, and with that I had some sympathy. The ability to admit to suffering quickens all the sensibilities. If we cannot admit to hurt—perhaps man's deepest experience—the whole self freezes. Joy is the first and self-expression the ultimate loss. I've found the spirit congealed and writing blocked in enough middle-class sons and daughters—black as well as white—to suspect a deeper problem than tests, television, or "English." The writing crisis is finally a crisis of identity in which tests and television, schools and a blur of culture conspire. The spell of advertisements, the plastic slipcovers, all those illusions of happiness in America so cheaply for sale—a culture of optimism ignoring complexity—all have wrought a denial of self. All those securities we use to hide from some dreadful truth muffle our ability to ask questions of the world, to react, to write.

Whenever I have found a profound writing problem in a student—writing little, never developing a thought, losing a thread in incoherence—it has been a problem of psyche or soul. A curtain has dropped between what the student admits and what his mind might tell him. A girl with much definition in her face, grace in her movement, the ability to concentrate, but unaccountably clumsy in her writing, pierced the chaos when she said of an unclear point, "I'm hiding from that." To teach writing is to provoke or cajole, to nurse or embarrass the American from his hiding place. It is to show him that he does have an identity—a way of looking at the world that is uniquely his and that in writing becomes a point of view, an organizing force. To get him to reveal himself is to get him to talk, in the classroom if possible—if necessary , to himself as he writes. To get him to talk is to show him that he has a language of his own that he can put to work in writing.

Occasionally breaking into a doubting smile, one black student never missed a class, but rarely wrote the assignments. Heavyset, wearing the white uniform of a student nurse, she wrote in a slow and tortured way; the words came out like drops from the last wringing of laundry. Asked to render an impression of something she had seen and thought about during the recent spring vacation, she sat immobile until the closing moments of the class and finally wrote:

Walking down 125th Street looking in all the African store windows, I started to dream.
  I saw my family in beautifully styled African clothes. We were living in Africa happy

and free. There were many tall beautiful trees and flowers of all sizes, all colors it was a breathtaking sight. There were children lots of children all happy laughing running and playing.

The women were shopping and working in their gardens with their vegetables and flowers. The men were working, some in politics others worked the mines some were computer operators. Many of the men worked in factories a few made their living in the sea. I have this dream many times it cheers me up.

In her vision of a black Eden she had reached into feeling and at last found the courage to write. Because she had found in her fantasy a subject that mattered to her, she had found balance in her writing. She had begun to use commas and periods, though not consistently.

As usual, the assignments were designed to help the student express his identity; in the SEEK classes self-expression rose easily, and if it found a meaningful subject, it glided toward literacy and sometimes way beyond. Elusive thing, identity had better be more than a gut reaction; at best it is expressed as an attitude, a way of looking at the world.

The next term a Puerto Rican girl brought irony and grievance to bear in a passage written in class. Short and olive-skinned, her hair a gleaming black, looking a bit like a girl not too far from her first communion, she seemed to move, to glide, in a world of feeling. Perhaps she would never write a scholarly paper on Jonathan Swift, but she too was a satirist of poverty.

In order for anyone to know why I behave the way I do he must know something about the beautiful place where I was born. I was born in the most beautiful place in the world where the sidewalks are lined with garbage cans and the people are all trouble free. Everyone wears a smile to hide the pain, the tears, and the disillusion. There is music and laughter everywhere so you won't hear the cries of anguish. I was born in "Harlem." It is very important for you to know this. I do not have the same morals as a middle class person would. We were born in different worlds. Worlds so close and yet so far. I have been made to understand the middle class values and yet my values have been ignored. They say we are sick, under-privileged. I say we are not the ones who are sick, you are. We have just adapted to life.

In middle-class students I had seen some morals I deplored, though perhaps not those she had in mind. Cheating occurred. I kept on getting term papers on "Capital Punishment" identical to ones that had been turned in before. Once I received a term paper on *Walden* so familiar that I could look it up; passage by passage, it was taken from a Brooks Atkinson introduction to Thoreau. I rose to a Puritan punishment. The girl had been an *A* student, but now all her work lay in the shadow of doubt. Just after turning in an *F* grade for her for the term, I met her in the hallway. "My mother gave it to me to turn in," she said of the paper. "My sister had used it once, and my mother said if it was good enough for her, why don't you turn it in, if you don't have anything else." She swore, as the tears threatened to come down, that all the other papers were hers alone. "I've got to get a good mark. My parents will kill me if I don't." After a brisk lecture which brought a vow of obedience from her, I remitted her *F* and gave her the gift of a *B*. A week later I got a thank-you card, white with embossed white lettering just signed with her name.

# Critical Thinking: Repackaging or Revolution?

*Marilyn Wilson*

While recently visiting the book exhibits at a national language arts conference, I overheard two teachers as they were busily sampling the wares being hawked by major publishers. "I know I have to do more with critical thinking skills in my reading class," sighed one. "Maybe I can find some good workbook exercises that will help me figure out what to do." Not an uncommon sentiment, I suspect, for teachers who have been told repeatedly over the last several years that they haven't been doing an adequate job of teaching their students to think, but who are uncertain about how it should be done.

When the National Assessment of Educational Progress released its results in the early and mid-eighties, it became apparent that the schools were falling short of their ability to teach certain skills. While students could read fairly well at the literal levels, they were having considerable difficulty with the "higher level thinking skills" of analysis, synthesis, application, and evaluation. Before long educators were united in their calls for increased focus on critical reading and critical thinking in America's classrooms. According to some educators, what has emerged

as a result of this concern is a revolution in the making; instead of students learning from rote, we have students engaged in questioning, supporting, analyzing, synthesizing, and applying. Rare is any teacher in any discipline who does not profess to be teaching students to think, or at least be concerned about how to go about teaching it. Equally rare is the current textbook or workbook that doesn't have at least one paragraph devoted to the need to help students read and think critically about the content of the material. One would consequently assume that the minds of students are now safely in the hands of right-thinking teachers who have taken Bloom's taxonomy to heart and who are intent on saving those minds from the damnation of literal thinking. Or so it appears.

## Issues of Critical Thinking/Literacy

While I applaud the shift from rote learning to critical thinking, I am admittedly uncertain about the gospel of critical literacy as it is being preached from every podium, every college of education, every publishing company across the country. Slickly packaged materials do not necessarily create good critical thinkers. Several questions need to be asked before we can even begin to evaluate the new materials on the market or the new strategies and techniques that purport to

Marilyn Wilson teaches in the English Department at Michigan State University. This article was originally published in *Language Arts* (65 [1988]: 543-551), a journal for elementary and high school teachers.

teach "higher-level thinking skills." The teacher looking for a convenient workbook may be able to make slight modifications in her approach to classroom learning, but more fundamental changes will need to occur before we turn out students who are critical thinkers of any significant magnitude. Do we know what we mean by critical thinking? Even if we can agree on a definition, is it something that can be taught? Can "critical thinking skills" be taught in the traditional classroom? Can they be taught in the abstract, and can they be transferred to other disciplines? What are the social/political implications for students raised to be critical thinkers, and does society as a whole really value people who dare to question and think and act on their beliefs? And finally, what are the implications for assessment, for standardized measures of competency, and for testing services that provide those standardized measures?

I raise these questions not because I don't value critical thinking but because they need to be discussed and answered before we can be clear about where we want to go and how we want to get there. I have the uneasy feeling that many riders on the critical thinking bandwagon have not considered them fully and may ultimately be disillusioned in their attempts to teach a set of skills. Teaching critical reading/thinking is more than selecting the right textbook or developing a more creative set of lesson plans. It needs to start with a reorientation to our students and to the subject we teach. It forces us to look critically at our own roles as teachers and at the nature of the learning that goes on in our classrooms. And beyond that, it forces us to look at the issue as a political one. We don't close the classroom door on the issue each afternoon at four o'clock, for it has implications far beyond the limits of the classroom as students develop new abilities and empower themselves as critical learners for the world at large. In short, developing students who read, write, and think critically demands nothing short of a revolution in the classroom. Reprocessed or repackaged skills lessons disguised as critical thinking skills will be a waste of time. And when they don't accomplish what we want them to, we'll be tempted to throw up our hands and condemn the latest theories that appear to have little application in the real world of the classroom.

This paper is not an attempt to explore all of the far-ranging issues suggested above. It is, rather, an attempt to begin the dialogue necessary to become critical thinkers about critical thinking. Too much of what passes as critical literacy/thinking suggests a search for easy definitions, for easy methods, and for formulas that will help us go from rote learning to critical thinking in one easy step without major restructuring. It is, of course, not that simple.

*Knowledge vs. Information*

In its most basic form, critical literacy/thinking suggests the need for learners to do more with texts than simply soak up bits and pieces of information. It advocates the use of strategies and techniques for helping learners think critically: such as predicting outcomes of parts of texts; formulating questions before and during reading; responding to statements in terms of student's own values and belief systems as they begin to read the text; making semantic maps of anticipated texts and modifying the maps as the text is being read; and responding to texts through a variety of creative writing experiences that ask readers to go beyond the confines of the text itself. Such strategies help readers/thinkers activate their stored knowledge, access it, and modify it as further information and knowledge are acquired. Furthermore they encourage readers to use that information for analyzing, synthesizing, and applying that knowledge to other situations. Critical thinking, then, at its most basic level, implies a reader/thinker who has some background knowledge to bring to the thinking task and who knows how to use that knowledge.

Much of the foregoing discussion emanates from schema theory and its focus on kinds of knowledge, how that knowledge is stored, and how it can be accessed and used by the reader/thinker in the process of comprehension. Schema theory is not new; it is an old concept, rejuvenated and newly named, that goes back to John Dewey, to Edmund Huey, and beyond. It's a concept that good teachers have been operating with for generations. But the very fact that it now has a label gives it a special focus. Researchers research it, models of learning are built on it, and teachers scramble to put the theory into practice. And, of course, herein lies the difficulty. Unless our understanding of schema theory and its relationship to the issues of critical reading/thinking is sufficiently complex, we are likely to look for exercises and pat formulas for its teaching. Too narrow a definition leads to a world of workbook exercises for distinguishing between fact and opinion, for identifying similes and metaphors, and for identifying kinds of propaganda techniques in expository prose, all in the name of critical thinking. The missing element is the substance, the sufficient background knowledge of the concepts being discussed, that enable readers/thinkers to make sense of text in order to do that kind of cognitive task.

*Substance vs. Form*

This focus is reminiscent of so much teaching that emphasizes form at the expense of substance and meaning—the English teacher teaching grammar on the assumption that knowledge of grammar will create better writers; the reading teacher who insists on knowledge of phonics rules in order for readers to read real texts; or the writing teacher who focuses first on paragraph indention, sentence structure, and outlining as prerequisites for writing. The skills or critical reading/thinking develop from the experience of reading/writing/thinking for real purposes. Like all psycholinguistic processes, critical thinking cannot be taught as a set of abstract rules about the process; it will develop as the reader/learner uses the process in real language activities that capture the reader's imagination and that provide real purposes for the learning. We will not be able to produce a grammar of critical/thinking whose instruction will inevitably lead to knowledge. A search for such a grammar is antithetical to the very basis of schema theory. It is the meaning base—the knowledge—that enables the language user/thinker to deal with the form and to recognize the structure in question, not the reverse. Unless readers possess adequate background knowledge and experience of the key concepts, ideals, and issues in the text as a whole, they will not be able to understand the parts, the bits and pieces that make up the whole. Self-questioning techniques, semantic mapping, etc., will work only if readers have sufficient background knowledge and experience with the concepts. It becomes easy to focus on the form of the strategies rather than on the underlying knowledge that readers bring to the reading experience. Critical reading/thinking cannot be taught as a series of skills in the way that mnemonic devices can be taught for memorizing dates and events; readers need to have sufficient schema and new knowledge related to that schema to critically think about.

Equally unworkable is the attempt by some teachers and programs to teach metacognitive skills, those skills of self-awareness and self-monitoring that help readers monitor their own comprehension processes during reading, unless readers have adequate background as the base. Readers need something to monitor before monitoring can occur. In the search for quick fixes, the form and technique take precedence over substance.

Unfortunately the previous assumptions about the acquisition and development of knowledge are perpetuated and strengthened by writers like E.D. Hirsch (1987), whose recommendations for developing a commonality of cultural knowledge are predicted on the assumption that the knowledge can be achieved from an accumulation of pieces of information. Despite his claims to the contrary, the very existence of a list of loosely connected terms, concepts, places, ideas, and people strongly suggests an approach to the dissemination of information through traditional means of teaching. While he devotes considerable time to the discussion of schema theory and the importance of schemata for comprehension, his discussion ignores knowledge of how schemata are developed. Information can be taught, to be sure. But knowledge—the integration of information into already existing schematic frameworks—cannot occur by so simplistic a means. Hirsch's list of unconnected terms, or ones similar to it, determined by self-proclaimed arbiters of cultural knowledge, will not result in the kinds of knowledge required for critical literacy/critical thinking. Learning does not occur in a vacuum. Learners develop schemata and the new knowledge available. Bussis (1982) describes the process of coming to "know" as follows:

Only when a person interprets information—however tentatively—does information qualify as knowledge. The interpretation need not be formulated in words: many experiences are represented in nonarticulate form. But an individual must note and interpret a pattern before he or she can be said to know something. In other words, information exists "out there" in the physical/social/cultural world or in physiological sensations arising from within the body. *Knowledge* exists in the mind. . . .An individual could conceivably attend to a par-

ticular kind of information for years without ever discerning a pattern that unifies the information or relates it to other meaningful patterns. Such a dismal outcome is not only theoretically possible but also quite probable, if the information an individual heeds consists primarily of isolated fragments of an event. Sufficient attention to information is an important and rather obvious condition of learning, but it guarantees nothing. (p. 239)

*Learning and Meaning Making*

A related question still remains. If we take the concept of schema theory seriously, whose meaning are we dealing with when we ask students to discuss their comprehension or interpretation of a text? And whose text is it that is the focus of discussion—the author's or the reader's? The reader/learner in current conceptualizations of schema theory is rightfully recognized as meaning maker in the process of reading, with the text no longer a fixed object but rather a fluid entity that, in part, is molded and shaped by a meaning-making reader. The text is only one of the components in the complex process of comprehension, along with the reader's prior knowledge and degree of reading proficiency, the nature of the reading task, the reader's purpose for reading, and the constraints of the reading context. In theory, at least, the text, as a guide and framework, has meaning potential that is realized only by a particular reader under a particular set of circumstances.

An understanding of schema theory in a much broader sense is necessary, then, for defining critical literacy/thinking. It calls for readers who recognize their rights to question the author's text and assert their own; who see their own experiences and backgrounds as legitimate factors in the creation of a meaning that may or may not be synonymous with the meaning created by others; who see the critic of a literary work as just another reader of the author's text, subject to the same limitations and liberties as the ordinary reader; and who value their own roles as readers/thinkers creating dialogue with fellow readers/thinkers in the learning community as a way to construct meaning for themselves. Comprehending/thinking is a particularistic experience that forces the question of the nature of meaning, where that meaning resides, and how that meaning is created by individual readers—questions that have implications on a broad scale. As Corcoran (1987) says about the particularity of the reading process: "The emphasis on particularity underscores the existence of culturally produced texts and readers, and points to transactive reading events which are structured by the placement of readers, texts, and teachers in a unique set of social, ideological, and institutional relationships" (p. 48). He goes on to say that readers forge rather than find meaning, not altogether a new idea, but a revolutionary one if acted upon. If we dare to give students that kind of authority and autonomy in reading comprehension, no longer will we be able to use traditional assessment measures of comprehension, either teacher-made or ETS-produced. Neither will we be satisfied with prepackaged materials from publishers who cannot possibly know the needs and the experiences of our own individual students. Do we really value readers/thinkers who ask real questions of texts, of authors of texts, and of us who teach these texts? Critical thinking calls for just that—a reformulation of learning and teaching the likes of which we have never seen. It is a revolutionary concept of literacy and learning far beyond the narrow definitions advocated by Hirsch.

Advocates of critical literacy/thinking are, in effect, making political statements about the reformulation of relationship in the classroom—teacher and student, student and student, student and text, teacher and text. The reformulation empowers learners to take responsibility for their own learning and to assert their authority as readers and meaning makers. Textbooks and workbooks that provide exercises for "teaching" critical thinking skills hardly have this concept of revolution in mind. In fact, for the most part, these exercises assume that meaning is entirely in the text. The responsibility of the reader is to use the skills necessary for ferreting out that meaning. While the reader is an active participant in the reading process, that activity functions primarily in information retrieval, with perhaps a cursory nod in the directions of analysis and synthesis. For real analysis, synthesis, and application to occur, the reader must be given the right of text creation growing out of the particularistic reading situation. Such a restructuring of classroom relationships takes some of the traditional control from the teacher in order to give it to the students who must take more responsibility for their own learning. The students, not the teacher, must do most of the cognitive work, a revolutionary concept, given the past several decades of traditional classroom practices.

## Affective and Cognitive Engagement

Engaging students' intellect, then, appears to be critical. But cognitive is always accomplished by affect, says Louise Rosenblatt (1978), one more element to be considered in the definition of critical literacy. Her transactive theory of reading comprehension suggests that reading involves the emotions as well as the intellect. If the reader is expected to take a stance toward the text that results in efferent reading only, a critical element of the reading experience is lost. Reading aesthetically, with the heart as well as with the head, will, according to Rosenblatt, fuse the cognitive and affective elements of consciousness into a personally lived-through reading experience. A reader's transaction with the text is richest when conceptual knowledge, linguistic knowledge, and affective response influence one another. If any one of these three elements is significantly restricted, the quality of the transaction will be diminished. It is perhaps naive to think that students are going to have the same "lived-through" experience with a text chapter on the Civil War that they might have with a poem or novel about the Civil War, but I think it is not unreasonable to assume that a reader's personal responses to the ideas and the substance of a piece of nonfiction prose can be encouraged, thereby giving the reading of the text a greater dimension and making it more personally relevant to the reader. Ideas and concepts divorced from personal relevance and response foster a limited engagement. Owning a text is as much a matter of emotional investment as it is an intellectual one. As a teacher we can't afford to ignore that side of experience. In fact, it may be that intellectual and emotional responses are reciprocal, each enhancing the other. We necessarily limit engagement by encouraging our students to focus on one at the expense of the other.

## Cultural Pluralism and a Community of Learners

This focus on the emotional as well as the intellectual calls for a more broadly-based concept of cultural literacy than Hirsch suggests. For real transactions to occur, readers need to bring their own cultural values, experiences, beliefs to bear on the texts they read. This calls for the validation of those widely divergent cultural backgrounds in American classrooms, not for the elimination of them. This kind of revolution would value cultural pluralism rather than denigrate it. Therefore, if proponents of schema theory like Hirsch are serious about their support, their views of schema theory must also include recognition and validation of those cultures, backgrounds, experiences brought to the classroom by *all* students, not just those representing the cultural majority.

Part of critical literacy/thinking, then, necessarily involves a view of learning as social. Students must be encouraged to share ideas, to formulate arguments with and for others, to discuss issues with each other in order to create a learning community that best fosters the development of critical literacy. Drawing on the works of Louise Rosenblatt (1979), who sees the text as the medium of communication, not only between author and reader but also among readers, Evans (1987) says, "Taken this way, we can understand more clearly how interchanges of views about the text will reveal different temperaments, different literary and lived-through experience, and how these can lead to increases in insight and perhaps sometimes to consensus" (p. 40). It is my contention that most of the real learning that occurs in classrooms results from the intellectual and emotional excitement generated from the group learning experience. Collaborative learning best reflects the concepts of critical literacy. Ideas do not develop, become modified, or solidify in a vacuum. Readers/thinkers need one another for those ideas to bloom.

## Accountability and Assessment

And finally, we need to look at the demand for accountability and to access its role in the issue of critical literacy. It is not accountability in and of itself that is the potential roadblock to programs supporting critical literacy/thinking. It is, rather, how that accountability is going to be achieved. We have seen a steady increase in the last several years in the use of standardized measures for student achievement and teacher accountability. In fact, commissions on excellence in education have specifically called for more standardized testing as a way of insuring "higher standards" (A Nation at Risk, 1983). Such measures rarely give students opportunities to argue points, to apply knowledge, to think. Nor do they allow for any kind of variation in response, interpretation, or meaning creation. Instead they encourage learning as an isolated phenomenon, accomplished primarily by individuals without the aid of learning communities. The very nature of such tests, rather than helping to uphold standards, may be contributing to their decline. Accountability measures in general contradict the notion of critical thinking. Educators who recognize this, however, have been powerless to change the system, given the push for "excellence" and the calls for accountability growing out of it. A critical thinking revolution will need to start with a reevaluation of the purposes for and means of assessment of student achievement, no small task considering the economic and political power wielded by major publishing companies and testing services who have a vested interest in maintaining the status quo.

If I have painted too gloomy a picture of the chances of critical thinking to succeed in American educational institutions, I can only respond by saying that we need to address the issues raised here as a profession if we are to go beyond simplistic conceptualizations of critical thinking. It is easy to find quick fixes in textbooks and workbooks that claim to be concerned with critical thinking. But I fear that those quick fixes are a far cry from what we really mean as critical thinking advocates. Getting students to think critically cannot be done by simply replacing one set of strategies with another in a traditional classroom or by finding a more adequate measure of assessment of student progress and achievement. Fundamental changes will be required within the structure of the classroom itself and in the relationship of readers/learners to teachers, to texts, and to each other, that will have profound effects on students' relationship to the world beyond the classroom doors. It will not be easy or painless. But we should not settle for less.

# References

Bussis, Anne M. " 'Burn it at the Casket': Research, Reading Instruction, and Children's Learning of the First R." *Phi Delta Kappan*, December 1982, pp. 237-241.

Corcoran, Bill. "Teachers Creating Readers." In *Readers, Text, Teachers*, edited by Bill Corcoran and Emrys Evans. Upper Montclair, New Jersey: Boynton/Cook Publishers, Inc., 1987.

Evans, Emrys. "Readers Recreating Texts." In *Readers, Texts, Teachers*, edited by Bill Corcoran and Emrys Evans. Upper Montclair, New Jersey: Boynton/Cook Publishers, Inc. 1987.

Hirsch, E. D., Jr. *Cultural Literacy: What Every American Needs to Know*, Boston, Mass.: Houghton Mifflin Company, 1987.

*A Nation at Risk: The Imperative for Educational Reform*. The National Commission on Excellence in Education, April, 1983.

Rosenblatt, Louise M., *The Reader, The Text, The Poem: The Transactional Theory of the Literary Work*. Carbondale, Illinois: Southern Illinois University Press, 1978.

Reading 2.11

# Is There Really a Language Crisis?

*Harvey Daniels*

The deathwatch over American English has begun again. After all the shocks and assaults of her long life, and after all of her glorious recoveries, the Mother Tongue now faces the final hour. Around the bedside cluster the mourners: Edwin Newman, John Simon, Clifton Fadiman, Tony Randall, and Ann Landers. In darkened ranks behind stand somber professors of freshman composition, a few school board members, a representative from the National Assessment of Educational Progress, and the entire usage panel of the *American Heritage Dictionary*. Like all deaths, this one evokes in the bereaved the whole range of human feeling; anger, frustration, denial, despair, confusion, and grim humor. It has been a long, degenerative disease and not pretty to watch.

Is there room for hope? Is it really, uh, terminal? The specialists leave no room for miracles—the prognosis is firm. The obituaries have been prepared and, in some cases, already published. Services will be announced. Memorials are referred to the Edu-

cational Testing Service. *Requiescat in pace* American English.

Yet, curiously, the language clings to life. She even weakly speaks from time to time, in delirium no doubt, for her words are in jargon, cant, argot, doublespeak, and various substandard dialects. She splits infinitives and dangles participles, and one of the watchers actually thought he heard her begin a sentence with *hopefully*. How can one so ill survive? It is torture to see this. It must end.

But it won't. If this is death in life, it is still the normal condition of American English and of all other human languages. As compelling as the medical metaphors may be, languages really are not very much like people, healthy or sick, and make poor candidates for personification. The illnesses, the abuses, the wounds, the sufferings of a language reside in the minds and hearts of its users, as do its glories, triumphs, and eras of progress. Our language is an essentially neutral instrument with which we communicate, more or less, and into which we pour an abundance of feeling. It is our central cultural asset and our cherished personal friend, but it is not, in many ways, what we think it is or would like it to be.

But here is another story about death which I believe does tell us something important about the present state of American English. In Chicago, during the Christmas season of 1978, twenty-six Spanish-speaking people were killed in a series of tragic fires. Many of them perished because they could not understand the instructions that firemen shouted in English. When the city promptly instituted a program to teach the firefighters a few emergency phrases in Spanish, a storm of protest arose. "This is America," proclaimed the head of the Chicago Firefighters Union, "let them speak English." A local newspaper columnist suggested, with presumably innocent irony: "Let's stop catering to the still-flickering nationalistic desires to perpetuate the Latin heritage." The city's top-rated television newscaster used his bylined editorial minute to inveigh against the Spanish-teaching program in the firehouse.

An exasperated resident wrote to the letters column of the *Chicago Tribune*: "I object to bilingual everything. It is a pretty low sort of person who wants to enjoy the benefits of this country while remaining apart from it, hiding in an ethnic ghetto." Another letter writer huffed: "What does it take to bring home to these stiff-necked Latinos that when they move to a foreign country the least they can do is learn this language? I, for one, am fed up with the ruination of the best country in the world." Still another correspondent was even more succinct: "If they can't understand two words—don't jump— they should go back where they came from." And after my own brief article on the language controversy appeared, an angry firefighter's wife wrote me to explain her husband's awful dilemma in being stationed in the Latino community. "Why should he risk his life for nothing?" she wondered.

What does this story, which concerns speakers of Spanish, tell us about the current state of English? It reminds us that our attitudes about the speechways of other people are as much a part of the linguistic environment as nouns, verbs, and adjectives—and that today these attitudes appear usually harsh and unforgiving. In the Chicago controversy, some otherwise decent people were willing to imply—and some plainly stated— that people who don't talk right can damn well take their chances in a burning building. And while the underlying hostilities that give rise to such sentiments may not begin with language, it is clear that we frequently use language as both a channel and an excuse for expressing some of our deepest prejudices. Admittedly, our unforgiving attitudes about certain kinds of language do not often decide matters of life and death. Judging by the angry reaction to the fire crisis in Chicago, it is a good thing that they don't.

It seems worth noting that this particular outpouring of linguistic intolerance occurred in the midst of a period of more general concern about the fate of the English language. For the last decade we have been increasingly hearing about the sudden and widespread corruption of our native tongue. Standard English is supposedly becoming an endangered species; jargon is rampant; the kids talk funny; politicians brutalize the language in their endless attempts to mislead us; bureaucrats pollute the environment with obfuscation and bluster; the verbal test scores of our school children are plunging, substandard dialects are often accepted or even encouraged in the schools; non-English speakers are infiltrating our cities; and no one in school or business can write a simple English sentence correctly.

We have been having a "literacy crisis"—a panic about the state of our language in all of its uses, reading and writing and speaking. Predictions of linguistic doom have become a growth industry. *Time* magazine asks: "Can't Anyone Here Speak English?" while *Newsweek* explains "Why Johnny Can't Write." *TV Guide* warns of "The New Illiteracy," *Saturday Review* bemoans "The Plight of the English Language," and even United Airline's *Mainliner Magazine* blusters "'Who's Been Messing Around with Our Mother Tongue?" Pop grammarians and language critics appear in every corner of the popular media, relentlessly detaining the latest abuses of language and pillorying individual abusers.

Blue-ribbon commissions are impaneled to study the declining language skill of the young, and routinely prescribe strong doses of "The Basics" as a remedy. Astute educational publishers crank out old-fangled grammar books. English professors offer convoluted explanations of the crisis and its causes, most of which lay the blame on public school English teachers. *The New York Times Magazine* adds Spiro Agnew's former speechwriter to its roster as a weekly commentator "On Language." The president of the United States goes on record as encouraging the "back-to-basics" movement generally and the rebirth of grammar instruction in particular. Scores of books on illiteracy are published, but none out-sells *Strictly Speaking*. Edwin Newman, house grammarian of the National Broadcasting Company has posed the question first, and apparently most frighteningly: "Will America be the death of English?" His answer was frightening too: "My mature, considered judgment is that it will."

It was in the midst of this ripening language panic that the Spanish courses were begun in a few Chicago firehouses. The resulting controversy and debate would surely have happened anyway, since the expression of linguistic prejudice is one of humankind's most beloved amusements. But I also believe that the dispute was broadened, extended, and made more explicitly cruel by the prevailing climate of worry about the overall deterioration of American English.

The public had repeatedly been informed that the language was in a mess, that it was time to draw the line, time to clean up the tongue, time to toughen our standards, time to quit coddling inadequate speakers. In Chicago, that line was drawn in no uncertain

terms. Obviously, the connections between the "language crisis," with its mythical Mother Tongue writhing on her deathbed, and the all-too-real events of that recent Chicago winter are subtle and indirect.

Language is changing, yes. People "misuse" language constantly—use it to lie, mislead, and conceal. Few of us write very well. Young people do talk differently from grownups. Our occupations do generate a lot of jargon. We do seem to swear more. I do not personally admire each of these phenomena. But reports of the death of the English language are greatly exaggerated.

English is not diseased, it has not been raped and ravaged, it is not in peril. A language cannot, by its very nature, suffer in such ways, In fact, it cannot suffer at all. One of the sternest of the pop grammarians, Richard Mitchell, has said in one of his calmer moments:

There is nothing wrong with English. We do not live in the twilight of a dying language. To say that our English is outmoded or corrupt makes as much sense as to say that multiplication has been outmoded by Texas Instruments and corrupted because we've all forgotten the times tables. You may say as often as you please that six times seven is forty-five, but arithmetic will not suffer.

Mitchell goes on to say that the real problem we face lies not in the language itself but in the ignorance and stupidity of its users. I agree, although my definition of ignorance and stupidity is quite different from his.

At least some of the ignorance from which we suffer is ignorance of the history of language and the findings of linguistic research. History shows us that language panics, some just as fierce as our present one, are as familiar a feature of the human chronicle as wars. In fact, one of the persistent characteristics of past crisis has been the inevitable sense that everything was fine until the moment at hand, 1965, or 1789, or 2500 B.C., when suddenly the language (be it

American English, British English, or Sumerian) began the final plunge to oblivion. Looking at the history of prior language crisis gives us a reassuring perspective for evaluating the current one.

But we need more than reassurance—we need facts, or at least the closest thing to them, about the nature of language and how it works. The study of linguistics, which has emerged only during the present century, provides just such crucial information. The fact that the sponsors of the language crisis almost unanimously condemn modern linguistics suggests the irreconcilable differences between the critic's and the linguist's view of language. The linguist's work is not to ridicule poor speakers and praise good ones; not to rank various languages according to their supposed superiority in expressing literary or scientific concepts; not to defend the Mother Tongue from real or imagined assaults. Instead, the linguist tries to understand and explain some of the wonderfully complex mechanisms which allow human beings to communicate with each other. This does not mean that linguists don't have opinions about good and bad language, or even that some of them won't cringe at a dangling *hopefully*. But their main business is not evaluative but explanatory, not prescriptive but descriptive—an orientation which is utterly alien to the work of the contemporary language critics.

Even if a review of the story of language and linguistic research does tend to deflate our sense of crisis, this does not mean that the widespread fear of linguistic corruption is meaningless. Far from it. Something is indeed going on, and the wordsmiths of our society have been able to spread their concern about it quite easily to people who do not make their living by teaching, writing, or editing English. In order to understand what is at stake, we will need to look closely at the assumptions of contemporary language

criticisms and the ways in which they have been shared with the public.

All this worry about a decline extends well beyond the speaking and writing of American English. It represents a much wider concern about the direction of our society, our culture, as a whole. We have displaced (to use some jargon) much of our anxiety about current cultural changes into concern for the language which of necessity reflects them. Today, as at certain other moments in the past, talking about language has become a way of talking about ourselves, and about what we mean by knowledge, learning, education, discipline, intelligence, democracy, equality, patriotism, and truth.

But there are problems, serious ones. Language itself cannot be asked to carry the weight of such grave issues alone. To the extent that we assign our problems mainly to language, and explain them mostly by reference to aspects of language, we often defeat our own purposes. The critics, in this sense, are actually compounding the problems they profess to solve. First, they are promulgating or reinforcing ideas about language that are just plain wrong. If language is as important as the critics unanimously claim, then we should at least try to tell the truth about it, even if the facts run counter to our favorite prejudices. Second, the ministrations of the critics, with their inaccurate notions about the workings of language, threaten to bring back old—or to inspire new—teaching curricula and techniques that will hinder, rather than enhance, our children's efforts to develop their reading and writing and speaking skills.

Third, the critics, ironically enough, often trivialize the study of language. Through their steadfast preoccupation with form—with spelling and punctuation and usage and adolescent jargon and bureaucratic bluster and political doublespeak—they deflect us from meaning. Of course we know that form and content are intimately related, as the study of political propaganda reveals. Yet the real study of propaganda involves penetrating beyond the surface features to the message which is being sent, to the messages unsent, and to the purposes of the senders. But much of the current scolding and fussing about language focuses on red-penciling and superficial niceties of written and spoken utterances, rather than on understanding where they come from and what they might mean.

For all their trivial obsessions, the critics do also offer a deeper, more general message. As they advise us to strengthen our democracy by cleaning up the language, they also encourage us to continue using minor differences in language as ways of identifying, classifying, avoiding, or punishing anyone whom we choose to consider our social or intellectual inferior. And this is the gravest problem which the language crisis has given us: it has reinforced and occasionally glorified some of the basest hatreds and flimsiest prejudices in our society. Surely this unfortunate side effect has been mainly inadvertent—but just as surely, it affects us all.

# In Short, Why Did the Class Fail?

*Henry F. Ottinger*

And now, like it or not, I'd like to say a few parting words.

As you know, I began the semester in a way that departed from the manner in which I had taught composition classes in the past. Much of my attitude at that time was influenced by Jerry Farber's book, *The Student as Nigger*. On the first day of class, I read to you the following:

School is where you let the dying society put its trip on you. Our schools may seem useful: to make children into doctors, sociologists, engineers—to discover things. But they're poisonous as well. They exploit and enslave students; they petrify society; they make democracy unlikely. And it's not *what* you're taught that does the harm, but *how* you're taught. Our schools teach you by pushing you around, by stealing your will and your sense of power, by making timid, apathetic slaves of you—authority addicts.

That sounded like a breath of fresh air back in February—and I suggested that we try to break the mold, that we could write papers on any subject we wanted, that we could spend class time discussing things—either "the burning issues of the day," or otherwise. You seemed to agree, and we spent a lot of time agreeing together that indeed Farber had *the* word and we would do what we could to break out of the mold.

Henry F. Ottinger was a graduate teaching assistant at the University of Missouri when he wrote this essay, which originally appeared in the *New York Times*.

Reprinted with permission from Henry Ottinger.

As you know, things went from initial ecstasy to final catastrophe. And recently, I fell back—no, you forced me back—into assigning general topics. As a result of that action, and several other factors, this semester has been the worst I've ever taught. In fact, I even debated with myself whether or not to go on teaching next year. But in some ways the semester was valuable because I learned something, if you didn't.

Let me share with you some of the things I learned: and keep in mind that this does not apply to all of you, but it does to the majority.

I learned that all this bull about "getting it together" or "working together" (be it for peace or a grade) is just that—bull. The 1950's were labeled by pop sociologists the "silent generation." I assure you they have nothing on you. Ten years ago, the people around the fountains wore saddle shoes and chinos, and had crewcuts. Now they're barefoot, wear Army fatigues, and have long hair. Big revelation: it's the same bunch of people.

Generally, this class has been the most silent, reticent, paranoid bunch of people in a group I have ever experienced. If you are indicative of the generation that's supposed to change things, good luck. Change is predicated on, among, other things, communication between people, "which in your case," as the poem "Naming of Parts" goes, "you have not got."

You had an opportunity to exchange ideas (which it often turned out "you have not got,'') and you were too embarrassed to do so.

You had an opportunity to find out about each other—you didn't. (Or perhaps you found out some of the same things I did: if so, congratulations: the semester has not been a waste for you.)

You had an opportunity to find out something about yourself. This, by the way, is the crux of education. And, as far as I can see, you found out very little.

You had an opportunity to explore ideas—on your own—and didn't. Most of the papers hashed over the usual cliché-ridden topics: abortion, the SST, the population explosion. One person went so far as to churn out a masterpiece on the pros and cons of fraternities, a topic that was really hot back around 1956.

Most of all, you had the opportunity to be free—free from the usual absurdities of a composition class where topics are assigned, thesis statements are submitted, and so on. You also had freedom of thought, as long as it was confined to the standards of formal English. You had the opportunity to be free—to be responsible to yourself—and you succeeded in proving to me and to yourself that Freedom is Slavery, a line from *1984* which I hope, for the sake of all of us, isn't prophetic.

But you protest! (Oh, how I wished you would): "We're incapable of handling all this freedom at once. You see, Mr. Ottinger, we've been conditioned; we're not used to all this!"

We'll, I read that in Farber, too, and it's bull. Rats and dogs are conditioned, and are usually incapable of breaking that conditioning. Human beings *can* break conditioning, if it's to their advantage. But here, it's too good an excuse to say, "I'm conditioned." Obviously, then, it's to your advantage *not* to break out of the mold.

*Why* is it to your advantage not to break the mold? In short, why did the class fail?

It failed because, as Dostoevski's "Underground Man" pointed out, thinking causes pain. And, like good little utilitarians, you want to avoid pain. No, it's much easier to come up with instant aesthetics, instant solutions, instant salvation, instant thoughts. After all, instant things, like breakfasts and TV dinners, are easily digestible—and easily regurgitated—and not terrible nourishing.

One of the more atrocious remarks I've heard this semester is, "Gosh, college is no fun," or when an idea is presented, "it doesn't turn me on."

If you don't believe that knowledge for its own sake is a valid and valuable goal, then you are in the wrong place, and you'd do much better in a vocational school, studying how to be a plumber or a beautician. And if you don't believe, along with Ezra Pound, that "real education must ultimately be limited to men who INSIST on knowing," you are definitely in the wrong place. You are merely clutter.

Granted, there are problems within the University itself—serious problems—that, despite what you may think, show some sign of possible solution. One step they could take (but probably won't) is to limit enrollment, and keep the forty-five percent of you out who don't belong here, because it's no fun.

Well, it's time, I suppose, to bring this to a halt, and let you go over to the Union, or wherever. Until then, I invite you to listen to the lyrics of the Beatles' "Nowhere Man," and if it fits, take it to heart.

Last, I will bid a good-bye (until the final) and say that if at any time some sly hint, or clue, or (God forbid) a half-truth slipped out of my unconscious and slid out the corner of my mouth and, pardon the expression, "turned one of you on," then we have not failed, you and I.

And, to paraphrase Theodore Roethke: I love you for what you might be; I'm deeply disturbed by what you are.

# Prologue: Horace's Compromise

*Theodore R. Sizer*

Here is an English teacher, Horace Smith. He's fifty-three, a twenty-eight-year veteran of high school classrooms, what one calls an old pro. He's proud, respected, and committed to his practice. He'd do nothing else. Teaching is too much fun, too rewarding, to yield to another line of work.

Horace has been at Franklin High in a suburb of a big city for nineteen years. He served for eight years as English department chairman, but turned the job over to a colleague, because he felt that even the minimal administrative chores of that post interfered with the teaching he loved best.

He arises at 5:45 A.M., careful not to awaken either his wife or grown daughter. He likes to be at school at 7:00, and the drive there from his home takes forty minutes. He wishes he owned a home near the school, but he can't afford it. Only a few of his colleagues live in the school's town, and they are the wives of executives whose salaries can handle the mortgages. His wife's job at the liquor store that she, he, and her brother own doesn't start until 10:00 A.M., and their daughter, a new associate in a law firm in the city, likes to sleep until the last possible minute and skip breakfast. He washes and dresses on tiptoe.

Horace prepares the coffee, makes some toast, and leaves the house at 6:20. He's not the first at school. The custodians and other, usually older, teachers are already there, "puttering around," one of the teachers says.

The teachers' room is large, really two rooms. The inner portion, windowless, is arranged in a honeycomb of carrels, one for each older teacher. Younger or newer teachers share carrels. Each has a built-in desk and a chair. Most have file cabinets. The walls on three sides, five feet high, are festooned with posters, photographs, lists, little sayings, notes from colleagues on issues long past. Horace: Call home. Horace: The following students in the chorus are excused from your Period 7 class— Adelson, Cartwright, Donato. . . .

Horace goes to his carrel, puts down his briefcase, picks up his mug, and walks to the coffee pot at the corner of the outer portion of the teachers' room, a space well lit by wide windows and fitted with a clutter of tables, vinyl-covered sofas, and chairs. The space is a familiar, comfortable jumble, fragrant with the smell of cigarettes smoked hours before. Horace lights up a fresh one, almost involuntarily, as a way perhaps to counteract yesterday's dead vapors. After pouring himself some coffee, he chats with some colleagues, mostly other English teachers.

Theodore R. Sizer is chairperson of the Education Department at Brown University. This essay is taken from his book, *Horace's Compromise: The Dilemma of American High Schools.*

The warning bell rings at 7:20. Horace smothers his cigarette, takes his still partly filled cup back to his carrel and adds it to the shuffle on his desk, collects some books and papers, and, with his briefcase, carries them down the hall to his classroom. Students are already clattering in, friendly, noisy, most of them ignoring him completely—not thoughtlessly, but without thinking. Horace often thinks of the importance of this semantic difference. Many adults are thoughtless about us teachers. Most students, however, just don't know we're here at all, people to think about. Innocents, he concludes.

7:30, and its bell. There are seventeen students here; there should be twenty-two. Bill Adams is ill; Horace has been told that by the office. Joyce Lezcowitz is at her grandmother's funeral; Horace hasn't been officially told that, but he knows it to be true. He marks Joyce "Ex Ab"—excused absence—on his attendance list. Looking up from the list, he sees two more students arrive, hustling to seats. You're late. Sorry . . . Sorry . . . The bus . . . Horace ignores the apologies and excuses and checks the two off on his list. One name is yet unaccounted for. Where is Jimmy Tibbetts? Silence. Tibbetts gets an "Abs" after his name.

Horace gets the class's attention by making some announcements about next week's test and about the method by which copies of the next play being read will be shared. This inordinately concerns some students and holds no interest for others. Mr. Smith, how can I finish the play when both Rosalie and I have to work after school? Mr. Smith, Sandy and I are on different buses. Can we switch partners? All these sorts of queries are from girls. There is whispering among some student. You got it? Horace asks, abruptly. Silence, signaling affirmation. Horace knows it is an illusion. Some character will come up two days later and guiltlessly assert that he has no play book, doesn't know how to get one, and has never heard of the plans to share the limited copies. Horace makes a mental note to inform Adams, Lezcowitz, and Tibbets of the text-sharing plan.

This is a class of juniors, mostly seventeen. The department syllabus calls for Shakespeare during this marking period, and *Romeo and Juliet* is the choice this year. The students have been assigned to read Act IV for this week, and Horace and his colleagues all get them to read the play out loud. The previous class had been memorable: Juliet's suicide had provoked much mirth. *Romeo, I come!* The kids thought it funny, clumsily melodramatic. Several, sniggering, saw a sexual meaning. Horace knew this to be inevitable; he had taught the play many times before.

We'll start at Scene Four. A rustle of books. Two kids looking helplessly around. They had forgotten their books, even though in-class reading had been a daily exercise for three weeks. Mr. Smith, I forgot my book. You've got to remember, Alice . . . *remember!* All this with a smile as well as honest exasperation. Share with George. Alice gets up and moves her desk next to that of George. They solemnly peer into George's book while two girls across the classroom giggle.

Gloria, you're Lady Capulet. Mary, the Nurse. George, you're old man Capulet. Gloria starts, reading without punctuation: *Hold take these keys and fetch more spices Nurse.* Horace: Gloria. Those commas. They mean something. Use them. Now, again. *Hold. Take these keys. And fetch more spices. Nurse.* Horace swallows. Better . . . Go on, Mary. *They call for dates and quinces in the pastry.* What's a quince? a voice asks. Someone answers, It's a fruit, Fruit! Horace ignores this digression but is reminded how he doesn't like this group of kids. Individually, they're nice, but the chemistry of them together doesn't work. Classes are too much a game for them. Go on . . . George?

*Come. Stir! Stir! Stir! The second cock hath crow'd.* Horace knows that reference to "cock" will give an opening to some jokester, and he squelches it before it can begin, by being sure he is looking at the class and not at his book as the words are read.

*The curfew bell hath rang. 'Tis three o'clock. Look to the bak'd meats, good Angelica . . .* George reads accurately, but with little accentuation.

Mary: *Go, you cot-quean, go . . .* Horace interrupts, and explains "cot-quean," a touch of contempt by the Nurse for the meddling Capulet. Horace does not go into the word's etymology, although he knows it. He feels that such a digression would be lost on this group, if not on his third-period class. He'll tell them. And so he returns: George, you're still Capulet. Reply to that cheeky Nurse.

The reading goes on for about forty minutes, to 8:15. The play's repartee among the musicians and Peter was a struggle, and Horace cut off the reading-out-loud before the end of the fifth scene. He assigns Act V for the next period and explains what will be on the *Romeo and Juliet* test. Mr. Smith, Ms. Viola isn't giving a test to her class. The statement is, of course, an accusing question. Well, we are. Ms. Viola's class will get something else, don't you worry. The bell rings.

The students rush out as the next class tries to push in. The newcomers are freshmen and give way to the eleventh-graders. They get into their seats expectantly, without quite the swagger of the older kids. Even though this is March, some of these students are still over-whelmed by the size of the high school.

There should be thirty students in this class, but twenty-seven are present. He marks three absences on his sheet. The students watch him; there is no chatter, but a good deal of squirming. These kids have the Wriggles, Horace has often said. The bell rings: 8:24.

Horace tells the students to open their textbooks to page 104 and read the paragraph at its top. Two students have no textbook. Horace tells them to share with their neighbors. *Always* bring your textbook to class. We never know when we'll need them. The severity in his voice causes quiet. The students read.

Horace asks: Betty, which of the words in the first sentence is an adverb? Silence. Betty stares at her book. More silence. Betty, what is an adverb? Silence. Bill, help Betty. It's sort of a verb that tells you about things. Horace pauses: Not quite, Bill, but close. Phil, you try. Phil: An adverb modifies a verb . . . Horace: O.K., Phil, but what does "modify" mean? Silence. A voice: "Darkly." Who said that? Horace asks. The sentence was "Heathcliff was a darkly brooding character." I did, Taffy says. O.K., Horace follows, you're correct, Taffy, but tell us why "darkly" is an adverb, what it does. Taffy: It modifies "character." No, Taffy, try again. Heathcliff? No. Brooding? Yes, now why? Is "brooding" a verb? Silence.

Horace goes to the board, writes the sentence, with chalk. He underlines *darkly*. Betty writes a note to her neighbor.

The class proceeds with this slow trudge through a paragraph from the textbook, searching for adverbs. Horace presses ahead patiently, almost dumbly at times. He is so familiar with the mistakes that ninth-graders make that he can sense them coming even before their utterance. Adverbs are always tougher to teach than adjectives. What frustrates him most are the partly correct answers; Horace worries that if he signals that a reply is somewhat accurate, all the student will think it is entirely accurate. At the same time, if he takes some minutes to sort out the truth from the falsity, the entire train of thought will be lost. He can never pursue any one student's errors to completion without losing all the others. Teaching grammar to classes like this is slow business, Horace feels. The bell rings. The students rush out, now more boisterous.

This is an Assembly Day, Horace remembers with pleasure. He leaves his papers on his desk, turns off the lights, shuts the door, and returns to the teachers' room. He can avoid assemblies; only the deans have to go. It's some student concert, in any event.

The teachers' room is full. Horace takes pleasure in it and wonders how his colleagues in schools in the city make do without such a sanctuary. Having a personal carrel is a luxury, he knows. He'd lose his here, he also knows, if enrollments went up again. The teachers' room was one happy consequence of the "baby bust."

The card game is going, set up on a square coffee table surrounded by a sofa and chairs. The kibitzers outnumber the players; all have coffee, some are smoking. The chatter is incessant, joshingly insulting. The staff members like one another.

Horace takes his mug, empties the cold leavings into the drain of the water fountain, and refills it. He puts a quarter in the large Maxwell House can supplied for that purpose, an honor system. He never pays for his early cup; Horace feels that if you come early, you get one on the house. He moves toward a clutch of fellow English and social studies teachers, and they gossip, mostly about a bit of trouble at the previous night's basketball game. No one was injured—that rarely happens at this high school—but indecorous words had been shouted back and forth, and Coke cans rolled on the gym floor. Someone could have been hurt. No teacher is much exercised about the incident. The talk is about things of more immediate importance to people: personal lives, essences even

more transitory, Horace knows, than the odors of their collective cigarettes.

Horace looks about for Ms. Viola to find out whether it's true that she's not going to give a test on *Romeo and Juliet*. She isn't in sight, and Horace remembers why: she is a nonsmoker and is offended by smoke. He leaves his groups and goes to Viola's carrel, where he finds her. She is put off by his query. Of course she is giving a test. Horace's lame explanation that a student told him differently doesn't help.

9:53. The third-period class of juniors. *Romeo and Juliet* again. Announcements over the public address system fill the first portion of the period, but Horace and a bunch of kids who call themselves "theater jocks" ignore them and talk about how to read Shakespeare well. They have to speak loudly to overpower the p.a. The rest of the class chatter among themselves. The readings from the play are lively, and Horace is able to exhibit his etymological talents with a disquisition on "cot-quean." The students are well engaged by the scene involving the musicians and Peter until the class is interrupted by a proctor from the principal's office, collecting absence slips for the first-class periods. Nonetheless, the lesson ends with a widespread sense of good feeling. Horace never gets around to giving out the assignment, talking about the upcoming test, or arranging for play books to be shared.

10:47, the Advanced Placement class. They are reading *Ulysses,* a novel with which Horace himself had trouble. Its circumlocutions are more precious than clever, he thinks, but he can't let on. Joyce is likely to be on the AP Exam, which will put him on a pedestal.

There are eighteen seniors in this class, but only five arrive. Horace remembers: This is United Nations Week at the local college, and a group of the high school's seniors is taking part, representing places like Mauritius and Libya. Many of the students in the UN Club are also those in Advanced Placement classes. Horace welcomes this remnant of five and suggests they use the hour to read. Although he is annoyed at losing several teaching days with this class, he is still quietly grateful for the respite this morning.

11:36. Lunch. Horace buys a salad on the cafeteria line—as a teacher he can jump ahead of students—and he takes it to the faculty dining room. He nods to the assistant principal on duty as he passes by. He takes a place at an empty table and is almost immediately joined by three physical education teachers, all of them coaches of varsity teams, who are noisily wrangling about the previous night's basketball game controversy. Horace listens, entertained. The coaches are having a good time, arguing with heat because they know the issue is really inconsequential and thus their disagreement will not mean much. Lunch is relaxing for Horace.

12:17. A free period. Horace checks with a colleague in the book storeroom about copies of a text soon to be used by the ninth-graders. Can he get more copies? His specific allotment is settled after some minutes' discussion. Horace returns to the teachers' room, to his carrel. He finds a note to call a Mrs. Altschuler, who turns out to be the stepmother of a former student. She asks, on behalf of her stepson, whether Horace will write a character reference for the young man to use in his search for a job. Horace agrees. Horace also finds a note to call the office. Was Tibbetts in your Period One class? No, Horace tells the assistant principal; that's why I marked him absent on the attendance sheet. The assistant principal overlooks this sarcasm. Well, he says, Tibbetts wasn't marked absent at any other class. Horace replies, That' someone else's problem. He was not in my class. The assistant principal: You're sure? Horace: Of course I'm sure.

The minutes of the free-period remaining are spent in organizing a set of papers that is to be returned to Horace's third junior English class. Horace sometimes alternates weeks when he collects homework so as not totally to bury himself. He feels guilty about this. The sixth-period class had its turn this week. Horace had skimmed these exercises—a series of questions on Shakespeare's life—and hastily graded them, but using only a plus, check, or minus. He hadn't had time enough to do more.

1:11. More *Romeo and Juliet.* This section is less rambunctious than the first-period group and less interesting than that of the third period. The students are actually rather dull, perhaps because the class meets at the end of the day. Everyone is ready to leave; there is little energy for Montagues and Capulets. However, as with other sections, the kids are responsive when spoken to individually. It is their blandness when they are in a group that Horace finds trying. At least they aren't hell raisers, the way some last-period-of-the-day sections can be. The final bell rings at 2:00.

Horace has learned to stay in his classroom at the day's end so that students who want to consult with him can always find him there. Several appear today. One wants Horace to speak on his behalf to a prospective employer. Another needs to get an assignment. A couple of other students come by actually just to come by. They have no special errand, but seem to like to check in and chat. These youngsters puzzle Horace. They always seem to need reassurance.

Three students from the Theater Club arrive with questions about scenery or the upcoming play. (Horace is the faculty adviser to the stage crew.) Their shared construction work on sets behind the scenes gives Horace great pleasure. He knows these kids and likes their company.

By the time Horace finishes in his classroom, it is 2:30. He drops his papers and books at his carrel, selecting some—papers given him by his Advanced Placement students two days previously that he has yet to find time to read—to put in his briefcase. He does not check in on the card game, now winding down, in the outer section of the teachers' room but, rather, goes briefly to the auditorium to watch the Theater Club actors starting their rehearsals. The play is Wilder's *Our Town*. Horace is both grateful and wistful that the production requires virtually no set to be constructed. The challenge for his stage crew, Horace knows, will be in the lighting.

Horace drives directly to his liquor store, arriving shortly after 4:00. He gives his brother-in-law some help in the stockroom and helps at the counter during the usual 4:30-to-6:30 surge of customers. His wife had earlier left for home and has supper ready for them both and their daughter at 7:45.

After dinner, Horace works for an hour on the papers he has brought home and on the Joyce classes he knows are ahead of him once the UN Mock Assembly is over. He has two telephone calls from students, one who has been ill and wants an assignment and another who wants to talk about the lighting for *Our Town*. The latter, an eager but shy boy, calls Horace often.

Horace turns in at 10:45, can't sleep, and watches the 11:00 news while his wife sleeps. He finally drifts off just before midnight.

Horace has high standards. Almost above all, he believes in the importance of writing, having his students learn to use language well. He believes in "coaching"—in having his students write and be criticized, often. Horace has his five classes of fewer than thirty students each, a total of 120. (He is lucky; his colleagues in inner cities like New York, San Diego, Detroit, and St. Louis have a school board-union negotiated "load" base of 175 students.) Horace believes that each student should write something for criticism at least twice a week—but he is realistic. As a rule, his students write once a week.

Most of Horace's students are juniors and seniors, young people who should be beyond sentence and paragraph exercises and who should be working on short essays, written arguments with moderately complex sequencing and, if not grace exactly, at least clarity. A page or two would be a minimum—but Horace is realistic. He assigns but one or two paragraphs.

Being a veteran teacher, Horace takes only fifteen to twenty minutes to check over each student's daily homework, to read the week's theme, and to write an analysis of it. (The "good" papers take a shorter time, usually, and the work of inept or demoralized students takes much longer.) Horace wonders how his inner-city colleagues, who usually have a far greater percentage of demoralized students, manage. Horace is realistic: even in his accommodating suburban school, fifteen minutes is too much to spend. He compromises, averaging five minutes for each student's work by cutting all but the most essential corners (the *reading* of the paragraphs in the themes takes but a few seconds; it is the thoughtful criticizing, in red ballpoint pen in the margins and elsewhere, that takes the minutes).

So, to check homework and to read and criticize one paragraph per week per student with the maximum feasible corner-cutting takes six hundred minutes, or ten hours, assuming no coffee breaks or flagging attention (which is some assumption, considering how enervating is most students' forced and misspelled prose).

Horace's fifty-some-minutes classes consume about twenty-three hours per week.

Administrative chores chew up another hour and a half. Horace cares about his teaching and feels that he should take a half-hour to prepare for each class meeting, particularly for his classes with old students, who are swiftly moving over quite abstract and unfamiliar material, and his class of ninth-graders, which requires teaching that is highly individualized. However, he is realistic. He will compromise by spending no more than ten minutes' preparation time, on average, per class. (In effect, he concentrates his "prep" time on the Advanced Placement class, and teaches the others from old notes.) Three of his sections are ostensibly of the same course, but because the students are different in each case, he knows that he cannot satisfactorily clone each lesson plan twice and teach to his satisfaction. (Horace is uneasy with this compromise but feels he can live with it.) Horace's class preparation time per week: four hours.

Horace loves the theater, and when the principal begged him to help out with the afternoon drama program, he agreed. He is paid $800 extra per year to help the student stage crews prepare sets. This takes him in all about four hours per week, save for the ten days before the shows, when he and his crew happily work for hours on end.

Of course, Horace would like time to work on the curriculum with his colleagues. He would like to visit their classes and to work with them on the English department program. He would like to meet his students' parents, to read in his field, and, most important for him, to counsel students as they need such counseling one on one. Being a popular teacher, he is asked to write over fifty recommendations for college admissions offices each year, a Christmas vacation task that usually takes three full days. (He knows he is good at it now. When he was less experienced, the reference writing used to take him a full week. He can now quickly crank

out the expected felicitous verbiage.) Yet Horace feels uneasy writing the crucial references for students with whom he has rarely exchanged ten consecutive sentences of private conversation. However, he is realistic: one does what one can and hopes that one is not sending the colleges too many lies.

And so before Horace assigns his one or two paragraphs per week, he is committed for over thirty-two hours of teaching, administration, class preparation, and extracurricular drama work. Collecting one short piece of writing per week from students and spending a bare five minutes per week on each student's weekly work adds ten hours, yielding a forty-two-hour work week. Lunch periods, supervisory duties frequently, if irregularly, assigned, coffee breaks, travel to and from school, and time for the courtesies, civilities, and biological necessities of life are all in addition.

For this, Horace, a twenty-eight-year veteran, is paid $27,300, a good salary for a teacher in his district. He works at the liquor store and earns another $8000 there, given a good year. The district adds 7 percent of his base salary to a nonvested pension account, and Horace tries to put away something more each month in an IRA. Fortunately, his wife also works at the store, and their one child went to the state university and its law school. She just received her J.D. Her starting salary in the law firm is $32,000.

Horace is a gentle man. He reads the frequent criticism of his profession in the press with compassion. Johnny can't read. Teachers have low Graduate Record Examination scores. We must vary our teaching to the learning styles of our pupils. We must relate to the community. We must be scholarly, keeping up with our fields. English teachers should be practicing, published writers. If they aren't all these things, it is obvious that *they don't care*. Horace is a trouper; he hides his bitterness. Nothing can be gained by showing it. The critics do not really want to hear him or to face facts. He will go with the flow. What alternative is there?

A prestigious college near Franklin High School assigns its full-time freshman expository writing instructors a maximum of two sections, totaling forty students. Horace thinks about his 120. Like these college freshmen, at least they show up, most of them turn in what homework he assigns, and they give him little hassle. The teachers in the city have 175 kids, almost half of whom may be absent on any given day but all of whom remain the teacher's responsibility. And those kids are a resentful, wary, often troublesome lot. Horace is relieved that he is where he is. He wonders whether any of those college teachers ever read any of the recommendations he writes each Christmas vacation.

Most jobs in the real world have a gap between what would be nice and what is possible. One adjusts. The tragedy for many high school teachers is that the gap is a chasm, not crossed by reasonable and judicious adjustments. Even after adroit accommodations and devastating compromises— only *five minutes per week* of attention of the written work of each student and an average of ten minutes of planning for each fifty-odd-minute class—the task is already crushing, in reality a sixty-hour work week. For this, Horace is paid a wage enjoyed by age-mates in semiskilled and low-pressure blue-collar jobs and by novices, twenty-five years his junior, in some other white-collar professions. Furthermore, none of these sixty-plus hours is spent in replenishing his own academic capital. That has to be done in addition, perhaps during the summer. However, he needs to earn more money then, and there is no pay for upgrading his teacher's skills. He has to take on tutoring work or increase his involvement at the liquor store.

Fortunately (from one point of view), few people seem to care whether he simply does not assign that paragraph per week, or whether he farms its criticisms out to other students. ("Exchange papers, class, and take ten minutes to grade your neighbor's essay.") He is a colorful teacher, and he knows that he can do a good job of lecturing, some of which can, in theory at least, replace the coaching that Horace knows is the heart of high school teaching. By using an overhead projector, he can publicly analyze the paragraphs of six of his students. But he will have assigned writing to all of them. As long as he does not let on which six papers he will at the last minute "pull" to analyze, he will have given real practice to all. There *are* tricks like this to use.

His classes are quiet and orderly, and he has the reputation in the community of being a good teacher. Accordingly, he gets his administrators' blessings. If he were to complain about the extent of his overload, he would find no seriously empathetic audience. Reducing teacher load is, when all the negotiating is over, a low agenda item for the unions and school boards. The administration will arrange for in-service days on "teacher burnout" (more time away from grading paragraphs) run by moonlighting education professors who will get more pay for giving a few "professional workshops" than Horace gets for a year's worth of set construction in the theater.

No one blames the system; everyone blames him. Relax, the consultants advise. Here are some exercises to help you get some perspective. Morphine, Horace thinks. It dulls my pain . . . Come now, he mutters to himself. Don't get cynical. . . . Don't keep insisting that these "experts" should try my job for a week. . . . They assure me that they *understand* me, only they say, "We hear you, Horace." I wonder who their English teachers were.

Horace's students will get into college, their parents may remember to thank him for the references he wrote for their offspring (unlikely), and the better colleges will teach the kids to write. The students who do not get the coaching at college, or who do not go to college, do not complain. No one seems upset. Just let it all continue, a conspiracy, a toleration of a chasm between the necessary and the provided and acceptance of big rhetoric and little reality. Horace dares not express his bitterness to the visitor conducting a study of high schools, because he fears he will be portrayed as a whining hypocrite.

# English, English Teaching and English Teachers: The Perceptions of 16-Year-Olds

*Brian Austin-Ward*

## Summary

As part of a study of language performance of 16-year-old students entering further education colleges, an attempt was made to discover the attitudes of these students towards English. The purpose was to find out what they thought of English at school, what they enjoyed and what they did not enjoy, of what importance they thought English to be and their reasons. To this end a questionnaire was drawn up and the responses may be summarized as follows.

The majority of students were critical of the English they were taught at secondary school, and saw little purpose in much of what they had done. They felt teachers had either concentrated on a few aspects of the subject, or attempted to cover so many aspects that they were unable to see any "core" in the subject. Teachers were described as having contradictory and conflicting approaches to English, particularly towards grammar, spelling and "correctness". This seemed to lead, in the minds of many students, to the strong conviction that English teachers were uncertain about their subject, and how to teach it. When comparisons were made with teachers of other subjects they were seen to be less professional, less competent and less well prepared. Many students gave the impression that much of what was done in English lessons made little sense, seemed of little relevance, and had given little pleasure or enjoyment. As a result, ten or eleven years of being taught English had left them with a strong sense of failure, a feeling of their own inadequacies and, above all, the conviction that "poor" English prevented academic success, restricted job opportunities, and caused others to see them as "uneducated".

## Background

Few school subjects arouse such passionate discussion as English. Controversy surrounds the whole area of English and English teaching, and has done so for more than 60 years. Indeed for most of this century the theory and practice of teaching English and the nature of the subject itself have been the center of debate. This debate, often fierce, has produced an abundance of material on the teaching of English. No school subject can have spawned as many text books as English. There has been no shortage of advice to teachers on what to teach and what not to teach, on methodology, on the

Brian Austin-Ward teaches in England at the Portsmouth Polytechnic School of Educational Studies.

From *Educational Research* 28 (1986): 32–42.
Reprinted with permission.

acquisition of language, on language and learning; indeed every aspect of the subject has been written about. Despite all this material we still know relatively little about what actually happens in the classroom: what is taught, how it is taught and, above all, how it was seen by those being taught. Even the official surveys and reports on the teaching of English have made few, if any, attempts to discover how the subject and those who teach it are observed by the learner.

There have been only two attempts to undertake a comprehensive and detailed investigation of the teaching of English. The first was the Newbolt Report (Board of Education, 1921). The report is of interest for the light it throws on the practice of English teaching in every sector of education. In fact, it provides what is conspicuously absent for most of the period 1900 to the present day, a picture of classroom practice based upon direct observation. The report found that no attempt had been made to establish a form, content and methodology appropriate to the subject. Teachers, it was felt, had failed to clarify their aims and tended to see English much as they saw other subjects: a narrow specific collection of topics or a series of detached and disparate subjects. The authors felt that many teachers saw English as synonymous with grammar and held a narrow utilitarian view of its nature and purpose.

More than 50 years later the Bullock Report (DES, 1975) found a similar situation and arrived at conclusions similar to those of the Newbolt Report. Bullock concluded that English was receiving "poor treatment" and expressed concern about the poor quality of English teaching to be found in secondary schools. It found a generally unsatisfactory level of teaching, much uncertainty and confusion over the nature of and content of English, a wide diversity of approaches and methodology and a lack of common aims and objectives. Bullock, too, found much class-room practice to be made up of a variety of separate topics and activities or concentration on a few areas. Bullock rejected the utilitarian concept of English which it found to be common among teachers and warned against the strong emphasis often placed upon the teaching of skills. It echoed the pleas of Newbolt that English should be seen not as just another subject but as the only truly liberal area of the curriculum. It found the wider role of English was seldom appreciated and rarely found in practice.

Subsequent investigations into the teaching of English have revealed a situation little changed. In a series of Working Papers, the HMI (DES, 1977, 1978, 1979) expressed dissatisfaction with the preparation given to young people for the language needs of their lives. In describing what happens in the classroom, they found the language experiences of most children in secondary school to be largely a matter of chance. They found the dominant modes to be exposition by teachers, questions and answers, the writing of notes and the writing of answers to work sheets. The pupils' own use of language they found to be subject to spasmodic correction. They conclude that the experience of many pupils must be that English itself and the language of school subjects become more and more alien during the years of secondary education and that, as a result, they participate less and less in its process.

In 1982 HMI produced a discussion paper (DES, 1982). The paper considers the effect on English teaching of the Bullock Report and of subsequent HMI surveys. The conclusions reached in this paper are based to a large extent on evidence gathered by the Inspectorate in its day-to-day work. The main conclusion it comes to is that many of the proposals made in Bullock and the suggestions in the HMI surveys have not been implemented and that the situation in English teaching remains much the same.

The Assessment of Performance Unit (APU) set out to survey language performance of 11-year-olds and 15-years-olds (Gorman *et al.*, 1981, 1982a, 1982b, 1983).

It is the conclusion of the APU that far too many pupils leave school unable to write at a level required in daily life. The APU findings support the concern expressed by the surveys and reports already mentioned.

The reports and investigations described briefly here centred almost exclusively on the teacher. This study centres on the learner. The young people who are the subject of this study confirm the conclusion drawn by the large-scale surveys and reports on the teaching of English. A majority of the sample expressed the conviction that teachers were uncertain and confused over the nature and content of English. They described a diversity of approaches and methodology and, as far as they were concerned, had not found obvious common aims and objectives in the teaching they had experienced. They held a narrow and utilitarian view of English and seemed unaware of any broader, more liberal approach to the subject. They expressed an increasing sense of alienation during their secondary schooling. Today's pupils, on the evidence of this study, seem to find the experience of English confusing and lacking in relevance.

## Sample

The students came from seven further education colleges, four in England, two in Scotland and one in Wales. These colleges represented a wide geographical spread, and ranged in size from a small rural college of further education to a very large college of technology in an inner city area. The students came from a large number of feeder schools, all comprehensive, and of differing sizes and geographical locations. A total of 487 students, aged between 16 and 17 years, who had left school within the previous year and had recently embarked on first-year craft courses in Motor Vehicle, Heavy Vehicle, Aeronautical, Marine, Electrical and General Engineering, Fabrication and Welding, Surface Finishing, Plumbing, Bricklaying, Road Construction and Building, Hairdressing and Office Studies, formed the sample.

## Procedure

A small pilot study suggested that the students would be willing and able to respond to a small number of simply worded questions. While it was appreciated that any test of attitude that included an attitude scale would provide data which could be analyzed statistically, it would inevitably restrain the responses of the students. They were therefore invited to respond in writing to five questions, and say as much or as little as they wished.

None of the questions in the questionnaire specifically asked for details of what the students had been taught in English lessons or for details of how they had been taught. However, the replies contained a great deal of information on both these areas, as well as information about the students themselves, their experiences, their perceptions of those who taught them, and their attitudes towards English. This paper summarizes not only the replies to the given questions in the questionnaire, but also the other information, comments, and opinions volunteered in the students' responses.

The questionnaire was administered during the early part of the first term of their courses in their FE colleges. Their lecturers explained the purpose of the questionnaire and made clear to the students that their names, the names of their secondary schools and present colleges would not be identified. The help given by the lecturers in the colleges is gratefully acknowledged.

195

The questions included in the questionnaire were as follows:

1. Did you like English lessons at secondary school? Please give your reasons.
2. Was English a popular subject in your class at school? Can you give any reasons?
3. Do you think English should be a compulsory subject at college? Please give your reasons.
4. What would you like to be included in classes in English at college?
5. Of what use do you think studying English will be to you in the future?

There was much common information offered in the responses to questions 1 and 2 and in the responses to questions 4 and 5. Therefore the responses to questions 1 and 2 are summarized together, as are the responses to questions 4 and 5. This summary includes extracts from the students' written responses, which are unaltered from the originals.

All the students in the sample responded to all the questions in the questionnaire. Questions 1, 2, and 3 were first classified according to affirmative/negative responses. The reasons offered in support of the affirmative/negative responses to these questions were analyzed. From this analysis a breakdown was produced. From the breakdown a number of categories emerged. These categories are used in Tables 1, 2, and 4. Questions 4 and 5 did not call for affirmative/negative responses. The preferences stated for the content of English classes at College were analyzed and categorized and are summarized in Table 3. The values the study of English were felt to have were analyzed and summarized as for questions 1, 2 and 3 (see Table 5). Although not asked to comment on English teachers, all students in the sample did so in responding to the questions. All references to English teachers were identified and analyzed and a breakdown of responses produced. From the breakdown a number of categories emerged. Tables 6 and 7 summarize the reasons given for English teachers being liked/disliked. A panel of three classifiers undertook the analysis of all responses. The panel consisted of the writer and two colleagues. Each member of the panel analyzed the responses independently. The results were compared and a final agreed analysis resulted.

## Findings

*Responses to Questions 1 and 2*

Some 55 per cent of the total sample (268) "liked" English at secondary school. This liking was, however, qualified, certain activities being enjoyed, liked, or considered useful, while others were not. Three main reasons for liking English emerged (Table 1). The first, and most popular one, seemed to be the extent to which they had been able to indulge their personal preferences; for example for discussions, for creative writing, or for spelling.

**Table 1:** Reasons for Liking English

| Reasons | Rank Order | n | % |
|---|---|---|---|
| Pupils allowed to say in choice of activities' | 1 | 173 | 65 |
| Popularity of teacher | 2 | 160 | 60 |
| Practical value of English lessons | 3 | 141 | 53 |
| Teacher explained what was being done and gave reasons | 4 | 106 | 40 |
| Lessons well organized/ planned | 6 | 93 | 35 |

## Table 1: *Continued*

| Reasons | Rank Order | n | % |
|---|---|---|---|
| Pupils' errors/mistakes explained and discussed by teacher | 6 | 93 | 35 |
| Written work commented on and discussed by teacher | 6 | 93 | 35 |
| Variety of activities in English lessons | 8 | 41 | 15 |
| Others* | 9 | 3 | 1 |

Total number of students who liked English: n = 268
*The category "others" includes a small number of
reasons not readily categorized and does not include any
single reason of particular significance.

The second, and also very popular reason for
liking English was a particular teacher. The
third reason was connected with what was
seen as the practical value that had been obtained from English lessons.

Few students expressed a liking for
English in all its various forms, their liking
tending to be limited to a small number of
activities, or in some instances, only one. A
view of English such as the one expressed by
this student, was rare:

"I liked English because there are so many different things to do, some are fun and some are
hard work, but there all interesting and useful."

Much more common were the following
views of English:

"English was lots of exercises, summaries, spelling, I liked that, I liked grammar, how to make
sentences, spelling, full stops";

"Answering questions on passages was good and
spelling tests and precis";

"Building and analyzing sentences I liked and how
to spell and using verbs";

"We did lots of essays, I liked that and we had
spelling games, I enjoyed them";

"I enjoy reading, writing, looking things up, we
did these things at school";

"We did very little discussions. I don't like
writing";

"I like doing drama";

"We were allowed to do topics on what we
wanted";

"I liked English when we did exercises';

"We had lots of discussions and watched TV
every week";

"the teacher let us sit quietly and read books";

"the teacher always asked us what we wanted to
do, other teachers don't;

"I enjoyed English because the teacher knew what
we should do".

It can be seen from these comments that the
students were far from united in what they
liked and enjoyed in English lessons. There
were some who enjoyed the learning of
"skills": spelling, punctuation, sentence building and summarizing, comprehension and essay
writing. The others, a slight majority, claimed
to have enjoyed less "formal," more
"creative" English: discussions, writing
stories and poems, reading fiction, drama and
watching films and television. It is clear from
responses to all the questions that the
majority saw the subject matter of English
lessons as a collection of discrete and disparate activities, often with little in common.

The comment *"It all depends on the
teacher"* sums up the second reason put forward for liking English. Whether English was
or was not liked seemed to depend on the
opinion held of the teacher. A number of
reasons were given for the popularity of a
teacher. Some are fairly obvious: he/she was
"kind", "approachable", "understanding",
"sympathetic", "understood my difficulties',
"helped me", and so on. Teachers who had
a sense of humour were liked, as, too, were

teachers who "trust" their pupils and treat them "properly". Some students liked English because the teacher allowed them the freedom to choose what they wanted to do, e.g.

"the teacher let groups of us teach the rest of the class";

"the teacher always asked us what we wanted to do";

the teacher let me do what I wanted".

However, for other students, English was liked because the teacher decided the content of the lesson:

"the teacher chose thing that were interesting";

"he never gave us boreing things";

"I was always happy to do what the teacher chose because it was always good";

"what ever she did was interesting because she new what she was doing".

These two views of the role of the teacher in deciding what was to be taught account for the same reason being put forward for liking and for disliking English lessons.

For others English was liked because it was felt to be practical and therefore useful. They showed a strong, if not always well-defined, conviction that the study of English would be of benefit to them. English, then, is enjoyed if it is seen to have relevance to the passing of examinations, success in other subjects and the obtaining of a job or a place in college. Lessons in which writing, spelling and the more "formal" aspects of language took place were considered enjoyable, although some students felt that "less formal" topics were also useful. Those who disliked English at school (45 per cent; 219) gave two main reasons (Table 2). One because it was perceived as "boring" and two, because the teacher was disliked. The word "boring" was used frequently when explaining why English had not been liked. High among the reasons given for this "boredom" was lack of variety in English lessons. This criticism

**Table 2:** Reasons for Disliking English

| *Reasons Order* | Rank | n | % |
|---|---|---|---|
| Unpopularity of teacher | 1 | 175 | 80 |
| Lack of variety of activities in English lessons | 2 | 164 | 75 |
| English lessons considered to have little practical value or relevance | 3 | 142 | 65 |
| No connection seen between different activities | 4 | 127 | 58 |
| Contradictory attitudes by teacher to marking and corrections | 5 | 109 | 50 |
| Lessons considered to be poorly planned and organized | 6 | 105 | 48 |
| Little opportunity for talk or discussion in English lessons | 7 | 100 | 46 |
| Pupils' problems/mistakes not discussed by teacher | 8 | 98 | 45 |
| Teacher considered to lack qualifications for teaching English | 9 | 26 | 12 |
| Lack of discipline in English lessons | 10 | 25 | 11 |
| Others* | 11 | 3 | 1 |

Total number of students who disliked English: n = 219
*The category "others" includes a small number of reasons not readily categorized and does not include any single reason of particular significance.

was levelled less against a particular activity than against what was seen as excessive concern with a particular activity, as can be seen from the following remarks:

"because what we did most of the time was to read books";

"boreing just writting";

it was the same old stuff every time we had English";

we had English to often";

we just did loads of writting";

we were always doing nouns and pronouns and things";

English was always grammer things";

answering questions on passages al the time".

Some of the "more creative" activities fared little better:

"always writing poems is boreing";

"I got sick of discussing and talking";

"we always to create, that was boring";

"we had a book with miserable things in it like starving, vandals, poor people and politics we had to taught and write about them daily".

It seems that it was not a particular aspect or topic which caused boredom, too much creative writing being as boring as too much grammar. Boredom resulted from lack of variety in English lessons. A further cause of boredom was what was felt to be lack of direction in the lessons:

"teacher couldn't discipline us so lessons were boreing";

"People got easily bored and this caused them to play the fool";

"we were all muking about and fed up";

"when the teachers were supposed to be teaching English, they sat in the tea room hiding";

"the teacher did not make us do proper work";

"I couldn't see why we were doing things";

"it didn't seem to lead anywhere".

Interestingly, both lessons controlled by the teacher and lessons in which the teacher exercised little control were criticized.

*Responses to Question 3*

Some 79 percent (384) of the total sample (487) thought English should be included in the courses they were following at college. The majority of these thought that studying English would help them in their careers (Table 3).

They saw English as a means to an end; it was considered to have little value beyond a strictly utilitarian one. The subject matter of English was also seen from a strictly utilitarian position. English was seen as a number of skills to be learned and mastered. The opinion was expressed time after time that studying English helps spelling, grammar and punctuation, and that English helps people to "speak properly", "use the right words", "lose your accent", "speak nicely", "be able to understand long words", and many other variations of these ideas. The ends to which these skills may be put were also narrow and limited, and restricted almost wholly to the needs of work and career. A competent command of written English was necessary to write reports, workcards, job sheets, letters, reports on patients in hospital, etc. Few students saw English as being of any help, other than in helping to cope with the demands of a job or in acquiring a better job. A good command of spoken language was also felt to be of help in the work situation:

"if you dont speak properly people will think your stupid";

"if you cant speak well theyll say you cant do the job";

"no one wants a secretary with a common way of speaking".

Many teachers of English would find these reasons narrow, unrealistic and possibly inappropriate. However, it is clear that many students had these expectations and felt that they had not been fulfilled at school.

**Table 3:** Reasons for Wanting to Continue to Study English

| Reasons | Rank Order | n | % |
|---|---|---|---|
| to learn to spell | 1 | 300 | 78 |
| to learn correct grammar | 2 | 295 | 77 |
| to learn to "speak properly" | 3 | 180 | 47 |
| to choose and use correct words | 4 | 174 | 45 |
| to lose accent | 5 | 150 | 39 |
| to gain self-confidence in speaking and writing | 6 | 140 | 36 |
| to express views and opinions | 7 | 130 | 34 |
| to write letters | 8 | 126 | 33 |
| to fill in forms | 9 | 100 | 26 |
| to avoid being thought uneducated | 10 | 92 | 24 |
| to acquire self respect | 11 | 69 | 18 |
| to get a "good job" | 12 | 60 | 16 |
| to impress people | 13 | 47 | 12 |
| to be thought the equal of others | 14 | 15 | 4 |

Total number of students who wanted to continue with English at college: n = 384

**Table 4:** Reasons for Rejecting the Study of English at College

| Reasons | Rank Order | n | % |
|---|---|---|---|
| English considered to have nothing to do with college course | 1 | 90 | 87 |
| English not needed in job/trade | 2 | 86 | 93 |
| English already done at school | 3 | 78 | 76 |
| English disliked in school | 4 | 75 | 73 |
| No good at English | 5 | 70 | 68 |
| Too late to improve English | 6 | 61 | 59 |
| No wish to repeat "failure" at school | 7 | 12 | 12 |

Total number of students who did not want to continue with English at College: n = 103.

It is possible to detect in some replies to this question the feeling that English may have something more to offer. A small number of replies, around ten per cent, referred to English as:

"the most important subject";

"without English you can't learn other subjects";

"you must understand your own language before you can learn others".

and even one reply in which it was stated that

"English is the most important think you learn, you need it for everything you do in life."

Twenty-one per cent (103) rejected the suggestion that English should be part of the course they were following at college. All were adamant in the belief that English would be of no help to them, and that it had nothing to do with the courses they were following (Table 4).

The responses to question 3 show many wanted to learn to "speak properly" and to lose their "accents". The opinion was expressed that having an accent would prove a disadvantage in obtaining a job and in being accepted as "educated". This concern is perhaps surprising and worrying. It is said that we are less concerned with accent than we once were. These students seem convinced that the way a person speaks is still important.

Having "done" English at school, they saw no value in doing it again. All had disliked English at school and were against the inclusion in their college courses of what they saw as another subject of the school curriculum. They seemed to have little idea of what English classes were intended to achieve:

"Its a waste of time and dosn't help a mechenic";

"We have done it at school lots of times";

"We should have learned enogh of it by now";

"I hate English, can't stand it never could".

A small number mentioned their own lack of success in English at school as a reason for rejecting the idea of continuing with English at college. They felt themselves to be very poor at English, and that to do English again would compound earlier failure. This is in contrast to the majority who gave lack of success in English as one of the main reasons for wanting to continue with English at college.

*Responses to Questions 4 and 5*

The majority of students wrote about the sort of English they thought would be of practical use to them (Table 5). About 60 per cent of replies concentrated on what can be described as the study of English for "profit", while around 20 per cent concentrated on English for "pleasure". Rather more expressed non-utilitarian attitudes in response to this question than in response to question 3. The remainder were opposed to the suggestion of compulsory English. "Discussions" were a popular choice across all courses. The attraction of "discussion" seemed to be the freedom to talk and to express their own ideas, and quite a number added that the subject must be

**Table 5:** Preferences for English Classes at College

| Preferences | Rank Order | n | % |
|---|---|---|---|
| Discussion/talk | 1 | 334 | 87 |
| Opportunities to express ideas | 2 | 327 | 85 |
| Spelling | 3 | 300 | 78 |
| Filling in forms | 4 | 249 | 65 |
| Eradicating accent | 5 | 245 | 64 |
| Learning to speak "correctly" | 6 | 240 | 63 |
| Plays | 7 | 23 | 6 |
| Reading and writing poetry | 8 | 20 | 5 |
| Going to the theatre | 9 | 15 | 4 |
| Discussing TV programmes | 10 | 10 | 3 |

Total number of students who wanted to continue with English at College: n = 384.

of the student's choice, and, perhaps unrealistically, that there should be little, preferably no, interference from the teacher. Other popular choices among the "utilitarian" aspects of English were spelling, filling in forms, learning to speak "properly" and the eradication of accents. The remaining choices were concerned largely with a desire to learn the mechanical skills of language and to acquire an acceptable standard of spoken and written English. No attempt was made to define what this standard is, but it was for many students as real as was their conviction that they fell short of the standard.

A few students (some ten per cent) expressed genuine enjoyment in plays, drama, reading and writing poetry, reading and writing stories, going to the theatre, seeing a Shakespeare play, and a whole variety of other subjects. The majority of students considered that English would be of use to them in their futures. Not one student suggested that English might help in living a happier, fuller life. For the majority of students the use that they thought English would be to them in the future can best be shown by the following quotations:

"It will do a great deal for me. I will be able to pronounce words properly write words down without having to think and above all to write words that my employers and Friends will understand";

"Fill up forms properly, write properly';

"communicate with different clases of people";

"not look a fool in front of educated people";

"get lots more knowledge so people will respect me";

"have my own bisiness one day-perhaps".

*Perceptions of English Teachers*

None of the questions made reference to teachers. However, all students commented on English teachers in their responses to questions 1, 2, 3 and 4. Tables 6 and 7 summarize the reasons put forward for the popularity and un-popularity of English teachers.

It is evident from the findings that the majority of students in the study were critical, to some degree, of the English teaching they had received in secondary school. The fault lay, in their eyes, with the teachers. A high standard of competence was expected and many students found this lacking.

Among the most frequently mentioned criticisms of English teachers were: that they dominated lessons, imposed their views, did not appreciate how difficult English was, did not explain what was to be done, or how, or why. Indeed it is clear that many students did not appreciate why they were doing particular aspects of English. They seemed just as unclear why they wrote essays, learned grammar, or wrote creatively. If their teach-

ers did attempt to discuss with their pupils the relevance and purpose of what they were doing, they seem to have been unsuccessful. In none of the comments was it possible to detect an awareness of the notion of "language across the curriculum".

**Table 6:** Reasons for Popularity of English Teachers

| *Reasons* | *Rank Order* | *n* | *%* |
|---|---|---|---|
| Teacher was kind/approachable/helpful | 1 | 425 | 87 |
| Teacher allowed pupils say in choice of activities | 2 | 420 | 86 |
| Teacher understood pupils' problems/difficulties with English | 3 | 415 | 85 |
| Teacher had clear idea of what to teach | 4 | 410 | 84 |
| Trusted pupils/treated them fairly | 5 | 400 | 82 |
| Teacher explained what was being done in lesson and gave reasons | 3 | 95 | 81 |
| Lessons planned/organized properly | 7 | 391 | 80 |
| Teacher sought pupils' views | 8 | 380 | 78 |
| Teacher respected pupils' views | 9 | 376 | 77 |
| Teacher was enthusiastic about English | 10 | 253 | 52 |
| Teacher made English lessons enjoyable | 11 | 210 | 43 |

| Reasons | Rank Order | n | % |
|---|---|---|---|
| Teacher was able to control class/keep discipline | 12 | 197 | 40 |
| Pupils were able to work hard and learn in English lessons | 13 | 100 | 21 |
| Teacher considered to like teaching | 14 | 50 | 10 |
| Teacher had sense of humour | 15 | 42 | 9 |

Total number of students who referred in their responses to teachers: n = 487

The criticism levelled against some of those who taught English was most explicit. Reference was made to lack of interest displayed by teachers:

"the teacher did not bother with us";

"he did not bother to correct them" (what they had written);

"the teacher did not explain what we were to do or why";

"they were interested in the bright kids really";

and to lack sympathy from teachers:

"we were pushed around so much, the teacher didn't understand how difficult English was";

and to the entire monopoly of the class by the teacher:

"She cared nothing for our views on anything. If we dared to question her she told us to shut up."

References were made time and again to the fact that English teachers seemed unclear as to what to teach, and that not only did they teach a variety of different things, but that different teachers seemed to have different views as to what constituted the subject mat-

**Table 7:** Reasons for the Unpopularity of English Teachers

| Reasons | Rank Order | n | % |
|---|---|---|---|
| Teacher felt to lack interest in subject | 1 | 429 | 88 |
| Teacher did not appreciate pupils' difficulties | 2 | 420 | 86 |
| Teacher thought to be unclear as to what to teach | 3 | 414 | 85 |
| Teacher monopolized lessons | 4 | 410 | 84 |
| Teacher imposed own views | 5 | 400 | 82 |
| Teacher corrected too harshly | 6 | 376 | 77 |
| Teacher did not correct written work | 7 | 370 | 76 |
| Teacher did not explain activities and why they were being done | 8 | 350 | 72 |
| Teacher did not discuss students' work | 9 | 300 | 62 |
| Teacher considered to be "unqualified" to teach English | 10 | 46 | 9 |

Total number of students who referred in their responses to teachers: n = 487

ter of English. A number of students were clearly confused by working with one teacher who seemed to concentrate on grammar, sentences and précis, and with another who spent much of the time asking the class to write poems, and perhaps with a third teacher who was following what they saw as a social studies syllabus, discussing "poverty, abortion, politics".

It is clear that, in the eyes of many, those who taught them English lacked credibility. Many expressed the opinion that they had not been taught by "proper" English teachers. Unfavourable comparisons were made between those who taught them English and those who taught them other subjects. Those who taught other subjects knew what to teach, "how to teach" and were therefore "better teachers". It was clear that a number shared this view:

"Our other teachers knew what they were going to do with for all term and some used to tell us. I think English teachers make up there lessons from day to day."

Also evident from many comments is the conviction that the pupils in higher streams, the top forms, the brighter pupils, get the best teachers.

## Discussion

Over the past few decades many school subjects have undergone some degree of self-questioning and re-definition. They seem to have emerged with new formulae, new directions and some measure of agreement among teachers. Few school subjects seem to have experienced the uncertainty of English about its nature, purpose and methodology. Indeed the question as to whether English should exist at all has been debated. These uncertainties can be found in almost all discussions about the teaching of English since the early 1950s.

Dixon (1967), in attempting to produce what he called a map of English teaching, defined three main models of English teaching. The first centres on skills, the second one stresses the transmission of cultural heritage, and the third focusses on personal growth. Dixon sees the "skills" model as concentrating on the teaching of spelling, punctuation, vocabulary, sentence building and comprehension. The "cultural heritage" model he sees as being based on the belief that by studying "great literature" pupils would experience a variety of models of good writing and thereby develop their own writing. The third model focusses on "personal growth" and stresses the need to re-examine the learning processes and the meaning to the individual of what he or she is doing in English lessons.

It is not possible to say which model is the dominant one today or indeed how many teachers may try to combine the three approaches. However, this study supports the findings of Bullock that teachers have not abandoned the teaching of skills. From the accounts of these students of what they were taught in English, just as many teachers see their aim to be the ensuring of the linguistic competence of their pupils, as see personal growth and development as their main aim (see Table 2). The number of pupils taught grammar, spelling and punctuation is almost equal to those who describe being taught "creative" English. That these two approaches exist side by side is well illustrated by the reactions of the young people in this study to marking and correction of written work. This aspect of English teaching was the one most clearly seen as confusing and contradictory. Criticism of the way teachers marked English work was made by many students (some 75 per cent). Complaints were divided equally against teachers who marked a lot and those who it was claimed seldom marked written work. Strict marking, it was felt, destroyed confidence, leading ultimately to the pupil giving up—many admitted to having done so. Teachers who did not explain why things were wrong and also teachers who used what were felt to be destructive comments came in for criticism. Just as many complaints were made against teachers who, it was claimed, did not mark, correct or comment on work. Students complained that they could not hope to improve unless they were given some idea of their weaknesses and mistakes. As one put it:

"All our stories were always goods, there was never anything wrong with them. We could not all be perfect."

Another complained he could not spell because,

"She would not tell us when our spelling was wrong so we never learnt it."

Not surprisingly those who had been exposed to both these approaches were confused and dissatisfied.

In reply to question 4, "What would you like to be included in English at college?", many students opted for discussion, talk, etc. Many complained at being given little opportunity to develop skill in speaking during English lessons. For others, high among the reasons for liking English lessons were the opportunities to speak, express their opinions and air their views. More than half the students who mentioned spoken English felt this had been a neglected area in their English lessons. It is this clear dichotomy in approach that creates the impression in the mind of the learner that English teachers are unclear as to what to teach and are therefore uncertain, confused and inept, and seem so when compared with teachers of other subjects. The "skills" versus "creativity" controversy which has bedevilled the teaching of English for more than two decades and the plethora of conflicting advice offered to those teaching English have resulted in uncertainty in the minds of teachers and confusion in the minds of their pupils.

The present confused state of English, so vividly illustrated by the experiences of pupils, is certainly due to uncertainty in the minds of those teaching English and disagreement amongst academics and experts. This situation may well be compounded by

findings of the Bullock Report that 30 per cent of those involved in English teaching in secondary schools have no qualification for teaching English; and that, of those teaching English, only 37 per cent spent all their time on it, 25 per cent were teaching it for more than half their time and 38 per cent less than half. The report concluded that no other secondary school subject is staffed by such a large number of teachers from other areas of the curriculum.

## Conclusions

The experiences and perceptions of the young people expressed in this study have confirmed the impressions given by successive reports and surveys. This study can claim to be unique in having obtained from the pupils their view of English and of English teaching.

It is surely important that we make ourselves aware of the expectations that our pupils have of us as teachers. It is important too that we attempt to discover and understand their perceptions of us as teachers and of our teaching. Pupils should not see English as just another subject. They should not view the subject matter of English solely in terms of skills. They should not measure success in English by the passing of examinations. It is the teacher who has the task of explaining to those he or she teaches what English is, what his/her aims are, and the reasons for the various activities the pupils are asked to experience. The idea of creative writing, personal growth and all the benefits associated with this approach need to be explained and discussed.

Pupils need to be told why, for example, spelling can be sometimes ignored in assessing a piece of personal writing and why at other times the teacher will correct misspellings. Tone, style, organization, presentation, sense of audience—all these areas may well be to the leaner imprecise and difficult to grasp and comprehend. They need to be explored and discussed with the learner. Teachers also need to show a greater sense of sensitivity to the language needs of their pupils and be aware of their self-consciousness. As this study shows, young people are only too aware of their real or imagined deficiencies and inadequacies. They need the right kind of encouragement and guidance in actively using the developing language, both spoken and written. To be convinced, as many of the young people in this study are, that after 11 years of English they are no good at their native language, and feel that when they write or speak they will expose their inadequacies to others, can do little for the development of a positive self concept.

# Sequence Three

## Race and Ethnicity in Our Families and Lives

We celebrate ethnic diversity in Chicago, yet we cannot deny that it is a divided city, often called the most segregated city in the United States. Indeed, one recent study made the point that the geographic and social isolation of ethnic groups in Chicago breeds continuing feelings of misunderstanding, suspicion, and stereotyping. A college or university, however, can function to counteract ethnic isolation. Its classrooms are the obvious places for members of different groups to become acquainted, establish a dialogue, and perhaps dispel some of the prejudices that they might harbor.

With the goal of establishing such a dialogue, this sequence invites you to examine your own and others' experiences of race and ethnicity. The sequence asks you to consider how difficult it might be to maintain an ethnic identity in the midst of mainstream American society, and it leads you to explore the ethnic dilemma: attempting to overcome isolation by assimilating into mainstream society can isolate a person from friends and relatives still immersed in the native cultures. As a possible solution to this problem, the sequence offers for you consideration the idea of multicultural education.

### Assignment One

*Readings:*

Ralph Ellison, "Prologue" to *Invisible Man.*
Simon J. Ortiz, ".,.;".".
Maxine Hong Kingston, "Girlhood Among Ghosts."
Alice Walker, "When the Other Dancer is the Self."

*Option One:* Race and ethnicity play determining roles in the lives of Maxine Hong Kingston, Simon Ortiz, Alice Walker, and Ralph Ellison's "invisible man." Write an essay in which you clarify how important race and ethnicity are to your identity and life. Consider the following questions, plus any others you think are pertinent to your essay: How conscious has your family been of your ethnic heritage? How have they shown this consciousness? How aware

are you about your race and cultural background? How, if at all, do you show your awareness and concern?

*Option Two:* Alice Walker, Maxine Hong Kingston, and Simon Ortiz all write about growing up different. Walker is African-American and has one blind eye. Kingston is Chinese-American in a white, English-speaking world. Ortiz is Native-American growing up with an oral language tradition. All three tell stories of isolation and sadness because they are somehow different. However, they grow up to be wonderful writers and role models. Who hasn't felt different at one point or another in his or her life? Write an essay in which you describe a time when you felt isolated or different—perhaps because of your language, your cultural background, your gender, or your ethnicity. For example, have you ever been the only woman in a room full of men? The only one in a group who didn't speak "good" English? The only African-American in an all-white neighborhood? The possibilities are limitless. Include in your essay details about the circumstances of your isolation, as well as details describing your feelings about those circumstances.

# Assignment Two

*Readings:*

David Mura, "Strangers in the Village."
Carlos Fuentes, "How I Started to Write."

As you read these essays, ask yourself questions about what happens when ethnic cultures come in contact with each other. Then proceed with either Option One or Option Two.

*Option One:* Write an essay in which you synthesize these two essays for a reader who hasn't read them. Consider the following questions, and any others you think may be pertinent. How do Fuentes and Mura describe the relationship between European cultural traditions and Third World (Latin American, Asian, African) cultural traditions? Does either author believe that either tradition is more important than the other to study? What did Fuentes' international upbringing in the U.S. Mexico, Chile, Argentina, and Switzerland teach him about cultures and their contact with one another? What did David Mura come to learn about the rage of the minorities and the guilt of the majority? Of what relevance to Mura's argument is the example with which he begins and ends the essay—the relationship between the middle class woman Barbra and her servant Bertha?

*Option Two:* Both Fuentes and Mura deal with discrimination as it affected their lives. When a person feels racial and ethnic discrimination, often he or she also feels isolated and alienated. Interview someone who has had to deal with these feelings, preferably someone who immigrated to the United States from another country. Write an essay for an audience of your peers in which you describe this person's experiences, his or her struggles to cope, and his or her ability (or lack of it) to adjust to mainstream American society. Before you conduct the interview, prepare specific questions about adjustment experiences. You may want to ask the person about how he or she adjusted to food, climate, clothing, customs, male-female interactions, schooling, language, or any other aspect you think is important.

# Assignment Three

*Reading:*

Samuel Betances, "Puerto Rican Youth."

*Option One:* All the authors you have read for Assignments One, Two, and Three explore distinctive features of different cultures: Chinese-American, Native American, African-American, and Puerto Rican. Write an essay in which you explain to your classmates one or more distinctive features of your ethnic heritage—for example, its beliefs, heroes, historical events and experiences, traditions, customs, folktales, sayings, holidays, foods, and so on. If you can, compare and contrast the feature or features you have chosen to the corresponding one(s) in "mainstream" American culture—for example, dating and marriage customs in your ethnic culture to those in "mainstream" America. The purpose of your essay is to enable your classmates to get to know you and your cultural background better and for them to see American ways from different perspectives.

*Option Two:* Samuel Betances writes that many second-generation Puerto Rican youth in the United States long for an identity—for a category to fit into. Some of the other authors you have read in this sequence, however, suggest an opposing tactic—namely that people who come from certain cultures want to isolate themselves and not fit into a predictable group. Write an essay in which you consider which is a better attitude. Should people with a strong sense of their ethnic culture try to share their identity with others who have things in common with them, or should they try to set themselves apart from such groups? Is there something in between. In your essay, refer to both your own ideas and experiences and to those developed in the readings for this sequence.

# Assignment Four

*Readings:*

Michael Novak, "White Ethnic."
Nathan Glazer, "A Happy Ending?"
Frederick Douglass, "Life as a Slave."

Thus far in this sequence you have examined the importance of race and ethnicity in your own life, studied what happens when people of different cultures come into contact with each other, and considered the degree to which people of all ethnic groups should try to "blend" into the mainstream culture. In this assignment, you need to confront the issue of racial and ethnic identity by proposing a course of action for education in the U.S. As you know, people of all backgrounds come together in America's schools. Consider whether you think some specific segment of American education—its elementary schools, its high schools, or its colleges and universities—or *all* of these segments should try to teach awareness of the many cultures represented by the students. What role, if any, should public education play in helping different ethnic groups preserve and promote their special features? Should the promotion of different ethnic and racial traditions be a feature of private education rather than public? Develop a specific plan for some segment of American education to incorporate your vision of multiculture education. Write an essay that would persuade the appropriate group of people—a group of teachers, a community group, a school board, a college or university department—to adopt your plan. Refer both to your own ideas and experiences and to any relevant points from the readings you have done for this sequence.

# Invisible Man

*Ralph Ellison*

## Prologue

I am an invisible man. No, I am not a spook like those who haunted Edgar Allan Poe; nor am I one of your Hollywood-movie ectoplasms. I am a man of substance, of flesh and bone, fiber and liquids—and I might even be said to possess a mind. I am invisible, understand, simply because people refuse to see me. Like the bodiless heads you see sometimes in circus sideshows, it is as though I have been surrounded by mirrors or hard, distorting glass. When they approach me they see only my surroundings, themselves, or figments of their imagination—indeed, everything and anything except me.

Nor is my invisibility exactly a matter of a biochemical accident to my epidermis. That invisibility to which I refer occurs because of a peculiar disposition of the eyes of those with whom I come in contact. A matter of the construction of their *inner* eyes, those eyes with which they look through their physical eyes upon reality. I am not complaining, nor am I protesting either. It is sometimes advantageous to be unseen, although it is most often rather wearing on the nerves. Then too, you're constantly being bumped against by those of poor vision. Or

Ralph Ellison is a novelist, critic, and cultural historian whose *Invisible Man* won the National Book Award in 1953.

again, you often doubt if you really exist. You wonder whether you aren't simply a phantom in other people's minds. Say, a figure in a nightmare which the sleeper tries with all his strength to destroy. It's when you feel like this that, out of resentment, you begin to bump people back. And, let me confess, you feel that way most of the time. You ache with the need to convince yourself that you do exist in the real world, that you're a part of all the sound and anguish, and you strike out with your fists, you curse and you swear to make them recognize you. And, alas, it's seldom successful.

One night I accidentally bumped into a man, and perhaps because of the near darkness he saw me and called me an insulting name. I sprang at him, seized his coat lapels and demanded that he apologize. He was a tall blond man, and as my face came close to his he looked insolently out of his blue eyes and cursed me, his breath hot in my face as he struggled. I pulled his chin down sharp upon the crown of my head, butting him as I had seen the West Indians do, and I felt his flesh tear and the blood gush out, and I yelled, "Apologize! Apologize!" But he continued to curse and struggle, and I butted him again and again until he went down heavily, on his knees, profusely bleeding. I kicked him repeatedly, in a frenzy because he still uttered insults though his lips were frothy with blood. Oh yes, I kicked him! And in my outrage I got out my knife and prepared to slit his throat, right there beneath the lamplight in the deserted street, holding him in the collar with one hand, and opening the knife with my teeth—when it occurred to me that the man had not *seen* me, actually; that he, as far as he knew, was in the midst of a walking nightmare! And I stopped the blade, slicing the air as I pushed him away, letting him fall back to the street. I stared at him hard as the lights of a car stabbed through the darkness. He lay there, moaning on the asphalt; a man almost killed by a phantom. It unnerved me. I was both disgusted and ashamed. I was like a drunken man myself, wavering about on weakened legs. Then I was amused: Something in this man's thick head had sprung out and beaten, him within an inch of his life. I began to laugh at this crazy discovery. Would he have awakened at the point of death? Would Death himself have freed him for wakeful living? But I didn't linger. I ran away into the dark, laughing so hard I feared I might rupture myself. The next day I saw his picture in the *Daily News,* beneath a caption stating that the had been "mugged." Poor fool, poor blind fool, I thought with sincere compassion, mugged by an invisible man!

Most of the time (although I do not choose as I once did to deny the violence of my days by ignoring it) I am not so overtly violent. I remember that I am invisible and walk softly so as not to awaken the sleeping ones. Sometimes it is best not to awaken them; there are few things in the world as dangerous as sleepwalkers. I learned in time though that it is possible to carry on a fight against them without their realizing it. For instance, I have been carrying on a fight with Monopolated Light & Power for some time now. I use their service and pay them nothing at all, and they don't know it. Oh, they suspect that power is being drained off, but they don't know where. All they know is that according to the master meter back there in their power station a hell of a lot of free cur-

rent is disappearing somewhere into the jungle of Harlem. The joke, of course, is that I don't live in Harlem but in a border area. Several years ago (before I discovered the advantages of being invisible) I went through the routine process of buying service and paying their outrageous rates. But no more. I gave up all that, along with my apartment, and my old way of life: That way based upon the fallacious assumption that I, like other men, was visible. Now, aware of my invisibility, I live rent-free in a building rented strictly to whites, in a section of the basement that was shut off and forgotten during the nineteenth century, which I discovered when I was trying to escape in the night from Ras the Destroyer. But that's getting too far ahead of the story, almost to the end, although the end is in the beginning and lies far ahead.

The point now is that I found a home—or a hole in the ground, as you will. Now don't jump to the conclusion that because I call my home a "hole" it is damp and cold like a grave; there are cold holes and warm holes. Mine is a warm hole. And remember, a bear retires to his hole for the winter and lives until spring; then he comes strolling out like the Easter chick breaking from its shell. I say all this to assure you that it is incorrect to assume that, because I'm invisible and live in a hole, I am dead. I am neither dead nor in a state of suspended animation. Call me Jack-the-Bear, for I am in a state of hibernation.

My hole is warm and full of light. Yes, *full* of light. I doubt if there is a brighter spot in all New York than this hole of mine, and I do not exclude Broadway. Or the Empire State Building on a photographer's dream night. But that is taking advantage of you. Those two spots are among the darkest of our whole civilization—pardon me, our whole *culture* (an important distinction, I've heard)—which might sound like a hoax, or a contradiction, but that (by contradiction, I mean) is how the world moves: Not like an arrow, but a boomerang. (Beware of those who speak of the *spiral* of history; they are preparing a boomerang. Keep a steel helmet handy.) I know; I have been boomeranged across my head so much that I now can see the darkness of lightness. And I love light. Perhaps you'll think it strange that an invisible man should need light, desire light, love light. But maybe it is exactly because I *am* invisible. Light confirms my reality, gives birth to my form. A beautiful girl once told me of a recurring nightmare in which she lay in the center of a large dark room and felt her face expand until it filled the whole room, becoming a formless mass while her eyes ran in bilious jelly up the chimney. And so it is with me. Without light I am not only invisible, but formless as well; and to be unaware of one's form is to live a death. I myself, after existing some twenty years, did not become alive until I discovered my invisibility.

That is why I fight my battle with Monopolated Light & Power. The deeper reason, I mean: It allows me to feel my vital aliveness. I also fight them for taking so much of my money before I learned to protect myself. In my hole in the basement there are exactly 1,369 lights. I've wired the entire ceiling, every inch of it. And not with fluorescent bulbs, but with the older, more-expensive-to-operate kind, the filament type. An act of sabotage, you know. I've already begun to wire the wall. A junk man I know, a man of vision, has supplied me with wire and sockets. Nothing, storm or flood, must get in the way of our need for light and ever more and brighter light. The truth is the light and light is the truth. When I finish all four walls, then I'll start on the floor. Just how that will go, I don't know. Yet when you have lived invisible as long as I have you develop a certain ingenuity. I'll solve the problem. And maybe I'll invent a gadget to place my coffee pot on the fire while I lie in bed, and even invent a gadget to warm my bed—like the fellow I saw in one of the picture magazines who made himself a gadget to warm his shoes! Though invisible, I am in the great American tradition of tinkers. That makes me kin to Ford, Edison and Franklin. Call me, since I have a theory and a concept, a "thinker-tinker." Yes, I'll warm my shoes; they need it, they're usually full of holes. I'll do that and more.

Now I have one radio-phonograph; I plan to have five. There is a certain acoustic deadness in my hole, and when I have music I want to *feel* its vibration, not only with my ear but with my whole body. I'd like to hear five recordings of Louis Armstrong playing and singing "What Did I Do to Be so Black and Blue"—all at the same time. Sometimes now I listen to Louis while I have my favorite dessert of vanilla ice cream and sloe gin. I pour the red liquid over the white mound, watching it glisten and the vapor rising as Louis bends that military instrument into a beam of lyrical sound. Perhaps I like Louis Armstrong because he's made poetry out of being invisible. I think it must be because he's unaware that he *is* invisible. And my own grasp of invisibility aids me to understand his music. Once when I asked for a cigarette, some jokers gave me a reefer, which I lighted when I got home and sat listening to my phonograph. It was a strange evening. Invisibility, let me explain, gives one a slightly different sense of time, you're never quite on the beat. Sometimes you're ahead and sometimes behind. Instead of the swift and imperceptible flowing of time, you are aware of its nodes, those points where time stands still or from which it leaps ahead. And you slip into the breaks and look around. That's what you hear vaguely in Louis' music.

Once I saw a prizefighter boxing a yokel. The fighter was swift and amazingly scientific. His body was one violent flow of rapid rhythmic action. He hit the yokel a hundred times while the yokel held up his arms in stunned surprise. But suddenly the yokel, rolling about in the gale of boxing gloves, struck one blow and knocked science, speed and footwork as cold as a well-digger's posterior. The smart money hit the canvas. The long shot got the nod. The yokel had simply stepped inside of his opponent's sense of time. So under the spell of the reefer I discovered a new analytical way of listening to music. The unheard sounds came through, and each melodic line existed of itself, stood out clearly from all the rest, said its piece, and waited patiently for the other voices to speak. That night I found myself hearing not only in time, but in space as well. I not only entered the music but descended, like Dante, into its depths. And *beneath the swiftness of the hot tempo there was a slower tempo and a cave and I entered it and looked around and heard an old woman singing a spiritual as full of Weltschmerz as flamenco, and beneath that lay a still lower level on which I saw a beautiful girl the color of ivory pleading in a voice like my mother's as she stood before a group of slaveowners who bid for her naked body, and below that I found a lower level and a more rapid tempo and I heard someone shout:*

*"Brothers and sisters, my text this morning is the 'Blackness of Blackness.' "*

*And a congregation of voices answered: "That blackness is most black, brother, most black . . ."*

*"In the beginning . . ."*

*"At the very start," they cried.*

*". . . there was blackness . . ."*

*"Preach it . . ."*

*". . . and the sun . . ."*

*"The sun, Lawd . . ."*

*". . . was bloody red . . ."*

*"Red . . ."*

*"Now black is . . ." the preacher shouted.*

*"Bloody . . ."*

*"I said black is . . ."*

*"Preach it, brother . . ."*

*". . . an' black ain't . . ."*

*"Red, Lawd, red: He said it's red!"*

*"Amen, brother . . ."*

*"Black will git you . . ."*

*"Yes, it will . . ."*

*"Yes, it will . . ."*

*". . . an' black won't . . ."*

*"Naw, it won't!"*

*"It do . . ."*

*"It do, Lawd . . ."*

*". . . an' it don't."*

*"Halleluiah . . ."*

*". . . It'll put you, glory, glory, Oh my Lawd, in the WHALE'S BELLY."*

*"Preach it, dear brother . . ."*

*". . . an' make you tempt . . ."*

*"Good God a-mighty!"*

*"Old Aunt Nelly!"*

*"Black will make you . . ."*

*"Black . . ."*

*". . . or black will un-make you."*

*"Ain't it the truth, Lawd?"*

*And at that point a voice of trombone timbre screamed at me, "Git out of here, you fool! Is you ready to commit treason?"*

*And I tore myself away, hearing the old singer of spirituals moaning, "Go curse your God, boy, and die."*

*I stopped and questioned her, asked her what was wrong.*

*"I dearly loved my master, son," she said.*

*"You should have hated him," I said.*

*"He gave me several sons," she said, "and because I loved my sons I learned to love their father though I hated him too."*

*"I too have become acquainted with ambivalence," I said. "That's why I'm here."*

*"What's that?"*

"Nothing, a word that doesn't explain it. Why do you moan?"

"I moan this way 'cause he's dead," she said.

"Then tell me, who is that laughing upstairs?"

"Them's my sons. They glad."

"Yes, I can understand that too," I said.

"I laughs too, but I moans too. He promised to set us free but he never could bring hisself to do it. Still I loved him . . ."

"Loved him? You mean . . .?"

"Oh yes, but I loved something else even more."

"What more?"

"Freedom."

"Freedom," I said. "Maybe freedom lies in hating."

"Naw, son, it's in loving. I loved him and give him the poison and he withered away like a frost-bit apple. Them boys woulda tore him to pieces with they homemade knives."

"A mistake was made somewhere," I said, "I'm confused." And I wished to say other things, but the laughter upstairs became too loud and moan-like for me and I tried to break out of it, but I couldn't. Just as I was leaving I felt an urgent desire to ask her what freedom was and went back. She sat with her head in her hands, moaning softly; her leather-brown face was filled with sadness.

"Old woman, what is this freedom you love so well?" I asked around a corner of my mind.

She looked surprised, then thoughtful, then baffled. "I done forgot, son. It's all mixed up. First I think it's one thing, then I think it's another. It gits my head to spinning. I guess now it ain't nothing but knowing how to say what I got up in my head. But it's a hard job, son. Too much is done happen to me in too short a time. Hit's like I have a fever. Ever' time I starts to walk my head gits to swirling and I falls down. Or if it ain't that, it's the boys; they gits to laughing and wants to kill up the white folks. They's bitter, that's what they is . . ."

"But what about freedom?"

"Leave me 'lone, boy; my head aches!"

I left her, feeling dizzy myself. I didn't get far.

Suddenly one of the sons, a big fellow six feet tall, appeared out of nowhere and struck me with his fist.

"What's the matter, man?" I cried.

"You made Ma cry!"

"But how?" I said, dodging a blow.

"Askin' her them questions, that's how. Git outa here and stay, and next time you got questions like that, ask yourself!"

He held me in a grip like cold stone, his fingers fastening upon my windpipe until I thought I would suffocate before he finally allowed me to go. I stumbled about dazed, the music beating hysterically in my ears. It was dark. My head cleared and I wandered down a dark narrow passage, thinking I heard his footsteps hurrying behind me. I was sore, and into my being had come a profound craving for tranquillity, for peace and quiet, a state I felt I could never achieve. For one thing, the trumpet was blaring and the rhythm was too hectic. A tom-tom beating like heart-thuds began drowning out the trumpet, filling my ears. I longed for water and I heard it rushing through the cold mains my fingers touched as I felt my way, but I couldn't stop to search because of the footsteps behind me.

"Hey, Ras," I called. "Is it you, Destroyer? Rinehart?"

No answer, only the rhythmic footsteps behind me. Once I tried crossing the road, but a speeding machine struck me, scraping the skin from my leg as it roared past.

Then somehow I came out of it, ascending hastily from this underworld of sound to hear Louis Armstrong innocently asking,

> *What did I do*
> *To be so black*
> *And blue?*

At first I was afraid; this familiar music had demanded action, the kind of which I was incapable, and yet had I lingered there beneath the surface I might have attempted to act. Nevertheless, I know now that few really listen to this music. I sat on the chair's edge in a soaking sweat, as though each of my 1,369 bulbs had everyone become a klieg light in an individual setting for a third degree with Ras and Rinehart in charge. It was exhausting—as though I had held my breath continuously for an hour under the terrifying serenity that comes from days of intense hunger. And yet, it was a strangely satisfying experience for an invisible man to hear the silence of sound. I had discovered unrecognized compulsions of my being—even though I could not answer "yes" to their promptings. I haven't smoked a reefer since, however; not because they're illegal, but because to *see* around corners is enough (that is not unusual when you are invisible). But to hear around them is too much; it inhibits action. And despite Brother Jack and all that sad, lost period of the Brotherhood, I believe in nothing if not in action.

Please, a definition: A hibernation is a covert preparation for a more overt action.

Besides, the drug destroys one's sense of time completely. If that happened, I might forget to dodge some bright morning and some cluck would run me down with an orange and yellow street car, or a bilious bus! Or I might forget to leave my hole when the moment for action presents itself.

Meanwhile I enjoy my life with the compliments of Monopolated Light & Power.

Since you never recognize me even when in closest contact with me, and since, no doubt, you'll hardly believe that I exist, it won't matter if you know that I tapped a power line leading into the building and ran it into my hole in the ground. Before that I lived in the darkness into which I was chased, but now I see. I've illuminated the blackness of my invisibility—and vice versa. And so I play the invisible music of my isolation. The last statement doesn't seem just right, does it? But it is; you hear this music simply because music is heard and seldom seen, except by musicians. Could this compulsion to put invisibility down in black and white be thus an urge to make music of invisibility? But I am an orator, a rabble rouser—Am? I *was*, and perhaps shall be again. Who knows? All sickness is not unto death, neither is invisibility.

I can hear you say, "What a horrible, irresponsible bastard!" And you're right. I leap to agree with you. I am one of the most irresponsible beings that ever lived. Irresponsibility is part of my invisibility; any way you face it, it is a denial. But to whom can I be responsible, and why should I be, when you refuse to see me? And wait until I reveal how truly irresponsible I am. Responsibility rests upon recognition, and recognition is a form of agreement. Take the man whom I almost killed: Who was responsible for that near murder—I? I don't think so, and I refuse it. I won't buy it. You can't give it to me. *He* bumped *me*, he insulted *me*. Shouldn't he, for his own personal safety, have recognized my hysteria, my "danger potential"? He, let us say, was lost in a dream world. But didn't *he* control that dream world—which, alas, is only too real!—and didn't *he* rule me out of it? And if he had yelled for a policeman, wouldn't *I* have been taken for the offending one? Yes, yes, yes! Let me agree with you, I was the irresponsible one; for I should have used my knife to protect the higher interests of society. Some day that

216

kind of foolishness will cause us tragic trouble. All dreamers and sleepwalkers must pay the price, and even the invisible victim is responsible for the fate of all. But I shirked that responsibility; I became too snarled in the incompatible notions that buzzed within my brain. I was a coward . . .

But what did *I* do to be so blue? Bear with me.

.   .   .

I don't remember a world without language. From the time of my earliest childhood, there was language. Always language, and imagination, speculation, utters of sound. Words, beginnings of words. What would I be without language? My existence has been determined by language, not only the spoken but the unspoken, the language of speech and the language of motion. I can't remember a world without memory. Memory, immediate and far away in the past, something in the sinew, blood, ageless cell. Although I don't recall the exact moment I spoke or tried to speak, I know the feeling of something tugging at the core of the mind, something unutterable uttered into existence. It is language that brings us into being in order to know life.

My childhood was the oral tradition of the Acoma Pueblo people—Aaquumeh hano—which included my immediate family of three older sisters, two younger sisters, two younger brothers, and my mother and father. My world was our world of the Aaquumeh in McCartys, one of the two villages descended from the ageless mother pueblo of Acoma. My world was our Eagle clan-people among

Simon Ortiz, an Acoma Pueblo Indian, teaches at Lewis and Clark University in Portland, Oregon.

Reprinted from I TELL YOU NOW: AUTOBIOGRAPHICAL ESSAYS BY NATIVE AMERICAN WRITERS, edited by Brian Swann and Arnold Krupat, by permission of the University of Nebraska Press. Copyright © 1987 by the University of Nebraska Press.

other clans. I grew up in Deetziyamah, which is the Aaquumeh name for McCartys, which is posted at the exit off the present interstate highway in western New Mexico. I grew up within a people who farmed small garden plots and fields, who were mostly poor and not well schooled in the American system's education. The language I spoke was that of a struggling people who held ferociously to a heritage, culture, language, and land despite the odds posed them by the forces surrounding them since 1540 A.D., the advent of Euro-American colonization. When I began school in 1948 at the BIA (Bureau of Indian Affairs) day school in our village, I was armed with the basic ABC's and the phrases "Good morning, Miss Oleman" and "May I please be excused to go to the bathroom," but it was an older language that was my fundamental strength.

In my childhood, the language we all spoke was Acoma, and it was a struggle to maintain it against the outright threats of corporal punishment, ostracism, and the invocation that it would impede our progress towards Americanization. Children in school were punished and looked upon with disdain if they did not speak and learn English quickly and smoothly, and so I learned it. It has occurred to me that I learned English simply because I was forced to, as so many other Indian children were. But I know, also, there was another reason, and this was that I loved language, the sound, meaning, and magic of language. Language opened up vistas of the world around me, and it allowed me to discover knowledge that would not be possible for me to know without the use of language. Later, when I began to experiment with and explore language in poetry and fiction, I allowed that a portion of that impetus was because I had come to know English through forceful acculturation. Nevertheless, the underlying force was the beauty and poetic power of language in its many forms that instilled in me the desire to become a user of language as a writer, singer, and storyteller. Significantly, it was the Acoma language, which I don't use enough of today, that inspired me to become a writer. The concepts, values, and philosophy contained in my original language and the struggle it has faced have determined my life and vision as a writer.

In Deetziyamah, I discovered the world of the Acoma land and people firsthand through my parents, sisters and brothers, and my own perceptions, voiced through all that encompasses the oral tradition, which is ageless for any culture. It is a small village, even smaller years ago, and like other Indian communities it is wealthy with its knowledge of daily event, history, and social system, all that make up a people who have a many-dimensional heritage. Our family lived in a two-room home (built by my grandfather some years after he and my grandmother moved with their daughters from Old Acoma), which my father added rooms to later. I remember my father's work at enlarging our home for our growing family. He was a skilled stoneworker, like many other men of an older Pueblo generation who worked with sandstone and mud mortar to build their homes and pueblos. It takes time, persistence, patience, and the belief that the walls that come to stand will do so for a long, long time, perhaps even forever. I like to think that by helping to mix mud and carry stone for my father and other elders I

managed to bring that influence into my consciousness as a writer.

Both my mother and my father were good storytellers and singers (as my mother is to this day—my father died in 1978), and for their generation, which was born soon after the turn of the century, they were relatively educated in the American system. Catholic missionaries had taken both of them as children to a parochial boarding school far from Acoma, and they imparted their discipline for study and quest for education to us children when we started school. But it was their indigenous sense of gaining knowledge that was most meaningful to me. Acquiring knowledge about life was above all the most important item; it was a value that one had to have in order to be fulfilled personally and on behalf of his community. And this they insisted upon imparting through the oral tradition as they told their children about our native history and our community and culture and our "stories." These stories were common knowledge of act, event, and behavior in a close-knit pueblo. It was knowledge about how one was to make a living through work that benefited his family and everyone else.

Because we were a subsistence farming people, or at least tried to be, I learned to plant, hoe weeds, irrigate and cultivate corn, chili, pumpkins, beans. Through counsel and advice I came to know that the rain which provided water was a blessing, gift, and symbol and that it was the land which provided for our lives. It was the stories and songs which provided the knowledge that I was woven into the intricate web that was my Acoma life. In our garden and our cornfields I learned about the seasons, growth cycles of cultivated plants, what one had to think and feel about the land; and at home I became aware of how we must care for each other: all of this was encompassed in an intricate relationship which had to be maintained in order that life continue. After supper on many occasions my father would bring out his drum and sing as we, the children, danced to themes about the rain, hunting, land, and people. It was all that is contained within the language of oral tradition that made me explicitly aware of a yet unarticulated urge to write, to tell what I had learned and was learning and what it all meant to me.

My grandfather was old already when I came to know him. I was only one of his many grandchildren, but I would go with him to get wood for our households, to the garden to chop weeds, and to his sheep camp to help care for his sheep. I don't remember his exact words, but I know they were about how we must sacredly concern ourselves with the people and the holy earth. I know his words were about how we must regard ourselves and others with compassion and love; I know that his knowledge was vast, as a medicine man and an elder of his kiva, and I listened as a boy should. My grandfather represented for me a link to the past that is important for me to hold in my memory because it is not only memory but knowledge that substantiates my present existence. He and the grandmothers and grandfathers before him thought about us as they lived, confirmed in their belief of a continuing life, and they brought our present beings into existence by the beliefs they held. The consciousness of that belief is what informs my present concerns with language, poetry, and fiction.

My first poem was for Mother's Day when I was in the fifth grade, and it was the first poem that was ever published, too, in the Skull Valley School newsletter. Of course I don't remember how the juvenile poem went, but it must have been certain in its expression of love and reverence for the woman who was the most important person in my young life. The poem didn't signal any prophecy of my future as a poet, but it must

have come from the forming idea that there were things one could do with language and writing. My mother, years later, remembers how I was a child who always told stories— that is, tall tales—who always had explanations for things probably better left unspoken, and she says that I also liked to perform in school plays. In remembering, I do know that I was coming to that age when the emotions and thoughts in me began to moil to the surface. There was much to experience and express in that age when youth has a precociousness that is broken easily or made to flourish. We were a poor family, always on the verge of financial disaster, though our parents always managed to feed us and keep us in clothing. We had the problems, unfortunately ordinary, of many Indian families who face poverty on a daily basis, never enough of anything, the feeling of a denigrating self-consciousness, alcoholism in the family and community, the feeling that something was falling apart though we tried desperately to hold it all together.

My father worked for the railroad for many years as a laborer and later as a welder. We moved to Skull Valley, Arizona, for one year in the early 1950s, and it was then that I first came in touch with a non-Indian, non-Acoma world. Skull Valley was a farming and ranching community, and my younger brothers and sisters and I went to a one-room school. I had never really had much contact with white people except from a careful and suspicious distance, but now here I was, totally surrounded by them, and there was nothing to do but bear the experience and learn from it. Although I perceived there was not much difference between *them* and *us* in certain respects, there was a distinct feeling that we were not the same either. This thought had been inculcated in me, especially by an Acoma expression—*Gnimun Mericano*—that spoke of the "fortune" of being an American. In later years as a social activist and committed writer, I would try to offer a strong positive view of our collective Indianness through my writing. Nevertheless, my father was an inadequately paid laborer, and we were far from our home land for economic-social reasons, and my feelings and thoughts about that experience during that time would become a part of how I became a writer.

Soon after, I went away from my home and family to go to boarding school, first in Santa Fe and then in Albuquerque. This was in the 1950s, and this had been the case for the past half-century for Indians: we had to leave home in order to become truly American by joining the mainstream, which was deemed to be the proper course of our lives. On top of this was termination, a U.S. government policy which dictated that Indians sever their relationship to the federal government and remove themselves from their lands and go to American cities for jobs and education. It was an era which bespoke the intent of U.S. public policy that Indians were no longer to be Indians. Naturally, I did not perceive this in any analytical or purposeful sense; rather, I felt an unspoken anxiety and resentment against unseen forces that determined our destiny to be un-Indian, embarrassed and uncomfortable with our grandparents' customs and strictly held values. We were to set our goals as American working men and women, singlemindedly industrious, patriotic, and unquestioning, building for a future which ensured that the U.S. was the greatest nation in the world. I felt fearfully uneasy with this, for by then I felt the loneliness, alienation, and isolation imposed upon me by the separation from my family, home, and community.

Something was happening; I could see that in my years at Catholic school and the U.S. Indian school. I remembered my grandparents' and parents' words: educate yourself in order to help your people. In that era and the generation who had the same experience I had, there was an unspoken vow: we were caught in a system inexorably, and we had to learn that system well in order to fight back. Without the motive of a fight-back we would not be able to survive as the people our heritage had lovingly bequeathed us. My diaries and notebooks began then, and though none have survived to the present, I know they contained the varied moods of a youth filled with loneliness, anger, and discomfort that seemed to have unknown causes. Yet at the same time, I realize now, I was coming to know myself clearly in a way that I would later articulate in writing. My love of language, which allowed me to deal with the world, to delve into it, to experiment and discover, held for me a vision of awe and wonder, and by then grammar teachers had noticed I was a good speller, used verbs and tenses correctly, and wrote complete sentences. Although I imagine that they might have surmised this as unusual for an Indian student whose original language was not English, I am grateful for their perception and attention.

During the latter part of that era in the 1950s of Indian termination and the Cold War, a portion of which still exists today, there were the beginnings of a bolder and more vocalized resistance against the current U.S. public policies of repression, racism, and cultural ethnocide. It seemed to be inspired by the civil rights movement led by black people in the U.S. and by decolonization and liberation struggles worldwide. Indian people were being relocated from their rural homelands at an astonishingly devastating rate, yet at the same time they resisted the U.S. effort by maintaining determined ties with their heritage, returning often to their native communities and establishing Indian centers in the cities they were removed to. Indian rural communities, such as Acoma Pueblo, insisted on their land claims and began to initiate legal battles in the areas of natural and social, political and economic human rights. By the retention and the inspiration of our native heritage, values, philosophies, and language, we would know ourselves as a strong and enduring people. Having a modest and latent consciousness of this as a teenager, I began to write about the experience of being Indian in America. Although I had only a romanticized image of what a writer was, which came from the pulp rendered by American popular literature, and I really didn't know anything about writing, I sincerely felt a need to say things, to speak, to release the energy of the impulse to help my people.

My writing in my late teens and early adulthood was fashioned after the American short stories and poetry taught in the high schools of the 1940s and 1950s, but by the 1960s, after I had gone to college and dropped out and served in the military, I began to develop topics and themes from my Indian background. The experience in my village of Deetziyamah and Acoma Pueblo was readily accessible. I had grown up within the oral tradition of speech, social and religious ritual, elders' counsel and advice, countless and endless stories, everyday event, and the visual art that was symbolically representative of life all around. My mother was a potter of the well-known Acoma clayware, a traditional art form that had been passed to her from her mother and the generations of mothers before. My father carved figures from wood and did beadwork. This was not unusual, as Indian people know; there was always some kind of artistic endeavor that people set themselves to, although they did not necessarily articulate it as ''Art'' in the sense of Western civilization. One lived and expressed an artful life, whether it was in ceremonial singing and dancing, architecture, painting, speaking, or in the way one's social-culture life was structured. When I turned my attention to my own heritage, I did

so because this was my identity, the substance of who I was, and I wanted to write about what that meant. My desire was to write about the integrity and dignity of an Indian identity, and at the same time I wanted to look at what this was within the context of an America that had too often denied its Indian heritage.

To a great extent my writing has a natural political-cultural bent simply because I was nurtured intellectually and emotionally within an atmosphere of Indian resistance. Aacquu did not die in 1598 when it was burned and razed by European conquerors, nor did the people become hopeless when their children were taken away to U.S. schools far from home and new ways were imposed upon them. The *Aaquumeh hano*, despite losing much of their land and surrounded by a foreign civilization, have not lost sight of their native heritage. This is the factual case with most other Indian peoples, and the clear explanation for this has been the fight-back we have found it necessary to wage. At times, in the past, it was outright armed struggle, like that of present-day Indians in Central and South America with whom we must identify; currently, it is often in the legal arena, and it is in the field of literature. In 1981, when I was invited to the White House for an event celebrating American poets and poetry, I did not immediately accept the invitation. I questioned myself about the possibility that I was merely being exploited as an Indian, and I hedged against accepting. But then I recalled the elders going among our people in the poor days of the 1950s, asking for donations—a dollar here and there, a sheep, perhaps a piece of pottery—in order to finance a trip to the nation's capital. They were to make another countless appeal on behalf of our people, to demand justice, to reclaim lost land even though there was only spare hope they would be successful. I went to the White House realizing that I was to do no less than they and those who had fought in the Pueblo Revolt of 1680, and I read my poems and sang songs that were later described as "guttural" by a Washington, D.C., newspaper. I suppose it is more or less understandable why such a view of Indian literature is held by many, and it is also clear why there should be a political stand taken in my writing and those of my sister and brother Indian writers.

The 1960s and afterward have been an invigorating and liberating period for Indian people. It has been only a little more than twenty years since Indian writers began to write and publish extensively, but we are writing and publishing more and more; we can only go forward. We come from an ageless, continuing oral tradition that informs us of our values, concepts, and notions as native people, and it is amazing how much of this tradition is ingrained so deeply in our contemporary writing, considering the brutal efforts of cultural repression that was not long ago outright U.S. policy. We were not to speak our languages, practice our spiritual beliefs, or accept the values of our past generations; and we were discouraged from pressing for our natural rights as Indian human beings. In spite of the fact that there is to some extent the same repression today, we persist and insist in living, believing, hoping, loving, speaking, and in our writing as Indians. This is embodied in the language we know and share in our writing. We have always had this language, and it is the language, spoken and unspoken, that determines our existence, that brought our grandmothers and grandfathers and ourselves into being in order that there be a continuing life.

# Girlhood Among Ghosts

*Maxine Hong Kingston*

Long ago in China, knot-makers tied string into buttons and frogs, and rope into bell pulls. There was one knot so complicated that it blinded the knot-maker. Finally an emperor outlawed this cruel knot, and the nobles could not order it anymore. If I had lived in China, I would have been an outlaw knot-maker.

Maybe that's why my mother cut my tongue. She pushed my tongue up and sliced the frenum. Or maybe she snipped it with a pair of nail scissors. I don't remember her doing it, only her telling me about it, but all during childhood I felt sorry for the baby whose mother waited with scissors or knife in hand for it to cry—and then, when its mouth was wide open like a baby bird's, cut. The Chinese say "a ready tongue is an evil."

I used to curl up my tongue in front of the mirror and tauten my frenum into a white line, itself as thin as razor blade. I saw no scars in my mouth. I thought perhaps I had had two frena, and she had cut one. I made other children open their mouths so I could compare theirs to mine. I saw perfect pink membranes stretching into precise edges that looked easy enough to cut. Sometimes I felt

Maxine Hong Kingston, a primary spokesperson for the Chinese-American experience, has written *Woman Warrior, China Men*, and most recently *Tripmaster Monkey*.

From *The Woman Warrior: Memoirs of a Girlhood Among Ghosts* by Maxine Hong Kingston. Copyright © 1975, 1976 by Maxine Hong Kingston. Reprinted by permission of Alfred A. Knopf, Inc.

very proud that my mother committed such a powerful act upon me. At other times I was terrified—the first thing my mother did when she saw me was to cut my tongue.

"Why did you do that to me, Mother?"

"I told you."

"Tell me again."

"I cut it so that you would not be tongue-tied. Your tongue would be able to move in any language. You'll be able to speak languages that are completely different from one another. You'll be able to pronounce anything. Your frenum looked too tight to do those things, so I cut it."

"But isn't 'a ready tongue an evil'?"

"Things are different in this ghost country."

"Did it hurt me? Did I cry and bleed?"

"I don't remember. Probably."

She didn't cut the other children's. When I asked cousins and other Chinese children whether their mothers had cut their tongues loose, they said, "What?"

"Why didn't you cut brothers' and sisters' tongues?"

"They didn't need it."

"Why not? Were theirs longer than mine?"

"Why don't you quit blabbering and get to work?"

If my mother was not lying she should have cut more, scraped away the rest of the frenum skin, because I have a terrible time talking. Or she should not have cut at all, tampering with my speech. When I went to kindergarten and had to speak English for the first time, I became silent. A dumbness—a shame—still cracks my voice in two, even when I want to say "hello" casually, or ask an easy question in front of the check-out counter, or ask directions of a bus driver. I stand frozen, or I hold up the line with the complete, grammatical sentence that comes squeaking out at impossible length. "What did you say?" says the cab driver, or "Speak up," so I have to perform again, only weaker the second time. A telephone call makes my throat bleed and takes up that day's courage. It spoils my day with self-disgust when I hear my broken broken voice come skittering out into the open. It makes people wince to hear it. I'm getting better, though. Recently I asked the postman for special-issue stamps; I've waited since childhood for postmen to give me some of their own accord. I am making progress, a little every day.

My silence was thickest—total—during the three years that I covered my school painting with black paint. I painted layers of black over houses and flowers and suns, and when I drew on the blackboard, I put a layer of chalk on top. I was making a stage curtain, and it was the moment before the curtain parted or rose. The teachers called my parents to school, and I saw they had been saving my pictures, curling and cracking, all alike and black. The teachers pointed to the pictures and looked serious, talked seriously too, but my parents did not understand English. ("The parents and teachers of criminals were executed," said my father.) My parents took the pictures home. I spread them out (so black and full of possibilities) and pretended the curtains were swinging open, flying up, one after another, sunlight underneath, mighty operas.

During the first silent year I spoke to no one at school, did not ask before going to the lavatory, and flunked kindergarten. My sister also said nothing for three years, silent in the playground and silent at lunch. There were other quiet Chinese girls not of our family, but most of them got over it sooner than we did. I enjoyed the silence. At first it did not occur to me I was supposed to talk or to pass kindergarten. I talked at home and to one or two of the Chinese kids in class. I made motions and even made some jokes. I drank out of a toy saucer when the water spilled out of the cup, and everybody laughed, pointing at me, so I did it some more. I didn't know that Americans don't drink out of saucers.

I liked the Negro students (Black Ghosts) best because they laughed the loudest and talked to me as if I were a daring talker too. One of the Negro girls had her mother coil braids over her ears Shanghai-style like mine; we were Shanghai twins except that she was covered with black like my paintings. Two Negro kids enrolled in Chinese school, and the teachers gave them Chinese names. Some Negro kids walked me to school and home, protecting me from the Japanese kids, who hit me and chased me and stuck gum in my ears. The Japanese kids were noisy and tough. They appeared one day in kindergarten, released from concentration camp, which was a tic-tac-toe mark, like barbed wire, on the map.

It was when I found out I had to talk that school became a misery, that the silence became a misery. I did not speak and felt bad each time that I did not speak. I read aloud in first grade, though, and heard the barest whisper with little squeaks come out of my throat. "Louder," said the teacher, who scared the voice away again. The other Chinese girls did not talk either, so I knew the silence had to do with being a Chinese girl.

Reading out loud was easier than speaking because we did not have to make up what to say, but I stopped often, and the teacher would think I'd gone quiet again. I

225

could not understand "I." The Chinese "I" has seven strokes, intricacies. How could the American "I," assuredly wearing a hat like the Chinese, have only three strokes, the middle so straight? Was it out of politeness that this writer left off strokes the way a Chinese has to write her own name small and crooked? No, it was not politeness; "I" is a capital and "you" is lower-case. I stared at that middle line and waited so long for its black center to resolve into tight strokes and dots that I forgot to pronounce it. The other troublesome word was "here," no strong consonant to hang on to, and so flat, when "here" is two mountainous ideographs. The teacher, who had already told me every day how to read "I" and "here," put me in the low corner under the stairs again, where the noisy boys usually sat.

When my second grade class did a play, the whole class went to the auditorium except the Chinese girls. The teacher, lovely and Hawaiian, should have understood about us, but instead left us behind in the classroom. Our voices were too soft or nonexistent, and our parents never signed the permission slips anyway. They never signed anything unnecessary. We opened the door a crack and peeked out, but closed it again quickly. One of us (not me) won every spelling bee, though.

I remember telling the Hawaiian teacher, "We Chinese can't sing 'land where our fathers died.'" She argued with me about politics, while I meant because of curses. But how can I have that memory when I couldn't talk? My mother says that we, like the ghosts, have no memories.

After American school, we picked up our cigar boxes, in which we had arranged books, brushes, and an inkbox neatly, and went to Chinese school, from 5:00 to 7:30 P.M. There we chanted together, voices rising and falling, loud and soft, some boys shouting, everybody reading together, reciting together and not alone with one voice. When we had a memorization test, the teacher let each of us come to his desk and say the lesson to him privately, while the rest of the class practiced copying or tracing. Most of the teachers were men. The boys who were so well behaved in the American school played tricks on them and talked back to them. The girls were not mute. They screamed and yelled during recess, when there were no rules; they had fistfights. Nobody was afraid of children hurting themselves or of children hurting school property. The glass doors to the red and green balconies with the gold joy symbols were left wide open so that we could run out and climb the fire escapes. We played capture-the-flag in the auditorium, where Sun Yat-sen and Chiang Kai-shek's pictures hung at the back of the stage, the Chinese flag on their left and the American flag on their right. We climbed the teak ceremonial chairs and made flying leaps off the stage. One flag headquarters was behind the glass door and the other on stage right. Our feet drummed on the hollow stage. During recess the teachers locked themselves up in their office with the shelves of books, copybooks, inks from China. They drank tea and warmed their hands at a stove. There was no play supervision. At recess we had the school to ourselves, and also we could roam as far as we could go—downtown, Chinatown stores, home—as long as we returned before the bell rang.

At exactly 7:30 the teacher again picked up the brass bell that sat on his desk and swung it over our heads, while we charged down the stairs, our cheering magnified in the stairwell. Nobody had to line up.

Not all of the children who were silent at American school found voice at Chinese school. One new teacher said each of us had to get up and recite in front of the class, who was to listen. My sister and I had memorized the lesson perfectly. We said it to each other at home, one chanting, one listening. The teacher called on my sister to recite first. It was the first time a teacher had called on the second-born to go first. My sister was scared. She glanced at me and looked away; I looked down at my desk. I hoped that she could do it because if she could, then I would have to. She opened her mouth and a voice came out that wasn't a whisper, but it wasn't a proper voice either. I hoped that she would not cry, fear breaking up her voice like twigs underfoot. She sounded as if she were trying to sing though weeping and strangling. She did not pause or stop to end the embarrassment. She kept going until she said the last word, and then she sat down. When it was my turn, the same voice came out, a crippled animal running on broken legs. You could hear splinters in my voice, bones rubbing jagged against one another. I was loud, though. I was glad I didn't whisper. There was one little girl who whispered.

# When the Other Dancer Is the Self

*Alice Walker*

It is a bright summer day in 1947. My father, a fat, funny man with beautiful eyes and a subversive wit, is trying to decide which of his eight children he will take with him to the country fair. My mother, of course, will not go. She is knocked out from getting us ready: I hold my neck stiff against the pressure of her knuckles as she hastily completes the braiding and then beribboning of my hair.

My father is the driver for the rich old white lady up the road. Her name is Miss May. She owns all the land for miles around, as well as the house in which we live. All I remember about her is that she once offered to pay my mother 75 cents for leaning her house, raking up piles of her magnolia leaves, and washing her family's clothes, and that my mother—she of no money, eight children, and a chronic earache—refused it. But I do not think of this in 1947. I am two-and-a-half years old. I want to go everywhere my daddy goes. I am excited at the prospect of riding in a car. Someone has told me fairs are fun. That there is room in the car for only three of us doesn't faze me at all. Whirling happily in my starchy frock, show-

ing off my biscuit polished patent leather shoes and lavender socks, tossing my head in a way that makes my ribbons bounce, I stand, hands on hips, before my father. "Take me, Daddy," I say with assurance, "I'm the prettiest!"

Later, it does not surprise me to find myself in Miss May's shiny black car, sharing the back seat with the other lucky ones. Does not surprise me that I thoroughly enjoy the fair. At home that night I tell all the unlucky ones about the merry-go-round, the man who eats live chickens, and the abundance of Teddy bears, until they say: that's enough, baby Alice. Shut up now, and go to sleep.

It is Easter Sunday, 1950. I am dressed in a green, flocked, scalloped-hem dress (handmade by my adoring sister Ruth) that has its own smooth satin petticoat and tiny hot-pink roses tucked into each scallop. My shoes, new T-strap patent leather, again highly biscuit polished. I am six years old and have learned one of the longest Easter speeches to be heard in church that day, totally unlike the speech I said when I was two: "Easter lilies/pure and white/blossom in/the morning light." When I rise to give my speech I do so on a great wave of love and pride and expectation. People in the church stop rustling their new crinolines. They seem to hold their breath. I can tell they admire my dress, but it is my spirit, bordering on sassiness (womanishness), they secretly applaud.

Alice Walker is the author of many works that explore the relationships between race and gender, including *In Search of Our Mothers' Gardens, Living by the Word, The Color Purple,* and most recently *The Temple of My Familiar.*

*"That girl's a little mess,"* they whisper to each other, pleased.

Naturally I say my speech without stammer or pause, unlike those who stutter, stammer, or, worst of all, forget. This is before the word "beautiful" exists in people's vocabulary, but 'Oh, isn't she the *cutest* thing!' frequently floats by my way. *"And got so much sense!"* they gratefully add . . . for which thoughtful addition I thank them to this day.

*It was great fun being cute. But then, one day, it ended.*

I am eight years old and a tomboy. I have a cowboy hat, cowboy boots, checkered shirt and pants, all red. My playmates are my brothers, two and four years older than me. Their colors are black and green, the only difference in the way we are dressed. On Saturday nights we all go to the picture show, even my mother; Westerns are her favorite movies. Back home, "on the ranch," we pretend we are Tom Mix, Hopalong Cassidy, Lash LaRue (we've even named one of our dogs Lash LaRue); we chase each other for hours rustling cattle, being outlaws, delivering damsels from distress. Then my parents decide to buy my brothers guns. These are not "real" guns. They shoot "BBs," copper pellets my brothers say will kill birds. Because I am a girl, I do not get a gun. Instantly I am relegated to the position of Indian. Now there appears a great distance between us. They shoot and shoot at everything with their new guns. I try to keep up with my bow and arrows.

One day while I am standing on top of our makeshift "garage"—pieces of tin nailed across some poles—holding my bow and arrow and looking out toward the fields, I feel an incredible blow in my right eye. I look down just in time to see my brother lower his gun.

Both brothers rush to my side. My eye stings, and I cover it with my hand. "If you tell," they say, "we will get a whipping. You don't want that to happen, do you?" I do not. "Here is a piece of wire," says the older brother, picking it up from the roof, "say you stepped on one end of it and the other flew up and hit you." The pain is beginning to start. "Yes," I say. "Yes, I will say that is what happened." If I do not say this is what happened, I know my brothers will find ways to make me wish I had. But now I will say anything that gets me to my mother.

Confronted by our parents we stick to the lie agreed upon. They place me on a bench on the porch and I close my left eye while they examine the right. There is a tree growing from underneath the porch, that climbs past the railing to the roof. It is the last thing my right eye sees. I watch as its trunk, its branches, and then its leaves are blotted out by the rising blood.

I am in shock. First there is intense fever, which my father tries to break using lily leaves bound around my head. Then there are chills: my mother tries to get me to eat soup. Eventually, I do not know how, my parents learn what has happened. A week after the "accident" they take me to see a doctor. "Why did you wait so long to come?" he asks, looking into my eye and shaking his head. "Eyes are sympathetic," he says. "If one is blind, the other will likely become blind too."

This comment of the doctor's terrifies me. But it is really how I look that bothers me most. Where the BB pellet struck there is a glob of whitish scar tissue, a hideous cataract, on my eye. Now when I stare at people—a favorite pastime, up to now—they will stare back. Not at the "cute" little girl, but at her scar. For six years I do not stare at anyone because I do not raise my head.

Years later, in the throes of a mid-life crisis, I ask my mother and sister whether I changed after the "accident." "No," they say, puzzled. "What do you mean?"

*What do I mean?*

I am eight, and for the first time, doing poorly in school, where I have been something of a whiz since I was four. We have just moved to the place where the "accident" occurred. We do not know any of the people around us because this is a different county. The only time I see the friends I knew is when we go back to our old church. My new school is the former state penitentiary. It is a large stone building, cold and drafty, crammed to overflowing with boisterous, ill-disciplined children. On the third floor there is a huge circular imprint of some partition that has been torn out.

"What used to be here?" I ask a sullen girl next to me on our way past it to lunch.

"The electric chair," says she.

At night I have nightmares about the electric chair, and about all the people reputedly "fried" in it. I am afraid of the school, where all the students seem to be budding criminals.

"What's the matter with your eye?" they ask, critically.

When I don't answer (I cannot decide whether it was an "accident" or not), they shove me, insist on a fight.

My brother, the one who created the story about the wire, comes to my rescue. But then brags so much about "protecting" me, I become sick.

After weeks of torture at the school, my parents decide to send me back to our old community to my old school. I live with my grandparents and the teacher they board. But there is no room for Phoebe, my cat. By the time my grandparents decide there is room, and I ask for my cat, she cannot be found. Miss Yarborough, the boarding teacher, takes me under her wing, and begins to teach me to play the piano. But soon she marries an African—a "prince," she says—and is whisked away to his continent.

At my old school there is at least one teacher who loves me. She is the teacher who "knew me before I was born" and brought my first baby clothes. It is she who makes life bearable. It is her presence that finally helps me turn on the one child at the school who continually calls me "one-eyed bitch." One day I simply grab him by his coat and beat him until I am satisfied. It is my teacher who tells me my mother is ill.

My mother is lying in bed in the middle of the day, something I have never seen. She is in too much pain to speak. She has an abscess in her ear. I stand looking down on her, knowing that if she dies, I cannot live. She is being treated with warm oils and hot bricks held against her cheek. Finally a doctor comes. But I must go back to my grandparents' house. The weeks pass, but I am hardly aware of it. All I know is that my mother might die, my father is not so jolly, my brothers still have their guns, and I am the one sent away from home.

"You did not change," they say.

*Did I imagine the anguish of never looking up?*

I am 12. When relatives come to visit I hide in my room. My cousin Brenda, just my age, whose father works in the post office and whose mother is a nurse, comes to find me. "Hello," she says. And then she asks, looking at my recent school picture which I did not want taken, and on which the "glob" as I think of it is clearly visible, "You still can't see out of that eye?"

"No," I say, and flop back on the bed over my book.

That night, as I do almost every night, I abuse my eye. I rant and rave at it, in front of the mirror. I plead with it to clear up before morning. I tell it I hate and despise it. I do not pray for sight. I pray for beauty.

"You did not change," they say.

I am 14 and baby-sitting for my brother Bill who lives in Boston. He is my favorite brother and there is a strong bond between us. Understanding my feelings of shame and ugliness, he and his wife take me to a local hospital where the "glob" is removed by a doctor named O. Henry. There is still a small bluish crater where the scar tissue was, but the ugly white stuff is gone. Almost immediately I become a different person from the girl who does not raise her head. Or so I think. Now that I've raised my head, I win the boyfriend of my dreams. Now that I've raised my head, I have plenty of friends. Now that I've raised my head, class work comes from my lips as faultlessly as Easter speeches did, and I leave high school as valedictorian, most popular student and *queen*, hardly believing my luck. Ironically, the girl who was voted most beautiful in our class (and was) was later shot twice through the chest by a male companion, using a "real" gun, while she was pregnant. But that's another story in itself. Or, is it?

"You did not change," they say.

It is now 30 years since the "accident." A gorgeous woman and famous journalist comes to visit and to interview me. She is going to write a cover story for her magazine that focuses on my last book. "Decide how you want to look on the cover," she says. "Glamorous or whatever,"

Never mind "glamorous," it is the "whatever" that I hear. Suddenly all I can think of is whether I will get enough sleep the night before the photography session: if I don't, my eye will be tired and wander, as blind eyes will.

At night in bed with my lover I think up reasons why I should not appear on the cover of a magazine. "My meanest critics will say I've sold out," I say. "My family will now realize I write scandalous books." But what's the real reason you don't want to do this?" he asks.

"Because in all probability," I say in a rush, "My eye won't be straight."

"It will be straight enough," he says. Then, "besides, I thought you'd made your peace with that."

And I suddenly realize that I have.

*I remember:*

I am talking to my brother Jimmy, asking if he remembers anything unusual about the day I was shot. He does not know I consider that day the last time my father, with his sweet home remedy of cool lily leaves, "chose" me, and that I suffered rage inside because of this. "Well," he says, "all I remember is standing by the side of the highway with Daddy, trying to flag down a car. A white man stopped, but when Daddy said he needed somebody to take his little girl to the doctor, he drove off."

*I remember:*

I am 33 years old. And in the desert for the first time. I fall totally in love with it. I am so overwhelmed by its beauty, I confront for the first time, consciously, the meaning of the doctor's words years ago: "Eyes are sympathetic. If one is blind, the other will likely become blind too." I realize I have dashed about the world madly, looking at this, looking at that, storing up images against the fading of the light. *But I might have missed seeing the desert!* The shock of that possibility—and gratitude for more than 25 years of sight—sends me literally to my knees. Poem after poem comes—which is perhaps how poets pray.

> I am so thankful I have seem
> The Desert
> And the creatures in The Desert
> And the desert Itself.
>
> The desert has its own moon
> Which I have seen
> With my own eye
>
> There is no flag on it.

Trees of the desert have arms
All of which are always up
That is because the moon is up
The sun is up
The stars
Clouds
None with flags.

If there *were* flags, I doubt
the trees would point.
Would you?

*But mostly, I remember this:*

I am 27, and my baby daughter is almost three. Since her birth I have worried over her discovery that her mother's eyes are different from other people's. Will she be embarrassed? I wonder. What will she say? Every day she watches a television program called "Big Blue Marble." It begins with a picture of the earth as it appears from the moon. It is bluish, a little battered-looking but full of light, with whitish clouds swirling around it. Every time I see it I weep with love, as if it is a picture of Grandma's house. One day when I am putting Rebecca down for her nap, she suddenly focuses on my eye. Something inside me cringes, gets ready to try to protect myself. All children are cruel about physical differences, I know from experience, and that they don't always mean to be is another matter. I assume Rebecca will be the same.

But no-o-o-o. She studies my face intently as we stand, her inside and me outside her crib. She even holds my face maternally between her dimpled little hands. Then, looking every bit as serious and lawyerlike as her father, she says, as if it may just possibly have slipped my attention: "Mommy, there's a *world* in your eye." (As in, "Don't be alarmed, or do anything crazy.") And then, gently, but with great interest: "Mommy, where did you *get* that world in your eye?"

For the most part, the pain left then. (So what if my brothers grew up to buy even more powerful pellet guns for their sons. And to carry real guns themselves. So what if a young "Morehouse man" once nearly fell off the steps of Trevor Arnett Library because he thought my eyes were blue.) Crying and laughing I ran to the bathroom, while Rebecca mumbled and sang herself off to sleep. Yes indeed, I realize, looking into the mirror. There *was* a world in my eye. And I saw that it was possible to love it: that in fact, for all it had taught me, of shame and anger and inner vision, I *did* love it. Even to see it drifting out of orbit in boredom, or rolling up out of fatigue, not to mention floating back at attention in excitement (bearing witness, a friend has called it), deeply suitable to my personality, and even characteristic of me.

That night I dream I am dancing to Stevie Wonder's song "Always." As I dance, whirling and joyous, happier than I've ever been in my life, another bright-faced dancer joins me. We dance and kiss each other and hold each other through the night. The other dancer has obviously come through all right, as I have done. She is beautiful, whole and free. And she is also me.

# Strangers in the Village

*David Mura*

Recently, in *The Village Voice*, a number of articles were devoted to the issue of race in America. Perhaps the most striking article, "Black Women, White Kids: A Tale of Two Worlds," was about Black women in New York City who take care of upper-middle-class and upper-class white children. Merely by describing the situation of these Black women and recording their words, the article pointed out how race and class affects these women's lives: "As the nanny sits in the park watching a tow-haired child play, her own kids are coming home from school; they will do their homework alone and make dinner."

None of the white people who employed these nannies seemed at all cognizant of the contradictions of this description. Instead the whites seemed to view the Black nannies as a natural facet of their lives, an expected privilege. Yet, on another less-conscious level, the whites appeared to have misgivings that they could not express. One of the nannies, named Bertha, talked about how she objected to the tone of voice her employer, Barbra, used: "You wait a minute here, Barbra. I'm not a child," Bertha would tell Barbra, "I can talk to you any way I want. This is a free country, it's not a commie country." Every time Bertha and Barbra have an argument, Barbra buys Bertha

David Mura, a poet and essayist, was a U.S.-Japan Fellowship winner and spent a year traveling in Japan.

presents: "She bought me shoes, a beautiful blouse, a Mother's Day present . . . she's a very generous person. She's got a good heart." But Bertha doesn't really like the presents. "It always made me feel guilty. To tell you the truth about it, I never had too many people give me presents, so it just made me feel bad.

"Another reason we don't get along," Bertha continues, "is she always trying to figure me out. See, I'm a very complicated person. I'm a very moody person . . . I'm independent. I figure I can deal with it myself. And we would sit there, I could just feel her eyes on me, and I'd have to get up and leave the room . . . She just wants you to be satisfied with her all the time . . . She wants me to tell her I love you. I just can't."

The author of the articles says that sometimes Barbra seems to want love and sometimes she seems to want forgiveness. "But perhaps for most white people, a black person's affection can never mean more than an act of absolution for historical and collective guilt, an affection desired not because of how one feels about that particular person but because that person is black."

As a middle-class third-generation Japanese-American, I read this article with mixed feelings. On one level, I have much more in common with Bertha's employer, Barbra, than I do with Bertha. Although at one time Japanese-Americans worked in jobs similar to Bertha's and were part of the lower class, by my generation this was not the case. I grew up in the suburbs of Chicago, went to college and graduate school, married a pediatrician who is three-quarters WASP and one-quarter Jewish. Although I will most likely assume a large portion of our child care when we have children, my wife and I will probably use some form of outside child care. Most likely, we would not employ a Black nanny, even if we lived in New York City, but I could not help feeling a sense of guilt and shame when I read the article. I could understand Barbra's wish to use acts of kindness to overlook inequalities of class and race; her desire to equate winning the affections of a Black servant with the absolution of historical and collective guilt. I would not, in the end, act like Barbra, but I do recognize her feelings.

At the same time, I also recognize and identify with the anger Bertha feels toward her white employer. In part, Bertha's anger is a recognition of how profoundly race has affected her and Barbra's lives, and also that Barbra does not truly understand this fact. Although generalizations like this can sometimes be misused—more about this later—American culture defines white middle-class culture as the norm. As a result, Blacks and other colored minorities, must generally know two cultures to survive—the culture of middle-class whites and their own minority culture. Middle-class whites need only to know one culture. For them, knowledge of a minority culture is a seeming—and I use the word "seeming" here purposely—luxury; they can survive without it.

On a smaller scale than Bertha I have experienced the inability of members of the white majority to understand how race has affected my life, to come to terms with the differences between us. Sometimes I can bridge this gap, but never completely; more often, a gulf appears between me and white friends that has previously been unacknowledged. I point out to them that the im-

ages I grew up with in the media were all white, that the books I read in school—from Dick and Jane onwards—were about whites and later, about European civilization. I point out to them the way beauty is defined in our culture and how, under such definitions, slanted eyes, flat noses, and round faces just don't make it. And as I talk, I often sense their confusion, the limits of their understanding of the world. They become angry, defensive. "We all have experiences others can't relate to," they reply and equate the issue of race with prejudice against women or Italians or rich people. Such generalizations can sometimes be used to express sympathy with victims of prejudice, but as used by many whites, it generally attempts to shut down racial anger by denying the distinct causes of that anger, thereby rendering it meaningless. Another form of this tactic is the reply, "I think of you just as a white person," or, a bit less chauvinistically, "I think of you as an individual." While, at one time in my life, I would have taken this for a compliment, my reply now is, "I don't want to be a white person. Why can't I be who I am? Why can't you think of me as a Japanese-American *and* as an individual?"

I'd like to leave these questions a moment and, because I'm a writer, take up these themes in terms of literature. In my talks with whites about race, I very quickly find myself referring to history. As many have pointed out, America has never come to terms with two fundamental historical events: enslavement of Blacks by whites and the taking of this continent by Europeans from the Native Americans and the accompanying policies of genocide. A third historical event that America hasn't come to terms with—and yet is closer to doing so than with the other two—is the internment of Japanese-Americans during World War II. Although some maintain that the camps were caused simply by wartime hysteria, the determining factors were racism and a desire for the property owned by the Japanese-Americans. Recently, in *War Without Mercy,* John Dower has demonstrated how the war in the Pacific, on both sides, took on racist overtones and used racist propaganda, while the Nazis were somehow kept separate from the rest of the German race, the Japanese, as a race, were characterized as lice and vermin. This racist propaganda was both caused by and intensified a phenomenon that led to the internment camps: A large number of white Americans were unable to distinguish between the Japanese as the enemy and Japanese-Americans.

Knowing the history behind the camps, knowing that during the internment the lives of many Japanese-Americans, particularly the Issei (first generation), were permanently disrupted; knowing the internment caused the loss of millions of dollars of property, I, as a Japanese-American, feel a kinship to both Blacks and Native Americans that I do not feel with white Americans. It is a kinship that comes from our histories as victims of injustice. Of course, our histories are more than simply being victims, and we must recognize that these histories are also separate and distinct, but there is a certain power and solace in this kinship.

This kinship in reinforced by our current position as minorities in a white-dominated culture. For instance, when Blacks or Native Americans or Chicanos complain about their image in the media, it is a complaint I easily understand. I myself have written a number of pieces about this subject, analyses of the stereotypes in such films as *Rambo* or *Year of the Dragon.* Recently, I read a play by a Sansei playwright, Philip Kan Gotanda, *Yankee Dawg You Die,* and I was struck by the similarities between this play about two Japanese-American actors and Robert Townsend's *Hollywood Shuffle,* a film about a Black actor trying to make it in Hollywood.

In both works, the actors must struggle with the battle between economics and integrity, between finding no parts or playing in roles that stereotype their minority. In *Hollywood Shuffle,* we see the hero, clearly a middle-class Black, trying and failing to portray a pimp in his bathroom mirror. Later in the film, there is a mock Black acting school where Black actors learn to talk in jive, to move like a pimp, to play runaway slaves, to shuffle their feet. In *Yankee Dawg You Die,* a young third-generation Japanese-American actor, Bradley, is fired at one point because he will not mix up his r's and l's when playing a waiter. Throughout the play, he keeps chastising an older Japanese-American actor for selling out, for playing stereotyped "coolie" and "dirty Jap" parts. Essentially, what Bradley is accusing Vincent of being is a Tom:

The Business. You keep talking about the business. The industry. Hollywood. What's Hollywood? Cutting up your face to look more white? So my nose is a little flat. Fine! Flat is beautiful. So I don't have a double fold in my eye-lid. Great! No one in my entire racial family has had it in the last 10,000 years.

My old girlfriend used to put scotch tape on her eyelids to get the double folds so she could look more "cau-ca-sian." My new girlfriend—she doesn't mess around, she got surgery. Where does it stop? "I never turned down a role." Where does it begin? Vincent? Where does it begin? All that self hate. You and your Charlie Chop Suey roles.

Vincent tells Bradley that he knows nothing about the difficulties he, Vincent, went through: "You want to know the truth? I'm glad I did it . . . in some small way it is a victory. Yes, a victory. At least an oriental was on the screen acting, being seen. We existed!" At this point, the scene slides into a father and son mode, where the father-figure, Vincent, tells Bradley that he should appreciate what those who went before him have done; it's east now for Bradley to spout the rhetoric of Asian-American consciousness, but in the past, such rhetoric was unthinkable. (Earlier in the play, when Vincent says, "I do not really notice, or quite frankly care, if someone is oriental or caucasian . . .") Bradley makes a certain connection between Asian-American rights and other liberation movements. "It's Asian, not oriental," he says. "Asian, oriental. Black, negro. Woman, girl. Gay, homosexual.")

But Bradley then gets on a soapbox and makes a cogent point, though a bit baldly, and I can easily imagine a young Black actor making a similar argument to an old Black actor who has done Stepin Fetchit roles:

You seem to think that every time you do one of those demeaning roles, all that is lost is your dignity . . . Don't you realize that every time you do a portrayal like that millions of people in their homes, in movie theatres across the country will see it. Be influenced by it. Believe it. Every time you do any old stereotypic role just to pay the bills, you kill the right of some Asian-American child to be treated as a human being. To walk through the school yard and not be called a "chinaman gook" by some taunting kids who just saw the last Rambo film.

By the end of the play, though, it's clear Bradley's been beaten down. After scrambling through failed audition after audition, wanting to make it in the business, he cries when he fails to get a role as a butler because he doesn't know kung fu. He also reveals he has recently had his nose fixed, á la Michael Jackson.

What do the similarities I've been pointing out mean for an Asian-American writer? Recently, there have been a spate of books, such as Allan Bloom's *The Closing of the American Mind*, which call for a return to the classics and a notion of a core-cultural tradition; these critiques bemoan the relativism and "nihilism" of the sixties and the multicultural movements which, in the name of "tolerance," have supposedly left our culture in a shambles. Unfortunately, such critics never really question the political and historical bases of cultural response. If they did, they would understand why, contrary to Allan Bloom, other minority writers represent a valuable resource for Asian-American writers and vice versa: our themes and difficulties are similar; we learn from each other things we cannot receive from a Saul Bellow or John Updike or even Rousseau or Plato.

It is not just the work of Asian-American writers like Gotanda that sustain me. I know a key point in my life was when I discovered the work of Frantz Fanon, particularly his book, *Black Skin, White Masks*. My experience with that work and others like it shows why multiculturalism, for a member of a racial minority, is not simply tolerance, but an essential key to survival.

In his work, Fanon, a Black psychologist, provides a cogent analysis of how a majority can oppress a minority through culture: it makes the victim or servant identify with the ruler and, in so doing, causes the victim to direct whatever anger he/she feels at the situation towards himself/herself in the form of self-hatred.

In the Antilles . . . in the magazines, the Wolf, the Devil, the Evil Spirit, the Bad Man, the Savage are always symbolized by Negroes or Indians; since there is always identification with the victor, the little Negro, quite as easily as the little white boy, becomes an explorer, an adventurer, a missionary "who faces the danger of being eaten by the wicked Negroes" . . . The black school boy . . . who in his lessons is forever talking about "our ancestors, the Gauls," identifies himself with the explorer, the bringer of civilization, the white man who carries truth to the savages—an all-white truth . . . the young Negro . . . invests the hero, who is white, with all his own aggression—at that age closely linked to sacrificial dedication, a sacrificial dedication permeated with sadism.

This passage can be taken as another version of Bradley's speech to Vincent on the effects of stereotypes on an Asian-American child.

Fanon was incredibly aware of how the economic, social, and political relations of power create and warp an individual's psychic identity. He was quick to point out that psychic sickness does not always find its source in the neuroses of an individual or that individual's family, but in the greater sickness of a society. In such cases, for the individual to become healthy, he or she must recognize that society is sick, and that the ideas he or she has received from that society are part of that sickness.

In short, what Fanon recognized and taught me was the liberating power of anger.

After reading Fanon and the Black French poet from Martinique, Aime Cesaire, I wrote a number of poems in which I chose to ally myself with people of color, anti-colonialist movements, and a non-Eurocentric consciousness. When writing these poems, I was aware of how such poems can often become vehicles for slogans and cheap rhetoric; still I tried to discover a language with a denseness which would prevent such reduction, increase thought, and turn words like "gook" and "nigger" against their original meaning, bending and realigning the slang of racism. Here is the ending of one of those poems:

. . . and we were all good niggers, good gooks and japs, good spics and rice eaters saying mem sab, sahib, bwana, boss-san, señor, father, heartthrob oh honored and most unceasing, oh devisor and provider of our own obsequious, ubiquitous ugliness, which stares at you baboon-like, banana-like, dwarf-like, tortoise-like, dirt-like, slant-eyed, kink-haired, ashen and pansied and brutally unredeemable, we are whirling about you, tartars of the air all the urinating, tarantula grasping, ant multiplying, succubused, hothouse hoards yes, it us, it us, we, we knockee, yes, sir, massa, boss-san, we tearee down your door!

I was scared at first by the anger of this poem, but I also saw it as an answer, an antidote to the depression I had been feeling, a depression brought on by a lack of self-worth and by my dropping out of English graduate school. As my therapist had told me, depression is the repression of anger and grief. In my diary I wrote about the unlocking of this repression:

In the first stages of such a process, one can enter a position where the destruction of one stereotype creates merely a new stereotype, and where the need to point out injustice overwhelms and leaves the writing with a baldness that seems both naive and sentimental. Still, the task must be faced, and what I am now trying to do in both my writing and my life is to replace self-hatred and self-negation with anger and grief over my lost selves, over the ways my cultural heritage has been denied to me, over the ways that people in America would assume either that I am not American or, conversely, that I am just like them; over the ways my education and the values of European culture have denied that other cultures exist. I know more about Europe at the time when my grandfather came to America than I know about Meiji Japan. I know Shakespeare and Donne, Sophocles and Homer better than I know Zeami, Bashō or Lady Murasaki. This is not to say I regret what I know, but I do regret what I don't know. And the argument that the culture of America is derived from Europe will not wipe away this regret.

I am convinced if I had not read Fanon, if I had not reached these insights, and gone on to explore beyond white European culture, I would have died as a writer and died spiritually and psychically as a person. I would have ended up denying who I am and my place in history. Thus, I think that to deny a people a right to determine their own cultural tradition is a type of genocide.

Of course, arguing for multiculturalism is not the same thing as saying that, as a minority writer, I don't need to read the works of European culture. It's not a case of either/or. As Carlos Feuntes remarked, "We [Latin Americans] have to know the cultures of the West even better than a Frenchman or an Englishman, and at the same time we have to know our own cultures. This sometimes means going back to the Indian cultures, whereas the Europeans feel they don't have to know our cultures at all. We have to know Quetzalcoatl and Descartes. They think Descartes is enough.'' I think Fuentes would agree with Jesse Jackson that there was something wrong with those students who greeted his appearance at Stanford with the chant, ''Hey hey, ho ho/Western culture's got to go.'' As Jackson pointed out, Western culture was their culture. It is difficult to strike an appropriate balance.

In the same issue of the *Village Voice* that the article about the Black nannies appeared, Stanley Couch wrote a perceptive, challenging critique of James Baldwin. Crouch argues that at the beginning of Baldwin's career, Baldwin was able to maneuver his way through subtleties of the Black writer's position. As an example of this, Crouch cites Baldwin's distinction between sociology and literature in evaluating the work of Richard Wright; Baldwin argues that despite the good intentions of protest novels, they cannot succeed if they are ''badly written and wildly improbable.'' Still Crouch maintains that very early Baldwin's vision began to blur, and cites this passage from the essay, ''Stranger in the Village,'' a depiction of Baldwin's visit to a Swiss town and his sense of alienation from its people:

These people cannot be, from the point of view of power, strangers anywhere in the world; they have made the modern world, in effect, even if they do not know it. The most illiterate among them is related, in a way that I am not, to Dante, Shakespeare, Michelangelo, Aeschylus, da Vinci, Rembrandt, and Racine; the cathedral at Chartres says something to them that it cannot say to me, as indeed would New York's Empire State Building, should anyone here ever see it. Out of their hymns and dances come Beethoven and Bach. Go back a few centuries and they are in their full glory—but I am in Africa, watching the conquerors arrive.

Crouch charges Baldwin with slipping into a simplistic dualistic thinking, with letting his rage create a we—they attitude which denies the complexity of the race situation:

Such thinking leads to the problems we still face in which too many so-called nonwhite people look upon ''the West'' as some catchall in which every European or person of European descent is somehow part of a structure bent solely on excluding or intimidating the Baldwins of the world. Were Roland Hayes, Marian Anderson, Leontyne Price, Jessye Norman, or Kiri Te Kanawa to have taken such a position, they would have locked themselves out of a world of music that originated neither among Afro-Americans nor Maoris. Further, his ahistorical ignorance is remarkable, and perhaps willful.

If Baldwin's position is that Afro-Americans cannot learn, or enjoy or perform European culture, or that European culture is worthless to an Afro-American, that is nonsense. But that is not Baldwin's position. He is simply arguing that his relationship to that culture is different from a white European; he views that culture through the experience of a Black American, and if he is to be faulted, it is because he does not give a detailed enough explanation of how his experience as a Black American informs his experience of European culture. But none of this—including the success of opera stars like Jessye Norman—negates the fact that, in American and Europe, European culture has political—that is, ideological—effects and one effect is to reinforce the political power of those of European descent and to promote a view of whites as superior to coloreds. (It is not the only effect of that culture, but again, neither Baldwin nor I am arguing that it is.)

Crouch goes on to argue that ''breaking through the mask of collective whiteness—collective guilt—that Baldwin imposes would demand recognition of the fact that, as history and national chauvinism prove, Europe is not a one-celled organism.'' I will say more about collective guilt a bit later, but it is interesting to note that Crouch refuses the concept of collectivity when it comes to guilt, yet at the same time charges that Baldwin refuses to entertain the possibility of "the international wonder of human heritage." Guilt can never be held collectively, but culture, specifically European culture, can be universal.

Yet, at the same time Crouch argues the non-exclusivity of European culture, he chastises Baldwin for taking the themes of third-World writers and adapting them to the context of America: "the denial by Europeans of non-Western cultural complexity—or parity; the social function of the inferiority complex colonialism threw over the native like a net; the alignment of Christianity and cruelty under colonialism, and the idea that world views were at odds, European versus the 'spirit of Bandung,' or the West in the ring with the Third World." How sharp the boundaries of culture should be is a difficult question; it may seem that both Crouch and Baldwin want things both ways: they just disagree on which cultures can attain universality, European culture or that of the Third World. To sort out the specifics of each of their cases requires us to connect attitudes towards culture with feelings about race, specifically the rage of Blacks and other colored minorities in America.

As I've already argued with my own reading of Frantz Fanon, I do think it is illuminating and useful to use Third-World problems in looking at the race issue in America. Still, I also agree with Crouch that there are fundamental differences between the position of Blacks in America and that of colonials in the Third World. To forget these differences in a desire to be at one with all oppressed peoples is both false and dangerous. And I recognize that when borrowing or learning from the language of Third-World peoples and American Blacks, Japanese-Americans, like myself, must still recognize fundamental differences between

our position and that of other people of color, whether here or in the third World.

Part of the danger is that if we ignore the specifics of the situation of our own minority group, in essence we both deny who we are and our own complexity. We also run the risk of using our victimhood as a mask for sainthood, of letting whatever sins the white race has committed against us become a permanent absolution for us, an excuse to forgo moral and psychological introspection. Crouch argues somewhat convincingly that this is exactly the trap that Baldwin fell into and cites as evidence Baldwin's remark that "Rage can only with difficulty, and never entirely, be brought under the domination of the intelligence and is therefore not susceptible to any arguments whatever." According to Crouch, Baldwin, as his career progressed, sold out to rage, despair, self-righteousness, and a will to scandalize:

In America . . . fat-mouthing Negroes . . . chose to sneer at the heroic optimism of the Civil Rights Movement; they developed their own radical chic and spoke of Malcom X as being beyond compromise, of his unwillingness to cooperate with the white man, and of his ideas of being too radical for assimilation. Baldwin was sucked into this world of intellectual airlessness. By *The Fire Next Time*, Baldwin is so happy to see white policemen made uncomfortable by Muslim rallies, and so willing to embrace almost anything that disturbs whites in general, that he starts competing with the apocalyptic tone of the Nation of Islam.

In focusing on Baldwin's inability to transform or let go his rage, I feel Crouch finally hits upon something. I also feel a shudder of self-recognition. Yet the condition Crouch pictures here is a bit more complex than he admits. Certainly, a convincing argument can be made that King's appeal to a higher yet common morality was and will be more effective than Malcom X's in changing the hearts and minds of whites in America, yet in his very approach to the problem, Crouch seems to put the burden for change upon the Black minority rather than on the white majority. There is something intellectually and morally dishonest about this. For whether one judges King's philosophy or Malcom X's as correct depends in part on a reading of the hearts and minds of white Americans. If those hearts and minds are fiercely unchanging, then Malcom X's might seem the more logical stance. Either way, it is a judgment call and it involves a great deal of uncertainty, especially since that judgment involves actions in the future. Yet nowhere in his argument does Crouch concede this.

Shaw called hatred the coward's revenge for ever having been intimidated, says Crouch, and Crouch sees this hatred as the basis of Baldwin's attitude towards whites and towards European culture. I find something skewed in Crouch's use of Shaw's quip here. Given the history of race in America, equating a Black man's sense of intimidation solely with cowardice seems a simplification; couldn't that intimidation in many cases be an acknowledgment of reality? Admittedly, there is in Baldwin that self-righteousness, that rage not quite under control. I know myself how easy it is to give in to it. But Crouch's approach to the dialectics of rage seems to me entirely unrealistic. In my poem, "Song For Artaud, Fanon, Cesaire, Uncle Tom, Tonto and Mr. Moto," I recognize a certain demagogic tone, a triumphant and self-righteous bitterness and rage. And yet, I also recognize that my rage needed to be released, that it had been held back in my own psyche for too many years, held back within my family, and held back within my race in America. That rage was liberating for me, just as it is for any oppressed people. As should be obvious to anyone, those who are oppressed cannot change their situation, cannot own themselves, unless they finally own their rage at their condition and those who have caused it. Crouch seems to have wanted Baldwin to overcome or stand above this

rage, but there is a certain wishful thinking in this. One does not overcome or stand above this rage: one first goes through it, and then leaves it behind.

The problem is that this process is both long and complicated and neither Crouch nor Baldwin quite understands what it entails: one must learn first how liberating anger feels, then how intoxicating, then how damaging, and in each of these stages, the reason for these feelings must be admitted and accurately described. It may be argued that Baldwin accomplished the first of these tasks—the liberation that comes from rage—and that he alluded or hinted at the second—the intoxication that comes from rage—and even at times alluded or hinted at the third, but for the most, because he never accurately described how intoxicating the rage he felt was, he could never see how damaging it was.

For it is intoxicating after years of feeling inferior, after years of hating oneself, it is so comforting to use this rage not just to feel equal to the oppressor, but superior, and not just superior, but simply blameless and blessed, one of the prophetic and holy ones. It is what one imagines a god feels like, and in this state one does feel like a god of history, a fate; one knows that history is on one's side, because one is helping to break open, to recreate history. And how much better it is to feel like a god after years of worshipping the oppressor as one.

But once one can clearly describe all this, one realizes that such a stance represents a new form of hubris, an intoxicating blindness: human beings are not gods, are not superior to other human beings. Human beings are fallible, cannot foresee the future, cannot demand or receive freely the worship of others. In aligning one's rage with a sense of superiority, one fails to recognize how this rage is actually fueled by a sense of inferiority: one's own version of history and views on equality need, on some level, the approval, the assent, the defeat of the oppressor. The wish for superiority is simply the reverse side of feeling inferior, not its cure. It focuses all the victim's problems on the other, the oppressor. Yet until it is recognized how one has contributed to this victimhood, the chains are still there, inside, are part of the psyche. Conversely, liberation occurs only when one is sure enough of oneself, feels good enough, to admit fault, admit their portion of blame.

Given the difficulty of this process, it's no wonder so many stumble in the process or stop midway through. And it is made much more difficult if the oppressor is especially recalcitrant, is implacable towards change. When this happens, fresh wound after fresh wound is inflicted, causing bundle after bundle of rage: bitterness then becomes too tempting; too much energy is required to heal. To his credit, Crouch shows some understanding of this fact in relationship to Baldwin: "Perhaps it is understandable that Baldwin could not resist the contemptuous pose of militance that gave focus to all of his anger for being the homely duckling, who never became a swan, the writer who would perhaps never have been read by so many Black people otherwise, and the homosexual who lived abroad most of his adult life in order to enjoy his preferences."

In the end, though, Crouch never comes to terms with the sources of Baldwin's rage. One reason for this is Crouch's belief that "collective whiteness—and *collective guilt*" were merely a mask, a simplification for Baldwin.

Part of Crouch's problem is that he distorts Baldwin's position. On the one hand, it is a simplification to pretend that collective whiteness and collective guilt are the *only* ways to view the race situation in America. But it is not a simplification to say that collective whiteness and collective white guilt

*do exist.* The superior economic and political power of whites as compared to colored minorities in this country is a fact, and on some level, every white in this country benefits from that power. Of course, this does not mean that every white has more economic and political power than every member of the colored minorities. But it is not just this inequality of power that makes collective white guilt a fact; it is the way that power was acquired and the way its sources have been kept hidden from the consciousness of both whites and colored minorities that makes this term applicable.

Here I return to the fundamental historical events I mentioned earlier in this essay: the enslavement of Blacks, the taking of Native American land and the genocidal policies that accomplished it. One can think of other related historical events: the internment camps, the Asian-Exclusion act, the conditions of the Asian workers building the American rail roads, the conditions of migrant farm workers and illegal aliens. The list could go on and on. But that is to point out the obvious. What is not so obvious is how the laws of property in our society have served to make permanent what was stolen in the past. Those who bought my grandparents' property for a song still benefit from that property today; there has been no compensation, just as there has been no compensation to Blacks for the institution of slavery or to Native Americans for the taking of a continent and the destruction of their peoples and culture. And as long as there is no movement toward a just compensation, the collective guilt will remain.

And yet I also recognize that a just compensation is not possible. The wrongs are too great, run too far back in history, and human beings are fallible and forgetful. Justice demands too high a price.

Therefore we must settle for less, for a compromise. The concept of white collective guilt reminds us of this compromise, that there has been and probably will always be a less than even settling of the debt. However whites protest that they want equality and justice, they are, in the end, not willing to pay the price. And when those they have wronged call for the price, the reaction of whites is almost always one of anger and resentment.

Now, in this situation, the whites have two choices. When they accept the concept of collective guilt, they admit that they feel unjustifiable anger and resentment at any measure that threatens any part of their privileged position, much less any of the measures that approach just compensation. When whites don't admit collective guilt, they try to blame racial troubles on those who ask for a just settlement and remain baffled at the anger and resentment of the colored minorities.

Whether in the area of culture or in economic relations, these choices remain. In the realm of culture in America, white European culture has held the floor for centuries; just as with any one-sided conversation, a balance can only be achieved if the speaker who has dominated speaks less and listens more. That is what conservative culture critics are unwilling to do; for them there is no such thing as collective guilt, much less the obligation such guilt bestows. It is not just that the colored minorities in America need to create and receive their own cultural images, nor that, for these minorities, the culture of the Third World and its struggles against white-dominated cultures pro-

vides insights into race in America that cannot be found in European literature. This much ought to seem obvious. But there is more: only when whites in America begin to listen to the voices of the colored minorities and the Third World will they come to understand not just those voices but also themselves and their world. Reality is not simply knowing who we think we are, but also what others think of us. And only with this knowledge will whites ever understand what needs to be done to make things equal.

The situation in the *Voice* article on nannies is not different: without admitting the concept of collective guilt, the white middle-class Barbra remains unable to comprehend her nanny Bertha, unable to understand what this Black woman feels. Ultimately, Barbra does not want to admit that the only way she is going to feel comfortable with Bertha is if they meet as equals; that society must be changed so that Barbra and her children will not enjoy certain privileges they have taken as rights. In short Barbra and other whites will have to give up power; that is what it means to make things equal. At the same time she must admit that no matter how much she works for change, how much society changes, there will never, on this earth, be a just settling of accounts. That is the burden she has to take up; she may think it will destroy her, but it will not. And, ultimately, this process would not only help Bertha to meet and know Barbra as an equal, but for Barbra to understand an accept who she is, to know herself.

# How I Started to Write

*Carlos Fuentes*

## I

I was born on November 11, 1928, under the sign I would have chosen, Scorpio, and on a date shared with Dostoevsky, Crommelynck, and Vonnegut. My mother was rushed from a steaming-hot movie house in those days before Colonel Buendia took his son to discover ice in the tropics. She was seeing King Vidor's version of *La Bohème* with John Gilbert and Lillian Gish. Perhaps the pangs of my birth were provoked by this anomaly: a silent screen version of Puccini's opera. Since then, the operatic and the cinematographic have had a tug-of-war with my words, as if expecting the Scorpio of fiction to rise from silent music and blind images.

All this, let me add to clear up my biography, took place in the sweltering heat of Panama City, where my father was beginning his diplomatic career as an attaché to the Mexican legation. (In those days, embassies were established only in the most important capitals—no place where the mean average year-round temperature was perpetually in the nineties.) Since my father was a convinced Mexican nationalist, the problem of where I was to be born had to be resolved

under the sign, not of Scorpio, but of the Eagle and the Serpent. The Mexican legation, however, though it had extraterritorial rights, did not have even a territorial midwife; and the minister, a fastidious bachelor from Sinaloa by the name of Ignacio Norris, who resembled the poet Quevedo as one pince-nez resembles another, would have none of me suddenly appearing on the legation parquet, even if the Angel Gabriel had announced me as a future Mexican writer of some, albeit debatable, merit.

So if I could not be born in a fictitious, extraterritorial Mexico, neither would I be born in that even more fictitious extension of the United States of America, the Canal Zone, where, naturally, the best hospitals were. So, between two territorial fictions—the Mexican legation, the Canal Zone—and a mercifully silent close-up of John Gilbert, I arrived in the nick of time at the Gorgas Hospital in Panama City at eleven that evening.

The problem of my baptism then arose. As if the waters of the two neighboring oceans touching each other with the iron fingertips of the canal were not enough, I had to undergo a double ceremony: my religious baptism took place in Panama, because my mother, a devout Roman Catholic, demanded it with as much urgency as Tristram Shandy's parents, although through less original means. My national baptism took place a few months later in Mexico City, where my father, an incorrigible Jacobin and priest-eater to the end, insisted that I be

Carlos Fuentes, a professor of Latin American Studies at Harvard University, is the author of several novels and collections of essays.

registered in the civil rolls established by Benito Juárez. Thus, I appear as a native of Mexico City for all legal purposes, and this anomaly further illustrates a central fact of my life and my writing: I am Mexican by will and by imagination.

All this came to a head in the 1930s. By then, my father was counselor of the Mexican Embassy in Washington, D.C., and I grew up in the vibrant world of the American thirties, more or less between the inauguration of Citizen Roosevelt and the interdiction of Citizen Kane. When I arrived here, Dick Tracy had just met Tess Trueheart. As I left, Clark Kent was meeting Lois Lane. You are what you eat. you are also the comics you peruse as a child.

At home, my father made me read Mexican history, study Mexican geography, and understand the names, the dreams and defeats of Mexico: a nonexistent country, I then thought, invented by my father to nourish my infant imagination with yet another marvelous fiction: a land of Oz with a green cactus road, a landscape and a soul so different from those of the United States that they seemed a fantasy.

A cruel fantasy: the history of Mexico was a history of crushing defeats, whereas I lived in a world, that of my D.C. public school, which celebrated victories, one victory after another, from Yorktown to New Orleans to Chapultepec to Appomattox to San Juan Hill to Belleau Wood: had this nation ever known defeat? Sometimes the names of United States victories were the same as the names of Mexico's defeats and humiliations: Monterrey. Veracruz. Chapultepec. Indeed: from the Halls of Montezuma to the shores of Tripoli. In the map of my imagination, as the United States expanded westward, Mexico contracted southward. Miguel Hidalgo, the father of Mexican independence, ended up with his head on exhibit on a lance at the city gates of Chihuahua.

Imagine George and Martha beheaded at Mount Vernon.

To the south, sad songs, sweet nostalgia, impossible desires. To the north, self-confidence, faith in progress, boundless optimism. Mexico, the imaginary country, dreamed of a painful past; the United States, the real country, dreamed of a happy future.

The French equate intelligence with rational discourse, the Russians with intense soul-searching. For a Mexican, intelligence is inseparable from maliciousness—in this, as in many other things, we are quite Italian: *furberia,* roguish slyness and the cult of appearances, *la bella figura,* are Italianate traits present everywhere in Latin America: Rome, more than Madrid, is our spiritual capital in this sense.

For me, as a child, the United States seemed a world where intelligence was equated with energy, zest, enthusiasm. The North American world blinds us with its energy; we cannot see ourselves, we must see *you.* The United States is a world full of cheerleaders, prize-giving, singin' in the rain: the baton twirler, the Oscar awards, the musical comedies cannot be repeated elsewhere; in Mexico, the Hollywood statuette would come dipped in poisoned paint; in France, Gene Kelly would constantly stop in his steps to reflect: *Je danse, donc je suis.*

Many things impressed themselves on me during those years. The United States—would you believe it?—was a country where things worked, where nothing every broke down: trains, plumbing, roads, punctuality, personal security seemed to function perfectly, at least on the eye level of a young Mexican diplomat's son living in a residential hotel on Washington's Sixteenth Street, facing Meridian Hill Park, where nobody was then mugged and where our superb furnished seven-room apartment cost us 110 pre-inflation dollars a month. Yes, in spite of all the problems, the livin' seemed easy during those long Tidewater summers when I became perhaps the first and only Mexican Calvinist: an invisible taskmaster called Puritanical Duty shadows my every footstep: I shall not deserve anything unless I work relentlessly for it, with iron discipline, day after day. Sloth is sin, and if I do not sit at my typewriter every day at 8 a.m. for a working day of seven to eight hours, I will surely go to hell. No *siestas* for me, alas and alack and *hélas* and *ay-ay-ay:* how I came to envy my Latin brethren, unburdened by the Protestant work ethic, and why must I, to this very day, read the complete works of Hermann Broch and scribble in my black notebook on a sunny Mexican beach, instead of lolling the day away and waiting for the coconuts to fall?

But the United States in the thirties went far beyond my person experience. The nation that Tocqueville had destined to share dominance over half the world realized that, in effect, only a continental state could be a modern state; in the thirties, the U.S.A. had to decide *what to do* with its new world-wide power, and Franklin Roosevelt taught us to believe that the first thing was for the United States to show that it was capable of living up to its ideals. I learned then—my first political lesson—that this is your true greatness, not, as was to be the norm of my lifetime, material wealth, not arrogant power misused against weaker peoples, not ignorant ethnocentrism burning itself out in contempt for others.

As a young Mexican growing up in the U.S., I had a primary impression of a nation of boundless energy, imagination, and the will to confront and solve the great social issues of the times without blinking or looking for scapegoats. It was the impression of a country identified with its own highest principles: political democracy, economic well-being, and faith in its human resources, especially in that most precious of all capital, the renewable wealth of education and research.

Franklin Roosevelt, then, restored America's self-respect in this essential way, not by macho posturing. I saw the United States in the thirties left itself by its bootstraps from the dead dust of Oklahoma and the gray lines of the unemployed in Detroit, and this image of health was reflected in my daily life, in my reading of Mark Twain, in the images of movies and newspapers, in the North American capacity for mixing fluffy illusion and hard-bitten truth, self-celebration and self-criticism: the madcap heiresses played by Carole Lombard coexisted with the Walker Evans photographs of hungry, old-at-thirty migrant mothers, and the nimble tread of the feet of Fred Astaire did not silence the heavy stomp of the boots of Tom Joad.

My school—a public school, nonconfessional and coeducational—reflected these realities and their basically egalitarian thrust. I believed in the democratic simplicity of my teachers and chums, and above all I believed I was, naturally, in a totally unself-conscious way, a part of that world. It is important, at all ages and in all occupations, to be "popular" in the United States; I have known no other society where the values of "regularity" are so highly prized. I was popular, I was "regular." Until a day in March—March 18, 1938. On that day, a man from another world, the imaginary country of my childhood, the president of Mexico, Lázaro Cárdenas, nationalized the holdings of foreign oil companies. The headlines in the North American press denounced the "communist" government of Mexico and its "red" president; they demanded the invasion of Mexico in the sacred name of private property, and Mexicans, under international boycott, were invited to drink their oil.

Instantly, surprisingly, I became a pariah in my school. Cold shoulders, aggressive stares, epithets, and sometimes blows. Children know how to be cruel, and the cruelty of their elders is the surest residue of the malaise the young feel toward things strange, things other, things that reveal our own ignorance or insufficiency. This was not reserved for me or for Mexico: at about the same time, an extremely brilliant boy of eleven arrived from Germany. He was a Jew and his family had fled from the Nazis. is shall always remember his face, dark and trembling, his aquiline nose and deep-set, bright eyes with their great sadness; the sensitivity of his hands and the strangeness of it all to his American companions. This young man, Hans Berliner, had a brilliant mathematical mind and he walked and saluted like a Central European; he wore short pants and high woven stocking, Tyrolean jackets and an air of displaced courtesy that infuriated the popular, regular, feisty, knickered, provincial, Depression-era little sons of bitches at Henry Cooke Public School on Thirteenth Street N.W.

The shock of alienation and the shock of recognition are sometimes one and the same. What was different made others afraid, less of what was different than of themselves, of their own incapacity to recognize themselves in the alien.

I discovered that my father's country was real. And that I belonged to it. Mexico was my identity yet I lacked an identity; Hans Berliner suffered more than I—headlines from Mexico are soon forgotten; another great issue becomes all-important for a wonderful ten days' media feast—yet he had an identity as a Central European Jew. I do not know what became of him. Over the years, I have always expected to see him receive a Nobel Prize in one of the sciences. Surely, if he lived, he integrated himself into North American society. I had to look at the photographs of President Cárdenas: he was a man of another lineage; he did not appear in the repertory of glossy, seductive images of

the salable North American world. He was a mestizo, Spanish and Indian, with a faraway, green, and liquid look in his eyes, as if he were trying to remember a mute and ancient past.

Was that past mine as well? Could I dream the dreams of the country suddenly revealed in a political act as something more than a demarcation of frontiers on a map or a hillock of statistics in a yearbook? I believe I then had the intuition that I would not rest until I came to grips myself with that common destiny which depended upon still another community: the community of time. The United States had made me believe that we live only for the future; Mexico, Cárdenas, the events of 1938, made me understand that only in an act of the present can we make present the past as well as the future: to be a Mexican was to identify a hunger for being, a desire for dignity rooted in many forgotten centuries and in many centuries yet to come, but rooted here, now, in the instant, in the vigilant time of Mexico I later learned to understand in the stone serpents of Teotihuacán and in the polychrome angels of Oaxaca.

Of course, as happens in childhood, all these deep musings had no proof of existence outside an act that was, more than a prank, a kind of affirmation. In 1939, my father took me to see a film at the old RKO-Keith in Washington. It was called *Man of Conquest* and it starred Richard Dix as Sam Houston. When Dix/Houston proclaimed the secession of the Republic of Texas from Mexico, I jumped on the theater seat and proclaimed on my own and from the full height of my nationalist ten years, "Viva México! Death to the gringos!" My embarrassed father hauled me out of the theater, but his pride in me could not resist leaking my first rebellious act to the *Washington Star*. So I appeared for the first time in a newspaper and became a child celebrity for the acknowledged ten-day span. I read Andy Warhol *avant l'air-brush:* Everyone shall be famous for at least five minutes.

In the wake of my father's diplomatic career, I traveled to Chile and entered fully the universe of the Spanish language, of Latin American politics and its adversities. President Roosevelt had resisted enormous pressures to apply sanctions and even invade Mexico to punish my country for recovering its own wealth. Likewise, he did not try to destabilize the Chilean radicals, communists, and socialists democratically elected to power in Chile under the banners of the Popular Front. In the early forties, the vigor of Chile's political life was contagious: active unions, active parties, electoral campaigns all spoke of the political health of this, the most democratic of Latin American nations. Chile was a politically verbalized country. It was no coincidence that it was also the country of the great Spanish-American poets Gabriela Mistral, Vicente Huidobro, Pablo Neruda.

I only came to know Neruda and became his friend many years later. This King Midas of poetry would write, in his literary testament rescued from a gutted house and a nameless tomb, a beautiful song to the Spanish language. The Conquistadors, he said, took our gold, but they left us their gold: they left us our words. Neruda's gold, I learned in Chile, was the property of all. One afternoon on the beach at Lota in southern Chile, I saw the miners as they came out, mole-like, from their hard work many feet under the sea, extracting the coal of the Pacific Ocean. They sat around a bonfire and sang, to guitar music, a poem from Neruda's *Canto General.* I told them that the author would be thrilled to know that his poem had been set to music.

What author? they asked me in surprise. For them, Neruda's poetry had no author, it came from afar, it had always been sung, like Homer's. It was the poetry, as Croce said of the *Iliad,* "d'un popolo intero poetante," of an entire poetizing people. It was the document of the original identity of poetry and history.

I learned in Chile that Spanish could be the language of free men. I was also to learn in my lifetime, in Chile in 1973, the fragility of both our language and our freedom when Richard Nixon, unable to destroy American democracy, merrily helped to destroy Chilean democracy, the same thing Leonid Brezhnev had done in Czechoslovakia.

An anonymous language, a language that belongs to us all, as Neruda's poem belonged to those miners on the beach, yet a language that can be kidnapped, impoverished, sometimes jailed, sometimes murdered. Let me summarize this paradox: Chile offered me and the other writers of my generation in Santiago both the essential fragility of a cornered langauge, Spanish, and the protection of the Latin of our times, the lingua franca of the modern world, the English language. At the Grange School, under the awesome beauty of the Andes, José Donoso and Jorge Edwards, Roberta Torretti, the late Luis Alberto Heyremans, and myself, by then all budding amateurs, wrote our first exercises in literature within this mini-Britannia. We all ran strenuous cross-country races, got caned from time to time, and recuperated while reading Swinburne; and we were subjected to huge doses of rugby, Ruskin, porridge for breakfast, and a stiff upper lip in military defeats. But when Montgomery broke through at El Alamein, the assembled school tossed caps in the air and hip-hip-hoorrayed to death. In South America, clubs were named after George Canning and football teams after Lord Cochrane; no matter that English help in winning independence led to English economic imperialism, from oil in Mexico to railways in Argentina. There was a secret thrill in our hearts: our Spanish conquerors had been beaten by the English; the defeat of Philip II's invincible Armada compensated for the crimes of Cortés, Pizarro, and Valdivia. If Britain was an empire, at least she was a democratic one.

In Washington, I had begun writing a personal magazine in English, with my own drawings, book reviews, and epochal bits of news. It consisted of a single copy, penciled and crayonned, and its circulation was limited to our apartment building. Then, at age fourteen, in Chile, I embarked on a more ambitious project, along with my schoolmate Roberto Torretti: a vast Caribbean saga that was to culminate in Haiti on a hilltop palace (Sans Souci?) where a black tyrant kept a mad French mistress in a garret. All this was set in the early nineteenth century and in the final scene (Shades of Jane Eyre! Reflections on Rebecca! Fans of Joan Fontaine!) the palace was to burn down, along with the world of slavery.

But where to begin? Torretti and I were, along with our literary fraternity at The Grange, avid readers of Dumas *père*. A self-respecting novel, in our view, had to start in Marseilles, in full view of the Chateau d'If and the martyrdom of Edmond Dantès. But we were writing in Spanish, not in French, and our characters had to speak Spanish. But, what Spanish? My Mexican Spanish, or Roberto's Chilean Spanish? We came to a sort of compromise: the characters would speak like Andalusians. This was probably a tacit homage to the land from which Columbus sailed.

The Mexican painter David Alfaro Siqueiros was then in Chile, painting the heroic murals of a school in the town of Chillán, which had been devastated by one of Chile's periodic earthquakes. He had been implicated in a Stalinish attempt on Trotsky's life in Mexico City and his commission to paint a mural in the Southern Cone was a kind of honorary exile. My father, as chargé d'affaires in Santiago, where his mission was to press the proudly independent Chileans to break relations with the Berlin-Rome Axis, rose above politics in the name of art and received Siqueiros regularly for lunch at the Mexican Embassy, which was a delirious mansion, worthy of William Beckford's follies, built by an enriched Italian tailor called Fallabella, on Santiago's broad Pedro de Valdivia Avenue.

This Gothic grotesque contained a Chinese room with nodding Buddhas, an office in what was known as Westminister Parliamentary style, Napoleonic lobbies, Louis XV dining rooms, Art Deco bedrooms, a Florentine loggia, many busts of Dante, and, finally, a vast Chilean vineyard in the back.

It was here, under the bulging Austral grapes, that I forced Siquiros to sit after lunch and listen to me read our by then 400-page-long opus. As he drowsed off in the shade, I gained and lost my first reader. The novel, too, was lost; Torretti, who now teaches philosophy of science at the University of Puerto Rico, has no copy; Siqueiros is dead, and, besides, he slept right through my reading. I myself feel about it like Marlowe's Barabbas about fornication: that was in another country, and, besides, the wench is dead. Yet the experience of writing this highly imitative melodrama was not lost on me; its international setting, its self-conscious search for language (or languages, rather) were part of a constant attempt at a breakthrough in my life. My upbringing taught me that cultures are not isolated, and perish when deprived of contact with what is different and challenging. Reading, writing, teaching, learning, are all activities aimed at introducing civilizations to each other. No culture, I believed unconsciously ever since then, and quite consciously today, retains its identity in isolation; identity is attained in contact, in contrast, in breakthrough.

Rhetoric, said William Butler Yeats, is the language of our fight with others; poetry is the name of our fight with ourselves. My passage from English to Spanish determined the concrete expression of what, before, in Washington, had been the revelation of an identity. I wanted to write and I wanted to write in order to show myself that my identity and my country were real: now, in Chile, as I started to scribble my first stories, even publishing them in school magazines, I learned that I must in fact write in Spanish.

The English language, after all, did not need another writer. The English language has always been alive and kicking, and if it ever becomes drowsy, there will always be an Irishman.

In Chile I came to know the possibilities of our language for giving wing to freedom and poetry. The impression was enduring; it links me forever to that sad and wonderful land. It lives within me, and it transformed me into a man who knows how to dream, love, insult, and write only in Spanish. It also left me wide open to an incessant interrogation: What happened to this universal language, Spanish, which after the seventeenth century ceased to be a language of life, creation, dissatisfaction, and personal power and became far too often a language of mourning, sterility, rhetorical applause, and abstract power? Where were the threads of my tradition, where could I, writing in mid-twentieth century in Latin America, find the direct link to the great living presences I was then starting to read, my lost Cervantes, my old Quevedo, dead because he could not tolerate one more winter, my Góngora, abandoned in a gulf of loneliness?

At sixteen I finally went to live permanently in Mexico and there I found the answers to my quest for identity and language, in the thin air of a plateau of stone and dust that is the negative Indian image of another highland, that of central Spain. But, between Santiago and Mexico City, I spent six wonderful months in Argentina. They were, in spite of their brevity, so important in this reading and writing of myself that I must give them their full worth. Buenos Aires was then, as always, the most beautiful, sophisticated, and civilized city in Latin America, but in the summer of 1944, as street pavements melted in the heat and the city smelled of cheap wartime gasoline, rawhide from the port, and chocolate éclairs from the *confiterias,* Argentina had experienced a succession of military coups: General Rawson had overthrown President Castillo of the cattle oligarchy, but General Ramirez had then overthrown Rawson, and now General Farrell had overthrown Ramirez. A young colonel called Juan Domingo Perón was General Farrell's up-and-coming minister of Labor, and I heard an actress by the name of Eva Duarte play the "great women of history" on Radio Belgrano. A stultifying hack novelist who went by the pen name Hugo Wast was assigned to the Ministry of Education under his real name, Martínez Zuviría, and brought all his anti-Semitic, undemocratic, profascist phobias to the Buenos Aires high-school system, which I had suddenly been plunked into. Coming from the America of the new Deal, the ideals of revolutionary Mexico, and the politics of the Popular Front in Chile, I could not stomach this, rebelled, and was granted a full summer of wandering around Buenos Aires, free for the first time in my life, following my preferred tango orchestras—Canara, D'-Arienzo, and Anibal Troilo, alias Pichuco—as they played all summer long in the Renoir-like shade and light of the rivers and pavilions of El Tigre and Maldonado. Now the comics were in Spanish: Mutt and Jeff were Benitín y Eneas. But Argentina had its own comic-book imperialism: through the magazines *Biliken* and *Patorozú,* all the children of Latin America knew from the crib that "las Malvinas son Argentinas."

Two very important things happened. First, I lost my virginity. We lived in an apartment building on the leafy corner of Callao and Quintana, and after 10 A.M. nobody was there except myself, an old and deaf Polish doorkeeper, and a beautiful Czech woman, aged thirty, whose husband was a film producer. I went up to ask her for her *Sintonía,* which was the radio guide of the forties, because I wanted to know when Evita was doing Joan of Arc. She said that had passed, but the next program was Madame Du Barry. I wondered if Madame Du Barry's life was as interesting as Joan of Arc's. She said it was certainly less saintly, and, besides, it could be emulated. How? I said innocently. And thereby my beautiful apprenticeship. We made each other very happy. And also very sad: this was not the liberty of love, but rather its libertine variety: we loved in hiding. I was too young to be a real sadist. So it had to end.

The other important thing was that I started reading Argentine literature, from the gaucho poems to Sarmiento's *Memories of Provincial Life* to Cané's *Juvenilia* to Güiraldes's *Don Segundo Sombra* to . . . to . . . to—and this was as good as discovering that Joan of Arc was also sexy—to Borges. I have never wanted to meet Borges personally because he belongs to that summer in B.A. He belongs to my personal discovery of Latin American literature.

# II

Latin American extremes: if Cuba is the Andalusia of the New World, the Mexican plateau is its Castile. Parched and brown, inhabited by suspicious cats burnt too many times by foreign invasions, Mexico is the sacred zone of a secret hope: the gods shall return.

Mexican space is closed, jealous, and self-contained. In contrast, Argentine space is open and dependent on the foreign: migrations, exports, imports, words. Mexican space was vertically sacralized thousands of years ago. Argentine space patiently awaits its horizontal profanation.

I arrived on the Mexican highland from the Argentine pampa when I was sixteen years old. As I said, it was better to study in a country where the minister of Education was Jaime Torres Bodet than in a country where he was Hugo Wast. This was not the only contrast, or the most important one. A land isolated by its very nature—desert, mountain, chasm, sea, jungle, fire, ice, fugitive mists, and a sun that never blinks— horizons, an arrow that wounds the sky but refuses the dangerous frontiers of the land, the canyons, the sierras without a human footprint, whereas the pampa is nothing if not an eternal frontier, the very portrait of the horizon, the sprawling flatland of a latent expansion awaiting, like a passive lover, the vast and rich overflow from that concentration of the transitory represented by the commercial metropolis of Buenos Aires, what Ezequiel Martínez Estrada called Goliath's head on David's body.

A well-read teenager, I had tasted the literary culture of Buenos Aires, then dominated by *Sur* magazine and Victoria Ocampo's enlightened mixture of the cattle oligarchy of the Pampas and the cultural clerisy of Paris, a sort of Argentinian cosmopolitanism. It then became important to appreciate the verbal differences between the Mexican culture, which, long before Paul Valéry, knew itself to be mortal, and the Argentine culture, founded on the optimism of powerful migratory currents from Europe, innocent of sacred stones or aboriginal promises. Mexico, closed to immigration by the TTT—the Tremendous Texas Trauma that in 1836 cured us once and for all of the temptation to receive Caucasian colonists because they had airport names like Houston and

Austin and Dallas—devoted its population to breeding like rabbits. Blessed by the Pope, Coatlicue, and Jorge Negrete, we are, all eighty million of us, Catholics in the Virgin Mary, misogynists in the stone goddesses, and *machistas* in the singing, pistol-packing *charro*.

The pampa goes on waiting: twenty-five million Argentinians today; scarcely five million more than in 1945, half of them in Buenos Aires.

Language in Mexico is ancient, old as the oldest dead. The eagles of the Indian empire fell, and it suffices to read the poems of the defeated to understand the vein of sadness that runs through Mexican literature, the feeling that words are identical to a farewell: "Where shall we go now, O my friends?" asks the Aztec poet of the Fall of Tenochtitlán: "The smoke lifts; the fog extends. Cry, my friends. Cry, oh cry." And the contemporary poet Xavier Villaurrutia, four centuries later, sings from the bed of the same lake, now dried up, from its dry stones:

In the midst of a silence deserted as a street before the crime
Without even breathing so that nothing may disturb my death
In this wall-less solitude
When the angels fled
In the grave of my bed I leave my bloodless statue.

A sad, underground language, forever being lost and recovered. I soon learned that Spanish as spoken in Mexico answered to six unwritten rules:

- Never use the familiar *tu*—thou—if you can use the formal you—*usted.*
- Never use the first-person possessive pronoun, but rather the second-person, as in "this is *your* home."
- Always use the first-person singular to refer to your own troubles, as in "Me fue del carajo, mano." But use the first-person plural when referring to your successes, as

in "During our term, we distributed three million acres."
- Never use one diminutive if you can use five in a row.
- Never use the imperative when you can use the subjunctive.
- And only then, when you have exhausted these ceremonies of communication, bring out your verbal knife and plunge it deep into the other's heart: "Chinga a tu madre, cabrón."

The language of Mexicans springs from abysmal extremes of power and impotence, domination and resentment. It is the mirror of an overabundance of history, a history that devours itself before extinguishing and then regenerating itself, phoenix-like, once again. Argentina, on the contrary, is a tabula rasa, and it demands a passionate verbalization. I do not know another country that so fervently—with the fervor of Buenos Aires, Borges would say—opposes the silence of its infinite space, its physical and mental pampa, demanding: Please, *verbalize* me! Martin Fierro, Carlos Gardel, Jorge Luis Borges: reality must be captured, desperately, in the verbal web of the gaucho poem, the sentimental tango, the meta-physical tale: the pampa of the gaucho becomes the garden of the tango becomes the forked paths of literature.

What is forked? What is said.

What is said? What is forked.

Everything: Space. Time. Language. History. Our history. The history of Spanish America.

I read *Ficciones* as I flew north on a pontoon plane, courtesy of Pan American Airways. It was wartime, we had to have priority; all cameras were banned, and glazed plastic screens were put on our windows several minutes before we landed. Since I was not an Axis spy, I read Borges as we splashed into Santos, saying that the best proof that the Koran is an Arab book is that not a single camel is mentioned in its pages.

I started thinking that the best proof that Borges is an Argentinian is in everything he has to evoke because it isn't there, as we glided into an invisible Rio de Janeiro. And as we flew out of Bahia, I thought that Borges invents a world because he needs it. I need, therefore I imagine.

By the time we landed in Trinidad, "Funes the Memorious" and "Pierre Ménard, Author of Don Quixote" had introduced me, without my being aware, to the genealogy of the serene madmen, the children of Erasmus. I did not know then that this was the most illustrious family of modern fiction, since it went, backwards, from Pierre Ménard to Don Quixote himself. During two short lulls in Santo Domingo (then, horrifyingly, called Ciudad Trujillo) and Port-au-Prince, I had been prepared by Borges to encounter my wonderful friends Toby Shandy, who reconstructs in his miniature cabbage patch the battlefields of Flanders he was not able to experience historically; Jane Austen's Catherine Moreland and Gustave Flaubert's Madame Bovary, who like Don Quixote believe in what they read; Dickens's Mr. Micawber, who takes his hopes to be realities; Dostoevsky's Myshkin, an idiot because he gives the benefit of the doubt to the good possibility of mankind; Pérez Galdós's Nazarín, who is mad because he believes that each human being can daily be Christ, and who is truly St. Paul's madman: "Let him who seems wise among you become mad, so that he might truly become wise."

As we landed at Miami airport, the glazed windows disappeared once and for all and I knew that, like Pierre Ménard, a writer must always face the mysterious duty of literally reconstructing a spontaneous work. And so I met my tradition: *Don Quixote* was a book waiting to be written. The history of Latin America was a history waiting to be lived.

## III

When I finally arrived in Mexico, I discovered that my father's imaginary country was real, but more fantastic than any imaginary land. It was as real as its physical and spiritual borders: Mexico, the only frontier between the industrialized and the developing worlds; the frontier between my country and the United States, but also between all of Latin America and the United States, and between the Catholic Mediterranean and the Protestant Anglo-Saxon strains in the New World.

It was with this experience and these questions that I approached the gold and mud of Mexico, the imaginary, imagined country, finally real but only real if I saw it from a distance that would assure me, because of the very fact of separation, that my desire for reunion with it would be forever urgent, and only real if I wrote it. Having attained some sort of perspective, I was finally able to write a few novels where I could speak of the scars of revolution, the nightmares of progress, and the perseverance of dreams.

I wrote with urgency because my absence became a destiny, yet a shared destiny: that of my own body as a young man, that of the old body of my country, and that of the problematic and insomniac body of my language. I could, perhaps, identify the former without too much trouble: Mexico and myself. But the language belonged to us all, to the vast community that writes and talks and thinks in Spanish. And without this language I could give no reality to either myself or my land. Language thus became the center of my personal being and of the possibility of forming my own destiny and that of my country into a shared destiny.

But nothing is shared in the abstract. Like bread and love, language and ideas are shared with human beings. My first contact with literature was sitting on the knees of Alfonso Reyes when the Mexican writer was

252

ambassador to Brazil in the earlier thirties. Reyes had brought the Spanish classics back to life for us; he had written the most superb books on Greece; he was the most lucid of literary theoreticians; in fact, he had translated all the Western culture into Latin American terms. In the late forties, he was living in a little house the color of the *mamey* fruit, in Cuernavaca. He would invite me to spend weekends with him, and since I was eighteen and a night prowler, I kept him company from eleven in the morning, when Don Alfonso would sit in a café and toss verbal bouquets at the girls strolling around the plaza that was then a garden of laurels and not, as it has become, of cement. I do not know if the square, ruddy man seated at the next table was a British consul crushed by the nearness of the volcano; but if Reyes, enjoying the spectacle of the world, quoted Lope de Vega and Garcilaso, our neighbor the *mescal* drinker would answer, without looking at us, with the more somber *stanze* of Marlowe and John Donne. Then we would go to the movies in order, Reyes said, to bathe in contemporary epic, and it was only at night that he would start scolding me: You have not read Stendhal yet? The world didn't start five minutes ago, you know.

He could irritate me. I read, against his classical tastes, the most modern, the most strident books, without understanding that I was learning his lesson: there is no creation without tradition; the "new" is an inflection on a preceding form; novelty is always a variation on the past. Borges said that Reyes wrote the best Spanish prose of our times. He taught me that culture had a smile, that the intellectual tradition of the whole world was ours by birthright, and that Mexican literature was important because it was literature, not because it was Mexican.

One day I got up very early (or maybe I came in very late from a binge) and saw him seated at five in the morning, working at his table, amid the aroma of the jacaranda and the bougainvillea. He was a diminutive Buddha, bald and pink, almost one of the elves who cobble shoes at night while the family sleeps. He liked to quote Goethe: Write at dawn, skim the cream of the day, then you can study crystals, intrigue at court, and make love to your kitchen maid. Writing in silence, Reyes did not smile. His world, in a way, ended on a funereal day in February 1913 when his insurrectionist father, General Bernardo Reyes, fell riddled by machine-gun bullets in the Zócalo in Mexico City, and with him fell what was left of Mexico's Belle Epoque, the long and cruel peace of Porfirio Díaz.

The smile of Alfonso Reyes had ashes on its lips. He had written, as a response to history, the great poem of exile and distance from Mexico: the poem of a cruel Iphigenia, the Mexican Iphigenia of the valley of Anáhuac:

I was another, being myself;
I was he who wanted to leave.
To return is to cry. I do not repent of this wide world.
It is not I who return,
But my shackled feet.

My father had remained in Buenos Aires as Mexican chargé d'affaires, with instructions to frown on Argentina's sympathies toward the Axis. My mother profited from his absence to enroll me in a Catholic school in Mexico City. The brothers who ruled this institution were preoccupied with something that had never entered my head: sin. At the start of the school year, one of the brothers would come before the class with a white lily in his hand and say: "This is a Catholic youth before kissing a girl." Then he would throw the flower on the floor, dance a little jig on it, pick up the bedraggled object, and confirm our worst suspicions: "This is a Catholic boy after . . ."

Well, all this made life very tempting. Retrospectively, I would agree with Luis Buñuel that sex without sin is like an egg without salt. The priests at the Colegio Francés made sex irresistible for us; they also made leftists of us by their constant denunciation of Mexican liberalism and especially of Benito Juárez. The sexual and political temptations became very great in a city where provincial mores and sharp social distinctions made it very difficult to have normal sexual relationships with young or even older women.

All this led, as I say, to a posture of rebellion that for me crystallized in the decision to be a writer. My father, by then back from Argentina, sternly said, Okay, go out and be a writer, but not at my expense. I became a very young journalist at the weekly *Siempre*, but my family pressured me to enter law school, or, in the desert of Mexican literature, I would literally die of hunger and thirst. I was sent to visit Alfonso Reyes in his enormous library-house, where he seemed more dimunitive than ever, ensconced in a tiny corner he saved for his bed among the Piranesi-like perspective of volume piled upon volume. He said to me: "Mexico is a very formalistic country. If you don't have a title, you are nobody: *nadie, ninguno.* A title is like the handle on a cup; without it, no one will pick you up. You must become a *licenciado,* a lawyer; then you can do whatever you please, as I did."

So I entered the School of Law at the National University, where, as I feared, learning tended to be by rote. The budding explosion in the student population was compounded by cynical teachers who would spend the whole hour of class taking attendance on the two hundred students of civil law, from Aguilar to Zapata. But there were great exceptions of true teachers who understood that the law is inseparable from culture, from morality, and from justice. Fore-most among these were the exiles from defeated Republican Spain, who enormously enriched Mexican universities, publishing houses, the arts, and the sciences. Don Manuel Pedroso, former dean of the University of Seville, made the study of law compatible with my literary inclinations. When I would bitterly complain about the dryness and boredom of learning the penal or mercantile codes by heart, he would counter: "Forget the codes. Read Dostoevsky, read Balzac. There's all you have to know about criminal or commercial law." He also made me see that Stendhal was right that the best model for a well-structured novel is the Napoleonic Code of Civil Law. Anyway, I found that culture consists of connections, not of separations: to specialize is to isolate.

Sex was another story, but Mexico City was then a manageable town of one million people, beautiful in its extremes of colonial and nineteenth-century elegance and the garishness of its exuberant and dangerous nightlife. My friends and I spent the last years of our adolescence and the first of our manhood in a succession of cantinas, brothels, strip joints, and silver-varnished nightclubs where the bolero was sung and the mambo danced; whores, mariachis, magicians were our companions as we struggled through our first readings of D. H. Lawrence and Aldous Huxley, James Joyce and André Gide, T. S. Eliot and Thomas Mann. Salvador Elizondo and I were the two would-be writers of the group, and if the realistic grain of *La Megión Más Transparente (Where the Air Is Clear)* was sown in this, our rather somnambulistic immersion in the spectral nightlife of Mexico City, it is also true that the cruel imagination of an instant in Elizondo's *Farabeuf* had the same background experience. We would go to a whorehouse oddly called El Buen Tono, choose a poor Mexican girl who usually said her name was Gladys and she came from Guadalajara, and go to our respective rooms. One time, a horrible scream was heard and Gladys from Guadalajara rushed out, crying and streaming blood. Elizondo, in the climax of love, had slashed her armpit with a razor.

Another perspective, another distance for approximation, another possibility of sharing a language. In 1950 I went to Europe to do graduate work in international law at the University of Geneva. Octavio Paz had just published two books that had changed the face of Mexican literature, *Libertad Bajo Palabra* and *El Laberinto de la Soledad.* My friends and I had read those books aloud in Mexico, dazzled by a poetics that managed simultaneously to renew our language from within and to connect it to the langauge of the world.

At age thirty-six, Octavio Paz was not very different from what he is today. Writers born in 1914, like Paz and Julio Cortázar, surely signed a Faustian pact at the very mouth of hell's trenches; so many poets died in that war that someone had to take their place. I remember Paz in the so-called existentialist nightclubs of the time in Paris, in discussion with the very animated and handsome Albert Camus, who alternated philosophy and the boogie-woogie in La Rose Rouge. I remember Paz in front of the large windows of a gallery on the Place Vendôme, reflecting Max Ernst's great postwar painting "Europe after the Rain," and the painter's profile as an ancient eagle; and I tell myself that the poetics of Paz is an art of civilizations, a movement of encounters. Paz the poet meets Paz the thinker, because his poetry is a form of thought and his thought is a form of poetry; and as a result of this meeting, an encounter of civilizations takes place. Paz introduces civilizations to one another, makes them presentable before it is too late, because behind the wonderful smile of Camus, fixed forever in the absurdity of death, behind the bright erosion of painting by Max Ernst and the crystals of the Place Vendôme, Octavio and I, when we met, could hear the voice of *el poeta Libra,* Ezra, lamenting the death of the best, "for an old bitch gone in the teeth, for a botched civilization."

Octavio Paz has offered civilizations the mirror of their mortality, as Paul Valéry did, but also the reflection of their survival in an epidemic of meetings and erotic risks. In the generous friendship of Octavio Paz, I learned that there were no privileged centers of culture, race, or politics; that nothing should be left out of literature, because our time is a time of deadly reduction. The essential orphanhood of our time is seen in the poetry and thought of Paz as a challenge to be met through the renewed flux of human knowledge, of *all* human knowledge. We have not finished thinking, imagining, acting. It is still possible to know the world; we are unfinished men and women.

I am not at the crossroads;
                              to choose
is to go wrong.

For my generation in Mexico, the problem did not consist in discovering our modernity but in discovering our tradition. The latter was brutally denied by the comatose, petrified teaching of the classics in Mexican secondary schools; one had to bring Cervantes back to life in spite of a school system fatally oriented toward the ideal of universities as sausage factories; in spite of the more grotesque forms of Mexican nationalism of the time. A Marxist teacher once told me it was un-Mexican to read Kafka; a fascist critic said the same thing (this has been Kafka's Kafkian destiny everywhere), and a rather sterile Mexican author gave a pompous lecture at the Belles Artes warning that readers who read Proust would proustitute themselves.

To be a writer in Mexico in the fifties, you had to be with Octavio Paz in the assertion that Mexico was not an isolated, virginal providence but very much part of the human race and its cultural tradition; we were all, for good or evil, contemporary with all men and women.

In Geneva, I regained my perspective, I rented a garret overlooking the beautiful old square of the Bourg-du-Four, established by Julius Caesar as the Forum Boarium two millennia ago. The square was filled with coffeehouses and old bookstores. The girls came from all over the world; they were beautiful, and they were independent. When they were kissed, one did not become a sullied lily. We had salt on our lips. We loved each other, and I also loved going to the little island where the lake meets the river, to spend long hours reading. Since it was called Jean-Jacques Rousseau Island, I took along my volume of the *Confessions*. Many things came together then. A novel was the transformation of experience into history. The modern epic had been the epic of the first-person singular, of the I, from St. Augustine to Abélard to Dante to Rousseau to Stendhal to Proust. Joyce de-Joyced fiction: Here comes everybody! But H.C.E. did not collectively save the degraded Ego from exhaustion, self-doubt, and, finally, self-forgetfulness. When Odysseus says that he is nonexistent, we know and he knows that he is disguised; when Beckett's characters proclaim their nonbeing, we know that "the fact is notorious": they are no longer disguised. Kafka's man has been forgotten; no one can remember K the land surveyor; finally, as Milan Kundera tells us, nobody can remember Prague, Czechoslovakia, history.

I did not yet know this as I spent many reading hours on the little island of Rousseau at the intersection of Lake Geneva and the Rhône River back in 1951. But I vaguely felt that there was something beyond the exploration of the self that actually made the idea of human personality possible if the paths be-

yond it were explored. Cervantes taught us that a book is a book is a book: Don Quixote does not invite us into "reality" but into an act of the imagination where all things are real: the characters are active psychological entities, but also the archetypes they herald and always the figures from whence they come, which were unimaginable, unthinkable, like Don Quixote, before they become characters first and archetypes later.

Could I, a Mexican who had not yet written his first book, sitting on a bench on an early spring day as the *bise* from the Jura Mountains quieted down, have the courage to explore for myself, with my language, with my tradition, with my friends and influences, that region where the literary figure bids us consider it in the uncertainty of its gestation? Cervantes did it in a precise cultural situation: he brought into existence the modern world by having Don Quixote leave his secure village (a village whose name has been, let us remember, forgotten) and take to the open roads, the roads of the unsheltered, the unknown, and the different, there to lose what he read and to gain what we, the readers, read in him.

The novel is forever traveling Don Quixote's road, from the security of the analogous to the adventure of the different and even the unknown. In my way, this is the road I wanted to travel. I read Rousseau, or the adventures of the I; Joyce and Faulkner, or the adventures of the We; Cervantes, or the adventures of the You he calls the Idle, the Amiable Reader: you. And I read, in a shower of fire and in the lightning of enthusiasm, Rimbaud. His mother asked him what a particular poem was about. And he answered: "I have wanted to say what it says there, literally and in all other senses." This statement of Rimbaud's has been an inflexible rule for me and for what we are all writing today; and the present-day vigor of the literature of the Hispanic world, to which

I belong, is not alien to this Rimbaudian approach to writing: Say what you mean, literally and in all other senses.

I think I imagined in Switzerland what I would try to write someday, but first I would have to do my apprenticeship. Only after many years would I be able to write what I then imagined; only years later, when I not only knew that I had the tools with which to do it, but also, and equally important, when I knew that if I did not write, death would not do it for me. You start by writing to live. You end by writing so as not to die. Love is the marriage of this desire and this fear. The women I have loved I have desired for themselves, but also because I feared myself.

# IV

My first European experience came to a climax in the summer of 1950. It was a hot, calm evening on Lake Zurich, and some wealthy Mexican friends had invited me to dinner at the elegant Baur-au-Lac Hotel. The summer restaurant was a floating terrace on the lake. You reached it by a gangplank, and it was lighted by paper lanterns and flickering candles. As I unfolded my stiff white napkin amid the soothing tinkle of silver and glass, I raised my eyes and saw the group dining at the next table.

Three ladies sat there with a man in his seventies. This man was stiff and elegant, dressed in double-breasted white serge and immaculate shirt and tie. His long, delicate fingers sliced a cold pheasant, almost with daintiness. Yet even in eating he seemed to me unbending, with a ramrod-back, military bearing. His aged face showed "a growing fatigue," but the pride with which his lips and jaws were set sought desperately to hide the fact, while the eyes twinkled with "the fiery play of fancy."

As the carnival lights of that summer's night in Zurich played with a fire of their own on the features I now recognized, Thomas Mann's face was a theater of implicit, quiet emotions. He ate and let the ladies do the talking; he was, in my fascinated eyes, a meeting place where solitude gives birth to beauty unfamiliar and perilous, but also to the perverse and the illicit. Thomas Mann had managed, out of this solitude, to find the affinity "between the personal destiny of [the] author and that of his contemporaries in general." Through him, I had imagined that the products of this solitude and of this affinity were named art (created by one) and civilization (created by all). He spoke so surely, in *Death in Venice,* of the "tasks imposed upon him by his own ego and the European soul" that as I, paralyzed with admiration, saw him there that night I dared not conceive of such an affinity in our own Latin American culture, where the extreme demands of a ravaged, voiceless continent often killed the voice of the self and made a hollow political monster of the voice of the society, or killed it, giving birth to a pitiful, sentimental dwarf.

Yet, as I recalled my passionate reading of everything he wrote, from *Blood of the Walsungs* to *Dr. Faustus,* I could not help but feel that, in spite of the vast differences between his culture and ours, in both of them literature in the end asserted itself through a relationship between the visible and the invisible worlds of narration. A novel should "gather up the threads of many human destinies in the warp of a single idea"; the I, the You, and the We were only separate and dried up because of a lack of imagination. Unbeknownst to him, I left Thomas Mann sipping his demitasse as midnight approached and the floating restaurant bobbed slightly and the Chinese lanterns quietly flickered out. I shall always thank him for silently teaching me that, in literature, you know only what you imagine.

The Mexico of the forties and fifties I wrote about in *La Región Más Transparente* was an imagined Mexico, just as the Mexico of the eighties and nineties I am writing about in *Cristóbal Nonato (Christopher Unborn)* is totally imagined. I fear that we would know nothing of Balzac's Paris and Dickens's London if they, too, had not invented them. When in the spring of 1951 I took a Dutch steamer back to the New World, I had with me the ten Bible-paper tomes of the Pléiade edition of Balzac. This phrase of his has been a central creed of mine: "Wrest words from silence and ideas from obscurity." The reading of Balzac—one of the most thorough and metamorphosing experiences of my life as a novelist—taught me that one must exhaust reality, transcend it, in order to reach, to try to reach, that absolute which is made of the atoms of the relative: in Balzac, the marvelous words of *Séraphita* or *Louis Lambert* rest on the commonplace words or *Père Goriot* and *César Birotteau.* Likewise, the Mexican reality of *Where the Air Is Clear* and *The Death of Artemio Cruz* existed only to clash with my imagination, my negation, and my perversion of the facts, because, remember, I had learned to imagine Mexico before I every knew Mexico.

This was, finally, a way of ceasing to tell what I understood and trying to tell, behind all the things I knew, the really important things: what I did not know. *Aura* illustrates this stance much too clearly, I suppose. I prefer to find it in a scene set in a cantina in *A Change of Skin*, or in a taxi drive in *The Hydra Head.* I never wanted to resolve an enigma, but to point out that there *was* an enigma.

I always tried to tell my critics: Don't classify me, read me. I'm a writer, not a genre. Do not look for the purity of the novel according to some nostalgic canon, do not ask for generic affiliation but rather for a dialogue, if not for the outright abolition, of genre; not for one language but for many languages at odds with one another; not, as Bakhtin would put it, for unity of style but for *heteroglossia,* not for monologic but for dialogic imagination. I'm afraid that, by and large, in Mexico at least, I failed in this enterprise. Yet I am not disturbed by this fact, because of what I have just said: language is a shared and shared part of culture that cares little about formal classifications and much about vitality and connection, for culture itself perishes in purity or isolation, which is the deadly wages of perfection. Like bread and love, language is shared with others. And human beings share a tradition. There is no creation without tradition. No one creates from nothing.

I went back to Mexico, but knew that I would forever be a wanderer in search of perspective: this was my real baptism, not the religious or civil ceremonies I have mentioned. But no matter where I went, Spanish would be the language of my writing and Latin America the culture of my language.

Neruda, Reyes, Paz; Washington, Santiago de Chile, Buenos Aires, Mexico City, Paris, Geneva; Cervantes, Balzac, Rimbaud, Thomas Mann: only with all the shared languages, those of my places and friends and masters, was I able to approach the fire of literature and ask it for a few sparks.

# Puerto Rican Youth

*Samuel Betances*

## Race and the Search for Identity

Puerto Ricans are sometimes white, they are sometimes black, and they are sometimes Puerto Ricans—and so they are quite often confused. This holds particularly true for the second generation Puerto Ricans in the U.S. mainland. The single most crucial issue burning deep in the souls of many young, second generation Puerto Ricans in the United States is that of the wider identity—the search for ethnicity.

Puerto Rican youth in America in search of their ethnic identity have often faced the stark reality of having to relate to critical issues solely on the basis of black and white. In other words, it becomes impossible simply to be "Puerto Rican" or "Latin" or a "Third World Type" or "Spanish" in a society that demands categories based on black and white.

To a large degree, Puerto Rican youth who come from a racially mixed background believe that in America they can choose whether they want to be black or white. Some have decided not to suffer the plight of becoming black. It is hard for them to be a Puerto Rican without becoming black as

Samuel Betances teaches sociology at Northeastern Illinois University in Chicago.

Excerpt from "Race and the Search for Identity" in *Borinquen: An Anthology of Puerto Rican Literature,* edited by Maria Teresa Dabin and Stan Steiner (New York: Vintage, 1974). Reprinted by permission of Samuel Betances.

well, the assumption being that one can choose with which group to relate.

Erik Erikson suggests that Negro creative writers are in a battle to reconquer for their people a "surrendered identity". He states:

I like this term because it does not assume total absence, as many contemporary writers do—something to be searched for and found, to be granted or given, to be created or fabricated—but something to be recovered. This must be emphasized because what is latent can become a living actuality, and thus a bridge from past to future.[1]

If what Erikson says is true, then the Puerto Rican adolescent's search for a wider identity becomes even more complicated in the light of some historical facts that are uniquely Puerto Rican.

Puerto Rico at present has no definite political status. The island is neither a state of the union, nor is it an independent nation. It is no more than a "perfume colony," as a critic of the present system has described it. Puerto Ricans are considered "Americans" by their Latin American cousins and "Latins" by the Americans. They have never been in control of their island and during a period of nineteen years, between 1898 and 1917, were citizens of no country.[2]

Dr. Roman Lopez Tames, a careful student of the Puerto Rican experience, has noted that there is insecurity in the island. Puerto Ricans are forever asking themselves, "What am I?" ("que soy?"), and "What are we?" ("que somos?"). He notes that "for the North Americans the island is hispanic, this is to say, strange sister to what they call Latin American." But on the other hand, "Latin American countries without having a very concrete notion about the island, quite frequently reject her considering her North Americanized, lost to the great family,"[3] Puerto Rico has been likened by Dr. Lopez Tames to the plight of the bat who is rejected by birds and by rodents, belonging to neither family in any concrete way, who is condemned to live a solitary life between two worlds, misunderstood by both.

To some degree, the seeds of insecurity toward ethnicity are already planted in the minds of first generation Puerto Ricans. Thus, a youngster who has parents who have some doubt as to their own identity has to face new problems which indicate further that he is neither black nor white. He is neither American nor Latin American. He comes from an island which is neither a state nor a nation. Is it possible for Puerto Ricans to find their "surrendered identity?" Or is it not a fact that to some degree the historical experience indicates that there is nothing there which is latent, nothing that can come alive, nothing that can serve as a bridge from the past to the future, since Puerto Rico, as a geographical entity, has been molded in an experience of dependency, first to Spain and then to the United States?

Confusion, ambivalency, and contradictions are present in the lives of Puerto Rican adolescents as they relate to the issue of race and color. Some Puerto Ricans learn English very quickly and refuse to speak Spanish in hopes of finding acceptance in the larger society. Others who are dark-skinned deliberately keep their Spanish, lest they be mistaken for American Negroes. Still others will hide their dark-skinned grandmother in the kitchen while introducing their potential spouses to their lighter-skinned parents.[4] The more successful the Puerto Rican, the more "European-looking" his wife tends to be. It's an interesting commentary that the first book[5] out of East Harlem, *Down These Mean Streets,* based on the second generation experience, was written by Piri Thomas, a Puerto Rican who is very concerned with the crucial issue of identity. One chapter in his book is entitled, "How to be a Negro Without Really Trying." Others are, "Hung Up Between Two Sticks" and "Brothers Under the Skin."

The migrant Puerto Rican, whose children are the focus of this paper, have brought with them certain experiences and outlooks on the issue of race and color that have influenced to some degree the lives of their children. The first generation grew up in an island which historically has experienced "whiteness" as a positive value and "blackness" as a negative one. "White is right," in Puerto Rico, too. While blackness may not be as negative as in America, it is still negative enough to be a source of embarrassment in many instances Puerto Rican life.

Puerto Rico has a problem of color; America has a problem of race.[6] That is the critical difference between discrimination in Puerto Rico and in the U.S. mainland.

Discrimination in Puerto Rico is based on color. As such, color is a physical characteristic which can be altered and/or changed in several generations. Marrying someone lighter-skinned than oneself immediately alters the way in which the offspring of such a union would be described. A Negro-Puerto Rican who marries a non-Negro Puerto Rican will have children which will be described as non-Negro.

If the pattern is continued through several generations, a Negro Puerto Rican can live to see his "white" great-grandchildren. The negative physical element, color, can be eliminated or be made to play a less embarrassing role in the lives of those who seek to make things "better for their children".[7]

Not so in America where discrimination is based on the concept of race. It has to do with a deep-seated conviction about one group being superior to another. In the United States, the element of racial inequality is prevalent. Racism has to do with the issue of the "purity of the blood," a kind of changeless, hereditary disease or blessing which is transmitted from parent to offspring. In America many gain their sense of being and power from their membership in the "superior" white race. The most deprived white man can think of himself as "better than any Nigger." It doesn't really matter what his position or educational background may be: "No matter how you dress him up, a Nigger is a Nigger," a racist will tell you.

To be black in America is such a serious handicap that a person with "one drop" of Negro blood is considered Negro. Negro blood is a kind of reverse and negative "black power," which haunts a person reminding him that he is inferior—at best, a mere shadow of white figure. Such are the "deep-seated, anxiety-rooted, sado-masochistic drives"[8] which account for much of the racial problems in America. Is it any wonder that in the United States inter-marriage is considered the unpardonable social sin?

Puerto Rico discrimination based on color as opposed to race can be labeled as a "milder" type of discrimination. It has, nevertheless, influenced the outlook of the people, including those who journeyed to the mainland with notions that blackness is a negative aspect in a person's life and whiteness is a positive value.

So that the non-Negroid Puerto Rican may look upon his darker skinned counterpart as a person with certain drawbacks, a descendant of slaves whose physical features, texture of hair and/or color of the skin may leave something to be desired. He is not necessarily someone to hate, to control, or to fear, but perhaps to avoid in certain social contexts.

And it is not always a matter of color that determines desirability in certain social contexts. Negroid features: full lips, kinky hair ("pelo malo") may play a much more crucial role in terms of desirability over light complexion in Puerto Rico. A man with "good" hair, but dark skin ("un trigueño de pelo bueno") may be more desirable than a light-skinned but kinky-haired individual. Color gives way to other physical characteristics at times. Distinction, however, may not be made verbally, so that when individuals refer to a person of "color," they may be really referring to "Negroid" features as opposed to complexion—although they may still relate to the question as one of "color".

Puerto Ricans believe that "trigueñas" or "morenas" (women of dark complexion) make better lovers than those who are non-dark. The belief that color plays a positive role in sex is somewhat different than the racist connotations found in such belief in America. One observer has noted, "this is not the expression of a neurotic fear of sexual insufficiency but an accepted and openly stated commonplace."[9]

Alex Rodríguez, a Puerto Rican spokesman in the city of Boston and past director of the Cooper Community Center in Lower Roxbury, was recently interviewed in the *Boston Globe* on the role of color and race in Puerto Rican life. Rodríguez noted that most Puerto Ricans, while identifying themselves as non-white, quickly learned the advantages of being "white" in a racist society. He suggests that in Puerto Rico, blackness is thought of as a beautiful trait. He used the following examples: "One of the most affectionate terms in Spanish is 'negra,' which means Dear or Darling, but literally translated means 'black one.' "

Rodríguez's example is used quite frequently by people of Latin America who would imply racial equality by citing it. The term "negrita" *does* imply intimacy and affection in the usage that Rodríguez gave it. But there is some difference between "intimacy" and "affection" with "equality" which should be considered. A Peruvian newspaper quoted Velarde who held to the same interpretation on this matter as Alex Rodríguez. Pitt-Rivers brings focus to that difference:

The implication of racial equality that he drew from his examples invites precision. Such terms do not find way into such context because they are flattering in formal usage, but because they are not. Intimacy is opposed to respect; because these terms are disrespectful, they are used to establish or stress a relationship where no respect is due. The word "Nigger" is used in this way among Negroes in the United States, but only among Negroes. Color has, in fact, the same kind of class connotation in the Negro community as in Latin America: pale-skinned means upper class. Hence, Nigger, in this context dark-skinned or lower class, implies a relationship that is free of obligation of mutual respect.[10]

It is true that Puerto Rico has never had a race riot. But the assertion made by Puerto Rican spokesman[11] that all is well in this matter of race and color in the island, or that Puerto Rico is one thousand years ahead of America on this issue is misleading. The fact that there is discrimination against those who would embrace the "Afro-Antillean cultured tradition"[12] or those who are dark-skinned, certainly enough discrimination to make those who are black wish that they were not, indicates all in not well in Puerto Rico.

Those who damned the United States race riots and point to the superior culture which does not have race riots in Puerto Rico, have not been as zealous in explaining the problem of color that does exist in the island. As a result many citizens on the mainland, including such noted sociologists as Nathan Glazer,[13] believe the problem to be less serious than in reality.

The point being suggested here is that the problem of color is serious enough in Puerto Rican life to complicate further the second generation's search for ethnicity in the mainland. As the second generation looks toward the island and toward their homes, they don't find people who have solved the problem of black and white. Instead they find further reasons for added anxiety, confusion, and feelings of uncertainty. Pointing out that Puerto Rico does not have race riots does not solve the problem of a youngster who must not only deal with a world outside of his home which is unsympathetic and at times cruel, but he also must confront his family and Puerto Rican neighbors who for reasons all their own seem to be making efforts toward concealment of color.

In the early part of 1970, sixty young second generation Puerto Ricans were interviewed concerning this issue of race and color as it affected their search for ethnicity in the U.S. mainland. Thirty of the youth resided in the South Bronx in New York City; fifteen of them resided in the Division Street area of Chicago's Northwest Side; and fifteen live in the South End of Boston. Their response to the questionnaire and their willingness to have their answers taped when requested, provided perspective in attempting to understanding this very crucial issue. A close look at their responses indicates the problem to be much more complicated than previously imagined.

One young Puerto Rican in Boston, when asked how she was perceived by other people in a downtown store or in a crowded bus or walking through the busy streets of Boston, answered that most people would consider her "white." She quickly added, "an Eastern European type or Italian."

When asked how she described herself—"say that you were applying for a job

262

and you had to fill out a blank which demanded some definition on your part"— she said, "Negro." Why? She explained that people on the streets tend to look at her very superficially. Since she has a light complexion and long, black hair, she could "pass" in that kind of situation. However, when applying for a job, she explained, employers tend to take a second look, even a third look, especially if the job requires one to be visible, like office work. By filing the blank "Negro," she felt the employer would probably say to himself that she was not really black. If he detected an accent, he would be sure that she was not really black. But he would probably be happy to hire such a nice, light-skinned, safe Negro.

On the other hand, if she filled in the blank "white," the employer would probably think her dishonest since she was not really white. He probably would not forgive her for trying to "pass." The chances of his objecting to one's describing oneself "Negro" are less than the other way around.

Here is a case of a nineteen-year-old Puerto Rican youth trying desperately to psyche out the society in which she lives, anticipating the moods of people she somehow must not offend if she is to make it in tense America in the 1970's. It is difficult to ascertain just what neurological price she and many like her are paying for their attempt to survive without arousing people's prejudices.

Several youths, when asked whether they thought people in America were prejudiced towards them because they were Puerto Ricans, answered, "no." They explained that prejudice stemmed from the face of their dark skin color. Somehow in their minds they had carefully separated their skin color from their Puerto Ricaness.

Answering another question, this time on the issue of inter-marriage between American Negroes and Puerto Ricans, one of the interviewees from New York answered:

Puerto Ricans are on the bottom of the social ladder in this country; blacks are even worse off. Blacks should not marry Puerto Ricans since two wrongs don't make a right!

While most of those interviewed said that when it comes to marriage it should really be up to the people involved, it would appear that the "two wrongs don't make a right" answer is closer to the feeling of those questioned. Deeper probing indicated that while most of them "prefer" not to marry American Negroes, they would not voice "opposition" to such marriages.

The question of intermarriage is a very difficult one for Puerto Rican youth to answer. Admitting that one has reservations, or voicing opposition to marriage with American Negroes, is in effect, admission of prejudice based on cultural and color differences. To agree even in principle with a stance against Negroes having a choice on who should be their potential spouses is to undermine the Puerto Rican position. If it is possible for a Puerto Rican to be prejudiced against Negroes in America, then it is possible for American-Anglos to be prejudiced towards Puerto Ricans, for similar reasons. This the second generation does not want.

What makes it difficult, then, is the fact that Puerto Ricans *do* express preferences in regard to skin color. Deep inside they know that Americans have "legitimate" reasons for prejudice toward Puerto Ricans since they have, perhaps themselves, reasons why they discriminate against blacks. The feelings of insecurity are there.

Interestingly enough, second generation Puerto Ricans believe that even marrying a darker Puerto Rican than oneself is not desirable. Most of the youth simply stated that they expected to marry someone lighter-skinned, but not darker than themselves. Most of them knew of Puerto Rican neighbors or had parents or relatives who would oppose their children marrying anyone, whether American Negro or Puerto Rican, who happened to be darker than they were, who could be described as "real black."

In the area of mutual cooperation with American Negroes in pursuit of better wages and against social discrimination, most Puerto Rican youth answered affirmatively. One youth in the Bronx voiced the opinion by stating that while Negroes experienced 100% prejudice, Puerto Ricans experienced about 99% prejudice; so they should work together. Five young Puerto Ricans in Chicago who had actually worked together in an organization with blacks were a little more cautious on the matter. They wanted to know what "together" meant. One young man in Chicago simply said that as long as there is a "fifty-fifty" cooperation at the top of such an organization that is all right, but not otherwise.

One response was somewhat bitter; a young man who obviously had some experience in black endeavors snapped at the question by saving:

When blacks need an extra pair of feet to march, they welcome the Puerto Rican cooperation. When they need an extra voice to shout against injustice, they welcome Puerto Rican cooperation. When they need another head to bleed in the struggle, cooperation is welcomed from their "Latin brothers." But when, as a result of the shouting, the marching, and the bloody head, there is an extra pocket to fill, the Puerto Ricans are suddenly not black enough.

When asked if Puerto Ricans should work with white Anglos in the same way that they would work with Negroes, most of them said, "yes." As one Puerto Rican put it, "Puerto Ricans should work with blacks and whites. The blacks have the power (aggressiveness) and the whites have the money; by working with both groups we can come out on top."

Another dimension in the trials of young Puerto Ricans' search for identity and ethnicity is the issue of just how black can a

Puerto Rican become? Afro-American youth see their ultimate unity revolving around the issue of "blackness." The cry is "I am black and beautiful." Puerto Ricans who participate in all black meetings find themselves apprehensive when the anti-white rhetoric reminds them that the "white devil" is just as much a part of his experience as the heritage and concern which make it possible for him to be allowed into such organizations. As Piri Thomas puts it, "It wasn't right to be ashamed of what one was. It was like hating Momma for the color she was and Poppa for the color he wasn't."[14]

If one can be a "Negro" without really trying as Thomas would suggest,[15] then it is quite another matter to be "black." The politics of race in the black movement at times make a distinction between those who are described as "colored," those who are described as "Negroes," and those who are "black." If the society at large determines that racially mixed Puerto Ricans are Negro (using the "one drop" formula), where will the black movement place them? Can Puerto Ricans ever be "black" enough for such groups and still be Puerto Rican?

Puerto Ricans in Chicago, those who had some experience in black organizations, complained that the "black power" movement is too obsessed with "blackness" and not enough with "power", thereby writing off some potential energy from Puerto Ricans who up to that time wanted to embrace their African heritage.

Most Puerto Rican youth interviewed expressed pessimism about their ability to resolve the issue of race and color and identity in their own lives. They have felt that for too long they have been in the middle of blacks and whites receiving the worst from both sides. They were relieved to learn that other Puerto Rican youth were having similar problems over the issue of identity. Some were also glad to hear that an adult, the interviewer, was having a difficult time as well; that while the problem has not been resolved, one can still function and have self-respect. Perhaps that in itself is a very important beginning at resolving the destructive trauma which creates so much confusion in the lives of second generation Puerto Rican adolescents.

It's a good feeling to know that one is not alone when facing critical problems. If more Puerto Rican adults would but share some of their ambivalency and their confusion and end "the conspiracy of silence," it could lead more second generation Puerto Ricans to the conclusion that given the historical experience of Puerto Ricans in the island and in the "barrios" in the mainland, confusion and ambivalency may not be abnormal as all that.

At a time when the governor of Puerto Rico is desperately trying to coin the phrase, "Puerto Rico is our fatherland, but the United States is our nation," confusion and ambivalecy may indeed not be as abnormal as all that!

# References

1. Erik H. Erikson, *Identity, Youth and Crisis* (New York, W. W. Horton and Company, Inc., 1968), p. 297 (emphasis added). The phrase "surrendered identity" was borrowed by Erikson from Van Woodward.

2. The U.S. Government declared the residents of Puerto Rico citizens on the eve of the First World War, in 1917.

3. Román López Tames, *El Estado Libre Asociado de Puerto Rico* (Oviedo: Publicaciones del Instituto Jurídico, 1965), pp. 14, 15.

4. Fortunato Vizcarrondo popularized the problem in his famous poem "Y tu agtieln onde ejta?" Literally translated, it means, "And your grandmother, where is she?"

5. While Jesús Colón's book, *A Puerto Rican in New York: And Other Sketches,* was published in 1961, several years before *Down These Mean Streets,* the treatment he gives his sketches suggests more of a first generation view of New York City rather than a second generation approach. Colón's formative years were spent in Puerto Rico; see pages 11 to 15 of his book.

6. Eric Williams, "Race Relations in Puerto Rico and the Virgin Islands," *Foreign Affairs* (1945, Vol. 23:308). As quoted in Renzo Sereno's, *Psychiatry,* "Cryptomelanism: A study of Color Relations and Personal Insecurity in Puerto Rico," Vol. X, 1947, p. 264.

7. "Color is an ingredient, not a determinant of class. It can, therefore, be traded for other ingredients. It is something that can be altered in the individual life, but it is something that can be put right in the next generation." Julian Pitt-Rivers, "Race, Color and Class in Central America and the Andes," *Daedalus: Journal of the American Academy of Arts and Sciences,* (Cambridge, Ma., Spring, 1967), Vol. 96, p. 556.

8. Pitt-Rivers: op cit., p. 547.

9. *Ibid., p. 550.*

10. Joseph Monserrat is guilty of this one-sided type of analysis. See his report, "School Integration: A Puerto Rican View" (New York, the Commonwealth of Puerto Rico, 1966), p. 5.

11. Gordon K. Lewis, *Puerto Rico: Freedom and Power in the Caribbean* (New York, Harper & Row Publ., 1963), P. 286.

12. For example, Nathan Glazer writes in his book: "The Puerto Rican introduced into the city a group that is intermediate in color, neither all white nor all dark, but having some of each, and a large number that show the physical characteristics of both groups. (They) carry new attitudes toward color—and attitudes that may be corrupted by continental color prejudice but it is more likely, since this is in harmony with terms that are making all nations of a single world community, that the Puerto Rican attitude to color, or something like it, will become the New York attitude." *Beyond the Melting Pot,* (Cambridge, Ma., M.I.T. Press, 1963), p. 132.

13. Piri Thomas, *Down These Mean Streets* (New York, Signet Book, The New American Library, Inc., 1967), p. 122.

14. *Ibid.,* pp. 124–126.

265

# White Ethnic
*Michael Novak*

Growing up in America has been an assault upon my sense of worthiness. It has also been a kind of liberation and delight.

There must be countless women in America who have known for years that something is peculiarly unfair, yet who have found it only recently possible, because of Women's Liberation, to give tongue to their pain. In recent months, I have experienced a similar inner thaw, a gradual relaxation, a willingness to think about feelings heretofore shepherded out of sight.

I am born of PIGS—those Poles, Italians, Greeks, and Slavs, non-English-speaking immigrants, numbered so heavily among the workingmen of this nation. Not particularly liberal, nor radical, born into a history not white Anglo Saxon and not Jewish—born outside what in America is considered the intellectual mainstream. And thus privy to neither power nor status nor intellectual voice.

Those Poles of Buffalo and Milwaukee—so notoriously taciturn, sullen, nearly speechless. Who has ever understood them? It is not that Poles do not feel emotion: what is their history if not dark passion, romanticism, betrayal, courage, blood? But where in America is there anywhere a language for

Michael Novak teaches at the State University of New York and has published essays in *Harper's* and *Saturday Review*.

voicing what a Christian Pole in this nation feels? He has no Polish culture left him, no Polish tongue. Yet Polish feelings do not go easily into the idiom of happy America, the America of the Anglo-Saxons and, yes, in the arts, the Jews. (The Jews have long been a culture of the word, accustomed to exile, skilled in scholarship and in reflection. The Christian Poles are largely of peasant origin, free men for hardly more than a hundred years.) Of what shall the man of Buffalo think, on his way to work in the mills, departing from his relatively dreary home and street? What roots does he have? What language of the heart is available to him?

The PIGS are not silent willingly. The silence burns like hidden coals in the chest.

All four of my grandparents, unknown to one another, arrived in America from the same country in Slovakia. My grandfather had a small farm in Pennsylvania; his wife died in a wagon accident. Meanwhile, a girl of fifteen arrived on Ellis Island, dizzy, a little ill from witnessing births and deaths and illnesses aboard the crowded ship, with a sign around her neck lettered "PASSAIC." There an aunt told her of the man who had lost his wife in Pennsylvania. She went. They were married. Inheriting his three children, each year for five years she had one of her own; she was among the lucky, only one died. When she was twenty-two, mother of seven, her husband died. And she resumed the work she had begun in Slovakia at the town home of a man known to us now only as "the Professor": she housecleaned and she laundered.

I heard this story only weeks ago. Strange that I had not asked insistently before. Odd that I should have such shallow knowledge of my roots. Amazing to me that I do not know what my family suffered, endured, learned, hoped these past six or seven generations. It is as if there were no project on which we all have been involved. As if history, in some way, began with my father and with me.

Let me hasten to add that the estrangement I have come to feel derives not only from a lack of family history. All my life, I have been made to feel a slight uneasiness when I must say my name. Under challenge in grammar school concerning my nationality. I had been instructed by my father to announce proudly: "American." When my family moved from the Slovak ghetto of Johnstown to the WASP suburb on the hill, my mother impressed upon us how well we must be dressed, and show good manners, and behave—people think of us as "different" and we mustn't give them any cause. "Whatever you do, marry a Slovak girl." was other advice to a similar end: "They cook. They clean. They take good care of you. For your own good."

When it was revealed to me that most movie stars and many other professionals had abandoned European names in order to feed American fantasies, I felt only a little sadness. One of my uncles, for business reasons and rather late in life, changed his name too, to a simple German variant. Not long, either, after World War II.

Nowhere in my schooling do I recall an attempt to put me in touch with my own history. The strategy was clearly to make an American of me. English literature. American literature: and even the history books, as I recall them, were peopled mainly by Anglo-Saxons from Boston (where most historians seemed to live). Not even my native Pennsylvania, let alone my Slovak forebears, counted for very many paragraphs. I don't remember feeling envy or regret: a feeling, perhaps, of unimportance, of remoteness, of not having heft enough to count.

The fact that I was born a Catholic also complicated life. What is a Catholic but what everybody else is in reaction against? Protestants reformed "the Whore of Babylon," others were "enlightened" from it, and Jews had reason to help Catholicism and the social structures it was rooted in to fall apart. My history books and the whole of education hummed in upon that point (during crucial years I attended a public, not a parochial, school): to be modern is decidedly not to be medieval: to be reasonable is not to be dogmatic; to be free is clearly not to live under ecclesiastical authority; to be scientific is not to attend ancient rituals, cherish irrational symbols, indulge in mythic practices. It is hard to grow up Catholic in America without becoming defensive, perhaps a little paranoid, feeling forced to divide the world between "us" and "them."

We had a special language all our own, our own pronunciation for words we shared in common with others (Augustine, contemplative), sights and sounds and smells in which few others participated (incense at Benediction of the Most Blessed Sacrament, Forty Hours, wakes, and altar bells at the silent consecration of the Host); and we had our own politics and slant on world affairs. Since earliest childhood, I have known about a "power elite" that runs America: the boys from the Ivy League in the State Department, as opposed to the Catholic boys from Hoover's FBI who, as Daniel Moynihan once put it, keep watch on them. And on a whole host of issues, my people have been, though largely Democratic, conservative: on censorship, on Communism, on abortion, on relig-

267

ious schools . . . Harvard and Yale long meant "them" to us.

The language of Spiro Agnew, the language of George Wallace, excepting its idiom, awakens childhood memories in me of men arguing in the barbershop, of my uncle drinking so much beer he threatened to lay his dick upon the porch rail and wash the whole damn street with steaming piss—while cursing the niggers in the mill, below, and the Yankees in the mill, above: millstones he felt pressing him. Other relatives were duly shocked, but everybody loved Uncle George: he said what he thought.

We did not feel this country belonged to us. We felt fierce pride in it, more loyalty than anyone could know. But we felt blocked at every turn. There were not many intellectuals among us, not even very many professional men. Laborers mostly. Small businessmen, agents for corporations perhaps. Content with a little, yes, modest in expectation. But somehow feeling cheated. For a thousand years the Slovaks survived Hungarian hegemony, and our strategy here remained the same: endurance and steady work. Slowly, one day, we would overcome.

A special word is required about a complicated symbol: sex. To this day my mother finds it hard to spell the word intact, preferring to write "s--." Not that much was made of sex in our environment. And that's the point: silence. Demonstrative affection, emotive dances, exuberance Anglo-Saxons seldom seem to share; but on the realities of sex, discretion. Reverence, perhaps; seriousness, surely. On intimacies, it is as though our tongues had been stolen. As though in peasant life for a thousand years the context had been otherwise. Passion yes: romance, yes; family and children, certainly: but sex, rather a minor part of life.

Imagine, then, the conflict in the generation of my brothers, sister, and myself. (The book critic for the *New York Times* reviews on the same day two new novels of fantasy: one a pornographic fantasy to end all such fantasies [he writes], the other about a mad family representing in some comic way the redemption wrought by Jesus Christ. In language and verve, the books are rated even. In theme, the reviewer notes his embarrassment in reporting a religious fantasy, but no embarrassment at all about the preposterous pornography.) Suddenly, what for a thousand years was minor becomes an all-absorbing investigation. It is, perhaps, one drama when the ruling classes (I mean subscribers to *The New Yorker*, I suppose) move progressively, generation by generation since Sigmund Freud, toward consciousness-raising sessions in Clit. Lib., but wholly another when we stumble suddenly upon mores staggering any expectation our grandparents ever cherished.

Yet more significant in the ethnic experience in America is the intellectual world one meets: the definition of values, ideas, and purposes emanating from universities, books, magazines, radio, and television. One hears one's own voice echoed back neither by spokesmen of "Middle America" (so complacent, smug, nativist, and Protestant), nor by "the intellectuals." Almost unavoidably, perhaps, education in America leads the student who entrusts his soul to it in a direction that, lacking a better word, we might call liberal: respect for individual conscience, a sense of social responsibility, trust in the free exchange of ideas and procedures of dissent, a certain confidence in the ability of men to "reason together" and to adjudicate their differences, a frank recognition of the vitality of the unconscious, a willingness to protect workers and the poor against the vast economic power of industrial corporations, and the like.

On the other hand, the liberal imagination has appeared to be astonishingly universalist, and relentlessly missionary. Perhaps the metaphor "enlightenment" offers a key.

One is initiated into light. Liberal education tends to separate children from their parents, from their roots, from their history, in the cause of a universal and superior religion. One is taught, regarding the unenlightened (even if they be one's Uncles George and Peter, one's parents, one's brothers perhaps), what can only be called a modern equivalent of *odium theologcum*. Richard Hofstadter described anti-intellectualism in America, more accurately in nativist America than in ethnic America, but I have yet to encounter a comparable treatment of anti-unenlightenment among our educated classes.

In particular, I have regretted and keenly felt the absence of that sympathy for PIGS that simple human feeling might have prodded intelligence to muster: that same sympathy that the educated find so easy to conjure up for black culture, Chicano culture, Indian culture, and other cultures of the poor. In such cases, one finds, the universalist pretensions of liberal culture are suspended: some groups, at least, are entitled to be both different and respected. Why do the educated classes find it so difficult to want to understand the man who drives a beer truck, or the fellow with a helmet working on a site across the street with plumbers and electricians, while their sensitivities race easily to Mississippi or even Bedford-Stuyvesant?

There are deep secrets here, no doubt, unvoiced fantasies and scarcely admitted historical resentments. Few persons, in describing "Middle Americans," "the Silent Majority," or Seammon and Wattenberg's "typical American voter," distinguish clearly enough between the nativist American and the ethnic American. The first is likely to be Protestant, the second Catholic. Both may be, in various ways, conservative, loyalist, and unenlightened. Each has his own agonies, fears, betrayed expectations. Neither is ready, quite, to become an ally of the other. Neither has the same history behind him here. Neither has the same hopes. Neither is living out the same psychic voyage. Neither shares the same symbols or has the same sense of reality. The rhetoric and metaphors differ.

There is overlap, of course. But country music is not a polka, a successful politician in a Chicago ward needs a very different "common touch" from the one used by the country clerk in Normal: the urban experience of immigration lacks that mellifluous, optimistic, biblical vision of the good America that springs naturally to the lips of politicians from the Bible Belt. The nativist tends to believe with Richard Nixon that he "knows America and the American heart is good." The ethnic tends to believe that every American who preceded him has an angle, and that he, by God, will one day find one too. (Often, ethnics complain that by working hard, obeying the law, trusting their political leaders, and relying upon the American Dream they now have only their own naïveté to blame for rising no higher than they have.)

It goes without saying that the intellectuals do not love Middle America, and that for all the good warm discovery of America that preoccupied them during the 1950's, no strong tide of respect accumulated in their hearts for the Yahoos, Babbitts, Agnews, and Nixons of the land. Willie Morris, in *North Toward Home,* writes poignantly of the chill, parochial outreach of the liberal sensibility, its failure to engage the humanity of the modest, ordinary little man west of the Hudson. The intellectual's map of the United States is distinct: "Two coasts connected by United Airlines."

Unfortunately, it seems, the ethnics erred in attempting to Americanize themselves, before clearing the project with the educated classes. They learned to wave the flag and to send their sons to war. (The Poles in World War I were 4 percent of the population but took 12 percent of the casualties.) They learned to support their President—an easy task, after all, for those accustomed abroad to obeying authority. And where would they have been if Franklin Roosevelt had not sided with them against established interests? They knew a little about Communism, the radicals among them in one way, and by far the larger number of conservatives in another. Not a few exchange letters to this day with cousins and uncles who did not leave for America when they might have, whose lot is demonstrably harder and less than free.

Finally, the ethnics do not like, or trust, or even understand the intellectuals. It is not easy to feel uncomplicated affection for those who call you "pig," "fascist," "racist." One had not yet grown accustomed not to hearing "Hunkie," "Polack," "Spic," "Mick," "Dago," and the rest. At no little sacrifice, one had apologized for foods that smelled too strong for Anglo-Saxon noses, moderated the wide swings of Slavic and Italian emotion, learned decorum, given oneself to education American style, tried to learn tolerance and assimilation. Each generation criticized the earlier for its authoritarian and European and old-fashioned ways. "Up-to-day" was a moral lever. And now when the process nears completion, when a generation appears that speaks without accent and goes to college, still you are considered pigs, fascists, and racists.

Racists? Our ancestors owned no slaves. Most of us ceased being serfs only in the last 200 years—the Russians in 1861. What have we got against blacks or blacks against us? Competition, yes, for jobs and homes and communities: competition, even, for political power. Italians, Lithuanians, Slovaks, Poles are not, in principle, against "community control," or even against ghettos of our own. Whereas the Anglo-Saxon model appears to be a system of atomic individuals and high mobility, our model has tended to stress communities of our own, at-

tachment to family and relatives, stability, and roots. We tend to have a fierce sense of attachment to our homes, having been homeowner's less than three generations: a home is almost fulfillment enough for one man's life. We have most ambivalent feelings about suburban assimilation and mobility. The melting pot is a kind of homogenized soup, and its mores only partly appeal to us: to some, yes, and to others, no.

It must be said that we think we are better people than the blacks. Smarter, tougher, harder working, stronger in our families. But maybe many of us are not so sure. Maybe we are uneasy. Emotions here are delicate. One can understand the immensely more difficult circumstances under which the blacks have suffered, and one is not unaware of peculiar forms of fear, envy, and suspicion across color lines. How much of all this we learned in America, by being made conscious of our olive skin, brawny backs, accents, names, and cultural quirks, is not plain to us. Racism is not our invention: we did not bring it with us; we found it here. And should we pay the price for America's guilt? Must all the gains of the blacks, long overdue, be chiefly at our expense? Have we, once again, no defenders but ourselves?

Television announcers and college professors seem so often to us to be speaking in a code. When they say "white racism," it does not seem to be their own traditions they are impugning. Perhaps it is paranoia, but it seems that the affect accompanying such words is directed at steelworkers, auto workers, truck drivers, and police—at us. When they say "humanism" or "progress," it seems to us like moral pressure to abandon our own traditions, our faith, our associations, in order to reap higher rewards in the culture of the national corporations—that culture of quantity, homogeneity, replaceability, and mobility. They want to grind off all the angles, hold us to the lathes, shape us to be objective, meritocratic, orderly, and fully American.

In recent years, of course, a new cleavage has sprung open among the intellectuals. Some seem to speak for technocracy—for that alliance of science, industry, and humanism whose heaven is "progress." Others seem to be taking the view once ascribed to ecclesiastical conservatives and traditionalists: that commitment to enlightenment is narrow, ideological, and hostile to the best interests of mankind. In the past, the great alliance for progress sprang from the conviction that "knowledge is power." Both humanists and scientists could agree on that, and labored in their separate ways to make the institutions of knowledge dominant in society: break the shackles of the Church, extend suffrage to the middle classes and finally to all, win untrammeled liberty for the marketplace of ideas. Today it is no longer plain that the power brought by knowledge is humanistic. Thus the parting of the ways.

Science has ever carried with it the stories and symbols of a major religion. It is ruthlessly universalist. If its participants are not "saved," they are nonetheless "enlightened," which isn't bad. And every single action of the practicing scientist, no matter how humble, could once be understood as a contribution to the welfare of the human race; each smallest gesture was invested with meaning, given a place in a scheme, and weighted with redemptive power. Moreover, the scientist was in possession of "the truth," indeed of the very meaning of and validating procedures for the word. His role was therefore sacred.

Imagine, then, a young strapping Slovak entering an introductory course in the Sociology of Religion at the nearby state university or community college. Is he sent back to his Slovak roots, led to recover paths of experience latent in all his instincts and reflexes, given an image of the life of his grandfather that suddenly, in recognition, brings tears to the eyes? Is he brought to a deeper appreciation of his Lutheran or Catholic heritage and its resonances with other bodies of religious experience? On the contrary, he is secretly taught disdain for what his grandfather *thought* he was doing when he acted or felt or imagined through religious forms. In the boy's psyche, a new religion is implanted: power over others, enlightenment, an atomic (rather than a communitarian) sensibility, a contempt for mystery, ritual, transcendence, soul, absurdity, and tragedy; and deep confidence in the possibilities of building a better world through scientific understanding. He is led to feel ashamed for the statistical portrait of Slovak immigrants which shows them to be conservative, authoritarian, not given to dissent, etc. His teachers instruct him with the purest of intentions, in a way that is value free.

To be sure, certain radical writers in America have begun to bewail "the laying on the culture" and to unmask the cultural religion implicit in the American way of science. Yet radicals, one learns, often have an agenda of their own. What fascinates *them* among working-class ethnics are the traces, now almost lost, of *radical* activities among the working class two or three generations ago. Scratch the resentful boredom of a classroom of working-class youths, we are told, and you will find hidden in their past some formerly imprisoned organizer for the CIO, some Sacco/Vanzetti, some bold pamphleteer for the IWW. All this is true. But supposing that a study of the ethnic past reveals that most ethnics have been, are, and wish to remain, culturally conservative? Supposed, for example, they wish to deepen their religious roots and defend their ethnic enclaves? Must a radical culture be "laid on" them?

America has never confronted squarely the problem of preserving diversity. I can remember hearing in my youth bitter arguments that parochial schools were "divisive." Now the public schools are attacked for their commitment to homogenization. Well, how *does* a nation of no one culture, no one language, no one race, no one history, no one ethnic stock continue to exist as one, while encouraging diversity? How can the rights of all, and particularly of the weak, be defended if power is decentralized and left to local interests? The weak have ever found strength in this country through local chapters of national organizations. But what happens when the national organizations themselves—the schools, the unions, the federal government—become vehicles of a new, universalistic, thoroughly rationalized, technological culture?

Still, it is not that larger question that concerns me here. I am content today to voice the difficulties in the way of saying what I wish to say, when I wish to say it. The tradition of liberalism is a tradition I have had to acquire, despite an innate skepticism about many of its structural metaphors (free marketplace, individual autonomy, reason naked and undisguised, enlightenment). Radicalism, with its bold and simple optimism about human potential and its anarchic tendencies, has been, despite its appeal to me as a vehicle for criticizing liberalism, freighted with emotions, sentiments, and convictions about men that I cannot bring myself to share.

In my guts, I do not feel that institutions are "repressive" in any meaning of the word that leaves it meaningful; the "state of nature" seems to me, emotionally, far less liberating, far more undifferentiated and confining. I have not dwelt for so long in the profession of the intellectual life that I find it easy to be critical and harsh. In almost everything I see or hear or read, I am struck first, rather undiscriminatingly, by all the things I like in it. Only with second effort can I bring myself to discern the flaws. My emotions and values seem to run in affirmative patterns.

My interest is not, in fact, in defining myself over against the American people and the American way of life. I do not expect as much of it as all that. What I should like to do is come to a better and more profound knowledge of who I am, whence my community came, and whither my son and daughter, and their children's children, might wish to head in the future: I want to have a history.

More and more, I think in family terms, less ambitiously, on a less than national scale. The differences implicit in being Slovak, and Catholic, and lower-middle class seem more and more important to me. Perhaps it is too much to try to speak to all peoples in this very various nation of ours. Yet it does not seem evident that by becoming more concrete, accepting one's finite and limited identity, one necessarily becomes parochial. Quite the opposite. It seems more likely that by each of us becoming more profoundly what we are, we shall find greater unity, in those depths in which unity irradiates diversity, than by attempting through the artifices of the American "melting pot" and the cultural religion of science to become what we are not.

There is, I take it, a form of liberalism not wedded to universal Reason, whose ambition is not to homogenize all peoples on this planet, and whose base lies rather in the imagination and in the diversity of human stories: a liberalism I should be happy to have others help me to find.

# A Happy Ending?

*Nathan Glazer*

A happy ending to a long story of forced assimilation? Perhaps. But there are still some troubling issues, as there always are when the regularities of state requirement enter a subtle and complex area of education, one that must be suited to individual and groups needs. There is something ironic about the government's mandating responsiveness to individual and group needs—and then issuing rigid guidelines as to how this is to be achieved. Thus, government specifies how students should be counted, what groups must be counted, the threshold number of students that will trigger a program, and so on. (As I pointed out, these "must" requirements derive from the extension of the notion of nondiscrimination, as provided in Title VI of the Civil Rights Act of 1964, by regulation and court rulings; the federal Bilingual Education Act only provides opportunities and does not mandate programs. But state programs may be mandatory.) The fact that these groups are as various as Navajo Indians and Greek immigrant children, or lower-class Puerto Ricans moving to and fro between island and mainland and middle-class Cubans committed to making a life in the United States, cannot be taken into account in

Nathan Glazer, a professor of sociology at Harvard University, has written many books about issues of race and ethnicity.

Reprinted by permission of the publishers from *Ethnic Dilemmas 1964–1982* by Nathan Glazer, Cambridge, Mass.: Harvard University Press. Copyright © 1983 by the President and Fellows of Harvard College.

government regulations, and one wonders whether it is taken into account by government compliance-review agents.

Ethnicity and race are subtle and complex matters; one doubts there are enough people in the country responsive to this complexity and to the variety of needs of different groups to do more than check whether pro forma requirements—some less than any group needs, some more than a group requires or desires—are being met in the over three hundred school districts investigated for compliance in 1975–1976. This number is up from seventy-four in 1973–1974, and even so is a small fraction of those districts with more than 5 percent linguistic minority children which must provide bilingual-bicultural programs according to the regulations.

In some communities—for example, one with a substantial Greek-origin population in Chicago—there has been resistance to the institution of a bilingual-bicultural program; these parents want their children educated in English. One notes that in Quebec there is severe resistance among immigrants, even among those speaking related languages such as Italian, to a requirement that their children must be educated in French rather than in English. In any group there will be division: there will be assimilationists, those who demand linguistic competence, those who want only maintenance of cultural attachment, those who insist on full education in language and culture. It is hard to see how school districts operating under governmental regulations will satisfy such a variety of interests.

Purely voluntary educational activities, conducted in private schools under only limited public authority, might respond to this variety of needs. In the case of Jewish education, for example, we have seen schools that are religious and secular. Orthodox (of several varieties), Conservative, and Reform, all-day, afternoon, and Sunday, variously emphasizing Hebrew, Yiddish, or English, reflecting a history of political tendencies including Zionism, diaspora nationalism, territorialism, anarchism, socialism, and communism. One wonders, after this history, what kind of bilingual-bicultural education established under public auspices and common central rules can possibly satisfy or be relevant to—to take one example—the children of Hebrew-speaking Israeli immigrants who are now coming to this country in substantial numbers. Or, to take another recent immigrant group, those from India and Pakistan; they speak a dozen languages, are in religion divided among Moslems, Hindus, Sikhs, Jains, and others, and reflect a variety of cultures. Will it now be up to school districts in which their numbers are substantial to provide a program? And even though their parents probably insist their education be in English, fully and completely?

The large question that multicultural education has not dealt with as yet is how very different are the desires and requirements of different groups in the area of bicultural and bilingual education. It is not possible for the state to legislate for each group separately, according to its needs and desires. That would run afoul of the state's need for general legislation, legislation that provides the "equal protection of the laws." Yet blacks, Mexican Americans, Puerto Ricans, American Indians, Cubans, Portuguese form the islands and the mainland, Frenchspeaking Canadians and Louisiana Cajuns, Jews, Chinese, Japanese, Poles, Italians, and so on need and want very different things. Some of these groups are concerned primarily with poor educational achievement: they want anything that will work, and if that means multicultural education and black English, so be it, but if it means the exact reverse, they will choose that. Some of these groups have only a transitional language problem and have no desire to maintain in a public school setting education in ancestral languages. Some want only to be recognized: if anything is to be done for any other groups, they want education in their own group's heritage, "equal time," but they may not even be sure they want their children to spend time taking it. And I have simplified the complexity, for in each group there are people with very different demands and needs.

Whether it is possible under state auspices to meet all these needs and requirements is a serious question. What tends to happen is that one model is created to deal with the most urgent needs—let us say, black studies for blacks to build up self-respect, and some teaching in Spanish to help bridge the transition to English. But then these initial model programs become models for others, too. They become the most extreme demands for some in each group who bargain for whatever any other group has, even if most people in the group do not recognize the need. The problem with state programs is that they must prescribe the same for everyone, even though the very essence of this situation is that each individual and each group has a rather different set of needs and wants something quite different from multicultural education.

The reason for this complexity derives directly from the American ethnic pattern. It is not a pattern of sharp lines of division between groups. If it were, if each individual were unambiguously a member of one group or another, then perhaps the same program could be prescribed for each. Some people want to see America this way, the way the early cultural pluralists saw it. Indeed, in this perspective, everyone is a member of an ethnic group, including those of Anglo-Saxon origin, and so we have proposals of ethnic studies for those who do not want them and do not need them simply because of someone's ideological commitment to the notion that every American must be a member of an ethnic group and must need the same things. So we have the outlandish discussions in educational journals of "white studies"—if we have black, brown, yellow, and red studies, why not white studies? But in fact some groups in this country are sharply distinguished by color and culture; others are not. Even so, many members of each of the sharply distinguished groups, through cultural change and intermarriage, move toward the boundaries of their group, and perhaps out of their group. And the overall hope for this country—a hope shaken in recent years—is that ultimately no group boundary will be important, that everyone will have the right to accept whatever he or she wants of ancestral culture and ethnic identity, and that this will be a private choice in which government will play no role, whether to encourage it or to discourage it. And it is still, I believe, part of the general expectation that a general American culture will prevail as the dominant one in our country, and one that does create national identity, loyalty, and commitment.

# Life As a Slave
*Frederick Douglass*

I was a slave—born a slave—and though the fact was incomprehensible to me, it conveyed to my mind a sense of my entire dependence on the will of *somebody* I had never seen; and, from some cause or another, I had been made to fear this somebody above all else on earth. Born for another's benefit, as the *firstling* of the cabin flock I was soon to be selected as a meet offering to the fearful and inexorable *demigod,* whose huge image on so many occasions haunted my childhood's imagination. When the time of my departure was decided upon, my grandmother, knowing my fears, and in pity for them, kindly kept me ignorant of the dreaded event about to transpire. Up to the morning (a beautiful summer morning) when we were to start, and, indeed, during the whole journey—a journey which, child as I was, I remember as well as if it were yesterday—she kept the sad fact hidden from me. This reserve was necessary; for, could I have known all, I should have given grandmother some trouble in getting me started. As it was, I was helpless, and she—dear woman!—led me along by the hand, resisting, with the reserve and solemnity of a priestess, all my inquiring looks to the last.

After escaping form slavery in 1838, Frederick Douglass joined the Massachusetts Anti-Slavery Society and toured the North lecturing on the brutality of slavery. His autobiography was published in 1865.

From "My Bondage and Freedom" © 1855.

The distance from Tuckahoe to Wye River—where my old master lived—was full twelve miles, and the walk was quite a severe test of the endurance of my young legs. The journey would have proved too severe for me, but that my dear old grandmother—blessings on her memory!—afforded occasional relief by "toting" me (as Marylanders have it) on her shoulder. My grandmother, though advanced in years—as was evident from more than one gray hair, which peeped from between the ample and graceful folds of her newly-ironed power and spirit. She was marvelously straight in figure, elastic, and muscular. I seemed hardly to be a burden to her. She would have "toted" me farther, but that I felt myself too much of a man to allow it, and insisted on walking. Releasing dear grandmamma from carrying me did not make me altogether independent of her, when we happened to pass through portions of the somber woods which lay between Tuckahoe and Wye river. She often found me increasing the energy of my grip, and holding her clothing, lest something should come out of the woods and eat me up. Several old logs and stumps imposed upon me, and got themselves taken for wild beasts. I could see their legs, eyes, and ears, or I could see something like eyes, legs, and ears, till I got close enough to them to see that the eyes were knots, washed white with rain, and the legs were broken limbs, and the ears, only ears owing to the point from which they were seen. Thus early I learned that the point from which a thing is viewed is of some importance.

As the day advanced the heat increased; and it was not until the afternoon that we reached the much dreaded end of the journey. I found myself in the midst of a group of children of many colors; black, brown, copper colored, and nearly white. I had not seen so many children before. Great houses loomed up in different directions, and a great many men and women were at work in the fields. All this hurry, noise, and singing was very different from the stillness of Tuckahoe. As a new comer, I was an object of special interest; and, after laughing and yelling around me, and playing all sorts of wild tricks, they (the children) asked me to go out and play with them. This I refused to do, preferring to stay with grandmamma. I could not help feeling that our being there boded no good to me. Grandmamma looked sad. She was soon to lose another object of affection, as she had lost many before. I knew she was unhappy, and the shadow fell from her brow on me, though I knew not the cause.

All suspense, however, must have an end; and the end of mine, in this instance, was at hand. Affectionately patting me on the head, and exhorting me to be a good boy, grandmamma told me to go and play with the little children. "They are kin to you,' she said; "go and play with them." Among a number of cousins were Phil, Tom, Steve, and Jerry, Nance and Betty.

Grandmother pointed out my brother PERRY, my sister SARAH, and my sister ELIZA, who stood in the group, I had never seen my brother nor my sisters before; and, though I had sometimes heard of them, and felt a curious interest in them, I really did not understand what they were to me, or I to them. We were brothers and sisters, but what of that? Why should they be attached to me, or I to them? Brothers and sisters we were by blood; but *slavery* had made us strangers. I heard the words brother and sisters, and knew they must mean something; but slavery had robbed these terms of their true meaning. The experience through which I was passing, they had passed through before. They had already been initiated into the mysteries of old master's domicile, and they seemed to look upon me with a certain degree of compassion; but my heart clave to my grandmother. Think it not strange, dear reader, that so little sympathy of feeling existed between us. The conditions of brotherly and sisterly feeling were wanting—we had never nestled and played together. My poor mother, like many slave-women, had *many children,* but NO FAMILY! The domestic hearth, with its holy lessons and precious endearments, is abolished in the case of a slave-mother and her children. "Little children, love one another," are words seldom heard in a slave cabin.

I really wanted to play with my brother and sisters, but they were strangers to me, and I was full of fear that grandmother might leave without taking me with her. Entreated to do so, however, and that, too, by my dear grandmother, I went to the back part of the house, to play with them and the other children. Play, however, I did not, but stood with my back against the wall, witnessing the playing of the others. At last, while standing there, one of the children, who had been in the kitchen, ran up to me, in a sort of roguish glee, exclaiming, "Fed, Fed! grandmammy gone! grandmammy gone!" I could not believe it, yet fearing the worst, I ran into the kitchen, to see for myself, and found it even so. Grandmammy had indeed gone, and was now far away, "clean" out of sight. I need not tell all that happened now. Almost heartbroken at the discovery, I fell upon the ground, and wept a boy's bitter tears, refusing to be comforted. My brother and sisters came around me, and said, "Don't cry," and gave me peaches and pears, but I flung them away, and refused all their kindly advances. I had never been deceived before; and I felt not only grieved at parting—as I supposed forever—with my grandmother, but indignant that a trick had been played upon me in a matter so serious.

It was now late in the afternoon. The day had been an exciting and wearisome one, and I knew not how or where, but I suppose I sobbed myself to sleep. There is a healing in the angel wing of sleep, even for the slave-boy; and its balm was never more welcome to any wounded soul than it was to mine, the first night I spent at the domicile of old master. The reader may be surprised that I narrate so minutely an incident apparently so trivial, and which must have occurred when I was not more than seven years old; but as I wish to give a faithful history of my experience in slavery, I cannot withhold a circumstance which, at the time, affected me so deeply. Besides, this was, in fact, my first introduction to the realities of slavery.

# Sequence Four

## Solving Problems and the Scientific Method

The discipline of science offers a set of rules for solving problems. To be a scientist, then, one must adhere to those rules. But one must also remember that the object of science, or any discipline, is not adhering to rules but solving problems, and that the rules are not an end but instead means to one. Keeping this in mind, the teacher of science must encourage students to adhere to the rules but also not discourage them from thinking unscientifically, from approaching and solving problems in novel ways.

While science enables us to solve problems, it also creates them. Praise and honors rightly go to those who make important scientific discoveries, invent useful new substances, and perfect new medical procedures. But advancement such as these sometimes occur so rapidly that our ability to assess their effects from a moral or philosophical perspective lags behind. When that happens, scientific issues become political ones, and scientific achievements not only provide answers, but also raise questions.

In this sequence, a look at science in both the narrow sphere of the classroom and the broader sphere of politics should enable us to gain a firmer understanding of scientific thinking, examine the advantages and disadvantages of adhering to rules, and speculate on the value of scientific achievements.

## Assignment One

*Readings:*

   Alexander Calandra, "Angels on a Pin."
   Karl Jaspers, "Is Science Evil?"

Jaspers asserts that "Within the purview of science there is no such thing as liberty." Write an essay in which you clarify for yourself how you feel about the difficulties the student in Calandra's essay encountered. Questions you may wish to address are: Did that student's teacher attempt to deny him liberty? Is denying liberty to a student of science necessary to maintain the "methodical, compellingly certain, and universally valid" nature of science? Do you think Calandra and his colleague treated the student fairly? How would you react, either as a student or a teacher, if confronted with a similar situation?

# Assignment Two

*Readings:*

Jonathan Schell, "What If the Bomb Hits Home?"
Helen Caldicott, " What You Must Know about Radiation."

In "Is Science Evil?" Jaspers wrote: "That modern science, like all things, contains its own share of corruption, that men of science only too often fail to live up to its standards, that science can be used for violent and criminal ends, that man will steal, plunder, abuse, and kill to gain knowledge—all this is no argument against science." He also asserts that science is "neither human nor inhuman." Yet, are the possibility of a nuclear explosion destroying New York City or increased incidence of cancers caused by careless handling of radioactive waste scientific issues or human ones? Schell provides a purely factual description of the destructive power of nuclear weapons, Caldicott, a factual account plus an emotional appeal. Both authors write to inform an audience, and both depend on scientific knowledge for the information they use to support their arguments. Write an essay in the style of either Schell or Caldicott, that is, purely factual or factual and emotional, in which you outline in detail what you think would happen if all students were allowed the liberty that the student in Calandra's essay attempted to take.

# Assignment Three

*Readings:*

Linda Bird Francke, "The Right to Choose."
Stephen Jay Gould, "Death Before Birth, or a Mite's *Nunc Dimittis*."

How does the way we present information influence the way we receive and evaluate it? At first glance one would gather that Gould's essay, judging by its title and its position next to Francke's essay, is about abortion. But that is incorrect. It is only the proximity of Gould's essay to Francke's that leads one to that judgment. Various writers and speakers have tried to portray abortion as either a scientific or a political issue. On the one hand, abortion is a relatively simple medical procedure, similar to, say, a tonsillectomy. On the other, it is a political issue filled with religious, emotional, and moral significance. Francke presents the physical details of her abortion but concentrates on the human factor, on her response as a person, not a patient. Consider whether you see the debate over abortion as a scientific issue, one that can be resolved with scientific information such as how old the fetus is, whether its heart is beating, whether it has brain activity, or as a moral dilemma that involves developing not only a non-scientific definition of life, but also a philosophy about rights and liberty. Then consider whether a doctor who performs abortions should be able to deal with the patient's emotions as well as perform the actual procedure. Write an essay in which you speculate on what kind of doctor Gould would be and why.

# Assignment Four

*Readings:*

    Charles Darwin, "On My Reading, Writing, and Thinking."
    Lewis Thomas, "How to Fix the Premedical Curriculum."

Darwin describes the many undesirable effects that years of scientific thinking have had on his mind. He laments having lost the ability to enjoy poetry and music and the conversion of his mind into "a kind of machine for grinding general laws out of large collections of facts," yet maintains that he has "steadily endeavored to keep [his] mind free." Thomas worries that premedical students never develop "higher aesthetic tastes" in college, and that by the time they matriculate to medical school, they already resemble Darwin's machine.

Perhaps worse, they lack the "love of natural science" that Darwin isolates as both his primary motivation and the primary factor in his success. Taking into account all the essays you have read for this sequence, write an essay in which you argue that an author of one of those essays would be Thomas's ideal student or ideal doctor. Questions to consider are: How broad an approach does each author take to his or her subject? Does this approach include both the scientific and the human perspective? After choosing an author, persuade your audience why he or she should be given the task of reconstructing the college curriculum. You are free to choose any author, but you must support your arguments.

# Angels on a Pin

*Alexander Calandra*

Some time ago, I received a call from a colleague who asked if I would be the referee on the grading of an examination question. He was about to give a student a zero for his answer to a physics question, while the student claimed he should receive a perfect score and would if the system were not set up against the student. The instructor and the student agreed to submit this to an impartial arbiter, and I was selected.

I went to my colleague's office and read the examination question: "Show how it is possible to determine the height of a tall building with the aid of a barometer."

The student had answered: "Take the barometer to the top of the building, attach a long rope to it, lower the barometer to the street, and then bring it up, measuring the length of the rope. The length of the rope is the height of the building."

I pointed out that the student really has a strong case for full credit, since he had answered the question completely and correctly. On the other had, if full credit were given, it could well contribute to a high grade for the student in his physics course. A high grade is supposed to certify competence in physics, but the answer did not confirm this. I suggested that the student have another try at answering the question. I was not surprised that my colleague agreed, but I was surprised that the student did.

I gave the student six minutes to answer the question, with the warning that his answer should show some knowledge of physics. At the end of five minutes, he had not written anything. I asked if he wished to give up, but he said no. He had many answers to this problem; he was just thinking of the best one. I excused myself for interrupting him, and asked him to please go on. In the next minute, he dashed off his answer, which read:

"Take the barometer to the top of the building and lean over the edge of the roof. Drop the barometer, timing its fall with a stop-watch. Then, using the formula $S = 1/2 \, at^2$, calculate the height of the building."

At this point, I asked my colleague if *he* would give up. He conceded, and I gave the student almost full credit.

In leaving my colleague's office, I recalled that the student had said he had other answers to the problem, so I asked him what they were. "Oh, yes," said the student. "There are many ways of getting the height of a tall building with the aid of a barometer. For example, you could take the barometer out on a sunny day and measure the height of the barometer, the length of its shadow, and the length of the shadow of the building, and the use of a simple proportion, determine the height of the building."

"Fine, " I said. "And the others?"

Reprinted with permission from Alexander Calandra. *Angels on a Pin* available in poster form from the author c/o Washington University, St. Louis, Mo. 63130

"Yes," said the student. "There is a very basic measurement method that you will like. In this method, you take the barometer and begin to walk up the stairs. As you climb the stairs, you mark off the length of the barometer along the wall. You then count the number of marks, and this will give you the height of the building in barometer units. A very direct method.

"Of course, if you want a more sophisticated method, you can tie the barometer to the end of a string, swing it as a pendulum, and determine the value of 'g' at the street level and at the top building. From the difference between the two values of 'g,' the height of the building can, in principle, be calculated."

Finally he concluded, there are many other ways of solving the problem. "Probably the best," he said, "is to take the barometer to the basement and knock on the superintendent's door. When the superintendent answers, you speak to him as follows: 'Mr. Superintendent, here I have a fine barometer. If you will tell me the height of this building, I will give you this barometer.'"

At this point, I asked the student if he really did not know the conventional answer to this question. He admitted that he did, but said that he was fed up with high school and college instructors trying to teach him how to think, to use the "scientific method," and to explore the deep inner logic of the subject in a pedantic way, as is often done in the new mathematics, rather than teaching him the structure of the subject. With this in mind, he decided to revive scholasticism as an academic lark to challenge the Sputnik-panicked classrooms of America.

# Is Science Evil?

*Karl Jaspers*

No one questions the immense significance of modern science. Through industrial technology it has transformed our existence, and its insights have transformed our consciousness, all this to an extent hitherto unheard of. The human condition throughout the millennia appears relatively stable in comparison with the impetuous movement that has now caught up mankind as a result of science and technology, and is driving it no one knows where. Science has destroyed the substance of many old beliefs and has made others questionable. Its powerful authority has brought more and more men to the point where they expect to be helped by science and only by science. The present faith is that scientific understanding can solve all problems and do away with all difficulties.

Such excessive expectations result inevitably in equally excessive disillusionment. Science has still given no answer to man's doubts and despair. Instead, it has created weapons able to destroy in a few moments that which science itself helped build up slowly over the years. Accordingly, there are today two conflicting viewpoints: first, the superstition of science, which holds scientific results to be as absolute as religious myths used to be, so that even religious movements are now dressed in the garments of pseudoscience. Second, the hatred of science, which

sees it as a diabolical evil of mysterious origin that has befallen mankind.

These two attitudes—both nonscientific—are so closely linked that they are usually found together, either in alternation or in an amazing compound.

A very recent example of this situation can be found in the attack against science provoked by the trial in Nuremberg of those doctors who, under Nazi orders, performed deadly experiments on human beings. One of the most esteemed medical men among German university professors has accepted the verdict on these crimes as a verdict on science itself, as a stick with which to beat "purely scientific and biological" medicine, and even the modern science of man in general: "this invisible spirit sitting on the prisoner's bench in Nuremberg, this spirit that regards men merely as objects, is not present in Nuremberg alone—it pervades the entire world." And he adds, if this generalization may be viewed as an extenuation of the crime of the accused doctors, that is only a further indictment of purely scientific medicine.

Anyone convinced that true scientific knowledge is possible only of things that *can* be regarded as objects, and that knowledge of the subject is possible only when the subject attains a form of objectivity; anyone who sees science as the one great landmark on the road to truth, and sees the real achievements of modern physicians as derived exclusively from biological and scientific medicine—

Karl Jaspers, "Is Science Evil?," from *Commentary* (1950). Reprinted with permission.

such a person will see in the above statements an attack on what he feels to be fundamental to human existence. And he may perhaps have a word to say in rebuttal.

In the special case of the crimes against humanity committed by Nazi doctors and now laid at the door of modern science, there is a simple enough argument. Science was not needed at all, but only a certain bent of mind for the perpetration of such outrages. Such crimes were already possible millennia ago. In the Buddhist Pali canon, there is the report of an Indian prince who had experiments performed on criminals in order to determine whether they had an immortal soul that survived their corpses: "You shall— it was ordered—put the living man in a tub, close the lid, cover it with a damp hide, lay on a thick layer of clay, put it in the oven, and make a fire. This was done. When we knew the man was dead, the tub was drawn forth, uncovered, the lid removed, and we looked carefully inside to see if we could perceive the escaping soul. But we saw no escaping soul." Similarly, criminals were slowly skinned alive to see if their souls could be observed leaving their bodies. Thus there were experiments on human beings before modern science.

Better than such a defense, however, would be a consideration of what modern science really genuinely is, and what its limits are.

First, it is *methodical* knowledge. I know something scientifically only when I also know the method by which I have this knowledge, and am thus able to ground it and mark its limits.

Second, it is *compellingly certain*. Even the uncertain—i.e., the probable or improbable—I know scientifically only insofar as I know it clearly and compellingly as such, and know the degree of its uncertainly.

Third, it is *universally valid*. I know scientifically only what is identically valid for every inquirer. Thus scientific knowledge spreads over the world and remains the same. Unanimity is a sign of universal validity. When unanimity is not attained, when there is a conflict of schools, sects, and trends of fashion, then universal validity becomes problematic.

This notion of science as methodical knowledge, compellingly certain, and universally valid, was long ago possessed by the Greeks. Modern science has not only purified this notion; it has also transformed it: a transformation that can be described by saying that modern science is *indifferent to nothing*. Everything—the smallest and meanest, the furthest and strangest—that is in any way and at any time *actual*, is relevant to modern science, simply because it *is*. Modern science wants to be thoroughly universal, allowing nothing to escape it. Nothing shall be hidden, nothing shall be silent, nothing shall be a secret.

In contrast to the science of classical antiquity, modern science is *basically unfinished*. Whereas ancient science had the appearance of something completed, to which the notion of progress was not essential, modern science progresses into the infinite. Modern science has realized that a finished and total world-view is scientifically impossible. Only when scientific criticism is crippled by making particulars absolute can a closed view of the world pretend to scientific validity—and then it is a false validity. Those great new unified systems of knowledge—such as modern physics—that have grown up in the scientific era, deal only with single aspects of reality. And reality as a whole has been fragmented as never before; whence the openness of the modern world in contrast to the closed Greek cosmos.

However, while a total and finished world-view is no longer possible to modern science, the idea of a unity of the sciences has now come to replace it. Instead of the cosmos of the world, we have the cosmos of the sciences. Out of dissatisfaction with all the separate bits of knowledge is born the desire to unite all knowledge. The ancient sciences remained dispersed and without mutual relations. There was lacking to them the notion of a concrete totality of science. The modern sciences, however, seek to relate themselves to each other in every possible way.

At the same time the modern sciences have increased their claims. They put a low value on the possibilities of speculative thinking, they hold thought to be valid only as part of definite and concrete knowledge, only when it has stood the test of verification and thereby become infinitely modified. Only superficially do the modern and the ancient atomic theories seem to fit into the same theoretical mold. Ancient atomic theory was applied as a plausible interpretation of common experience; it was a statement complete in itself of what might possibly be the case. Modern atomic theory has developed through experiment, verification, refutation: that is, through an incessant transformation of itself in which theory is used not as an end in itself but as a tool of inquiry. Modern science, in its question, pushes to extremes. For example: the rational critique of appearance (as against reality) was begun in antiquity, as in the concept of perspective and its application to astronomy, but it still had some connection with immediate human experiences; today, however, this same critique, as in modern physics for instance, ventures to the very extremes of paradox, attaining a knowledge of the real that shatters any and every view of the world as a closed and complete whole.

So it is that in our day a scientific attitude has become possible that addresses itself inquisitively to everything it comes across, that is able to know what it knows in a clear and positive way, that can distinguish between the known and the unknown, and that has acquired an incredible mass of knowledge. How helpless was the Greek doctor or the Greek engineer! The ethos of modern science is the desire for reliable knowledge based on dispassionate investigation and criticism. When we enter its domain we feel as though we were breathing pure air, and seeing the dissolution of all vague talk, plausible opinions, haughty omniscience, blind faith.

But the greatness and the limitations of science are inseparable. It is a characteristic of the greatness of modern science that it comprehends its own limits:

1. Scientific, objective knowledge is not a knowledge of Being. This means that scientific knowledge is particular, not general, that it is directed toward specific objects, and not toward Being itself. Through knowledge itself, science arrives at the most positive recognition of what it does *not* know.
2. Scientific knowledge or understanding cannot supply us with the aims of life. It cannot lead us. By virtue of its very clarity it directs us elsewhere for the sources of our life, our decisions, our love.
3. Human freedom is not an object of science, but is the field of philosophy. Within the purview of science there is no such thing as liberty.

These are clear limits, and the person who is scientifically minded will not expect from science what it cannot give. Yet science has become, nevertheless, the indispensable element of all striving for truth, it has become the premise of philosophy and the basis in general for whatever clarity and candor are today possible. To the extent that it succeeds in penetrating all obscurities and unveiling all secrets, science directs to the most profound, the most genuine secret.

The unique phenomenon of modern science, so fundamentally different from anything in the past, including the science of the Greeks, owes its character to the many sources that were its origin; and these had to meet together in Western history in order to produce it.

One of these sources was Biblical religion. The rise of modern science is scarcely conceivable without its impetus. Three of the motives that have spurred research and inquiry seem to have come from it:

1. The ethos of Biblical religion demanded truthfulness at all costs. As a result, truthfulness became a supreme value and at the same time was pushed to the point where it became a serious problem. The truthfulness demanded by God forbade making the search for knowledge a game or amusement, an aristocratic leisure activity. It was a serious affair, a calling in which everything was at stake.

2. The world is the creation of God. The Greeks knew the cosmos as that which was complete and ordered, rational and regular, eternally subsisting. All else was nothing, merely material, not knowable and not worth knowing. But if the world is the creation of God, then everything that exists is worth knowing, just because it is God's creation; there is nothing that ought not to be known and comprehended. To know is to reflect upon God's thought. And God as creator is—in Luther's words—present even in the bowels of a louse.

The Greeks remained imprisoned in their closed world-view, in the beauty of their rational cosmos, in the logical transparency of the rational whole. Not only Aristotle and Democritus, but Thomas Aquinas and Descartes, too, obey this Greek urge, so

paralyzing to the spirit of science, toward a closed universe. Entirely different is the new impulse to unveil the totality of creation. Out of this there arises the pursuit through knowledge of that reality which is not in accord with previously established laws. In the Logos itself [the Word, Reason] there is born the drive toward repeated self-destruction—not as self-immolation, but in order to arise again and ever again in a process that is to be continued infinitely. This science springs from a Logos that does not remain closed within itself, but is open to an anti-Logos which it permeates by the very act of subordinating itself to it. The continuous, unceasing reciprocal action of theory and experiment is the simple and great example and symbol of the universal process that is the dialectic between Logos and anti-Logos.

This new urge for knowledge sees the world no longer as simply beautiful. This knowledge ignores the beautiful and the ugly, the good and the wicked. It is true that in the end, *omne ens est bonum* [all Being is good], that is, as a creation of God. This goodness, however, is no longer the transparent and self-sufficient beauty of the Greeks. It is present only in the love of all existent things as created by God, and it is present therefore in our confidence in the significance of inquiry. The knowledge of the createdness of all worldly things replaces indifference in the face of the flux of reality with limitless questioning, an insatiable spirit of inquiry.

But the world that is known and knowable is, as created Being, Being of the second rank. For the world is unfathomable, it has its ground in another, a Creator, it is not self-contained and it is not containable by knowledge. The Being of the world cannot be comprehended as definitive, absolute reality but points always to another.

The idea of creation makes worthy of love whatever is, for it is God's creation; and it makes possible, by this, and intimacy with reality never before attained. But at the same time it give evidence of the incalculable distance from that Being which is not merely created Being but Being itself, God.

3. The reality of this world is full of cruelty and horror for men. "That's the way things are," is what man must truthfully say. If, however, God is the world's creator, then he is responsible for his creation. The question of justifying God's way becomes with Job a struggle with the divine for the knowledge of reality. It is a struggle against God, for God. God's existence is undisputed and just because of this the struggle arises. It would cease if faith were extinguished.

This God, with his unconditional demand for truthfulness, refuses to be grasped through illusions. In the Bible, he condemns the theologians who wish to console and comfort Job with dogmas and sophisms. This God insists upon science, whose content always seems to bring forth an indictment of him. Thus we have the adventure of knowledge, the furtherance of unrestricted knowledge—and at the same time, a timidity, an awe in the face of it. There was an inner tension to be observed in many scientists of the past century, as if they heard: God's will is unconfined inquiry, inquiry is in the service of God—and at the same time: it is an encroachment on God's domain, all shall not be revealed.

This struggle goes hand in hand with the struggle of the man of science against all that he holds most clear, his ideals, his beliefs; they must be proven, newly verified, or else transformed. Since God could not be believed in if he were not able to withstand all the questions arising from the facts of reality, and since the seeking of God involves the painful sacrifice of all illusions, so true inquiry is the struggle against all personal desires and expectations.

This struggle finds its final test in the struggle of the scientist with his own theses. It is the determining characteristic of the modern scientist that he seeks out the strongest points in the criticism of his opponents and exposes himself to them. What in appearance is self-destructiveness becomes, in this case, productive. And it is evidence of degradation of science when discussion is shunned or condemned, when men imprison themselves and their ideas in a milieu of like-mined savants and become fanatically aggressive to all outside it.

That modern science, like all things, contains its own share of corruption, that men of science only too often fail to live up to its standards, that science can be used for violent and criminal ends, that man will steal, plunder, abuse, and kill to gain knowledge—all this is no argument against science.

To be sure, science as such sets up no barriers. As science, it is neither human nor inhuman. So far as the well-being of humanity is concerned, science needs guidance from other sources. Science in itself is not enough—or should not be. Even medicine is only a scientific means, serving an eternal ideal, the aid of the sick and the protection of the healthy.

When the spirit of a faithless age can become the cause of atrocities all over the world, then it can also influence the conduct of the scientist and the behavior of the physician, especially in those areas of activity where science itself is confused and unguided. It is not the spirit of science but the spirit of its vessels that is depraved. Court Keyserling's dictum—"The roots of truth seeking lie in primitive aggression"—is as little valid for science as it is for any genuine truth seeking. The spirit of science is in no way primarily aggressive, but becomes so only when truth is prohibited; for men rebel against the glossing over of truth or its suppression.

In our present situation the task is to attain to that true science which knows what it knows at the same time that it knows what cannot know. This science shows us the ways to the truth that are the indispensable precondition of every other truth. We know what Mephistopheles knew when he thought he had outwitted Faust:

*Verachte nur Vernunft und Wissenschaft*
Des Menschen allerhöchste Kraft
So habe ich Dich schon unbedingt.
(Do but scorn Reason and Science
Man's supreme strength
Then I'll have you for sure.)

# What If the Bomb Hits Home?

*Jonathan Schell*

One way to begin to grasp the destructive power of present-day nuclear weapons is to describe the consequences of the detonation of a one-megaton bomb, which possesses 80 times the explosive power of the Hiroshima bomb, on a large city, such as New York. Burst some 8,500 feet above the Empire State Building, a one-megaton bomb would gut or flatten almost every building between Battery Park and 125th Street, or within a radius of four and four-tenths miles, or in a area of 61 square miles, and would heavily damage building between the northern tip of Staten Island and the George Washington Bridge, or within a radius of about eight miles, or in an area of about 200 square miles.

A conventional explosive delivers a swift shock, like a slap, to whatever it hits, but the blast wave of a sizable nuclear weapon endures for several seconds and can surround and destroy whole buildings. People, of course, would be picked up and hurled away from the blast along with the rest of the debris. Within the 61 square miles, the walls, roofs and floors of any buildings that had not been flattened would be collapsed, and the people and furniture inside would be swept down onto the street. (Technically, this zone would be hit by various over-pressures of at least five pounds per square inch. Over-

pressure is defined as the pressure in excess of normal atmospheric pressure.)

As far away as 10 miles from ground zero, pieces of glass and other sharp objects would be hurled about by the blast wave at lethal velocities. In Hiroshima, where buildings were low and, outside the center of the city, were often constructed of light materials, injuries from falling building were often minor. But in New York, where the buildings are tall and are constructed of heavy materials, the physical collapse of the city would certainly kill millions of people.

The streets of New York are narrow ravines running between the high walls of the city's buildings. In a nuclear attack, the walls would fall and the ravines would fill up. The people in the buildings would fall to the street with the debris of the buildings, and the people in the street would be crushed by this avalanche of people and buildings.

At a distance of two miles or so from ground zero, winds would reach 400 miles an hour, and another two miles away they would reach 180 miles an hour. Meanwhile, the fireball would be growing, until it was more than a mile wide, and rocketing upward to a height of over six miles. For ten seconds, it would broil the city below. Anyone caught in the open within nine miles of ground zero would receive third-degree burns and would probably be killed; closer to the explosion, people would be charred and killed instantly.

From Greenwich Village up to Central Park, the heat would be great enough to melt metal and glass. Readily inflammable materials, such as newspapers and dry leaves, would ignite in all five boroughs (though in only a small part of Staten Island) and west to the Passaic River, in New Jersey, within a radius of about nine and a half miles from ground zero, thereby creating an area of more than 180 square miles in which mass fires were likely to break out.

If it were possible (as it would not be) for someone to stand at Fifth Avenue and Seventy-second Street (about two miles from ground zero) without being killed instantly, he would see the following sequence of events. A dazzling white light from the fireball would illumine the scene, continuing for perhaps 30 seconds. Simultaneously, searing heat would ignite everything flammable and start to melt windows, cars, buses, lampposts, and everything else made of metal or glass. People in the street would immediately catch fire, and would shortly be reduced to heavily charred corpses.

About five seconds after the light appeared, the blast wave would strike, laden with the debris of a now nonexistent midtown. Some buildings might be crushed, as though a giant fist had squeezed them on all sides, and others might be picked up off their foundations and whirled uptown with the other debris. On the far side of Central Park, the West Side skyline would fall from south to north. The 400-mile-an-hour wind would blow from south to north, die down after a few seconds, and then blow in the reverse direction with diminished intensity. While these things were happening, the fireball would be burning in the sky for the 10 seconds of the thermal pulse. Soon huge, thick clouds of dust and smoke would envelop the scene, and as the mushroom cloud rushed overhead (it would have a diameter of about 12 miles), the light from the sun would be blotted out, and day would turn to night.

Within minutes, fires, ignited both by the thermal pulse and by broken gas mains, tanks of gas and oil, and the like, would begin to spread in the darkness, and a strong, steady wind would begin to blow in the direct of the blast. As at Hiroshima, a whirlwind might be produced, which would sweep through the ruins, and radioactive rain, generated under the meteorological conditions created by the blast, might fall.

Before long, the individual fires would coalesce into a mass fire, which depending largely on the winds, would become either a conflagration or a firestorm. In a conflagration, prevailing winds spread a wall of fire as fire as there is any combustible material to sustain it; in a firestorm, a vertical updraft caused by the fire itself sucks the surrounding air in toward a central point, and the fires therefore converge in a single fire of extreme heat. A mass fire of either kind renders shelters useless by burning up all the oxygen in the air and creating toxic gases, so that anyone inside the shelters is asphyxiated, and also by heating the ground to such high temperatures that the shelters turn, in effect, into ovens, cremating the people inside them.

In Dresden, several days after the firestorm raised there by Allied conventional bombing, the interiors of some bomb shelters were still so hot that when they were opened the in-rushing air caused the contents to burst into flame. Only those who had fled their shelters when the bombing started had any chance of surviving. (It is difficult to predict in a particular situation which form the fires will take. In actual experience, Hiroshima suffered a firestorm and Nagasaki suffered a conflagration.)

In this vast theatre of physical effects, all the scenes of agony and death that took place at Hiroshima would again take place, but now involving millions of people rather than hundreds of thousands.

# What You Must Know about Radiation

*Helen Caldicott*

All radiation is dangerous. No radiation is safe, and we live with a certain amount of background radiation all the time. It comes from the sun, and from cosmic rays that originate in outer space. Now, eons of time ago, when we were just amoebae and paramecia and other small organisms and when the ozone layer in the atmosphere was very thin, a lost of radiation came through, and the radiation changed our genes—and genes, I remind you, are they very essence of life; they control everything about us. So as radiation poured in from the sun eons of time ago, the structure and functions of the genes in the amoebae and the paramecia and other small organisms were changed and a process of evolution began, eventually producing fish, birds, plants and living animals, including human beings.

Now, a change in a gene is called "mutation." And there were some mutations that were good. They allowed fish to develop lungs and birds to develop wings—that sort of thing. But there also were mutations that created disease and deformities, that made many organisms unfit to survive in their environment. Those organisms died off. The others lived. Many people call this process of separation of the fit creatures from the unfit ones an illustration of the Darwinian theory of the "survival of the fittest." In any case,

that's how we think human beings evolved, But radiation continues to produce mutations in cells. Some of these mutations cause changes—"cancer."

Today the background radiation from the sun is much lesser that it was in the beginning, millions of years ago. That's because the ozone layer is thicker—it tends to strain out a lot of the radiation—and we live more or less in equilibrium with background radiation, though we do get a certain amount of cancer from it.

Although we get radiation from natural sources—from air, rocks and our own body cells—we also, in modern times, get it from man made sources. X-rays, administered in doctor's offices and hospitals, are the commonest source today.

It has been estimated that 40 to 50 percent of all medical x-rays are unnecessary, and since the effect of all radiation is cumulative—that is, each exposure increases the risk of getting cancer—you must never have an x-ray without knowing absolutely why and without being assured that it is truly necessary. If you are a heavy smoker, obviously you will need more chest x-rays than a nonsmoker. Or if you cough up blood or have pneumonia or break your arm, you really need an x-ray. The risk from one x-ray is minimal, and the benefit can be great if it is truly necessary. But keep in mind that doctors often order x-rays without thinking much about it. X-rays have become routine. Instead of putting his hand on a patient's belly, palpating it and working out a clinical diagnosis, a doctor may order an x-ray. And some doctors may simply want to have an x-ray for their files as part of your record.

Then there are dental x-rays. You don't need a dental x-ray every six months; you don't even need one every year. When I was a child my dentist didn't have an x-ray machine, and I've got well-filled teeth. Very occasionally, if you have severe pain or you have a root abscess or something like that, you need a tooth x-rayed. But you see, like doctors, some dentists do not think of the dangers. And some buy x-ray machines and pay for them by taking a lot of x-rays and charging the patients for them.

When a doctor or dentist suggests an x-ray, ask, "Why? What you going to find out from this x-ray?" Get the doctor to draw a picture and explain the pathology so that you understand; *you* make the decision. But don't ever have an unnecessary x-ray.

The reason for care is that human beings are more sensitive to the effects of radiation than any other animal. We get cancer more readily. We don't know why. And children and fetuses are about 10 to 20 times more sensitive than adults because their cells are rapidly dividing and growing. It is during the time when a child is growing and the cells are multiplying that radiation damage to the genes can have its most devastating effect.

The British epidemiologist Dr. Alice Stewart has shown that one x-ray of a pregnant abdomen increases the risk of eventual leukemia in the baby by 40 percent about the normal incidence. Fortunately, we don't often x-ray pregnant abdomens nowadays. We use ultrasound to determine where the fetal head is. But if you *have* had an x-ray while pregnant, let me reassure you: The increased incidence of 40 percent isn't much, because

normally only about 1 in 40,000 children develop leukemia.

I have been talking about natural radiation and x-ray radiation. Now let us talk about nuclear radiation. This is the kind that comes from atomic bombs and is developed in nuclear energy plants.

In order to run the atomic reactors that produce energy and make nuclear bombs, we need uranium. Uranium is a natural ore that is found int the ground, and it's safe enough if it's left in the ground. But when it is mined, it emits radioactive byproducts—radium and a radioactive gas called "radon." Unfortunately, uranium is worth a lot of money; both the Government and private utilities pay a very good price for it.

Large-scale uranium mining in the United States started in the '40's, during World War II, in connection with the Manhattan Project, which was created to produce the first atomic bombs. Many of the miners who were doing this work inhaled the radon gas, which attaches itself to tiny dust particles and lodges in the terminal air passages in the lungs. Nothing happened to these men at the time, but 15, 25, 30 years later some of these men found themselves coughing up blood or having other symptoms of chest disease. This time x-rays, and on each x-ray plate there was a big mass—a big white mass. It was cancer.

Now, what happened? Well, here are the cells in the lung and here is the radon, which has been continuously emitting its radioactive alpha particles. Inside each cell is a nucleus, which is the "brain" of the cell. In the nucleus are chromosomes, and on the chromosomes are the genes. Now, in every cell in the body there's a gene that controls the rate of cell division, and that is called the "regulatory gene." And what happened to the men who got cancer from the radon gas was that one of the alpha particles in the gas by chance hit the regulatory gene in one of the cells and damaged it. And the cell sat very quietly for all those years until one day, instead of dividing to produce just two daughter cells as it should, it went berserk and produced millions and trillions of daughter cells—a clone of abnormal cells—and that is cancer. In other words, it may actually take only one alpha particle emitted from one atom, to hit one cell and one gene, to initiate the cancer cycle. And this is very serious, because in this country right now, a lot of the men who mined uranium in the past are dying of lung cancer.

It is a terrible thing that when uranium mining first began in this country none of the big companies paid any attention to the need for safety precautions, in site of the fact that it was known that men in Europe who had mined other ores that contained some uranium died of cancer. So now there is a epidemic of lung cancer among former American uranium miners. The same kind of indifference to human welfare exists in industries that produce dangerous nonradioactive chemicals.

Regulations of the Environmental Protection Agency are being watered down because of the tremendous pressure that is exerted on government by industry. Industry makes hundred of new chemicals every year. Very few are tested for their potential as causes of cancer. They are just dumped into the environment, as they were in Love Canal, Niagara Falls, New York, and in many other places around the country, where they become concentrated in the food chains, in our air, in our water, in our soil. Our whole world is rapidly becoming polluted with substances we haven't even looked at from the medical point of view. All to make money, to produce useless objects like plastic bottles that we throw away.

After uranium is mined it is taken to a milling plant. There it is crushed and chemically treated. The uranium is then removed and the stuff produced as a byproduct, called "uranium tailings," is discarded. These tailings, a sandy material, contain the radioactive products of radium and thorium, which continue to emit radon gas for hundreds of thousands of years. If you live next to a uranium tailings dump, you have double the risk of getting cancer, compared to a nonexposed population.

There are millions of tons of tailings lying around in this country. There's a huge pile of uranium tailings right next to Grants, New Mexico. Just last spring the Navaho Indians, many of whom were uranium miners in the early 1950s and are dying of lung cancer, staged an antinuclear demonstration a few miles from Grants. At the same time the people of Grants, which bills itself as "the Uranium Capital of the United States," staged a different demonstration. It was a huge pronuclear parade and rally, which included more than 15 floats, many of them provided my milling and mining companies in the area. One of the floats bore the following statement: "This community lives from uranium—it's our bread and butter." And all the time, tailings were being blown over Grants from the lethal pile, and the people in that area have a double risk of getting lung cancer. But they don't know; they really don't understand the dangers.

They didn't understand the dangers in other places either. In some places tailings were used as landfill, and homes, stores and other structures were built on top of them. In other places tailings were simply dumped. Salt Lake city has a uranium tailings dump of 1.7 million tons. It is called the "Vitro Dump," after the city's Vitro Chemical Company mill. In New Jersey there are tow churches that stand on or next to areas where tailings were dumped. In addition, because tailings are like sand and were free for the taking, contractors and builders used them in concrete mix; and in Grand Junction, Colorado, there are thousands of structures in which tailings were used—among them two schools, three shopping malls, an airport and many, many houses.

Obviously the people were never told that the tailings might be dangerous, and all the time they were emanating radiation. Then, about 1971, a pediatrician, Dr. Robert M. Ross, Jr., sounded an alarm: He was finding too many birth defects and too much cancer among his young patients. A committee composed of doctors and researchers was appointed to investigate, and some months later they compared statistics from Mesa County, where Grand Junction is located, with those of the whole state. They found that the death rate from birth defects in Mesa county was more than 50 percent higher than in all of Colorado from 1965 to 1968. Cleft lip and cleft palate were nearly twice as common in Mesa County as in all of Colorado, and death from cancer was significantly higher in the Grand Junction area than in the rest of the state. Though there was controversy about those figures, and there still is, another statistic was recently added by Dr. Stanley W. Ferguson, of the Colorado State Health Department: Between 1970 and 1976, the incidence of leukemia in Grand Junction more than doubled. Efforts to remedy this situation began in 1972 and are still going on, but it's a patchwork affair predicated on "permissible levels of radiation." Of course, I'm convinced that no level of radiation is safe, and since its effects are cumulative, we'll probably be hearing of case after case of cancer in that area in the years to come.

It was only about a year ago that the United States Congress passed a bill making mandatory that all the millions of tons of tailings in this country be disposed of properly—a practically hopeless task because so much of the stuff has accumulated. In the meantime a great deal of harm has been done.

The next step in the nuclear cycle is enrichment. It takes a full ton of uranium ore to make four pounds of pure uranium, and about 99 percent of this pure uranium is unfissionable—not usable for making energy. This is called Isotope Uranium-238. About a half ounce out of the four pounds is fissionable; this is called Uranium-235. Uranium-235 is what is used for nuclear power, but the 0.7 percent that is got from the natural ore must be enriched to 3.0 percent to be used in a reactor. If it is enriched to 20 percent or more, it is suitable for making atomic bombs. The bomb used on Hiroshima was a uranium bomb it was call "Little Boy." They have nice names for their bombs.

After enrichment comes fabrication. If you've seen the film *The China Syndrome,* you know that the enriched uranium is made into little pellets like aspirin tablets and packed into hollow rods that are about three quarters of an inch thick and about 12 feet long. When this has been done the rods are taken to the nuclear plant, where they are packed into the core of the nuclear reactor. When they have finished there are 100 tons of uranium in the reactor core, at which point they submerge it all in water. Now, when you pack uranium so densely and in such a way, it reaches "critical mass." That means that the atoms spontaneously start breaking apart, and this action produces about 200 new radioactive elements called "fission products," which are the broken-down products of the original uranium atoms. These fission products are the same materials that are formed when an atom bomb explodes.

An atom bomb explodes as the uranium fissions because it is an uncontrolled reaction. But in a nuclear power plant this process is controlled and the fissioning uranium doesn't explore. Instead, the heat produced by the fission process boils the water in which the uranium-bearing rods have been submerged, and the steam that is formed turns a turbine that makes electricity.

So in fact, all a nuclear reactor does is boil water. It's a very sophisticated way to boil water. Because inside of each 1,000-megawatt reactor is as much radioactive material as would be released by the explosion of 1,000 bombs of the size of the one that was dropped on Hiroshima.

The reason we are discussing all this is that something happened at Three Mile Island, near Harrisburg, Pennsylvania, last spring. What happened? Well, accident, certainly human error and possibly mechanical failure caused large quantities of water to escape from the container holding the immensely hot uranium rods. Apparently the operators of the plant were unaware of the escaping water. Because the water wasn't immediately replaced, the rods became uncovered and remained uncovered for at least 50 minutes. Looking back at it now, most nuclear engineers can't understand what kept the uranium fuel in the uncovered rods from melting down.

What would have happened if there had been a meltdown? The low water level an subsequent inefficient cooling of the rods would have allowed the intrinsic heat of the fission products in the uranium to melt the 100 tons of uranium into a globular mass. It then would have continued to melt right through the bottom of the container and—nuclear experts say—hundreds of feet into the earth "toward China"! That's what is called the "China syndrome" by the nuclear industry.

If a meltdown had occurred at Three Mile Island, a massive steam explosion would have ruptured the reactor container and released all the radiation—as much as 1,000 Hiroshima-sized bombs—into the air. It would not have been an atomic explosion, but it would have contaminated an area the size of Pennsylvania for thousands of years.

Nobody could have lived there any more for thousands of years! And depending on the direction of the wind, other huge areas could have been contaminated.

Such an accident would cost about $17 billion in property damage. And what about human damage? Let's say that as many as 10 million people would have been exposed—that would be entirely possible. Well, some statisticians report that almost immediately about 3,300 people would die of lethal radiation exposure. Two or three weeks later about 10,000 to 100,000 more could die of what is called acute radiation illness. First they'd go bald. Their hair would drop out; we saw this for the first time after the bomb was dropped on Hiroshima. Then they would begin to hemorrhage under the skin. They would develop skin ulcers, awful ulcers in their mouths, vomiting and diarrhea, and they'd die of bleeding or infection.

That would happen in a relatively short time, but there are long-term effects too. Hundreds of thousands of men would be rendered sterile from the radiation damage to their testicles. Hundreds of thousands of women would stop menstruating, many permanently. Thousands of people would develop hypothyroidism. With their thyroid glands damaged, their metabolic rate would slow down, they would become constipated, they would be unable to think properly, they'd lose their appetites and at the same time become fat.

Thousands more would have acute respiratory impairment, the radiation having damaged their lungs. Thousands of babies affected by radiation while still in their mothers' wombs would be born with microcephaly, or with very small heads—"pinheads," they called them in Hiroshima, where this happened after the bomb fell. Thousands more would be born cretins, with ablated thyroids and neurological damage.

And five, ten, 20, 30 years later, hundreds of thousands of cases of cancer would occur, to say nothing of the varieties of genetic defects—dwarfism, mental retardation, hemophilia, and others—that would develop and be passed on and on through future generations.

My list of sick, dying and dead comes to just less than half a million people. Possibly the estimate could be for a few less, since Three Mile Island had been in operation for only three months before the accident and had only 80 percent of the inventory of radioactive products that a normal, long-term operating, 1,000-megawatt reactor would contain. But it would have been a catastrophe such as the world has never seen, because only 200,000 people died in Hiroshima and Nagasaki, though the incidence of cancer is still increasing among the bomb survivors there.

Now, what I want to know is, why doesn't our Government tell us of the dangers to which we are being exposed? Why hasn't it told us what a meltdown would mean? What can we expect as a result of the careless dumping of nuclear wastes, which, if not as swiftly devastating as a meltdown or a bomb, can be just as deadly over a period of time? Where does the allegiance of our elected representatives belong—to the utility companies to us? Did Dwight Eisenhower, when he was President and they were testing hydrogen bombs in Nevada in 1953, set a permanent policy when he told the Atomic Energy Commission to "keep the public confused" about radioactive fallout? (The AEC certainly was receptive to Eisenhower's advice. Recently declassified commission records show that it repeatedly brushed aside questions about health hazards; and in February, 1955, Willard F. Libby, a member of the commission, said: "People have got to learn to live with facts of life, and part of the facts of life is fallout.")

The accident at Three Mile Island in Pennsylvania revealed still other alarming things. People operating the nuclear plant for Metropolitan Edison didn't know what they were doing. In the first 48 hours after the accident, primary coolant (water that surrounds the rods) was vented into the atmosphere as steam. Rule number one in the nuclear energy business is, Never vent primary coolant! It's like, if you are a surgeon, you never cut off a head—you just don't do that! But the primary coolant was vented after the cladding of many of the rods had melted and released highly radioactive fission products into the water. They weren't measuring anything in the first 48 hours, either, so they don't know exactly what they let out—plutonium? strontium? cesium? radioactive iodine? That's the first thing. The second thing is that a whole lot of radioactive water from the primary coolant spilled onto the reactor floor. An attempt was made to transfer some of this to a tank in an auxiliary building that stands beside the reactor, but the tank already contained radioactive water—perhaps not so radioactive as the primary coolant, but radioactive just the same. To make room for the primary coolant, 4,000 gallons of radio active water from the tank was emptied into the Susquehanna River.

Now, water from that tank is routinely emptied into the Susquehanna, but first, as Government spokesman would say, it has to be tested and diluted to a "permissible level of radio activity." As I see it, no level of radioactivity is permissible, so that's bad enough. But during those first critical 48 hours, the 4,000 gallons of radioactive water they emptied into the river weren't even tested. They also released a lot of radio active gases into the air, many of which are precursors of products such as Strontium-90, Cesium-137 and Radioactive Iodine-131.

More proof that the people operating that plant didn't know what they were doing: Not only did they make "a series of errors"—I quote the *New York Times*—"in the operation of the plant," but when the accident occurred they continued to make errors. A very serious problem. And because Metropolitan Edison doesn't know how much radioactive stuff was emptied into the environment, there is no hard data on which to make predictions about what will happen to people int he Harrisburg area in the future. And yet Joseph A. Califano, Jr., then Secretary of the Department of Health, Education and Welfare, said that only one person—at worst, ten people—would die of cancer as a result of the accident. He had no primary data on which to base the announcement. It's very worrying.

Let me tell you about Strontium-90. Strontium-90 stays poisonous for 600 years. Released into the atmosphere, it settles on the grass from the air, the rain and the dew, and its potency gets compounded many times over the concentration that is in the air. When this happens in dairying areas, cattle eat the grass and the Strontium-90 is concentrated in cow's milk, which both calves and babies drink. It concentrates most highly in human breast milk, and it gets there when pregnant women and nursing mothers eat dairy products that are contaminated by Strontium-90. Now, anybody who ingests a radioactive substance can be affected, but it's very important to know that babies are inordinately sensitive to the effects of radiation. You can't taste the radiation. It's odorless, invisible and tasteless, and when a baby drinks milk containing Strontium-90 the body treats it as if it were calcium; it's deposited in the growing bones. It causes bone cancer. It also causes leukemia—many of those children die.

Between January, 1951, and October 1958, when a large number of atomic and hydrogen bombs were tested in the Nevada desert, the winds carried the fallout to agricultural as well as populated ares in Utah and Strontium-90 was found in milk. At that time the Nobel Prize-winning scientist Linus Pauling said if babies drank milk containing Strontium-90, they might get leukemia later. And the Government said Pauling was wrong. Then early this year the New England Journal of Medicine published a paper saying that the incidence of leukemia in Utah children in the "high fallout" counties who were under 14 at the time of the testing had increased nearly two and a half times above normal level.

Radioactive Iodine-131 also concentrates in milk, and if there are bodies of water nearby, it concentrates in fish. Although it is active for only a few weeks, once it get into milk or fish its potency is compounded thousands of times. And its effect, when ingested by humans, is vicious and lasting. Taken up by the thyroid, it can cause thyroid cancer. Keep in mind that I have named only three or four dangerous elements. Actually almost 200 of those dangerous elements that are made in nuclear reactors are contained in nuclear waste.

Nuclear waste. Garbage. Nobody needs it. Nobody wants it. And nobody knows what to do with it. And it has to be disposed of, isolated from the environment, because many of those elements remain potent for one million years. If those materials leak, they get into our air, they get into our water, they get into our food chain and get recycled through human bodies for hundreds and thousands of years, causing cancers after cancers after cancers, to say nothing of birth deformities and genetic disease.

Now, by present methods of technology, nuclear waste, which is active up to one million years, can be safely stored for only ten to 20 years. But even before that the containers begin to corrode; there are leaks; it gets into all parts of our environment. Even if the most brilliant scientist we have should think he's found the answer for storing nuclear wastes, he'll be dead long before his hypothesis can be verified. This is the heritage we are leaving to our descendants.

You can imagine our descendants, like the people at Love Canal, Niagara Falls, New York, where non-nuclear but dangerous chemicals were dumped, waking up one morning with their food already contaminated, their kids already being born deformed and dying of leukemia and cancer, and with adults too dying of cancer. It will be too late. But we're risking millions of lives so we can turn our lights on. And to keep the economy running. And because government and big business have invested a lot of money.

In the nuclear industries they say, "Don't worry, we're scientists; we'll find the answer." That's like my saying to a patient, "you have cancer; you have about six months to live; but don't worry, I'm a good doctor and by 1995 I might find a cure."

Now lets's talk about plutonium, out of which both atomic and hydrogen bombs are made. That's one of the most dangerous elements known. It is manmade in a nuclear reactor; it didn't exist until we fissioned uranium. And it's named, appropriately, after Pluto, the god of the underworld. It is so incredibly toxic that a millionth of a gram—and a gram is about the size of a grape—can cause cancer. When plutonium is exposed to the air it produces particles as fine as talcum powder that are totally invisible. And if you inhale any of those particles, they will almost certainly give you lung cancer.

If you took just ten pounds of plutonium and put a speck of it in every human lung, that would be enough to kill every single person on earth. Ten pounds! And each nuclear reactor makes 500 pounds of it every year. Five hundred pounds! What's worse, plutonium remains toxic for a half a

million years. It is not biodegradable, that is, it doesn't decompose; so the plutonium-contaminated waste remains toxic all that time.

There are areas around Denver, Colorado, that are contaminated by plutonium radiation, and the testicular cancer rate in a suburb next to Rock Flats, about 13 miles from the center of Denver, is 140 percent higher than the normal incidence. You see, plutonium lodges in the testicles and it's in the testicles that the sperm are, where the genes for future generations are! Plutonium also crosses the placental barrier, where it can damage the developing fetus. It can kill a cell that's going to form the left side of a baby's brain, or, say, the left arm, or whatever. Do you remember what thalidomide did? Plutonium is thalidomide forever! It will damage fetus after fetus after fetus, down the generations, virtually for the rest of time. And, of course, its effects are not limited to the unborn. It causes lung cancer. It causes bone cancer. It causes liver cancer, and more.

The nuclear reactor was first designed as part of the Manhattan Project to make plutonium, the plutonium to be used in making nuclear weapons. And in making bombs and other atomic weapons they have produced 74 million gallons of high-level radioactive waste, and scientists and engineers and environmental specialists all have studied the problem—and nobody seems to know what to do with it.

Nobody has devised a foolproof, leak proof, fail-safe place to sequester those wastes over the thousands and thousands of years they remain dangerous. At the present time, wastes, contained in large carbon-steel tanks, are being stored on the site of the Government's Hanford Reservation, a nuclear complex near Richland, Washington. They are also being stored on the site of the Savannah River Plant, another Government facility that produces nuclear weapons materials, near Aiken, South Carolina. At Hanford the tanks have already leaked 450,000 gallons of poisonous radioactive waste into the soil near the Columbia River. Eventually these radioactive elements will probably enter the Columbia River, where they will become concentrated in the fish we eat, in the water we drink and, if the water is used for irrigation, in plants and animals.

The dangers of nuclear power are not only accidental meltdowns, escaping radiation and all the radioactive wastes we don't know how to dispose of. The dangers are even greater because it is a small step from nuclear power to nuclear weaponry.

When Robert Strange McNamara was U.S. Secretary of Defense he figured out that if the United States had 400 nuclear weapons, we could wipe out one third of the Soviet population and destroy two thirds of the industry—and that would be a deterrent. The United States now has at least 30,000 nuclear warheads and can kill every human being on earth 12 times over. *Overkill*—that's the Pentagon term. The Russians can overkill Americans 20 times.

Do you know that probably every town and city in this country with a population of 25,000 or more is targeted at this instant with a nuclear weapon? The same is true for towns and cities in the U.S.S.R., China, Europe and England. From the moment that a button in other countries are pressed in retaliation, it would take about one-half hour to two hours to complete the war. And that would be the end of civilization as we know it. Shelters would be useless. People in shelters would be asphyxiated. That's because a 20-megaton bomb produces a fire storm of 3.000 square miles that uses up all the oxygen, including that in the shelter.

It is known that the man who had his finger on the button in this country five and half years ago was not what any psychiatrist would term psychiatrically stable at the end of his term in office. Leonid Brezhnev had

been a sick man and, people say, has been treated with cortisone. A good drug. But occasionally it can induce acute psychosis. Not long ago, while still in power, the dictator Idi Amin, of Uganda, who is not exactly given to good judgment, let alone respect for human life, bragged that he would have an atomic bomb in a few years. Granted that some leaders seem more stable that others, but ask yourself: Who is there that any of us would entrust with the safety of the world?

There are now 35 countries that have nuclear weapons capability because they have been sold nuclear reactors—some small, some large—by this country and by others. And since each 1,000-megawatt reactor produces about 500 pounds of plutonium every year, so theoretically, many of those 35 countries could made 50 atomic bombs every year from each 1,000-megawatt reactor.

Albert Einstein said, "The splitting of the atom has changed everything save man's mode of thinking; thus we drift toward unparalleled catastrophe."

What would happen if all the weapons were used? One, the synergistic effects could be so great, with the ozone destroyed, icecaps melting, radiation everywhere, and so on, that probably not an organism would survive. Maybe the cockroaches would survive because they're 400,000 times more radiation-resistant that humans. Or if you did survive—if there had been no fire storm to eat up all the oxygen in your shelter—and you stayed in your shelter for at least two weeks (otherwise you would die from the intense radiation) what would you find when you came out? There would be countless dead and dying—Guyana, where the earth was covered with the dead, would have nothing on us. There would be no doctors, drugs or hospital beds in big cities, because those are targeted. You might find some doctors in small communities, but what could they do? Disease would be rampant. And you can imagine the earth inhabited by bands of roving mutant humanoids generations hence. This would be like no science fiction story ever invented.

Look at the changing seasons—the spring and the flowers and the trees coming into leaf. Look at the fall of the year and the leaves turning gold. Look at our growing children. One child. One baby. We're fantastic species. We're capable of such creativity, love and friendship.

I've got three children. And I am a doctor who treats children, a great many of them having the commonest genetic disease of childhood—cystic fibrosis. I live with dying children. I live with grieving parents. I understand the value of every single human life.

The ultimate in preventive medicine is to eliminate nuclear power and nuclear wea-pons. I look on this as a religious issue too. Because what is our responsibility to God but to continue creation?

Someone said, "Evil flourishes only when good men and women do nothing." And there are many of us—good men and women—and we can do a lot.

We have only a short time to turn the destructive powers around. A short time. I appeal especially to women to do this work because we understand the genesis of life. Our bodies are built to nurture life. We have wombs; we have breasts; we have periods to remind us that we can produce life! We also have won a voice in the affairs of the world and are becoming more influential every day. I beg you—do what you can today.

# The Right to Choose

*Linda Bird Francke*

"Jane Doe," thirty-eight, had an abortion in New York City in 1973. The mother of three children, then three, five, and eleven, Jane had just started a full-time job in publishing. She and her husband, an investment banker, decided together that another baby would add an almost unbearable strain to their lives, which were already overfull. What Jane had not anticipated was the guilt and sadness that followed the abortion. She wrote about the experience shortly thereafter and filed the story away. Three years later she reread it and decided it might be helpful to other women who experience the ambivalence of abortion. The *New York Times* ran it on their Op-Ed page in May 1976. This is what she wrote:

We were sitting in a bar on Lexington Avenue when I told my husband I was pregnant. It is not a memory I like to dwell on. Instead of the champagne and hope which had heralded the impending births of the first, second, and third child, the news of this one was greeted with shocked silence and Scotch. "Jesus," my husband kept saying to himself, stirring the ice cubes around and around. "Oh, Jesus."

Oh, how we tried to rationalize it that night as the starting time for the movie came and went. My husband talked about his plans for a career change in the next year, to stem the staleness that fourteen years with the same investment-banking firm had brought him. A new baby would preclude that option.

The timing wasn't right for me either. Having juggled pregnancies and child care with what freelance jobs I could fit in between feedings, I had just taken on a full-time job. A new baby would put me right in the nursery just when our youngest child was finally school age. It was time for us, we tried to rationalize. There just wasn't room in our lives now for another baby. We both agreed. And agreed. And agreed.

How very considerate they are at the Women's Services, known formally as the Center for Reproductive and Sexual Health. Yes, indeed, I could have an abortion that very Saturday morning and be out in time to drive to the country that afternoon. Bring a first morning urine specimen, a sanitary belt and napkins, a money order or $125 cash—and a friend.

My friend turned out to be my husband, standing awkwardly and ill at ease as men always do in places that are exclusively for women, as I checked in at nine A.M. Other men hovered around just as anxiously knowing they had to be there, wishing they weren't. No one spoke to each other. When I would be cycled out of there four hours later, the same men would be slumped in their same seats, locked downcast in their cells of embarrassment.

The Saturday morning women's group was more dispirited than the men in the waiting room. There were around fifteen of us, a mixture of races, ages and backgrounds. Three didn't speak English at all and a fourth, a pregnant Puerto Rican girl around eighteen, translated for them.

There were six black women and hodge-podge of whites, among them a T-shirted teenager who kept leaving the room to throw up and a puzzled middle-aged woman from Queens with three grown children.

"What form of birth control were you using?" the volunteer asked each one of us. The answer was inevitably "none." She then went on to describe the various forms of birth control available at the clinic, and offered them to each of us.

The youngest Puerto Rican girl was asked through the interpreter which she'd like to use: the loop, diaphragm, or pill. She shook her head "no" three times. "You don't want to come back here again, do you?" the volunteer pressed. The girl's head was so low her chin rested on her breastbone. "Si," she whispered.

We had been there two hours by that time, filling out endless forms, giving blood and urine, receiving lectures. But unlike any other group of women I've been in, we didn't talk. Our common denominator, the one which usually floods across language and economic barriers into familiarity, today was one of shame. We were losing life that day, not giving it.

The group kept getting cut back to smaller, more workable units, and finally I was put in a small waiting room with just two other women. We changed into paper bathrobes and paper slippers, and we rustled whenever we moved. One of the women in my room was shivering and an aide brought her a blanket.

"What's the matter?" the aide asked her. "I'm scared," the woman said. "How much will it hurt?" The aide smiled. "Oh, nothing worse than a couple of bad cramps," she said. "This afternoon you'll be dancing a jig."

I began to panic. Suddenly the rhetoric, the abortion marches I'd walked in, the telegrams sent to Albany to counteract the Friends of the Fetus, the Zero Population Growth buttons I'd worn, peeled away, and I was all alone with my microscopic baby. There were just the two of us there, and soon, because it was more convenient for me and my husband, there would be one again.

How could it be that I, who am so neurotic about life that I step over bugs rather than on them, who spend hours planting flowers and vegetables in the spring even though we rent out the house and never see them, who make sure the children are vaccinated and inoculated and filled with vitamin C, could so arbitrarily decide that this life shouldn't be?

"It's not a life," my husband had argued, more to convince himself than me. "It's a bunch of cells smaller than my fingernail."

But any woman who has had children knows that certain feeling in her taut, swollen breasts, and the slight but constant ache in her uterus that signals the arrival of a life. Though I would march myself into blisters for a woman's right to exercise the option of motherhood, I discovered there in the waiting room that I was not the modern woman I thought I was.

When my name was called, my body felt so heavy the nurse had to help me into the examining room. I waited for my husband to burst through the door and yell "stop," but of course he didn't. I concentrated on three black spots in the acoustic ceiling until they grew in size to the shape of saucers, while the doctor swabbed by insides with antiseptic.

"You're going to feel a burning sensation now," he said, injecting Novocaine into the neck of the womb. The pain was swift and severe, and I twisted to get away from him. He was hurting my baby, I reasoned, and the black saucers quivered in the air. "Stop," I cried. "Please stop." He shook his head, busy with his equipment. "It's too late to stop now," he said. "It'll just take a few more seconds."

What good sports we women are. And how obedient. Physically the pain passed even before the hum of the machine signaled that the vacuuming of my uterus was completed, my baby sucked up like ashes after a cocktail party. Ten minutes start to finish. And I was back on the arm of the nurse.

There were twelve beds in the recovery room. Each one had a gaily flowered draw sheet and a soft green or blue thermal blanket. It was all very feminine. Lying on these beds for an hour or more were the shocked victims of their sex, their full wombs now stripped clean, their futures less encumbered.

It was very quiet in that room. The only voice was that of the nurse, locating the new women who had just come in so she could monitor their blood pressure, and checking out the recovered women who were free to leave.

Juice was being passed about, and I found myself sipping a Dixie cup of Hawaiian Punch. An older woman with tightly curled bleached hair was

303

just getting up form the next bed. "That was no goddamn snap," she said, resting before putting on her miniskirt and high white boots. Other women came and went, some walking out as dazed as they had entered, others with a bounce that signaled they were going right back to Bloomingdale's.

Finally then, it was time for me to leave. I checked out, making an appointment to return in two weeks for a IUD insertion. My husband was slumped in the waiting room, clutching a single yellow rose wrapped in a wet paper towel and stuffed into a baggie.

We didn't talk the whole way home, but just held hands very tightly. At home there were more yellow roses and a tray in bed for me and the children's curiosity to divert.

It had certainly been a successful operation. I didn't bleed at all for two days just as they had predicted and then bled only moderately for another four days. Within a week my breasts had subsided and the tenderness vanished any my body felt mine again instead of the eggshell it becomes when it's protecting someone else.

My husband and I are back to planning our summer vacation and his career switch.

And it certainly does make more sense not to be having a baby right now—we say that to each other all the time. But I have this ghost now. A very little ghost that only appears when I'm seeing something beautiful, like the full moon on the ocean last weekend. And the baby waves at me. And I wave at the baby. "Of course, we have room," I cry to the ghost. "Of course, we do."

I am "Jane Doe." Using a pseudonym was not the act of cowardice some have said it was, but rather an act of sympathy for the feelings of my family. My daughters were too young then to understand what an abortion was, and my twelve-year-old son (my husband's stepson) reacted angrily when I even broached the subject of abortion to him. Andrew was deeply moralistic, as many children are at that age, and still young enough to feel threatened by the actions of adults; his replies to my "suppose I had an abortion" queries were devastating. "I think abortion is okay if the boy and girl aren't married, and they just made a mistake," he

said. "But if you had an abortion, that would be different. You're married, and there is no reason for you not to have another baby. How could you just kill something—no matter how little it is—that's going to grow and have legs and wiggle its fingers?

"I would be furious with you if you had an abortion. I'd lose all respect for you for being so selfish. I'd make you suffer and remind you of it all the time. I would think of ways to be mean. Maybe I'd give you the silent treatment or something.

"If God had meant women to have abortions, He would have put buttons on their stomachs."

I decided to wait until he was older before we discussed it again.

There were other considerations as well. My husband and I had chosen not to tell our parents about the abortion. My mother was very ill at the time and not up to a barrage of phone calls from her friends about "what Linda had written in the newspaper." And there were my parents-in-law, who had always hoped for a male grandchild to carry on the family name. So I avoided the confessional and simply wrote what I though would be a helpful piece for other women who might have shared my experience.

The result was almost great enough to be recorded on a seismograph. Interpreting the piece as anti-abortion grist, the Right-to-Lifers reproduced it by the thousands and sent it to everyone on their mailing lists. In one Catholic mailing, two sentences were deleted from the article: one that said I was planning to return to the clinic for an IUD insertion, and the other the quote from a middle aged woman, "That was no goddamn snap." Papers around the country and in Canada ran it, culminating in its appearance in the Canadian edition of the *Reader's Digest*, whose staff took it upon their editorial selves to delete the last paragraph about the "little ghost" because they considered it "mawkish." They also changed the title from "There Just Wasn't Room in Our Lives for Another Baby" to "A Successful Operation" in hopes that it would change their magazine's pro-abortion image.

Hundreds of letters poured into the *New York Times*, some from Right-to-Lifers, who predictably called me a "murderer," and others from pro-choice zealots who had decided the article was a "plant" and might even have been written by a man. Women wrote about their own abortions, some of which have been positive experiences and some disastrous. One women even wrote that she wished her own mother had an abortion instead of subjecting her to a childhood that was "brutal and crushing." Many of the respondents criticized me, quite rightly, for not using birth control in the first place. I was stunned, and so was the *New York Times*. A few weeks later they ran a sampling of the letters and my reply, which follows:

The varied reactions to my abortion article do not surprise me at all. They are all right. And they are all wrong. There is no issue so fundamental as the giving of life, or the cessation of it. These decisions are the most personal one can ever make and each person facing them reacts in her own way. It is not black-and-white as the laws governing abortion are forced to be. Rather it is the gray area whose core touches our definition of ourselves that produces "little ghosts" in some, and a sense of relief in others.

I admire the woman who chose not to bear her fourth child because she and her husband could not afford to give that child the future they felt necessary. I admire the women who were outraged that I had failed to use any form of contract of contraception. And I ache for the woman whose mother had given birth to her even though she was not wanted, and thus spent an empty, lonely, childhood. It takes courage to take the life of someone else in your own hands, and even more courage to assume responsibility for your own.

I had my abortion over two years ago. And I wrote about it shortly thereafter. It was only recently, however, that I decided to publish it. I felt it was important to share how one person's abortion had affected her, rather than just sit by while the pro and con groups haggled over legislation.

The effect has indeed been profound. Though my husband was very supportive of me, and I, I think, of him, our relationship slowly faltered. As our children are girls, my husband anguished at the possibility that I had been carrying a son. Just a case of male macho, many would argue. But still, that's the way he feels, and it is important. I hope we can get back on a loving track again.

Needless to say, I have an IUD now, instead of the diaphragm that is too easily forgotten. I do not begrudge my husband his lack of contraception. Condoms are awkward. Neither do I feel he should have a vasectomy. It is profoundly difficult for him to face the possibility that he might never have that son. Nor do I regret having the abortion. I am just as much an avid supporter of children by choice as I ever was.

My only regret is the sheer irresponsibility on my part to become pregnant in the first place. I pray to God that it will never happen again. But if it does, I will be equally thankful that the law provides women the dignity to choose whether to bring a new life into the world or not.

# Death Before Birth, or a Mite's *Nunc Dimittis*

*Stephen Jay Gould*

Can anything be more demoralizing than parental incompetence before the most obvious and innocent of children's questions: why is the sky blue, the grass green? Why does the moon have phases? Our embarrassment is all the more acute because we thought we knew the answer perfectly well, but hadn't rehearsed it since we ourselves had received a bumbled response in similar circumstances a generation earlier. It is the things we think we know—because they are so elementary, or because they surround us— that often present the greatest difficulties when we are actually challenged to explain them.

One such question, with an obvious and incorrect answer, lies close to our biological lives: why, in humans (and in most species familiar to us), are males and females produced in approximately equal numbers? (Actually, males are more common than females at birth in humans, but differential morality of males leads to a female majority in later life. Still, the departures from a one to one ratio are never great.) At first glance, the answer seems to be, as in Rabelais's motto, "plain as the nose on a man's face."

After all, sexual reproduction requires a mate; equal numbers imply universal mating—the happy Darwinian status of maximal reproductive capacity. At second glance, it isn't so clear at all, and we are drawn in confusion to Shakespeare's recasting of the smile: "A jest unseen inscrutable, invisible, as a nose on a man's face." If maximal reproductive capacity is the optimal state for a species, then why make equal numbers of males and females? Females, after all, set the limit upon numbers of offspring, since eggs are invariably so much larger and less abundant than sperm in species familiar to us— that is, each egg can make an offspring, each sperm cannot. A male can impregnate several females. If a male can mate with nine females and the population contains a hundred individuals, why not make ten males and ninety females? Reproductive capacity will certainly exceed that of a population composed of fifty males and fifty females. Populations made predominantly of females should by their more rapid rates of reproduction, win any evolutionary race with populations that maintain equality in numbers between the sexes.

What appeared obvious is therefore rendered problematical and the question remains: why do most sexual species contain approximately equal numbers of males and females? The answer, according to most evolutionary biologists, lies in a recognition that

Darwin's theory of natural selection speaks only of struggle among *individuals* for reproductive success. It contains no statement about the good of populations, species, or ecosystems. The argument for ninety females and ten males was framed in terms of advantages for populations as a whole—the usual, congenial, and dead wrong, way in which most people think of evolution. If evolution worked for the good of populations as a whole, then sexual species would contain relatively few males.

The observed equality of males and females, in the face of obvious advantages for female predominance if evolution worked upon groups, stands as one of our most elegant demonstrations that Darwin was right—natural selection works by the struggle of individuals to maximize their own reproductive success. The Darwinian argument was first framed by the great British mathematical biologist R.A. Fisher. Suppose, Fisher argued, that either sex began to predominate. Let us say, for example, that fewer males than females are born. Males now begin to leave more offspring than females since their opportunities for mating increase as they become rarer—that is, they impregnate more than one female on average. Thus, if any genetic factors influence the relative proportion of males born to a parent (and such factors do exist), then parents with a genetic inclination to produce males will gain a Darwinian advantage—they will produce more than an average number of grandchildren thanks to the superior reproductive success of their predominantly male offspring. Thus, genes that favor the production of males will spread and male births will rise in frequency. But, this advantage for males fades out as male births increase and it disappears entirely when males equal females in number. Since the same argument works in reverse to favor female births when females are rare, the sex ratio is driven by Darwinian

processes to its equilibrium value of one to one.

But how would a biologist go about testing Fisher's theory of sex ratio? Ironically, the species that confirm its predictions are no great help beyond the initial observation. Once we frame the basic argument and determine that the species we know best have approximately equal numbers of males and females, what do we achieve by finding that the next thousand species are similarly ordered? Sure, it all fits, but we do not gain an equal amount of confidence each time we add a new species. Perhaps the one to one ratio exists for another reason.

To test Fisher's theory, we must look for exceptions. We must seek unusual situations in which the premises of Fisher's theory are not met—situations that lead to a specific prediction about how sex ratio should depart from one to one. If change of premises leads to a definite and successful prediction of altered outcome, then we have an independent test that strongly boosts our confidence. This method is embodied in the old proverb that "the exception proves the rule," although many people misunderstood the proverb because it embodies the less common meaning of "prove." Prove comes from the Latin *probare*—to test or to try. Its usual, modern meaning refers to final and convincing demonstration and the motto would seem to say that exceptions establish indubitable validity. But in another sense, closer to its root, "prove" (as in "proving ground" or printer's "proof") is more like its cognate "probe"— a test or an exploration. It is the exception that probes the rule by testing and exploring its consequences in altered situations.

Here nature's rich diversity comes to our aid. The stereotyped image of a birder assiduously adding the rufous-crowned, peg-legged, speckle-backed, cross-billed, and cross-eyed towhee to his life list gives, in unwarranted ridicule, a perverted twist to the actual use made by naturalist of life's diversity. It is nature's richness that permits us to establish a science of natural history in the first place—for the variety virtually guarantees that appropriate exceptions can be found to probe any rule. Oddities and weirdnesses are tests of generality, not mere peculiarities to describe and greet with awe or a chuckle.

Fortunately, nature has been profligate in providing species and modes of life that violate the premises of Fisher's argument. In 1967, British biologist W.D. Hamilton (now at the University of Michigan) gathered the cases and arguments into an article entitled "Extraordinary sex ratios." I will discuss in this essay only the clearest and most important of these probing violations.

Nature rarely heeds our homilies in all cases. We are told, and with good reason, that mating of brothers and sisters should be avoided, lest too many unfavorable recessive genes gain an opportunity to express themselves in double dose. (Such genes tend to be rare, and chances are small that two unrelated parents will both carry them. But the probability that two sibs carry the same gene is usually fifty percent.) Nonetheless, some animals never heard the rule and indulge, perhaps exclusively, in sib mating.

Exclusive sib mating destroys the major premise of Fisher's argument for one to one sex ratios. If females are always fertilized by their brothers, then the same parents manufacture both partners of any mating. Fisher assumed that the males had different parents and that an undersupply of males awarded genetic advantages to those parents that could produce males preferentially. But if the same parents produce *both* the mothers and fathers of their grandchildren, then they have an equal genetic investment in each grandchild, no matter what percentage of males and females they produce among their children. In this case, the reason for an equal

balance of males and females disappears and the previous argument for female predominance reasserts itself. If each pair of grandparents has a limited store of energy to invest in offspring, and if grandparents producing more offspring gain a Darwinian edge, then grandparents should make as many daughters as possible, and produce only enough sons to ensure that all their daughters will be fertilized. In fact, if their sons can muster sufficient sexual prowess, then parents should make just one son and use every bit of remaining energy to produce as many daughters as they can. As usual, bountiful nature comes to our aid with numerous exceptions to probe Fisher's rule: indeed, species with sib mating also tend to produce a minimal number of males.

Consider the curious life of a male mite in the genus *Adactylidium,* as described by E.A. Albadry and M. S. Tawfik in 1966. It emerges from its mother's body and promptly dies within a few hours, having done apparently nothing during its brief life. It attempts, while outside its mother, neither to feed nor to mate. We know about creatures with short adult lives—the mayfly's single day after a much lengthier larval life, for example. But the mayfly mates and insures the continuity of its kind during these few precious hours. The males of *Adactylidium* seem to do nothing at all but emerge and die.

To solve the mystery, we must study the entire life cycle and look inside the mother's body. The impregnated female of *Adactylidium* attaches to the egg of a thrips. That single egg provides the only source of nutrition for rearing all her offspring—for she will feed on nothing else before her death. This mite, so far as we know, engages exclusively in sib mating; thus, it should produce a minimal number of males. Moreover, since total reproductive energy is so strongly constrained by the nutritional resources of a single thrips' egg, progeny are strictly limited, and the more females the better. Indeed, *Adactylidium* matches our prediction by raising a brood of five to eight sisters accompanied by a single male who will serve as both brother and husband to them all. But producing a single male is chancy; if it dies, all sisters will remain virgins and their mothers's evolutionary life is over.

If the mite takes a chance on producing but a single male, thus maximizing its potential brood of fertile females, two other adaptations might lessen the risk—providing both protection for the male and guaranteed proximity to his sisters. What better than to rear the brood entirely within a mother's body, feeding both larvae and adults within her, and even allowing copulation or occur inside her protective shell. Indeed, about forty-eight hours after she attaches to the thrips' egg, six to nine eggs hatch within the body of a female *Adactylidium*. The larvae feed on their mother's body, literally devouring her from inside. Two days later, the offspring reach maturity, and the single male copulates with all his sisters. By this time, the mother's tissues have disintegrated, and her body space a mass of adult mites, their feces, and their discarded larval and nymphal skeletons. The offspring then cut holes through their mother's body wall and emerge. The females

must now find a thrips' egg and begin the process again, but the males have already fulfilled their evolutionary role before "birth." They emerge, react however a mite does to the glories of the outside world, and promptly die.

But why not carry the process one stage further? Why should the male be born at all? After copulating with its sisters, its work is done, it is ready to chant the acarine version of Simeon's prayer, *Nunc dimittis*— Oh Lord, now lettest thou thy servant depart in peace. Indeed, since everything that is possible tends to occur at least once in the multifarious world of life, a close relative of *Adactylidium* does just this. *Acarophenax tribolii* also indulges exclusively in sib mating. Fifteen eggs, including but a single male, develop within the mother's body. The male emerges within his mother's shell, copulates with all his sisters, and dies before birth. It may not sound like much of a life, but the male *Acarophenax* does as much for its evolutionary continuity as Abraham did in fathering children into his tenth decade.

Nature's oddities are more than good stories. They are material for probing the limits of interesting theories about life's history and meaning.

# On My Reading, Writing, and Thinking

*Charles Darwin*

I have now mentioned all the books which I have published, and these have been the milestones in my life, so that little remains to be said. I am not conscious of any change in my mind during the last thirty years, excepting in one point presently to be mentioned; nor indeed could any change have been expected unless one of general deterioration. But my father lived to his eighty-third year with his mind as lively as ever it was, and all his faculties undimmed; and I hope that I may die before my mind fails to a sensible extent. I think that I have become a little more skillful in guessing right explanations and in devising experimental tests; but this may probably be the result of mere practice, and of a larger store of knowledge. I have as much difficulty as ever in expressing myself clearly and concisely; and this difficulty has caused me a very great loss of time; but it has had the concisely; and this difficulty has caused me a very great loss of time; but it has had the compensating advantage of forcing me to think long and intently about every sentence, and thus I have been often led to see errors in reasoning and in my own observations or those of others.

There seems to be a sort of fatality in my mind leading me to put at first my statement and proposition in a wrong or awkward form. Formerly I used to think about my sentences before writing them down; but for several years I have found that it saves time to scribble in a vile hand whole pages as quickly as I possibly can, contracting half the words; and then correct deliberately. Sentences thus scribbled down are often better ones than I could have written deliberately.

Having said this much about my manner of writing, I will add that with my larger books I spend a good deal of time over the general arrangement of the mater. I first make the rudest outline in two or three pages, and then a larger one in several pages, a few words or one word standing for a whole discussion or series of facts. Each of these headings is again enlarged and often transformed before I being to write *in extenso.* As in several of my books facts observed by others have been very extensively used, and as I have always had several quite distinct subjects in hand at the same time, I may mention that I keep from thirty to forty large portfolios, in cabinets with labelled shelves, into which I can at once put a detached reference or memorandum. I have brought many books and at their ends I make an index of all the facts that concern my work; or, if the book is not my own, write out a separate abstract, and of such abstracts I have a large drawer full. Before beginning on any subject I look to all the short indexes and make a general and classified index, and by taking the one or more proper portfolios I have all the information collected during my life ready for use.

I have said that in one respect my mind has changed during the last twenty or thirty years. Up to the age of thirty, or beyond it, poetry of many kinds, such as the works of Milton, Gray, Byron, Wordsworth, Coleridge, and Shelley, gave me great pleasure, and even as a schoolboy I took intense delight in Shakespeare, especially in the historical plays. I have also said that formerly pictures gave me considerable, and music very great delight. But now for many years I cannot endure to read a line of poetry: I have tried lately to read Shakespeare, and found it so intolerably dull that it nauseated me. I have also almost lost any taste for pictures or music.—Music generally sets me thinking too energetically on what I have been at work on, instead of giving me pleasure. I retain some taste for fine scenery, but it does not cause me the exquisite delight which it formerly did. On the other hand, novels which are works of imagination, though not of a very high order, have been for years a wonderful relief and pleasure to me, and I often bless all novelists. A surprising number have been read aloud to me, and I like all if moderately good, and if they do not end unhappily—against which a law ought to be passed. A novel, according to my taste, does not come into the first class unless it contains some person whom one can thoroughly love, and if it be a pretty woman all the better.

This curious and lamentable loss of the higher aesthetic tastes is all the odder, as books on history, biographies and travels (independently of any scientific facts which they may contain), and essays on all sorts subjects interest me as much as ever they did. My mind seems to have become a kind of machine for grinding general laws out of large collections of facts, but why this should have caused the atrophy of that part of the brain alone, on which the higher tastes depend, I cannot conceive. A man with a mind more highly organized or better constituted than mine, would not I suppose have thus suffered; and if I had to live my life again I would have made a rule to read some poetry and listen to some music at least once every week; for perhaps the parts of my brain now atrophied could thus have been kept active through use. The loss of these tastes is a loss of happiness, and may possibly be injurious to the intellect, and more probably to the moral character, by enfeebling the emotional part of our nature.

My books have sold largely in England, have been translated into many languages, and passed through several editions in foreign countries. I have heard it said it that the success of a work abroad is the best test of its enduring value. I doubt whether this is at all trustworthy; but judged by this standard my name ought to last for a few years. Therefore it may be worth while for me to try to analyze the mental qualities and the conditions on which my success has depended; though I am aware that no man can do this correctly.

I have no great quickness of apprehension or wit which is so remarkable in some clever men, for instance Huxley. I am therefore a poor critic: a paper or book, when first read, generally excites my admiration, and it is only after considerable reflection that I perceive the weak points. My power to follow a long and purely abstract train of thought is very limited; I should, moreover, never have succeeded with metaphysics or mathematics. My memory is extensive, yet hazy: it suffices to make me cautious by vaguely telling me that I have observed or read something opposed to the conclusion which I am drawing, or a time I can generally recollect where to search for my authority. So poor in one sense is my memory, that I have never been able to remember for more than a few days a single date or a line of poetry.

Some of my critics have said, "Oh, he is a good observer, but has no power of reasoning." I do not think that this can be true, for the *Origin of Species* is one long argument from the beginning to the end, and it has convinced not a few able men. No one could have written it without having some power of reasoning. I have a fair share of invention and of common sense or judgement, such as every fairly successful lawyer or doctor must have, but not I believe, in any higher degree.

On the favorable side of the balance, I think that I am superior to the common run of men in noticing things which easily escape attention, an in observing them carefully. My industry has been nearly as great as it could have been in the observation and collection of facts. What is far more important, my love of natural science has been steady and ardent. This pure love has, however, been much aided by the ambition to be esteemed by my fellow naturalists. From my early youth I have had the strongest desire to understand or explain whatever I observed,— that is, to group all facts under some general laws. These causes combined have given me the patience to reflect or ponder for any number of years over any unexplained problem. As far as I can judge, I am not apt to follow blindly the lead of other men. I have steadily endeavored to keep my mind free, so as to give up any hypothesis, however much beloved (and I cannot resist forming one on every subject), as soon as facts are shown to

be opposed to it. Indeed I have had no choice but to act in this manner, for with the exception of the Coral Reefs, I cannot remember a single first-formed hypothesis which had not after a time to be given up or greatly modified. This has naturally led me to distrust greatly deductive reasoning in the mixed sciences. On the other hand, I am not very skeptical,—a frame of mind which I believe to be injurious to the progress of science; a good deal of skepticism in a scientific man is advisable to avoid much loss of time; for I have met with not a few men, who I feel sure have often thus been deferred from experiment or observations, which would have proved directly or indirectly serviceable. . . .

My habits are methodical, and this has been of not a little use for a particular line of work. Lastly, I have had ample leisure from not having to earn my own bread. Even ill-health, though it has annihilated several years of my life, has saved me from the distractions of society and amusement.

Therefore, my success as a man of science, whatever this may have amounted to, has been determined, as far as I can judge, by complex and diversified mental qualities and conditions. Of these the most important have been—the love of science— unbounded patience in long reflecting over any subject—and a fair share of invention as well as of common-sense. With such moderate abilities as I possess, it is truly surprising that thus I should have influenced to a considerable extent the beliefs of scientific men on some important points.

# How to Fix the Premedical Curriculum

*Lewis Thomas*

The influence of the modern medical school on liberal-arts education in this country over the last decade has been baleful and malign, nothing less. The admission policies of the medical schools are at the root of the trouble. If something is not done quickly to change these, all the joy of going to college will have been destroyed, not just for that growing majority of undergraduate students who draw breath only to become doctors, but for everyone else, all the students, and all the faculty as well.

The medical schools used to say they wanted applicants as broadly educated as possible, and they used to mean it. The first two years of medical school were given over entirely to the basic biomedical sciences, and almost all entering students got their first close glimpse of science in those years. Three chemistry courses, physics, and some sort of biology were all that were required from the colleges. Students were encouraged by the rhetoric of medical-school catalogues to major in such nonscience disciplines as history, English, philosophy. Not many did so; almost all premedical students in recent generations have had their majors in chem-

istry or biology. But anyway, they were authorized to spread around in other fields if they wished.

There is still some talk in medical deans' offices about the need for general culture, but nobody really means it, and certainly the premedical students don't believe it. They concentrate on science.

They concentrate on science with a fury, and they live for grades. If there are courses in the humanities that can be taken without risk to class standing they will line up for these, but they will not get into anything tough except science. The so-called social sciences have become extremely popular as stand-ins for traditional learning.

The atmosphere of the liberal-arts college is being poisoned by premedical students. It is not the fault of the students, who do not start out as a necessarily bad lot. They behave as they do in the firm belief that if they behave any otherwise they won't get into medical school.

I have a suggestion, requiring for its implementation the following announcement from the deans of all the medical schools: henceforth, any applicant who is self-labeled as a "premed," distinguishable by his course selection form his classmates, will have his dossier placed in the third stack of three. Membership in a "premedical society" will, by itself, be grounds for rejection. Any college possessing something called a "premedical curriculum," or maintaining offices for people called "premedical advisers," will be excluded from recognition by the medical schools

Now as to grades and class standing. There is obviously no way of ignoring these as criteria for acceptance, but it is the grades *in general* that should be weighed. And, since so much of the medical-school curriculum is, or ought to be, narrowly concerned with biomedical science, more attention should be paid to the success of students in other nonscience disciplines before they are admitted, in order to assure the scope of intellect needed for a physician's work.

Hence, if there are to be MCAT tests, the science part ought to be made the briefest, and weigh the least. A knowledge of literature and languages ought to be the major test, and the scariest. History should be tested, with rigor.

The best thing would be to get rid of the MCATs, once and for all, and rely instead, wholly, on the judgment of the college faculties.

You could do this if there were some central, core discipline, universal within the curricula of all the colleges, which could be used for evaluating the free range of a student's mind, his tenacity and resolve, his innate capacity for understanding of human beings, and his affection for the human condition. For this purpose, I propose that classical Greek be restored as the centerpiece of undergraduate education. The loss of Homeric and Attic Greek from American college life was one of this century's disasters. Putting it back where it once was would quickly make up for the dispiriting impact which generations of spotty Greek in translation have inflicted on modern thought. The capacity to read Homer's language closely enough to sense the terrifying poetry in some of the lines could serve as a shrewd test for the qualities of mind and character needed in a physician.

If everyone had to master Greek, the college students aspiring to medical school would be placed on the same footing as everyone else, and their identifiability as a separate group would be blurred, to everyone's advantage. Moreover, the currently depressing drift on some campuses toward special courses for prelaw students, and even prebusiness students, might be inhibited before more damage is done.

Latin should be put back as well, but not if it is handled, as it ought to be, by the secondary schools. If Horace has been absorbed prior to college, so much for Latin. But Greek is a proper discipline for the college mind.

English, history, the literature of at least two foreign languages, and philosophy should come near the top of the list, just below Classics, as basic requirements, and applicants from medical school should be told that their grades in these courses will count more than anything else.

Students should know that if they take summer work as volunteers in the local community hospital, as ward aides or laboratory assistants, this will not necessarily be held against them, but neither will it help.

Finally, the colleges should have much more a say about who goes on to medical school. If they know, as they should, the students who are generally bright and also respected, this judgment should carry the heaviest weight for admission. If they elect to use criteria other than numerical class standing for recommending applicants, this evaluation should hold.

The first and most obvious beneficiaries of this new policy would be the college students themselves. There would no longer be anywhere they could be recognized as a coherent group, the "premeds," that most detestable of all cliques eating away at the heart of the college. Next to benefit would be the college faculties, once again in possession of the destiny of their own curriculum, for better or worse. And next in line, but perhaps benefiting the most of all, are the basic-science faculties of the medical schools, who would once again be facing classrooms of students who are ready to be started and excited by a totally new and unfamiliar body of knowledge, eager to learn, unpreoccupied by the notions of relevance that are paralyzing the minds of today's first-year medical students already so surfeited by science that they want to start practicing psychiatry in the first trimester of the first year.

Society would be the ultimate beneficiary. We could look forward to a generation of doctors who have learned as much as anyone can learn, in our colleges and universities, about how human beings have always lived out their lives. Over the bedrock of knowledge about our civilization, the medical schools could then construct as solid as structure of medical science as can be built, but the bedrock would always be there, holding everything else upright.

# Sequence Five

# Public Art and the Public Eye

Controversial works of art have been in the news a great deal in recent years, all over the U.S. and particularly in Chicago. In the spring of 1988, a painting depicting the late Mayor Harold Washington in a way that many people found offensive was displayed in the student gallery of the School of the Art Institute. The following year, another student at the same school included in an exhibit an American flag laid on the floor. More recent controversies outside Chicago involved the display of sexually explicit or otherwise controversial photographs by Robert Mapplethorpe and Andres Serrano. These incidents and others have led various government bodies to propose funding cuts for, or even prohibit, some kinds of artistic expression. The debates surrounding these works have focused on complicated issues of freedom of expression, artistic integrity, public funding for the arts, and censorship. Whatever one's stand on these issues, it must be taken into account that all of these works were exhibited privately. Members of the public were able to *choose* whether or not they wanted to view them.

This is not true of works of art or architecture displayed in public places, especially public buildings. Such works raise additional questions: Should the public be "subjected" to—and, as taxpayers, asked to pay for—works of public art they find offensive, meaningless, unpleasant to look at, or simply inconvenient to have around? Should artists have to consult public understanding and taste when they plan their works? Is the role of the artist to educate the public about art? Should the design of public buildings be guided mainly by the artist's sense of artistic integrity, or must the public's comfort and convenience be taken into account? Who should make these decisions? How should they be made?

In this sequence, you will explore your own experiences with public art and architecture, consider the issues raised by a number of controversial works, and present your own analysis of a particular work or building. In addition, you will be invited to think about the relationship between the plastic arts—sculpture and architecture—and writing as forms of individual and public expression.

# Assignment One

*Readings:*

Robert Sommer, "Hard Architecture."
Albert Elsen, "Public Rights and Critics' Failures."
Sylvia Hochfield, "The Moral Rights (and Wrongs) of Public Art."

*Option One:* In these readings you will find examples of how art and architecture affect the quality of life for people who come into contact with them. How do you respond to art and architecture? Think of a place where you spend lots of time. It could be public or private: your bedroom or the dormitory lounge, a library or an open field, your family room or the chemistry lab. Write an essay in which you describe the purpose of and your feelings about this place. How do the construction, size, and furnishings suit this purpose? What about the space, colors, shapes, and textures specifically makes this space appealing or unappealing to you?

*Option Two:* Design a study lounge for yourself. Explain why you made your choices in terms of aesthetics, purpose, and your opinion of how people relate to their surroundings.

# Assignment Two

*Readings:*

Calvin Tomkins, "Tilted Arc."
"The Storm in the Plaza."
Elizabeth Hess, "A Tale of Two Memorials."

*Option One:* In addition to reading these three selections, interview a person who lived in Chicago during the late 1960s when the Picasso statue was being commissioned and constructed in what is now Daley Plaza. In his article on the "Tilted Arc," Calvin Tomkins states that most people acknowledge the existence of modern art but "in general they seem to feel that it has nothing to do with them and can be ignored." Write an essay in which you explain how you think the general public interacts with art. Do you agree with Tomkins that people ignore art? If they generally do, why have such works as "Tilted Arc," the Vietnam War Memorial, and the Picasso provoked controversy? What do you think makes a work of public art succeed or fail with the public?

*Option Two:* The "Tilted Arc" sculpture was removed from Federal Plaza in New York City after a public outcry was raised against it. Richard Serra, the artist who designed it, now considers the sculpture destroyed. Write an imaginary dialogue in which Richard Serra and an employee in the Federal Plaza Building who wanted "Tilted Arc" removed discuss the fate of the sculpture and the public's role in deciding that fate. Should artists consider the public when creating their works? Is the role of the artist to educate the public about art, to challenge perceptions of what is good art? Or do such presuppositions preempt the "voice of the people?" Use the readings to make yourself familiar with these issues and to provide information for your dialogue.

# Assignment Three

*Readings:*

Jim Murphy, "2000 and Beyond: The State of Illinois Center: Infamous, a Noble Effort, or Both?"

Nora Richter Greer, "Look What Landed in the Loop: State of Illinois Center, Chicago."

Paul Gapp, "Jahn's State of Illinois Center Revisited: Strong Enough to Survive the Storm."

*Option One:* In Jim Murphy's article, Helmut Jahn, the architect of the State of Illinois Center, claims that the context in which a public building is constructed in not as important a standard of judgment as the aesthetic qualities of the building itself. Others claim that the surroundings of a building as well as the people who use it should be consulted as standards for judging whether a public building is a success or not. After you read these selections, visit the State of Illinois Center. Observe it carefully, inside and out. Look at its surroundings. Then write an essay in which you either agree or disagree with Jahn.

*Option Two:* Write an essay in which you present an argument about some building or work of public art, either one you have already read and written about or another. You may advocate some specific action: removing, changing, protecting, or restoring the work or building. Or you may argue more generally about its good and/or bad qualities. In either case, your argument should take into account the rights and the design of the artist or architect, the people who use the building or view the art, and the surrounding area.

# Assignment Four

*Readings:*

James Burns, "University of Illinois, Chicago Campus: Transition, Tradition, or New Approach."

Nory Miller, "Evaluation: The University of Illinois' Chicago Circle Campus as Urban Design."

Paul Gapp, "Library Design Keeps City a Step Ahead."

Blair Kamin, "Jurors Take a Look Back to Pick New Library Design."

*Option One:* Choose a word used by all three architects quoted in James Burns' article. Discuss how each of the architects uses the word in the context of the UIC, then define the word as *your* experience with UIC campus has led you to think about it. Compare and contrast your definition with one of the architects with whom you differ, or find parallels between your definition and one of the architects with whom you agree.

*Option Two:* Write an essay in which you explain the kind of language the press uses to describe architecture. Select either Paul Gapp's or Blair Kamin's article and ask yourself the following questions about it: What words are used to describe the realm of aesthetics and utility? What is the article's tone—its attitude toward the subject at hand? What is the article's purpose—to inform, to persuade, to describe? What role does language play in achieving that purpose? What role does language play in suggesting the audience that the author had in mind for this article?

# Hard Architecture

*Robert Sommer*

Prison fixtures are being installed in the restrooms of city parks. According to the manufacturers' statements, they are supposed to be vandal-proof. One advertisement shows a man attacking a toilet with a sledgehammer. According to Sacramento, California, Recreation Director Solon Wishmam, Jr., "There is no exposed plumbing in the new buildings. The external fixtures are made of cast aluminum covered with hard epoxy. The buildings themselves are made of concrete blocks rather than wood or brick."[1] This same trend toward hard buildings is evident in public facilities across the country. Picnic tables are being cast of concrete rather than built of wood and are embedded several feet into the ground. It isn't possible to move these tables to a shady place or combine two tables to accommodate a large group, but that is an inconvenience for the users rather than the park officials. The older wood and metal tables remaining from a happier era are chained to blocks of concrete or steel posts.

The original inspiration for the park restroom, the prison cell, illustrates the hard facts of hard architecture. Human beings are enclosed in steel cages with the bare minimum of furnishings or amenities. In some cells there may be no furniture whatever except for the furthest advance in the field of vandal-proof plumbing, the hole in the concrete floor, otherwise known as a Chinese toilet. Because nothing is provided that the inmate might destroy, he may have to sleep on a bare concrete floor without mattress or blanket. I am not talking about the Middle Ages or some backward part of the nation. I have a clear image of an isolation cell circa 1973 with a man in a steel cage for 23 hours a day with nothing to do but pace the floor and curse the guard watching him through the slit in a steel door. The architecture of the isolation cell is based on a variant of Murphy's Law—if something can be destroyed, it will be destroyed.[2] In mental hospitals of the early 1950s, the line was, "If you give the patients anything nice, they won't take care of it." For public housing tenants it went "If you provide good architecture they won't appreciate it." There is the same denigrating we/they dichotomy in all these assessments of people's response to their surroundings. We know what's best for them and they don't. Even if we provide what they say they'd like, they won't take care of it and will probably destroy it. Ergo, it is best for everyone, especially the taxpayers who foot the bill, to design things that cannot be destroyed.

The result is that architecture is designed to be strong and resistant to human

Robert Sommer was teaching psychology and environmental studies at the University of California at Davis when he wrote *Tight Spaces: Hard Architecture and How to Humanize It.*

Robert Sommer, "Hard Architecture," from *Tight Spaces: Hard Architecture and How to Humanize It* (pp. 7-19, 103, and 111-114), as excerpted in *The Little Brown Reader,* eds. Marcia Stubbs and Sylvan Barnet, 4th ed, 1986 pp. 121-135. Reprinted with permission.

imprint. To the inhabitants it seems impervious, impersonal, and inorganic. Lady Allen, who pioneered the adventure playground in Great Britain, was appalled at American play yards which she described as "an administrator's heaven and a child's hell . . . asphalt barracks yards behind wire mesh screen barriers" built primarily for ease and economy of maintenance.[3] There is a whole industry built around supplying steel cages for prisons, wire mesh fences for city parks, and graffiti-resistant paint for public buildings. On a larger scale, the hardening of the landscape is evident in the ever-growing freeway system, the residential and second-home subdivisions pushing aside orchards and forests, the straightening and cementing of river beds, the walled and guarded cities of suburbia, and the TV cameras in banks and apartment buildings.

Another characteristic of hard architecture is a lack of permeability between inside and out. Often this means an absence of windows, a style referred to in Berkeley as postrevolutionary architecture. At first glance the Bank of America on Berkeley's Telegraph Avenue seems to have windows but these are really reflecting metal surfaces. The new postal center in Oakland, with its tiny slit windows, looks as if it were intended for urban guerilla warfare. Older buildings that still have plate glass use steel shutters and gates that can be drawn across the exterior in a matter of minutes. Some corporations are moving their data-processing machinery underground where they are less vulnerable to attack. The fact that employees must work underground forty hours a week is a minor cost borne by the employees rather than the architect.

Hard architecture means wall surfaces that resist human imprint. Dark colors and rough cement were satisfactory prior to the advent of the aerosol can. The counter response of the hard-line designers has taken two forms. The first is the legal effort to remove aerosol cans from the hands of potential graffitists. Ordinances have been proposed to make it illegal to carry open aerosol cans on city streets. A New York State Senator has proposed a bill to make it illegal for people under eighteen to purchase cans of spray paint. The other approach is to develop vandal-resistant surfaces and stronger kinds of paint remover. In a six-month period New York City purchased 7,000 gallons of a yellow jelly called DWR (dirty word remover) from a Moorestown, N. J., manufacturer of industrial chemicals. The remover comes in two strengths and the heavier duty version is optimistically called Enzitall.[4] Planners of President Nixon's inauguration sprayed the trees alongside the motorcade route with a material that prevented birds from roosting there. They didn't want the president being embarrassed by an occasional bird-dropping. The two-year interval during which the birds would be unable to roost on these trees is a minor inconvenience again borne by the users.

Most of these efforts to harden the environment have had the avowed purpose of increasing security. Frequently this reason is a coverup for a desire to maintain order, discipline, or control. Although these motives are related to security, there are important differences between security and control that must be recognized and heeded if a democratic society is to continue. . . .

## Ideological Supports for Hard Buildings

Any effort to soften hard buildings and improve the lot of the public housing tenant, the prisoner, or the park user will encounter the popular prejudice against "frills" in public facilities. As they say about army buildings, "It doesn't have to be cheap, it just has to look cheap." The taxpayer doesn't want to believe that people living in public housing are better off than he is. Almost every prison official advocates individual cells for prisoners. The logic behind single cells is compelling; it includes the physical protection of weaker inmates, reduces homosexual relationships, enables better control of inmates in single cells, as well as increased privacy and personal dignity. However, whenever prison officials argue for single cells, they are accused of coddling convicts. The apocryphal question from the state legislature is how single rooms can be justified for people who have broken the law when army recruits are compelled to live in open barracks. Is it reasonable to provide more amenities for law breakers than for draftees?

There are several good answers to this question. First we can turn to Florence Nightingale's dictum that the first requisite of a hospital is that it do the patients no harm. The minimum criterion of a prison should be that an inmate emerges no worse than when he entered. At present this is not the case and prisons are accurately described as breeding grounds for criminal behavior. When someone is hurt and angry, there is no reason to believe that putting him in a degrading and dehumanizing environment will improve his outlook or behavior. Indeed there is every reason to suppose that this will worsen whatever antisocial attitudes presently exist.

The logic of subjecting the poor, the criminal, and the deviant to degrading conditions is also based on a puritanical attitude toward comfort. A belief in the redemptive value of hard work and frugality pervades much of our thinking about people who are public charges. The first American prison was developed in Pennsylvania in response to demands for the humane treatment of criminals by the Quaker sect, a group characterized both by its humane impulses and a disdain for anything beyond the minimum in personal comfort. Following Quaker precepts, lawbreakers were confined to solitary cells with ample time to consider their transgressions and become penitent. The cells were quite large and the inmate remained in his cell most of the day apart from a one-hour exercise period. Later, when large-scale workshops proved more efficient than individual craft work performed in a single cell, the solitary system of the Pennsylvania prison was replaced by the silent system of the Auburn Prison, in which inmates also lived in single cells but came together to work and eat but had to remain silent. The idea that an ascetic life would help to rehabilitate prisoners was used against any effort to humanize the institutions.

Even today, efforts to improve the drab conditions of army life, to permit recruits to personalize their sleeping quarters or choose their own hair styles, are regarded by many senior officers as responsible for breakdowns in order and discipline. Not too long ago architects who planned college classrooms and dormitories were advised against making the furnishings too pleasant or comfortable lest the students become distracted or fall asleep. Guidebooks for undergraduate students still warn against too many amenities in the student's room. Here is a sampling of advice on dormitory furnishing: "Choose a straight backed chair rather than a very comfortable one. . . ." "All of the votes are in favor of a simple, rugged, straightbacked chair with no cushion. You study best when you are not too comfortable or relaxed. . . ." "For obvious reasons, avoid studying on a couch, easy chair, or in bed. . . ." "A bed is no place to study. Neither is a sofa, nor a foam rubber lounge chair. When you are too relaxed and comfortable physically, your concentration also relaxes. A straight-backed wooden chair is best for most students; it allows them to work at maximum concentration for longer periods." Before analyzing the attitudes behind these recommendations, let me state emphatically that there is no evidence that people work better when they are uncomfortable. Let the reader examine his or her own circumstances while reading this book. Are you sitting bolt upright in a straight-backed chair or lying on a couch with your head against a cushion? My own observations of the way students read suggest that when a couch or easy chair is available, it will be chosen almost every time over the rugged, virtuous, and uncomfortable straight-backed chair.

Another ideological prop behind hard architecture is neo-behaviorism. Providing decent housing for public charges would be "rewarding" poverty or criminal behavior. The argument goes beyond the accusation of simply coddling convicts to the idea that improved conditions will actually "reinforce" criminal tendencies. Neo-behaviorism maintains that people won't be deterred from crime if the consequences are not sufficiently dire. This requires some form of punishment—if not actual torture then at least confinement without amenity. The critical question is whether confinement and removal from society constitute sufficient punishment or whether the transgressor must be punished still further during confinement. There is no evidence to indicate that such punishment exerts any positive influences on an inmate's character. Instead it increases his alienation from and his bitterness toward society. There is not much basis for believing that dehumanizing public housing will help to reduce welfare rolls, juvenile delinquency, or anything else society considers bad. Poor housing lowers the self-image of the tenant and helps to convince him how little society cares about his plight. This is not a terribly important consideration to a philosophy that is unabashedly beyond freedom and dignity. Hard, hard, hard, ain't it hard? Yet it is. But does it

work? No, it doesn't. City officials across the country will testify that there is no such thing as a vandal-proof restroom or picnic bench. If restrooms are built out of concrete they will be dynamited and have concrete poured down the toilet holes. Vandals, thousands of helmeted Huns riding out of the East, have managed to dig out concrete blocks and haul away picnic tables weighing hundreds of pounds. Bolt cutters and wire snippers can sever any chain-link fence manufactured today. In the People's Park disturbance of 1972, the metal poles for the fence were used to break up the macadam of the parking lot. Local police were very cooperative in carting away the broken macadam pieces lest they in turn be used to break the windows of local stores. The harder the architecture, the greater its potential as a weapon if it is used against the authorities. Prison inmates have learned how to make deadly knives from steel bedsprings. Hard architecture also costs more to adapt or remove. Pennsylvania's Eastern Penitentiary, built in 1829, was closed down in 1966, but has yet to be removed from the site because of the high razing expense. The extra costs of hard architecture are manifold; first in the initial purchase price because it costs twice as much as ordinary items, second in its potential for abuse once it is destroyed as well as the greater cost in repairing or removing a heavy and rigid item designed to be installed permanently, and finally the human costs resulting from being in cold, ugly, and impersonal buildings.

Challenge people to destroy something and they will find a way to do it. Many people prefer to ignore the great amount of technological ingenuity released in wartime. Although only sketchy accounts of the automated battle field have been made public, it is evident that the Vietnam War has produced the most sophisticated gadgetry in the history of warfare. If city agencies use remote sensors and infrared photography to detect the presence of people in the parks after closing time, it is likely that such methods will have the same success in New York parks that they had in Vietnam. Authorities who go the route of vandal-proof facilities are deluding themselves. They are short-range thinkers who cost everyone money in the long run. Adversity puts human ingenuity to the test and the prison inmate naked in his strip cell is tested more severely. By law the California authorities are required to provide even strip-cell inmates with their own Bibles. The result is that the Bible has become a weapon in a manner unintended by the most ardent missionary. Inmates stuff the pages into the ventilator shaft and use the covers to stop up the Chinese toilet. Think of what the inmate could do if he had a table and chair to work with! An advisory committee on dental hygiene ran into problems when it suggested to the California Department of Corrections that inmates should be allowed to use dental floss. Prison officials pointed out that dental floss "when coated with an abrasive substance, could be as effective as metal blades in cutting through iron bars."[5]

The major defects of hard architecture are that it is costly, dehumanizing, and it isn't effective. Besides that, it doesn't look very nice. The prototype of hard architecture is the strip cell in the maximum security prison containing nothing but reinforced concrete poured over a steel cage without any amenities. If we can develop ways of humanizing the prison cell, perhaps we can also do so for schools, parks, and other public facilities.

The rationale of the hard prison is that the inmate will destroy anything that is provided for him. It is easy to prove the correctness of this view by giving a wooden chair to an inmate in a strip cell. It is likely that he will bang the chair against the wall until the legs have come loose and he has several clubs in his possession. Give him a mattress and sooner or later the authorities will have a fire or smoke problem on their hands. Just what does this prove? One can also supply numerous examples of maximum security cells that are equally secure and full of amenities including rugs, tables, desks, television sets, and stereo systems. In prison disturbances, where inmates are rampaging against virtually every part of the prison building, television sets purchased with inmate welfare funds remain undisturbed. Nor do inmates destroy the paintings made by their fellow prisoners.

The arguments against providing amenities for inmates do not discuss the costs of denying a human existence to the lawbreakers. I have never heard anyone maintain that the inmate's mental or physical health is improved by a bare, unheated cell with no exercise yard or outside stimulation. This experience does not teach him a greater respect for the law or the society that maintains him under such dehumanizing conditions. However, guards legitimately object to providing chairs for inmates who are going to break them apart and fashion clubs from the pieces. The typical solution has been to harden prison furnishings with indestructible materials and attach them to the walls. But human ingenuity can always find a way to destroy things that are physically or spiritually oppressive.

Another assumption behind hard architecture is that security through steel, concrete, and electronic surveillance is cheaper and more effective than security through public access. Stated another way, security can be gained through technological control of the environment. This is perhaps valid when one is working *with* people rather than against them. To design a highway to minimize ambiguity, error, and accidents increases everyone's sense of security. I feel more comfortable riding my bike on a well-planned bicycle path than on a street or highway that was designed with automobiles in mind. However, we have not been discussing situations in which everyone gains from good design, but rather those in which hard architecture is used by one group to exclude or oppress another.

The emulation of the prison as a security environment is the more ironic because the prison is a failing institution from everyone's standpoint. It provides no security for inmates, guards, wardens, and visitors. It does provide a short-run protection to outside society by segregating offenders for brief periods, but this must be weighed against the corrosive effects of incarceration in an oppressive and unnatural environment.

## Soft Architecture

If experience has shown that hard architecture isn't working from the standpoint of economics, aesthetics, or human dignity, what then is the answer? The solution, I believe, is to reverse course and make buildings more rather then less responsive to their users. Instead of hardening things to resist human imprint, let us design buildings, parks, and cities to welcome and reflect the presence of human beings—let us abandon the fruitless and costly search for ever more secure cell furnishings. There is another alternative to the completely empty cell. This would involve materials such as foam and inflatables as well as other types of plastics. Provided one selects materials that are fire proof, the security implications of an inexpensive air mattress or styrofoam chair are virtually zero, or at least they are considerably less than with ordinary prison furnishings. There is no justification for inmates in maximum security cells sleeping on hard concrete floors when the wholesale cost of an air mattress is twenty cents. At least an in-

mate should be offered a choice between the bare concrete floor and an air mattress which he can destroy if he chooses. If he elects to destroy the air mattress, the security implications to the guard as well as the cost to the taxpayers are minimal. However, if he does not destroy it, an equally inexpensive foam chair might be tried next. In this way a valid transaction between the inmate and the authorities regarding cell furnishings could be established.

Soft architecture can change the relationship between keeper and inmate. New Jersey State Penitentiary in Leesburg was deliberately built by the architects to include breakable materials; a necessary adjunct to a humane environment. Glass abounds and each cell has natural light with an exterior window in addition to the glazed walls separating cells from courtyards. Locally some people refer to this medium security facility as "the glass house." All windows face the interior courtyards and exterior security is provided by the back wall of the residential units, a deep overhang of the roof to prevent climbing, and a cyclone fence surrounding the entire site. However the interior of the prison contains a great amount of breakable material requiring inmates and guards to reach a mutually satisfactory accommodation, because any burst of anger would result in shattered glass.[6] It would indeed be difficult to run a repressive prison in "the glass house." On the other hand, it requires tremendous tact, patience, and sensitivity to run such a prison. Let the reader answer whether he or she would prefer to work (or be confined) in Leesburg or in a traditional institution.

Several years ago, the dormitories on my campus had strict rules against students hanging pictures or posters on the walls. There were constant inspections by university officials who removed illegal posters and fined the offenders. The basis for these regulations was that the tacks or tape used to mount these posters would scratch the walls. The prohibition against decorating dormitory rooms continued for years even though it was a constant irritant as well as being costly and ineffective. Besides the inspections there was the annual repainting bill, which mounted steadily over the years. Eventually the administration decided that it would be cheaper and happier for everyone to let students hang anything they wanted on their walls. The housing office now provides paint at the beginning of the year so that students can erase anything done by the previous occupants and have the colors they want. Students living on the same floor can decide jointly how the corridors and stairwells are to be painted. New dormitories now contain soft wall materials such as cork or burlap on wood so that students can hang pictures, mobiles, or macrame without marring the surface. They are built to be largely maintained by the users. This has proven cheaper and more satisfying than the previous arrangement of bare walls accompanied by constant inspections, fines, and reprimands, as well as periodic repainting by the maintenance staff. It costs $15 per room to allow students to do the painting themselves, compared to $75 charged by the physical plant office. In 1970, the repaint rate was 10 percent—that is, only one out of ten rooms was repainted by the subsequent occupant.[7]

On any college campus there is always a shortage of study space, particularly around exam time. There is also a great deal of unused space in the evenings, in the form of academic offices, laboratories, and even cafeterias, but it is difficult to get these opened for student use. I don't know of a single campus where faculty offices are available in the evenings as study space—the territorial feelings of the faculty toward their offices are too strong. However, on a number of campuses there have been successful campaigns to open up the cafeterias in the evenings. These campaigns have been successful only sporadically and probably less than one-third of university cafeterias are routinely opened for evening studiers, another third are opened during examination periods, and the remainder are locked and available only during specified meal hours. The arguments against opening up cafeterias are custodial and security-oriented—the students will disturb the table arrangements and will steal the utensils and perhaps even the chairs and tables themselves. At a large university in Los Angeles where the silverware is automatically returned to the locked kitchen after meals, the explanation for closing the cafeteria in the evenings is that the students would steal the salt and pepper shakers. Like the belief that mental patients will flush magazines down the toilets, prisoners will destroy decent furnishings if they have them or park users will chop up wooden benches, a few instances can always be cited, but the trade-offs in social utility and aesthetics are rarely considered. The best counter argument for opening up college cafeterias for evening studiers is that the system works on scores of campuses across the nation. The loss of twenty salt and pepper shakers and perhaps an extra $10 per evening in janitorial services to open up two cafeterias for around-the-clock use might provide the campus with an additional 15,000 feet of prime study space already equipped with tables and chairs. If need be, the student government or some dormitory organization can provide proctors or monitors in the late evening hours.

In all such illustrations—magazines for mental patients, amenities for prisoners, and study space for college students—the security and custodial opposition is largely specious, but this is obvious only to someone knowledgeable about the situation elsewhere. The argument that mental patients will immediately tear up magazines and flush them down the toilet has at least minimal logic unless one has worked on a psychiatric ward where magazines and newspapers are freely available. The arguments against amenity for prisoners seem equally ridiculous if one has seen maximum security cells equipped with carpets, stereos, green plants, and tropical fish. To the criticism that inmates will hide knives and drugs in flower pots and stereos, one can cite the fact that inmates presently secrete weapons and contraband even in the barest of cells and sometimes as suppositories. It is also true that the majority of stabbings and other serious injuries have occurred at the most security-conscious institutions. The explanation always returns to the "type of inmate" and never to the type of place. The mental patients who had free access to newspapers and magazines and didn't flush them down the toilets were presumably a "better class of patients." Similarly, students at University A who have access to cafeterias for evening study and leave the salt and pepper shakers undisturbed are a "better class of students." This "class logic" treats people apart from their surroundings, as if there is some intrinsic self independent of the environment. This is a false model of any natural process, including person/environment transactions. There is no behavior apart from environment even *in utero*. People adapt themselves to their surroundings in diverse and complex ways. When those surroundings are cold and oppressive, people who can will avoid them. Unfortunately many people, for economic, social, or statutory reasons, cannot avoid places that oppress them. The result may be somatic disorders, anxiety, and irritation, but the probable outcome will be numbness to one's surroundings, with psychological withdrawal substituting for physical avoidance. . . .

The dream of a society in which people who share common goals will trust and respect one another is being suffocated in a torrent of concrete, steel, and sophisticated security equipment. I would feel less strongly if windowless buildings, barbed-wire fences, and electronic surveillance equipment were infrequent aberrations of paranoid homeowners and public officials, but they are not. Housing projects, schools, playgrounds, courtrooms, and commercial buildings reveal the hardening process at an advanced stage. If there is truth to Churchill's dictum that the building we shape will eventually shape us, then the inevitable result of hard buildings will be withdrawn, callous, and indifferent people. A security emphasis is being poured into concrete that will harden our children's children fifty years from now. . . .

## Personalization

There is no single best arrangement of office furniture and no way for a designer, building manager, or psychologist to intuit someone's space needs without meeting the person, seeing the sort of job he or she has to do, and how he or she does it. Every faculty office on my campus comes equipped with a standard complement of furniture—a desk, filing cabinet, table, two or three bookcases, coat rack, and so on. Because all these people have the same job title (professor) and the size and shape of all office pieces are identical, one could conceive of standardized office arrangements. However, a walk down the hallways reveals a great diversity of arrangements. One man has placed his bookcase between his desk and the door for maximum privacy. Another has joined together his desk and table to yield a large work area and writing surface as well as considerable distance from any visitor, and a third has placed all furniture against the walls to remove any barriers between himself and the students. Numerous attempts at personalization are evident. Out of their own pocket, faulty purchased rugs, drapes, wall-hangings, and pictures of every description, as well as artifacts and symbols of their respective professions. The same diversity of arrangements is evident in the student dormitories, which also come equipped with a standardized complement of similar furniture. Sometimes I think I have seen every conceivable arrangement of two desks, two beds, two chairs, and two dressers, but invariably I am surprised to find a novel pattern.

Instead of guessing "user needs" one should aim at providing access to a pool or selection of furnishings and allow people to arrange their office areas as they see fit. During the occupation of the administration building during Berkeley's Free Speech Movement crisis in 1964, it was reported that the students had broken into and ransacked the office of President Emeritus Robert Gordon Sproul. When the police had removed the demonstrators, they found Sproul's office in disarray with papers strewn about the floor. The situation was resolved when Sproul's secretary reported that her employer often worked on the floor and left papers strewn about.

The idea that people should be able to control and personalize their work spaces is well within the technical capability of the building industry. It does call for a reversal of the tendency to centralize services and decision-making regarding the physical environment. In the short run it may be cheaper to omit the light switches in an office building, but this makes it difficult to show slides and it is also terribly wasteful of electric power. The same point applies to heating, air conditioning, and humidity controls. There is something tragic about an employee who is officially reprimanded for placing cardboard over her air conditioning vent or a poster on the wall to brighten an otherwise drab office. There is no contradiction between central design and local control provided one develops an overall design scheme that makes allowance for local inputs. One can design a soft building in which each occupant controls his own temperature—hotels and motels do this routinely—or one can design a hard building in which the custodian controls everyone's temperature. In the work on classroom seating . . . it was found that janitors arranged chairs in accordance with their educational philosophies. They also followed their own standards of temperature, humidity, and illumination. The custodian in my building has a clear conception of where my desk and chair belong. Every morning I move my chair over to the side of the room and every evening he returns it to my desk. He arranges the room according to his scheme and I to mine. Fortunately the rules allow me to move my chair. I visited a conference room in one government agency and found taped to the wall under the President's picture a diagram specifying how every item of furniture in the room was to be arranged.

Pleas for personalizing offices and work spaces are academic and even precious until one sees the drab and impersonal conditions under which many people work. At the offices of a large insurance company I found hundreds of clerk's desks in straight rows in a large open room with phones ringing, people scurrying about, and no one having any control over the thermal, acoustical, or visual environment. A federal agency building is liable to be a maze of offices of identical size, shape, and decor. All the furniture, including desks and bookcases, is government-issue grey and on every wall there is a framed photograph of the President and the agency director. A few executives are able to place maps on the walls for visual relief, but that is all. The quest for stimulating and attractive work places, the right to personalize one's own spaces and control temperature and illumination and noise are not academic issues to people who must spend eight hours a day in these settings. I don't feel it is necessary to "prove" that people in colorful offices will type more accurately, stay healthier, or buy more government bonds than people in drab offices. People should have the right to attractive and humane working conditions. Somehow the onus of the argument for a decent environment always falls upon the person who wants to improve things; the custodians and the rest of the grey wall crowd never have to defend drab and unresponsive buildings. This is a curious double standard. If an employee hangs up a poster by his desk, he is imposing his values and artistic tastes on the other employees, but if the management paints all the walls in the building grey or institutional green, that is part of the natural order. We eventually tune them out and thereby become alienated from the very buildings in which we spend our daylight hours.

Ugly and drab furnishings cannot be justified economically. For a corporation or government agency, colored items would cost only slightly more than grey ones and on a large order the difference would disappear entirely. There is some poetic justice that many of the drab furnishings of state office buildings are manufactured by the state prison system. In private corporations, which buy their furniture in the free market where a wide variety of styles and colors is available, standardization is less a result of economics or efficiency than of insensitivity and deliberate unconcern. There is also more than a hint of authoritarianism in the idea that each employee must accept the specific furniture arrangement provided by the company. In a large corporation or agency it would be feasible to give each employee a choice of desk, chair, file cabinet, table, and waste basket from a central furniture pool, not only at the time of employment, but every six months if the person felt like changing things around. This may sound utopian but it isn't. It doesn't take all that long to move furniture. The main objective is not so much to keep the furniture moving as it is to sensitize people to the connection between themselves and their surroundings and counteract the pervasive numbness and apathy. The idea of so many millions of people singlemindedly going to dingy little work stations in large skyscrapers, completely turned off to other people and places, is profoundly disturbing. This kind of numbness to one's surroundings can become a life style.

## Notes

1. Jeff Raimundo, "Park Facilities Are Still Vulnerable," Sacramento *Bee,* February 8, 1973, p. B1.
2. Murphy's Law No. 1: If something can go wrong, it will. Law No. 2: The toast always falls butter side down.
3. Lady Allen of Hurtwood, *Planning for Play* (Cambridge: M.I.T. Press, 1968).
4. "Help Arrives," Cincinnati *Enquirer,* April 23, 1972.
5. Sacramento *Bee,* May 8, 1973, p. B2.
6. Suzanne Stephens, "Pushing Prisons Aside," *The Architectural Forum* (March 1973), pp. 28-51.
7. Robbie Hart, "Room Painting in the Residence Halls," Unpublished report, University of California, Davis Housing Office, 1970.

# Public Rights and Critics' Failures

*Albert Elsen*

A secretary arrives at her office one day to find that her employer has hung a painting over her desk that shows a woman copulating with a vacuum cleaner. Students and members of the public using a corridor in a university student union are confronted by an exhibition of pictures of nudes in which male and female genitalia are emphasized in clinical detail. The Indian community in a western state discovers installed in front of the state university campus a large painted sculpture that caricatures a shoot-out between a cowboy and an Indian. Employees who work in a federal office building in New York find themselves suddenly faced with a long, rusting steel sculpture that cuts across the plaza they must traverse daily to get to and from work.

In all of these instances, the offended members of the public took action, and in all but one case they succeeded in having the art they found offensive removed. Were these removals egregious violations of the artists' right of free speech and blatant acts of censorship?

Those who believe that freedom of speech for artists is absolute will answer in the affirmative. Others will ask, however, what rights members of the public have when they are offended by public art. They may

Albert Elsen teaches art history and art law at Stanford University.

not always succeed, but members of the public have the right to complain to and petition the responsible authorities to remove what they find offensive. Disgruntled taxpayers also have the right to vote against, or try to recall, elected officials with whose taste in public at they disagree. (The public siting of a Henry Moore cost a mayor of Toronto his office.)

The most compelling argument against the absolute right of free speech for artists is that the captive audience suffers an invasion of privacy by unwilling exposure to what it considers offensive art. As stated by the judge who ordered the closing of the student union exhibition, "Freedom of speech must recognize, at least within limits, freedom not to listen."

Whether censorship was involved in all of the examples cited above is questionable. In no instance was the artwork sequestered, destroyed, or legally prohibited from being shown elsewhere. The artists were not permanently denied access to an audience for their art in other locations. All of the artists whose works were removed availed themselves of the opportunity to relocate their art in more appropriate or hospitable environs. The case of the sculpture in New York is still unresolved. In Paris, however, citizens of the 13th arrondissement, outraged by the presence of a similar work by the same artist, followed the example of the New Yorkers and petitioned the mayor to have the piece removed from the center of a much-loved public park.

Rare is the professional art critic who, for fear of offending the art world, takes the public's interest into account. One prominent critic who wrote glowingly of the Paris piece apparently never even considered asking members of the community what they thought of the sudden intrusion of huge, rusting steel, graffiti-inviting presence into their park. Nor did he write a follow-up review that considered whether the sculpture he admired so much added to the quality of life in the community—in the view of the people who lived there. Having lived in that part of Paris last year for eight months and having experienced the communal hatred for this piece, I was vividly reminded by this critic's review of how enthusiasm for an otherwise controversial public work is often directly proportional to the writer's distance from the site.

Art critics usually don't consider public art in terms of its purpose—what its impact is, good and bad, on the quality of life in a community. They treat it purely aesthetically, as if it were in a gallery or museum, or they see the site as an abstraction, not in terms of how people relate to it. As in the case of a temporary gallery show, reviews of public art are written right after it is installed, and no awareness is shown of how a work affects its audience—those who must see it daily.

Critics are averse to returning to the scene of what is sometimes artistically, a civic crime. But if they have a choice, they should voluntarily refrain from writing about public art until several months after its installation, or impose on themselves the requirement of writing a follow-up review at least a year later so that they can get a better sense of the community's reaction as well as their own.

Critics seem to regard the public as unregenerately philistine. But by its acceptance of, and often enthusiasm for, so many modern artworks in civic spaces across the country, the public has earned the right to be taken seriously. Consider the number of cities like Seattle, Baltimore, and Portland that pride themselves on programs of tax-supported public art. In Chicago and Grand Rapids, sculptures by Picasso and Calder have become civic logos. Many communities are developing sculpture parks on municipal land.

The public as well as the art world successfully supported George Sugarman against the Baltimore judges who would have prevented the installation of his General Services Administration commission in front of a courthouse. Testimony by members of the public against Richard Serra's *Titled Arc* was as eloquent as, and often more compelling than, that of its supporters from the art community, some of whom acted out of loyalty rather than conviction. Popular reaction against *Tilted Arc* did not, as many predicted it would, set off a wave of similar negative reactions to the more than 200 G.S.A. works already installed in public places.

In many ways, artists have learned to credit the public with more sophistication than have critics. Modern public art has come of age, but professional art critics—and their editors—have not. Theirs is a failure of imagination, courage, and courtesy. Until such time as we get more conscientious and enlightened critical writing, the public must exert its right to say no to what it considers offensive public art.

# The Moral Rights and Wrongs of Public Art

*Sylvia Hochfield*

The mosaic mural on the facade of the new city hall in Edwardsville, Illinois, was a source of civic pride when it was dedicated in 1967. It was designed by the architect himself, who was also an artist well thought of in the area. Its subject was chosen by a panel of citizens appointed by the mayor, which worked with the artist in shaping the final design. The whole town pitched in to raise funds. Everybody, it seemed, thought the mural was a civic adornment.

Twenty years later, a city commission demanded that part of the mural be destroyed and replaced. The city council refused. The artist, who had no more say in the matter than anyone else, was very angry; some people thought the dispute hastened his death a few months later. The conflict enveloped everyone in Edwardsville. A prominent member of the local arts community protested that changing the mural would violate its integrity, but opponents weren't interested in sophisticated theories of moral right. Finally, after over a year of heated public discussion, the city council agreed that the mural would be partially destroyed and remade.

The dispute arose because one segment of the community—the 10 percent of Edwardsville's population of 16,000 that is

black—didn't have a very loud voice in 1967, when the mural by Edward A. Kane, Sr., was dedicated. Nobody else objected then to the scenes from Edwardsville history that were its subject. Twenty years later, the black community's voice was a little bit louder, and the city's Human Relations Commission was listening. What the black community objected to was one figure in the mural, described as follows by the artist in 1967: "A Negro, a rope of bondage having been cut, symbolical of the slaves that were freed in Edwardsville by one of the early governors of Illinois."

Tim Earley, chairman of the Human Relations Commission and a community activist, describes the figure somewhat differently: "The complaint was that the image of the black person was done in the Stepin Fetchit tradition," he says. "He's standing there with slumped shoulders, hands out, and a watermelon-eating grin on his face." Black people, Earley continues, were deeply offended by the figure. "Many people in this community were and had been for years burdened by their humiliation every time they walked past city hall and saw the way their ancestors had been portrayed."

David C. Huntley, director of university museums at Southern Illinois University, in Edwardsville, has another point of view. He doesn't deny that the figure is a stereotype, but he thinks that revising it would be like

Sylvia Hochfield is editor-at-large of *ARTnews*.

From *ARTnews* (May 1988): 143–146. Copyright © by Sylvia Hochfield. Reprinted by permission of *ARTnews*.

rewriting history. "We can't go back and change the ideas of artists from the past," he says. "This mural is not a great work of art, but it is an honest and legitimate expression of an individual. It has been presented to the public; it is in a public place, adorning a public building, and that in itself should give it some stature."

Earley completely disagrees: "The reactionary forces have often been the so-called protectors of art," who uphold "an ideology of art—that nothing can be changed, that art is sacrosanct, that art is permanent," he says. "My point of view is that art doesn't have any more right to deeply offend people than people have to deeply offend people."

Earley's position prevailed. The eight-member (six white, two black) city council, surprised and shocked at the extent of the controversy, voted unanimously to let the Human Relations Commission change the mural, and a local artist was chosen to transform the freed slave into a dignified figure holding farm implements, symbolic of the early black settlers of Edwardsville, many of whom were farmers. And then, in March, when everyone thought the dispute was over, Edward A. Kane, Jr., the artist's son, filed for an injunction to prevent the change on the ground that "allowing any such alteration would constitute a deprivation of the right to artistic communication without governmental influence, interference, censorship, or suppression."

To Earley, and to most of the people in Edwardsville, the dispute over the mural had nothing to do with esthetics and everything to do with ideology, which made it a throwback to the kind of controversy over public art that was not unusual in this country before the rise of abstraction. The great public-art battles of the early 20th century usually pitted a radical artist against a more conservative patron or public. With the vic-

tory of abstraction, the battleground changed. The ideologies that were brought to bear in defense of Richard Serra's *Tilted Arc* in New York City were the esthetic ideologies of the art world; the issue for the public was whether you liked the sculpture or not. But the Edwardsville conflict may have been the first in which the art community, defending a work of art against public opposition, could be labeled "reactionary forces."

As works of art proliferate in public places, the controversies surrounding them multiply as well. In New York, Richard Serra lost his suit to prevent the removal of *Tilted Arc* from Federal Plaza in downtown Manhattan to another location and announced that he would appeal the decision. In the meantime, a panel appointed by the National Endowment for the Arts to pick another site for the sculpture recommended that it remain where it is. In Chicago, frescoes painted by Irene Siegel in a library in a working-class neighborhood so enraged local people that they formed a group called Uprave and sued, unsuccessfully, to stop the work. In St. Louis, a city bureaucrat acting entirely on her own had an environmental sculpture by Alan Sonfist bulldozed into the ground.

Washington State has been a particularly heated battleground. In Seattle, proposals to use percent-for-art funds for sculpture to decorate a jail provoked seven years of controversy between local politicians and the county arts commission. In Tacoma, a neon mural by Stephen Antonakos almost precipitated a public revolt when it was installed in the sports arena. The lights remain, but angry voters repealed the city's percent-for-art ordinance. In Olympia, murals by Michael Spafford and Alden Mason in the state capitol were attacked—Spafford's semi-abstract images by legislators who thought they were obscene, and Mason's symbolic landscapes by an interior decorator who was refurbishing the building and said they clashed with

333

his new color scheme. A suit to save the murals was unsuccessful. Mason's will be unbolted from the walls and put into storage; Spafford's, which can't be removed, are hidden behind curtains.

Such controversies aren't limited to the United States. In France, Jean Dubuffet sued the Renault auto company in 1975, when the company's new president decided to halt construction of a half-completed environmental sculpture it had commissioned for its new headquarters near Paris. The court ruled for the sculptor, saying that Renault had to allow him to complete his work. Having won his point, Dubuffet said he had no desire to force anything on the company that it didn't want and gave up the project. In Toronto, Michael Snow sued to force a shopping center to remove the Christmas decorations that had been draped over his sculpture *Flight Stop*. Snow didn't care that the decorations were temporary, he said that decking his work with ribbons was like dressing the Venus de Milo in dangling earrings.

Dubuffet won his case because French law, like that of most European countries, recognizes the "moral right" of the artist. Snow won his case because Canada is a signatory to the Berne Convention for the Protection of Literary and Artistic Works, which also gives creators certain moral rights over their works, even after those works are sold or otherwise transferred to others. One of the most important components of the moral right is the right of integrity of the work of art, which, as it is explained by John Henry Merryman and Albert E. Elsen in their book *Law, Ethics, and the Visual Arts* (University of Pennsylvania Press), is based on the idea that the work of art is an expression of the artist's personality. Distortion or misrepresentation of the work, according to Merryman, "mistreats an expression of the artist's personality, affects his artistic identity, personality and honor, and thus impairs

a legally protected personality interest." Another component of the moral right is the right of paternity—the right of the artist to insist that his work be associated with his name or, conversely, to insist that his name not be associated with works that are not his.

A bill is now pending in Congress to bring the United States into the Berne Convention. Until that happens, only five states have any kind of moral-rights legislation. The California Art Preservation Act was passed in 1979, and the New York Artists' Authorship Rights Act in 1983. Laws in Massachusetts, Pennsylvania, and Louisiana are based on the California statute.

The California law is concerned with protecting works of fine art, and it recognizes that "there is a public interest in preserving the integrity of cultural and artistic creations." The New York law, on the other hand, is concerned entirely with protecting the artist's reputation. It doesn't prohibit the mutilation or destruction of artworks, as the California law does. It merely gives the artist the right to disclaim authorship and to block the public exhibition of a work that has been altered by anyone else without his consent if he believes that the altered work would damage his reputation.

If the New York law had been in force in 1980, it would not have helped Isamu Noguchi when the Bank of Tokyo destroyed a sculpture it had commissioned from him for the lobby of its Wall Street branch. To remove the sculpture, which some employees and clients didn't like, the bank chopped it up. There was nothing Noguchi could do to prevent its destruction, since he had transferred all of his rights in the sculpture to the bank. And the New York Artists's Authorship Rights Act would have allowed him only to block the display of the work if the bank had wanted to exhibit it in its mutilated condition in a public place in New York State. The California and New York laws are so different, legal scholars point out, that somebody could deliberately mutilate an artwork in New York and then exhibit it in California without breaking the law in either state.

The California law is confined to works of art of "recognized quality," so that a Sunday painter can't sue if one of his creations is destroyed or a parent protest if a child's finger painting is thrown away. But legal scholars speculate that there may be problems with the definition of "recognized quality," which the law says shall be determined by "the opinions of artists, art dealers, collectors of fine art, curators of art museums, and other persons involved with the creation or marketing of the art." This requirement, according to Franklin Feldman and Stephen E. Weil in their book *Art Law* (Little, Brown), might conceivably turn the courtroom into a forum "where quality and one's view of artistic merit becomes the dominant issue." To some degree, they point out, a similar situation exists in New York, since an artist asserting that his reputation is damaged by the display of his work in an altered form may find himself in the position of having to prove that he has a reputation and that it can be damaged.

The first case brought under the New York law was that of Robert Newmann, who was sandblasting a mural into the back of the Palladium Theatre in Manhattan when the building's owner, Delmar Realty Co., leased it to the Muidallap Corporation. Muidallap wasn't interested in Newmann's mural. In 1984 Newmann sued for the right to finish his work, which the court granted. The decision, however, was based only tangentially on the moral-rights statute; the court decided that Newmann had a contractual right to finish the mural, even if it were to be demolished immediately upon completion. A few months later, Newmann discovered that workmen had punched two holes through the back wall of the building so that construction materials could be passed through. He went back to court, claiming that the holes constituted an alteration to the "negative space" surrounding his work, which was an integral part of the work itself. This time the court disagreed with him.

The first major case brought under the California legislation is expected to go to trial this year, according to Los Angeles attorney Allen I. Neiman, who is representing the artist, Tom Van Sant. Van Sant was commissioned in 1967 to paint a 120-foot-long mural for the lobby of the new Crocker Citizens Plaza in Los Angeles. In 1982 the Crocker National Bank sold the building to Mitsui Fudosan Inc., and in 1984 Mitsui leased it to AT&T. To accommodate the new tenant, Mitsui remodeled parts of the building, mutilating the mural in the process, although, according to Van Sant, it is painted on a freestanding, lightweight wall that could easily have been removed.

Another case being closely watched by art lawyers is that of Alan Sonfist. When St. Louis accepted his proposal for an environmental sculpture, the mayor presented him with the key to the city, and the dedication ceremony, in 1986, was a festive occasion complete with marching bands and balloons. Sonfist calls his *Time Landscape of St. Louis* a "celebration of the land": on a stretch of parkland next to an abandoned railroad station in an area slated for urban renewal, he created a wedge-shaped "primeval forest," about a block long, of native Missouri trees. It was elevated on a mound, symbolic of the region's Indian heritage, and surrounded by a French formal garden, a reminder of the city's French founders. The cost of the work was about $100,000. There was no controversy about the project; critical reaction was highly favorable, and Sonfist says that ordinary people liked it and seemed to understand it.

But last year, only 17 months after the dedication ceremony, *Time Landscape* was bulldozed into oblivion by a newly appointed parks commissioner, Evelyn O. Rice. Rice acted entirely alone, a day after informing members of the city's arts commission of what she intended to do. St. Louis has a public-arts policy that calls for establishing a panel to review public artworks before they are removed, but Rice ignored it because "I didn't want people making promises just to force further delays." Sonfist was given no warning that the work was about to be destroyed; he heard the news from a friend a few days afterward.

Rice said she acted because *Time Landscape* was so badly maintained that it had come to look like a construction site. But the city had agreed when it accepted Sonfist's proposal that the parks department would be responsible for maintenance. The artist says he provided a meticulously detailed two-year maintenance plan to take care of the sculpture until it became self-maintaining, and that it was Rice's responsibility, as parks commissioner, to carry out the work.

Rice also complained that homeless people had taken over the site and were hanging their laundry from the trees. Sonfist replies that there are homeless people all over St. Louis. "I saw them sleeping on the steps of city hall. Does that mean city hall should be pulled down?"

Sonfist says he is outraged that a single bureaucrat acting on her own could arbitrarily destroy a work of art. He is planning to sue the city, asking for the reconstruction of *Time Landscape* and for a public apology.

The multiplication of public-art controversies has given rise to a new art-law specialty dealing with art in public places. New York attorney Barbara Hoffman, who headed a subcommittee on public-art law for the Association of the Bar of the City of New York, says that many issues are still to be resolved. "You have the government owning works of art, so the question is: What limitations, if any, are imposed on the government as an owner of private property when that property is art? Are there limitations that arise from artists' rights? Are there limitations that arise from community concerns? We're talking about defining private-property concepts as they relate to government ownership of artworks, and that definition has to include considerations of public interest as well as the interests of the artists." Until such problems are resolved, the controversies are likely to continue.

# Tilted Arc

*Calvin Tomkins*

The climate of acceptance in which new art flourishes today is deceptive. Although the accepting public is much larger than it used to be, it is still, in relative terms, infinitesimal. Most people have never really accepted modern art, much less its contemporary ("postmodern") manifestation. They acknowledge its existence, but in general they seem to feel that it has nothing to do with them and can therefore be ignored. When a work of contemporary art proves impossible to ignore, the result is sometimes big trouble.

The recent brouhaha over Richard Serra's "Tilted Arc" is a case in point. "Tilted Arc" is a Minimalist sculpture in the form of an enormous steel wall, a hundred and twenty feet long and twelve feet high, that bisects the plaza in front of the Jacob K. Javits Federal Building, in lower Manhattan. Viewed from above—from the height, say, of a tenth-floor office window—it makes a graceful, curving line across the space and sets up a contrapuntal relationship with the plaza's only other feature, a circular fountain that never seems to have water in it. Seen from ground level, the "Arc" is an overwhelming, intimidating mass. The wall's height shuts off the view of Foley Square and its architectural monuments—McKim,

Calvin Tomkins is a regular contributor to *The New Yorker*.

Mead & White's soaring Municipal Building, Cass Gilbert's neoclassic United States Courthouse, and other souvenirs of a bygone era. The sculpture is made of Cor-Ten steel, a "weathering" metal that is supposed to acquire a rich dark-brown patina of rust; in this case, however, the constant battle against graffiti has left the surface mottled and scuffed. The wall is set into the paving stones of the plaza at a slight angle, so that it leans toward the Federal Building. Pedestrians on that side sometimes have the disorienting sensation that it is about to fall on them.

The sculpture was commissioned by the General Services Administration, the federal agency responsible for the construction of all new government office buildings throughout the United States. The G.S.A.'s Art-in-Architecture Program authorizes the spending of one-half of one percent of a building's construction budget for a work (or works) of art, and Serra's "Arc" was the work chosen for the Federal Building. Following well-established procedures, in 1979 the G.S.A. invited Serra to make a proposal for the plaza. The agency approved his plan for "Tilted Arc," reaffirmed its approval at all stages of the design-review process, and executed a contract awarding the artist a hundred and seventy-five thousand dollars for the finished work, which was installed in the spring of 1981. Ever since, irate citizens have been trying to get rid of it. Petitions, letters, and other forms of protest have made it clear that a great many people *hate* "Tilted Arc." Last December, after nearly four years of agitation, the G.S.A.'s regional administrator for the New York area, William Diamond, decided on his own to schedule public hearings on the issue of the sculpture's "relocation." Thus the stage was set for one of those infrequent battles between the minority that accepts modern art and the majority that does not.

The three days of public hearings, on March 6th, 7th, and 8th, generated more heat than light. Fifty-six people spoke against the sculpture, voicing complaints that by this time were well known: that it was ugly; that it spoiled the view; that it prevented the plaza from being used for concerts, performances, or social gatherings; that it attracted graffiti; that it made access to the building difficult. One woman, a G.S.A. employee whose job involved the building's security, testified that the "Arc" would make a terrorist bomb attack more destructive: "The sculpture could vent an explosion inward and in an angle toward the buildings," she said. Although Mr. Diamond had reiterated that the G.S.A.'s decision would reflect no "aesthetic judgment" but only "the most effective use of the plaza," the subtext of a great many anti-"Arc" statements was that "Tilted Arc" was not art—it was "that rusted steel wall," that barrier, that piece of junk.

Richard Serra, one of the country's most highly regarded sculptors, had mobilized the international art world to resist the philistines. A hundred and eighteen people rose to defend his sculpture—fellow-artists, writers, musicians, filmmakers, museum curators, and public figures, including Joan Mondale, Senator Howard Metzenbaum, and Mrs. Jacob Javits, the Senator's wife, who read a statement by her husband about art and political freedom. The pro-"Arc" statements were more complicated than the anti-"Arc" ones but no less predictable: Serra was a major artist; he had a legal contract with the G.S.A., which the G.S.A. had no right to renege on; a public hearing was an improper forum, and Mr. Diamond had prejudged the case by making public statements in favor of relocating the sculpture; since "Tilted Arc" was a "site-specific" work, having been designed for that particular space, to relocate it would be to destroy it; important new art was often disturbing at first, and anyway, as the artist Robert Murray put it, "we cannot have public art by plebiscite." Any number of speakers argued that if the G.S.A. gave in to public pressure and removed the work the entire Art-in-Architecture Program would be placed in jeopardy: other communities would demand the removal of government-sponsored artworks, and self-respecting artists would refuse to undertake G.S.A. commissions.

Relatively few pro-"Arc" speakers defended the sculpture on aesthetic grounds. Some of Serra's most fervent supporters actually dislike the piece, and feel considerable sympathy for the office workers who have to look at it every day. They argued as they did because of the larger issues that seemed to be involved—issues of artistic freedom and the government's role in support of the arts. Serra, who dressed for the hearings in a heavy wool shirt and workmen's pants, emphasized those issues in his own rostrum-thumping statement at the hearings. As he phrased it, freedom of creative expression implies that once an artist has been selected and commissioned by the government "the artist's work must be uncensored, respected, and tolerated, although deemed abhorrent, or perceived as challenging, or experienced as threatening." The G.S.A. has commissioned more than two hundred works of art during the last twenty years, at a cost of seven million dollars. Some of these works have generated vehement opposition among local

338

groups, but the G.S.A., until now, has stood firmly behind its commissioned artists, and the Arts-in-Architecture Program has been widely praised by the professional art establishment for its enlightened and respectful attitude toward contemporary art. One rumor going around at the hearings was that the entire Art-in-Architecture Program was in trouble, a potential victim of the Reagan Administration's reactionary tilt.

Some of the points, both pro and con, that were raised at the hearings might have been hard to sustain. Had the plaza, a meager and ungainly space in a noisy, crowded section of town, really been deprived of festive social gatherings by the somber presence of the "Arc"? Would relocating the sculpture in another setting really destroy it as a work of art? (A great many Renaissance altarpieces now in American museums were originally "site-specific.") In all the verbiage, however, one statement stood out like a beacon. It was by Alvin S. Lane, a lawyer active in a number of arts organizations, and in it he asked several searching questions. "Is the purpose of the Art-in-Architecture Program to benefit the artist or the community?" was one of them. "Should an artist have the right to impose his values and taste on a public that now rejects his taste and values?" was another. "In the selection of art, even the greatest experts will make mistakes from time to time," Lane went on to say. "If it is a private matter, the mistake can be rectified by not showing the work of art. Where it is a public matter, should there be a different standard?" Speaking personally, Lane said that he did not like "Tilted Arc" and would welcome its removal. But Mr. Diamond and the four men he had appointed to preside at the hearings were not, he felt, the right people to rule on that. Instead, he recommended that they use the hearings "for the purpose of formulating recommendations for legislation that would establish a fair procedure for reevaluating all public works of living artists."

Mr. Lane's questions went unanswered at the hearings, but they bear thinking about. To my knowledge, he was the only speaker to suggest that a work of art in a public space ought not to be judged by the same criteria that are applied to works of art in museums or in private collections. A great many people have to look at "Tilted Arc" every day, whether they want to or not, and a significant number of them seem to feel that it is an unwelcome imposition on their values and taste. They don't think it's art, and they don't see why they have to put up with it. If asked, they would almost certainly say that in this case the G.S.A. acted for the benefit of the artist, not the community.

It is not enough simply to dismiss this as a philistine attitude. The problem is that today there is no general agreement or understanding about art's social function. During the Renaissance, people might disagree about the relative merits of a new altarpiece or an equestrian statue but they did not question the tradition that placed such works in public places. It is the absence of any such tradition that causes trouble when modern art (which has been largely a private matter) attempts to go public, as it increasingly tends to do these days. More and more artists are being commissioned to provide works for public spaces. Quite a few of them have made serious efforts to think about the social implications of public art, and their thinking has led them, often enough, to jettison the idea of sculpture, monumental or otherwise, in favor of a process of collaboration with architects, designers, landscape architects, engineers, and local community groups of all kinds, with a view to making the public space itself a work of art. The G.S.A.'s Art-in-Architecture Program began, about three years ago, to move in a similar direction. Before an artist is even approached for a commission now, the G.S.A. tries to establish contact with a broad cross-section of people in the community where the new government building is going up. The mayor's office, local civic and arts organizations, and neighborhood groups are all consulted about the possibility of commissioning a work of art, and recommendations are solicited for people to serve on the design-review panel. Artists who live in the area receive special attention in the selection process, and once an artist has been commissioned the G.S.A. encourages him or her to meet with the local groups, answer their questions, and let them in on the aesthetic thinking behind the work. According to Donald Thalacker, the highly respected director of the Art-in-Architecture Program, this has slowed the whole process down considerably but it has also helped to convince a lot of people that the program is working for the community, not just for the artist.

The community-minded approach to public art is shared by artists with widely divergent interests, and methods, among them Siah Armajani, Scott Burton, Nancy Holt, Mary Miss, Elyn Zimmerman, and Richard Fleischner. It is not shared by Richard Serra. In a 1980 interview, Serra stated his position with customary bluntness. "Placing pieces in an urban context is not synonymous with an interest in a large audience even though the work will be seen by many people who wouldn't otherwise look at art," he said, "The work I make does not allow for experience outside the conventions of sculpture as sculpture. My audience is necessarily very limited."

Nobody with a serious interest in contemporary art questions Serra's reputation as a major artist. His work has consistently advanced the concept of sculpture in powerful and provocative ways, as his forthcoming retrospective at the Museum of Modern Art will demonstrate. (It is scheduled to open early in 1986.) Serra was one of the first artists to explore the contemporary notion of "site-specific" sculpture. His main interest now is in making outdoor urban sculptures that relate in terms of size, scale, placement, and structure to their surroundings. His work is usually so dynamic and so aggressive in its use of heavyweight industrial materials that it significantly alters the way those surroundings look to others, and that is part of the plan. One of Serra's primary goals is to force people to see their surroundings in a new way—to make them experience sculpture as place, and place as sculpture. In another 1980 interview, soon after he had been commissioned to do the piece for the Federal Building, Serra announced that he had "found a way to dislocate or alter the decorative function of the plaza and actively bring people into the sculpture's context." The sculpture, he said, would change the space of the plaza. "After the piece is created, the space will be understood primarily as a function of the sculpture."

On Serra's terms, "Tilted Arc" is a huge success. It certainly changed the plaza, making it wholly subservient to the sculptural context. The trouble is that not many office workers want a sculptural experience twice a day (four times if they go out for lunch). Not this particular sculptural experience, at any rate. As Serra said, his audience is a limited one. And I think it is perfectly legitimate to question whether public spaces and public funds are the right context for work that appeals to so few people—no matter how far it advances the concept of sculpture.

What should be done, then, about "Tilted Arc"? What *has* been done is clearly lamentable—public hearings called by an administrator who had said in advance that he favored the sculpture's removal. Mr. Diamond's panel decided, after deliberating, that the sculpture should be removed, and this recommendation was duly forwarded to

Dwight Ink, the G.S.A.'s acting administrator in Washington (the previous acting administrator, Ray Kline, had retired from office the day before the hearings began). Mr. Ink, whom nobody seems to know much about, will shortly decide on the sculpture's fate. Serra has let it be known that if the G.S.A. decides for removal he will seek an injunction claiming breach of contract. A lot of his time would then be spent in litigation, and a lot of money would be made by lawyers. This sorry state of affairs seems to cry out for redress—something along the lines, perhaps, of Alvin Lane's suggestion that the G.S.A. set up a fair procedure for reevaluating its controversial commissions.

Even if you feel, though, that the G.S.A. made a mistake in commissioning "Tilted Arc" (as I think it did), there is something to be said for the hated monster. In its rough, confrontational way, it has pushed the whole notion of public art—what it is, what it could or should be—into clearer focus for a great many people. It is already a landmark, and it will continue to be one for years to come, even if it goes away.

# Storm in the Plaza

*From a hearing in New York City in March on the issue of whether to relocate Richard Serra's* Tilted Arc, *a sculpture commissioned by the federal government for the plaza of the Jacob Javits Federal Building in lower Manhattan. The hearing was convened by William Diamond, regional administrator of the General Services Administration, in response to the demand by many of the people who work in the building that the sculpture be removed. In April, Diamond recommended that* Tilted Arc *be relocated. A final decision by the GSA is pending. The testimony below has been edited for space.*

REPRESENTATIVE TED WEISS: Imagine, if you will, this curved slab of welded steel twelve feet high, 120 feet long, and weighing over seventy-three tons bisecting the street in front of your house, and you can imagine the reaction to *Tilted Arc* of those who live and work in the area.

Adding to the shock effect is the sculpture's natural oxide coating, which gives it the appearance of a rusted metal wall. Many who first viewed Tilted Arc regarded it as an abandoned piece of construction material, a relic perhaps too large and cumbersome to move.

The artist is said to have intended with this piece to "alter and dislocate the decorative function of the plaza." If that was the intent, one may conclude from the sculpture's harsh, disorienting effect that the artist has eloquently succeeded.

But what of those who live and work nearby? The sculpture cuts a huge swath across the center of the plaza, dividing it in two and acting as a barrier to the building's main doorways. Access to the building is awkward and confusing, and the normal walking patterns of those who enter and exit the building are disrupted.

The time has come to find a new location for *Tilted Arc.*

Mr. Serra argues that because his work is site specific, moving it to another location would destroy it. It has, he maintains, a proprietary claim upon the plaza just as real as that of a painting to its canvas. I suggest that there are other valid claims upon the plaza that conflict with Mr. Serra's, and that the scales tip in their favor. The community—those thousands of people who live and work in the area—has the right to reclaim this small oasis for the respite and relaxation for which it was intended.

Mr. Serra, I do not wish to see your work destroyed. I simply would like to see it in a more felicitous location.

RICHARD SERRA: My name is Richard Serra and I am an American sculptor.

I don't make portable objects. I don't make works that can be relocated or site adjusted. I make works that deal with the environmental components of given places. The scale, size, and location of my site-specific works are determined by the topography of the site, whether it be urban, landscape, or an architectural enclosure. My works become part of and are built into the structure of the site, and they often restructure, both conceptually and perceptually, the organization of the site.

My sculptures are not objects for the viewer to stop and stare at. The historical purpose of placing sculpture on a pedestal was to establish a separation between the sculpture and the viewer. I am interested in creating a behavioral space in which the viewer interacts with the sculpture in its context.

One's identity as a person is closely connected with one's experience of space and place. When a known space is changed through the inclusion of a site-specific sculpture, one is called upon to relate to the space differently. This is a condition that can be engendered only by sculpture. This experience of space may startle some people.

When the government invited me to propose a sculpture for the plaza it asked for a permanent, site-specific sculpture. As the phrase implies, a site-specific sculpture is one that is conceived and created in relation to the particular conditions of a specific site, and only to those conditions.

To remove *Tilted Arc*, therefore, would be to destroy it.

The final decision to install *Tilted Arc* was based upon the GSA's full knowledge of the sculpture, and the agency made an explicit commitment that the work would not be removed or dismantled.

It has been suggested that the public did not choose to install the work in the first place. In fact, the choice of the artist and the decision to install the sculpture permanently in the plaza were made by a public entity: the GSA. Its determination was made on the basis of national standards and carefully formulated procedures, and a jury system ensured impartiality and the selection of art of lasting value. The selection of this sculpture was, therefore, made by, and on behalf of, the public.

The agency made its commitments and signed a contract. If its decision is reversed in response to pressure from outside sources, the integrity of governmental programs related to the arts will be compromised, and artists of integrity will not participate. If the government can destroy works of art when confronted with such pressure, its capacity to foster artistic diversity and its power to safeguard freedom of creative expression will be in jeopardy.

JUDGE DOMINICK DICARLO: I had my first encounter with *Tilted Arc* after learning that I was being considered for appointment to the United States Court of International Trade. I was driving on Centre Street when I saw it. What is it? It's a 120-foot-by-twelve-foot rusted piece of iron. Having just returned from visiting our embassies in Rome, Islamabad, Rangoon, and Bangkok, I concluded that this rusted iron object was an anti-terrorist barricade, part of a crash program to protect United States government buildings against terrorist activities. But why such a huge barricade? Was this an overreaction? Why in cities where terrorist activity is much greater are comparatively attractive high-way dividers and concrete pillars sufficient to do the job?

After my appointment to the court, I was told that this was art. Was it a thing of beauty? Could be, since beauty is in the eyes of the beholder. Could its maker be making a political statement? Perhaps it was a discarded and rusted piece of the iron curtain. Or perhaps its author was expressing his views on trade policy. This is the Court of International Trade. Was his iron barrier symbolic of a protectionist viewpoint?

We don't have to guess why the iron wall was placed in the plaza. Those responsible have told us. It was to alter and dislocate the decorative function of the plaza, to redefine the space, to change the viewers' experience of that plaza. Simply put, their intention was to destroy the plaza's original artistic concept, the concept of its architects.

To object to the removal of the iron wall on the basis of an honest, moral right to preserve the integrity of the work is astounding, since the sculptor's intent was to destroy another artistic creation.

This may top the usual example of chutzpa: the person who kills his mother and father and then asks for mercy on the grounds that he is an orphan.

PETER HIRSCH: I am the research director and legal counsel for the Association of Immigration Attorneys. We are constantly at 26 Federal Plaza, since that is where the Immigration Service is located.

My membership has authorized me to say that we are entirely opposed to *Tilted Arc*. My own personal view is that a good place to put *Tilted Arc* would be in the Hudson River. That is not a facetious comment. Westway is about to be built, and I am told that they are going to have to put artificial things in the river to provide shelter for the striped bass. I think *Tilted Arc* would make a very fine shelter.

FRED HOFFMAN: I am an art historian and curator of contemporary art associated with many of the leading cultural organizations in Los Angeles.

We can learn more about ourselves, about the nature of our social relations, and about the nature of the spaces we inhabit and depend upon by keeping *Tilted Arc* than we

ever could by languishing in the alleged pleasures of a Serra-less plaza.

One of the fundamental realities about an important work of art such as *Tilted Arc* is that it does not simply sit down, roll over, and play dead. This work does not have as its intention pleasing, entertaining, or pacifying. By structuring an experience that is continually active, dynamic, and expansive, *Tilted Arc* makes sure that we do not fall asleep, mindless and indifferent to our destiny and to the increasing scarcity of freedom in an increasingly banal, undifferentiated, and style-oriented world.

VICKIE O'DOUGHERTY: I am a physical security specialist for the Federal Protection and Safety Division of the GSA.

My main purpose here is to present the security angle, which affects us in the execution of our duties. I consider *Tilted Arc* to be a security hazard, or disadvantage.

My main contention is that it presents a blast wall effect. It's 120 feet long, twelve feet high, and angled toward two federal buildings. The front curvature of the design is such that it could vent an explosion both upward and at an angle toward both buildings.

In the past, there have been several terrorist explosions on federal property. Many times a wall or something like it was used to vent the explosion against the building.

Another problem is graffiti. That wall—pardon, *Tilted Arc*—is used more for graffiti purposes than any of the other walls. And most of the graffiti is on the far side, where we cannot see the graffiti artists at work.

Basically, we feel that if *Tilted Arc* stays, we can adapt. But if there was an explosion on our side of the sculpture, there would be a great deal of property damage in the form of shattering glass. If it happened during the day, this could mean loss of life.

WILLIAM RUBIN: I am director of the Department of Painting and Sculpture at the Museum of Modern Art.

Like many creations of modern art, *Tilted Arc* is a challenging work that obliges us to question received values in general and the nature of art and of art's relation to the public in particular.

About one hundred years ago the Impressionists and post-Impressionists (Monet, Gauguin, Cézanne, for example), artists whose works are today prized universally, were being reviled as ridiculous by the public and the established press. At about the same time, the Eiffel Tower was constructed, only to be greeted by much the same ridicule. Leading architects of the day as well as writers and philosophers, to say nothing of the man on the street, condemned the tower as a visual obscenity.

As these examples suggest, truly challenging works of art require a period of time before their artistic language can be understood by the broader public.

I must say that I have never heard of a decision to remove a public monument being settled by popular vote. If that is what is being contemplated here, it seems to me a most dangerous precedent. Moreover, the decision should, it seems to me, involve the sentiments of a much wider circle than simply those who work in the immediate neighborhood. For society as a whole has a stake in such works of art.

Certainly the consideration of any such move should not be a response to pressure tactics and, above all, should not take place before the sculpture's artistic language can become familiar.

I therefore propose that consideration of this issue be deferred for at least ten years.

JOEL KOVEL: I am a writer and a professor at the New School for Social Research.

This very hearing proves the subversiveness, and hence the value, of *Tilted Arc.* Its very tilt and rust remind us that the gleaming and heartless steel and glass structures of the state apparatus can one day pass away. It therefore creates an unconscious sense of opposition and hope.

This opposition is itself a creative act, as, indeed, this hearing is a creative act. I would submit that the true measure of a free and democratic society is that it permits opposition of this sort. Therefore, it is essential that this hearing result in the preservation of Serra's work as a measure of the opposition this society can tolerate.

JOSEPH LIEBMAN: I am the attorney in charge of the International Trade Field Office, Civil Division, U.S. Department of Justice, with offices located at 26 Federal Plaza.

I have worked at 26 Federal Plaza since 1969. While the plaza never fulfilled all my expectations, until 1980 I regarded it as a relaxing space where I could walk, sit, and contemplate in an unhurried manner. Every now and then rays of sunshine bathed the plaza, creating new vistas and moods for its vibrant, unchallenged space.

I remember those moments. I remember the cool spray of the fountain misting the hot air. I remember the band concerts. I remember the musical sounds of neighborhood children playing on the plaza while their mothers rocked baby carriages. I remember walking freely in the plaza, contemplating the examination of a witness, undisturbed by the presence of other people engaged in conversation or young lovers holding hands. I also remember my dreams of additional seating areas, more cultural events, temporary outdoor exhibits of painting and sculpture, and ethnic dance festivals.

All of those things are just memories now.

Regardless of the thoughtfulness and artistic accomplishment of its creator, *Tilted*

345

*Arc* fails to add significant value to the plaza. The arc has condemned us to lead emptier lives. The children, the bands, and I no longer visit the plaza. Instead, the arc divides space against itself. Whatever artistic value the arc may have does not justify the disruption of the plaza and our lives.

The arc, a creation of mortal hand, should yield. Relocate it in another land. Reprieve us from our desolate condemnation.

DOUGLAS CRIMP: I am a critic and the managing editor of the cultural journal *October*. I want to speak here not as a professional, however, but as a member of the public.

What makes me feel manipulated here today is that I am being forced to argue for art as against some other social function. I am asked to line up on the side of sculpture and against those who are on the side of, say, concerts, or maybe picnic tables. But of course all of these things have social functions. It is a measure of the meager nature of our public social life that we are asked, in a travesty of democratic procedure, to fight it out over the crumbs of social experience.

I believe that we have been polarized here so that we do not notice the real issue: the fact that our social experience is deliberately and drastically limited by our public officials.

The view that those who have convened this hearing hold of us, the public, can be discerned from a passage in a letter written by chief Judge Edward Re, who has been leading the fight to remove *Tilted Arc* since the day it was erected. After a long list of complaints against *Tilted Arc* (including the absolutely surreal claim that it causes rat problems) Judge Re writes, and I quote, "Finally, but by no means of minor importance, is the loss of efficient security surveillance. The placement of this wall across the plaza obscures the view of security personnel, who have no way of knowing what is taking place on the other side of the wall."

Well, I would submit that it is we, the public, who are on the other side of this wall, and that it is *we* who Judge Re so fears and despises that he wants that wall torn down in order that we may be properly subjected to surveillance.

It is no small measure of the success of *Tilted Arc* that it has elicited this repugnant view of the public and brought it into the public realm.

I urge that this wall be kept in place and that we construct our social lives in relation to it: that is, out of sight of those who would conceive of social life as something to be feared, despised, and surveyed.

DONALD JUDD: We need to revive a secular version of sacrilege to categorize the attempt to destroy Richard Serra's work in Federal Plaza in Manhattan.

Art is not to be destroyed, either old or new. It is visible civilization. Those who want to ruin Serra's work are barbarians.

MICHAEL HALL: I am head of the sculpture department at the Cranbrook Academy of Art, Detroit.

Perhaps the public agencies that generate and institute public art projects have failed to execute their mandate completely. In a simple analogy, I would expect a public health agency to undertake a broad educational program in any community where it expected to begin mass immunization programs. People rarely submit to injections of vaccine without some idea of why a needle is being pushed into their skin.

Evolving art, because it is witness to evolving thought, pricks our emotional and intellectual skin. The vaccine is not ineffective just because the injection is uncomfortable. This is not simply to assert that because it tastes bad, it's good for you. On the other hand, appetites *are* cultivated, and the arc is a part of a banquet that is being served up for our pleasure and our nutrition.

346

An agency and an idea may well have failed here, rather than an artist and a sculpture.

HOLLY SOLOMAN: I had a gallery in SoHo and now I've moved to Fifty-seventh Street. I don't feel qualified to discuss the law part of this and I don't feel I have time to discuss the taste or the art historical importance of this piece. I can only tell you, gentlemen, that this is business, and to take down the piece is bad business. Mr. Serra is one of the leading sculptors of our time. I sell many paintings. I try very hard to reach people about contemporary art, but the bottom line is that this has financial value, and you really have to understand that you have a responsibility to the financial community. You cannot destroy property.

PHIL LA BASI: I have been a federal employee for twenty-two years, about eleven years in this building.

First of all, I would like to say that I really resent the implication that those of us who oppose this structure are cretins or some sort of reactionaries.

It seems to be very typical of self-serving artists and so-called pseudointellectuals that when they disagree with something someone else has to say, they attack the person. So I am not going to attack the artist.

What I see there is something that looks like a tank trap to prevent an armed attack from Chinatown in case of a Soviet invasion. In my mind it probably wouldn't even do that well, because one good Russian tank could probably take it out.

To be very serious, I wouldn't call it *Tilted Arc*. To me it looks like crooked metal or bent metal. I think we can call anything art if we call that art. I think any one of these people here could come along with an old broken bicycle that perhaps got run over by a car, or some other piece of material, and pull it up and call it art and name it something. I think that was what was done here.

The poor federal employees, us cretins, us reactionaries, us poor slobs that work at 26 Federal Plaza, are given a bad name because we are not intellectual and we don't appreciate art. Well, many of us have art in our homes and many of us appreciate it, but that thing out there—by no stretch of the imagination, so help me God—I could not call that art if you paid me to call it art.

SHIRLEY PARIS: I am here as a private citizen, although I work in the area.

*Tilted Arc* is in my opinion the Berlin Wall of Foley Square, and like its prototype, it should have been knocked down during construction.

This gigantic strip of rust is an arrogant, nose-thumbing gesture at the government, at the civil servants who serve the government, and at those of us who make up much of the regular daytime population of Foley Square.

It is bad enough for the government and its civil servants to be the perennial targets of the public and the press alike, but for us to be denigrated by artists as well is, to say the least, to compound the insult.

It should be noted that many of the people who visit this building are going to the Immigration and Naturalization Service to apply for citizenship. They are eager to become citizens of our great nation and leave behind their original, and often oppressive, homelands. Yet as they enter the building from which they hope to emerge with the promise of a brighter future, they are compelled to circumvent this rusty reminder of totalitarianism.

FRANK STELLA: In the matter under discussion here the government and the artist, Richard Serra, have acted in good faith and have executed their responsibilities in exemplary fashion.

347

The objections to their efforts are without compelling merit. The objections are singular, peculiar, and idiosyncratic. The government and the artist have acted as the body of society attempting to meet civilized, one might almost say civilizing, goals—in this case, the extension of visual culture into public spaces.

The attempt to reverse their efforts serves no broad social purpose and is contrary to the honest, searching efforts that represent the larger and truer goals of society.

Satisfaction for the dissenters is not a necessity. The continued cultural aspirations of the society are a necessity, as is the protection of these aspirations.

The dissenters have accomplished enough by having their objections heard, discussed, and publicized. Whatever merit their case may have, it is now part of the public record and will have its proper influence in future decisions involving matters of this kind.

To destroy the work of art and simultaneously incur greater public expense in that effort would disturb the status quo for no gain. Furthermore, the precedent set can only have wasteful and unnecessary consequences.

There is no reason to encourage harassment of the government and the artist working toward a public good. There are no circumstances here to warrant further administrative or judicial action. If the matter stands as it is, no one will experience any serious harm or duress and one more work of art will be preserved.

This dispute should not be allowed to disrupt a successful working relationship between government agencies and citizen artists.

Finally, no public dispute should force the gratuitous destruction of any benign, civilizing effort.

DANNY KATZ: My name is Danny Katz and I work in this building as a clerk. My friend Vito told me this morning that I am a philistine. Despite that, I am getting up to speak.

Listen fast, because I hear seconds being counted and tempers are high.

The blame falls on everyone involved in this project from the beginning for forgetting the human element. I don't think this issue should be elevated into a dispute between the forces of ignorance and art, or art versus government. I really blame government less because it has long ago outgrown its human dimension. But from the artists I expected a lot more.

I didn't expect to hear them rely on the tired and dangerous reasoning that the government has made a deal, so let the rabble live with the steel because it's a deal. That kind of mentality leads to wars. We had a deal with Vietnam.

I didn't expect to hear the arrogant position that art justifies interference with the simple joys of human activity in a plaza. It's not a great plaza by international standards, but it is a small refuge and place of revival for people who ride to work in steel containers, work in sealed rooms, and breathe recirculated air all day. Is the purpose of art in public places to seal off a route of escape, to stress the absence of joy and hope? I can't believe that this was the artistic intention, yet to my sadness this for me has been the dominant effect of the work, and it's all the fault of its position and location.

I can accept anything in art, but I can't accept physical assault and complete destruction of pathetic human activity.

No work of art created with a contempt for ordinary humanity and without respect for the common element of human experience can be great. It will always lack a dimension.

I don't believe the contempt is in the work. The work is strong enough to stand alone in a better place. I would suggest to Mr. Serra that he take advantage of this opportunity to walk away from this fiasco and demand that the work be moved to a place where it will better reveal its beauty.

# A Tale of Two Memorials

*Elizabeth Hess*

*War memorials may be too important to leave simply to artists and architects.*
—Congressman Henry J. Hyde

Advocates of modernism and realism often have difficulty appreciating each other. As old as our century, the conflict between these two points of view has recently been elevated to a new stage—the nation's capital—where two memorials for Vietnam veterans, one abstract and the other realistic, will soon be permanently at war with each other. The bitter Washington debate surrounding the erection of these two monuments has itself been warlike. What began as a clearly defined project to memorialize Americans who died in Vietnam has become, during the past two years, a battlefield echoing with the same rhetoric once heard at Kent State. So far there have been no casualties in this art war, only compromises.

Original plans had called for a single memorial to be built on Washington's prestigious mall between the Lincoln Memorial and the Washington Monument. Its design was to be selected by a jury of specialists from participants in a nation-wide competition. In May of 1981 the judges unanimously chose as their $20,000 prize-winner the entry of Maya Ying Lin, then a 21-year-old Yale undergraduate. But soon after Lin's moder-

nist design for an austerely simple, V-shaped wall was made public, extremely vocal protests began to be heard in Washington, and within a short time a small group of influential men—some in government and some private citizens—launched a noisy, finally unsuccessful campaign to block construction of Lin's memorial. In spite of their efforts, ground was broken in March of 1982 and seven months later the memorial was on its site.

But the opponents of Lin's design did not admit defeat; though they could not prevent the erection of her monument, they did manage to arrange for the addition of a second memorial. A larger-than-life-size realistic statue of three GIs in battle dress, designed by Frederick Hart, a figurative sculptor from Washington, D.C., is presently under construction. Accompanied by a 50-foot flagpole, Hart's statue (which has thus far only been seen in maquette form) will be placed on the memorial site by Veterans Day, 1983.

The story of the two memorials begins with Jan Scruggs, who was born in Washington, D.C., graduated from high school and went straight to Vietnam. Half of his company, the U.S. Army Light Infantry Brigade, was killed or wounded between 1969 and 1970, and Scruggs himself landed in the hospital for two months. Upon his return to the U.S., Scruggs enrolled at American University and became deeply involved in the problems of the demobilized Vietnam troops.

Elizabeth Hess is a freelance writer living in Washington, D.C. She is currently writing a book on feminist art.

From *Art in America* (April 1983): 120–126. Reprinted by permission of *Art in America*.

Eventually attending graduate school, he completed a study on the psychological adjustments facing Vietnam veterans, and in 1976 presented his findings to a Senate subcommittee. Scruggs's sincere if somewhat naive aspiration was to replace the veteran's nightmare with the American Dream.

In 1979, Scruggs incorporated the Vietnam Veterans Memorial Fund (VVMF) of which he remains president. Its specific and only purpose was to erect a national monument honoring those who had died in the war. According to a press release issued by the Fund, the monument was to be "without political content," and it was to be funded by contributions from private sources. That year legislation was introduced in Congress to allocate land for the planned memorial and the project was eventually signed into law by President Carter in 1980. As is usual in such matters, all considerations for the memorial—design, landscape, planning, esthetics—would have to be approved by the National Capital Planning Commission (NCPC), the Commission of Fine Arts (CFA) and the Department of the Interior. (Those familiar with the process of trying to get anything built in the District of Columbia know that it is at best an extremely arduous procedure.)

The VVMF members decided to select a design by holding a juried competition open to all American citizens over 18, even though the Fund would thereby lose control over the final result. Advised by landscape architect Paul Spreiregen, the VVMF placed the decision in the hands of eight men: landscape architects Hideo Sasaki and Garrett Eckbo; architects Harry Weese and Pietro Belluschi; sculptors Costantino Nivola, James Rosati and Richard H. Hunt; and Grady Clay, editor of *Landscape Architecture*. The seed money to launch the contest was provided by Texas computer millionaire H. Ross Perot. (Ironically, Perot would later be among those who would attempt to dismantle the entire competition process.)

There were two design requirements stipulated by the VVMF that severely limited all entries. First, the names of the 57,939 Americans who died, or are still missing, in Vietnam had to be engraved somewhere on the memorial. Second, contestants were required to be sensitive to the Washington Monument and the Lincoln Memorial, which would bracket the site. Constitution Gardens, as the area is called, is the President's backyard—it's sacred territory. These considerations pretty much ruled out a vertical monument, and a wall of some sort would obviously be necessary for the names.

The competition, which was announced in October, 1980, received 1,421 entries, a surprisingly large response. In accord with contest rules, no names were attached to any of the proposals. Thus, when Maya Lin's design was selected in May of the following year, everyone was astonished to find the winner was female, Chinese-American and an undergraduate. Lin's competition-winning design was a combination Minimalist sculpture-earthwork. It consisted of two walls—each 250 feet long and made of 140 panels—which met at a 125-degree angle; beginning at ground level at each extreme, both walls gradually rose to a height of 10 feet at the monument's center, or the apex of the angle. Working within and taking full advantage of the Fund's guidelines, Lin made some innovational decisions: she chose polished black granite as her material, thus turning the walls into mirrors; and she decided to list the 57,939 Vietnam casualties not alphabetically, as is customary, but in the order in which they were killed. ("I wanted to return the vets to the time-frame of the war," Lin explains, "and in the process, I wanted them to see their own reflection in the names.") Furthermore, rather than simply setting the two walls on top of the ground, Lin's design proposed to build them into a rise in the landscape, with only their inscribed sides visible. The spectator, walking downward along the length of either wall, would thus have the dramatic sensation of descending into the earth. In view of the response that Lin's walls would later provoke, it is amusing to speculate that initially her design was probably chosen because of its utter modesty—its simple, straight lines, its unobtrusive character. The jurors may well have thought that Lin's proposal was least likely to make waves in the ultrasensitive District of Columbia.

On Oct. 13, 1981, Lin attended one of the regular monthly meetings of the Board of Directors of the CFA, prepared to discuss granite samples. The CFA's chairman, J. Carter Brown, who has been called Washington's "arbiter of excellence," is also the director of the National Gallery. This commission, originally established by Congress in 1910, was created to give expert advice on works of art or architecture acquired or commissioned by the government. At an earlier meeting, Brown had already echoed the jurors' unanimous approval of Lin's design, and the October meeting included on its agenda various details of a largely site-specific character. As are all CFA monthly meetings, the Oct. 13 session was open to the public and transcripts were made of the proceedings for the record. There was an unexpected guest at this meeting—Tom Carhart, a member of the VVMF and a former infantry platoon leader with two Purple Hearts. Carhart had helped raise funds for the memorial and, in his enthusiasm for the project, had even entered a design in the competition himself—the first art work he had ever attempted.

Carhart was not happy with Lin's design. He characterized it as "the most insulting and demeaning memorial to our experience that was possible." He passionately argued that it was a memorial to "the war at home" rather than to the one in Southeast Asia: "When I came home from Vietnam in 1968," he said, "I was literally spat upon as I walked through the Chicago airport in my uniform by some girl in a band of hippies. That spit hurt." Carhart charged that Lin's design was geared to "those who would still spit," and he called the proposed monument a "degrading ditch." He was the first to publicly attack the color of the stone: "Black," he said, is "the universal color of shame, sorrow and degradation in all races, all societies worldwide." Carhart demanded a white memorial.

Ross Perot in Texas was also unhappy with Lin's design. A legendary and somewhat enigmatic figure, even in a state known for its cowboy capitalists, Perot is notorious for such expensive ventures as his unsuccessful hiring of a group of mercenaries to bring home POWs from North Vietnam and his financing of a surveillance mission into Iran during the hostage crisis. No one in Washington has been anxious to articulate Perot's exact role in the memorial controversy. Off the record, however, many people have targeted him as the organizer of the opposition to Lin's design. ("When powerful people are against you," Scruggs whispered to me over the phone, "it may not be in your interest to answer questions.") Perot, himself, was more than willing to talk to me about his side of the story in a telephone interview. To him, Lin's memorial was "a slap in the face." But he says he wasn't surprised that the memorial looked like a "tombstone" since "Maya did design it in a class on funereal architecture at Yale."

Rumor has it that when Perot's money talks, people listen. After contributing $160,000 towards funding the memorial, Perot may have expected to have some say in its final disposition. His strategy for overturning the decision of the jurors was to create the impression that the veterans them-selves had rejected Lin's design. Scruggs be-lieves that Perot flew in veterans from around the country to lobby against the jurors' choice. The Texan flatly denies this and says that all he did was "try to get the Fund off their ego trip long enough to remember their constituency of two million vets." To do so, he personally financed a poll of 587 POWs. According to Perot's poll, 67 percent of those polled disliked the original design; 70 percent thought the color of the memorial should be white; 96 percent thought the American flag should be prom-inently displayed on the memorial site. Though on the basis of Perot's statistics it seemed as if the majority of veterans were against the design, the memorial's supporters have charged that, since POWs are probably a good deal more conservative than the average veteran, the survey was skewed. Moreover, Scruggs claims that when he had the poll checked by an expert, he was told that it wasn't worth the paper it was written on. Perot, on the other hand, brushes aside these objections, saying, "Losers always dis-credit the winners." He insists that the poll was sent to POWs only as a test mailing.

Meanwhile in Washington during the fall of 1981, Maya Lin was beginning to be viewed as something of a radical. Her work, which had initially been praised by the CFA because it was "apolitical," was now labeled subversive. James Webb, for example, a highly decorated marine and author of a Vietnam novel titled *Fields of Fire*, called it a "wailing wall for anti-draft demon-strators." In some quarters, the monument's V-shape was being interpreted as the symbol of the antiwar movement. Carhart had al-ready referred to the black stone as a "black" spot in American history." Though one critic honorifically described the listing of names in nonalphabetical order as "a profoundly metaphoric twist with universal implications," Carhart called it a "random scattering . . . such that neither brother nor father nor lover nor friend could ever be found." The fact that it was possible from one vantage point to see the monument as sinking into the earth was interpreted by some commentators as an admission of guilt—an acknowledgment that we had com-mitted crimes in Vietnam.

The VVMF, too, was under attack. In Scrugg's view, "The memorial's enemies were mostly members of the New Right" and they were pressuring the Fund to com-promise their original plan. According to *The Washington Post*, it was Senator Jeremiah Denton who led the fight against Lin's memorial on Capitol Hill, and the campaign picked up considerable steam on its way to the White House. Even Phyllis Schlafly be-came an art-critic-for-a-day, calling the memorial a "tribute to Jane Fonda" in the pages of the *Washington Inquirer,* the Moral Majority's weekly newspaper. As the flak got heavier, Jan Scruggs admits that he began to suffer from battle fatigue. It seemed to him that if he wanted to dedicate the memorial by Veterans Day, 1982—then less than a year away—a compromise was the only way out.

It was clear to most observers that the battle over the memorial was being fought entirely with political ammunition. Attempt-ing, as one Senator put it, "to neutralize this apolitical statement," the opponents of Lin's memorial could at most hope for additions to the site. They could not block construction completely nor even censor Lin's design without angering the press and the art world. It was also evident that James Watt, the Secretary of the Interior, held the final card, since his authorization was required before the VVMF could break ground. Watt, who would subsequently make his position clear in a carefully worded letter to the CFA, was refusing to grant permission until suitable ad-ditions to the memorial were agreed upon by the Fund, the CFA and the National Capital Planning Commission.

By January '82, the debate suddenly moved behind closed doors. A loosely organized committee, chaired by Senator John Warner and including, among other conservatives, Milton Copulos—a Vietnam veteran and currently an energy expert with the Heritage Foundation (a well-known right-wing think-tank)—was formed and Scruggs was invited to meet with them in face-to-face combat in order to settle the dispute. The press was not invited to this kangaroo court and no public record of proceedings exists. But according to a statement issued by the VVMF more than a year later, the group, which had convened on Jan. 27, 1982, agreed, after a nasty fight, to support the addition to the memorial site of a sculpture and a flag, but "with no location specified." The opponents of Lin's memorial also agreed "to cease their political effort to block approval of the design and to allow the planned March groundbreaking to occur on schedule." A second meeting was planned to "consider various alternative designs for the sculpture."

Now that the opponents of Lin's memorial had won their first major battle, they turned their attention to the strategic placement of the statue and the flag. According to members of the Fund, when Senator Warner's group reconvened in March of '82 to discuss designs for the sculpture, it was Ross Perot who changed the committee's agenda. Realizing that placement of the sculpture would be a crucial issue, he urged the group to agree about it at once. When a vote was taken, the majority of those present wanted the flag placed on top of the memorial, at the vertex of the walls, and the sculpture placed on the ground below, at the middle of the V. According to the Fund's printed statement, this majority opinion was not surprising: "As at the prior meeting, the handful of VVMF representatives were far outnumbered by the group of opponents which Mr. Perot and others had organized to attend the meeting." But the votes taken at this meeting were not final. All decisions still had to go through Watt, the CFA and the NCPC.

What was most significant about these meetings was that the VVMF had been convinced to sponsor the additional sculpture and flag. Realizing that it was the only way to get Lin's piece built, Scruggs presented the VVMF's new proposal to the proper authorities, and in March work on the monument finally began. In April, without Maya Lin's knowledge, a sculpture panel was chosen by the VVMF to select an artist for the second memorial; it was comprised entirely of Vietnam veterans who had been involved in the dispute and included two people who supported Lin's memorial—Arthur Mosley and William Jayne—and two who opposed it—James Webb and Milton Copulos. In July, Frederick Hart was commissioned by the VVMF (for a fee neither party will make public) to design another Vietnam memorial, and by September Hart's maquette for the statue was unveiled.

The conservatives had wanted a statue in the tradition of the Iwo Jima memorial, which was based on an actual photograph. But Hart knew that there were few heroic moments in the Vietnam War. (After all, one of the most memorable photographs in the entire Vietnam debacle was of the shot taken at point-blank range into a guerrilla's head by Nguyen Ngoc Loan, then chief of police in Saigon.) Hart's model is a competent homage to an abstraction called "vets"—as traditional as a Hallmark card. Three young men, one of whom is black, stand on a small base. All three look to their right, perhaps (depending on their final sitting) towards Lin's walls. There is nothing to identify these soldiers specifically with Vietnam other than their uniforms; the realism lies in the details of their military garb, in the gun thrown over a shoulder, the ammunition around a waist. The facial expressions of these soldiers are somewhat peculiar; they look stunned—more bewildered than heroic—but, of course, their features may change when the statue is executed at the projected scale of 8 feet.

When the maquette was made public last fall, its placement was still a matter of dispute. The members of Warner's committee who wanted the statue in the center of Lin's walls—in effect, penetrating her V—now began to fight an extended battle over the location of the second memorial. The issue was not settled until February, 1983, when after a great deal of acrimonious debate, it was finally decided that both Hart's statue and the flag would be placed 120 feet from Lin's walls, near the entrance to the memorial site. Hart himself supported this decision, understanding quite well that the two works of art would clash if placed too close together.

The decision to add a second memorial to the site has not been popular everywhere in Washington. Some of the negative feelings were expressed at last October's meeting of the CFA, when many witnesses testified against acceptance of Hart's model. Among them was Paul Spreiregen, the Washington landscape architect who was advisor to the original contest. "Imagine Arlington Cemetery," Spreiregen said, "with groups of larger-than-life soldiers, in various combat outfits, winding their way through the trees, coming up on headstones." Robert Lawrence, president of the American Institute of Architects, called the compromise a "concerted effort . . . by a few individuals unhappy with the design," even though Lin's design had been "applauded almost unanimously."

As many at the CFA meeting pointed out, the battle went beyond the memorial's design to the Vietnam war itself. Indeed, what the rhetoric of the memorial controver-sy reflected was the impossibility of separating the issue of Lin's design from opinions concerning the war; the controversy also revealed the naiveté of those members of the VVMF who had thought the memorial could be isolated from the war, and who had mandated the impossible—a "neutral" memorial.

Throughout this period, the VVMF and Lin's supporters tried to prove that there was nothing radical about her design, but Lin's enemies continued to see red reflected in the memorial's slick black walls. It was not simply the fact that the monument was abstract and black that angered them. Lin's memorial ran counter to tradition in several other important ways: it appeared to be sinking into the ground rather than towering above the site; it had an unconventional system of listing names; it was completely unheroic, totally nonaggressive. It could, in fact, be read as a pacifist piece. To add insult to injury, the eight male jurors had chosen a memorial with a distinctly female character, placing at the base of Washington's giant phallus a wide V-shape surrounded by a grassy mound. The memorial was hardly a "black gash of shame," but it could indeed be read as a radical statement about the war, and even as the expression of a female sensibility. The vast number of names inscribed on the wall comes across as a powerful antiwar statement. As a woman standing in front of the memorial remarked, "What an unbelievable waste."

And facing the myriad names, it is difficult for anyone *not* to question the purpose of the war. The reawakening of old conflicts about Vietnam has inevitably disturbed members of the Reagan administration; such reopened battle scars are too likely to suggest parallels with our current involvements in, for example, El Salvador. Lin's memorial functions as a powerful reminder of the potential consequences of our current foreign policy.

Towards the end of the memorial battle, Benjamin Forgey in *The Washington Post* underlined the essentially nonesthetic nature of the conflict. "Adding the sculpture and the flag," he wrote, "clearly was a political not an esthetic necessity." Even those critics who argued that Lin's memorial was too abstract for popular taste were attacking it from a political perspective. Tom Wolfe, who published a well-timed article in *The Washington Post* on the same day that the CFA heard testimony on the proposed additions, is a case in point. Calling Lin's memorial "non-bourgeois art," or art "that baffled the general public," Wolfe compared Lin's experience to that of Carl Andre in Hartford and Richard Serra in downtown Manhattan. He concluded that her memorial, too, was abstract and elitist. Yet no one, including Wolfe, has actually been baffled by the memorial. While Wolfe predictably lambasted the "Mullahs of Modernism," he also used this occasion to add the antiwar movement to his enemy list. Having referred to the memorial as a "perverse prank," he ended his vituperative piece with the already familiar phrase, "A tribute to Jane Fonda!"

If Lin's memorial is a tribute to Fonda, then Hart's is a tribute to John Wayne. It salutes the military establishment—the representatives of the American Legion, the Marine Corps League, the Naval Association and the Military Order of the Purple Heart—all of whom demanded an alternative to Lin's piece. What Hart's statue is not, however, is a tribute to the troops. In fact, no one has been anxious to hear from *them.* It is no secret that returning veterans were not welcomed home with open arms. There were no ticker-tape parades for an army that now has the highest suicide rate of any population of ex-GIs. "A few moments of honest conversation with any [veteran]," wrote critic Peter Marin in *The Nation,* "put to shame the versions of the war produced by our filmmakers,

novelists and many journalists." The veterans are as divided as the rest of the population about Vietnam—and about the memorial. "I can't imagine anyone being proud of what we did over there," commented John VanZwieten, who returned home and joined the Vietnam Veterans Against the War. Although he now lives in Washington, VanZwieten doesn't even want to see the memorial—not because it's a tribute to Jane, but in fact for quite the opposite reason. As one veteran put it in *About Face,* a newspaper handed out at the dedication ceremony, "Buttering up Vietnam veterans as 'forgotten heroes' is a slap in the face directed at millions in this country who resisted the war."

Thanks to the battle over the Vietnam memorial, Constitution Gardens will present two very different interpretations of the war. Though initially Lin's memorial may have had a certain political ambiguity, its juxtaposition with Hart's conservative statue will clearly emphasize its radical edge. Scrugg's original contention that America owed the veterans was neither radical nor conservative. It was a centrist position shared by millions of Americans including the families of those who came home in body bags. These are the thousands who flooded Washington for last year's dedication: one monument was more than enough for them. Veterans have been weeping in front of Lin's black walls. Their families have been eager to touch a name or take a rubbing. Visitors have left flowers, clothes, snapshots and personal treasures belonging to the dead. The reception to this cold, black, abstract object has in fact been overwhelmingly warm. As *The Washington Post* noted in its editorial column, "The argument over the memorial dissolves the moment you get there." When Hart's statue is in place, the two memorials will inevitably challenge each other with contrary points of view. But this is one confrontation that Maya Lin should easily win.

# 2000 and Beyond

## The New State of Illinois Center: Infamous, a Noble Effort, or Both?

*James Murphy*

Chicago is unique. Any student of architecture can recite the litany of Adler & Sullivan, Holabird & Roche, Burnham & Root, Jenney, Wright, and Mies that makes the city preeminent. Nor have its architectural awareness and spirit waned over the decades since these greats made history. Brash new ideas are a way of life in Chicago.

Enter a governor and an architect with a common desire to make a noticeable blip in this distinguished timeline. The result is Helmut Jahn's State of Illinois Center (SOIC), the building that provokes epithets or praise from polarized Chicagoans, and from many other quarters as well. There is reason for both. However, this does not preclude a combination of thoughts about this built paradox.

Chicago's grid plan is modified by the nonconforming Chicago river and parts of Wacker Drive. South and east of these diversions, the North Loop's grid is a given condition for most blocks, including the SOIC site, bounded by Clark, Randolph, LaSalle, and

James Murphy is Profession and Industry editor of *Progressive Architecture* and a Fellow in the American Institute of Architects.

"2000 and Beyond: The New State of Illinois Center: Infamous, a Noble Effort, or Both?," by James Murphy, from *Progressive Architecture* 66 (December 1985): 72–79. Copyright 1985 Penton Publishing. Reprinted with permission.

Lake Streets. The last few decades have been marked, in Chicago and other major cities, by the proliferation of urban plazas; Chicago's are often described as windswept and virtually deserted in winter and as inhospitable baking sheets in summer. Most are formal in geometry and orthogonal in relation to buildings and the grid.

Helmut Jahn designed this structure in a joint venture of Murphy/Jahn and Lester B. Knight & Associates. It has always been important to Jahn to hold the street line where applicable, and to draw other design parameters from various sources, whether in physical proximity or philosophical content. Priorities for SOIC included expressing its governmental status, relating to the height and scale of the adjacent City/County Building, providing direct links for surrounding government buildings with subway and elevated transit lines, and combining a sense of importance, vitality, and energy efficiency. It is intended that it provide a humane, stimulating environment, thus reestablishing "the social role of architecture."

In choosing the rotunda form, Jahn sought to imply *government,* recalling domed buildings historically associated with such facilities. On the west, north, and part of the east edges of the site, the street line was held. The height of the building and the material of its arcade are responses to the

City/County Building. The left over corner court is seen as an element, symbolically enclosed, leading into the main event, the atrium. Linkage with the elevated transit line parallel to the north facade will include a new station, yet to begin construction under a separate contract.

Several major programmatic directions, in many ways interrelated, have provided lively topics for discussion. "Open office" planning was taken to either new heights or ridiculous extremes, depending on who is asked. As a big symbolic step toward assuring the public of government's accessibility and aboveboard intentions, much of the upper-level office space is open to the atrium and has few walls elsewhere. Energy considerations are cited as part of the reason for a low-rise atrium solution with a combination of reflective and clear glazing, providing significant natural illumination. "Active" energy design includes an ice-making capability for handling cooling loads. Double glazing was part of the original scheme of things.

Beyond these most obvious influences, the intended layers and imagery get more complex. Jahn is not unsympathetic to the use of historical referents in his work, but he has interjected a distance in their expression. He cannot, he says, bring himself to be literal in his references. His goal has been to reinterpret or restate them in modern materials, to arrive at a new syntax. To date, SOIC has been his most ambitious built attempt at that synthesis of future and past. A truncated dome, keystones expressed in colored glass, and stone arcade piers that either "freestand" or fail to touch ground all play representational roles as interpreted by today's thesaurus. This building design sets forth enormous and, in many respects, worthy goals.

Does it "fit in?" How does it relate to its neighbors, its heritage, the grid and plazas of Chicago, or its stated intentions? Helmut Jahn does not like the word "contextual," citing its obvious overuse by architects to justify what they do. If the term, like Post-Modern, has lost whatever edge of specificity it had, it is still useful for getting a handle on relatively broad issues. The issue at SOIC is its "comfort factor" with its venerable or not-so-venerable adjacencies. To the City/County Building, acknowledgement of heights and, minimally, to materials, is present. To the Richard J. Daley Center it judiciously makes no noticeable gesture other than the grand foil of its curved corner/facade.

It is the combination of this sloped-back curve, the free-form plaza elements, the relatively low (17-story) height of the overall structure, and the majority of its surface cladding that gives SOIC its otherworldly aura. At present, it can be seen from Wacker Drive and the river, across cleared city lots. From this vantage point, it has an abstract beauty, the slope and the curves of its sliced east facade counterthrusting amid the staid boxes around it. However, at the closer range of the streets around it, it takes on a heavier, less graceful—albeit still alien—aspect. In Jahn's view, if a building can be contextual, SOIC is more so than most recent and more overt attempts. Contextual, it seems is in the eye of. . . .

Strict adherence to the street line on the west, north, and east reinforces the grid and the canyonlike aspects of LaSalle and Lake Streets. The plaza at the south and east makes the entry hierarchy obvious and is a reasonable transition on the way to the interior experience. The dematerializing arcade members that march on to define the antespace, however, were far more bewitching as a paper concept than as reality. The poetry and imagery are diminished. There is something about a stone ruin supported by lollipop-stick columns that disappoints.

Commentary about the appearance of the glass cladding, its color, and its detailing has almost become a bore in its abundance. If you don't like these shades of blue and salmon, you will have trouble with this building. Color is hard to be objective about; the details are easier. The curved wall is beautiful, while the design of other elements of the curtain wall succumbs to a combination of influences, many producing less than positive results.

Possibly one of the most exciting prospects held out by a handful of architects in the past few years has been that of polychromy through glass variations. Tried in other places by other architects, the technique has produced less than promised. Jahn has put a whole lot of faith in this approach and has come away with good results, even if the gradations are not all that obvious to the casual observer. Fading from medium dark below to almost white at the top, from reflective to transparent to opaque, the glazing at SOIC—in all of its shades and types—has top billing. The darkest blue, incidentally, represents the maximum allowable amount of blue pigment in the ceramic frit applied to the glass; while applied to "clear" glass results in a green cast. Glass keystones, stripes, and bands perform at least a fair measure of their abstract role.

Silicone glazing, producing the nearly seamless curved wall, was the architects' first choice for the whole building. At the time the specifics were being refined, however, a limit on the liability the manufacturers were willing to accept also limited the area of silicone glazing. It is pleasant, if pointless, to speculate on how the color variations in the glass skin would have looked, uninterrupted by mullions. At the least, a higher degree of elegance on the straight walls would have been a vast improvement. Brought down to people level, concern over the heavy detailing is overshadowed by thoughts of snow removal equipment being deftly choreographed to thread its way around and between glass planes.

From the outside, the prospect of a magnificent interior space is conveyed dramatically by the clear glass slice at the center of the curved wall. Not since Saarinen's Ford Foundation went up in New York has a building displayed such a dramatic atrium to busy city streets in this way. Upon entering, even the most seasoned veteran of the atrium revolution will gawk. A 17-story-high space topped by a rotunda 160 feet in diameter causes that reaction, even if it is involuntary.

Ringed at the lower levels by shops and restaurants, and on the upper tiers by state offices, this space is what the building is really about. The reason for the steel columns outside becomes clearer, if not more desirable, from inside. Here, a very elegant and spidery structure enfolds the void and becomes the matrix on which everything is hung. Layers of office floor trays encircle the atrium, and the mechanics of getting up and down are celebrated. Seemingly freestanding elevator banks and articulated suspended stairways lend an air of kinetic sculpture, an impression compounded almost to limitless degrees by the kaleidoscopic reflective spandrel rings. These segmented bands turn the reflections of moving people into ever changing Duchamp paintings. The views, whether from top, middle, or ground floor, are spectacular and endlessly changing.

Also celebrated are the nuts and bolts that make the assemblage stand up and function. This ethic is at its peak around the elevators, where bolts, clamps, ducts, wiring, cables, and counterweights all parade their properties. Contrasted with this gutsy display are the pristine details of the elevator cabs, and the elevator car button and ash tray panels. In reviewing steps taken to get this far, a visitor may begin to realize the purposeful playoff between bones and skin that characterizes this building. It is constructivist and high tech simultaneously, with tightly controlled historical references.

Politics and unions and contracts are, if anything, more pronounced factors of doing anything in Chicago than in many cities. With the maze of separate contracts covering SOIC, the objections raised by city building officials (overruled in some cases because it was a state job), and the unusual nature of the project, it is no wonder that it is still not completely finished. The magnitude of these and other obstacles can only be mentioned in passing, and they still go on. The three lower retail levels are the province of the City of Chicago, with a whole new layer of complex contracts.

In addition to, and partly because of, aesthetic considerations, the building's detractors jump gleefully on two aspects, the comfort and the cost of the facility. Occupants have indeed been subjected to temperatures in excess of 90 degrees when ice-making failed to keep up with the outside weather. Jahn asserts that a lack of understanding of this sophisticated system was compounded by operators who flushed the atrium with very hot summer night air. No doubt the single glazing substituted as a show of good budget-cutting intentions hurts daytime performance as well. The building and its complexities *are* still in a shakedown period.

Talk of doubling the initial budget costs, rampant in Chicago, are uninformed and highly misleading, Jahn says. The original funding requested by enthusiastic Governor Jim Thompson was not the "budget," he points out, and the $80 million was never intended to include such things as land, fees, furnishings, etc. The much publicized final cost of $172 million includes all of that and more, and should not be compared with the cost of other buildings when they include building costs only.

Because he has tried for so much, Jahn has risked being on a limb that the public—and certain architects—might wish to saw off. It *is* the Chicago tradition to dare. If SOIC has its glaring faults, and it has, many seem to stem from a stiffening process (and budget compromises) on the way from concept to reality. Despite the avowed gesture to humane design, there is a certain lack of joy in many of the materials and in their detailing. The building is denied the richness that goes with warm materials while at the same time it fairly bristles with another type of richness—activity. It is exciting to be in the atrium, on the balconies, and in the office trays, even with complaints of noise and too little enclosure. It is, if anything, too rich at this level, being vibrant almost to the point of overload.

Possibly the last time an architect produced anything this audacious and self-contained in a major city was 1959, when Wright's Guggenheim Museum in New York was completed. It has long since taken its place, but then, Fifth Avenue has more trees and Wrights' composition and grace are those of a mature master. Jahn is not Wright and SOIC is not the Guggenheim; but the Chicago heritage of testing and exceeding the comfortable, established limits continues at the hand of a talented and prolific architect. SOIC is a courageous attempt that wins some, loses some, and raises the ante.

# Look What Landed in the Loop
## State of Illinois Center, Chicago
*Nora Richter Greer*

Occupying an entire block in Chicago's North Loop is a huge, squat, wedge-shaped, polychromatic glass and steel building with a distinctive, sliced-off cylindrical crown that seems to have popped through the roof. It is neither of modern nor post-modern genre, but is a synthesis of old and new forms, abstraction and functionalism, purity and pizazz. Eclectically futuristic, it stands in a tense relationship with its more traditional neighbors.

It is the State of Illinois Center, a $118 million building housing 3,000 state employees and 150,000 square feet of commercial space. (Rather than creating a typical government office building that is deserted after 5 o'clock and on weekends, the State of Illinois insisted on a mixed use facility.) The architect is Helmut Jahn, AIA, of the Chicago firm Murphy/Jahn. The design was the most radical (and Jahn's favorite) of three submitted to Gov. James R. Thompson, the others being a more conventional, triangular-shaped office tower and a 17-story building similar to the scheme chosen but fashioned out of rectangular planes.

Nora Richter Greer is editor of *Preservation Forum*, a publication of the National Trust for Historic Preservation.

Nora Richter Greer, "Look What Landed in the Loop: State of Illinois Center, Chicago," from *Architecture* 74:1 (November 1985):40–45. Reprinted with permission.

In the design chosen, Jahn took a low-rise (17 story) Miesian glass box and transformed one of the short sides (the south end at Randolph Street) into a sweeping curve that twice steps inward as it rises. Instead of simply pulling the curve from the southwest to southeast corners, the glass skin is tautly stretched from the southwest corner to halfway along the east side, giving the curve greater volume. The result is the most spectacular rounded facade in the city, one that seems to drastically change shape when seen from different vantage points. At times it appears smooth and graceful; others, bulky and distorted.

Curving the structure frees a portion of the southeast corner for a small plaza, in which now stands a Jean Dubuffet sculpture and which announces the building's front entrance. The placement of the curve and that entrance orients the center toward other government offices—the City/County Building to the south (a 1906, 10-story, classical building with huge Corinthian columns rising from a granite base) and the Richard J. Daley Civic Center (a 31-story, glass and cor-ten steel building designed in the early '60s by Murphy/Jahn's predecessor firm C. F. Murphy). In the process of creating this tripodal relationship, however, an awkward thing happens: The State of Illinois Center with its tremendous bulk (1.2 million square feet) overwhelms the two older buildings.

In sharp contrast to the curve are the three rectilinear facades. On the south side (Lake Street), down the middle of which run elevated tracks, the wall rises straight up and serves as a backdrop for the elevated trains. On the east and west sides (Clark and La-Salle Streets, respectively), the curtain wall is raised two stories by columns, the space beneath becoming a covered arcade. Jahn brought the colonnaded west side to the curb to maintain LaSalle Street's canyon. And to echo the curving facade's inward motion, both the LaSalle and Clark elevations twice step slightly back as they rise. Where these elevations hit the curve, the edges are slightly scalloped.

Jahn has described the treatment of the center's facade as "a play between what is transparent, translucent, and opaque—not always conscious, sometimes unconscious and totally unintended." The center of the curve is transparent—clear glass with four, thin vertical strips of reflective glass. Through this portion hints of the interior can be gleaned. At either end of the curve, the surface becomes more translucent; here 2.5-foot panes of clear glass vertically alternate with the same sized panes of reflective glass. On the remaining three facades the vertical stripping becomes even more opaque, as blue glass panes, alternate with clear. The almost garish blue panes on the facades' lower third lighten each time the building steps back. The blue hues are actually quite fickle, changing significantly as the intensity and the direction of the light alters.

Juxtaposed against the skin are salmon-colored columns. The arcade has salmon and white patterns on its storefront surface and its ceiling. And placed next to the columns are pink and gray granite "mock" columns that march away from the building as it curves and that diminish in size as they move down Randolph and Clark streets. Meant to be whimsically metaphorical, at points the granite hits the ground, at others it is suspended, sometimes it is on the street side of the columns, other times on the inside, and at the LaSalle Street entrance it make an arch with a keystone of glass.

Like the curving facade, this ornamentation is most successful when seen in isolated vignettes. When all exterior elements are seen together, the effect is dizzying. New York *Times* architecture critic Paul Goldberger calls it "hyperactive . . . architecture on amphetamines, a building that is so utterly relentless that is seems never to let you go."

Enter the building, though, and the atmosphere changes to one of congenial exuberance. At its heart is a 17-story, 160-foot-diameter atrium topped by that sliced-off cylindrical protrusion. Opening onto the atrium is a soaring antechamber, a triangular-shaped space the hypotenuse of which is actually part of the curving facade. Together, the skylight and the ante-chamber let in abundant natural light, which is patterned by the steel space frame  and bounces off mirrored glass walls in the atrium.

The grand atrium—the largest and most exhilarating in Chicago—was conceived by Jahn as a modern-day rotunda, modeled after those found in turn-of-the-century government buildings. Jahn also wanted to reflect the feeling of an Italian piazza albeit sheltered from Chicago's brutal winter climate and rendered in high-tech aesthetic. The necessary ingredients, besides light, were shops and restaurants and motion and color.

While the shops are located mainly on the first and second floors, the restaurants are below on the concourse level. A large circular hole cut in the center of the atrium floor lets light and views of the space above into the concourse, opening up what otherwise would have been a dark, closed environment.

Motion and color are everywhere. Across the atrium from the main entrance are two exposed elevator shafts, each with six glass enclosed cabs that race up and down, one nine floors and the other 16. From the elevators, clip-on walkways lead to the offices, the balconies of which open onto and ring more than two-thirds of the atrium. Down on the main floor, escalators immediately in front of the entrance lead to and from the concourse level; escalators to the right and left lead to the second floor balcony. Above these side escalators are staircases that seem to precariously hand off the office balconies. In addition, there is a steady flow of people: tourists visiting what is fast becoming the city's biggest attraction, Chicagoans there for state business or simply to cut through the building on their way to or from the "L" of subway, others to browse in the shops or eat. Repeated are the blues and salmons of the exterior, again the tones at the lowest levels fading to pastels above. The steel space frame is red. The result is a series of richly complex images that shift as one moves through the building, the most dynamic being the view from the top balcony down to the elaborately patterned granite floors on the first and concourse levels.

In this new state office building, Governor Thompson wanted to create a new focal point in the North Loop. What Jahn gave the state is a highly dynamic and idiosyncratic building, one that since its conception half a decade ago has been the subject of a heated public debate.

# Jahn's State of Illinois Center Revisited: Strong Enough to Survive the Storm

*Paul Gapp*

A humorous greeting card depicting State of Illinois Center went on sale in Chicago stores not long ago. The card's cover bears a cartoon likeness of the glassy, wedge-shaped building designed by Helmut Jahn. Its printed message reads, "Forgive Me. Everyone Makes Mistakes."

This unkind jest is interesting because of two obvious marketing assumptions: That Chicagoans recognize the building instantly and hardly anyone can look at it without smiling—or worse.

It is not really true that Jahn's building is unanimously mocked, however. Furthermore, the card is not the sort of thing you would send to someone who has never been to Chicago. State of Illinois Center hasn't achieved the level of national recognition attained by the work of such Postmodern architects in the East as Michael Graves.

Still, the greeting card reinforces the truth that State of Illinois Center has become the most esthetically controversial office building ever constructed in Chicago. Its functional problems are also turning it into a textbook example of architecture that is scandalously short on user comfort. For these and

Paul Gapp is architecture critic for the *Chicago Tribune*.

other reasons, it is time for another critical assessment of this extraordinary building that opened 15 months ago.

The most highly visible element belatedly added to the structure is a curtain of water that flows down a grubby slab of plastic from the lobby to the concourse level, where it runs across four shallow basins before disappearing. The water display makes a pleasant sound but is otherwise a lackluster failure.

Permanent directional graphics in the building are adequate, and the information kiosks in the lobby are essential even if a bit intrusive, since tourists from all over the world swarm through the building every day (overtaxing the elevators, which were not intended to accommodate so many gawkers).

Ugly pedestal signs used by some of the building's commercial tenants are a blight that ought to be banned. If the state cannot figure out how to display a large abstract lobby sculpture without surrounding it with a rope, the sculpture should be removed. Still, these problems are overshadowed by more major concerns.

When an architect designs any sort of structure, he sets up short and long-term maintenance challenges. Interior housekeeping at the state building seems to be coping fairly well with Jahn's lavish use of glass likely to be touched. Outdoors, however, the thin and brightly colored metal that covers the building's circular columns is already dented, scraped, and smudged.

The state building's most famous and frequently publicized problem, of course, is still summer heat against which the air conditioning system is powerless. Dozens of old-fashioned electric fans set up by building managers and individual office workers offer a touch of relief on hot days, yet in some areas there never seems to be enough chilled air.

State of Illinois Center was designed and engineered by a joint venture team comprised of Murphy/Jahn and Lester B. Knight & Associates. At this point, it appears that someone made the profound error of grossly underestimating how much air conditioning tonnage it would take to cool the building. This is far more serious than installing a system that is mechanically balky.

Air conditioning specialists have been trying to remedy the cooling deficiency ever since last summer.

Summertime sun glare has been particularly intolerable in State of Illinois Center offices where it roasts the occupants while creating blinding reflections on their computer screens. Several workers tried to solve the problem with sun umbrellas—a gesture not intended as a joke.

Some 1,600 sets of venetian blinds were recently hung on windows in the curved section of the building wall facing southeast. Fixed at a permanent angle, they are practically invisible except at close range. The blinds have cut computer screen glare and reduced air conditioning needs by several hundred tons (a typical central air conditioning unit in a house puts out about three tons). Still, the cooling system remains deficient by a large margin.

In Chicago, at least, the cooling mess has tended to blur public judgment about other aspects of the building. More than ever now, some people perceive the building's huge atrium as "wasteful" when it is actually one of the grandest and most visually successful spatial gestures any architect ever made in this city. Happily, the atrium is also getting intensive use as a year-round ceremonial and performance space.

But while the interior of State of Illinois Center is a brilliant visual success, the building still fails as a chunky and graceless object on the cityscape.

# University of Illinois, Chicago Campus: Transition, Tradition, or New Approach?

*James Burns*

The new Chicago campus of the University of Illinois by Walter Netsch, Jr., of Skidmore, Owings & Merrill raises significant questions concerning the design and planning of the contemporary institution of higher education. Not since SOM's Air Force Academy has there been an educational project of such scope, and the Academy was a unique problem. At the Chicago campus, the architect was confronted with the problems of creating a university that was integrated with the urban fabric yet that at the same time possessed its own identity as a seat of learning; of providing facilities and spaces appropriate for today's instructional methods, which must be adapted to different methods as they appear on the fast-changing educational scene; of creating an atmosphere, an ambience, that will have a deep meaning

In the fall of 1965, when the new UIC campus opened at its present site, the journal *Progressive Architecture* sponsored a discussion among Walter Netsch, the primary architect of the campus; Edward Dart, an architect from another firm; Leonard Currie, then dean of the UIC's School of Art and Architecture; and James Burns, senior editor of *Progressive Architecture*. This article contains highlights of that discussion.

for the commuting student body and the faculty; of re-examining the instructional structure of a university and developing buildings and pedagogical areas that reflect a much less hidebound, departmentalized system than has the traditional school.

To examine these questions and others as they pertain to the new campus and to future campuses, P/A Senior Editor James Burns went to Chicago for a lengthy discussion with Walter Netsch, Edward Dart of Loebl, Schlossman, Bennett & Dart, and Leonard Currie, Dean of the School of Architecture and Art on the new campus. Presented here are the highlights of that discussion, touching generally on the large problem of new university design as sparked by the University of Illinois Chicago campus, and specifically on Netsch's campus, its planning and its architecture.

"At the Chicago campus of the University of Illinois we have, in reality," Dart said, "a traditional campus. By a traditional campus, I mean a series of buildings related to each other in an interesting manner around a mall or the like. I believe this originated from the practice of individual donors giving buildings, and those buildings having to be things apart. There are beginning to be campuses for everything: for colleges, for elementary schools, for industrial parks, for businesses; before you know it, there will be campuses for houses, where we'll have to go outside to get from the living room to the dining room. In a climate as unkind as ours in Chicago, this campus maybe could have taken the approach of a more original concept, one less in conformity to tradition. As far as I am concerned, Walter, this comes back to a discussion you and I and several others had some time ago: that it would be great if we architects could get together now and again and criticize each other's work, hoping for a better thing. We never have, and that's why I am glad about the discussion."

"Your point on campuses is interesting for two reasons," replied Netsch. "You referred to the placing of buildings on a traditional campus for individual donors. The placing of buildings here in Chicago also had reasons in the previous placement of utilities and the economics of the project. The bridges that connect everything here represent a systematized effort to make major and minor connections to enforce what we agree is the goal—a unified totality—and to develop a network. Obviously, the center of the campus is not the village green; it is distinctly urban in setting. The lecture center that supports the central plaza joins the library and the student union, and then the classrooms surrounding it, obviously in a matrix system. It's a problem of phasing from 5000 now to 20,000 with the original educational program, and of changing with future educational programs. One of the important problems is not only the *acceleration* of school design, but also the capability of growth to almost infinite limits in certain changes of educational patterns. The Architecture and Art Building will be the last building on campus and in many respects is the synthesis of what we have learned about intercommunication."

Currie commented, "I agree with Ed in his general desire to get a more concentrated urban campus, and I certainly agree with his general definition of traditional campuses— individual buildings set in a green. But this campus had deviated greatly from that tradition of the American university. This is a campus that ultimately will service 20,000 undergraduate students, so it is going to be almost as large as any other single campus in the country. The academic core here—leaving out some of the parking areas, landscaped areas, and play areas—is 34 acres, whereas the traditional state university campus or land-grant college is apt to have about 150 acres doing the same job. I see this concept as a very urban one; in the heart of the campus we have, instead of the green, this paved plaza, which is more reminiscent to me of the *agora* of the Greek city or the Piazza San Marco."

"This scheme was developed in about six months," Netsch said, "and, if I may be conceited, I feel the group we were working with was strongly forward-looking, considering the complexities of phasing (to a larger student body) and economics. This is a transitional campus that *stems* from tradition, that has some radical departures, but that is not the completely systems-organized single building we had actually hoped to do. If you will look back at the evolution of the central plaza design, you will see we had trees on top of the plaza. I showed this to Bush-Brown and he gave me hell for it. We came back to the idea that trees, like human beings, should be where there is dirt going all the way down. And we took the trees off the plaza, and that also made us think about people. On the original presentation, I think you will see benches all around the edge, a linear thing, kind of park benches in a row. We came to a more spontaneous thing—the plaza and its 'excedra'—out of a greater effort at social communication. This has been an additive, and I think the lecture center and plaza are elements in the nontraditional sense.''

"The elevated walkway, which is the spine of the design, done in granite rather than green, is still the same concept of a central sort of space," Dart insisted. "My only urban disturbance in this is that, in our damn climate, this thing will be vacated between December and March."

"Well," retorted Netsch, "you use the lower level, and go into a controlled climate inside. Then we have the times when you don't have to sit in the air-conditioned climate and you can sit in the open and let the wind blow in your hair. It's a seasonal kind of thing that I think all of us want."

Dart replied, "I am not talking about a hermetically sealed, canned environment where there is nothing but air-conditioning. I just feel that this circulation is a very strong part of the design—its spine—and that all the efforts that have been made to make this a plaza in some way should have made it a more useful plaza."

"I walked on it last winter," Currie stated. "It was cold; it was unpleasant. It was not always a happy situation. But I don't think it was any different than it would have been walking along those other sidewalks in that same terrible weather in Chicago. I am not sure that when the wind is blowing I would not rather be up there than underneath where you get a wind weir effect. I might walk underneath on a very hot day to get shade, or when it is raining, to get protection, but when you're talking about the cold winter wind of Chicago, it's going to blow on you whether you're on Michigan Avenue, or on top of that ramp, or below it."

"This reinforces the desire I have of making this even more compact than it is," Dart urged. "An example is the school Aalto did, or is doing, in Finland at Otariemi. It is a compact university complex in a climate worse than ours. Not that this is the total

solution to the problem, but I sincerely think that this is the direction in which to go."

Netsch expanded, "The interesting issue between European and American planning is the problem of scale. Ed refers to the centrality of the scheme. There will be 20,000 students on this campus. We have 10-minute walking distances between classes. We have a commuter campus, where men and women go to work as well as go to school. There are 4300 seats in the lecture center in 16 different kinds of lecture rooms. There will be 6000 seats in the library. The Student Union is designed for the campus as a whole. So if there is a centrality, it does go back in a sense to the Greeks, where the areas of social communications were concentrated.

"We made several studies before we arrived at this solution. One of them was of four separate colleges. The centrality in that case would have been those things shared by all four—the technological, library, and the rest. We discovered in doing that that we also set up numerous separate departments— English, mathematics, and so forth. The university made a study and found that the problem in acquiring enough staff at the rate of four heads of everything plus even the faculty salary problem when we're trying to get seven universities going in the state was not possible.

"This is the difference in the way our scale works. The real, basic things we have to ask ourselves as we move forward on every front—not only increasing opportunities but increasing scale and increasing performances and increasing demands—is how far can we go, where can we go, how can we recognize the individual in this; so this becomes a problem to be worked out with each solution. All of us, architects and educators alike, will learn a lot when more of these universities—California and New York

367

State, for instance— are finished and evaluations can be made.''

"About the spine," Currie reiterated. "I find it quite a departure and quite a unique thing. You can get on the subway in front of the SOM office at the Inland Steel Building downtown and in four minutes you can get off at the university station, go up the escalator, get on the pedestrian ramp, and go anyplace on this campus and never cross vehicular traffic. To do this in a city the size of Chicago is an entirely different thing than we have ever done before, and I don't care if you're walking on grass or mud or granite or whatnot. From the traffic and circulation point of view this is quite different and quite important, and a significant step in taming the automobile.''

"This really defines the difference between this walkway and the walkway you find in a shopping center, which is related to the store," observed Netsch. "This is a systems-oriented pedestrian communications network that says: I want to go to the classroom; I want to go to the high-rise; I want to go to the library. No one is trying to appeal to me to go to the drugstore. The walkway is performing a very different function than the one we traditionally find. If it could be a single matrix, then it would be even more clearly articulated.''

Burns asked, "What about the problem of an existing urban campus such as New York University in Greenwich Village, where Philip Johnson has been called on to try to tie it together and has used a large 'galleria' to get people out of Washington Square and off the sidewalks and into the school proper?''

"I think there are going to be a lot more of these," Currie replied. "Take the problems they have at Columbia and here at Roosevelt University—using existing buildings and converting them and tying them together in a meaningful complex in the heart of the city. Walter's campus is an urban renewal—urban development—thing.''

"This is an 'instant' campus," added Dart, "The others perhaps just grew.''

"As an urban renewal problem and an urban campus problem," Burns continued, "if the city and the state tell you they have a certain amount of land, do you have to take all the land? Can't it be used otherwise? Can you simply say, 'I want this much' and make it denser and more compact—perhaps higher?''

"We made two studies," Netsch explained. "Since the university was not originally an urban campus, they made the original assumption there would be no highrise buildings, there would be walk-ups. We were asked to determine the acreage in that case; it was 150 acres. And we didn't get 150 acres. So obviously that demand of theirs had to give way. The other study was how small an acreage could we develop, and we developed a single building and it took about 10 acres. It was interesting in this case that, to move 20,000 people on this 50-minute class cycle, which is not an ordinary urban system (it was like a small town or a baseball park changing over every 50 minutes), involved a system of skip-floor escalators and the cost would have been absolutely prohibitive.''

"Don't get me wrong," cautioned Dart; "I'm not talking of a huge Pentagon-type building. I'm just wondering if some of these academic spaces, which are at least connected by covered walkways, could not be more interconnected.

"I agree," agreed Netsch, "and that is why I say that it is a transitional solution and that the proposed Architecture Building is a refinement in the direction you are talking about.

"The real problem in this area, aside from the utilities that we could not move on this campus, is the problem of moving in almost 1,000,000 sq. ft. increments. That, again, is an example of the American scale that even those of us who accept such projects know that this is still a transitional type of thing. We should think about that, if this is the scale in which the city is going; then this campus is a microcosm of an urban environment, and we can understand the reasons and ways of handling this change of scale in the manner we have been talking about with all its complexities. Maybe then we'll have begun to solve the problem of urban environments. It doesn't have to be the single building of immense square footage; that, again, is a kind of transitional solution. When we slide over to the last building on the campus, Architecture, then we are perhaps going in that direction. A series of forms that are individually articulated, but less definite and with a kind of growth capability that goes beyond the individual buildings. This is, of course, a perceivable problem—250,000 sq. ft.—but how do you make 3,000,000 sq. ft. perceivable with diverse social goals?''

Dart replied, ''Your statements about growth intrigue me most, because I think you could have an organism—that is, an organism as a plan—that grows, that has the capability of growth, not so much as the annular rings of a tree, but in which disciplines might be rooted, so to speak, in a common core or service area, yet that have the ability to grow individually as their needs dictate.''

''It's interesting that your description is linear,'' Netsch said, ''Take just the problem of science and engineering here. We have to realize these people have problems in proximity. This campus is unique in developing just five centers of interest, instead of the traditional 30. They have divided the programs into systems, energy, physics; there are five, and even with those five, we have some wonderful three-dimensional mathematics in their growth. These university people are interested in environment and have

been the resource for architectural advances. The methods with which areas like the energy boys are expanding—their needs for their own proximities—I could project into a beautiful three-dimensional Swiss cheese, where the expansion has to recoil and then come back. One vital element is the system of umbilical cords that furnish the utilities and energy supply to one kind of room versus another. These vary extremely. So we're asking for the machine that has this tremendous capability and we're all on this threshold; and industry, which has the human environment, has not been pushing these kind of expansive capabilities to reach these goals.''

''But the expansion here on this campus is still linear,'' Dart insisted. ''The Engineering is, the architecture also.''

''I'm talking ideally,'' retorted Netsch: ''we have to move things. It would be unfair to ask scientists to establish limits; none of us want to establish limits. But I think if you sat down to a problem where you said every 'limit' worked to infinity, you'd have a difficult problem to put it in finite terms. An interdisciplinary character has to eventually evolve into the three-dimensional matrix I referred to, rather like three-dimensional chess. I will accept the criticism that the science and engineering building is in essence still linear, but I think that your proposal is still linear also.

''At the new campus, I have described the scheme as a drop of water with the intensity in the middle. As you go out, there is less intensity in terms of communication— the three-hour lab versus the 50-minute lecture hall. We're not talking about Harvard when we're talking about these state universities of 20,000. We're talking about techniques that are going to go into television, into teaching machines, into trying to give the individual his choice in time, and by preserving the professor's opportunity to work with the students at the seminar level in which the basic communication on a particular discipline has already been engendered in the student. In the lecture center, the four radical lecture rooms occur around a round room in the middle. Albeit designed as an acoustical experience at this time, it eventually will lodge technological equipment that will permit simultaneous showing of four different things in those lecture rooms. So it would be the equivalent of an all-night movie in the future, and you could take your English at three o'clock in the morning.''

"Walter referred to the great new industry of mass education and communication,' observed the Dean. "In a way it is, and in a way it is a very forward-looking industry. But it is also a traditional industry, and while many of the people in a given discipline are pushing the edges of knowledge in their own fields, they are often reluctant to change their environment and the whole set of relationships they are used to in the university.''

"Are you saying that we're stuck with the traditional form I described?'' asked Dart.

"No,'' Currie replied. "I'm saying only that we have residual resistance to change within the university community.''

"I appreciate the three-dimensional qualities of this school,'' Dart stated. "I just wonder how some relationships, such as architecture and science-engineering, which are at opposite nodes of the campus, could have been improved in this context.''

"Well,'' proposed Netsch, "if we consider it as the palm of the hand with fingers able to make it a circle, it might be more clear. Also realize that the vestigial utilities plans we had to work with—plus substations—are legacies of Daniel Burhnam's plan.

"This is really the third civilization on this campus. There was pre-Chicago fire, post-Chicago fire, and now this. More freedom from this imposed restriction might have led to another kind of solution, but I would like to point out that your previous suggestion is in the same general character as the linear organization.''

"This has been compared to the 'celestial' architecture of Maharajah Sawai Jai Singh in Jaipur,—you know, the more-than-life-size astronomical instruments built in the 18th Century,'' Burns said. "While this is admittedly a superficial look on the part of casual observers, what do you think of the monumental aspect of the campus?''

"Well, the width of the granite walkways looks terribly big now that they are practically empty,'' Netsch replied. "The ultimate number was determined not by me but by someone who was knowledgeable about traffic conditions.

"What would be nice, when the walkways and plaza get too crowded, would be to be able to say 'Stop!' and go build another place as they did in previous times. But that isn't going to be possible, and, looking at it now, none of us have seen the campus in its fully-utilized appearance.''

"Even now, though, those connections to the three-unit classroom clusters have gotten pretty jammed up,'' Currie observed.

"A good point,'' agreed Netsch. "We have already recognized that, and are probably going to have to complete the loop of the classroom clusters back to the walkways. But that is one thing we think the scheme has—this adaptability.''

"One of the things I have noticed is the 'expressway' quality of the granite walkways,'' Currie added. "You see someone you know, and you can wave to them, but you can't stop and talk to them. So I think we are going to have increasing use of the central plaza as a socializing space. Perhaps if the walkways had had little nodes coming off them. . . .''

"Cost was one factor there," Netsch pointed out, "but if you will look at the drawing on the lower level, you will see that this is where the perambulating area is—where the gardens and the colonnades are."

Burns asked, "This is not really a 'lolling' campus anyway, is it? It seems to me a very fast campus—you go to the classes, the library, the student union, and leave."

"The kind of organic (pardon the expression) or nucleus campus I am proposing might have better chance of a controlled architectural expression," Dart mused. "You know, I wonder if what has happened at Yale and many other campuses, where each building that each architect does becomes his 'terminal' expression—the building to end all buildings—I wonder if the traditional campus doesn't *breed* this sort of architectural gymnastics."

"That's true, but I don't think it's necessarily bad to have the kind of variety that has gone on at Yale," Currie opined.

"Oh, I think Yale's a mess," Dart insisted.

"Well, Yale's a mess," Currie granted, "but when Yale was all collegiate Gothic, or when the University of Chicago was all collegiate Gothic, I don't think we were too happy with that either. There was an architectural unity, a homogeneity about it, but it was deadly."

"Well, I don't mind Stiles and Morse and I don't even mind the Colonial things, because they are college enclaves within the whole university," said Dart. "I do object to the Yale whale and the Art and Architecture building and things of that nature that are personal statements or platforms."

"Let's look at the University of Illinois campus," Netsch compared, "where I think Charles Murphy Associates did not attempt to make a personal statement with the student union, and I think Harry Weese's design for the future gymnasium is very polite. You can see it working here, I believe. On the usual streetline urban campus or city university, it is going to take a tremendous amount of self-discipline on the part of the architect not to become personal. But where we get into single objects in a particular, existing environment, we're really going to get into attitudes of taste."

"There has been some criticism of the new campus as not being related to the community," Currie stated, "but when you're thinking of an all-purpose university of large size in a city like Chicago, you might say the relation to the close-by community is more important than the relation to the entire city or metropolitan region."

"I get the feeling, on experiencing this campus, that you draw these commuting students into it and create kind of a feeling that this university is in relation to Chicago as the amphitheater is to the university," Burns said. "And you bring them in more closely even than that, into the courts and into the classrooms, which are either under the central plaza-roof or behind a pronounced sculptural window treatment."

"Yes," agreed Netsch, "this was an effort to try to relate scale. This was not the problem of the Air Force Academy, where you have 2600 cadets marching en masse here and there. So we tried, in the little plazzas near the classrooms, to attempt to let 50 people get together and feel their dimensions versus the larger scale in the big plaza with its excedra. In one other space, which will not be complete until the gardens are, we will have individual chairs, where you will be able to take a chair and sit in the sun or sit in the shade or go off by yourself and say people are no damn good."

"The scale of the buildings is fine; the relationships are swell," conceded Dart. "I am concerned about the scale of the high-rise, which reads as a landmark from a distance but doesn't read from the campus, because it doesn't come down to the ground.''

"This is where it is not traditional, like a campanile; if it occupied," Netsch replied. "We didn't want the feeling of Big Brother watching you; it would have been unfortunate to have the high-rise dominating the plaza. We wanted to identify it with the expressway, not with the campus, but the students still feel it relates to them.''

"Incidentally, in the town and gown problem, we may have a fortuitous break on this campus. Since it was planned as a commuter campus, if it ever goes residential, the residences have got to go into the heart of the city, and will not be isolated. You might say this is a beneficial by-product of an extremely difficult situation.''

"I feel that after one acknowledges the delight and interest of some of the ground space levels between the buildings," said Dart, "the ingenuity of the structure of the elevated granite walkways, the remarkable quality of the exposed concrete surfaces, and the charm of the lecture theaters below the elevated plaza in the center, one must face the disconcerting nervousness in the detail of the buildings. The capricious and thoroughly unconvincing fenestration of the classroom buildings, for example, indicates a sort of ferocious compulsion to have to do something to everything for effect.''

"You object to the seeming uniqueness of the window design on the classrooms and the high-rise because it becomes architecturally very strong in the environment," Netsch rejoined. "We had two problems that lead to a search for a solution. One: Since this is an all air-conditioned campus, and it is not done on a rent basis, you couldn't knock that off the income tax, but it comes from tax dollars that you and I pay. We had to find a way of reducing the amount of glass so the air conditioning load would be less. Second: There was a feeling on our part that

we did not want to do enclosed, interior classrooms. This brought up the grave problem of what do you do to reduce the amount of glass on your facade in terms of heat gain, and still provide an opportunity for looking out. There was also the maintenance aspect of who owns the Venetian blinds, who cleans them, who repairs them, who leaves them up and who leaves them down. So we also wanted to get rid of Venetian blinds. Thus, we have, in essence, five different kinds of transparencies of glass. In the window design you see with the vertical slit, there are various intensities in various buildings. The middle portion is always the same—about 3 percent transmission, allowing you to look out even in bright sunlight. The upper portion and the lower portion vary in intensity— 11 percent, 28 percent, and 55 percent— depending where we thought there would be need for projection, when you would just turn out the lights. The biggest response we have had against this has been in the high-rise building. I think we made an aesthetic decision there that was in error—not that the window is wrong, but that the color of the storage walls is wrong. We have a window wall which, following this theme of looking out and loss of transmission, has a very elegant texture of the acid-etched concrete. But when we also picked a dark value for the storage wall, which gives a dichotomy in relatively small rooms between looking at the storage wall and looking at the window wall. It is, I would say, a controversial aspect of the design. But I want to stress it was not a search for uniqueness. There were some very real problems. It was like the evolution of the ground concrete block in the classroom: how could we develop a surface that was pleasant, real, and at the same time not involve maintenance.''

"This is personal," Dart replied: "I feel very depressed in the rooms. On an August day, you feel as though it were

February 15. Windows, I think, are things to let the light in and look out of, even at the risk of having to pull blinds and increase the air-conditioning load. I just wanted to make that point—that the fenestration has a formal thing to it that is pulling strongly at the design."

"It might be that there could have been a little more variety in these window walls," Currie suggested, "that if this concrete frame that goes on so long and so often had been interrupted with areas that do not appear obstructed."

"I disagree," Dart exclaimed. "There's too much variety!"

"I too; I feel quite the contrary," Burns concurred.

"We tried more than one solution to solve it," Netsch resumed. "On the library, you'll notice our windows are perpendicular to the outside, and this exposes the column in the sense of sections. On Architecture and Art, we have the big windows such as in the studio room, as an effort. I have to admit, too, that it is not a perfect solution. The effort was, shall we say, heavy in trying to solve it. The results have satisfied many of the basic criteria. Many people respond to it. And there are those who respond negatively."

Dart admitted, "When it comes to fenestration, I'm a dyed-in-the-wool traditionalist, really.

"The whole design thing is this remarkable choice you have to make. To bring off a great thing, you must bring it up to a precarious point, a precipice. Go too far one way, and it topples into ostentation or the sort of 'personal statement' we were talking about. Don't take it far enough, and it can slide back into something not fully realized."

"One of the things we have tried to do on the campus is provide a sense of being in touch with reality," Netsch said. "We have done the campus using natural materials: concrete, brick, wood. One thing we have done in the structure is to set about to use standard-strength concrete and minimum steel. If a column is big, or a beam or a girder, it is because it had to do a particular job."

"This is the thing that comes off—the quality of the concrete and your attention to detail, and the texture between concrete and brick in the materials," Dart observed. "Those are things in this campus that are real. . . . And scale: when I speak of scale, you can touch it, you can feel it. Damn good to the touch."

"On the whole," Netsch concluded, "I think education and architecture have changed; are changing. The young people are probably more aware of the larger context of civilization. You can be young and spend a summer in Mississippi and have quite a different attitude toward planning and architecture than people had in the past. Really quite a different attitude than our saying, 'I lived through the Depression.' One is *living through*, the other is *participating in*. This is the real problem when we talk about an increase of scale and the different capacity of the individual to understand a more complex problem, then contrasting that with the capabilities of technology to create a new myriad of opportunities and freedoms if properly used. This is the kind of great question that even the Great Society hasn't gotten into, because they are interested in establishing the Great Society first and then worrying about how we can do the technical details. But that's one of the critical details of our times: technological capability contrasted with the capability of individuation in relation to a project. And this is something that *none* of us has yet resolved."

# Evaluation: The University of Illinois' Chicago Circle Campus as Urban Design

*Nory Miller*

At the time, it captured everyone's imagination. The University of Illinois' Chicago Circle campus was what the 20th century was all about. It had a mission, a democratic American mission. This was no Ivy League school; it was low-cost, take-a-subway, get-your-equal-opportunity-here education for everyone, including a stratum of society that has never been to college before.

No more revolutions in the cafe, this was government talking and it was talking big—118 acres; $177 million: 20,000 students, maybe 30,000.

For years, the university's Chicago branch had been stuffed into makeshift quarters on an old shipping pier. But the St. Lawrence Seaway was opening and the pier had asked for its freedom. Circle's time had come. It was the late '50s and provincial, gangling America had become the richest, most powerful country in the world.

Nory Miller has written several books and articles about architecture and urban design. This article was published 12 years after the UIC campus opened.

Nory Miller, "Evaluation: The University of Illinois' Chicago Circle Campus as Urban Design," from *AIA Journal* 66:1 (Jan. 1977): 24–31. Reprinted with permission.

When the University of Chicago was built, 60 years before, it painstakingly modeled itself after Oxford, even choosing limestone that would weather and "look established" quickly. But America had gained confidence since then and Circle was not only new, it was to look new. *And improved.*

For architect, planner mastermind, the university chose Walter A. Netsch Jr., FAIA, of Skidmore, Owings & Merrill. Still young, Netsch already had been involved in two huge planning projects—the wartime atomic research community at Oak Ridge, Tenn., and the Air Force Academy in Colorado Springs.

The site was Congress Circle in Chicago's Little Italy and Greektown neighborhoods, urban renewal land previously scheduled for housing. The site was fed by every manner of highway and public transportation not far from downtown and prepaid largely from federal and city coffers.

After five years of master-planning and three years of construction, the doors opened in 1965 to the first 9,000 students. The second building phase had only just begun, yet the campus captured an honor award from the local AIA chapter and a total design award from the National Society of Interior Designers.

*Architectural Forum* devoted 25 pages to the campus in its September 1965 issue—more pages than it had ever devoted before to a single project. The magazine described Circle as "a slightly scaled-down model of what a 20th century city might be."

And that is the point of taking a second look at the urban design of Circle campus, 11 years later. It is not entirely farfetched to think of Circle as the product of the "best and brightest" of its moment. It is the campus, the new town, the downtown. It is urban renewal and total design. It is, perhaps, what we knew then.

Netsch's game plan reads a little like the International Congresses for Modern Architecture (CIAM) Athens Charter, at the time the profession's most sincere and serious urban design manifesto, although he rejects the comparison. As CIAM was dedicated to recognizing and separating the four basic activities of mankind into homogeneous zones, Netsch proposed grouping campus functions—lecture halls, classrooms, labs, offices, etc.—into similarly separate buildings. As CIAM was evangelical on the subject of separating trucks from cars and cars from people, so Netsch "pedestrianized" his campus and created an elaborate double walkway system.

These were Netsch's main planning innovations, but there were many complicated urban design decisions, both by Netsch and his client. Equally complex are the contemporary reactions by the "users" of Circle campus.

Today, clearly the most common complaint—by professor, student or staff—is that in 11 years, a campus "community" has failed to gel. It's a tricky problem. A commuter school means somewhere else is home. And most students have outside jobs besides. So does a number of faculty.

However, say the user-critics—and the overwhelming majority of people interviewed were disaffected with the campus—there were mistakes in physical planning that aggravate the situation.

Circle was to be new and improved and the old ideas of organizing a university into colleges or into disciplines were ideas from other centuries with other economies and other missions. At Circle, classrooms were all in classroom buildings, offices were all in a high-rise office building, lecture halls were all in the lecture center, lounges were all in the student union. One advantage, Netsch argues, is that this forces faculty to do most of the traveling between classes while students just head across the hall. Since there are fewer faculty than students, congestion is avoided.

It also permits heavier use of fewer physical facilities. The same room can be scheduled for chemistry, psychology and American literature all in one morning.

As a planning idea, this only got to first base. By the time the first phase of buildings opened, it was already clear that the second phase was going a different route. The faculty was dead set against the original plan. And it was also becoming apparent that instead of the estimated 300–400 graduate students, Circle was headed toward 3,000–4,000, maybe more. Graduate students, architect and client agreed, need their labs, faculty offices, libraries, etc., close together.

But the first phase buildings, designed for lower division students, *are* grouped by function—the lecture center with different-sized halls, the central library, student union, the little classroom buildings. And both the present director of physical plant and head of auxiliary services are still enthusiastic. The goals of efficiency and traffic control have been well served.

Some faculty comments: "It is disastrous academically; there is little rapport between students and teachers"; "We don't have a community, we have an hourly changing of the guards."

Students are also resentful. Frequently, one hears a variation of the comment: "This place is like a factory which turns out graduates instead of products."

A survey completed in 1970, using a sample of 1,000 returned questionnaires from students, gives a fuller explanation. The majority of the students answered that not enough space had been provided for studying (66 percent), having fun (60 percent) or being alone (80 percent). It turned out that students infrequently used the student center lounges or the vending machine "mini-centers" in the classroom buildings or the TV rooms. Students also answered that they infrequently talked to an instructor outside of class. The survey indicated that the library was the main place for studying and the student union cafeterias were the main places to socialize and that these weren't enough.

Thus two problems emerge. One is how spaces are grouped, the other is what spaces were provided at all and at what scale. One cannot very well be alone in a corral-sized lounge.

The administration is well aware of these problems and is trying to correct them. Says Vice-Chancellor Eugene Eidenberg: "We have a very efficient physical plant—but that doesn't work as a commuter campus." So the process now is to convert other rooms, as widely distributed on campus as possible, into lounges, nap facilities or study halls and to add recreation like ice skating (actually part of Netsch's plan that got cost-cut), indoor tennis and a rathskeller—to the limited extent that money and space are still flexible.

All seem to agree that whether offices or libraries or labs are spread throughout the different campus buildings, the "residual" spaces should definitely have been.

Netsch had hoped that the out-of-doors would provide many of these residual spaces. He planned to punctuate the grounds with "urban events" that would capture one's attention on the way somewhere for a moment of rest or conversation. "What happens between classes," said Netsch in 1965, "came to be regarded as being as important as what happens in classes."

One of the observations that the 1970 student survey indicated was that students turn out to spend very little time outdoors at Circle.

Some of Netsch's plans were never realized. His ice skating rink was trimmed off the budget. And one of his corner-of-the-campus gardens became a parking lot instead. His two tree gardens equipped with four kiosks each—one for garbage, one for folding chairs and two for hot dog and ice cream stands—sit calmly in the middle of campus with the garbage still waiting for the chairs and the food.

Yet the reaction to what was realized is less than favorable, with the exception of the classroom building courtyards.

Absolute center of the campus is what Netsch calls Circle's agora. It is the roof of the lecture center—ground plane to the second-level walkways. In each corner is a sunken excedra and in the middle, a full-scale amphitheater. It was to be a place for intellectual discourse or socializing, taking a nap, soap-boxing, plays and concerts.

Even in nice weather, say the students, this is cold and forbidding. Says a chemistry prof: "It was great during the 1969 demonstrations but now it's not used much. We're down to Jews vs. Arabs once a year." Vice-Chancellor Eidenberg volunteers: "It ain't like sitting on grass."

It ain't like an agora, either. Instead of a bustling marketplace with hundreds of reasons to be there, what Circle has is a left over roof with some crater-like dents in it.

Much of what is greenery on campus is hedged off from the students and exists only as a foil to the buildings. The one real garden is at such a far corner of the campus that many students don't know it's there.

"There are lots of spaces between buildings," observes one professor, "but few function as social spaces." "The voids are leavings, not places," observes another.

Like St. Elia's classic sketches, Circle campus has highways in the sky. Not for cars, though. Cars are banned from "the city"; they are left in parking lots around its edge. The highways are for pedestrians. Netsch calls them pedestrian expressways.

They are large, organized on a grid and built in granite where it could be afforded and concrete where not. At ground level is another circulation system for pedestrians—a series of intimately scaled, asphalt paths curving from one building to the next. Wherever possible, the upper walkways shelter the lower ones from rain and snow.

Netsch created the double circulation system to relieve traffic congestion between classes. Not one person interviewed mentioned any problem with congestion. On the other hand, not one person admitted to using the "expressways" more than rarely.

In winter, everyone agrees, the skyways ice up and are dangerous. During good weather, most of which occurs during the lower enrollment summer program anyway, they just aren't that convenient. Why not?

- "The walkways aren't the shortest way to go from one building to another."
- "You walk to University Hall on the walkway and all you get to is a windy, empty platform where you wait for an elevator. It's cold and it's dangerous."
- There are doors at the second levels of buildings but lobby activities are at the first. So why go up to go down?

Meanwhile, maintenance people complain that the walkways weren't designed for efficient snow removal. Snow has to be knocked off and then picked up again from the ground, they say. Students complain of getting an avalanche of snow from above in the process.

Others find that the structures cut them off from the rest of the campus and make it difficult to get around. "They block any clear view of the campus," says one student.

Most agree they do work as shelter for the ground paths except to the classrooms where, for esthetic reasons, the ground path enters on one side and the walkway on another. "It was a clear case of conflict between classic form and linear system," says Netsch.

"When the structure of the walkways weakens," says the director of physical plant, "we'll tear them down. No one uses them anyway."

While pedestrian is separated from pedestrian with the two systems of walkways, one thing that is not separated from anyone is the servicing of buildings. Trucks use the same ground paths as people and loading docks and garbage bins frequently adorn main entrances. Garbage also is a charter tenant in the kiosk of the two tree gardens. An education professor exclaimed: "I have never been so aware of garbage in my life."

Says the director of physical plant: "The campus was planned without enough attention to deliveries and refuse removal. Until we put in an extra driveway to University Hall, toilet paper and garbage had to be hauled 150 feet in and out on the janitor's back."

Circle is built as a series of small buildings dotting the landscape rather than a continuous sheltered space. Netsch still has hopes that the buildings can eventually be joined by galleries in which the walkways would simply be upper corridors.

He grouped the buildings according to his "drop of water" theory which means that generalized, heavily trafficked functions occur in the center of the campus—things like the library, lecture hall and student union—with specialization increasing as one goes outward. The layout is axial and gridded. Netsch may have been led to the grid by early intentions of using existing utilities. But even in his earliest criteria, he emphasized the importance of an understandable relationship between each element and the whole."

The buildings are all walk-up, no more than four stories, with two exceptions. Largest is the faculty and administrative office building—University Hall—a 28-story highrise. Netsch thinks of University Hall as a symbolic and navigational landmark for the campus.

Amazingly, nearly everyone grumbles about getting lost—even longtime employees. Although Circle's ground plan is almost classically clear in aerial view, it apparently is not so in the thick of things. Teachers and students alike groused about "constantly walking into blank walls"; having to "walk all the way around to get into a building"; there not being "a system you can learn like street patterns." It is a situation not helped by the almost total absence of exterior signage. Says one art instructor, visiting for a semester: "The thing is, you can't even ask directions. No one knows how to explain where buildings are except by other buildings. There are no visual reference points."

The relative location of generalized and specialized buildings seems to have been successful and the compactness of the layout is appreciated. Most of the buildings are located on about one-third of the site.

There is no agreement about a series of buildings instead of one enclosed space. Some like trudging through the snow to class, others protest. Many, however, suggest that the gales on campus are indeed formidable, and suspect the buildings of accentuating wind velocities.

Lowrise appears to have been absolutely the right decision, but many add that Netsch didn't go far enough. Twenty-eight-story University Hall is a very unpopular building. On the one hand, even though it is reserved for office space, there is sufficient student traffic to overwhelm the elevators. On registration days, it is a spectacle.

On the other hand, there is quite a number of faculty who claim only to go there once a semester—registration day—and to live out of their pockets the rest of the year.

One English teacher said the tower made her feel like she was in a medieval castle frowning down on the serf students—"the opposite of the professed democratic mission of the urban campus."

The 28th floor is the office of the chancellor and vice-chancellor. Netsch calls it the campus "ivory tower." Current Chancellor Donald Riddle, as every chancellor before him, calls it embarrassing.

There is a separate elevator from the 27th to the 28th floor. "It isolates the top administration," says Riddle. He wants to move out and turn the place into a faculty club.

Previous chancellors have wanted to turn it into a museum, a graduate library and a student center for the humanities.

Circle is now doing a new master plan. It's a complicated situation. Netsch worked out what kinds of spaces to build based on elaborate projections of student enrollment. Then the enrollment changed—more professional school trainees than expected.

In addition, a number of buildings and extensions from phase two and three never got built. A Nixon Administration cutoff of aid to higher education, the end of the baby boom and a broke Illinois legislature didn't help.

"It's not that we don't have enough space," says the vice-chancellor. "It's that we don't have the right kind of space for our current needs. But the state won't give us building funds because we have all the square footage our enrollment justifies.

"The problem is that the mode of construction is pretty unyielding. It's a major expense to adapt anything to a different use. I don't think anyone could really have predicted the future, but it's foolish to freeze an academic program by building so inflexibly."

A widely disliked symbol of this inflexibility is classroom seating that resists rearrangement by either faculty or students. Other hard to change ways in which the plan has not proved out:

- No one foresaw the need for "defensive" design necessitated by the escalating rates of crime and vandalism.
- The technical wizardry of closed-circuit TV for every lecture hall goes practically unused. Students didn't like it. There is also a deck washing system "with pump and everything" that has not been used.
- The computer center is in far more demand than it can handle. It was geared for scientists but is now overwhelmed by the social researchers.
- The library has had to be retrofitted for electronic information retrieval.
- The energy crunch and price rise have made maintenance and budget administrators antagonistic to the inoperable windows and reheat coils of the HVAC system.
- The same people grouse about the custom details which make replacing a few floor tiles or a door a major expense and headache.
- When Circle was planned, the trustees made a conscious decision not to design for the handicapped because the university's main campus in Urbana was fully equipped. Since then, the Occupational Safety and Health Administration has made things pretty hot.
- Netsch himself pointed out another. In the early buildings he used rough materials inside to discourage graffiti. "But spray paint is something else entirely," he admits, "and we found for the later buildings that plaster makes the most sense because it can be repainted."

Somewhere along the line, urban design means: How does the campus fit into the neighborhood? Once upon a time that was a very tense question. The Italians and Greeks living in Circle's neighborhood had so little use for a huge university on home turf that they went to court. To the Supreme Court. And they lost. The Greeks moved to another part of Chicago. So did a lot of Italians.

The university had such fondness for the guy next door that it instructed the architect to build a wall—solid brick in some places, fence in others—around the whole campus.

The animosity, say the faculty and administration, is just beginning to die down now. Now the biggest argument is how to keep the students from using up all the street parking.

There is no question, of course, but that the animosity had to do with wrenching a piece of land away from people who wanted to hold onto it. As a result, the neighborhood has really never "come back," none of the neighborhood things like cafes and little stores and sandwich places that usually adorn a college area has sprung up. That frequent attempts to proffer campus facilities to community organizations have met with only limited success may indicate the serious and destructive aspects of this kind of radical urban surgery. Yet it is too soon to really tell what the full cycle will bring.

The physical design seems to be a deterrent to community relations, as well. Neighbors complain of the wall, the stretches of parking lot between it and them and the "different" and "mean" look of the campus.

What is of more concern to on-campus people is the fact the Circle is deserted by 4 P.M. weekdays and on weekends. It is so deserted that it is not only susceptible to criminals but to packs of dogs. There is little physically to be done at this point—Circle is a large single-purpose environment, separated from its neighborhood. Administrators are instead working on extending classes into evening hours and catalyzing the erection of student housing nearby.

Circle campus was built with ambition and a sense of adventure by both client and architect. Its disfavor today almost mirrors the disfavor in which the general planning implements and goals of the mid-century are held.

There are shortcomings that might have been predicted even at the time; the redundancy of a second pedestrian circulation system; the resistance to use of the upper-level system; the visibility of garbage; most important, the unsuitability of a fixed program for anything as volatile as education.

But many of the roots of the problems at Circle campus are the same as in our cities. That single-use zoning, expressways through urban center and large-scale urban renewal "islands" are in disrepute is apparent in city council chambers across the country.

The disillusionment is not so much with technology—for not many are willing to give up washing machines, electricity or even computers—but with an environment that calls up the image of the machine. If TV teaching and highrises are unpopular on Circle campus, it is the images of impersonality and power that are no longer so attractive.

# Library Design Keeps City a Step Ahead

*Paul Gapp*

Thomas Beeby's library competition victory fits the Chicago tradition of staying out in the forefront of American architectural leadership, not lagging behind.

It also reinforces the continuing Chicago movement away from the International Style that was brought to perfection here by Ludwig Mies van der Rohe.

Finally, it certifies that government officials—not private enterprise—exert the most profound effect on large-scale buildings in Chicago nowadays.

Beeby's 500,000-square-foot Neoclassical library, if it is built as planned, will be the largest Postmodern structure in the United States serving a complex set of operational and technical demands.

Far taller commercial buildings have been constructed under the stylistic barrier of Postmodernism, which borrows from styles of the past and reshapes them in combination with contemporary technology and materials. Still, most such buildings are mere slipcovers for office space. None has been so programmatically complicated as the Chicago library.

Chicago architects were slow to embrace the sometimes quick look of Postmodernism when it first came into vogue in the early 1970s at the hands of Robert Ven-

tura of Philadelphia and Philip Johnson of New York.

Beeby, though, was among the first of the city's designers to make a philosophical breakaway from strict adherence to International Style dogma. He was one of the so-called "Chicago Seven," a group of architects who in 1976 declared the need for more openness in design.

In the year since, Beeby has turned out no tall buildings of the sort that sometimes lead to instant fame. He has, however, been widely honored for such work as the Sulzer Regional Library at 4455 N. Lincoln Ave; an elegant addition to North Shore Congregation Israel in Glencoe; and the Champaign Public Library. The new south wing of the Art Institute of Chicago, designed by Beeby, is scheduled to open in September.

The library design choice recalls that Postmodernism made a sensational arrival in the Loop only a few years ago. That was when Helmut Jahn turned out the State of Illinois Center, whose soaring atrium and dizzying color scheme made it the most sensational building constructed in Chicago since World War II. The decision to accept the daring design was made by Gov. James Thompson—who could have chosen one of the less startling options offered by Jahn.

The library competition jury and city officials are carrying on in the bold tradition of cutting edge public architecture paid for by the taxpayers.

Beeby's library looks like a building that might have been constructed a century ago in Paris, London—or Chicago. Yet it is the very revival of the Classical style that makes it audacious, particularly in Chicago.

The "Chicago School" of architecture was born around the turn of the century. Its simple lines expressed the muscular frames of buildings, a stylistic practice that also marked the work of Mies van der Rohe many years later.

Three of the losing library design competitors—Jahn, Dick Lohan and Adrian Smith—paid close attention to the Chicago tradition with their schemes. Beeby turned his back on the tradition.

Still, the Beeby library has been well-liked at the grass-roots level since a model of it went on display several weeks ago. It looks much the way many libraries used to look, and most Chicagoans are likely to feel visually comfortable with it.

Except for placing some perhaps excessive ornamentation at the library's summit, Beeby did not indulge himself in the kind of whimsy that draws the fire of anti-Postmodernists. His library is a serious building, stylistically and functionally. It demonstrates that there is room under the postmodern umbrella for conservatism and traditional values as well as cartoon architecture.

Some may read too much into Beeby's victory. It does not signal any drastic turn-around in the Chicago design scene. Yet the new library will draw global attention among architects and scholars who have long looked to Chicago as the departure point of so much that has been important to American building in the last century.

# Jurors Take a Look Back to Pick New Library Design

*Blair Kamin*

An 11-member jury Monday selected a design for Chicago's new central library that is a throwback to turn-of-the-century classical monuments and a sinking departure from the city's internationally renowned glass-look architecture.

The panel of 10 men and 1 woman chose the proposal by the team of Thomas Beeby and Chicago developer U.S. Equities Realty Inc. over entries by four other groups of architects, designers and contractors.

Its decision represents a marked shift from the steel-and-glass boxes of such Chicago architectural giants as Ludwig Mies van der Rohe.

In contrast to those sleek structures, which often stand aloof from their surroundings, the exterior of Beeby's design is unabashedly historical and tries to blend comfortably with the redeveloping South Loop area.

"Our main concern was building a first-class building within the historic context," said Beeby, 46, a partner in the Chicago architectural firm of Hammond Beeby & Babka and dean of the Yale University School of Architecture.

This $140 million library is scheduled to open in mid-1991 at the corner of State

and Van Buren Streets. With an interior of about 500,000 square feet, the 10-story structure will be the largest municipal library ever built in the United States.

Under the glass-domed ceiling of the Chicago Public Library Cultural Center, jury chairman Norman Ross announced at 9:33 A.M. that the vote was 9–2 in favor of Beeby's proposal.

"It was a tough call," Ross said at a press conference attended by Mayor Eugene Sawyer.

Another juror said that the panel's second choice was the granite- and marble-covered design by Chicago architect Helmut Jahn. It was one of two proposals that would have spanned the Chicago Transit Authority elevated tracks on Van Buren Street.

"We all liked his design very much," said the juror, who requested anonymity. But the juror said that Beeby's design won because it "would be more flexible and function better."

Following Monday's announcement, the Library Policy Review Committee voted unanimously to accept the jury's recommendation. Library Board officials said they would vote Tuesday on the recommendation.

Approval is considered likely because Library Policy Review Committee members constitute a majority of the Library Board. If approval is granted, city officials said, construction could begin next fall.

Blair Kamin is a reporter for the *Chicago Tribune*.

Faced with a gamut that ranged from the futuristic proposal of Canadian architect Arthur Erickson to Beeby's traditional design, thousands of Chicagoans voiced their opinions after the entries were unveiled in May.

The vociferous debate stemmed from Chicago's reputation as a center of American architecture and from the long-running civic embarrassment of having most of the library's 2.3 million volumes housed in a dingy warehouse at 425 N. Michigan Ave.

Their placement there, which was supposed to be temporary, has lasted 12 years as city officials dickered over various proposals for downtown library sites.

The low point came in 1986 when officials abandoned a plan to place the new central library in the vacated Goldblatt Bros. department store at 333 S. State St.

Sawyer alluded to the library's troubled past when he congratulated the winners on Monday. "There's a light at the end of the tunnel, and it's the light of learning," the mayor said.

Beeby's design calls for the library to rise on the southern block of a block-and-a-half urban renewal site in the South Loop. Now occupied by a parking lot, the block is bounded by Congress Parkway on the south, State Street on the east, Van Buren Street on the north and Plymouth Court on the west.

Its classical design is based on such Chicago landmarks as the Art Institute, the Auditorium Building (now Roosevelt University), the Rookery Building and the Chicago Public Library Cultural Center. That building was Chicago's central library when it opened in 1897.

While most of the exterior would be a departure from steel and glass modern architecture, Beeby said that its interior would use as a takeoff point the modular design of modern buildings.

Beeby sought to create large, flexible storage areas on working library floors by moving small reading areas and service functions such as fire escape stairs to the perimeter of the building.

# Sequence Six

# Boundaries of the Individual

This above all: to thine own self be true,
And it must follow, as the night the day,
Thou canst not then be false to any man.

Shakespeare, *Hamlet*

Be yourself. Know yourself. Think for yourself. These are some of the dozens of truisms that most of us have grown up with.

An elusive thing, the self. It is difficult to define, much less to find or act upon. You may finish this sequence asking, "Is the self even there?" To confront this difficult question, this sequence examines some of the ways people talk about the self.

Here in the United States, we often think of ourselves as a nation of individuals, pioneering new vistas in solitary effort. But how far does this individualism go? How important is it? Where does the self end and the rest of the world begin?

The amount of time we spend interacting with various organizations and structures in our society says something about the kind of individuals we are. The way we feel about work and government and how large a role they should play in our lives indicates our priorities and our philosophies of life. Should the individual self be recognized within the family? In the workplace? In government? How do different cultural or religious traditions affect the way we think about ourselves and the way we act?

Students often protest that asking questions like this is "just philosophical." It can seem of little value to write, often at great length, about what seems to be an abstract topic. But the answers to questions about the self are not merely an excuse to "be philosophical." Through this sequence of reading and writing assignments, you can see that these questions pose real-world problems. The solutions offered to these problems throughout history have shaped our homes, our families, our educations, our occupations, our forms of government, and then, like a circle, our ideas about ourselves.

This sequence offers a chance to discover directly something about writing that is often frustrating, always difficult, but sometimes almost magical—a chance to discover a part of "thine own self."

# Assignment One

*Readings:*

    May Sarton, "The Rewards of Living a Solitary Life."
    Carson McCullers, "Loneliness: An American Malady."
    Margaret Mead, "Rage, Rhythm, and Autonomy."

# The Self

Carson McCullers and May Sarton both seem to believe that a conflict exists between the "self" and the world of others. McCullers thinks that what the human struggle is all about is the need to lose our sense of isolated identity so that we might "belong to something larger and more powerful than the weak, lonely self." Sarton believes that before we can be ready to "belong" to anything, we must first take time to nurture a strong sense of self in solitude. Margaret Mead's study of the Manus Islanders offers an interesting contrast. She reports that a child's development of a strong, autonomous self depends on the ways family and community members consider the child an integrated, connected part of the social structure in his or her early years.

*Option One:* Write an essay in which you clarify for yourself the ways your own sense of individuality has come into conflict with the needs or expectations of others. You might want to ask yourself some of the following questions (or come up with your own) to help give a focus to your writing: Do you seek solitude or go somewhere in particular when you feel the need to consider yourself as an individual? Have there been times when you have purposely gone against a rule or the status quo because you felt it was wrong or it dampened your style? Have there been times when what you have wanted hasn't been what another person you care about wanted? Have there been times when you have made yourself stand out in a crowd by the way you have looked or acted? Do you hold beliefs that seem unique to you, that your friends and family members do not hold? Do you believe that you are special in some way that others do not acknowledge?

*Option Two:* Mart Twain wrote, "We are creatures of *outside influences*—we originate *nothing* within. Whenever we take a new line of thought and drift into a new line of belief and action, the impulse is *always* suggested from the *outside.*" To prepare for this part of the assignment, jot down some of the special talents or abilities you have developed over the years. These might include (but are in no way limited to) a talent for art or music, a special ability in sports, a proclivity toward the love of nature, or perhaps simply the desire to spend time alone or to help others. Then, write an essay in which you clarify for yourself the ways other people or particular events in your life have helped to shape that special quality you possess.

# Assignment Two

*Readings:*

Virginia Woolf, from *A Room of One's Own.*
Marc Feigen Fasteau, "Friendships Among Men."

## The Self and Others

Virginia Woolf creates the imaginary Judith Shakespeare to demonstrate how women's subordinate status historically has prevented them from the kinds of creative achievements that men have accomplished. According to Woolf, this status relegated we men to the role of help-mates, rather than independent persons in their own right. Marc Feigen Fasteau points out that gender stereotypes are deeply imbedded in our social structure, and we have difficulty escaping their influence, even when it becomes apparent that they severely limit us. In the first assignment, you explored your own individuality. In this assignment, you will look at how stereotypes influence our determinations of ourselves and others.

*Option One:* Think about some of the programs that are currently on television. Do they do a good job of mirroring modern stereotypes of men and women? In your opinion, are those stereotypes positive or negative? Write an essay in which you inform your readers whether or not you believe television portrays authentic images of men and women. Be sure to include plenty of examples from a variety of programming. Be aware that before you can explain how gender stereotypes show up on television, you need to define how they manifest themselves in real life.

*Option Two:* Interview someone you know who you think has surpassed his or her traditional gender role—for instance, a woman who excels at a job that was once considered strictly a man's domain, or a man who has overcome the masculine stereotype that Fasteau describes. Write an essay in which you inform your readers about what you think is the secret of that person's success. What specific cultural biases did this person have to overcome? What personal qualities enabled him or her to overcome them? Before your interview, either on your own or with classmates, compile a good list of questions to ask during the interview. Keep in mind that you may want to quote directly or paraphrase some of the things the person says in the interview, so bring a tape recorder or a sturdy pad for taking notes to the interview.

# Assignment Three

*Readings:*

John Paul II, "On Human Work."
Huston Smith, "The Hindu Way to God Through Work."
Barbara Ehrenreich, "Farewell to Work."

# The Self and Work

Christianity and Hinduism offer two very different reasons for working, but both declare that work, or activity, is a natural drive in humans. Ehrenreich argues that work is simply part of an economic power struggle—it's not "natural" at all. As you prepare for this assignment, consider some of the consequences of each of these philosophies. We spend a great deal of time at work, and the type of work we choose often defines us for others. So far in this sequence, you have considered your individuality and investigated how stereotypes affect you. In this assignment, think about how your attitudes toward work affect who you are.

*Option One:* Write an essay explaining what has made you want to become educated for a particular career. Even if you haven't yet chosen a career, do you feel the need to do so? Why or why not? In your essay, demonstrate the importance—or unimportance—of choosing the "right" career. You may want to think about some of these questions as you prepare to write: What are the factors you consider when thinking about a career? Which of these factors are most important? Why? Is this level of importance dictated by you or someone else? Would you like the process of choosing a career to be different? If so, how and why?

*Option Two:* Write an essay in which you first explain America's work ethic. Is the typical American worker hungry for power? Does he or she simply have an urge to be active? Is he or she driven by an urge to make the world a better place? Are there other explanations for the work ethic? Then evaluate the work ethic. Should it be different or the same? Why? You may want to consider some of these questions: What should be of the utmost importance where work is concerned, the good of the individual or the good of the community? Why? Should they be of equal importance? Can such a division even be drawn? How would your vision of an ideal work ethic play itself out in real-world terms, in real consequences?

# Assignment Four

# The Self and Government

While some governments give special groups preferential treatment, other try to determine what is best for all groups. Either of these practices can create conflict for any particular individual. As you work on this assignment, keep in mind what you have determined about the way a person's sense of self is influenced by stereotypes and by work. For this assignment, you will explore the areas where the self and government come into contact.

*Option One:* Socrates and Martin Luther King both try to change the way people think. Socrates uses his skills as a teacher and philosopher to encourage critical thinking in Plato and the Athenian youth. King uses his talent as a writer and minister to try to change the narrow-mindedness of bigotry and the laws that allow it. But Socrates and King differ over the role that government should play in our activities. How far should the government be allowed to control what we do to persuade others? Is there a distinction between physical and verbal persuasion? If a statement or work of art has the potential to harm certain people or incite dangerous behavior, should censorship be allowed? Write a letter about censorship to a newspaper of your choice. Try to persuade its readers that the government should or should not be allowed to censor, and under what conditions. Use examples from both the readings for this assignment and from your own ideas and experiences.

*Option Two:* Both Socrates and Martin Luther King were jailed for doing something they thought right. Socrates argues that even though he thinks his sentence is wrong, to be a good citizen he must accept it. King, on the other hand, feels that, as an upright person, he cannot accept what he views as the injustice of his sentence. Thus, the two men disagree about who determines the standards of justice. Does the government know what is best for us, or does the individual? Write an essay in which you try to persuade your classmates that either the government or the individual should decide what justice is and who should be served by it. Use examples from both essays to support your ideas.

# The Rewards of Living a Solitary Life

*May Sarton*

The other day an acquaintance of mine, a gregarious and charming man, told me he had found himself unexpectedly alone in New York for an hour or two between appointments. He went to the Whitney and spent the "empty" time looking at things in solitary bliss. For him it proved to be a shock nearly as great as falling in love to discover that he could enjoy himself so much alone.

What had he been afraid of, I asked myself? That, suddenly alone, he would discover that he bored himself, or that there was, quite simply, no self there to meet? But having taken the plunge, he is now on the brink of adventure; he is about to be launched into his own inner space, space as immense, unexplored, and sometimes frightening as outer space to the astronaut. His every perception will come to him with a new freshness and, for a time, seem startlingly original. For anyone who can see things for himself with a naked eye becomes, for a moment or two, something of a genius. With another human being present vision becomes double vision, inevitably. We are busy won-

May Sarton is a poet, essayist, and novelist whose works include *Faithful are the Wounds*, *Mrs. Stevens Hears the Mermaids Singing*, and *Kinds of Love*.

dering, what does my companion see or think of this, and what do I think of it? The original impact gets lost, or diffused.

"Music I heard with you was more than music." Exactly. And therefore music *itself* can only be heard alone. Solitude is the salt of personhood. It brings out the authentic flavor of every experience.

"Alone one is never lonely: the spirit adventures, walking/In a quiet garden, in a cool house, abiding single there."

Loneliness is most acutely felt with other people, for with others, even with a lover sometimes, we suffer from our differences of taste, temperament, mood. Human intercourse often demands that we soften the edge of perception, or withdraw at the very instant of personal truth for fear of hurting, or of being inappropriately present, which is to say naked, in a social situation. Alone we can afford to be wholly whatever we are, and to feel whatever we feel absolutely. That is a great luxury!

For me the most interesting thing about a solitary life, and mine has been that for the last twenty years, is that it becomes increasingly rewarding. When I can wake up and watch the sun rise over the ocean, as I do most days, and know that I have an entire day ahead, uninterrupted, in which to write a few pages, take a walk with my dog, lie down in the afternoon for a long think (why does one think better in a horizontal position?), read and listen to music, I am flooded with happiness.

I am lonely only when I am overtired, when I have worked too long without a break, when for the time being I feel empty and need filling up. And I am lonely sometimes when I come back home after a lecture trip, when I have seen a lot of people and talked a lot, and am full to the brim with experience that needs to be sorted out.

Then for a little while the house feels huge and empty, and I wonder where my self is hiding. It has to be recaptured slowly by watering the plants, perhaps, and looking again at each one as though it were a person, be feeding the two cats, by cooking a meal.

It takes a while, as I watch the surf blowing up in fountains at the end of the field, but the moment comes when the world falls away, and the self emerges again from the deep unconscious, bringing back all I have recently experienced to be explored and slowly understood, when I can converse again with my hidden powers, and so grow, and so be renewed, till death do us part.

# Loneliness . . . An American Malady

*Carson McCullers*

This city, New York—consider the people in it, the eight million of us. An English friend of mine, when asked why he lived in New York City, said that he liked it here because he could be so alone. While it was my friend's desire to be alone, the aloneness of many Americans who live in cities is an involuntary and fearful thing. It has been said that loneliness is the great American malady. What is the nature of this loneliness? It would seem essentially to be a quest for identity.

To the spectator, the amateur philosopher, no motive among the complex ricochets of our desires and rejections seems stronger or more enduring than the will of the individual to claim his identity and belong. From infancy to death, the human being is obsessed by these dual motives. During our first weeks of life, the question of identity shares urgency with the need for milk. The baby reaches for his toes, then explores the bars of his crib; again and again he compares the difference between his own body and the objects around him, and in the wavering, infant eyes there comes a pristine wonder.

Consciousness of self is the first abstract problem that the human being solves. Indeed, it is this self-consciousness that removes us from lower animals. This primitive grasp of identity develops with constantly shifting emphasis through all our years. Perhaps maturity is simply the history of those mutations that reveal to the individual the relation between himself and the world in which he finds himself.

After the first establishment of identity there comes the imperative need to lose this new-found sense of separateness and to belong to something larger and more powerful than the weak, lonely self. The sense of moral isolation is intolerable to us.

In *The Member of the Wedding,* the lonely 12-year-old girl, Frankie Addams, articulates this universal need: "The trouble with me is that for a long time I have just been an *I* person. All people belong to a *We* except me. Not to belong to a *We* makes you too lonesome."

Love is the bridge that leads from the *I* sense to the *We,* and there is a paradox about personal love. Love of another individual opens a new relation between the personality and the world. The lover responds in a new way to nature and may even write poetry. Love is affirmation; it motivates the *yes* responses and the sense of wider communication. Love casts out fear, and in the security of this togetherness we find contentment,

Carson McCullers, a Southern novelist and essayist, wrote *The Heart is a Lonely Hunter, The Ballad of the Sad Cafe,* and *A Member of the Wedding.*

courage. We no longer fear the age-old haunting questions: "Who am I?" "Why am I?" "Where am I going?"—and having cast out fear, we can be honest and charitable.

For fear is a primary source of evil. And when the question "Who am I?" recurs and is unanswered, then fear and frustration project a negative attitude. The bewildered soul can answer only: "Since I do not understand 'Who I am,' I only know what I am *not.*" The corollary of this emotional incertitude is snobbism, intolerance, and racial hate. The xenophobic individual can only reject and destroy, as the xenophobic nation inevitably makes war.

The loneliness of Americans does not have its source in xenophobia; as a nation we are an outgoing people, reaching always for immediate contacts, further experience. But we tend to seek out things as individuals, alone. The European, secure in his family ties and rigid class loyalties, knows little of the moral loneliness that is native to us Americans. While the European artists tend to form groups or aesthetic schools, the American artist is the eternal maverick—not only from society in the way of all creative minds, but within the orbit of his own art.

Thoreau took to the woods to seek the ultimate meaning of his life. His creed was simplicity and his *modus vivendi* the deliberate stripping of external life to the Spartan necessities in order that his inward life could freely flourish. His objective, as he put it, was to back the world into a corner. And in that way did he discover "What a man thinks of himself, that it is which determines, or rather indicates, his fate."

On the other hand, Thomas Wolfe turned to the city, and in his wanderings around New York he continued his frenetic and lifelong search for the lost brother, the magic door. He too backed the world into a corner, and as he passed among the city's millions, returning their stares, he experienced "That silent meeting [that] is the summary of all the meetings of men's lives."

Whether in the pastoral joys of country life or in the labyrinthine city, we Americans are always seeking. We wander, question. But the answer waits in each separate heart— the answer of our own identity and the way by which we can master loneliness and feel that at last we belong.

# Rage, Rhythm, and Autonomy

*Margaret Mead*

We may now turn to the way in which children born to Manus parents develop a character within which anger is both so ready and so disapproved that exhortations against anger can become the focus of a whole local religious system.

In describing the way Manus character is formed, it is not possible to go back to a comparison of the way the newborn was treated in 1928. For, in 1928, no woman who had not herself borne a child was permitted to witness a birth, and I believed then, as I do now, that in field work it is essential not to deceive those from whom one wishes to learn the truth. I had never had a child and so I saw no childbirth. None of the accounts which I was given told me anything of importance about the way in which a child's introduction to the world foreshadowed the future course of its development.

When I returned to Peri in 1953, having fulfilled the necessary requirements for 1928, I found them no longer necessary. Husbands and even small children were now freely admitted to a birth.

For the birth of a Peri child, it is necessary to have three women present besides the expectant mother, one of whom is a representative of the husband's family, two from her own family. Of these three, two should be experienced older women. Inexperience may mean an incorrectly cut cord or a long delay in expelling the afterbirth. No preparations are made for a birth except to accumulate coconuts which will be made into a special dish for the new mother after the baby is born. These coconuts are provided by the mother's brother, and cooked by her brother's wife, one of the three women who ideally participate in the birth.

Today, children are born in the little old-style houses which are built out over the sea for the old women, who are given a chance to live as they have always lived, close to the shifting tides, and who also provide hospital care both for obstetric cases and for any illness which makes it difficult for the patient to walk about. These little houses do not differ from the houses of long ago, except that they are very tiny and flimsy and the fear of the house collapsing if a crowd gathers is more intense. The fireplace is still a framed square of ashes on the floor, and the expectant mother lies on a mat beside the fire; a second mat is hung up to shield her from the chance gaze of the men in the house. The walls of these houses are made of leaf thatch attached to very slender supports. For something against which the expectant woman can push her feet, an extra post or board will be fastened firmly in the wall.

Then the three helping women seat themselves, one on each side and one behind

Margaret Mead was an anthropologist and social psychologist who studied and wrote about the tribal customs of primitive societies.

the woman in labour. Each old woman has a slightly different style, but the pattern is the same. The expectant mother hooks one leg over the leg of the midwife—this gives her human support—and presses with the other against the wall. The women behind and beside her support her and, as each pain passes, she again relaxes and lies quietly on her mat, while the three women also relax, smoke, chew betel, or possibly one of them nurses her own baby, laying it down or passing it to someone else when the next pain comes. From time to time, the midwife suggests that the expectant mother lie on her side, and she and her vis-à-vis change sides. The expectant mother then hooks her other leg over the midwife's other leg in the reciprocal of her previous position. This may be done twenty or thirty times during the course of labour, each position being the replica of the previous one until one has almost the sense of an impersonal machine-like exactitude, a mobile unit in which each piece plays a set role.

When the experienced old midwife realizes that the moment of birth is near, all three women go into action, backing up the mother, literally and emotionally, in the act of getting the baby born, efficiently, quickly. At the moment of birth they form a hollow square, each part flexible, determined, strong, within which the baby arrives and is picked up by the woman on the other side. Cord uncut, the baby is held facing the mother and completing the square. Then, two things happen together: the midwife and the woman behind the mother redouble their efforts to get her to expel the afterbirth, and the nurse, holding the baby, begins to sing a lullaby in time with the baby's birth wail. As the baby wails and the midwife and her assistant exhort the mother to greater and greater effort, the nurse's voice rises into a crescendo and the new baby becomes part of the rhythm of the world about it. Only if the afterbirth is delayed for ten or fifteen minutes or more are more drastic methods necessary, and the cord will be cut before the expulsion of the afterbirth. Once the afterbirth is out, the cord is pinched clear of matter and tied so that "no blood will run back into the belly," then cut, and the helping women—by this time there may be several more—set to work on the post-delivery tasks, bathing the baby in sea water, preparing a hot coconut soup for the mother.

The baby characteristically shrieks at being bathed, and is then settled into a nest made of an old grass skirt, a nest that is slightly prickly but soft and yielding and from which it can gaze about in the flickering lights of the room, lit from the doorway and by light that comes through the slats in the floor. Whenever it cries, there is the lullaby echoing its cry in exact rising cadence, interspersed with the words, "Some day you'll be a fisherman, you'll sail the seas, you'll catch fish," if the baby is a boy, and with, "You'll grow big, you'll bear children," if a girl. The new baby is not fed until it "cries for food," which may be several hours after birth, when it is given milk by the woman who has given birth most recently. Thus the Manus baby's introduction to the world, its first contact, is not an oral one, but is muscular and auditory, as its nurse moves and (I hesitate to use the word *sing*, for the lullaby is more like a noisy roar modelled on an infant's wail) lulls it, taking her time cues from its voice. Instead of initially communicating with the world through a nipple from which comes the food and comfort, it moves with a world that moves with it. And the cue the child gives is a real cue, not an imputed one, a real cry which the adult imitates. It has begun a life of autonomy in which others will respond to its strength, its initiative, its will to move, to make sounds, to grasp food.

So from the moment that a Manus baby is born, it is caught into a system which emphasizes the active rhythmic reciprocity with the world about it, de-emphasizes differences in size and strength and sex, and stresses its existence as an independent organism. Before the cord is cut, the old woman who takes care of the newborn starts to lull it in time to its own crying, so that the sound it makes and the sounds it hears are as nearly one as it is possible to make them.

Nursing is not done in a way which makes the infant into either a passive receptor or into a demanding little monarch to whom the mother passively offers herself through the breast. Instead, the complementary relationship, in which the strong, large mother with milk gives her breast to the small, passive, hungry baby, is converted by the Manus into a kind of reciprocal exchange in which the breast is treated more like a connecting piece of tubing between mother and child than as a part of the mother. From the earliest suckling the mother handles her breast in this detached way, and the child soon learns to treat it in the same way, pulling, dragging, stretching the breast about to suit its needs.

During the first month or so of a child's life, the mother stays close to the baby. It is held on her outstretched legs, or laid near by to sleep, always on its side, propped up by pillows, or picked up, fed, kept warm and clean, and given every attention. The hands that hold it—twenty-five years ago they were women's hands only, today fathers also take part in the care of very small babies—are alert for every sign of strength, of potential autonomy, for its ability to rear its head, reach out its hand, sit with support, go through the gestures of walking with support. Every slight advance is taken advantage of.

This treatment results in very marked differences between babies who continue to gain rapidly after the first couple of months and turn into very active assertive happy babies, and the babies who grow less well

and are not as easily stimulated into activity, who tend to develop into more passive, whining babies, less willing to go to others, less attractive to a crowd of young aunts, uncles, and cousins. These weaker babies are more of a drain on the mother, who is crosser and more irritable, thus in turn reinforcing in her child its pettishness, fretfulness, and intolerance of others.

The active, growing baby forges ahead, refuses to be handfed, but instead insists on taking its lumps of taro in its own hands, is active every single moment that it is awake, and is terrifically tiring to care for. Where the fretful, passive baby demands to be carried most of the time, the active happy baby will also prefer human arms and attention to sitting on the floor or playing by itself. Twenty-five years ago, babies were left more to themselves, laid on mats on the floor, while their mothers did elaborate hand work of beads or string. But today, the mothers do no hand work, most of the year they do not even have to go for water, and their housework takes at most a couple of hours a day. For the rest of the time they have no excuse not to hold a child except that they are already holding another one. It is a common sight to see a woman with a small child in her arms and a knee baby* holding on to her back. Before they can walk, children become accustomed to adults turning themselves into human pedestals and transportation systems. If the baby wants to see, it is lifted up; if it leans toward something, the adult leans with it; if it wants to go toward something, the adult carries it. At every turn the adult makes up to the child for its lesser strength and size, holding it high, carrying it because its legs are too weak or too slow.

This desire to move is underwritten by the care with which the adults seize on each forward movement, and yet never force a

*Second child, displaced child, or "child whose nose is out of joint."

396

child, never make it sit without support before its back is strong enough. However much it is put through walking paces, its arms are held firmly and no weight inhibits the playful walking movements until the legs are ready to carry it. Every bit of motor freedom is anticipated, rehearsed with enthusiasm. But there is no forcing and no pushing, no attribution to the child of a strength which it does not have. This is in strong contrast with the behaviour of the American mother who says she can do "nothing" with her two-year-old, confusing her desire for him to be wilful and independent with a totally spurious physical strength. When it is necessary, Manus adults simply pick up children of any age and lift them to where they want them to go, in spite of their articulate howls and kicks. There is no real attempt to keep them from howling and kicking, although the parent will repeat the reason why the force is being exerted. But any discipline is a genuine trial of strength, not a spurious one, so that the child is not confused about its own strength, which has been tested again and again, realistically, against the hands and arms and wills of adults who know their own capacities. As a result, a very angry three-year-old girl can often be handled only by an adult, and a twelve-year-old girl or boy who attempts to lift and carry a screaming three-year-old child may be kicked and unable to keep the child from squirming away. The adults teach the child autonomy, conveying by their every act the admonitions: Be as strong as you can. We will back you up, give you every help, admire every step, turn away our eyes from your mistakes. So a small child's learning to walk has also the qualities of a coming-out party; there are always willing hands to help it practise and a group of spectators to exclaim with delight.

This combination of a premium on autonomy, on realistic precocity, and a will-

ingness to stand the strain and work involved in letting a child be as active as it wishes to be, produces a child who is highly sensitive to activity in others and extremely ready to imitate the behaviour of others who have, in many cases, picked up its behaviour to imitate initially. All action—walking, swimming, talking, dancing—is a reciprocal interweaving between adult and child in which every discrepancy in size, strength, and knowledge that can be minimized is minimized, as adult and child exchange the same word, fifty or sixty times, and the child sees itself mirrored, not in a looking glass, but in the strong, sure accents of adulthood. This mirroring has as an accompaniment a tendency for one to respond immediately to the acts of others. Any Manus group is an organized tense pattern in which people on one side of a room respond, either by direct imitation or contrapuntally, to people on the other, or in which groups are formed around some activity, like sailing a canoe, delivering a woman, caulking a hull, etc. Response to the activity of others is built into the activity system. The minimizing of differences between adult and child minimizes any tendency toward a refusal to imitate. Manus children can be stubborn and mutinous to verbal commands and respond with negative activity, but this does not seem to be accompanied by emotional withdrawal. As they experience imitation as a free act, so they also feel free to go their own way. Later, in adult life, the slightest diminution of ability to move, a strained muscle, a sprained ankle, a swollen shoulder, immediately arouses anxiety, brooding, and depression. The sense of the self as a zestful, active person is dependent upon movement, upon the ability to move freely and to get out of any uncomfortable situation by running away. The adults in turn work to circumscribe the area of safe running away; all political differences used to be solved by part of the group running away.

But in contrast to running away, people saw themselves as freely choosing everything that they were free to choose. The old Sir Ghost system, which simply channelled and drove this activity, was felt to be externally coercive.

In developmental terms, the Manus emphasize as the tasks of the toddler control of the body and sphincter control. The dominant emotional mood is anger. Even fear is expressed as anger, so that if a parent takes a child into a frightening situation, the child expresses its fear by beating the parent with its fists, demanding to be lifted off the ground or taken out of the frightening situation. Demanding assertiveness up to the limits of one's strength pitted against adult strength evokes in the adult a conflict between the desire to indulge the child and fatigue from the child's demands, and leads to frequent outbursts of anger. A mother sitting with a fifteen-month-old child in her arms and two older children playing about is engaged in a continuous active struggle as the children climb, push, and pull at each other with her body as the stage. Not infrequently, the observer is unable to distinguish between love and anger, play and punishment, as a mother breast-feeds a child, paddles it on its little behind, or shouts a lullaby which imitates the child's recent screams. The amount of screaming that goes on is roughly in inverse relation to the number of hands free to hold and amuse the child.

# From *A Room of One's Own*

*Virginia Woolf*

. . . Nothing is known about women before the eighteenth century. I have no model in my mind to turn about this way and that. Here am I asking why women did not write poetry in the Elizabethan age, and I am not sure how they were educated; whether they were taught to write; whether they had sitting-rooms to themselves; how many women had children before they were twenty-one; what, in short, they did from eight in the morning till eight at night. They had no money evidently; according to Professor Trevelyan they were married whether they liked it or not before they were out of the nursery, at fifteen or sixteen very likely. It would have been extremely odd, even upon this showing, had one of them suddenly written the plays of Shakespeare, I concluded, and I thought of that old gentleman, who is dead now, but was a bishop, I think, who declared that it was impossible for any woman, past, present, or to come, to have the genius of Shakespeare. He wrote to the papers about it. He also told a lady who applied to him for information that cats do not as a matter of fact go to heaven, though they have, he added, souls of a sort. How much thinking those old gentlemen used to save

one! How the borders of ignorance shrank back at their approach! Cats do not go to heaven. Women cannot write the plays of Shakespeare.

Be that as it may, I could not help thinking, as I looked at the works of Shakespeare on the shelf, that the bishop was right at least in this; it would have been impossible, completely and entirely, for any woman to have written the plays of Shakespeare in the age of Shakespeare. Let me imagine, since facts are so hard to come by, what would have happened had Shakespeare had a wonderfully gifted sister, called Judith, let us say. Shakespeare himself went, very probably—his mother was an heiress—to the grammar school, where he may have learnt Latin—Ovid, Virgil and Horace—and the elements of grammar and logic. He was, it is well known, a wild boy who poached rabbits, perhaps shot a deer, and had, rather sooner then he should have done, to marry a woman in the neighbourhood, who bore him a child rather quicker than was right. That escapade sent him to seek his fortune in London. He had, it seemed, a taste for the theatre; he began by holding horses at the stage door. Very soon he got work in the theatre, became a successful actor, and lived at the hub of the universe, meeting everybody, knowing everybody, practising his art on the boards, exercising his wits in the streets, and even getting access to the palace of the queen. Meanwhile his extraordinarily gifted sister, let us suppose, remained at home. She was as adven-

Virginia Woolf, a novelist, essayist, and critic, was one of the most influential modern British writers. She died in 1941.

turous, as imaginative, as agog to see the world as he was. But she was not sent to school. She had no chance of learning grammar and logic, let alone of reading Horace and Virgil. She picked up a book now and then, one of her brother's perhaps, and read a few pages. But then her parents came in and told her to mend the stockings or mind the stew and not moon about with books and papers. They would have spoken sharply but kindly, for they were substantial people who knew the conditions of life for a woman and loved their daughter—indeed, more likely than not she was the apple of her father's eye. Perhaps she scribbled some pages up in an apple loft on the sly, but was careful to hide them or set fire to them. Soon, however, before she was out of her teens, she was to be betrothed to the son of a neighbouring wool-stapler. She cried out that marriage was hateful to her, and for that she was severely beaten by her father. Then he ceased to scold her. He begged her instead not to hurt him, not to shame him in this matter of her marriage. He would give her a chain of beads or a fine petticoat, he said; and there were tears in his eyes. How could she disobey him? How could she break his heart? The force of her own gift alone drove her to it. She made up a small parcel of her belongings, let herself down by a rope one summer's night and took the road to London. She was not seventeen. The birds that sang in the hedge were not more musical than she was. She had the quickest fancy, a gift like her brother's, for the tune of words. Like him, she had a taste for the theatre. She stood at the stage door; she wanted to act, she said. Men laughed in her face. The manager—a fat, loose-lipped man—guffawed. He bellowed something about poodles dancing and women acting— no woman, he said, could possibly be an actress. He hinted—you can imagine what. She could get no training in her craft. Could she even seek her dinner in a tavern or roam the streets at midnight? Yet her genius was for fiction and lusted to feed abundantly upon the lives of men and women and the study of their ways. At last—for she was very young, oddly like Shakespeare the poet in her face, with the same grey eyes and rounded brows—at last Nick Greene the actor-manager took pity on her; she found herself with child by that gentleman and so— who shall measure the heat and violence of the poet's heart when caught and tangled in a woman's body?—killed herself one winter's night and lies buried at some cross-roads where the omnibuses now stop outside the Elephant and Castle.

That, more or less, is how the story would run, I think, if a woman in Shakespeare's day had had Shakespeare's genius. But for my part, I agree with the deceased bishop, if such he was—it is unthinkable that any woman in Shakespeare's day should have had Shakespeare's genius. For genius like Shakespeare's is not born among labouring, uneducated, servile people. It was not born in England among the Saxons and the Britons. It is not born today among the working classes. How, then, could it have been born among women whose work began, according to Professor Trevelyan, almost before they were out of the nursery, who were forced to it by their parents and held to it by all the power of law and custom? Yet genius of a sort must have existed among women as it must have existed among the working classes. Now and again an Emily Brontë or a Robert Burns blazes out and proves its presence. But certainly it never got itself on to paper. When, however, one reads of a witch being ducked, of a woman possessed by devils, of a wise woman selling herbs, or even of a very remarkable man who had a mother, then I think we are on the track of a lost novelist, a suppressed poet, of some mute and inglorious Jane Austen, some Emily Brontë who dashed her brains out on the moor or mopped and mowed about the highways crazed with the torture that her gift had put her to. Indeed, I would venture to guess that Anon, who wrote so many poems without signing them, was often a woman. It was a woman Edward Fitzgerald, I think, suggested who made the ballads and the folksongs, crooning them to her children, beguiling her spinning with them, or the length of the winter's night.

This may be true or it may be false—who cay say?—but what is true in it, so it seemed to me, reviewing the story of Shakespeare's sister as I had made it, is that any woman born with a great gift in the sixteenth century would certainly have gone crazed, shot herself, or ended her days in some lonely cottage outside the village, half witch, half wizard, feared and mocked at. For it needs little skill in psychology to be sure that a highly gifted girl who had tried to use her gift for poetry would have been so thwarted and hindered by other people, so tortured and pulled asunder by her own contrary instincts, that she must have lost her health and sanity to a certainty. No girl could have walked to London and stood at a stage door and forced her way into the presence of actor-managers without doing herself a violence and suffering an anguish which may have been irrational—for chastity may be a fetish invented by certain societies for unknown reasons—but were none the less inevitable. Chastity had then, it has even now, a religious importance in a woman's life, and has so wrapped itself round with nerves and instincts that to cut it free and bring it to the light of day demands courage of the rarest. To have lived a free life in London in the sixteenth century would have meant for a woman who was poet and playwright a nervous stress and dilemma which might well have killed her. Had she survived, whatever she had written would have been twisted and deformed, issuing from a strained and morbid imagination.

And undoubtedly, I thought, looking at the shelf where there are no plays by women, her work would have gone unsigned. That refuge she would have sought certainly. It was the relic of the sense of chastity that dictated anonymity to women even so late as the nineteenth century. Currer Bell, George Eliot, George Sand, all the victims of inner strife as their writings prove, sought ineffectively to veil themselves by using the name of a man. Thus they did homage to the convention, which if not implanted by the other sex was liberally encouraged by them (the chief glory of a woman is not to be talked of, said Pericles, himself a much-talked-of man), that publicity in women is detestable. Anonymity runs in their blood. The desire to be veiled still possesses them. They are not even now as concerned about the health of their fame as men are, and, speaking generally, will pass a tombstone or a signpost without feeling an irresistible desire to cut their names on it, as Alf, Bert or Chas. must do in obedience to their instinct, which murmurs if it sees a fine woman go by, or even a dog, Ce chien est à moi. And, of course, it may not be a dog, I thought, remembering Parliament Square, the Sieges Allee and other avenues; it may be a piece of land or a man with curly black hair. It is one of the great advantages of being a woman that one can pass even a very fine negress without wishing to make an Englishwoman of her.

That woman, then, who was born with a gift of poetry in the sixteenth century, was an unhappy woman, a woman at strife against herself. All the conditions of her life, all her own instincts, were hostile to the state of mind which is needed to set free whatever is in the brain. But what is the state of mind that is most propitious to the act of creation, I asked. Can one come by any notion of the state that furthers and makes possible that strange activity? Here I opened the volume containing the Tragedies of Shakespeare.

What was Shakespeare's state of mind, for instance, when he wrote *Lear* and *Antony and Cleopatra?* It was certainly the state of mind most favourable to poetry that there has ever existed. But Shakespeare himself said nothing about it. We only know casually and by chance that he "never blotted a line." Nothing indeed was ever said by the artist himself about his state of mind until the eighteenth century perhaps. Rousseau perhaps began it. At any rate, by the nineteenth century self-consciousness had developed so far that it was the habit for men of letters to describe their minds in confessions and autobiographies. Their lives also were written, and their letters were printed after their deaths. Thus, though we do not know what Shakespeare went through when he wrote *Lear,* we do know what Carlyle went through when he wrote the *French Revolution;* what Flaubert went through when he wrote *Madame Bovary;* what Keats was going through when he tried to write poetry against the coming of death and the indifference of the world.

And one gathers from this enormous modern literature of confession and self-analysis that to write a book of genius is almost always a feat of prodigious difficulty. Everything is against the likelihood that it will come from the writer's mind whole and entire. Generally material circumstances are against it. Dogs will bark; people will interrupt; money must be made; health will break down. Further, accentuating all these difficulties and making them harder to bear is the world's notorious indifference. It does not ask people to write poems and novels and histories; it does not need them. It does not care whether Flaubert finds the right word or whether Carlyle scrupulously verifies this or that fact. Naturally, it will not pay for what it does not want. And so the writer, Keats, Flaubert, Carlyle, suffers, especially in the creative years of youth, every form of dis-traction and discouragement. A curse, a cry of agony, rises from those books of analysis and confession. "Mighty poets in their misery dead"—that is the burden of their song. If anything comes through in spite of all this, it is a miracle, and probably no book is born entire and uncrippled as it was conceived.

But for women, I thought, looking at the empty shelves, these difficulties were infinitely more formidable. In the first place, to have a room of her own, let alone a quiet room or a sound-proof room, was out of the question, unless her parents were exceptionally rich or very noble, even up to the beginning of the eighteenth century.

• • •

The indifference of the world which Keats and Flaubert and other men of genius have found so hard to bear was in her case not indifference but hostility. The world did not say to her as it said to them, Write if you choose; it makes no difference to me. The world said with a guffaw, Write? What's the good of your writing?

• • •

Let us suppose that a father from the highest motives did not wish his daughter to leave home and become writer, painter or scholar. . . . Even if her father did not read out loud these opinions, any girl could read them for herself; and the reading, even in the nineteenth century, must have lowered her vitality, and told profoundly upon her work. There would always have been that assertion—you cannot do this, you are incapable of doing that—to protest against, to overcome. Probably for a novelist this germ is no longer of much effect; for there have been women novelists of merit. But for painters it must still have some sting in it; and for musicians, I imagine, is even now active and poisonous in the extreme. The woman composer stands where the actress stood in the time of Shakespeare. Nick Greene, I thought, remembering the story I had made about Shakespeare's sister, said that a woman acting put him in mind of a dog dancing. Johnson repeated the phrase two hundred years later of women preaching. And here, I said, opening a book about music, we have the very words used again in this year of grace, 1928, of women who try to write music. "Of Mlle. Germaine Tailleferre one can only repeat Dr. Johnson's dictum con-cerning a woman preacher, transposed into terms of music. 'Sir, a woman's composing is like a dog's walking on his hind legs. It is not done well, but you are surprised to find it done at all.' "[1] So accurately does history repeat itself.

## Notes

1. *A Survey of Contemporary Music,* Cecil Gray, p. 246.

# Friendships Among Men

*Marc Feigen Fasteau*

There is a long-standing myth in our society that the great friendships are between men. Forged through shared experience, male friendship is portrayed as the most unselfish, if not the highest form, of human relationship. The more traditionally masculine the shared experience from which it springs, the stronger and more profound the friendship is supposed to be. Going to war, weathering crises together at school or work, playing on the same athletic team, are some of the classic experiences out of which friendships between men are believed to grow.

By and large, men do prefer the company of other men, not only in their structured time but in the time they fill with optional, nonobligatory activity. They prefer to play games, drink, and talk, as well as work and fight together. Yet something is missing. Despite the time men spend together, their contact rarely goes beyond the external, a limitation which tends to make their friendships shallow and unsatisfying.

My own childhood memories are of doing things with my friends—playing games or sports, building walkie-talkies, going camping. Other people and my relationships to them were never legitimate subjects for attention. If someone liked me, it was an opaque, mysterious occurrence that bore no analysis. When I was slighted, I felt hurt. But relationships with people just happened. I certainly had feelings about my friends, but I can't remember a single instance of trying consciously to sort them out until I was well into college.

For most men this kind of shying away from the personal continues into adult life. In conversations with each other, we hardly ever use ourselves as reference points. We talk about almost everything except how we ourselves are affected by people and events. Everything is discussed as though it were taking place out there somewhere, as though we had no more felt response to it than to the weather. Topics that can be treated in this detached, objective way become conversational mainstays. The few subjects which are fundamentally personal are shaped into discussions of abstract general questions. Even in an exchange about their reactions to liberated women—a topic of intensely personal interest—the tendency will be to talk in general, theoretical terms. Work, at least its objective aspects, is always a safe subject. Men also spend an incredible amount of time rehashing the great public issues of the day. Until early 1973, Vietnam was the workhorse topic. Then came Watergate. It doesn't seem to matter that we've all had a hundred similar conversations. We plunge in for another round, trying to come up with a new angle as much as to impress the others with

Marc Feigen Fasteau is a lawyer who actively works for legislation to eliminate sex discrimination.

Excerpt from *The Male Machine* (New York: McGraw-Hill, 1974 [pp. 6–17]). Reprinted by permission of the publisher.

what we know as to keep from being bored stiff.

Games play a central role in situations organized by men. I remember a weekend some years ago at the country house of a law-school classmate as a blur of softball, football, croquet, poker, and a dice-and-board game called Combat, with swimming thrown in on the side. As soon as one game ended, another began. Taken one at a time, these "activities" were fun, but the impression was inescapable that the host, and most of his guests, would do anything to stave off a lull in which they would be together without some impersonal focus for their attention. A snapshot of almost any men's club would show the same thing, 90 percent of the men engaged in some activity—ranging from backgammon to watching the tube—other than, or at least as an aid to, conversation.[1]

My composite memory of evenings spent with a friend at college and later when we shared an apartment in Washington is of conversations punctuated by silences during which we would internally pass over any personal or emotional thoughts which had arisen and come back to the permitted track. When I couldn't get my mind off personal matters, I said very little. Talks with my father have always had the same tone. Respect for privacy was the rationale for our diffidence. His questions to me about how things were going at school or at work were asked as discreetly as he would have asked a friend about someone's commitment to a hospital for the criminally insane. Our conversations, when they touched these matters at all, to say nothing of more sensitive matters, would veer quickly back to safe topics of general interest.

In our popular literature, the archetypal male hero embodying this personal muteness is the cowboy. The classic mold for the character was set in 1902 by Owen Wister's novel *The Virginian* where the author spelled out, with an explicitness that was never again necessary, the characteristics of his protagonist. Here's how it goes when two close friends the Virginian hasn't seen in some time take him out for a drink.

All of them had seen rough days together, and they felt guilty with emotion.
"It's hot weather," said Wiggin.
"Hotter in Box Elder," said McLean. "My kid has started teething."
Words ran dry again. They shifted their positions, looked in their glasses, read the labels on the bottles. They dropped a word now and then to the proprietor about his trade, and his ornaments.

One of the Virginian's duties is to assist at the hanging of an old friend as a horse thief. Afterward, for the first time in the book, he is visibly upset. The narrator puts his arm around the hero's shoulders and describes the Virginian's reaction:

I had the sense to keep silent, and presently he shook my hand, not looking at me as he did so. He was always very shy of demonstration.

And, for explanation of such reticence, "As all men know, he also knew that many things should be done in this world in silence, and that talking about them is a mistake."

There are exceptions, but they only prove the rule.

One is the drunken confidence. "Bob, ole boy, I gotta tell ya—being divorced isn't so hot. . . . [ and see, I'm too drunk to be held responsible for blurting it out.]" Here, drink becomes an excuse for exchanging confidences and a device for periodically loosening the restraint against expressing a need for sympathy and support from other men—which may explain its importance as a male ritual. Marijuana fills a similar need.

Another exception is talking to a stranger—who may be either someone the speaker doesn't know or someone who isn't in the same social or business world. (Several black friends told me that they have been on the receiving end of personal confidences from white acquaintances that they were sure had not been shared with white friends.) In either case, men are willing to talk about themselves only to other men with whom they do not have to compete or whom they will not have to confront socially later.

Finally, there is the way men depend on women to facilitate certain conversations. The women in a mixed group are usually the ones who make the first personal reference, about themselves or others present. The men can then join in without having the onus for initiating a discussion of "personalities." Collectively, the men can "blame" the conversation on the women. They can also feel in these conversations that since they are talking "to" the women instead of "to" the men, they can be excused for deviating from the masculine norm. When the women leave, the tone and subject invariably shift away from the personal.

The effect of these constraints is to make it extraordinarily difficult for men to really get to know each other. A psychotherapist who has conducted a lengthy series of encounter groups for men summed it up:

With saddening regularity [the members of these groups] described how much they wanted to have closer, more satisfying relationships with other men: "I'd settle for having one really close man friend. I supposedly have some close men friends now. We play golf or go for a drink. We complain about our jobs and our wives. I care about them and they care about me. We even have some physical contact—I mean we may even give a hug on a big occasion. But it's not enough."

The sources of this stifling ban on self-disclosure, the reasons why men hide from each other, lie in the taboos and imperatives of the masculine stereotype.

To begin with, men are supposed to be functional, to spend their time working or otherwise solving or thinking about how to solve problems. Personal reaction, how one feels about something, is considered dysfunctional, at best an irrelevant distraction from the expected objectivity. Only weak men, and women, talk about—i.e., "give in," to their feelings. "I group my friends in two ways," said a business executive:

those who have made it and don't complain and those who haven't made it. And only the latter spend time talking to their wives about their problems and how bad their boss is and all that. The ones who concentrate more on communicating . . . are those who have realized that they aren't going to make it and therefore they have changed the focus of attention.

In a world which tells men they have to choose between expressiveness and manly strength, this characterization may be accurate. Most of the men who talk personally to other men *are* those whose problems have gotten the best of them, who simply can't help it. Men not driven to despair don't talk about themselves, so the idea that self-disclosure and expressiveness are associated with problems and weakness becomes a self-fulfilling prophecy.

Obsessive competitiveness also limits the range of communication in male friendships. Competition is the principal mode by which men relate to each other—at one level because they don't know how else to make contact, but more basically because it is the way to demonstrate, to themselves and others, the key masculine qualities of unwavering toughness and the ability to dominate and control. The result is that they inject competition into situations which don't call for it.

In conversations, you must show that you know more about the subject than the other man, or at least as much as he does. For example, I have often engaged in a contest that could be called My Theory Tops Yours, disguised as a serious exchange of ideas. The proof that it wasn't serious was that I was willing to participate even when I was sure that the participants, including myself, had nothing fresh to say. Convincing the other person—victory—is the main objective, with control of the floor an important tactic. Men tend to lecture at each other, insist that the discussion follow their train of thought, and are often unwilling to listen. As one member of a men's rap group said,

When I was talking I used to feel that I had to be driving to a point, that it had to be rational and organized, that I had to persuade at all times, rather than exchange thoughts and ideas.

Even in casual conversation some men hold back unless they are absolutely sure of what they are saying. They don't want to have to change a position once they have taken it. It's "just like a woman" to change your mind, and, more important, it is inconsistent with the approved masculine posture of total independence.

Competition was at the heart of one of my closest friendships, now defunct. There was a good deal of mutual liking and respect. We went out of our way to spend time with each other and wanted to work together. We both had "prospects" as "bright young men" and the same "liberal but tough" point of view. We recognized this about each other, and this recognition was the basis of our respect and of our sense of equality. That we saw each other as equals was important— our friendship was confirmed by the reflection of one in the other. But our constant and all-encompassing competition made this equality precarious and fragile. One way or another, everything counted in the measuring process. We fought out our tennis matches as though our lives depended on it. At poker, the two of us would often play on for hours after the others had left. These *mano a mano* poker marathons seem in retrospect especially revealing of the competitiveness of the relationship: playing for small stakes, the es-

sence of the game is in outwitting, psychologically beating down the other player—the other skills involved are negligible. Winning is the only pleasure, one that evaporates quickly, a truth that struck me in inchoate form every time our game broke up at four A.M. and I walked out the door with my five-dollar winnings, a headache, and a sense of time wasted. Still, I did the same thing the next time. It was what we did together, and somehow it counted. Losing at tennis could be balanced by winning at poker; at another level, his moving up in the federal government by my getting on the *Harvard Law Review.*

This competitiveness feeds the most basic obstacle to openness between men, the inability to admit to being vulnerable. Real men, we learn early, are not supposed to have doubts, hopes and ambitions which may not be realized, things they don't (or even especially do) like about themselves, fears and disappointments. Such feelings and concerns, of course, are part of everyone's inner life, but a man must keep quiet about them. If others know how you really feel you can be hurt, and that in itself is incompatible with manhood. The inhibiting effect of this imperative is not limited to disclosures of major personal problems. Often men do not share even ordinary uncertainties and half-formulated plans of daily life with their friends. And when they do, they are careful to suggest that they already know how to proceed—that they are not really asking for help or understanding but simply for particular bits of information. Either way, any doubts they have are presented as external, carefully characterized as having to do with the issue as distinct from the speaker. They are especially guarded about expressing concern or asking a question that would invite personal comment. It is almost impossible for men to simply exchange thoughts about matters involving them personally in a comfortable, non-crisis atmosphere. If a friend tells you of his concern that he and a colleague are always disagreeing, for example, he is likely to quickly supply his own explanation—something like "different professional backgrounds." The effect is to rule out observations or suggestions that do not fit within this already reconnoitered protective structure. You don't suggest, even if you believe it is true, that in fact the disagreements arise because he presents his ideas in a way which tends to provoke a hostile reaction. It would catch him off guard; it would be something he hadn't already thought of and accepted about himself and, for that reason, no matter how constructive and well-intentioned you might be, it would put you in control for the moment. He doesn't want that; he is afraid of losing your respect. So, sensing he feels that way, because you would yourself, you say something else. There is no real give-and-take.

It is hard for men to get angry at each other honestly. Anger between friends often means that one has hurt the other. Since the straightforward expression of anger in these situations involves an admission of vulnerability, it is safer to stew silently or find an "objective" excuse for retaliation. Either way, trust is not fully restored.

Men even try to let it show when they feel good. We may report the reasons for our happiness, if they have to do with concrete accomplishments, but we try to do it with straight face, as if to say, "Here's what happened, but it hasn't affected my grown-up unemotional equilibrium, and I am not asking for any kind of response." Happiness is a precarious, "childish" feeling, easy to shoot down. Others may find the event that triggers it trivial or incomprehensible, or even threatening to their own self-esteem—in the sense that if one man is up, another man is down. So we tend not to take the risk of expressing it.

What is particularly difficult for men is seeking or accepting help from friends. I, for one, learned early that dependence was unacceptable. When I was eight, I went to a summer camp I disliked. My parents visited me in the middle of the summer and, when it was time for them to leave, I wanted to go with them. They refused, and I yelled and screamed and was miserably unhappy for the rest of the day. That evening an older camper comforted me, sitting by my bed as I cried, patting me on the back soothingly and saying whatever it is that one says at times like that. He was in some way clumsy or funny-looking, and a few days later I joined a group of kids in cruelly making fun of him, an act which upset me, when I thought about it, for years. I can only explain it in terms of my feeling, as early as the age of eight, that by needing and accepting his help and comfort I had compromised myself, and took it out on him.

"You can't express dependence when you feel it," a corporate executive said, "because it's a kind of absolute. If you are loyal 90 percent of the time and disloyal 10 percent, would you be considered loyal? Well, the same happens with independence, you are either dependent or independent; you can't be both." "Feelings of dependence," another explained, "are identified with weakness or 'untoughness' and our culture doesn't accept those things in men." The result is that we either go it alone or "act out certain games or rituals to provoke the desired reaction in the other and have our needs satisfied without having to ask for anything."

Somewhat less obviously, the expression of affection also runs into emotional barriers growing out of the masculine stereotype. When I was in college, I was suddenly quite moved while attending a friend's wedding. The surge of feeling made me uncomfortable and self-conscious. There was nothing inherently difficult or, apart from the fact of being moved by a moment of tenderness, "unmasculine" about my reaction. I just did not know how to deal with or communicate what I felt. "I consider myself a sentimentalist," one man said, "and I think I am quite able to express my feelings. But the other day my wife described a friend of mine to some people as my best friend and I felt embarrassed when I heard her say it."

A major source of these inhibitions is the fear of being, of being thought, homosexual. Nothing is more frightening to a heterosexual man in our society. It threatens, at one stroke, to take away every vestige of his claim to a masculine identity—something like knocking out the foundation of a building—and to expose him to the ostracism, ranging from polite tolerance to violent revulsion, of his friends and colleagues. A man can be labeled as homosexual not just because of overt sexual act but because of almost any sign of behavior which does not fit the masculine stereotype. The touching of another man, other than shaking hands, or, under emotional stress, an arm around the shoulder, is taboo. Women may kiss each other when they meet; men are uncomfortable when hugged even by close friends. Onlookers might misinterpret what they saw, and more important, what would we think of ourselves if we feel a twinge of sexual pleasure from the embrace.

Direct verbal expressions of affection or tenderness are also something that only homosexuals and women engage in. Between "real" men affection has to be disguised in gruff, "you old son-of-a-bitch" style. Paradoxically, in some instances, terms of endearment between men can be used as a ritual badge of manhood, dangerous medicine safe only for the strong. The flirting with homosexuality that characterizes the initiation rites of many fraternities and men's clubs serves this purpose. Claude Brown wrote about black life in New York City in the 1950s:

The term ["baby"] had a hip ring to it. . . . It was like saying, "Man, look at me. I've got masculinity to spare. . . . I can say 'baby' to another cat and he can say 'baby' to me, and we can say it with strength in our voices." If you could say it, this meant that you really had to be sure of yourself, sure of your masculinity.

Fear of homosexuality does more than inhibit the physical display of affection. One of the major recurring themes in the men's groups led by psychotherapist Don Clark was:

"A large segment of my feelings about other men are unknown or distorted because I am afraid they might have something to do with homosexuality. Now I'm lonely for other men and don't know how to find what I want with them."

As Clark observes, "The specter of homosexuality seems to be the dragon at the gateway to self-awareness, understanding, and acceptance of male-male needs. If a man tries to pretend the dragon is not there by turning a blind eye to erotic feelings for all other males, he also blinds himself to the rich variety of feelings that are related."

The few situations in which men do acknowledge strong feelings of affection and dependence toward other men are exceptions which prove the rule. With "cop couples," for example, or combat soldier "buddies," intimacy and dependence are forced on the men by their work—they have to ride in the patrol car or be in the same foxhole with somebody—and the jobs themselves have such highly masculine images that the man can get away with behavior that would be suspect under any other conditions.

Furthermore, even these combat-buddy relationships, when looked at closely, turn out not to be particularly intimate or personal. Margaret Mead has written:

During the last war English observers were confused by the apparent contradiction between American soldiers' emphasis on the buddy, so grievously exemplified in the breakdowns that followed a buddy's death, and the results of detailed inquiry which showed how transitory these buddy relationships were. It was found that men actually accepted their buddies as derivatives from their outfit, and from accidents of association, rather than because of any special personality characteristics capable of ripening into friendship.

One effect of the fear of appearing to be homosexual is to reinforce the practice that two men rarely get together alone without a reason. I once called a friend to suggest that we have dinner together. "O.K.," he said. "What's up?" I felt uncomfortable telling him that I just wanted to talk, that there was no other reason for the invitation.

Men get together to conduct business, to drink, to play games and sports, to re-establish contact after long absences, to participate in heterosexual social occasions—circumstances in which neither person is responsible for actually wanting to see the other. Men are particularly comfortable seeing each other in groups. The group situations defuses any possible assumptions about the intensity of feeling between particular men and provides the safety of numbers— "All the guys are here." It makes personal communication, which requires a level of trust and mutual understanding not generally shared by all members of a group, more difficult and offers an excuse for avoiding this dangerous territory. And it provides what is most sought after in men's friendships: mutual reassurance of masculinity.

## Notes

1. Women may use games as a reason for getting together—bridge clubs, for example. But the show is more for the rest of the world—to indicate that they are doing *something*—and the games themselves are not the only means of communication.

Reading 6.6

# On Human Work

*John Paul II*

## A Particular Task for the Church

It is right to devote the last part of these reflections about human work, on the occasion of the ninetieth anniversary of the Encyclical *Rerum novarum,* to the spirituality of work in the Christian sense. Since work in its subjective aspect is always a personal action, an *actus personae,* it follows that *the whole person, body and spirit,* participates in it, whether it is manual or intellectual work. It is also to the whole person that the word of the living God is directed, the evangelical message of salvation, in which we find many points which concern human work and which throw particular light on it. These points need to be properly assimilated: an inner effort on the part of the human spirit, guided by faith, hope and charity, is needed in order that through these points the *work* of the individual human being may *be given the meaning which it has in the eyes of God* and by means of which work enters into the salvation process on a par with the other ordinary yet particularly important components of its texture.

The Church considers it her duty to speak out on work from the viewpoint of its human value and of the moral order to which it belongs, and she sees this as one of her important tasks within the service that she renders to the evangelical message as a whole. At the same time she sees it as her particular duty *to form a spirituality of work* which will help all people to come closer, through work, to God, the Creator and Redeemer, to participate in His salvific plan for man and the world and to deepen their friendship with Christ in their lives by accepting, through faith, a living participation in His three-fold mission as Priest, Prophet and King, as the Second Vatican Council so eloquently teaches.

## Work as a Sharing in the Activity of the Creator

As the Second Vatican Council says, "throughout the course of the centuries, men have labored to better the circumstances of their lives through a monumental amount of individual and collective effort. To believers, this point is settled: considered in itself, such human activity accords with God's will. For man, created to God's image, received a mandate to subject to himself the earth and all that it contains, and to govern the world with justice and holiness; a mandate to relate himself and the totality of things to Him who was to be acknowledged as the Lord and Creator of all. Thus, by the subjection of all things to man, the name of God would be wonderful in all the earth."

The word of God's revelation is profoundly marked by the fundamental truth that *man,* created in the image of God, *shares by his work in the activity of the Creator* and

Pope John Paul II was chosen leader of the world's Catholics in 1978, the first non-Italian pope in 400 years.

(c) Vatican Translation.

that, within the limits of his own human capabilities, man in a sense continues to develop that activity, and perfects it as he advances further and further in the discovery of the resources and values contained in the whole of creation. We find this truth at the very beginning of Sacred Scripture, in the book of Genesis, where the creation activity itself is presented in the form of "work" done by God during "six days," "resting" on the seventh day. Besides, the last book of Sacred Scripture echoes the same respect for what God has done through His creative "work" when it proclaims: "Great and wonderful are your deeds, O Lord God the Almighty"; this is similar to the book of Genesis, which concludes the description of each day of creation with the statement: "And God saw that it was good."

This description of creation, which we find in the very first chapter of the book of Genesis, is also *in a sense the first "gospel of work."* For it shows what the dignity of work consists of: it teaches that man ought to imitate God, his Creator, in working, because man alone has the unique characteristic of likeness to God. Man ought to imitate God both in working and also in resting, since God Himself wished to present His own creative activity under the form of *work and rest.* This activity by God in the world always continues, as the words of *Christ attest: "My Father is working still. . .":* He works with creative power by sustaining in existence the world that He called into being from nothing, and He works with salvific power in the hearts of those whom from the beginning He has destined for "rest" in union with Himself in His "Father's house." Therefore man's work too not only requires a rest every "seventh day," but also cannot consist in the mere exercise of human strength in external action; it must leave room for man to prepare himself, by becoming more and more what in the will of God he ought to be, for the

*"rest" that the Lord reserves for His servants and friends.*

Awareness that man's work is a participation in God's activity ought to permeate, as the Council teaches, even *"the most ordinary everyday activities.* For, while providing the substance of life for themselves and their families, men and women are performing their activities in a way which appropriately benefits society. They can justly consider that by their labor they are unfolding the Creator's work, consulting the advantages of their brothers and sisters, and contributing by their personal industry to the realization in history of the divine plan."

This Christian spirituality of work should be a heritage shared by all. Especially in the modern age, the *spirituality* of work should show the *maturity* called for by the tensions and restlessness of mind and heart. "Far from thinking that works produced my man's own talent and energy are in opposition to God's power, and that the rational creature exists as a kind of rival to the Creator, Christians are convinced that the triumphs of the human race are a sign of God's greatness and the flowering of His own mysterious design. For the greater man's power becomes, the farther his individual and community responsibility extends. . . . People are not deterred by *the Christian message* from building up the world, or impelled to neglect the welfare of their fellows. They are, rather, more stringently bound to do these very things."

The knowledge that by means of work man shares in the work of creation constitutes the most profound *motive* for undertaking it in various sectors. "The faithful, therefore," we read in the Constitution *Lumen gentium,* "must learn the deepest meaning and the value of all creation, and its orientation to the praise of God. Even by their secular activity they must assist one another to live holier lives. In this way the world will be permeated by the spirit of Christ and more effectively achieve its purpose in justice, charity and peace. . . . Therefore, by their competence in secular fields and by their personal activity, elevated from within by the grace of Christ, let them work vigorously so that by human labor, technical skill, and civil culture created goods may be perfected according to the design of the Creator and the light of His Word.''

• • •

# The Hindu Way to God Through Work

*Huston Smith*

The path toward God, intended for persons of active bent, is *karma yoga,* the path toward God through work.

An examination of the anatomy and physiology of the human organism discloses an interesting fact. All organs of digestion and respiration serve to feed the blood with nutritive materials. The circulatory apparatus delivers this nourishing blood throughout the body maintaining bones, joints, and muscles. Bones provide a framework without which the muscles could not operate while joints supply the flexibility needed for movement. The brain envisions the movements that are to be made and the spinal nervous system executes them. The vegetative nervous system helped by the endocrine system maintains the harmony of the viscera on which the motor muscles depend. In short, the entire body except for its reproductive apparatus converges toward muscles and their movements. All human life when looked at from the angle of the body converges on action. "The human machine," writes a contemporary physician, "seems indeed to be made *for action.*"

Work is the staple of human life. The point is not simply that all but the few who are born into the truly leisure class have to

Huston Smith is Thomas J. Watson Professor of Religion, Emeritus, at Syracuse University.

work. Ultimately, the impulse to work is psychologically, not economically, motivated. Forced to be idle most persons become irritable; forced to retire they decline. Included are the Marthas trotting from chore to chore, as well as captains of industry. To such persons Hinduism says, You don't have to retire to a cloister to realize God. You can find him in the world of everyday affairs as readily as anywhere. Throw yourself into your work with everything you have, only do so wisely, in a way that will bring the highest rewards, not just trivia. Learn the secret of work by which every movement can carry you Godward even while other things are being accomplished, like a wristwatch that winds itself as other duties are being attended to.

How this is to be done depends on other components in the worker's nature. By assuming this path he has already indicated his predominantly active disposition, but there remains the question of whether in other respects he is inclined more in a reflective or affective direction. The path of work has alternate routes depending on whether it is approached philosophically or in the attitude of love. In the language of the four *yogas, karma yoga* can be practiced under the mode either of *jnana* (knowledge) or *bhakti* (devotion).

As we have seen, the point of life is to transcend the smallness of the finite self.

This can be done either by shifting the center of interest and affection to a personal God experienced as distinct from oneself or by identifying oneself with the impersonal Absolute that resides at the core of one's being. The first is the way of the *bhakta*, the second the *jnani*. Work can be a vehicle for self-transcendence by either approach. For according to Hindu doctrine every action performed upon the external world has its correlative internal reaction upon the doer. If I chop down a tree that blocks my view, each stroke of the ax unsettles the tree but leaves its mark on me as well, driving deeper into my being my determination to have my way in the world. Every deed I do for the sake of my own private welfare adds another coating to the ego and in thus thickening it insulates it further from God within or without. Correlatively, every act done without thought of self diminishes self-centeredness until finally no barrier remains to cloud one from the divine.

The best way for the emotionally inclined to render his work selfless is to bring his ardent and affectionate nature into play and work for God's sake instead of his own. "He who performs actions without attachment, resigning them to God, is untainted by their effects as the lotus leaf by water." Such a one is just as active as before, but he works for a completely different reason. His whole orientation toward the tasks of his daily life has become one of devotion. Every act of his diurnal routine is performed without concern for its effect upon himself. Not only is it performed as a service to God; it is regarded as prompted by God's will, executed for God's sake, and transacted by God's own energy which is being channeled through the devotee. "Thou art the Doer, I the instrument." Performed in this spirit actions lighten the ego instead of encumbering it. Each task becomes a sacred ritual, lovingly fulfilled as a living sacrifice to God and his glory without thought of profit that might redound to the individual. "Whatever you do, whatever you eat, whatever you offer in sacrifice, whatever you give away, whatever austerity you practice, O Son of Kunti, do this as an offering to Me. Thus shall you be free from the bondages of actions that bear good and evil results." They have no desire for the fruits of their actions," echoes the *Bhagavata Purana*: "These persons would not accept even . . . the state of union with Me; they would always prefer My service."

A young man, newly married and in love, works not for himself alone. As he works the thought of his beloved is in the back of his mind giving meaning and purpose to all his labors. So too with a devoted servant. He claims nothing for himself. Regardless of personal cost he does his duty for his master's satisfaction. Just so is God's will the sole joy and satisfaction of the devotee. Surrendering himself to the Lord of all, he remains untouched by the uncertainties of life over which he has no control. Such persons' backs never break. They never grow discouraged for they do not ask to win; they ask only to be on the side where they belong. They know that if history ever changes it will not be men who will change it but its Author—when men come to the point that they want it changed. Men in history lose their centering in eternity when they grow anxious for the outcome of their deeds. As long as they rest them on the knees of the Living God they are released by them from the bondages of the sea of death. "Do without attachment the work you have to do. . . . Surrendering all action to Me . . . freeing yourself from longing and selfishness, fight—unperturbed by grief."

Once he has forsaken every claim on his acts including all claims for success, the *karma yogi's* deeds no longer boomerang to litter and increase his ego. They leave no mark on his mind to produce future effects, good or evil. In this way he works out the accumulated impressions of previous deeds without acquiring new ones. Whatever one's reaction to this imagery, it is not difficult to see the psychological truth of such a description. A man who is completely at the disposal of others does not exist. When Negro slaves accidently hurt their feet or their hands, they used to say wryly, "It does not matter, it is the master's foot, the master's hand." He who has no sense of possessiveness around which selfhood can crystallize does not exist. The Spanish put the point nicely: "Would you like to become invisible? Have no thought of yourself for two years and no one will notice you."

Work as a path toward God takes a different turn for persons whose dispositions are more reflective than emotional. For these too the key is work done unselfishly, but the psychological framework is different. Philosophers tend to find the idea of Infinite Being at the center of one's self more meaningful than the thought of a personal Heavenly Father who stands over and above men and the world ruling them with a love that is eternal. It is only intelligent, therefore, that their approach to work should be adapted to this perspective.

The secret of this *jnana* approach to work consists in discrimination. Specifically it consists in drawing a sharp line between the empirical self immersed in action and the eternal self which stands aloof from it. Man's usual interest in work relates to the consequences it will have for his empirical self, the pay or acclaim it will bring. Such interests obviously inflate the ego and thicken the insulation between our conscious selves and the Infinite that is beneath them.

The way that leads to enlightenment is work performed in the spirit of complete detachment, almost dissociation, from the empirical self. Identifying himself securely with the Eternal, the worker goes about his duties, but as these are being effected by his empirical self, his True Self is in no way involved with them. "The knower of Truth, [being] centered [in the Self] should think, 'I do nothing at all'—though seeing, hearing, touching, smelling, eating, going, sleeping, breathing, speaking, letting go, holding, opening and closing the eyes—convinced that it is the senses that move among sense objects."

As the *yogi's* identification shifts from his finite to his infinite self, he will become increasingly indifferent to the consequences that flow from his work for the former. More and more he will recognize the truth of the *Gita's* dictum: "To work you have the right, but not the fruits thereof." Duty for duty's sake becomes his sole concern in action.

> He who does the task
> Dictated by duty,
> Caring nothing
> For the fruit of the action,
> He is a yogi.

Hence the story of the *yogi* who as he sat meditating on the banks of the Ganges saw a scorpion fall into the water before him. He scooped it out, only to have it bite him. Presently the scorpion fell into the river again. Once more the *yogi* rescued him, only to be bitten a second time. The sequence was repeated twice more, whereupon a bystander asked the *yogi*, "Why do you keep rescuing that scorpion when the only gratitude it shows is to bite you?" It is the nature of *yogis* to help others when they can."

The *karma yogi* will try to do each thing as it comes as if it were the only thing he has to do, and having done it or being forced to leave it to go on to another duty, to do so in the same spirit. He will seek to concentrate fully and calmly on each duty as it presents itself, resisting all impatience, excitement, and the vain attempt to do or think of half a dozen things at once. Into the various tasks that fall to his lot he will put

all the strokes he can, for to do otherwise
would be to yield to laziness which is simply
a variety of selfishness; but once he has done
this he will dissociate himself from the act
and let the chips fall where they may.

One to me is loss or gain,
One to me is fame or shame,
One to me is pleasure, pain.

# A Farewell to Work

*Barbara Ehrenreich*

The media just buried the last yuppie, a pathetic creature who had not heard the news that the great pendulum of public consciousness has just swung from Greed to Compassion and from Tex-Mex to meatballs. Folks lined up outside the mausoleum bearing many items he had hoped to take with him, including a quart bottle of raspberry vinegar and the Cliffs notes for *The Wealth of Nations*. I also brought something to throw onto the funeral pyre—the very essence of yupdom, its creed and its meaning. Not the passion for money, not even the lust for tiny vegetables, but the work ethic.

Yes, I realize how important the work ethic is. I understand that it occupies the position in the American constellation of values once held by motherhood and Girl Scout cookies. But yuppies took it too far; they *abused* it.

One of the reasons they only lived for three years (1984–1987) was that they *never* rested, never took the time to chew between bites or gaze soulfully past their computer screens. What's worse, the mere rumor that someone—anyone—was not holding up his or her end of the work ethic was enough to send them into tantrums. They blamed lazy workers for The Decline of Productivity.

Barbara Ehrenreich writes columns and essays about popular culture and social history for a wide variety of magazines, including *The Nation, Ms.,* and *Mother Jones.*

From *Mother Jones* (May 1988). Reprinted by permission of *Mother Jones.*

They blamed lazy welfare mothers for The Budget Deficit. Their idea of utopia (as once laid out in that journal of higher yup thought, the *New Republic*) was the "Work Ethic State": no free lunches, no handouts, and too bad for all the miscreants and losers who refuse to fight their way up to the poverty level by working 80 hours a week at Wendy's.

Personally, I have nothing against work, particularly when performed, quietly and unobtrusively, by someone else. I just don't happen to think it's an appropriate subject for an "ethic." As a general rule, when something gets elevated to apple-pie status in the hierarchy of American values, you have to suspect that its actual monetary value is skidding toward zero. Take motherhood: nobody ever thought of putting it on a moral pedestal until some brash feminists pointed out, about a century ago, that the pay is lousy and the career ladder nonexistent. Same thing with work: would we all be so reverent about the "work ethic" if it weren't for the fact that the average working stiff's hourly pay is shrinking, year by year, toward the price of a local phone call?

In fact, let us set the record straight: the work ethic is not a "traditional value." It is a johnny-come-lately value, along with thin thighs and nonsmoking hotel rooms. In ancient times, work was considered a disgrace inflicted upon those who had failed to amass a nest egg through imperial conquest or other forms of organized looting. Only serfs, slaves, and women worked. The yuppies of ancient Athens—which we all know was a perfect cornucopia of "traditional values"—passed their time rubbing their bodies with olive oil and discussing the Good, the True, and the Beautiful.

The work ethic came along a couple of millennia later, in the form of Puritanism—the idea that the amount of self-denial you endured in this life was a good measure of the amount of fun awaiting you in the next. But the work ethic only got off the ground with the Industrial Revolution and the arrival of the factory system. This was—let us be honest about it—simply a scheme for extending the benefits of the slave system into the age of emancipation.

Under the new system (aka capitalism, in this part of the world), huge numbers of people had to be convinced to work extra hard, at pitifully low wages, so that the employing class would not have to work at all. Overnight, with the help of a great number of preachers and other well-rested propagandists, work was upgraded from an indignity to an "ethic."

But there was a catch: the aptly named *working* class came to resent the *resting* class. There followed riots, revolutions, graffiti. Quickly the word went out from the robber barons to the swelling leisure class of lawyers, financial consultants, plant managers, and other forerunners of the yuppie: Look busy! Don't go home until the proles have punched out! Make 'em think *we're* doing the work and that they're lucky to be able to hang around and help out!

The lawyers, managers, etc., were only too happy to comply, for as the perennially clever John Kenneth Galbraith once pointed out, they themselves constituted a "new leisure class." Of course, they "work," but only under the most pleasant, air-conditioned, centrally heated, and fully carpeted conditions, and then only in a sitting position. It was in their own interest to convince the working class that what looks like lounging requires intense but invisible effort.

The yuppies, when they came along, had to look more righteously busy than anyone, for the simple reason that they did nothing at all. Workwise, that is. They did not sow, neither did they reap, but rather sat around pushing money through their modems in games known as "corporate takeover" and "international currency speculation." Hence their rage at anyone who actually works—the "unproductive" American worker, or the woman attempting to raise a family on welfare benefits set below the average yuppie's monthly spa fee.

So let us replace their cruel and empty slogan—"Go for it!"—with the cry that lies deep in every true worker's heart: "Gimme a break!" What this nation needs is not the work ethic, but a *job* ethic: if it needs doing—highways repaired, babies changed, fields plowed—let's get it done. Otherwise, take five. Listen to some new wave music, have a serious conversation with a three-year-old, write a poem, look at the sky. Let the yuppies Rest in Peace. The rest of us deserve a break.

419

# CRITO

*Plato*

*About the time of Socrates' trial, a state galley had set out on an annual religious mission to Delos and while it was away no execution was allowed to take place. So it was that Socrates was kept in prison for a month after the trial. The ship has now arrived at Cape Sunium in Attica and is thus expected at the Piraeus momentarily. So Socrates' old and faithful friend, Crito, makes one last effort to persuade him to escape into exile, and all arrangements for this plan have been made. It is this conversation between the two old friends that Plato professes to report in this dialogue. It is, as Crito plainly tells him, his last chance, but Socrates will not take it, and he gives his reasons for his refusal. Whether this conversation took place at this particular time is not important, for there is every reason to believe that Socrates' friends tried to plan his escape, and that he refused. Plato more than hints that the authorities would not have minded much, as long as he left the country.*

SOCRATES: Why have you come so early, Crito? Or is it not still early?

CRITO: It certainly is.

S: How early?

C: Early dawn.

Plato, who lived between the fifth and fourth centuries B.C., was the most famous of the ancient Greek philosophers.

Pages 45–56 of *Five Dialogues,* translated by G. M. A. Grube, 1981. With the permission of Hackett Publishing Co., Indianapolis, IN, and Cambridge, MA.

S: I am surprised that the warder was willing to listen to you.

C: He is quite friendly to me by now, Socrates. I have been here often and I have given him something.

S: Have you just come, or have you been here for some time?

C: A fair time.

S: Then why did you not wake me right away but sit there in silence?

C: By Zeus no, Socrates. I would not myself want to be in distress and awake so long. I have been surprised to see you so peacefully asleep. It was on purpose that I did not wake you, so that you should spend your time most agreeably. Often in the past throughout my life, I have considered the way you live happy, and especially so now that you bear your present misfortune so easily and lightly.

S: It would not be fitting at my age to resent the fact that I must die now.

C: Other men of your age are caught in such misfortunes, but their age does not prevent them resenting their fate.

S: That is so. Why have you come so early?

C: I bring bad news, Socrates, not for you, apparently, but for me and all your friends the news is bad and hard to bear. Indeed, I would count it among the hardest.

S: What is it? Or has the ship arrived from Delos, at the arrival of which I must die?

C: It has not arrived yet, but it will, I believe, arrive today, according to a message brought by some men from Sunium, where they left it. This makes it obvious that it will come today, and that your life must end tomorrow.

S: May it be for the best. If it so please the gods, so be it. However, I do not think it will arrive today.

C: What indication have you of this?

S: I will tell you. I must die the day after the ship arrives.

C: That is what those in authority say.

S: Then I do not think it will arrive on this coming day, but on the next. I take to witness of this a dream I had a little earlier during this night. It looks as if it was the right time for you not to wake me.

C: What was your dream?

S: I thought that a beautiful and comely woman dressed in white approached me. She called me and said: "Socrates, may you arrive at fertile Phthia[1] on the third day."

C: A strange dream, Socrates.

S: But it seems clear enough to me, Crito.

C: Too clear it seems, my dear Socrates, but listen to me even now and be saved. If you die, it will not be a single misfortune for me. Not only will I be deprived of a friend, the like of whom I shall never find again, but many people who do not know you or me very well will think that I could have saved you if I were willing to spend money, but that I did not care to do so. Surely there can be no worse reputation than to be thought to value money more highly than one's friends, for the majority will not believe that you yourself were not willing to leave prison while we were eager for you to do so.

S: My good Crito, why should we care so much for what the majority think? The most reasonable people, to whom one should pay more attention, will believe that things were done as they were done.

C: You see, Socrates, that one must also pay attention to the opinion of the majority. Your present situation makes clear that the majority can inflict not the least but pretty well the greatest evils if one is slandered among them.

S: Would that the majority could inflict the greatest evils, for they would then be capable of the greatest good, and that would be fine, but now they cannot do either. They cannot make a man either wise or foolish, but they inflict things haphazardly.

C: That may be so. But tell me this, Socrates, are you anticipating that I and your other friends would have trouble with the informers if you escape from here, as having stolen you away, and that we should be compelled to lose all our property or pay heavy fines and suffer other punishment besides? If you have any such fear, forget it. We would be justified in running this risk to save you, and worse, if necessary. Do follow my advice, and do not act differently.

S: I do have these things in mind, Crito, and also many others.

C: Have no such fear. It is not much money that some people require to save you and get you out of here. Further, do you not see that those informers are cheap, and that not much money would be needed to deal with them? My money is available and is, I think, sufficient. If, because of your affection for me, you feel you should not spend any of mine, there are those strangers here ready to spend money. One of them, Simmias the Theban, has brought enough for this very purpose. Cebes, too, and a good many others. So, as I say, do not let this fear make you hesitate to save yourself, nor let what you said in court trouble you, that you would not know what to do with yourself if you left Athens, for you would be welcomed in many places to which you might go. If you want to go to Thessaly, I have friends there who will greatly appreciate you and keep you safe, so that no one in Thessaly will harm you.

Besides, Socrates, I do not think that what you are doing is right, to give up your life when you can save it, and to hasten your fate as your enemies would hasten it, and indeed have hastened it in their wish to destroy you. Moreover, I think you are betraying your sons by going away and leaving them, when you could bring them up and educate them. You thus show no concern for what their fate may be. They will probably have the usual fate of orphans. Either one should not have children, or one should share with them to the end the toil of upbringing and education. You seem to me to choose the easiest path, whereas one should choose the path a good and courageous man would choose, particularly when one claims throughout one's life to care for virtue.

I feel ashamed on your behalf and on behalf of us, your friends, lest all that has happened to you be thought due to cowardice on our part: the fact that your trial came to court when it need not have done so, the handling of the trial itself, and now this absurd ending which will be thought to have got beyond our control through some cowardice and unmanliness on our part, since we did not save you, or you save yourself, when it was possible and could be done if we had been of the slightest use. Consider, Socrates, whether this is not only evil, but shameful, both for you and for us. Take counsel with yourself, or rather the time for counsel is past and the decision should have been taken, and there is no further opportunity, for this whole business must be ended tonight. If we delay now, then it will no longer be possible, it will be too late. Let me persuade you on every count, Socrates, and do not act otherwise.

S: My dear Crito, your eagerness is worth much if it should have some right aim; if not, then the greater your keenness the more difficult it is to deal with. We must therefore examine whether we should act in this way or not, as not only now but at all times I am the kind of man who listens only to the argument that on reflection seems best to me. I cannot, now that this fate has come upon me, discard the arguments I used; they seem to me much the same. I value and respect the same principles as before, and if we have no better arguments to bring up at this moment, be sure that I shall not agree with you, not even if the power of the majority were to frighten us with more bogeys, as if we were children, with threats of incarcerations and executions and confiscation of property. How should we examine this matter most reasonably? Would it be by taking up first your argument about the opinions of men, whether it is sound in every case that one should pay attention to some opinions, but not to others? Or was that well-spoken before the necessity to die came upon me, but now it is clear that this was said in vain for the sake of argument, that it was in truth play and nonsense? I am eager to examine together with you, Crito, whether this argument will appear in any way different to me in my present circumstances, or whether it remains the same, whether we are to abandon it or believe it. It was said on every occasion by those who thought they were speaking sensibly, as I have just now been speaking, that one should greatly value some people's opinions, but not others. Does that seem to you a sound statement?

You, as far as a human being can tell, are exempt from the likelihood of dying tomorrow, so the present misfortune is not likely to lead you astray. Consider then, do you not think it a sound statement that one must not value all the opinions of men, but some and not others, nor the opinions of all men, but those of some and not of others? What do you say? Is this not well said?

C: It is.

S: One should value the good opinions, and not the bad ones?

C: Yes.

S: The good opinions are those of wise men, the bad ones those of foolish men?

C: Of course.

S: Come then, what of statements such as this: Should a man professionally engaged in physical training pay attention to the praise and blame and opinion of any man, or to those of one man only, namely a doctor or trainer?

C: To those of one only.

S: He should therefore fear the blame and welcome the praise of that one man, and not those of the many?

C: Obviously.

S: He must then act and exercise, eat and drink in the way the one, the trainer and the one who knows, thinks right, not all the others?

C: That is so.

S: Very well. And if he disobeys the one, disregards his opinion and his praises while valuing those of the many who have no knowledge, will he not suffer harm?

C: Of course.

S: What is that harm, where does it tend, and what part of the man who disobeys does it affect?

C: Obviously the harm is to his body, which it ruins.

S: Well said. So with other matters, not to enumerate them all, and certainly with actions just and unjust, shameful and beautiful, good and bad, about which we are now deliberating, should we follow the opinion of the many and fear it, or that of the one, if there is one who has knowledge of these things and before whom we feel fear and shame more than before all the others. If we do not follow his directions, we shall harm and corrupt that part of ourselves that is improved by just actions and destroyed by unjust actions. Or is there nothing in this?

C: I think there certainly is, Socrates.

S: Come now, if we ruin that which is improved by health and corrupted by disease by not following the opinions of those who know, is life worth living for us when that is ruined? And that is the body, is it not?

C: Yes.

S: And is life worth living with a body that is corrupted and in bad condition?

C: In no way.

S: And is life worth living for us with that part of us corrupted that unjust action harms and just action benefits? Or do we think that part of us, whatever it is, that is concerned with justice and injustice, is inferior to the body?

C: Not at all.

S: It is more valuable?

C: Much more.

S: We should not then think so much of what the majority will say about us, but what he will say who understands justice and injustice, the one, that is, and the truth itself. So that, in the first place, you were wrong to believe that we should care for the opinion of the many about what is just, beautiful, good, and their opposites. "But," someone might say "the many are able to put us to death."

C: That too is obvious, Socrates, and someone might well say so.

S: And, my admirable friend, that argument that we have gone through remains, I think, as before. Examine the following statement in turn as to whether it stays the same or not, that the most important thing is not life, but the good life.

C: It stays the same.

S: And that the good life, the beautiful life, and the just life are the same; does that still hold, or not?

C: It does hold.

S: As we have agreed so far, we must examine next whether it is right for me to try to get out of here when the Athenians have not acquitted me. If it is seen to be right, we will try to do so; if it is not, we will abandon the idea. As for those questions you raise about money, reputation, the upbringing of children, Crito, those considerations in truth belong to those people who easily put men to death and would bring them to life again if they could, without thinking; I mean the majority of men. For us, however, since our argument leads to this, the only valid consideration, as we were saying just now, is whether we should be acting rightly in giving money and gratitude to those who will lead me out of here, and ourselves helping with the escape, or whether in truth we shall do wrong in doing all this. If it appears that we shall be acting unjustly, then we have no need at all to take into account whether we shall have to die if we stay here and keep quiet, or suffer in another way, rather than do wrong.

C: I think you put that beautifully, Socrates, but see what we should do.

S: Let us examine the question together, my dear friend, and if you can make any objection while I am speaking, make it and I will listen to you, but if you have no objection to make, my dear Crito, then stop now from saying the same thing so often, that I must leave here against the will of the Athenians. I think it important to persuade you before I act, and not to act against your wishes. See whether the start of our enquiry is adequately stated, and try to answer what I ask you in the way you think best.

C: I shall try.

S: Do we say that one must never in any way do wrong willfully, or must one do wrong in one way and not in another? Is to do wrong never good or admirable, as we have agreed in the past, or have all these former agreements been washed out during the last few days? Have we at our age failed to notice for some time that in our serious discussions we were no different from children? Above all, is the truth such as we used to say it was, whether the majority agree or not, and whether we must still suffer worse things than we do now, or will be treated more gently, that nonetheless, wrongdoing is in every way harmful and shameful to the wrongdoer? Do we say so or not?

C: We do.

S: So one must never do wrong.

C: Certainly not.

S: Nor must one, when wronged, inflict wrong in return, as the majority believe, since one must never do wrong.

C: That seems to be the case.

S: Come now, should one injure anyone or not, Crito?

C: One must never do so.

S: Well then, if one is oneself injured, is it right, as the majority say, to inflict an injury in return, or is it not?

C: It is never right.

S: Injuring people is no different from wrongdoing.

C: That is true.

S: One should never do wrong in return, nor injure any man, whatever injury one has suffered at his hands. And Crito, see that you do not agree to this, contrary to your belief. For I know that only a few people hold this view or will hold it, and there is no common ground between those who hold this view and those who do not, but they inevitably despise each other's views. So then consider very carefully whether we have this view in common, and whether you agree, and let this be the basis of our deliberation, that neither to do wrong or to return a wrong is ever right, not even to injure in return for an injury received. Or do you disagree and do not share this view as a basis for discussion? I have held it for a long time and still hold it now, but if you think otherwise, tell me now. If, however, you stick to our former opinion, then listen to the next point.

C: I stick to it and agree with you. So say on.

S: Then I state the next point, or rather I ask you: when one has come to an agreement that is just with someone, should one fulfill it or cheat on it?

C: One should fulfill it.

S: See what follows from this: if we leave here without the city's permission, are we injuring people whom we should least injure? And are we sticking to a just agreement, or not?

C: I cannot answer your question, Socrates. I do not know.

S: Look at it this way. If, as we were planning to run away from here, or whatever one should call it, the laws and the state came and confronted us and asked: "Tell me, Socrates, what are you intending to do? Do you not by this action you are attempting intend to destroy us, the laws, and indeed the whole city, as far as you are concerned? Or do you think it possible for a city not to be destroyed if the verdicts of its courts have no force but are nullified and set at naught by private individuals?" What shall we answer to this and other such arguments? For many things could be said, especially by an orator on behalf of this law we are destroying, which orders that the judgments of the courts shall be carried out. Shall we say in answer, "The city wronged me, and its decision was not right." Shall we say that, or what?

C: Yes, by Zeus, Socrates, that is our answer.

S: Then what if the laws said: "Was that the agreement between us, Socrates, or was it to respect the judgments that the city came to?" And if we wondered at their words, they would perhaps add: "Socrates, do not wonder at what we say but answer, since you are accustomed to proceed by question and answer. Come now, what accusation do you bring against us and the city, that you should try to destroy us? Did we

not, first, bring you to birth, and was it not through us that your father married your mother and begat you? Tell us, do you find anything to criticize in those of us who are concerned with marriage?" And I would say that I do not criticize them. "Or in those of us concerned with the nurture of babies and the education that you too received? Were those assigned to that subject not right to instruct your father to educate you in the arts and in physical culture?" And I would say that they were right. "Very well," they would continue, "and after you were born and nurtured and educated, could you, in the first place, deny that you are our offspring and servant, both you and your forefathers? If that is so, do you think that we are on an equal footing as regards the right, and that whatever we do to you it is right for you to do to us? You were not on an equal footing with your father as regards the right, nor with your master if you had one, so as to retaliate for anything they did to you, to revile them if they reviled you, to beat them if they beat you, and so with many other things. Do you think you have this right to retaliation against your country and its laws? That if we undertake to destroy you and think it right to do so, you can undertake to destroy us, as far as you can, in return? And will you say that you are right to do so, you who truly care for virtue? Is your wisdom such as not to realize that your country is to be honoured more than your mother, your father and all your ancestors, that it is more to be revered and more sacred, and that it counts for more among the gods and sensible men, that you must worship it, yield to it and placate its anger more than your father's? You must either persuade it or obey its orders, and endure in silence whatever it instructs you to endure, whether blows or bonds, and if it leads you into war to be wounded or killed, you must obey. To do so is right, and one must not give way or retreat or leave one's post, but both in war and in courts and everywhere else, one must obey the commands of one's city and country, or persuade it as to the nature of justice. It is impious to bring violence to bear against your mother or father, it is much more so to use it against your country." What shall we say in reply, Crito, that the laws speak the truth, or not?

C: I think they do.

S: "Reflect now, Socrates," the laws might say, "that if what we say is true, you are not treating us rightly by planning to do what you are planning. We have given you birth, nurtured you, educated you, we have given you and all other citizens a share of all the good things we could. Even so, by giving every Athenian the opportunity, after he has reached manhood and observed the affairs of the city and us the laws, we proclaim that if we do not please him, he can take his possessions and go wherever he pleases. Not one of our laws raises any obstacle or forbids him, if he is not satisfied with us or the city, if one of you wants to go and live in a colony or wants to go anywhere else, and keep his property. We say, however, that whoever of you remains, when he sees how we conduct our trials and manage the city in other ways, has in fact come to an agreement with us to obey our instructions. We say that the one who disobeys does wrong in three ways, first because in us he disobeys his parents, also those who brought him up, and because, in spite of his agreement, he neither obeys us nor, if we do something wrong, does he try to persuade us to do better. Yet we only propose things, we do not issue savage commands to do whatever we order; we give two alternatives, either to persuade us or to do what we say. He does neither. We do say that you too, Socrates, are open to those charges if you do what you have in mind; you would be among, not the least, but the most guilty of the Athenians." And if I

should say "Why so?" they might well be right to upbraid me and say that I am among the Athenians who most definitely came to that agreement with them. They might well say: "Socrates, we have convincing proofs that we and the city were congenial to you. You would not have dwelt here most consistently of all the Athenians if the city had not been exceedingly pleasing to you. You have never left the city, even to see a festival, nor for any other reason except military service; you have never gone to stay in any other city, as people do; you have had no desire to know another city or other laws; we and our city satisfied you.

"So decisively did you choose us and agree to be a citizen under us. Also, you have had children in this city, thus showing that it was congenial to you. Then at your trial you could have assessed your penalty at exile if you wished, and you are now attempting to do against the city's wishes what you could then have done with her consent. Then you prided yourself that you did not resent death, but you chose, as you said, death in preference to exile. Now, however, those words do not make you ashamed, and you pay no heed to us, the laws, as you plan to destroy us, and you act like the meanest type of slave by trying to run away, contrary to your undertakings and your agreement to live as a citizen under us. First then, answer us on this very point, whether we speak the truth when we say that you agreed, not only in words but by your deeds, to live in accordance with us." What are we to say to that, Crito? Must we not agree?

C: We must, Socrates.

S: "Surely," they might say, "you are breaking the undertakings and agreements that you made with us without compulsion or deceit, and under no pressure of time for deliberation. You have had seventy years during which you could have gone away if you did not like us, and if you thought our agreements unjust. You did not choose to go to Sparta or to Crete, which you are always saying are well governed, nor to any other city, Greek or foreign. You have been away from Athens less than the lame or the blind or other handicapped people. It is clear that the city has been outstandingly more congenial to you than to other Athenians, and so have we, the laws, for what city can please without laws? Will you then not now stick to our agreements? You will, Socrates, if we can persuade you, and not make yourself a laughing-stock by leaving the city.

"For consider what good you will do yourself or your friends by breaking our agreements and committing such a wrong? It is pretty obvious that your friends will themselves be in danger of exile, disfranchisement and loss of property. As for yourself, if you go to one of the nearby cities—Thebes or Megara, both are well governed—you will arrive as an enemy to their government; all who care for their city will look on you with suspicion, as a destroyer of the laws. You will also strengthen the conviction of the jury that they passed the right sentence on you, for anyone who destroys the laws could easily be thought to corrupt the young and the ignorant. Or will you avoid cities that are well governed and men who are civilized? If you do this, will your life be worth living? Will you have social intercourse with them and not be ashamed to talk to them? And what will you say? The same as you did here, that virtue and justice are man's most precious possession, along with lawful behaviour and the laws? Do you not think that Socrates would appear to be an unseemly kind of person? One must think so. Or will you leave those places and go to Crito's friends in Thessaly? There you will find the greatest license and disorder, and they may enjoy hearing from you how absurdly you escaped from prison in some disguise, in a leather jerkin or some other things in which escapees wrap themselves, thus altering your appearance. Will there be no one to say that you, likely to live but a short time more, were so greedy for life that you transgressed the most important laws? Possibly, Socrates, if you do not annoy anyone, but if you do, many disgraceful things will be said about you.

"You will spend your time ingratiating yourself with all men, and be at their beck and call. What will you do in Thessaly but feast, as if you had gone to a banquet in Thessaly? As for those conversations of yours about justice and the rest of virtue, where will they be? You say you want to live for the sake of your children, that you may bring them up and educate them. How so? Will you bring them up and educate them by taking them to Thessaly and making strangers of them, that they may enjoy that too? Or not so, but they will be better brought up and educated here, while you are alive, though absent? Yes, your friends will look after them. Will they look after them if you go and live in Thessaly, but not if you go away to the underworld? If those who profess themselves your friends are any good at all, one must assume that they will.

"Be persuaded by us who have brought you up, Socrates. Do not value either your children or your life or anything else more than goodness, in order that when you arrive in Hades you may have all this as your defence before the rulers there. If you do this deed, you will not think it better or more just or more pious here, nor will any one of your friends, nor will it be better for you when you arrive yonder. As it is, you depart, if you depart, after being wronged not by us, the laws, but by men; but if you depart after shamefully returning wrong for wrong and injury for injury, after breaking your agreement and contract with us, after injuring those you should injure least—yourself, your friends, your country and us—we shall be angry with you while you are still alive, and our brothers, the laws of the underworld, will not receive you kindly, knowing that you tried to destroy us as far as you could. Do not let Crito persuade you, rather than us, to do what he says."

Crito, my dear friend, be assured that these are the words I seem to hear, as the Corybants seem to hear the music of their flutes, and the echo of these words resounds in me, and makes it impossible for me to hear anything else. As far as my present beliefs go, if you speak in opposition to them, you will speak in vain. However, if you think you can accomplish anything, speak.

C: I have nothing to say, Socrates.

S: Let it be then, Crito, and let us act in this way, since this is the way the god is leading us.

## Notes

1. A quotation from the ninth book of the *Iliad* (363). Achilles has rejected all the presents of Agamemnon for him to return to the battle, and threatens to go home. He says his ships will sail in the morning, and with good weather he might arrive on the third day "in fertile Phthia" (which is his home). The dream means, obviously, that on the third day Socrates' soul, after death, will find its home. As always, counting the first member of a series, the third day is the day after tomorrow.

# Letter from Birmingham Jail

*Martin Luther King, Jr.*

April 16, 1963

MY DEAR FELLOW CLERGYMEN:[1]

While confined here in the Birmingham city jail, I came across your recent statement calling my present activities ''unwise and untimely.'' Seldom do I pause to answer criticism of my work and ideas. If I sought to answer all the criticisms that cross my desk, my secretaries would have little time for anything other than such correspondence in the course of the day, and I would have no time for constructive work. But since I feel that you are men of genuine good will and that your criticisms are sincerely set forth, I want to try to answer your statement in what I hope will be patient and reasonable terms.

I think I should indicate why I am here in Birmingham, since you have been influenced by the view which argues against ''outsiders coming in.'' I have the honor of serving as president of the Southern Christian Leadership Conference, an organization operating in every southern state, with headquarters in Atlanta, Georgia. We have some eighty-five affiliated organizations across the South, and one of them is the Alabama Christian Movement for Human Rights. Fre-

quently we share staff, educational, and financial resources with our affiliates. Several months ago the affiliate here in Birmingham asked us to be on call to engage in a nonviolent direct-action program if such were deemed necessary. We readily consented, and when the hour came we lived up to our promise. So I, along with several members of my staff, am here because I was invited here. I am here because I have organizational ties here.

But more basically, I am in Birmingham because injustice is here. Just as the prophets of the eighth century B.C. left their villages and carried their ''thus saith the Lord'' far beyond the boundaries of their home towns, and just as the Apostle Paul left his village of Tarsus and carried the gospel of Jesus Christ to the far corners of the Greco-Roman world, so am I compelled to carry the gospel of freedom beyond my own home town. Like Paul, I must constantly respond to the Macedonian call for aid.

Moreover, I am cognizant of the interrelatedness of all communities and states. I cannot sit idly by in Atlanta and not be concerned about what happens in Birmingham. Injustice anywhere is a threat to justice everywhere. We are caught in an escapable network of mutuality, tied in a single garment of destiny. Whatever affects one directly, affects all indirectly. Never again can we afford to live with the narrow, provincial, ''outside agitator'' idea. Anyone who lives

Martin Luther King, Jr., was the most influential leader of the civil rights movement in the United States in the late 1950s and 1960s. He was assassinated in 1968.

''Letter from Birmingham Jail'' from WHY WE CAN'T WAIT by Martin Luther King, Jr. Copyright © 1963, 1964 by Martin Luther King, Jr. Reprinted by permission of Harper & Row, Publishers, Inc.

inside the United States can never be considered an outsider anywhere within its bounds.

You deplore the demonstrations taking place in Birmingham. But your statement, I am sorry to say, fails to express a similar concern for the conditions that brought about the demonstrations. I am sure that none of you would want to rest content with the superficial kind of social analysis that deals merely with effects and does not grapple with underlying causes. It is unfortunate that demonstrations are taking place in Birmingham, but it is even more unfortunate that the city's white power structure left the Negro community with no alternative.

In any nonviolent campaign there are four basic steps: collection of the facts to determine whether injustices exist; negotiation; self-purification; and direct action. We have gone through all these steps in Birmingham. There can be no gainsaying the fact that racial injustice engulfs this community. Birmingham is probably the most thoroughly segregated city in the United States. Its ugly record of brutality is widely known. Negroes have experienced grossly unjust treatment in the courts. There have been more unsolved bombings of negro homes and churches in Birmingham than in any other city in the nation. These are the hard brutal facts of the case. On the basis of these conditions, Negro leaders sought to negotiate with the city fathers. But the latter consistently refused to engage in good-faith negotiation.

Then, last September, came the opportunity to talk with leaders of Birmingham's economic community. In the course of the negotiations, certain promises were made by the merchants—for example, to remove the stores' humiliating racial signs. On the basis of these promises, the Reverend Fred Shuttlesworth and the leaders of the Alabama Christian Movement for Human Rights agreed to a moratorium on all demonstrations. As the weeks and months went by, we realized that we were the victims of a broken promise. A few signs, briefly removed, returned; the others remained.

As in so many past experiences, our hopes had been blasted, and the shadow of deep disappointment settled upon us. We had no alternative except to prepare for direct action, whereby we would present our very bodies as a means of laying our case before the conscience of the local and the national community. Mindful of the difficulties involved, we decided to undertake a process of self-purification. We began a series of workshops on nonviolence, and we repeatedly asked ourselves: "Are you able to accept blows without retaliating?" "Are you able to endure the ordeal of jail?" We decided to schedule our direct-action program for the Easter season, realizing that except for Christmas, this is the main shopping period of the year. Knowing that a strong economic-withdrawal program would be the by-product of direct action, we felt that this would be the best time to bring pressure to bear on the merchants for the needed change.

Then it occurred to us that Birmingham's mayoral election was coming up in March, and we speedily decided to postpone action until after election day. When we discovered that the Commissioner of Public Safety, Eugene "Bull" Connor, had piled up enough votes to be in the run-off, we decided again to postpone action until the day after the run-off so that the demonstrations could not be used to cloud the issues. Like many others, we waited to see Mr. Connor defeated, and to this end we endured postponement after postponement. Having aided in this community need, we felt that our direct-action program could be delayed no longer.

You may well ask, "Why direct action? Why sit-ins, marches, and so forth? Isn't negotiation a better path?" You are quite right in calling for negotiation. Indeed, this is the very purpose of direct action. Nonviolent direct action seeks to create such a crisis and foster such a tension that a community which has constantly refused to negotiate is forced to confront the issue. It seeks so to dramatize the issue that it can no longer be ignored. My citing the creation of tension as part of the work of the nonviolent register may sound rather shocking. But I must confess that I am not afraid of the word "tension." I have earnestly opposed violent tension, but there is a type of constructive, nonviolent tension which is necessary for growth. Just as Socrates felt that it was necessary to create a tension in the mind so that individuals could rise from the bondage of myths and half truths to the unfettered realm of creative analysis and objective appraisal, so must we see the need for nonviolent gadflies to create the kind of tension in society that will help men rise from the dark depths of prejudice and racism to the majestic heights of understanding and brotherhood.

The purpose of our direct-action program is to create a situation so crisis-packed that it will inevitably open the door to negotiation. I therefore concur with you in your call for negotiation. Too long has our beloved Southland been bogged down in a tragic effort to live in monologue rather than dialogue.

One of the basic points in your statement is that the action that I and my associates have taken in Birmingham is untimely. Some have asked: "Why didn't you give the new city administration time to act?" The only answer that I can give to this query is that the new Birmingham administration must be prodded about as much as the outgoing one, before it will act. We are sadly mistaken if we feel that the election of Albert Boutwell as mayor will bring the millennium to Brimingham. While Mr. Boutwell is a much more gentle person than Mr. Connor,

they are both segregationists, dedicated to maintenance of the status quo. I have hoped that Mr. Boutwell will be reasonable enough to see the futility of massive resistance to desegregation. But he will not see this without pressure from devotees of civil rights. My friends, I must say to you that we have not made a single gain in civil rights without determined legal and nonviolent pressure. Lamentably, it is an historical fact that privileged groups seldom give up their privileges voluntarily. Individuals may see the moral light and voluntarily give up their unjust posture; but, as Reinhold Niebuhr has reminded us, groups tend to be more immoral than individuals.

We know through painful experience that freedom is never voluntarily given by the oppressor; it must be demanded by the oppressed. Frankly, I have yet to engage in a direct-action campaign that was "well-timed" in the view of those who have not suffered unduly from the disease of segregation. For years now I have heard the word "Wait!" It rings in the ear of every Negro with piercing familiarity. This "wait" has almost always meant "Never." We must come to see, with one of our distinguished jurists, that "justice too long delayed is justice denied."

We have waited for more than 340 years for our constitutional and God-given rights. The nations of Asia and Africa are moving with jet-like speed toward gaining political independence, but we still creep at horse-and-buggy pace toward gaining a cup of coffee at a lunch counter. Perhaps it is easy for those who have never felt the stinging darts of segregation to say, "Wait." But when you have seen vicious mobs lynch your mothers and fathers at will and drown your sisters and brothers at whim; when you have seen hate-filled policemen curse, kick, and even kill your black brothers and sisters; when you see the vast majority of your twenty million Negro brothers smothering in an airtight cage of poverty in the midst of an affluent society; when you suddenly find your tongue twisted and your speech stammering as you seek to explain to your six-year-old daughter why she can't go to the public amusement park that has just been advertised on television, and see tears welling up in her eyes when she is told that Funtown is closed to colored children, and see ominous clouds of inferiority beginning to form in her little mental sky, and see her beginning to distort her personality by developing an unconscious bitterness toward white people; when you have to concoct an answer for a five-year-old son who is asking "Daddy, why do white people treat colored people so mean?"; when you take a cross-country drive and find it necessary to sleep night after night in the uncomfortable corners of your automobile because no motel will accept you; when you are humiliated day in and day out by nagging signs reading "white" and "colored"; when your first name becomes "nigger," your middle name becomes "boy" (however old you are) and your last name becomes "John," and your wife and mother are never given the respected title "Mrs."; when you are harried by day and haunted by night by the fact that you are a Negro, living constantly at tiptoe stance, never quite knowing what to expect next, and are plagued with inner fears and outer resentments; when you are forever fighting a degenerating sense of "nobodiness"—then you will understand why we find it difficult to wait. There comes a time when the cup of endurance runs over, and men are no longer willing to be plunged into the abyss of despair. I hope, sirs, you can understand our legitimate and unavoidable impatience.

You express a great deal of anxiety over our willingness to break laws. This is certainly a legitimate concern. Since we so diligently urge people to obey the Supreme Court's decision of 1954 outlawing segregation in the public schools, at first glance it may seem rather paradoxical for us consciously to break laws. One may well ask: "How can you advocate breaking some laws and obeying others?" The answer lies in the fact that there are two types of laws: just and unjust. I would be the first to advocate obeying just laws. One has not only a legal but a moral responsibility to obey just laws. Conversely, one has a moral responsibility to disobey unjust laws. I would agree with St. Augustine that "an unjust law is no law at all."

Now, what is the difference between the two? How does one determine whether a law is just or unjust? A just law is a man-made code that squares with the moral law or the law of God. An unjust law is a code that is out of harmony with the moral law. To put it in the terms of St. Thomas Aquinas: An injust law is a human law that is not rooted in eternal law and natural law. Any law that uplifts human personality is just. Any law that degrades human personality is unjust. All segregation statutes are unjust because segregation distorts the soul and damages the personality. It gives the segregator a false sense of superiority and the segregated a false sense of inferiority. Segregation, to use the terminology of the Jewish philosopher Martin Buber, substitutes an "I-it" relationship for an "I-thou" relationship and ends up relegating persons to the status of things. Hence segregation is not only politically, economically, and sociologically unsound, it is morally wrong and sinful. Paul Tillich has said that sin is separation. Is not segregation an existential expression of man's tragic separation, his awful estrangement, his terrible sinfulness? Thus it is that I can urge men to obey the 1954 decision of the Supreme Court, for it is morally right; and I can urge them to disobey segregation ordinances, for they are morally wrong.

Let us consider a more concrete example of just and unjust laws. An unjust law is a code that a numerical or power majority group compels a minority group to obey but does not make binding on itself. This is *difference* made legal. By the same token, a just law is a code that a majority compels a minority to follow and that it is willing to follow itself. This is *sameness* made legal.

Let me give another explanation. A law is unjust if it is inflicted on a minority that, as a result of being denied the right to vote, had no part in enacting or devising the law. Who can say that the legislature of Alabama which set up that state's segregation laws was democratically elected? Throughout Alabama all sorts of devious methods are used to prevent Negroes from becoming registered voters, and there are some counties in which, even though Negroes constitute a majority of the population, not a single Negro is registered. Can any law enacted under such circumstances be considered democratically structured?

Sometimes a law is just on its face and unjust in its application. For instance, I have been arrested on a charge of parading without a permit. Now, there is nothing wrong in having an ordinance which requires a permit for a parade. But such an ordinance becomes unjust when it is used to maintain segregation and to deny citizens the First Amendment privilege of peaceful assembly and protest.

I hope you are able to see the distinction I am trying to point out. In no sense do I advocate evading or defying the law, as would the rabid segregationist. That would lead to anarchy. One who breaks an unjust law must do so openly, lovingly, and with a willingness to accept the penalty. I submit that an individual who breaks a law that conscience tells him is unjust, and who willingly accepts the penalty of imprisonment in order to arouse the conscience of the community over its injustice, is in reality expressing the highest respect for law.

Of course, there is nothing new about this kind of civil disobedience. It was evidenced sublimely in the refusal of Shadrach, Meshach, and Abednego to obey the laws of Nebuchadnezzar, on the ground that a higher moral law was at stake. It was practiced superbly by the early Christians, who were willing to face hungry lions and the excruciating pain of chopping blocks rather than submit to certain unjust laws of the Roman Empire. To a degree, academic freedom is a reality today because Socrates practiced civil disobedience. In our own nation, the Boston Tea Party represented a massive act of civil disobedience.

We should never forget that everything Adolf Hitler did in Germany was "legal" and everything the Hungarian freedom fighters did in Hungary was "illegal." It was "illegal" to aid and comfort a Jew in Hitler's Germany. Even so, I am sure that, had I lived in Germany at the time, I would have aided and comforted my Jewish brothers. If today I lived in a Communist country where certain principles dear to the Christian faith are suppressed, I would openly advocate disobeying that country's antireligious laws.

I must make two honest confessions to you, my Christian and Jewish brothers. First, I must confess that over the past few years I have been gravely disappointed with the white moderate. I have almost reached the regrettable conclusion that the Negro's great stumbling block in his stride toward freedom is not the White Citizen's Counciler or the Ku Klux Klanner, but the white moderate, who is more devoted to "order" than to justice; who prefers a negative peace which is the absence of tension to a positive peace which is the presence of justice; who constantly says, "I agree with you in the goal you seek, but I cannot agree with your methods of direct action"; who paternalistically believes he can set the timetable for another man's freedom; who lives by a mythical concept of time and who constantly advises the Negro to wait for a "more convenient season." Shallow understanding from people of good will is more frustrating than absolute misunderstanding from people of ill will. Lukewarm acceptance is much more bewildering than outright rejection.

I had hoped that the white moderate would understand that law and order exist for the purpose of establishing justice and that when they fail in this purpose they become the dangerously structured dams that block the flow of social progress. I had hoped that the white moderate would understand that the present tension in the South is a necessary phase of the transition from an obnoxious negative peace, in which the Negro passively accepted his unjust plight, to a substantive and positive peace, in which all men will respect the dignity and worth of human personality. Actually, we who engage in nonviolent direct action are not the creators of tension. We merely bring to the surface the hidden tension that is already alive. We bring it out in the open, where it can be seen and dealt with. Like a boil that can never be cured so long as it is covered up but must be opened with all its ugliness to the natural medicines of air and light, injustice must be exposed, with all the tension its exposure creates, to the light of human conscience and the air of national opinion, before it can be cured.

In your statement you assert that our actions, even though peaceful, must be condemned because they precipitate violence. But is this a logical assertion? Isn't this like condemning a robbed man because his possession of money precipitated the evil act of robbery? Isn't this like condemning Socrates because his unswerving commitment to truth and his philosophical inquiries precipitated the act by the misguided populace in which

they made him drink hemlock? Isn't this like condemning Jesus because his unique God-consciousness and never-ceasing devotion to God's will precipitated the evil act of crucifixion? We must come to see that, as the federal courts have consistently affirmed, it is wrong to urge an individual to cease his efforts to gain his basic constitutional rights because the quest may precipitate violence. Society must protect the robbed and punish the robber.

I had also hoped that the white moderate would reject the myth concerning time in relation to the struggle for freedom. I have just received a letter from a white brother in Texas. He writes: "All Christians know that the colored people will receive equal rights eventually, but it is possible that you are in too great a religious hurry. It has taken Christianity almost two thousand years to accomplish what it has. The teachings of Christ take time to come to earth." Such an attitude stems from a tragic misconception of time, from the strangely irrational notion that there is something in the very flow of time that will inevitably cure all ills. Actually, time itself is neutral; it can be used either destructively or constructively. More and more I feel that the people of ill will have used time much more effectively than have the people of good will. We will have to repent in this generation not merely for the hateful words and actions of the bad people, but for the appalling silence of the good people. Human progress never rolls in on wheels of inevitability; it comes through the tireless efforts of men willing to be co-workers with God, and without this hard work, time itself becomes an ally of the forces of social stagnation. We must use time creatively, in the knowledge that the time is always ripe to do right. Now is the time to make real the promise of democracy and transform our pending national elegy into a creative psalm of brotherhood. Now is the time to lift our national policy from the quicksand of racial injustice to the solid rock of human dignity.

You speak of our activity in Birmingham as extreme. At first I was rather disappointed that fellow clergymen would see my nonviolent efforts as those of an extremist. I began thinking about the fact that I stand in the middle of two opposing forces in the Negro community. One is a force of complacency, made up in part of Negroes who, as a result of long years of oppression, are so drained of self-respect and a sense of "somebodiness" that they have adjusted to segregation; and in part of a few middle-class Negroes who, because of a degree of academic and economic security and because in some ways they profit by segregation, have become insensitive to the problems of the masses. The other force is one of bitterness and hatred, and it comes perilously close to advocating violence. It is expressed in the various black nationalist groups that are springing up across the nation, the largest and best known being Elijah Muhammad's Muslim movement. Nourished by the Negro's frustration over the continued existence of racial discrimination, this movement is made up of people who have lost faith in America, who have absolutely repudiated Christianity, and who have concluded that the white man is an incorrigible "devil."

I have tried to stand between these two forces, saying that we need emulate neither the "do-nothingism" of the complacent nor the hatred and despair of the black nationalist. For there is the more excellent way of love and nonviolent protest. I am grateful to God that, through the influence of the Negro church, the way of nonviolence became an integral part of our struggle.

If this philosophy had not emerged, by now many streets of the South would, I am convinced, be flowing with blood. And I am further convinced that if our white brothers dismiss as "rabble-rousers" and "outside agitators" those of us who employ nonviolent direct action, and if they refuse to support our nonviolent efforts, millions of Negroes will, out of frustration and despair, seek solace and security in black nationalist ideologies—a development that would inevitably lead to a frightening racial nightmare.

Oppressed people cannot remain oppressed forever. The yearning for freedom eventually manifests itself, and that is what has happened to the American Negro. Something within has reminded him of his birthright of freedom, and something without has reminded him that it can be gained. Consciously or unconsciously, he has been caught up by the *Zeitgeist*, and with his black brothers of Africa and his brown and yellow brothers of Asia, South America, and the Caribbean, the United States Negro is moving with a sense of great urgency toward the promised land of racial justice. If one recognizes this vital urge that has engulfed the Negro community, one should readily understand why public demonstrations are taking place. The Negro has many pent-up resentments and latent frustrations, and he must release them. So let him march; let him make prayer pilgrimages to the city hall; let him go on freedom rides—and try to understand why he must do so. If his repressed emotions are not released in nonviolent ways, they will seek expression through violence; this is not a threat but a fact of history. So I have not said to my people, "Get rid of your discontent." Rather, I have tried to say that this normal and healthy discontent can be channeled into the creative outlet of nonviolent direct action. And now this approach is being termed extremist.

But though I was initially disappointed at being categorized as an extremist, as I continued to think about the matter I gradually gained a measure of satisfaction from the label. Was not Jesus an extremist for love: "Love your enemies, bless them that curse you, do good to them that hate you, and pray for them which despitefully use you, and persecute you.'' Was not Amos an extremist for justice: ''Let justice roll down like waters and righteousness like an ever-flowing stream.'' Was not Paul an extremist for the Christian gospel: ''I bear in my body the marks of the Lord Jesus.'' Was not Martin Luther an extremist: ''Here I stand; I cannot do otherwise, so help me God.'' And John Bunyan: ''I will stay in jail to the end of my days before I make a butchery of my conscience.'' And Abraham Lincoln: ''This nation cannot survive half slave and half free.'' And Thomas Jefferson: ''We hold these truths to be self-evident, that all men are created equal. . . .'' So the question is not whether we will be extremists, but what kind of extremists we will be. Will we be extremists for hate or for love? Will we be extremists for the preservation of injustice or for the extension of justice? In that dramatic scene on Calvary's hill three men were crucified. We must never forget that all three were crucified for the same crime—the crime of extremism. Two were extremists for immorality, and thus fell below their environment. The other, Jesus Christ, was an extremist for love, truth, and goodness, and thereby rose above his environment. Perhaps the South, the nation, and the world are in dire need of creative extremists.

I had hoped that the white moderate world would see this need. Perhaps I was too optimistic; perhaps I expected too much. I suppose I should have realized that few members of the oppressor race can understand the deep groans and passionate yearnings of the oppressed race, and still fewer have the vision to see that injustice must be rotted out by strong, persistent, and determined action. I am thankful, however, that some of our white brothers in the South have grasped the meaning of this social revolution and committed themselves to it. They are still all too few in quantity, but they are big in quality. Some—such as Ralph McGill, Lillian Smith, Harry Golden, James McBride Dabbs, Ann Braden, and Sarah Patton Boyle—have written about our struggle in eloquent and prophetic terms. Others have marched with us down nameless streets of the South. They have languished in filthy, roach-infested jails, suffering the abuse and brutality of policemen who view them as ''dirty nigger-lovers.'' Unlike so many of their moderate brothers and sisters, they have recognized the urgency of the moment and sensed the need for powerful ''action'' antidotes to combat the disease of segregation.

Let me take note of my other major disappointment. I have been so greatly disappointed with the white church and its leadership. Of course, there are some notable exceptions. I am not unmindful of the fact that each of you has taken some significant stands on this issue. I commend you, Reverend Stallings, for your Christian stand on this past Sunday, in welcoming Negroes to your worship service on a non-segregated basis. I commend the Catholic leaders of this state for integrating Spring Hill College several years ago.

But despite these notable exceptions, I must honestly reiterate that I have been disappointed with the church. I do not say this as one of those negative critics who can always find something wrong with the church. I say this as a minister of the gospel, who loves the church; who was nurtured in its bosom; who has been sustained by its spiritual blessings and who will remain true to it as long as the cord of life shall lengthen.

When I was suddenly catapulted into the leadership of the bus protest in Montgomery, Alabama, a few years ago, I felt we would be supported by the white church. I felt we would be supported by the white church. I felt that the white ministers, priests, and rabbis of the South would be among our strongest allies. Instead, some have been outright opponents, refusing to understand the freedom movement and misrepresenting its leaders; all too many others have been more cautious than courageous and have remained silent behind the anesthetizing security of stained-glass windows.

In spite of my shattered dreams, I came to Birmingham with the hope that the white religious leadership of this community would see the justice of our cause and, with deep moral concern, would serve as the channel through which our just grievances could reach the power structure. I had hoped that each of you would understand. But again I have been disappointed. . . .

There was a time when the church was very powerful—in the time when the early Christians rejoiced at being deemed worthy to suffer for what they believed. In those days the church was not merely a thermometer that recorded the ideas and principles of popular opinion; it was a thermostat that transformed the mores of society. Whenever the early Christians entered a town, the people in power became disturbed and immediately sought to convict the Christians for being "disturbers of the peace" and "outside agitators." But the Christians pressed on, in the conviction that they were "a colony of heaven," called to obey God rather than man. Small in number, they were big in commitment. They were too God intoxicated to be "astronomically intimidated." By their effort and example they brought an end to such ancient evils as infanticide and gladiatorial contests.

Things are different now. So often the contemporary church is a weak, ineffectual voice with an uncertain sound. So often it is an arch-defender of the status quo. Far from being disturbed by the presence of the church, the power structure of the average community is consoled by the church's silent—and often even vocal—sanction of things as they are.

But the judgment of God is upon the church as never before. If today's church does not recapture the sacrificial spirit of the early church, it will lose its authenticity, forfeit the loyalty of millions, and be dismissed as an irrelevant social club with no meaning for the twentieth century. Every day I meet young people whose disappointment with the church has turned into outright disgust.

Perhaps I have once again been too optimistic. Is organized religion too inextricably bound to the status quo to save our nation and the world? Perhaps I must turn my faith to the inner spiritual church, the church within the church, as the true *ekklesia* and the hope of the world. But again I am thankful to God that some noble souls from the ranks of organized religion have broken loose from the paralyzing chains of conformity and joined us as active partners in the struggle for freedom. They have left their secure congregations and walked the streets of Albany, Georgia, with us. They have gone down the highways of the South on torturous rides for freedom. Yes, they have gone to jail with us. Some have been dismissed from their churches, have lost the support of their bishops and fellow ministers. But they have acted in the faith that right defeated is stronger than evil triumphant. Their witness has been the spiritual salt that has preserved the true meaning of the gospel in these troubled times. They have carved a tunnel of hope through the dark mountain of disappointment.

I hope the church as a whole will meet the challenge of this decisive hour. But even if the church does not come to the aid of justice, I have no despair about the future. I have no fear about the outcome of our struggle in Birmingham, even if our motives are at present misunderstood. We will reach the goal of freedom in Birmingham and all over the nation, because the goal of America is freedom. Abused and scorned though we may be, our destiny is tied up with America's destiny. Before the pilgrims landed at Plymouth, we were here. Before the pen of Jefferson etched the majestic words of the Declaration of Independence across the pages of history, we were here. For more than two centuries our forebears labored in this country without wages; they made cotton king; they built the homes of their masters while suffering gross injustice and shameful humiliation—and yet out of a bottomless vitality they continued to thrive and develop. If the inexpressible cruelties of slavery could not stop us, the opposition we now face will surely fail. We will win our freedom because the sacred heritage of our nation and the eternal will of God are embodied in our echoing demands.

Before closing I feel impelled to mention one other point in your statement that has troubled me profoundly. You warmly commended the Birmingham police force for keeping "order" and "preventing violence." I doubt that you would have so warmly commended the police force if you had seen its dogs sinking their teeth into unarmed, nonviolent Negroes. I doubt that you would so quickly commend the policemen if you were to observe their ugly and inhumane treatment of Negroes here in the city jail; if you were to watch them push and curse old Negro women and young Negro girls; if you were to see them slap and kick old Negro men and young boys; if you were to observe them, as they did on two occasions, refuse to give us food because we wanted to sing our grace together. I cannot join you in your praise of the Birmingham police department.

It is true that the police have exercised a degree of discipline in handling the demonstrators. In this sense they have conducted themselves rather "nonviolently" in public. But for what purpose? To preserve the evil system of segregation. Over the past few years I have consistently preached that nonviolence demands that the means we use must be as pure as the ends we seek. I have tried to make clear that it is wrong to use immoral means to attain moral ends. But now I must affirm that it is just as wrong, or perhaps even more so, to use moral means to preserve immoral ends. Perhaps Mr. Connor and his policemen have been rather nonviolent in public, as was Chief Pritchett in Albany, Georgia, but they have used the moral means of nonviolence to maintain the immoral end of racial injustice. As T. S. Eliot has said, "The last temptation is the greatest treason: To do the right deed for the wrong reason."

I wish you had commended the Negro sit-inners and demonstrators of Birmingham for their sublime courage, their willingness to suffer, and their amazing discipline in the midst of great provocation. One day the South will recognize its real heroes. They will be the James Merediths, with the noble sense of purpose that enables them to face jeering and hostile mobs, and with the agonizing loneliness that characterizes the life of the pioneer. They will be old, oppressed, battered Negro women, symbolized in a seventy-two-year-old woman in Montgomery, Alabama, who rose up with a sense of dignity and with her people decided not to ride segregated buses, and who responded with ungrammatical profundity to one who inquired about her weariness: "My feets is tired, but my soul is at rest." They will be the young high school and college students, the young ministers of the gospel and a host of their elders, courageously and nonviolently sitting in at lunch counters and willingly going to jail for conscience' sake. One day the South will know that when these disinherited children of God sat down at lunch counters, they were in reality standing up for what is best in the American dream and for the most sacred values in our Judaeo-Christian heritage, thereby bringing our nation back to those great wells of democracy which were dug deep by the founding fathers in their formulation of the Constitution and the Declaration of Independence.

Never before have I written so long a letter. I'm afraid it is much to long to take your precious time. I can assure you that it would have been much shorter if I had been writing from a comfortable desk, but what else can one do when he is alone in a narrow jail cell, other than write long letters, think long thoughts, and pray long prayers?

If I have said anything in this letter that overstates the truth and indicates an unreasonable impatience, I beg you to forgive me. If I have said anything that understates the truth and indicates my having a patience that allows me to settle for anything less than brotherhood, I beg God to forgive me.

I hope this letter finds you strong in the faith. I also hope that circumstances will soon make it possible for me to meet each of you, not as an integrationist or a civil rights leader but as a fellow clergyman and a Christian brother. Let us all hope that the dark clouds of racial prejudice will soon pass away and the deep fog of misunderstanding will be lifted from our fear-drenched communities, and in some not too distant tomorrow the radiant stars of love and brotherhood will shine over our great nation with all their scintillating beauty.

Yours in the cause of
Peace and Brotherhood,

MARTIN LUTHER KING, JR.

## Notes

1. This response to a published statement by eight fellow clergymen from Alabama [Bishop C. C. J. Carpenter, Bishop Joseph A. Durick, Rabbi Hilton L. Grafman, Bishop Paul Hardin, Bishop Holan B. Harmon, the Reverend George M. Murray, the Reverend Edward V. Ramage and the Reverend Earl Stallings] was composed under somewhat constricting circumstances. Begun on the margins of the newspaper in which the statement appeared while I was in jail, the letter was continued on scraps of writing paper supplied by a friendly Negro trusty, and concluded on a pad my attorneys were eventually permitted to leave me. Although the text remains in substance unaltered, I have indulged in the author's prerogative of polishing it for publication. [King's note]